Query Processing in Parallel Relational Database Systems

Query Processing in Parallel Relational Database Systems

Hongjun Lu
Beng-Chin Ooi
Kian-Lee Tan

IEEE Computer Society Press
Los Alamitos, California
Washington • Brussels • Tokyo

Library of Congress Cataloging-in-Publication Data

Query Processing in Parallel Relational Database Systems / [edited by] Hongjun Lu, Beng-Chen Ooi, Kian-Lee Tan.
p. cm.
Includes bibliographical references.
ISBN 0-8186-5452-X (case). — ISBN 0-8186-5451-1 (fiche)
1. Relational databases. 2. Parallel processing (Electronic computers) 3. Database searching.
I. Lu, Hongjun II. Ooi, Beng-Chin, 1961- . III. Tan, Kian-Lee
QA76.9.D3Q475 1994
005.75'6 — dc20 93-45665
CIP

Published by the
IEEE Computer Society Press
10662 Los Vaqueros Circle
P.O. Box 3014
Los Alamitos, CA 90720-1264

IEEE Computer Society Press Order Number 5452-01
IEEE Catalog Number EH0391-3
Library of Congress Number 93-45665
ISBN 0-8186-5451-1 (microfiche)
ISBN 0-8186-5452-X (case)

Additional copies can be ordered from

IEEE Computer Society Press
Customer Service Center
10662 Los Vaqueros Circle
P.O. Box 3014
Los Alamitos, CA 90720-1264
Tel: (714) 821-8380
Fax: (714) 821-4641
Email: cs.books@computer.org

IEEE Service Center
445 Hoes Lane
P.O. Box 1331
Piscataway, NJ 08855-1331
Tel: (908) 981-1393
Fax: (908) 981-9667

IEEE Computer Society
13, avenue de l'Aquilon
B-1200 Brussels
BELGIUM
Tel: +32-2-770-2198
Fax: +32-2-770-8505

IEEE Computer Society
Ooshima Building
2-19-1 Minami-Aoyama
Minato-ku, Tokyo 107
JAPAN
Tel: +81-3-3408-3118
Fax: +81-3-3408-3553

Technical Editor: Sudha Ram
Production Editor: Lisa O'Conner
Printed in the United States of America by Braun-Brumfield, Inc.

The Institute of Electrical and Electronics Engineers, Inc.

Contents

Preface

Along with the availability of inexpensive commodity microprocessors, memories, and disks, parallel database systems have become a very promising approach to meet the performance demands of database applications that uniprocessor systems are unable to satisfy. Although parallel computing has been an active research area for the last two decades, most of the work concentrated on the parallel processing of computational-intensive tasks, and less attention was paid to database operations in which large volumes of data are stored on disks and shared among a large number of users.

In relational database management systems (RDBMS), queries are expressed in high-level declarative query languages, such as SQL. The query processor, or query optimizer, is responsible for generating query execution plans that are sequences of primitive operations. It is also responsible for supporting efficient processing of these primitive operations. The performance of a database system is determined largely by the effectiveness of algorithms used to evaluate the primitive operations and the optimality of procedural execution plans generated for user queries. The introduction of parallel processing into database systems that feature large volumes of persistent data and concurrent access by large numbers of users engenders many new and important technical issues that must be solved before high-performance parallel database systems can be designed and implemented. Query processing and optimization is one such issue. Since parallel database systems utilize more resources, they provide more optimization opportunities and hence introduce new challenges to researchers and developers. Our objectives in preparing this tutorial are to provide readers with a background knowledge of parallel database query processing and optimization and to cover recent developments in the field.

The first two chapters give some background information about parallel database systems in general. Chapter 1 is an introduction that provides an overview of parallel database systems and major technical issues other than query processing.

The focus of this book, parallel database query processing, depends greatly on other components of a database management system, especially the low-level storage management and access methods. In parallel database systems, the system architecture — that is, how the major resources used in query processing are connected — plays a critical role in the design and implementation of a query processor. Chapter 2 gives a general review of the architectures of parallel database systems, which provides a foundation for our discussion on query processing and optimization.

In relational systems, the user queries are typically written in relational calculus-based languages, and the low-level execution plans are typically in some form of relational algebra, with selected access paths. An algebraic operation accepts as input one to two relations and produces as output a resultant relation. For each operation, different implementation strategies may be used, and some of these methods may require their input to be sorted in order to be efficient. In addition, sorting has also been used to remove duplicates from the output of an operation and to facilitate other operations such as join and aggregation. Therefore, sorting is important to parallel query processing, and we present three papers concerning sorting in parallel database systems in Chapter 3.

Join is one of the most frequently used and time-consuming operations in relation database systems. Although join has been well researched in the uniprocessor environment, these conventional join strategies cannot be applied efficiently and directly to parallel database systems. One of the problems is that in a parallel database system, a relation has a high possibility of being partitioned horizontally into multiple subrelations and stored in different processors. Parallel processing of unary relational operations such as selection and projection are quite straightforward, but parallel processing of join is not as easy because correlations exist among subrelations. Chapter 4 briefly reviews conventional join strategies and approaches in parallelizing such joins, and presents four papers on parallelizing joins for different system architectures.

Linear speedup is one of the objectives of designing parallel processing algorithms. However, in real applications, linear speedup is hardly achievable. In addition to communications overhead and interference among connected hardware components, load imbalance among the participating processors and disks can degrade the effectiveness of parallel processing. One major source of load imbalance is the distribution of data. The techniques employed to balance skewed data are discussed in Chapter 5.

The first step of query processing is to transform a user query expressed in some high-level, nonprocedural language into a procedural query execution plan (QEP). It is essential for high-performance database systems that the obtained QEP is optimal or near-optimal. In parallel database systems where various types of parallelism can be explored, the optimization search space is much larger compared to uniprocessor relational systems. Chapter 6 discusses the query optimization strategies proposed for parallel database systems.

Chapter 7 concludes the tutorial with a brief discussion of a few issues related to parallel database query processing and optimization that need to be addressed before the field can be considered mature.

Parallel database query processing is an active research topic; it would be impossible to cover all aspects of it in a single volume. A bibliography is included for further reference.

It is our hope that this book, as a tutorial, will serve as an introduction to those who are interested in knowing more about recent developments in the field and as a summary for those who have been working in this area, so that new issues can be further identified and solved.

Hongjun Lu, Beng-Chin Ooi, and Kian-Lee Tan
National University of Singapore
February, 1994

Chapter 1: Introduction

Relational database systems have dominated the commercial market for the last decade, and relational technologies have penetrated new application areas, such as engineering databases for CAD/CAM, geographic information systems (GIS), multimedia (text, image, voice, video) information systems, scientific databases, and others. Compared to business applications, these so-called nonconventional database applications feature more complex data types, much larger volumes of data, and more complex queries. While the basic requirements for data processing (high performance, high reliability and availability, and high extensibility) remain the same, the new applications make these requirements more difficult to achieve because of the new environment. A large amount of research has been conducted to meet the challenges in almost all subareas of database management systems (DBMS). Parallel database systems (PDBS) attempt to exploit recent multiprocessor computer architectures in order to build database systems with high performance, high availability, and high extensibility.

Parallel database systems

A parallel database system can be loosely defined as a DBMS implemented on a tightly coupled multiprocessor.[1] It attempts to achieve high performance by parallelism. The set-oriented nature of the relational data model and the high-level, declarative query languages used in relational systems facilitate parallel processing. In parallel database systems, two types of parallelism can be explored at the query level: intraquery parallelism and interquery parallelism. With intraquery parallelism, several processors cooperate to concurrently execute a single query; interquery parallelism permits multiple queries to be simultaneously executed by the processors. As a single database query typically consists of a number of primitive relational operations, parallelism can be further explored at the operator level. First, a number of processors can be assigned to concurrently execute one single operation, which is commonly known as intraoperator parallelism. Second, several operators may be processed concurrently by splitting the processors to clusters such that each cluster will execute one operator. This form of parallelism is called interoperator parallelism. Within each cluster, intraoperator parallelism can also be explored. One limitation of interoperator parallelism is that the concurrently executed operations must be independent of each other. When a number of operations must be executed in a certain order, another type of parallelism, pipeline parallelism, can be explored. In other words, the results of an operation are immediately directed to the set of processors that are assigned to execute the next operation, and a number of such operations form a pipeline. Because of such large-scale parallelism, parallel database systems are expected to be able to deliver very high performance even for complex queries with very large volumes of data.

Parallel database systems versus database machines

Parallel database systems are not the first attempt in the database community to meet the high-performance requirement for some database applications. A large amount of research work on developing special-purpose database machines was done in the late 1970s and early 1980s. In the traditional approach to database systems, the data are stored on the secondary storage; the DBMS runs on the same computer as the user programs. It is necessary to move the data to the processing unit for processing and determine what portion of them are needed to respond to a user's query. The basic concept of database machines is to offload the database management functions onto a special processor, the database machine, to relieve the host computer system of the work of managing the database. One approach taken in database machines is to add a certain level of computing capacity to the storage devices so that it is feasible to decide whether a given set of data will be useful in the evaluation of a query without having to transfer the data to the processing unit. One design of such an approach is to associate a processor with each track of a fixed-head disk or with each read/write head of a moving-head disk. Data from the track (or head) are processed by the associated processor, and data from all tracks (heads) can be processed simultaneously. However, the return from the efforts spent in this direction was small. Besides the high costs of special or customized hardware, limited extensibility is another major reason for the failure of database machines using special hardware components. Only by using standard hardware components can the continuing technology improvements be integrated into the system with minimal costs and delay. A few successful database machines, such as the DBC/1012 database computer from Teradata, adopted the same approach as that of the current parallel database systems: to develop software-oriented solutions that exploit massive numbers of fast and cheap commodity disks, processors, and memories.

Parallel query processing versus distributed query processing

Another related effort to improve the performance, reliability and availability, and extendibility of database systems is distributed database systems (DDBSs). In DDBSs, the database is stored on several computers (sites) that communicate with one another through various communication media. If a query involves data at several sites, it may be possible to split the query into subqueries that can be executed in parallel. To further increase parallelism, relations in a DDBS can be horizontally and/or vertically fragmented so that a number of sites can concurrently process one operation (such as selection) on different portions of a relation. A join that involves two relations stored on two different sites can also be implemented using semi-join methods to realize some form of parallelism. However, DDBSs are not considered as parallel database systems in general. Following are a few important differences between PDBS and DDBS:

- The sites or nodes in a DDBS are autonomous computers. They do not share main memory or disks. They run under independent operating and database management systems. Processors in PDBSs, on the other hand, are usually not autonomous computers and are controlled by a single operating system and DBMS. These processors may share main memory and/or disks.

- Being able to share data stored in computers that are geographically distributed (more than a few thousand miles apart) is one of the main features of DDBSs not shared by PDBSs. Processors in a PDBS are often tightly coupled using a fast interconnection network or bus.

- The number of sites in a DDBS are relatively small compared to the number of processors in parallel database systems. As a result, much higher parallelism can be achieved in PDBSs than in DDBSs.

These basic differences give rise to different technical issues and potential application areas for DDBSs and PDBSs.

Parallel database query processing versus general parallel processing

As mentioned earlier, PDBSs explore parallelism to achieve high performance. The process of translating a user query expressed in a certain high-level language, such as SQL, into an efficient execution plan and executing the plan in parallel is referred to as parallel database query processing. Although parallel processing has been a very active research area in computer science for the last two decades, the problems to be addressed here, or the focus of research in parallel query processing, are quite different. One of the most important differences is that most of the well-known parallel processing systems and architectures, such as Hypercubes, Butterfly, and connection machines, were developed to solve computation-intensive problems, with few of them considering disk I/O, one important factor that cannot be ignored in database applications. These parallel processing systems and algorithms usually assume that both the program (instructions) and data are in memory. However, for most database operations, the operand — that is, the data — is originally stored on disks. The disks have to be fetched into memory first to make them available to the processors. The results of operations are usually written back to the disks. The disk I/O time is often comparable to or longer than the processing time. In other words, for parallel database query processing, the problems to be solved are also data-intensive. Another important difference is that the language used, such as SQL, in database systems is of a declarative nature and is usually at a higher level than the languages used in general parallel computing systems. Parallel database systems not only control the parallel execution of operations but also need to generate optimal plans (that is, the sequence of the operations) for high-level query statements. This query optimization process is often more complex because of the large search space provided by the potential of high parallelism.

Papers in this chapter

Although the theme of this book, parallel query processing and optimization, is one of the subareas in parallel database systems, three papers are included in this introductory chapter to help readers grasp the overview of parallel database systems.

The first paper by DeWitt and Gray, "Parallel Database Systems: The Future of High Performance Database Systems," provides solid arguments in favor of parallel database systems. It also discusses the basic implementation techniques and surveys existing state-of-the-art commercial and research systems.

The second paper, "Parallelism in Relational Data Base Systems: Architectural Issues and Design Approaches," by Pirahesh, Mohan, Cheng, Liu, and Selinger, addresses the issues of supporting intraquery parallelism in a relational DBMS. Arguments for and against the commonly used parallel architectures are presented. The design of parallel algorithms and their impact on different components of a relational DBMS are also discussed. Also, this paper identifies the stages of query processing where the efforts of parallelism will provide big returns.

The optimization of queries is addressed by the third paper, "Optimizing SQL Queries for Parallel Execution" by Bultzinsloewen. This paper is among the first to highlight the major issues in developing optimization techniques for parallel database systems. Key issues include the need to refine the objective of optimization to suit a parallel environment, the search strategy that the optimizer should employ, the kind of scheduling information that the plan should contain, and the need for efficient heuristics to generate a near-optimal, if not optimal, parallel execution plan.

Reference

1. P. Valduriez, "Parallel Database Systems: Open Problems and New Issues," *Distributed and Parallel Databases,* Vol. 1, No. 2, Apr. 1993, pp. 137-166.

Parallel Database Systems: The Future of High Performance Database Systems

Highly parallel database systems are beginning to displace traditional mainframe computers for the largest database and transaction processing tasks. The success of these systems refutes a 1983 paper predicting the demise of database machines [3]. Ten years ago the future of highly parallel database machines seemed gloomy, even to their staunchest advocates. Most database machine research had focused on specialized, often trendy, hardware such as CCD memories, bubble memories, head-per-track disks, and optical disks. None of these technologies fulfilled their promises; so there was a sense that conventional CPUs, electronic RAM, and moving-head magnetic disks would dominate the scene for many years to come. At that time, disk throughput was predicted to double while processor speeds were predicted to increase by much larger factors. Consequently, critics predicted that multiprocessor systems would soon be I/O limited unless a solution to the I/O bottleneck was found.

While these predictions were fairly accurate about the future of hardware, the critics were certainly wrong about the overall future of parallel database systems. Over the last decade Teradata, Tandem, and a host of startup companies have successfully developed and marketed highly parallel machines.

David DeWitt and Jim Gray

Parallel Database Systems

Why have parallel database systems become more than a research curiosity? One explanation is the widespread adoption of the relational data model. In 1983 relational database systems were just appearing in the marketplace; today they dominate it. Relational queries are ideally suited to parallel execution; they consist of uniform operations applied to uniform streams of data. Each operator produces a new relation, so the operators can be composed into highly parallel dataflow graphs. By streaming the output of one operator into the input of another operator, the two operators can work in series giving *pipelined parallelism.* By partitioning the input data among multiple processors and memories, an operator can often be split into many independent operators each working on a part of the data. This partitioned data and execution gives *partitioned parallelism* (Figure 1).

The dataflow approach to database system design needs a message-based client-server operating system to interconnect the parallel processes executing the relational operators. This in turn requires a high-speed network to interconnect the parallel processors. Such facilities seemed exotic a decade ago, but now they are the mainstream of computer architecture. The client-server paradigm using high-speed LANs is the basis for most PC, workstation, and workgroup software. Those same client-server mechanisms are an excellent basis for distributed database technology.

Mainframe designers have found it difficult to build machines powerful enough to meet the CPU and I/O demands of relational databases serving large numbers of simultaneous users or searching terabyte databases. Meanwhile, multiprocessors based on fast and inexpensive microprocessors have become widely available from vendors including Encore, Intel, NCR, nCUBE, Sequent, Tandem, Teradata, and Thinking Machines. These machines provide more total power than their mainframe coun-

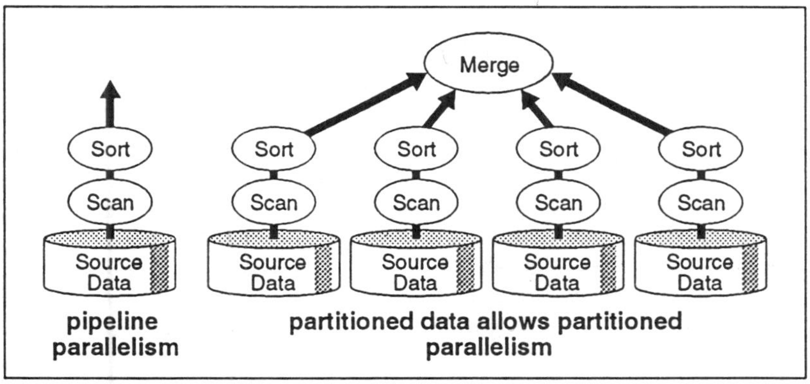

Figure 1.
The dataflow approach to relational operators gives both pipelined and partitioned parallelism. Relational data operators take relations (uniform sets of records) as input and produce relations as outputs. This allows them to be composed in dataflow graphs that allow *pipeline parallelism* (left) in which the computation of one operator proceeds in parallel with another, and *partitioned parallelism* in which operators (sort and scan in the diagram at the right) are replicated for each data source, and the replicas execute in parallel.

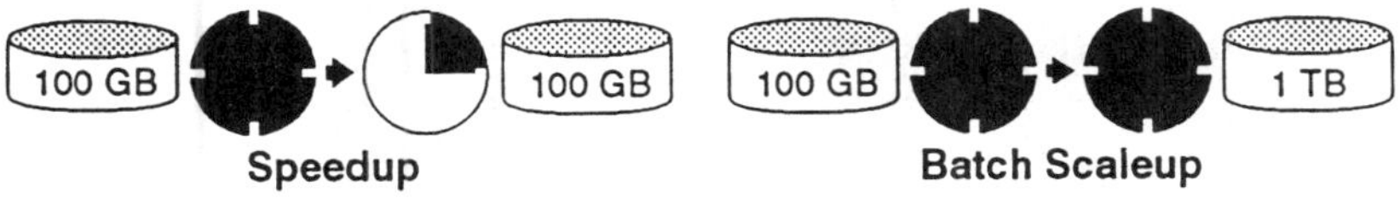

Figure 2.
Speedup and Scaleup. A speedup design performs a one-hour job four times faster when run on a four-times larger system. A scaleup design runs a ten-times bigger job is done in the same time by a ten-times bigger system.

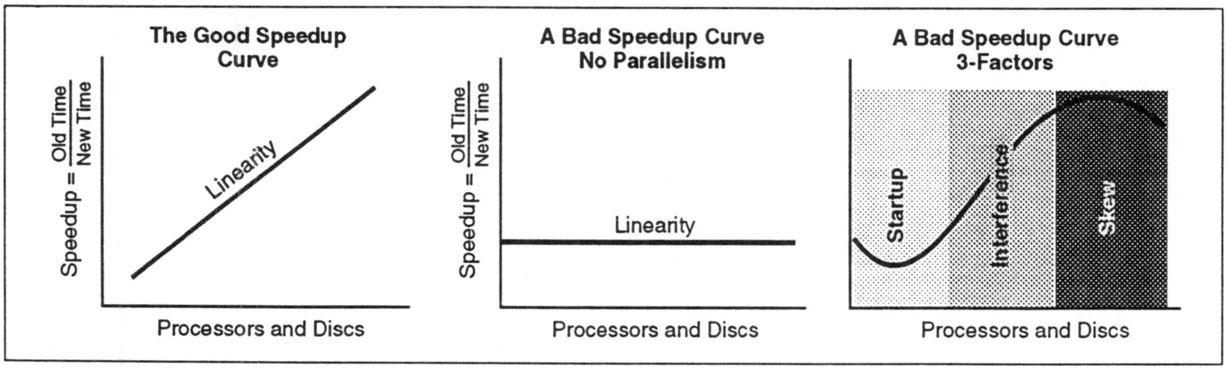

Figure 3.
Good and bad speedup curves. The standard speedup curves. The left curve is the ideal. The middle graph shows no speedup as hardware is added. The right curve shows the three threats to parallelism. Initial startup costs may dominate at first. As the number of processes increase, interference can increase. Ultimately, the job is divided so finely, that the variance in service times (skew) causes a slowdown.

terparts at a lower price. Their modular architectures enable systems to grow incrementally, adding MIPS, memory, and disks either to speedup the processing of a given job, or to scaleup the system to process a larger job in the same time.

In retrospect, special-purpose database machines have indeed failed; but parallel database systems are a big success. The successful parallel database systems are built from conventional processors, memories, and disks. They have emerged as major consumers of highly parallel architectures, and are in an excellent position to exploit massive numbers of fast-cheap commodity disks, processors, and memories promised by current technology forecasts.

A consensus on parallel and distributed database system architecture has emerged. This architecture is based on a *shared-nothing* hardware design [29] in which processors communicate with one another only by sending messages via an interconnection network. In such systems, tuples of each relation in the database are *partitioned (declustered)* across disk storage units[1] attached directly to each processor. Partitioning allows multiple processors to scan large relations in parallel without needing any exotic I/O devices. Such architectures were pioneered by Teradata in the late 1970s and by several research projects. This design is now used by Teradata, Tandem, NCR, Oracle-nCUBE, and several other products currently under development. The research community has also embraced this shared-nothing dataflow architecture in systems like Arbre, Bubba, and Gamma.

The remainder of this article is organized as follows: The next section describes the basic architectural concepts used in these parallel database systems. This is followed by a brief presentation of the unique features of the Teradata, Tandem, Bubba, and Gamma systems in the following section, entitled "The State of the Art." Several areas for future research are described in "Future Directions and Research Problems" prior to the conclusion of this article.

Basic Techniques for Parallel Database Machine Implementation

Parallelism Goals and Metrics: Speedup and Scaleup

The ideal parallel system demonstrates two key properties: (1) *linear speedup:* Twice as much hardware can perform the task in half the elapsed time, and (2) *linear scaleup:* Twice as much hardware can perform twice as large a task in the same elapsed time (see Figures 2 and 3).

More formally, given a fixed job run on a small system, and then run on a larger system, the *speedup* given by the larger system is measured as:

$$Speedup = \frac{small\_system\_elapsed\_time}{big\_system\_elapsed\_time}$$

Speedup is said to be linear, if an N-times large or more expensive system yields a speedup of N.

Speedup holds the problem size constant, and grows the system. Scaleup measures the ability to grow both the system and the problem. *Scaleup* is defined as the ability of an N-times larger system to perform an N-times larger job in the same elapsed time as the original system. The scaleup metric is:

$$Scaleup = \frac{small\_system\_elapsed\_time\_on\_small\_problem}{big\_system\_elapsed\_time\_on\_big\_problem}$$

If this scaleup equation evaluates to 1, then the scaleup is said to be linear[2]. There are two distinct kinds of scaleup, batch and transactional. If the job consists of performing many small independent requests submitted by many clients and operating on a shared database, then scaleup consists of N-times as many clients, submitting N-times as many requests against an N-times larger database. This is the scaleup typically found in transaction processing systems and timesharing systems. This form of scaleup is used by the Transaction Processing Performance Council to scaleup their transaction processing benchmarks [36]. Consequently, it is called *transaction scaleup.* Transaction scaleup is ideally suited to parallel systems since each transaction is typically a small independent job that can be run on a separate processor.

A second form of scaleup, called *batch scaleup,* arises when the scaleup task is presented as a single large job. This is typical of database queries and is also typical of scientific simulations. In these cases, scaleup consists of using an N-times larger computer to solve an N-times larger problem. For database systems batch scaleup translates to the same query on an N-times larger database; for scientific problems, batch scaleup translates to the same calculation on an N-times finer grid or on an N-times longer simulation.

The generic barriers to linear speedup and linear scaleup are the triple threats of:

startup: The time needed to start a parallel operation. If thousands of processes must be started, this can easily dominate the actual computation time.

interference: The slowdown each new process imposes on all others when accessing shared resources.

skew: As the number of parallel steps increases, the average size of each step decreases, but the variance can well exceed the mean. The service time of a job is the service time of the slowest step of the job. When the variance dominates the mean, increased parallelism improves elapsed time only slightly.

The subsection "A Parallel

[1]The term disk is used here as a shorthand for disk or other nonvolatile storage media. As the decade proceeds, nonvolatile electronic storage or some other media may replace or augment disks.

[2]The execution cost of some operators increases super-linearly. For example, the cost of sorting n-tuples increases as *nlog(n).* When n is in the billions, scaling up by a factor of a thousand, causes *nlog(n)* to increase by 3,000. This 30% deviation from linearity in a three-orders-of-magnitude scaleup justifies the use of the term *near-linear* scaleup.

Dataflow Approach to SQL Software" describes several basic techniques widely used in the design of shared-nothing parallel database machines to overcome these barriers. These techniques often achieve linear speedup and scaleup on relational operators.

Hardware Architecture, the Trend to Shared-Nothing Machines

The ideal database machine would have a single infinitely fast processor with an infinite memory with infinite bandwidth—and it would be infinitely cheap (free). Given such a machine, there would be no need for speedup, scaleup, or parallelism. Unfortunately, technology is not delivering such machines—but it is coming close. Technology is promising to deliver fast one-chip processors, fast high-capacity disks, and high-capacity electronic RAM. It also promises that each of these devices will be very inexpensive by today's standards, costing only hundreds of dollars each.

So, the challenge is to build an infinitely fast processor out of infinitely many processors of finite speed, and to build an infinitely large memory with infinite memory bandwidth from infinitely many storage units of finite speed. This sounds trivial mathematically; but in practice, when a new processor is added to most computer designs, it slows every other computer down just a little bit. If this slowdown (interference) is 1%, then the maximum speedup is 37 and a 1,000-processor system has 4% of the effective power of a single-processor system.

How can we build scaleable multiprocessor systems? Stonebraker suggested the following simple taxonomy for the spectrum of designs (see Figures 4 and 5) [29][3]:

shared-memory: All processors share direct access to a common global memory and to all disks. The IBM/370, Digital VAX, and Sequent Symmetry multiprocessors typify this design.

shared-disks: Each processor has a private memory but has direct access to all disks. The IBM Sysplex and original Digital VAXcluster typify this design.

shared-nothing: Each memory and disk is owned by some processor that acts as a server for that data. Mass storage in such an architecture is distributed among the processors by connecting one or more disks. The Teradata, Tandem, and nCUBE machines typify this design.

Shared-nothing architectures minimize interference by minimizing resource sharing. They also exploit commodity processors and memory without needing an incredibly powerful interconnection network. As Figure 5 suggests, the other architectures move large quantities of data through the interconnection network. The shared-nothing design moves only questions and answers through the network. Raw memory accesses and raw disk accesses are performed locally in a processor, and only the filtered (reduced) data is passed to the client program. This allows a more scaleable design by minimizing traffic on the interconnection network.

Shared-nothing characterizes the database systems being used by Teradata [33], Gamma [8, 9], Tandem [32], Bubba [1], Arbre [21], and nCUBE [13]. Significantly, Digital's VAXcluster has evolved to this design. DOS and UNIX workgroup systems from 3com, Borland, Digital, HP, Novell, Microsoft, and Sun also adopt a shared-nothing client-server architecture.

The actual interconnection networks used by these systems vary enormously. Teradata employs a redundant tree-structured communication network. Tandem uses a three-level duplexed network, two levels within a cluster, and rings connecting the clusters. Arbre, Bubba, and Gamma are independent of the underlying interconnection network, requiring only that the network allow any two nodes to communicate with one another. Gamma operates on an Intel Hypercube. The Arbre prototype was implemented using IBM 4381 processors connected to one another in a point-to-point network. Workgroup systems are currently making a transition from Ethernet to higher speed local networks.

The main advantage of shared-nothing multiprocessors is that they can be scaled up to hundreds and probably thousands of processors that do not interfere with one another. Teradata, Tandem, and Intel have each shipped systems with more than 200 processors. Intel is implementing a 2,000-node hypercube. The largest shared-memory multiprocessors currently available are limited to about 32 processors.

These shared-nothing architectures achieve near-linear speedups and scaleups on complex relational queries and on on-line transaction processing workloads [9, 10, 32]. Given such results, database machine designers see little justification for the hardware and software complexity associated with shared-memory and shared-disk designs.

Shared-memory and shared-disk systems do not scale well on database applications. Interference is a major problem for shared-memory multiprocessors. The interconnection network must have the bandwidth of the sum of the processors and disks. It is difficult to build such networks that can scale to thousands of nodes. To reduce network traffic and to minimize latency, each processor is given a large private cache. Measurements of shared-memory multiprocessors running database workloads show that loading and flushing these caches considerably degrades processor performance [35]. As parallelism increases, interference on shared resources limits performance. Multiprocessor systems

[3] Single Instruction stream, Multiple Data stream (SIMD) machines such as ILLIAC IV and its derivatives like MASSPAR and the "old" Connection Machine are ignored here because to date they have few successes in the database area. SIMD machines seem to have application in simulation, pattern matching, and mathematical search, but they do not seem to be appropriate for the multiuser, I/O intensive, and dataflow paradigm of database systems.

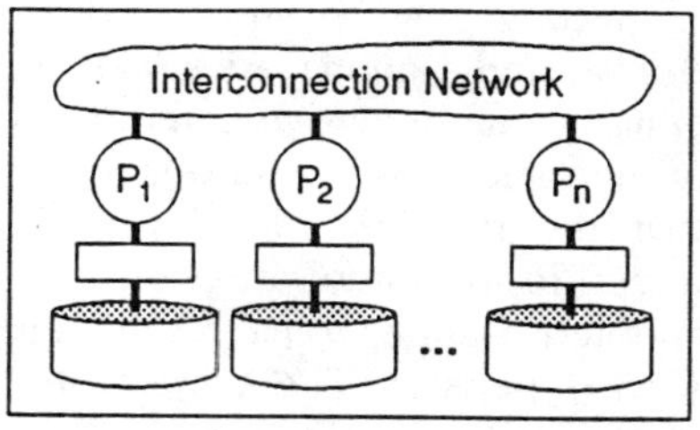

Figure 4.
The basic shared-nothing design. Each processor has a private memory and one or more disks. Processors communicate via a high-speed interconnect network. Teradata, Tandem, nCUBE, and the newer VAXclusters typify this design.

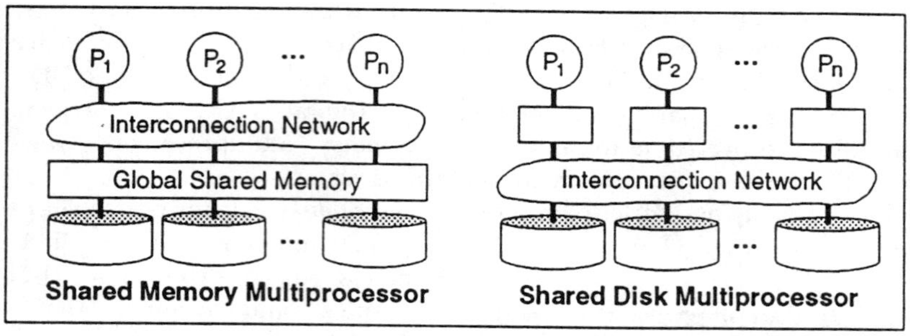

Figure 5.
The shared-memory and shared-disk designs. A shared-memory multiprocessor connects all processors to a globally shared memory. Multiprocessor IBM/370, VAX, and Sequent computers are typical examples of shared-memory designs. Shared-disk systems give each processor a private memory, but all the processors can directly address all the disks. Digital's VAXcluster and IBM's Sysplex typify this design.

Figure 6.
Example of a scan of a telephone relation to find the phone numbers of all people named Smith.

```
SELECT  telephone_number        /* the output attribute(s) */
FROM    telephone_book          /* the input relation      */
WHERE   last_name = 'Smith';    /* the predicate           */
```

often use an affinity scheduling mechanism to reduce this interference; giving each process an affinity to a particular processor. This is a form of data partitioning; it represents an evolutionary step toward the shared-nothing design. Partitioning a shared-memory system creates many of the skew and load balancing problems faced by a shared-nothing machine; but reaps none of the simpler hardware interconnect benefits. Based on this experience, we believe high-performance shared-memory machines will not economically scale beyond a few processors when running database applications.

To ameliorate the interference problem, most shared-memory multiprocessors have adopted a shared-disk architecture. This is the logical consequence of affinity scheduling. If the disk interconnection network can scale to thousands of disks and processors, then a shared-disk design is adequate for large read-only databases and for databases where there is no concurrent sharing. The shared-disk architecture is not very effective for database applications that read and write a shared database. A processor wanting to update some data must first obtain the current copy of that data. Since others might be updating the same data concurrently, the processor must declare its intention to update the data. Once this declaration has been honored and acknowledged by all the other processors, the updator can read the shared data from disk and update it. The processor must then write the shared data to disk so that subsequent readers and writers will be aware of the update. There are many optimizations of this protocol, but they all end up exchanging reservation messages and exchanging large physical data pages. This creates processor interference and delays. It creates heavy traffic on the shared interconnection network.

For shared database applications, the shared-disk approach is much more expensive than the shared-nothing approach of exchanging small high-level logical questions and answers among clients and servers. One solution to this interference has been to give data a processor affinity; other processors wanting to access the data send messages to the server managing the data. This has emerged as a major application of transaction processing monitors that partition the load among partitioned servers, and is also a major application for remote procedure calls. Again, this trend toward the partitioned data model and shared-nothing architecture on a shared-disk system reduces interference. Since the shared-disk system interconnection network is difficult to scale to thousands of processors and disks, many conclude that it would be better to adopt the shared-nothing architecture from the start.

Given the shortcomings of shared-disk and shared-memory architectures, why have computer architects been slow to adopt the shared-nothing approach? The first answer is simple, high-performance, low-cost commodity components have only recently become available. Traditionally, commodity components provided relatively low performance and low quality.

Today, old software is the most significant barrier to the use of parallelism. Old software written for uniprocessors gets no speedup or scaleup when put on any kind of multiprocessor. It must be rewritten to benefit from parallel processing and multiple disks. Database applications are a unique exception to this. Today, most database programs are written in the relational language SQL that has been standardized by both ANSI and ISO. It is possible to take standard SQL applications written for uniprocessor systems and execute them in parallel on shared-nothing database machines. Database systems can automatically distribute data among multiple processors. Teradata and Tandem routinely port SQL applications to their system and demonstrate near-linear speedups and scaleups. The following subsection explains the basic techniques used by such parallel database systems.

A Parallel Dataflow Approach to SQL Software

Terabyte on-line databases, consisting of billions of records, are becoming common as the price of online storage decreases. These databases are often represented and manipulated using the SQL relational model. The next few paragraphs give a rudimentary introduction to relational model concepts needed to understand the remainder of this article.

A relational database consists of *relations* (*files* in COBOL terminology) that in turn contain *tuples* (*records* in COBOL terminology). All the tuples in a relation have the same set of *attributes* (*fields* in COBOL terminology).

Relations are created, updated, and queried by writing SQL statements. These statements are syntactic sugar for a simple set of operators chosen from the relational algebra. *Select-project,* here called *scan,* is the simplest and most common operator—it produces a row-and-column subset of a relational table. A scan of relation R using predicate P and attribute list L produces a relational data stream as output. The scan reads each tuple, t, of R and applies the predicate P to it. If $P(t)$ is true, the scan discards any attributes of t not in L and inserts the resulting tuple in the scan output stream. Expressed in SQL, a scan of a telephone book relation to find the phone numbers of all people named Smith would be written as shown in Figure 6. A scan's output stream can be sent to another relational operator, returned to an application, displayed on a terminal, or printed in a report. Therein lies the beauty and utility of the relational model. The uniformity of the data and operators allow them to be arbitrarily composed into dataflow graphs.

The output of a scan may be sent to a *sort* operator that will reorder the tuples based on an attribute sort criteria, optionally eliminating duplicates. SQL defines several *aggregate* operators to summarize attributes into a single value, for example, taking the sum, min, or max of an attribute, or counting the number of distinct values of the attribute. The *insert* operator adds tuples from a stream to an existing relation. The *update* and *delete* operators alter and delete tuples in a relation matching a scan stream.

The relational model defines several operators to combine and compare two or more relations. It provides the usual set operators *union, intersection, difference,* and some more exotic ones like *join* and *division.* Discussion here will focus on the *equi-join* operator (here called *join*). The join operator composes two relations, A and B, on some attribute to produce a third relation. For each tuple, ta, in A, the join finds all tuples, tb, in B whose attribute values are equal to that of ta. For each matching pair of tuples, the join operator inserts into the output stream a tuple built by concatenating the pair.

Codd, in a classic paper, showed that the relational data model can represent any form of data, and that these operators are complete [5]. Today, SQL applications are typically a combination of conventional programs and SQL statements. The programs interact with clients, perform data display, and provide high-level direction of the SQL dataflow.

The SQL data model was originally proposed to improve programmer productivity by offering a nonprocedural database language. Data independence was an additional benefit; since the programs do not specify how the query is to be executed, SQL programs continue to operate as the logical and physical database schema evolves.

Parallelism is an unanticipated benefit of the relational model. Since relational queries are really just relational operators applied to very large collections of data, they offer many opportunities for parallelism. Since the queries are presented in a nonprocedural language, they offer considerable latitude in executing the queries.

Relational queries can be executed as a dataflow graph. As mentioned in the first section of this article, these graphs can use both pipelined parallelism and partitioned parallelism. If one operator sends its output to another, the two operators can execute in parallel giving potential speedup of two.

The benefits of pipeline parallelism are limited because of three factors: (1) Relational pipelines are rarely very long—a chain of length ten is unusual. (2) Some relational operators do not emit their first output until they have consumed all their inputs. Aggregate and sort operators have this property. One cannot pipeline these operators. (3) Often, the execution cost of one operator is much greater than the others (this is an example of skew). In such cases, the speedup obtained by pipelining will be very limited.

Partitioned execution offers much better opportunities for speedup and scaleup. By taking the large relational operators and partitioning their inputs and outputs, it is possible to use divide-and-conquer to turn one big job into many independent little ones. This is an ideal situation for speedup and scaleup. Partitioned data is the key to partitioned execution.

Data Partitioning. Partitioning a relation involves distributing its tuples over several disks. Data partitioning has its origins in centralized systems that had to partition files, either because the file was too big for one disk, or because the file access rate could not be supported by a single disk. Distributed databases use data partitioning when they place relation fragments at different network sites [23]. Data par-

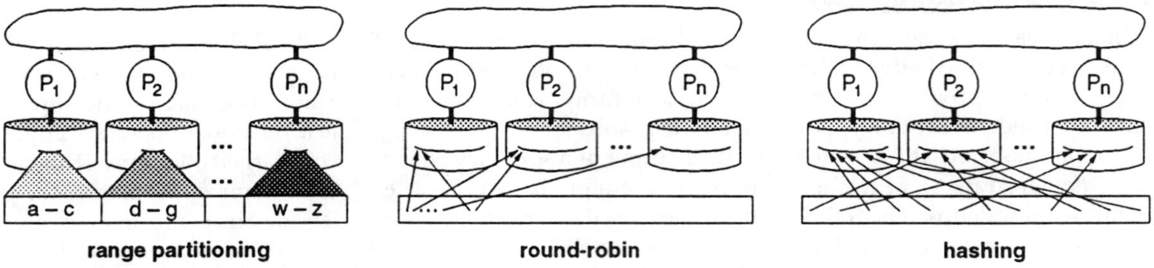

Figure 7.
The three basic partitioning schemes. Range partitioning maps contiguous attribute ranges of a relation to various disks. Round-robin partitioning maps the i'th tuple to disk i **mod** n. Hashed partitioning maps each tuple to a disk location based on a hash function. Each of these schemes spreads data among a collection of disks, allowing parallel disk access and parallel processing.

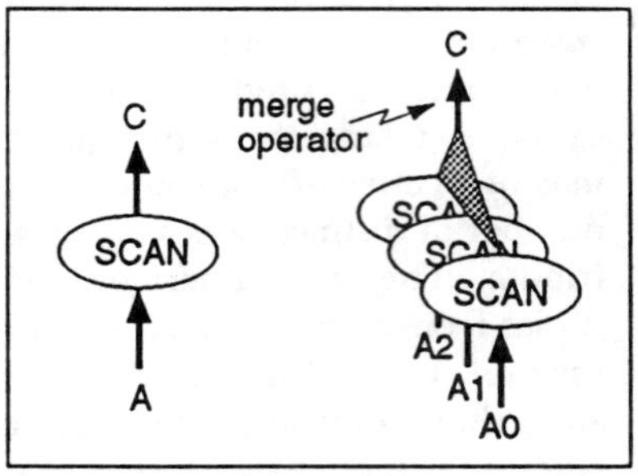

Figure 8.
Partitioned data parallelism. A simple relational dataflow graph showing a relational scan (project and select) decomposed into three scans on three partitions of the input stream or relation. These three scans send their output to a merge node that produces a single data stream.

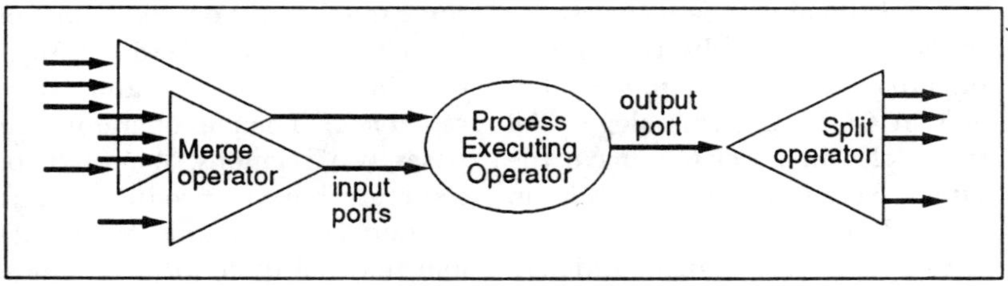

Figure 9.
Merging the inputs and partitioning the output of an operator. A relational dataflow graph showing a relational operator's inputs being merged to a sequential stream per port. The operator's output is being decomposed by a split operator in several independent streams. Each stream may be a duplicate or a partitioning of the operator output stream into many disjoint streams. With the split and merge operators, a web of simple sequential dataflow nodes can be connected to form a parallel execution plan.

titioning allows parallel database systems to exploit the I/O bandwidth of multiple disks by reading and writing them in parallel. This approach provides I/O bandwidth superior to RAID-style systems without needing any specialized hardware [22, 24].

The simplest partitioning strategy distributes tuples among the fragments in a *round-robin* fashion. This is the partitioned version of the classic entry-sequence file. Round-robin partitioning is excellent if all applications want to access the relation by sequentially scanning all of it on each query. The problem with round-robin partitioning is that applications frequently want to associatively access tuples, meaning that the application wants to find all the tuples having a particular attribute value. The SQL query looking for the Smiths in the phone book shown in Figure 6 is an example of an associative search.

Hash partitioning is ideally suited for applications that want only sequential and associative access to the data. Tuples are placed by applying a *hashing* function to an attribute of each tuple. The function specifies the placement of the tuple on a particular disk. Associative access to the tuples with a specific attribute value can be directed to a single disk, avoiding the overhead of starting queries on multiple disks. Hash partitioning mechanisms are provided by Arbre, Bubba, Gamma, and Teradata.

Database systems pay considerable attention to clustering related data together in physical storage. If a set of tuples is routinely accessed together, the database system attempts to store them on the same physical page. For example, if the Smiths of the phone book are routinely accessed in alphabetical order, then they should be stored on pages in that order, these pages should be clustered together on disk to allow sequential prefetching and other optimizations. Clustering is very application-specific. For example, tuples describing nearby streets should be clustered together in geographic databases, tuples describing the line items of an invoice should be clustered with the invoice tuple in an inventory control application.

Hashing tends to randomize data rather than cluster it. *Range partitioning* clusters tuples with similar attributes together in the same partition. It is good for sequential and associative access, and is also good for clustering data. Figure 7 shows range partitioning based on lexicographic order, but any clustering algorithm is possible. Range partitioning derives its name from the typical SQL range queries such as

latitude BETWEEN 38° AND 39°

Arbre, Bubba, Gamma, Oracle, and Tandem provide range partitioning.

The problem with range partitioning is that it risks *data skew*, where all the data is placed in one partition, and *execution skew* in which all the execution occurs in one partition. Hashing and round-robin are less susceptible to these skew problems. Range partitioning can minimize skew by picking non-uniformly-distributed partitioning criteria. Bubba uses this concept by considering the access frequency *(heat)* of each tuple when creating partitions of a relation; the goal being to balance the frequency with which each partition is accessed (its *temperature*) rather than the actual number of tuples on each disk (its volume) [6].

Table 1.
Sample Split Operators.
Each split operator maps tuples to a set of output streams (ports of other processes) depending on the range value (predicate) of the input tuple. The split operator on the left is for the relation A scan in Figure 10, while the table on the right is for the relation B scan. The tables partition the tuples among three data streams.

Relation A Scan Split Operator		Relation B Scan Split Operator	
Predicate	**Destination Process**	**Predicate**	**Destination Process**
"A-H"	(CPU #5, Process #3, Port #0)	"A-H"	(CPU #5, Process #3, Port #1)
"I-Q"	(CPU #7, Process #8, Port #0)	"I-Q"	(CPU #7, Process #8, Port #1)
"R-Z"	(CPU #2, Process #2, Port #0)	"R-Z"	(CPU #2, Process #2, Port #1)

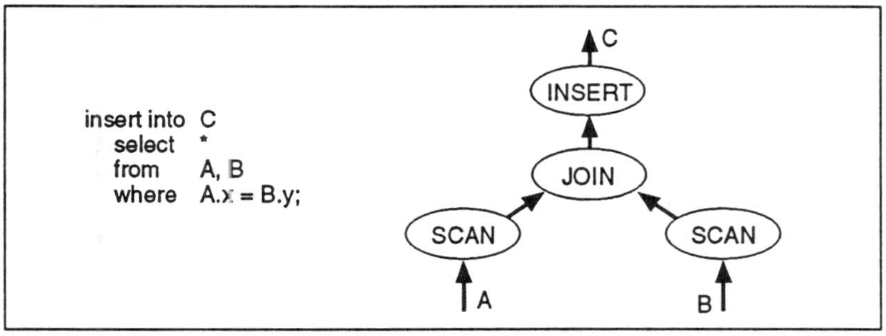

Figure 10.
A simple SQL query and the associated relational query graph. The query specifies that a join is to be performed between relations A and B by comparing the x attribute of each tuple from the A relation with the y attribute value of each tuple of the B relation. For each pair of tuples that satisfy the predicate, a result tuple is formed from all the attributes of both tuples. This result tuple is then added to the result relation C. The associated logical query graph (as might be produced by a query optimizer) shows a tree of operators, one for the join, one for the insert, and one for scanning each input relation.

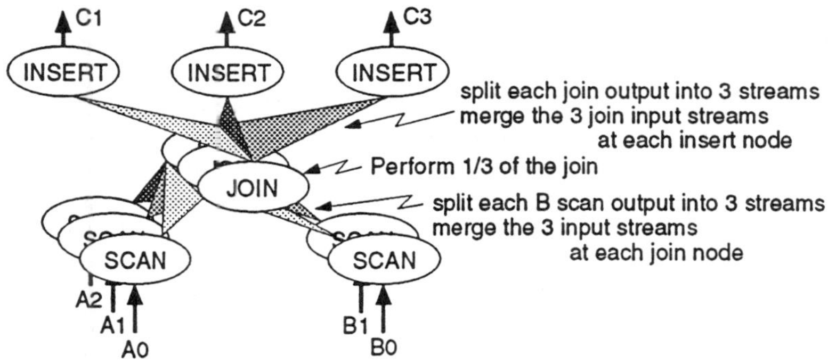

Figure 11.
A simple relational dataflow graph. It shows two relational scans (project and select) consuming two input relations, A and B and feeding their outputs to a join operator that in turn produces a data stream C.

While partitioning is a simple concept that is easy to implement, it raises several new physical database design issues. Each relation must now have a partitioning strategy and a set of disk fragments. Increasing the degree of partitioning usually reduces the response time for an individual query and increases the overall throughput of the system. For sequential scans, the response time decreases because more processors and disks are used to execute the query. For associative scans, the response time improves because fewer tuples are stored at each node and hence the size of the index that must be searched decreases.

There is a point beyond which further partitioning actually increases the response time of a query. This point occurs when the cost of starting a query on a node becomes a significant fraction of the actual execution time [6, 11].

Parallelism Within Relational Operators. Data partitioning is the first step in partitioned execution of relational dataflow graphs. The basic idea is to use parallel data streams instead of writing new parallel operators (programs). This approach enables the use of unmodified, existing sequential routines to execute the relational operators in parallel. Each relational operator has a set of *input ports* on which input tuples arrive and an *output* port to which the operator's output stream is sent. The parallel dataflow works by partitioning and merging data streams into these sequential ports. This approach allows the use of existing sequential relational operators to execute in parallel.

Consider a scan of a relation, A, that has been partitioned across three disks into fragments A0, A1, and A2. This scan can be implemented as three scan operators that send their output to a common merge operator. The merge operator produces a single output data stream to the application or to the next relational operator. The parallel query executor creates the three scan processes shown in Figure 8 and directs them to take their inputs from three different sequential input streams (A0, A1, A2). It also directs them to send their outputs to a common merge node. Each scan can run on an independent processor and disk. So the first basic parallelizing operator is a *merge* that can combine several parallel data streams into a single sequential stream.

The merge operator tends to focus data on one spot. If a multistage parallel operation is to be done in parallel, a single data stream must be split into several independent streams. A *split operator* is used to partition or replicate the stream of tuples produced by a relational operator. A split operator defines a mapping from one or more attribute values of the output tuples to a set of destination processes (see Figure 9).

As an example, consider the two split operators shown in Table 1 in conjunction with the SQL query shown in Figure 10. Assume that three processes are used to execute the join operator, and that five other processes execute the two scan operators—three scanning partitions of relation A while two scan partitions of relation B. Each of the three relation A scan nodes will have the same split operator, sending all tuples between "A-H" to port 1 of join process 0, all between "I-Q" to port 1 of join process 1, and all between "R-Z" to port 1 of join process 2. Similarly the two relation B scan nodes have the same split operator except that their outputs are merged by port 1 (not port 0) of each join process. Each join process sees a sequential input stream of A tuples from the port 0 merge (the left-scan nodes) and another sequential stream of B tuples from the port 1 merge (the right-scan nodes). The outputs of each join are, in turn, split into three streams based on the partitioning criterion of relation C.

To clarify this example, consider the first join process in Figure 11 (processor 5, process 3, ports 0 and 1 in Table 1). It will receive all the relation A "A-H" tuples from the three relation A scan operators merged as a single stream on port 0, and will get all the "A-H" tuples from relation B merged as a single stream on port 1. It will join them using a hash-join, sort-merge join, or even a nested join if the tuples arrive in the proper order.

If each of these processes is on an independent processor with an independent disk, there will be little interference among them. Such dataflow designs are a natural application for shared-nothing machine architectures.

The split operator in Table 1 is just an example. Other split operators might duplicate the input stream, or partition it round-robin, or partition it by hash. The partitioning function can be an arbitrary program. Gamma, Volcano, and Tandem use this approach [14]. It has several advantages including the automatic parallelism of any new operator added to the system, plus support for many kinds of parallelism.

The split and merge operators have flow control and buffering built into them. This prevents one operator from getting too far ahead in the computation. When a split-operator's output buffers fill, it stalls the relational operator until the data target requests more output.

For simplicity, these examples have been stated in terms of an operator per process. But it is entirely possible to place several operators within a process to get coarser grained parallelism. The fundamental idea though is to build a self-pacing dataflow graph and distribute it in a shared-nothing machine in a way that minimizes interference.

Specialized Parallel Relational Operators. Some algorithms for relational operators are especially appropriate for parallel execution, either because they minimize data flow, or because they better tolerate data and execution skew. Improved algorithms have been found for most of the relational operators. The evolution of join operator algorithms is sketched here as an example of these improved algorithms.

Recall that the join operator combines two relations, A and B, to produce a third relation containing all tuple pairs from A and B with matching attribute values. The conventional way of computing the join is to sort both A and B into new relations ordered by the join attribute. These two intermediate relations are then compared in sorted order, and matching tuples are inserted in the output stream. This algorithm is called *sort-merge* join.

Many optimizations of sort-merge join are possible, but since sort has execution cost *nlog(n)*, sort-merge join has an *nlog(n)* execution cost. Sort-merge join works well in a parallel dataflow environment unless there is data skew. In case of data skew, some sort partitions may be much larger than others. This in turn creates execution skew and limits speedup and scaleup. These skew problems do not appear in centralized sort-merge joins.

Hash-join is an alternative to sort-merge join. It has linear execution cost rather than *nlog(n)* execution cost, and it is more resistant to data skew. It is superior to sort-merge join unless the input streams are already in sorted order. Hash join works as follows. Each of the relations A and B are first hash partitioned on the join attribute. A hash partition of relation A is hashed into memory. The corresponding partition of table relation B is scanned, and each tuple is compared against the main-memory hash table for the A partition. If there is a match, the pair of tuples are sent to the output stream. Each pair of hash partitions is compared in this way.

The hash join algorithm breaks a big join into many little joins. If the hash function is good and if the data skew is not too bad, then there will be little variance in the hash bucket size. In these cases hash-join is a linear-time join algorithm with linear speedup and scaleup. Many optimizations of the parallel hash-join algorithm have been discovered over the last decade. In pathological skew cases, when many or all tuples have the same attribute value, one bucket may contain all the tuples. In these cases no algorithm is known to speedup or scaleup.

The hash-join example shows that new parallel algorithms can improve the performance of relational operators. This is a fruitful research area [4, 8, 18, 20, 25, 26, 38, 39]. Although parallelism can be obtained from conventional sequential relational algorithms by using split and merge operators, we expect that many new algorithms will be discovered in the future.

The State of the Art

Teradata

Teradata quietly pioneered many of the ideas presented in this article. Since 1978 they have been building shared-nothing highly-parallel SQL systems based on commodity microprocessors, disks, and memories. Teradata systems act as SQL servers to client programs operating on conventional computers.

Teradata systems may have over 1,000 processors and many thousands of disks. The Teradata processors are functionally divided into two groups: Interface Processors (IFPs) and Access Module Processors (AMPs). The IFPs handle communication with the host, query parsing and optimization, and coordination of AMPs during query execution. The AMPs are responsible for executing queries. Each AMP typically has several disks and a large memory cache. IFPs and AMPs are interconnected by a dual redundant, tree-shaped interconnect called the Y-net [33].

Each relation is hash partitioned over a subset of the AMPs. When a tuple is inserted into a relation, a hash function is applied to the primary key of the tuple to select an AMP for storage. Once a tuple arrives at an AMP, a second hash function determines the tuple's placement in its fragment of the relation. The tuples in each fragment are in hash-key order. Given a value for the key attribute, it is possible to locate the tuple in a single AMP. The AMP examines its cache, and if the tuple is not present, fetches it in a single disk read. Hash secondary indices are also supported.

Hashing is used to split the outputs of relational operators into intermediate relations. Join operators are executed using a parallel sort-merge algorithm. Rather than using pipelined parallel execution, during the execution of a query, each operator is run to completion on all participating nodes before the next operator is initiated.

Teradata has installed many systems containing over 100 processors and hundreds of disks. These systems demonstrate near-linear speedup and scaleup on relational queries, and far exceed the speed of traditional mainframes in their ability to process large (terabyte) databases.

Tandem NonStop SQL

The Tandem NonStop SQL system is composed of processor clusters interconnected via 4-plexed fiber-optic rings. Unlike most other systems discussed in this article, the Tandem systems run the applications on the same processors and operating system as the database servers. There is no front-end/back-end distinction between programs and machines. The systems are configured at a disk per MIPS, so each 10-MIPS processor has about 10 disks. Disks are typically duplexed [2]. Each disk is served by a set of processes managing a large shared RAM cache, a set of locks, and log records for the data on that disk pair. Considerable effort is spent on optimizing sequential scans by prefetching large units, and by filtering and manipulating the tuples with SQL predicates at these disk servers. This minimizes traffic on the shared interconnection network.

Relations may be range partitioned across multiple disks. Entry-sequenced, relative, and B-tree organizations are supported. Only B-tree secondary indices are supported. Nested join, sort-merge join, and hash join algorithms are provided. Parallelization of operators in a query plan is achieved by inserting split and merge operators between operator nodes in the query tree. Scans, aggregates, joins, updates, and deletes are executed in parallel. In addition, several utilities use parallelism (e.g., load, reorganize, . . .) [31, 39].

Tandem systems are primary designed for on-line transaction processing (OLTP)—running many simple transactions against a large shared database. Beyond the parallelism inherent in running many independent transactions in parallel, the main parallelism feature for OLTP is parallel index update. SQL relations typically have five indices on them, although it is not uncommon to see 10 indices on a relation. These indices speed reads, but slow down inserts, updates, and deletes. By doing the index maintenance in parallel, the maintenance time for multiple indices can be held almost constant if the indices are spread among many processors and disks.

Overall, the Tandem systems demonstrate near-linear scaleup on transaction processing workloads, and near-linear speedup and scaleup on large relational queries [10, 31].

Gamma

The current version of Gamma runs on a 32-node Intel iPSC/2 Hypercube with a disk attached to each node. In addition to round-robin, range and hash partitioning, Gamma also provides hybrid-range partitioning that combines the best features of the hash and range partitioning strategies [12]. Once a relation has been partitioned, Gamma provides both clustered and nonclustered indices on either the partitioning or nonpartitioning attributes. The indices are implemented as B-trees or hash tables.

Gamma uses split and merge operators to execute relational algebra operators using both parallelism and pipelining [9]. Sort-merge and three different hash join methods are supported [7]. Near-linear speedup and scaleup for relational queries has been measured on this architecture [9, 25, 26].

The Super Database Computer

The Super Database Computer (SDC) project at the University of Tokyo presents an interesting contrast to other database systems [16, 20]. SDC takes a combined hardware and software approach to the performance problem. The basic unit, called a processing module (PM), consists of one or more processors on a shared memory. These processors are augmented by a special-purpose sorting engine that sorts at high speed (3MB/second at present), and by a disk subsystem [19]. Clusters of processing modules are connected via an omega network that provides both non-blocking NxN interconnect and some dynamic routing minimize skewed data distribution during hash joins. The SDC is designed to scale to thousands of PMs, and so considerable attention is paid to the problem of data skew.

Data is partitioned among the PMs by hashing. The SDC software includes a unique operating system, and a relational database query executor. The SDC is a shared-nothing design with a software dataflow architecture. This is consistent with our assertion that current parallel database machines systems use conventional hardware. But the special-purpose design of the omega network and of the hardware sorter clearly contradict the thesis that special-purpose hardware is not a good investment of development resources. Time will tell whether these special-purpose components offer better price performance or peak performance than shared-nothing designs built of conventional hardware.

Bubba

The Bubba prototype was implemented using a 40-node FLEX/32 multiprocessor with 40 disks [4]. Although this is a shared-memory multiprocessor, Bubba was designed as a shared-nothing system and the shared-memory is only used for message passing. Nodes are divided into three groups: Interface Processors for communicating with external host processors and coordinating query execution; Intelligent Repositories for data storage and query execution; and Checkpoint/Logging Repositories. While Bubba also uses partitioning as a storage mechanism (both range and hash partitioning mechanisms are provided) and dataflow processing mechanisms, Bubba is unique in several ways. First, Bubba uses FAD rather than SQL as its interface language. FAD is an extended-relational persistent programming language. FAD provides support for complex objects via several type constructors including shared subobjects, set-oriented data manipulation primitives, and more traditional language constructs. The FAD compiler is responsible for detecting operations that can be executed in parallel according to how the data objects being accessed are partitioned. Program execution is performed using a dataflow execution paradigm. The task of compiling and parallelizing a FAD program is significantly more difficult than parallelizing a relational query. Another Bubba feature is its use of a single-level store mechanism in which the persistent database at each node is mapped to the virtual memory address space of each process executing at the node. This is in contrast to the traditional approach of files and pages. Similar mechanisms are used in IBM's AS400 mapping of SQL databases into virtual memory, HP's mapping of the Image Database into the operating system virtual address space, and Mach's mapped file [34] mechanism. This approach simplified the implementation of the upper levels of the Bubba software.

Other Systems

Other parallel database system prototypes include XPRS [30], Volcano [14], Arbre [21], and the PERSIST project under development at IBM Research Labs in Hawthorne and Almaden. While both Volcano and XPRS are implemented on shared-memory multiprocessors, XPRS is unique in its exploitation of the availability of massive shared-memory in its design. In addition, XPRS is based on several innovative techniques for obtaining extremely high performance and availability.

Recently, the Oracle database system has been implemented atop a 64-node nCUBE shared-nothing system. The resulting system is the first to demonstrate more than 1,000 transactions per second on the industry-standard TPC-B benchmark. This is far in excess of Oracle's performance on conventional mainframe systems—both in peak performance and in price/performance [13].

The NCR Corporation has announced the 3600 and 3700 product lines that employ shared-nothing architectures running System V R4 of Unix on Intel 486 and 586 processors. The interconnection network for the 3600 product line uses an enhanced Y-Net licensed from Teradata while the 3700 is based on a new multistage interconnection network being developed jointly by NCR and Teradata. Two software offerings have been announced. The first, a port of the Teradata software to a Unix environment, is targeted toward the decision-support marketplace. The second, based on a parallelization of the Sybase DBMS, is intended primarily for transaction processing workloads.

Database Machines and Grosch's Law

Today shared-nothing database machines have the best peak performance and best price performance available. When compared to traditional mainframes, the Tandem system scales linearly well beyond the largest reported mainframes on the TPC-A transaction processing benchmark. Its price/performance on these benchmarks is three times cheaper than the comparable mainframe numbers. Oracle on an nCUBE has the highest reported TPC-B numbers, and has very competitive price performance [13, 36]. These benchmarks demonstrate linear scaleup on transaction processing benchmarks.

Gamma, Tandem, and Teradata have demonstrated linear speedup and scaleup on complex relational database benchmarks. They scale well beyond the size of the largest mainframes. Their performance and price performance is generally superior to mainframe systems.

These observations defy Grosch's law. In the 1960s, Herb Grosch observed that there is an economy-of-scale in computing. At that time, expensive computers were much more powerful than inexpensive computers. This gave rise to super-linear speedups and scaleups. The current pricing of mainframes at \$25,000/MIPS and \$1,000/MB of RAM reflects this view. Meanwhile, microprocessors are selling for \$250/MIPS and \$100/MB of RAM.

By combining hundreds or thousands of these small systems, one can build an incredibly powerful database machine for much less money than the cost of a modest mainframe. For database problems, the near-linear speedup and scaleup of these shared-nothing machines allows them to outperform current shared-memory and shared disk mainframes.

Grosch's law no longer applies to database and transaction processing problems. There is no economy of scale. At best, one can expect linear speedup and scaleup of performance and price/performance. Fortunately, shared-nothing database architectures achieve this near-linear performance.

Future Directions and Research Problems

Mixing Batch and OLTP Queries

The second section of this article, "Basic Techniques for Parallel Database Machine Implementation", concentrated on the basic techniques used for processing complex relational queries in a parallel database system. Concurrently running a mix of both simple and complex queries concurrently presents several unsolved problems.

One problem is that large relational queries tend to acquire many locks and tend to hold them for a relatively long time. This prevents concurrent updates of the data by simple on-line transactions. Two solutions are currently offered: give the ad-hoc queries a fuzzy picture of the database, not locking any data as they browse it. Such a "dirty-read" solution is not acceptable for some applications. Several systems offer a versioning mechanism that gives readers a consistent (old) version of the database while updators are allowed to create newer versions of objects. Other, perhaps better, solutions for this problem may also exist.

Priority scheduling is another mixed-workload problem. Batch jobs have a tendency to monopolize the processor, flood the memory cache, and make large demands on the I/O subsystem. It is up to the underlying operating system to quantize and limit the resources used by such batch jobs to ensure short response times and low variance in response times for short transactions. A particularly difficult problem is the *priority inversion problem,* in which a low-priority client makes a request to a high-priority server. The server must run at high priority because it is managing critical resources. Given this, the work of the low-priority client is effectively promoted to high priority when the low-priority request is serviced by the high-priority server. There have been several ad-hoc attempts at solving this problem, but considerably more work is needed.

Parallel Query Optimization

Current database query optimizers do not consider all possible plans when optimizing a relational query. While cost models for relational queries running on a single processor are now well-understood [27] they still depend on cost estimators that are a guess at best. Some dynamically select from among several plans at run time depending on, for example, the amount of physical memory actually available and the cardinalities of the intermediate results [15]. To date, no query optimizers consider all the parallel algorithms for each operator and all the query tree organizations. More work is needed in this area.

Another optimization problem relates to highly skewed value distributions. Data skew can lead to high variance in the size of intermediate relations, leading to both poor query plan cost estimates and sublinear speedup. Solutions to this problem are an area of active research [17, 20, 37, 38].

Application Program Parallelism

The parallel database systems offer parallelism within the database system. Missing are tools to structure application programs to take advantage of parallelism inherent in these parallel systems. While automatic parallelization of applications programs written in COBOL may not be feasible, library packages to facilitate explicitly parallel application programs are needed. Ideally the SPLIT and MERGE operators could be packaged so that applications could benefit from them.

Physical Database Design

For a given database and workload there are many possible indexing and partitioning combinations. Database design tools are needed to help the database administrator select among these many design options. Such tools might accept as input a description of the queries comprising the workload, their frequency of execution, statistical information about the relations in the database, and a description of the processors and disks. The resulting output would suggest a partitioning strategy for each relation plus the indices to be created on each relation. Steps in this direction are beginning to appear.

Current algorithms partition relations using the values of a single attribute. For example, geographic records could be partitioned by longitude or latitude. Partitioning on longitude allows selections for a longitude range to be localized to a limited number of nodes, selections on latitude must be sent to all the nodes. While this is acceptable in a small configuration, it is not acceptable in a system with thousands of processors. Additional research is needed on multidimensional partitioning and search algorithms.

On-line Data Reorganization and Utilities

Loading, reorganizing, or dumping a terabyte database at a megabyte per second takes over 12 days and nights. Clearly parallelism is needed if utilities are to complete within a few hours or days. Even then, it will be essential that the data be available while the utilities are operating. In the SQL world, typical utilities create indices, add or drop attributes, add constraints, and physically reorganize the data, changing its clustering.

One unexplored and difficult problem is how to process database utility commands while the system remains operational and the data remains available for concurrent reads and writes by others. The fundamental properties of such algorithms are that they must be *online* (operate without making data unavailable), *incremental* (operate on parts of a large database), *parallel* (exploit parallel processors), and *recoverable* (allow the operation to be canceled and return to the old state).

Summary and Conclusions

Like most applications, database systems want cheap, fast hardware. Today that means commodity processors, memories, and disks. Consequently, the hardware concept of a *database machine* built of exotic hardware is inappropriate for current technology. On the other hand, the availability of fast microprocessors, and small inexpensive disks packaged as standard inexpensive but fast computers is an ideal platform for *parallel database systems*. A shared-nothing architecture is relatively straightforward to implement and, more importantly, has demonstrated both speedup and scaleup to hundreds of processors. Furthermore, shared-nothing architectures actually simplify the software implementation. If the software techniques of data partitioning, dataflow, and intra-operator parallelism are employed, the task of converting an existing database management system to a highly parallel one becomes relatively straightforward. Finally, there are certain applications (e.g., data mining in terabyte databases) that require the computational and I/O resources available only from a parallel architecture.

While the successes of both commercial products and prototypes demonstrate the viability of highly parallel database machines, several research issues remain unsolved including techniques for mixing ad-hoc queries with on-line transaction processing without seriously limiting transaction throughput, improved optimizers for parallel queries, tools for physical database design, on-line database reorganization, and algorithms for handling relations with highly skewed data distributions. Some application domains are not well supported by the relational data model. It appears that a new class of database systems based on an object-oriented data model is needed. Such systems pose a host of interesting research problems that require further examination. ■

References

1. Alexander, W., et al. Process and dataflow control in distributed data-intensive systems. In *Proceedings of ACM SIGMOD Conference* (Chicago, Ill., June 1988) ACM, NY, 1988.
2. Bitton, D. and Gray, J. Disk shadowing. In *Proceedings of the Fourteenth International Conference on Very Large Data Bases* (Los Angeles, Calif., August, 1988).
3. Boral, H. and DeWitt, D. Database machines: An idea whose time has passed? A critique of the future of database machines. In *Proceedings of the 1983 Workshop on Database Machines.* H.-O. Leilich and M. Missikoff, Eds., Springer-Verlag, 1983.
4. Boral, H. et al. Prototyping Bubba: A highly parallel database system. *IEEE Knowl. Data Eng. 2,* 1, (Mar. 1990).
5. Codd, E.F. A relational model of data for large shared databanks. *Commun. ACM 13,* 6 (June 1970).
6. Copeland, G., Alexander, W., Boughter, E., and Keller, T. Data placement in Bubba. In *Proceedings of ACM-SIGMOD International Conference on Management of Data* (Chicago, May 1988).
7. DeWitt, D.J., Katz, R., Olken, F., Shapiro, D., Stonebraker, M. and Wood, D. Implementation techniques for main memory database systems. In *Proceedings of the 1984 SIGMOD Conference,* (Boston, Mass., June, 1984).
8. DeWitt, D., et al. GAMMA—A high performance dataflow database machine. In *Proceedings of the 1986 VLDB Conference* (Japan, August 1986).
9. DeWitt, D., et al. The Gamma database machine project. *IEEE Knowl. Data Eng. 2,* 1 (Mar. 1990).
10. Engelbert, S, Gray, J., Kocher, T., and Stah, P. A benchmark of non-stop SQL Release 2 demonstrating near-linear speedup and scaleup on large databases. Tandem Computers, Technical Report 89.4, Tandem Part No. 27469, May 1989.
11. Ghandeharizadeh, S., and DeWitt, D.J. Performance analysis of alternative declustering strategies. In *Proceedings of the Sixth International Conference on Data Engineering* (Feb. 1990).
12. Ghandeharizadeh, S., and Dewitt, D.J. Hybrid-range partitioning strategy: A new declustering strategy for multiprocessor database machines. In *Proceedings of the Sixth International Conference on Very Large Data Bases,* (Melbourne, Australia, Aug. 1990).
13. Gibbs, J. Massively parallel systems, rethinking computing for business and science. *Oracle 6,* 1 (Dec. 1991).
14. Graefe, G. Encapsulation of parallelism in the Volcano query processing system. In *Proceedings of 1990*

ACM-SIGMOD International Conference on Management of Data (May 1990).

15. Graefe, G., and Ward, K. Dynamic query evaluation plans. In *Proceedings of the 1989 SIGMOD Conference*, (Portland, Ore., June 1989).
16. Hirano, M.S. et al. Architecture of SDC, the super database computer. In *Proceedings of JSPP '90*. 1990.
17. Hua, K.A. and Lee, C. Handling data skew in multiprocessor database computers using partition tuning. In *Proceedings of the Seventeenth International Conference on Very Large Data Bases*. (Barcelona, Spain, Sept. 1991).
18. Kitsuregawa, M., Tanaka, H., and Moto-oka, T. Application of hash to data base machine and its architecture. *New Generation Computing 1*, 1 (1983).
19. Kitsuregawa, M., Yang, W., and Fushimi, S. Evaluation of 18-stage pipeline hardware sorter. In *Proceedings of the Third International Conference on Data Engineering* (Feb. 1987).
20. Kitsuregawa, M., and Ogawa, Y. A new parallel hash join method with robustness for data skew in super database computer (SDC). In *Proceedings of the Sixteenth International Conference on Very Large Data Bases*. (Melbourne, Australia, Aug. 1990).
21. Lorie, R., Daudenarde, J., Hallmark, G., Stamos, J., and Young, H. Adding intra-transaction parallelism to an existing DBMS: Early experience. *IEEE Data Engineering Newsletter 12*, 1 (Mar. 1989).
22. Patterson, D. A., Gibson, G. and Katz, R. H. A case for redundant arrays of inexpensive disks (RAID). In *Proceedings of the ACM-SIGMOD International Conference on Management of Data*. (Chicago, May 1988).
23. Ries, D. and Epstein, R. Evaluation of distribution criteria for distributed database systems. UBC/ERL Technical Report M78/22, UC Berkeley, May, 1978.
24. Salem, K. and Garcia-Molina, H. Disk-striping. Department of Computer Science, Princeton University Technical Report EEDS-TR-322-84, Princeton, N.J., Dec. 1984.
25. Schneider, D. and DeWitt, D. A performance evaluation of four parallel join algorithms in a shared-nothing multiprocessor environment. In *Proceedings of the 1989 SIGMOD Conference* (Portland, Ore., June 1989).
26. Schneider, D. and DeWitt, D. Tradeoffs in processing complex join queries via hashing in multiprocessor database machines. In *Proceedings of the Sixteenth International Conference on Very Large Data Bases*. (Melbourne, Australia, Aug., 1990).
27. Selinger P. G., et al. Access path selection in a relational database management system. In *Proceedings of the 1979 SIGMOD Conference* (Boston, Mass., May 1979).
28. Stonebraker, M. Muffin: A distributed database machine. ERL Technical Report UCB/ERL M79/28, University of California at Berkeley, May 1979.
29. Stonebraker, M. The case for shared nothing. *Database Eng. 9*, 1 (1986).
30. Stonebraker, M., Katz, R., Patterson, D., and Ousterhout, J. The design of XPRS. In *Proceedings of the Fourteenth International Conference on Very Large Data Bases*. (Los Angeles, Calif., Aug. 1988).
31. Tandem Database Group. NonStop SQL, a distributed, high-performance, high-reliability implementation of SQL. Workshop on High Performance Transaction Systems, Asilomar, CA, Sept. 1987.
32. Tandem Performance Group. A benchmark of non-stop SQL on the debit credit transaction. In *Proceedings of the 1988 SIGMOD Conference* (Chicago, Ill., June 1988).
33. Teradata Corporation. DBC/1012 Data Base Computer Concepts & Facilities. Document No. C02-0001-00, 1983.
34. Tevanian, A., et al. A Unix interface for shared memory and memory mapped files under Mach. Dept. of Computer Science Technical Report, Carnegie Mellon University, July, 1987.
35. Thakkar, S.S. and Sweiger, M. Performance of an OLTP application on symmetry multiprocessor system. In *Proceedings of the Seventeenth Annual International Symposium on Computer Architecture*. (Seattle, Wash., May, 1990).
36. *The Performance Handbook for Database and Transaction Processing Systems*. J. Gray, Ed., Morgan Kaufmann, San Mateo, Ca., 1991.
37. Walton, C.B., Dale, A.G., and Jenevein, R.M. A taxonomy and performance model of data skew effects in parallel joins. In *Proceedings of the Seventeenth International Conference on Very Large Data Bases*. (Barcelona, Spain, Sept. 1991).
38. Wolf, J.L., Dias, D.M., and Yu, P.S. An effective algorithm for parallelizing sort-merge joins in the presence of data skew. In *Proceedings of the Second International Symposium on Parallel and Distributed Systems*. (Dublin, Ireland, July, 1990).
39. Zeller, H.J. and Gray, J. Adaptive hash joins for a multiprogramming environment. In *Proceedings of the 1990 VLDB Conference* (Australia, Aug. 1990).

CR Categories and Subject Descriptors: B.5.1 [**Register-Transfer-Level Implementation**]: Design-style (e.g., parallel, pipelined, special-purpose); C.1.2 [**Computer Systems Organization**]: Processor Architectures—*Multiple Data Stream Architectures (Multiprocessors)*; F.1.2 [**Computation by Abstract Devices**]: Modes of Computation—*Parallelism*; H.2.1 [**Information Systems**]: Database Management—*Logical design*; H.2.8 [**Information Systems**]: Database Management—*Database Applications*; H.3 [**Information Systems**]: Information Storage and Retrieval

General Terms: Design, Measurement

Additional Keywords and Phrases: Parallelism, parallel database systems, parallel processing systems.

About the Authors:

DAVID DEWITT is a professor in the Computer Sciences Department at the University of Wisconsin. His current research interests include parallel database systems, object-oriented database systems, and database performance evaluation. **Author's Present Address:** Computer Sciences Department, University of Wisconsin, 1210 West Dayton Street, Madison, WI 53706; email: dewitt@cs.wisc.edu

JIM GRAY is a staff member with the Digital Equipment Corporation. His current research interests include databases, transaction processing, and computer architecture. **Author's Present Address:** San Francisco Systems Center, Digital Equipment Corporation, 455 Market Street—7th Floor, San Francisco, CA 94105-2403; email: gray@sfbay.enet.dec.com

This research was partially supported by the Defense Advanced Research Projects Agency under contract N00039-86-C-0578, by the National Science Foundation under grant DCR-8512862, and by research grants from Digital Equipment Corporation, IBM, NCR, Tandem, and Intel Scientific Computers.

Parallelism in Relational Data Base Systems: Architectural Issues and Design Approaches

Hamid Pirahesh, C. Mohan, Josephine Cheng*, T.S. Liu*, Pat Selinger

Data Base Technology Institute, IBM Almaden Research Center, San Jose, CA 95120, USA
{pirahesh, mohan, pat}@ibm.com

*Data Base Technology Institute, IBM Santa Teresa Laboratory, San Jose, CA 95150, USA

Abstract With current systems, some important complex queries may take days to complete because of: (1) the volume of data to be processed, (2) limited aggregate resources. Introducing parallelism addresses the first problem. Cheaper, but powerful computing resources solve the second problem. According to a survey by Brodie,[1] only 10% of computerized data is in data bases. This is an argument for both more variety and volume of data to be moved into data base systems. We conjecture that the primary reasons for this low percentage are that data base management systems (DBMSs) still need to provide far greater functionality and improved performance compared to a combination of application programs and file systems. This paper addresses the issues and solutions relating to *intra-query* parallelism in a relational DBMS supporting SQL. Instead of focussing only on a few algorithms for a subset of the problems, we provide a broad framework for the study of the numerous issues that need to be addressed in supporting parallelism efficiently and flexibly. We also discuss the impact that parallelization of complex queries has on short transactions which have stringent response time constraints. The pros and cons of the *shared nothing*, *shared disks* and *shared everything* architectures for parallelism are enumerated. The impact of parallelism on a number of components of an industrial-strength DBMS are pointed out. The different stages of query processing during which parallelism may be gainfully employed are identified. The interactions between parallelism and the traditional systems' pipelining technique are analyzed. Finally, the performance implications of parallelizing a specific complex query are studied. This gives us a range of sample points for different parameters of a parallel system architecture, namely, I/O and communication bandwidth as a function of aggregate MIPS.

1. Introduction

The widespread adoption of the easy-to-use products of the relational technology has led to greater expectations on the part of the data base user community. Support for high level ad hoc query languages like SQL has replaced the weeks or months of coding required in the case of the prerelational systems with a few days of coding in order to produce programs which access the data base management system (DBMS) to generate complex reports. Along with this has come the expectation that the responses to the queries should also be received faster than before, especially because the queries may be posed by a user at a terminal rather than by a batch program, as in the past. Coupled to this is the fact that the volumes of data to be dealt with also grow by leaps and bounds as the years go by and computerization goes into full swing. Already there are customers who would like to store more than 100 gigabytes of data in a *single table* and keep it all online all the time! The amount of data kept in a single large relational data base is expected to be in the terabyte range in the coming decade. These trends cause the queries to become *data-intensive*. Furthermore, there is growing emphasis on supporting newer, nonstandard data base applications like VLSI CAD, Computer Aided Software Engineering (CASE), etc., where the volumes of data are enormous compared to the traditional business data processing arena [HaSS88].

With competition intensifying in various sectors of the economy (due to, e.g., deregulation in the airline

Reprinted from *Second Int'l Symp. Databases in Parallel and Distributed Systems,* 1990, pp. 4-29.

0-8186-5452-X/94 $3.00 © 1990 IEEE

industry), and direct-mail marketing becoming more and more common, the complexity of the queries that are being posed is also growing. Ad hoc interactions with the new generation DBMSs are commonly performed through high-level user interfaces, allowing complex queries to be specified very easily by users, where the users may not even be aware of the complexity of their requests! Often, a high-level interface query results in many complex DBMS queries, which must have a short response time due to the interactive nature of the user interface. This increases both the complexity and the traffic rate of DBMS queries. The same phenomenon occurs in interfaces between high level programming languages, such as Prolog, and DBMSs (i.e., data base support for logic programming also has this effect) [Wolf88]. These programming environments allow programmers to write applications which initiate many complex DBMS queries. These trends cause the queries to become *logic-intensive*.

The processing power of affordable parallel computers is expected to be over 1000 MIPS shortly. The combination of massive amounts of data plus enormous processing power creates the opportunity for much more complex queries. Hence, we expect that future DBMSs will have to deal with applications which are increasingly data-intensive and logic-intensive.

Today's relational query languages typically do not have the functions for statistical analysis and structural (complex objects, record structures, etc.) expressibility, which are crucial for data summation and engineering data bases, respectively. We expect the functionality provided by such query languages to grow considerably. More of the application logic will be moved inside the DBMS, both for better performance (bringing function to data) and for better sharing of data among applications (better protection of data by encapsulation). Note that bringing function to data would be a good thing even in a nonparallel system just because it would avoid dragging up to the application level numerous records which subsequently get disqualified by the application when it applies some fancy predicates. Given that applications tend to be sequential, in a parallel DBMS, applying the fancy predicates within the DBMS would allow parallelism to be exploited in evaluating those predicates also, thereby potentially reducing the response time tremendously.

DBMSs will have to deal with a much larger set of data types and operations. From the application performance viewpoint, this is valuable since it allows more type specific operations to be specified in search predicates, so that, possibly, massive amounts of irrelevant data does not pass through the different layers of the DBMS to the applications. This is particularly significant since the data rate of the output from DBMSs is typically much less than the data rate of storage devices from which data is retrieved. Operations such as outer join, recursion, and sampling [OlRo89] should be handled by DBMSs for the same reason.

The problems that the query optimization and the query execution logic must handle are expanding because the nature of the queries that DBMSs must handle is expanding. In most cases, one can hope to get realtime responses to data and logic intensive queries only by exploiting parallelism. This may come as a surprise to some people who might be led to think that the way to attack the response time requirement is to stay with the simpler strategy of no intra-query parallelism, but use faster processors, and larger and larger amounts of memory. The limitations to the improvement of response time via faster processors and larger memories alone relate to the following observations:

- Based on the trends of the recent past, it is clear that the growth in the processing capacity of a uniprocessor or a closely-coupled multiprocessor is not going to be sufficient to provide realtime responses to certain types of complex queries using such systems. At least today, it appears that the $/MIPS (Million Instructions Per Second) cost of the very powerful machines is much higher than the $/MIPS cost of smaller, microprocessor-based machines.

- Even though the price of main memory keeps declining rapidly and the sizes of the memories that are attachable to a single processor keep growing, the volume of data to be handled keeps growing also. Further, with some architectures, there are limits on the amount of main memory that may be attached to a single machine (e.g., 2GB of real memory due to the 31-bit *real* memory addressing used on the IBM/370).

- As the processors become more and more powerful (even in the smaller microprocessor-based machines), the gap between the CPU processing speed and the I/O capacity of a single device becomes wider and wider. (We will return to this

1 Presented at the ACM-SIGMOD International Conference on Management of Data. Chicago, May 1988.

point in the section "2.5. I/O Versus CPU Versus Communication Parallelism".) This is at present necessitating the use of techniques like disk striping [CABK88, SaGa86] and disk arrays [PaGK88] to improve the I/O bandwidth. For a long time, systems like IBM's TPF [Hobs87, Scru87, Siwi77] used disk striping in software to improve *inter*-transaction parallelism. But now, striping is needed for supporting *intra*-transaction and query parallelism as well. Disk striping, if done in software, already demands parallelism at least at the I/O level to access the multiple disks in parallel.

Therefore, in order to gain price-performance advantages and response time improvements, the trend is towards building a data base machine consisting of a large number of smaller machines and exploiting intra-query parallelism.

2. Overall System Architecture Options

2.1. Shared Everything Versus Shared Disks Versus Shared Nothing

One approach to improving the capacity and availability characteristics of a single-system DBMS is to use multiple systems. There are three major architectures in use in the multisystem environment [Bhid88]: (1) ***shared disks (SD)*** or also called ***data sharing*** [DIRY89, Haer88, MoNa90, MoNP90, Rahm87, Rahm88, Rahm89b, Shoe86], (2) ***shared nothing (SN)*** or also called ***partitioned*** [Bora88a, Ston86], and (3) ***shared everything***.

With SD, all the disks containing the data bases are shared amongst the different systems and each system has its own buffer pool. Every system that has an instance of the DBMS executing on it may access and modify any portion of the data base on the shared disks. Since each instance has its own buffer pool and because conflicting accesses to the same data may be made from different systems, the interactions amongst the systems must be controlled via various synchronization protocols. This necessitates global locking and protocols for the maintenance of buffer coherency. SD is the approach used in IBM's IMS/VS Data Sharing product [CaHS85, ObSW83, PeSt83, StUW82], TPF product [Hobs87, Scru87, Siwi77] and the Amoeba research project [MoNa90, MoNP90, SNOP85], in DEC's VAX DBMS[2] and VAX Rdb/VMS products [JoRo89, KrLS86, ReSW89], and in NEC's DCS [SMMTG84]. These systems are using the SD architecture for *inter*-transaction parallelism rather than *intra*-transaction parallelism.

With SN, each system owns a portion of the data base and only that portion may be directly read or modified by that system. That is, the data base is partitioned amongst the multiple systems. The kind of synchronization protocols mentioned before for SD are not needed for SN. But, a transaction accessing data in multiple systems would need a form of two-phase commit protocol (e.g., the Presumed Abort protocol of [MoLO86]) to coordinate its activities. This is the approach taken in Tandem's Encompass[2] and NonStop SQL[2] [BoPu88, Borr81, Borr84, EGKS89, Tand87, Tand88], Teradata's DBC/1012[2] [DeSB87, Nech86, Tera88], MCC's Bubba [AlCo88, Bora88b, CABK88], and the University of Wisconsin's Gamma [DeGS88, GeDe87, ScDG89].

In the shared everything approach, memory, in addition to disks, is also shared across the processors. University of California - Berkeley's XPRS system has adopted this approach [SKPO88, StAS89]. It has been pointed out in [StAS89] that shared everything has scalability problems. But, it is attractive *within* a node of an SD or SN system. It helps reduce the number of nodes, making system management and load balancing easier. DB2 [CLSW84, HaJa84], for example, is able to very nicely exploit a shared everything machine like an IBM 3090-600J which has 6 processors.

Arguments in favor of SD are given in [HaSS89] in the context of complex objects and parallelism. For complex objects, it is said that partitioning the data, as is required with SN, is a big problem.

2.2. Transaction Monitors

In discussing an overall architecture, the role of data communications [Duqu87, Sche87, SSSHD87] and the transaction monitor (like IMS/DC [McGe77], TUXEDO [AnCK89] or CICS [Serl89]) cannot be ignored. Most online transactions are executed in the environment of a transaction monitor. The monitors provide support for terminal interactions, message queue management, logging, program libraries, etc. They are in essence an extension of the base operating system.

2 IBM, AS/400, and OS/2 are trademarks of the International Business Machines Corp. Encompass, NonStop SQL, and Tandem are trademarks of Tandem Computers, Inc. DEC, VAX DBMS, VAX, VAXcluster, and Rdb/VMS are trademarks of Digital Equipment Corp. DBC/1012 is a trademark of Teradata Corp. SYBASE is a registered trademark of Sybase, Inc.

Supporting the transaction monitor and the environment that it needs is essential even in a parallel architecture system. Any existing large application base which relies on such an environment must be accounted for. Resources (CPU, I/O, communication) used in the nonDBMS part of transactions (i.e., in transaction monitors and applications) are very significant. Hence, it is important to provide a parallel environment for both applications and transaction monitors. Tandem's Encompass and NonStop SQL provide such an environment. This is the so called ***peer-peer*** configuration.

If the adopted approach is one in which the monitor would run on one or more frontend machines and the actual data management would be done in a backend (the so called ***frontend-backend*** configuration) where parallelism would be exploited using machines of a different nature from the frontend machines, then two issues must be addressed. First, the cost of the interactions between the frontend and the backend must be taken into account in evaluating the performance implications of this approach on the transaction workload. This division of labor between the frontend and the backend is bound to increase the overall pathlength of a transaction. This increase will be felt especially in the case of the short transactions of the transaction workload. One way to attack this problem is to support the notion of stored procedures (as in the Sybase[2] DBMS [Corn88, Epst88]) and make the frontend issue a single call to the backend to execute a sequence of SQL statements.

The second issue is related to pushing more application functions down into the lower layers of the DBMS, either in the form of operations on abstract data types, function libraries (for scientific routines, statistical routines, etc.), methods on objects stored in the data base (as in the object-oriented DBMSs), or rules (as in rule-based systems). This trend essentially pushes for a more uniform runtime environment for applications and DBMSs, thereby allowing functions to move from applications into DBMS more easily. As a result, it may not be a good idea to have a very special-purpose operating system in the backend.

2.3. *Interconnection Technologies and Requirements*

The technology used for interconnecting the processors and the storage devices plays a crucial role in determining the communication bandwidth that can be sustained between the processors themselves, and between the processors and the storage devices. While fiber-optic [Ross89] switches can sustain high bandwidths and cover more distances compared to copper interconnects, costs of fiber-optic interface and switching devices are still rather high.

In the case of the SD approach, the storage devices must be attached through a switch since any processor must be capable of accessing any of the devices. This means that the switch should support high bandwidth communication. The processor to processor communications will be less in this environment, if parallelism for a given transaction is going to be handled within a system by utilizing a multiprocessor like the 6-way IBM 3090/600J. Most of the processor to processor communication is likely to be messages relating to global locking and buffer coherency protocols [CaHS85, MoNa90, MoNP90, ObSW83, Rahm88, ReSW89].

With SN, the devices may be locally attached to the *owning* processors, perhaps using cheaper technologies. In this case, the processor to processor communications can be significant if a given complex query is accessing data owned by multiple systems.

2.4. *Short Transactions and Complex Queries*

It is very important that the system architecture that is chosen be such that it can accommodate complex queries as well as short transactions against the *same* data. That is, it should be possible to pose ad hoc queries against the same data on which the "bread and butter" applications of the customers are also performing online, short transactions which may be updating as well as reading the data. The former is called the ***query workload*** and the latter is called the ***transaction workload***. In modern applications, mostly the transaction workload transfers new data from the real world into data bases. Hence, they are the *producers* of the data from the data base viewpoint. Examples are: transactions originating from Automated Teller Machines, point of sale transactions, stock exchange transactions. Complex queries are usually *consumers* of data. Sharing between producers and consumers of data is a fundamental phenomenon. Good performance for the transaction workload must be guaranteed since those transactions have more stringent response time constraints.

Traditionally, users have been forced to deal with this problem of handling the transaction and query workloads properly by maintaining two different data bases on two different systems. One of the data bases is the most up-to-date one and it is against that one that the transaction workload is run. The other data base is an extracted version of the first one and it is on this extracted data base that the complex queries are executed. Not all users are happy with this solution. In addition to the problems of having to maintain two different systems, the disk storage requirements are doubled.[3] Additionally, there is the expensive extraction process which needs to be performed periodically and which only gives out-of-date data to the ad hoc query users. Some of the advantages of this two data base strategy are: (1) the two types of workloads are on different machines and hence could hopefully be more easily managed, and (2) since the second data base is a read-only one, different access paths and buffer management policies (or even a different DBMS) may be defined for it to improve the performance of complex queries. Some of these users with dual data bases may have an IMS or TPF [Hobs87, Scru87, Siwi77] system which is running the older transaction workload and from which they are unable to migrate away quickly due to performance and/or application rewrite cost reasons. They may extract data from such a system and put it into a DB2 or Teradata system for the benefit of their newer decision support applications.

When both sets of workloads are brought into the same system, great care must be exercised to ensure that the exploitation of parallelism by the complex queries does not consume too much resources (CPU, I/O, and memory) at the expense of the short transactions. This requires that the system, at the least, support a priority concept for treating different users or data base requests differently. Some server-based systems do not have such a concept, which leads to very unpredictable response times and wide variances. A resource governor would also be essential to control "runaway" queries. DB2 V2R1, for example, introduced such a governor for controlling the resource consumption of dynamic SQL queries.

There is also a concurrency versus locking overhead dilemma with respect to mixing these workloads with very different characteristics. In order to maximize concurrency for the transaction workload, the application would be highly tempted to choose fine-granularity (e.g., record) locking [MHLPS89, MoPi90]. But this will make the query workload incur significant locking overhead since queries in general access large number of records. Apart from the overhead concern, the major problem may be that the locks held by the complex queries will delay the transaction workload from performing updates. Typically, this problem is dealt with by executing the complex queries with the isolation level of ***cursor stability*** (***CS*** - degree 2 consistency of System R [Gray78]). That is, the read locks are given up as the cursor moves from one record to the next. Even though many DBMSs (like DB2, the OS/2 Extended Edition[2] Database Manager [ChMy88], SQL/DS [ChGY81], and NonStop SQL) support CS, the research literature has concentrated only on repeatable read (***RR*** - degree 3 consistency of System R). More implications of CS on data accesses have been discussed in [MHWC90, Moha89, MoLe89].

The locking pathlength overhead problem is normally addressed using different solutions, with each one compromising on some functionality or the other. Two of the solutions are:

- **Unlocked Reads** Run the queries without locking and use latches [MHLPS89, MHWC90] to assure physical consistency of the pages being read. IMS supports this type of access via what is called *GO processing*. Relational systems like Tandem's NonStop SQL and IBM's AS/400[2] [AnCo88] also support such accesses. This solution avoids not only the locking overhead but also the undesirable lock conflicts between the two types of workloads. This approach has the disadvantage that uncommitted data may be exposed to the transactions that are not obtaining locks. In particular, integrity constraint violations may be noticed by the unlocked readers. For statistical queries (e.g., market analysis queries), this exposure usually causes little or no problem. But there is a concern regarding queries dealing with structured (e.g., CAD/CAM) objects, where inconsistent data close to the root of the object may result in retrieving a very different, and possibly invalid set of children objects. In fact, this problem, to a lesser degree, also occurs with cursor stability. Retrieval of the children at two different times during the course of a query may result in two different sets since the read data is locked only briefly and the data might have been updated in between the two retrievals.

- **Transient Versioning** In this approach, for data that is being modified, one or more older versions of it may be maintained [AgSe89, ChGr85, Reed78, Weih87]. With this support, the query workload would be able to read without locking. Just for

[3] It should be mentioned that, for large data bases, even if only one copy of the data is stored, the total cost of the disks used for storing the data base is a major portion of the cost of the complete system configuration.

data that is being modified, a slightly older, but a committed version of that data will be exposed to such transactions. The advantage is that the data base that is being exposed will be internally consistent. The concerns may be that not all the exposed data is up to date and the slight increase in storage consumption and complexity to keep multiple copies of some of the data. But the major problem may be that typically in such schemes the transactions that are not locking are not allowed to do any updates and such transactions must predeclare themselves to be read-only.

[Moha90] presents a technique, called **Commit_LSN**, for eliminating, most of the time, the need for locking when CS accesses are made. This technique takes advantage of some information (e.g., the log sequence number [MHLPS89, MoPi90]) that is tracked, for recovery purposes, on every page to conclude, without locking, that all the data in a page is in the committed state. It turns out to be of help in reducing the locking overhead even for update transactions, when record locking is in effect. Concurrency is also improved in conjunction with index concurrency control methods like ARIES/IM [MoLe89]. Many applications of the Commit_LSN technique are described in detail in [Moha90].

2.5. I/O Versus CPU Versus Communication Parallelism

Query processing in a parallel environment requires four major resource types: CPU, I/O, memory, and communication. Some form of parallelism is needed for large scale use of any of these resources. Disk arrays [PaGK88] provide both large amounts of storage as well as many read/write arms for higher bandwidth (they may also improve availability by striping different bits of a byte on different devices and by storing some parity bits in a similar fashion). Main memory subsystems with many ports and many memory modules provide similar features. Likewise, communication systems with switches at different levels and many ports provide high bandwidth. The degree of parallelism needed in each resource type (e.g., CPU) depends on the load on that resource type and the speed of a component of that resource type (e.g., a CPU). As a result, different degrees of parallelism are needed for different resource types. Here, we study the relationship between parallelism of two major resource types in DBMSs: CPU and I/O.

Our objective function is: minimize the response time up to a threshold, where the constraint is the amount of given resources. ***Threshold*** is defined as that response time below which minimization is not significant. In other words, we want to *maximize* use of the given *limited* resources to *minimize* the response time up to a threshold.[4] Different degrees of parallelism may satisfy this objective. Suppose we can fully utilize the CPU resource with 100 tasks or with 1000 tasks. One question is what the degree of parallelism should be. We argue that it is important to find the *minimal* degree of parallelism, while satisfying our objective function. The higher the degree of parallelism, the harder the load balancing would be. By *increasing* the number of tasks across which work is being distributed, we are *decreasing* the number of tuples that each task handles. In other words, we have fragmented the processing, and made it *less set oriented*, hence potentially compromising one of the major benefits that the relational model provides us. As a result, the processing may become less efficient. For example, we may lose the efficiency of sequential prefetch [TeGu84] because each task does not access enough pages to take full advantage of sequential prefetch in terms of amortizing the cost of an I/O call across a large number of pages.

Inefficiency can also arise in accessing data through *nonclustered* indices. In sequential processing, we extract the ***TIDs*** (tuple identifiers) of qualified tuples from the index, sort the TIDs by page IDs, and then do the I/Os [MHWC90]. Hence, each relevant data page is retrieved only once. If many tasks do this in parallel, often the *same page* may be retrieved many times, because, for a given page, more than one task may be interested in different tuples in it. Each task has a certain fixed cost associated with operations such as opening and closing scans, and sort initialization (e.g., initialization of the tournament trees when tournament sorts are used). This cost is multiplied by the degree of task parallelism. In addition to the wastage of CPU cycles, other resources like memory, and channel capacity may also be wasted. Contention for disk arms and channels may also be increased.

We would like to study the relationship between CPU and I/O parallelism. One concern that we have

4 *Maximize* must be interpreted more carefully in the context of a multiuser environment. As we see shortly, sometimes too much parallelism may lead to too much wastage of resources, and may not decrease the response time significantly. We must avoid these cases for the benefit of other users of the system.

is that often there is a significant mismatch between the degree of parallelism needed for CPU and that needed for the I/O subsystem. One reason for this is that the speed of I/O devices has not increased as fast as that of CPUs. To study the relationship between I/O and CPU parallelism, consider the problem of accessing, directly or through indices, the base tables. If all the data fits in main memory, then each task is CPU bound, and we need only one task per CPU. Hence, degree of parallelism is the number of available CPUs. If data is on disks, the tasks can be I/O bound if one disk arm at a time is used. This causes a significant mismatch between the degrees of parallelism needed for CPU and I/O. The reason is that the speeds of the available disks are too low compared to the power of the currently available CPUs, especially the mainframe ones. Therefore, we need to have numerous disk arms, as in disk arrays, to keep up with each CPU. Let's go through an example. We assume that the processing capacity of each CPU is 30 MIPS. We consider two types of disks:

1. **Slower disks**: 3MBPS (megabytes per second) bandwidth; 20 ms average seek plus search (i.e., rotational latency) time.

2. **Faster disks**: higher bandwidth, moderately lower seek plus search time. Let's assume that these disks are an order of magnitude better in bandwidth (30MBPS) and half order of magnitude better in average seek plus search time (7 ms).

Let's consider two types of queries:

- **Type 1**: complex queries with numerous sequential table scans;

- **Type 2**: complex queries with numerous TID list data accesses, as explained above (mostly doing random I/Os).

The second type of access is chosen when the table is very big and the predicates are very selective. Hence, we may be heavily using even nonclustered indices (one index, or several, with index ANDing and/or ORing [MHWC90]). The queries of the first type mainly do sequential I/Os. Hence, for each I/O, the seek/search cost is incurred once for a set of pages (e.g., 64 pages). In this case, the limiting factor is mostly the data transfer bandwidth of the disk. The second type of queries mainly do random I/Os. Hence, the seek/search time delay is usually incurred for every page. In this case, the seek/search time is the limiting factor.

Let's study this more quantitatively. Suppose, for a given query, let *L* be the total pathlength and *I* the total number of pages retrieved from disk. *L* includes CPU instructions for performing I/O, locking, predicate evaluation, sort, join, etc. The ratio ***L / I*** is the average number of instructions of CPU processing incurred for each page retrieved from the disk. This ratio is a good means of characterizing a workload, and we use it to study the balance between CPU and I/O. The value of this ratio depends on the type of a query. Later, in the section "5. A More Quantitative Analysis", we will discuss the details of the performance of a complex query, called ***5fanj***. For this query, which is of type 1, the ratio *L / I* is about 20K. For queries that have mostly very selective predicates supported by indices, this ratio is typically less than 1K. These queries perform a significant amount of random I/Os. They essentially retrieve one tuple out of every accessed page. For queries that perform significant amount of random I/Os and also significant amount of processing (e.g., sorts, joins, aggregation, etc.) on the retrieved data, the ratio increases significantly.

In a mixed query and transaction workload, we must also consider the effect of transaction workloads on the balance of CPU and I/O. Transaction workloads also perform a significant amount of random I/Os. The *L / I* ratio for TP1 transactions [Anon85] is roughly 50K.[5] As we will comment later, these ratios also depend on the buffer sizes. [FTSN89] reports 15 to 45 I/Os per second per MIPS for users of DEC computers. Assuming a page size of 4K bytes, we get *L / I* equal to 13 to 34 (this is after converting VAX MIPS to IBM/370 MIPS using the formula given in the reference).

Figure 1 gives the degree of I/O parallelism for each CPU (more precisely, for a task that fully utilizes a CPU) for different *L / I* ratios.

For *L / I* = 20 (***5fanj*** type 1 query), the ratio of degree of parallelism of I/O and CPU is about 2.5 for slower disks. This number is about 0.3 for faster disks. In this case, there is not much mismatch between the

5 Typically, accessing the account table incurs one I/O for the index leaf page, and one I/O for the data page. Updating of the account table incurs one I/O. Each transaction benefits from the caching of teller and branch tables. Also, I/Os for the journal table and log (assuming *group commit* [GaKi85] is used) are compensated across multiple transactions. The actual number of I/Os for this heavily depends on the buffer sizes. If we assume one more I/O for all of these, and a pathlength of about 200K instructions, we get 50K per I/O.

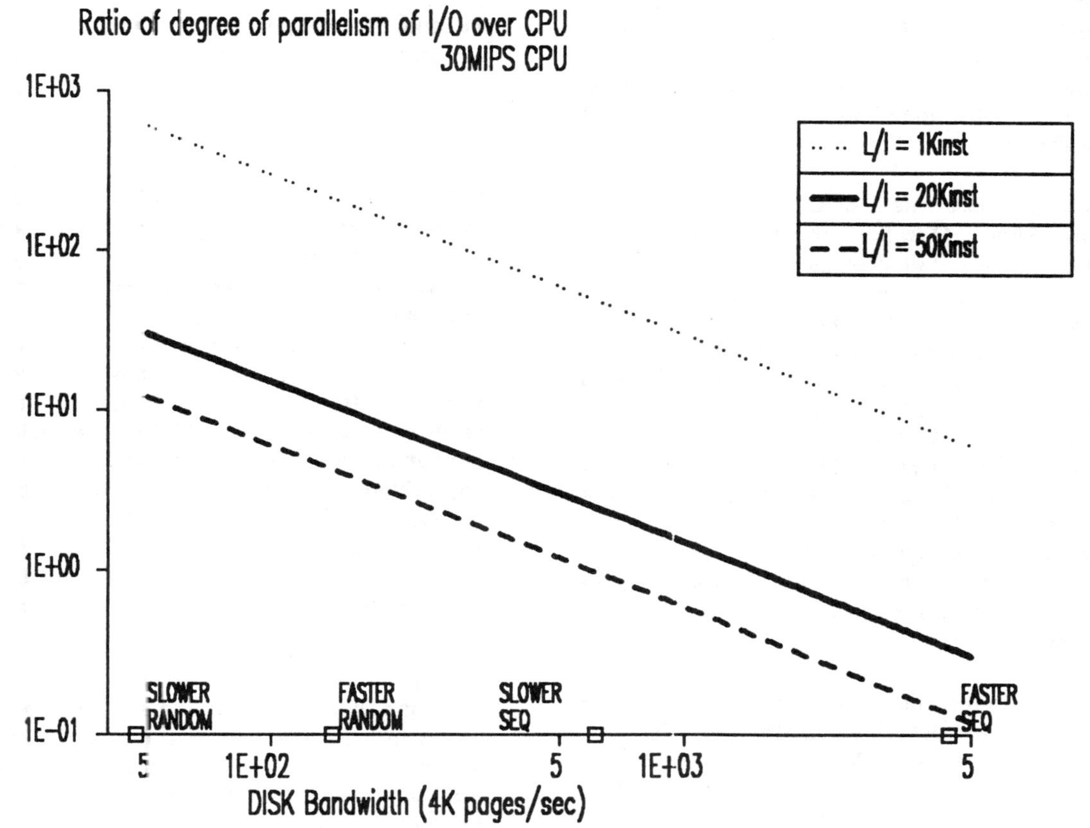

Figure 1: I/O Versus CPU Parallelism

degree of parallelism needed for CPU and I/O. If this query is of type 2 and has the same *L / I* ratio, the degree of parallelism of I/O and CPU is about 31 for slower disks. This number is about 10 for faster disks. In this case, the degree of I/O parallelism needed is more than an order of magnitude greater than that of CPU, hence there is a significant mismatch between degree of parallelism of CPU and I/O resources.

As the I/O speed increases, we need less parallelism in the I/O subsystem. There are two interesting cases:

1. Degrees of parallelism for CPU and I/O are close to each to other.

2. Degree of parallelism for I/O is much more than that for CPU (more than an order of magnitude in the above example).

In case 1, the system is not significantly CPU or I/O bound. Each task spends roughly equal time using CPU or I/O resources. Suppose each task does asynchronous disk page prefetch, where the task starts the I/O for the next set of pages at the time it starts working on the current set of pages. Under these conditions, each task becomes CPU bound, and it is sufficient to have as many tasks as CPUs. I/O parallelism follows from (happens as a result of) CPU parallelism, and no special mechanism is needed for I/O parallelism.

For case 2, we have two possibilities:

1. Use the same approach as above, where I/O parallelism follows from CPU parallelism. In this case, each task is now mostly I/O bound (even with I/O overlap). We need to increase the degree of CPU parallelism to that of I/O, hence allowing better utilization of resources,

such as CPU. The problem with this approach is that it artificially increases the CPU parallelism significantly (an order of magnitude in our example). This may not be acceptable because as we argued above, we want to decrease the degree of parallelism in CPU as much as possible for better load balancing and reduction of overheads.

2. Decouple parallelism of CPU and I/O subsystems. Allow I/O to have more parallelism than CPU. This is the desired approach. An example of such an approach is the use of disk arrays where different blocks of data are scattered on different disks. Note that we mostly need this for random I/O, allowing different disk arms to work on different blocks of data. As explained before (and in [MHWC90]), a CPU task accesses the index and forms a list of pages to be retrieved. This list is given to the I/O subsystem (via the STARTIO instruction). Suppose these pages are stored in a DASD array. The control unit of the DASD array is responsible to initiate I/O (tasks) on different disk devices in parallel to retrieve the pages.

As we increase the efficiency of the DBMS software (more efficient predicate evaluation, sort, join, etc.), the ratio L/I is reduced. As a result, the curve in Figure 1 moves toward the right, thereby increasing the amount of I/O parallelism that is needed. The same happens when the speed of CPUs increases. The curve moves toward the left with the availability of more main memory which results in less I/Os, or with faster I/O systems. This decreases the amount of needed I/O parallelism. Also, the same happens as the queries become more logic intensive, i.e., as more processing is done on the retrieved pages. Examples are queries with large number of predicates, predicates involving expensive methods on complex data types (e.g., geographic data), and large number of joins (with pipelining).

3. Parallel Algorithms

In this section we will discuss ways of parallelizing a query, load balancing issues, and what parallelization impact is on different components of a relational DBMS.

3.1. Targets of Parallelization

There are two (orthogonal) ways of parallelizing complex queries:

- Program Parallelism (PP)
- Data Parallelism (DP)

PP and DP are possible in both the SD and SN architectures.

3.1.1. Program Parallelism (PP)

Let us consider an example which involves joining the four tables T0, T1, T2, and T3. A possible execution strategy is one in which the join of T0 and T1 is performed in parallel with the join of T2 and T3. We call this ***independent task execution.*** Another possible execution strategy is one in which the join of T0 and T1 is performed by task S1 which then sends the result records incrementally to task S2 to perform the join with T2. S2 then sends its result records incrementally to S3 to do the join with T3. We call this the ***asynchronous pipeline***. The reasoning behind the name has to do with the fact that the tuples are piped between tasks. But, unlike the *synchronous* pipelining used in sequential plans (e.g., as in System R [SACL79]), here different stages of the pipeline are not executed in a lock-step fashion.

The queue between the producer and consumer tasks is called a ***table queue*** since its contents are tuples in (composite) tables. Obviously, some sort of flow control is needed between the producer(s) and consumer(s) of a table queue in order to reduce the overflow of the queue to disk, if the queue gets too large due to a slow consumer. This kind of asynchronous pipelining is also proposed in [Grae90], and is also useful in distributed data base management systems and was used in the R* prototype [LMHDL85, SeAd80]. In the latter, the communication network protocols provided the pacing between the producer and the consumer.

An execution plan is a partially ordered set of operators [HFLP89]. Examples of operators are index or data access and predicate evaluators, sort, join, aggregation, etc. The number of operators depends on the complexity of queries. Obviously, the degree of parallelism obtainable by PP is limited by the number of operators used in a query. In fact, the actual degree of parallelism attainable is usually much less than this upper bound due to the dependencies between operators. For example, the merge join of T1 and T2 cannot start until the access and sort of T1 and T2 are completed. In most of the cases, PP is not sufficient to provide a degree of parallelism in the 100s or 1000s. However, PP is more useful in conjunction with DP which is discussed more below. Furthermore, the cost of inter-task communication between operators in two different tasks is considerably higher than that between operators within the same task. In fact, in systems like DB2 [CLSW84], (in most of the cases) the tuples are not copied when they go through synchronous pipelines between operators. This cost is particularly high if tasks are in different processors which are not sharing memory. Analysis of the 5fanj query in the context of a model based on projected pathlengths of MVS and DB2 shows that the pathlength more than doubles if all *synchronous* pipelines are replaced by *asynchronous* pipelines. The extra pathlengths are mostly due to the costs of forming tuples, inserting them into and retrieving them from table queues.

3.1.2. Data Parallelism (DP)

DP is the key to supporting a high degree of parallelism. Currently, even in a system which does not employ parallelism within a query (beyond doing sequential prefetching of data using system tasks in anticipation of future requests from the user's query processing task [TeGu84]), a table may be divided up into a number of partitions (one such system, DB2, allows up to 64 partitions, for example). Each partition may be stored on a different device (maybe of even different types) and reorganized independently. DB2's partitioning is based on nonoverlapping key ranges, as specified by the creator of the table. In contrast, systems like TPF, Bubba, DBC/1012, and Grace [KiTM83] use hashing to assign tuples to different partitions.

A hybrid approach is one that combines DP and PP. The extreme case of the hybrid approach is the one where we associate one task with each operator for each data partition. That is, we employ full DP and full PP. We call it the ***parallel asynchronous pipeline***. The parallel asynchronous pipeline approach is undesirable from the viewpoint of the tremendous increase in pathlength that it would cause. Hence, if DP provides the desired parallelism, then use synchronous pipeline as much as possible for each partition and run different partitions in parallel. This scheme is called the ***parallel synchronous pipeline***.

Pipelining helps reduce peaks in data communications and disk I/O. If pipelining is not used, in a SN architecture, the data from the producer is transferred across the network and put on disk at the consumer's system. This may cause a peak in communication [GeDe87], if the producer does not have much work to do (e.g., it is reading the local workfiles and distributing them across the network). But, if the data is piped to the consumer, then usually it is the consumer who is the bottleneck due to the processing (e.g., join) that needs to be performed on the incoming data, and also may be due to the lower priority assigned to it. As a result, the data transfer is spread over a longer period of time, thereby reducing the peak in the communication traffic. In the section "5. A More Quantitative Analysis", we will revisit this phenomenon. An asynchronous approach and a synchronous approach are presented in [SMLC86] for controlling and managing query pipelines.

3.2. Load Balancing Issues

As discussed earlier, the key elements of parallelism are data and computation partitioning. Different methods of data partitioning (e.g., key range partitioning) and computation partitioning (e.g., program and data parallelism) were discussed before. Computation partitioning must be done such that the load is spread as evenly as possible amongst the different tasks and different physical resources involved in the computation. Two kinds of load balancing are important: (1) physical resource level (e.g., load balancing of CPU nodes across many simultaneous applications), (2) task level (e.g., load balancing of different tasks accessing a table in parallel). Other discussions on load balancing can be found in [DGRS89, Rahm89a].

3.2.1. Physical Resource Level

Here, we consider load balancing among the CPU nodes. Load balancing of I/O and communication resources are not considered. In the partitioned architecture, the data from a disk must be retrieved through the CPU node that the disk is attached to. This node does I/O and locking, applies the local predicates, and extracts the qualified tuples, and sends them to the next stage of computation, which may be in another node. A node may become overloaded if there is too much demand for the data under its control.[6] To reduce the load on this node, we might consider the following alternatives:

1. **Off-loading Predicate Evaluation and Tuple Extraction.** This requires sending raw pages to the destination nodes. Locking is essentially at the page level because the source node cannot distinguish between qualified and unqualified tuples. Another alternative is for the destination node to do the locking. But this requires a

6 Note that the source node also has to deal with updates, causing further load imbalance.

global locking mechanism, as in the SD architecture.[7] The effective communication bandwidth required may also go up considerably because the tuples are not filtered at the source. With this, the SN architecture comes closer to the SD architecture, where raw pages are shared amongst the nodes. But unlike in SD, no buffer coherency protocols are needed.

2. **Data Redistribution.** We can redistribute the data to avoid this situation. This is possible if different pages, or different tuples within pages are demanded from the different nodes. Also, it requires *a priori* knowledge of the data usage pattern. Further, the usage pattern must not change too often (e.g., between day and night). Note that the SD architecture can handle this very well.

3. **Orthogonal Data Distribution.** In this approach, the correlation between distribution of data placement and data usage is minimized. An example of this is random data placement. This approach is the best for avoiding skews. However, it does not allow the clustering of data to minimize I/O and locking costs. This is particularly a drawback for handling of complex objects. Also, the overhead may be too much for "small" queries - if request has 15 tuple result, it probably will involve at least 15 tasks on 15 nodes.

It is possible that the same set of tuples are demanded from different nodes. If the data is only read most of the time, then data replication can reduce contention. Otherwise, the data must be granularized more through schema changes, or new lock modes (such as increment/decrement locks) must be introduced to reduce contention. Also, the *Commit_LSN* technique of [Moha90] may be used to reduce contention and to avoid a significant amount of locking overhead.

3.2.2. Task Level

With data parallelism, each operator is assigned a portion of the work. Load balancing among tasks still requires extensive research. Here, we briefly mention some of the main issues. Access operators usually have some local predicates, which must be considered in assignment of work to different tasks. For example, if a **sales** table is partitioned on the value of the month column and a query is issued in which the predicate on month is such that only the December tuples are required, then we need data parallelism at a finer level for processing this query. Each task may handle the data for a particular day. Unfortunately, there may be more data for some days than for others, causing an imbalance in the work to be performed. This situation is worse if we do not know at compile time what month of the year the predicate will specify. This usually happens when the binding for the month variable comes from the application or other parts of the query (e.g., it is a correlation variable passed to a subquery, or it is part of a join column used during access of the inner table).

Similar cases exist for other operators. [IyDi90, IyRV89, LoYo89] address the load balancing issues for the sort operator.

3.3. System Components-Level Impact

Providing support for intra-query parallelism in a system designed initially without parallelism in mind requires making changes to a number of components in the system. These are the changes that we would like to address in this section.

Using the System R terminology, we call the upper part of the system that deals with query optimization and plan generation the relational data system (***RDS***). The lower part of the system that deals with buffer management, concurrency control, recovery, record management, and space management is called the data management system (***DMS***). We will discuss the enhancements that need to be done at the RDS and DMS levels (corresponding to System R's RDS and RSS levels).

Enhancements to the SQL language are necessary to make more parallelism possible within the DBMS. Some implementations of SQL allow the application to provide only one tuple at a time to the DBMS for insertion. As a result, there is little chance for parallelism for such insert operations.[8] We must allow the application to specify a set of tuples and insert them using one SQL command, as is done in SQL/DS. The same is true for the SQL statements *update* or *delete where current of cursor*. Only one tuple at a time can be updated or deleted in this case. We must allow the application to specify update/delete

7 In partitioned architectures, usually all the locking is done locally.

8 Parallelism is limited to the updating of indices, and subquery execution for symmetric views with subqueries, where subquery tables are affected by the insert.

for a set of tuples in one SQL command.[9] Enhancements to the application program interface (API) are also required to interface DBMS applications which have many parallel pieces.

The optimizer may be designed to deal with the questions relating to the degree of parallelism and the assignment of work to the different tasks solely at the time of query compilation. This would be what we call the ***compile-time or static optimization***. Another possible approach is the one in which, in addition to doing the compile-time determination of the number of tasks, etc., enough intelligence is built into the run-time support and the plans themselves to dynamically adapt the execution plan based on information about the loads on the different processors, characteristics (size, data distribution, etc.) of the intermediate results, the availability of memory, etc. As can be imagined, this ***dynamic optimization*** is more difficult than the static optimization approach.

Complexity of optimization is already a major problem in relational DBMSs, and parallelism makes this problem even bigger. One question is whether there is a compromise approach to optimization without increasing the complexity too much. One idea is a two-phase static optimizer. First, optimize the query ignoring parallelism (i.e., act as if the query will be run in a sequential DBMS). Then, take the query plan chosen above and optimize it further for parallelism. This is the approach chosen in XPRS [StAS89]. This approach is particularly attractive, if we want to parallelize an existing DBMS. The two-phase optimization approach also reduces the search space of optimization.

Obviously, there will be cases for which this approach does not produce an optimal plan due to the fragmentation of optimization. Suppose the first phase chooses plan alternative P1 and rejects plan alternative P2. If P2 is much more expensive than P1, then usually we are not interested in the parallelized version of P2 either. The reason is that it wastes a significant amount of resources and such wastage is not acceptable in a multiuser environment. Furthermore, there is a good chance that its response time will be worse than that of P1. If the resource consumption of P1 is not very different and the parallelized version of P2 is better than the parallelized version of P1 then this approach loses. Suppose P1 uses a nonpartitioned index scan and P2 uses a partitioned table scan then P2 may be preferable because it is usually easier to parallelize.

One may consider giving hints to the sequential optimizer to choose alternatives that are easier to parallelize.

As argued above, the parallel optimization of a query depends on how much resources are available. This is usually known at runtime. However, one source of complexity of dynamic optimization is the need for the modification of the plan at runtime, particularly during the execution of the plan. One way to avoid this is for the static optimizer to optimize the query based on the maximum amount of available resources. Then, at runtime, the degree of parallelism of each part of the plan can be changed based on the actual amount of available resources. This usually does not require complex plan changes at runtime.

Another change that would be desirable to the RDS component is the consideration of bushy joins (i.e., composite inner tables) in addition to the System R approach of considering only noncomposite inners. Otherwise, we would be restricted to pipelining as the only means of getting program parallelism amongst the join operations. Join pipelining is feasible only if no sort needs to be performed on the result of one join before the next join can be performed.

As we will see in the section "5. A More Quantitative Analysis", runtime part of a parallel DBMS must support starting/stopping of tasks, monitoring their progress, and communicating runtime errors. The papers on Gamma [ScDG89] and PROSPECT [DGRSZ88] discuss examples of such support. In a multiuser environment, only a portion of the resources are allocated to a given query. Parallel queries have the potential of using the entire system resources, such as CPU, I/O, etc. Therefore, there is a need for a runtime mechanism to limit resource usage rate of queries to the assigned values. This usually requires cooperation with the (operating) system resource manager.

Enhancements may be necessary at the DMS level for the following:

- Handling of large buffer sizes, and possibly multiple buffer pools [TeGu84]
- Parallelism
  - I/O parallelism
  - Task structure
- Locking support for parallelized update queries.

---

9 To some extent, this is expected to be addressed in the context of *scrollable cursor* support by ANSI SQL standard committee [SQL23].

4. Details of Relational Operators

Parallelism is enhanced if we (1) reduce dependencies between operations (e.g., by deferring application of join predicates), and (2) make even the lower level DBMS functions more set oriented (e.g., by performing aggregation during sort).

Access refers to accessing permanent tables or workfiles. This operation also includes acquiring any locks, applying the eligible predicates and performing projections. An access may be via indexes or by table scans. When access via index is chosen, more than one index may be used for accessing the records of a single table [MHWC90].

The *join* operation involves taking the results of accessing two or more tables and applying the join predicates. If parallelism amongst accesses and the join is being maximized, then, during the access of the inner table, we cannot take advantage of those predicates on the inner table that involve columns of the outer table. The effect is as if the nested loop join method is not being used and the accesses are more like those performed in the sort-merge join method.

Ideally, aggregation should be combined with the sort and merge phases of the SQL *Group By* operation, instead of being performed as a separate operation after the merge is completed and we have a completely sorted stream. Combining aggregation with other operations will cut down the number of passes through the data by one. More importantly, in most cases, it will reduce the number of records to be dealt with in the merge phases, thereby potentially reducing the CPU and I/O overheads.

Duplicate elimination also should be combined with sort and merge operations. Of course, if the columns of interest in the result constitute the key of a nonunique index, then it would be highly preferable to make the index manager itself return only nonduplicate values. Under these conditions, retrieving all the keys and then eliminating duplicates in the index manager's caller would be much more expensive since indexes typically store duplicate keys in a compressed form which can drastically reduce the number of comparisons required to select only one instance of each duplicate key. It may also reduce the number of locks that are acquired, depending on what the objects of locking are (see [Moha89, Moha90, MoLe89] for more discussions). This will be especially beneficial in the SD environment where the locks are global locks. While the above points are applicable even without parallelism coming into the picture, they become extremely important in the context of a data base machine since adopting them could lead to a drastic reduction in communication traffic also.

In the case of the set-oriented insert, delete, and update operations, the selection of the records to be dealt with can go on in parallel with the insert, delete, or update operation. Depending on the consistency level used (RR or CS) during the retrievals, by the time the delete or update operation is executed, the records which previously qualified may no longer qualify for the delete or update due to the activities of other transactions. This has to be dealt with carefully to avoid inconsistencies. This sort of problem arises even when there is no intra-transaction parallelism, but the data access is postponed until the index accesses are finished and cursor stability is used during the index access (see [MHWC90, Moha90] for more discussions).

The *union* operation will not have much work to do, unless (1) duplicates are to be eliminated and/or (2) an Order By clause exists. If duplicate elimination is required, then, unless multiquery optimization is going to be performed and somehow the queries constituting the operands of the union are going to be combined, the elimination of the postprocessing done to remove duplicates would not be possible in most cases.

5. A More Quantitative Analysis

A comprehensive quantitative analysis is required to give us the resource requirements of various workloads, and provide us the effect of resource limitations. A comprehensive performance evaluation requires a definition of a benchmark data base and a set of queries for a particular workload. As mentioned before, we are more interested in a complex query workload as opposed to a transaction workload. However, a transaction workload is needed to study the performance of a mix of query and transaction workloads. There has been a substantial effort in the past to define a transaction workload [Anon85, TPC89]. However, work in defining a complex query workload is still in a preliminary stage. Such a workload must include queries with large number of predicates, joins, and aggregations etc. The data base of such a benchmark must be scalable to several terabytes. The recent efforts [Onei89, TuOB89] are steps in this direction. We have introduced a set of such queries using a scaled up version of the DB2 benchmark data base described in [Loos86]. These queries cover the major DBMS operations as far as parallelism is concerned, including predicate evaluation, sort, join, aggregation, and set (and multiset) operations.

An in-depth study of such a benchmark is beyond the scope of this paper. However, we feel it is important to report some results from our effort in this area to give a more quantitative feel about the amounts of different resources needed for complex queries, and what the balance is between these resources. We will explain some of the key observations that arise from studying a complex query, called ***5fanj***, and will comment on variations of it. We will give the results of modeling and simulation of 5fanj query, including the CPU, I/O, and communications requirements. We assume a shared nothing system with aggregate CPU power of 10000MIPS, consisting of 334 CPUs each with a processing power of 30 MIPS. We increase the degree of parallelism such that all the CPU power is used. Based on these, we derive the aggregate effective communication and I/O bandwidths.

The SQL formulation of 5fanj query is (also see Figure 3):

```
SELECT ITMTABLN, ITPTBALN, PURTABLN,
        ITLTABLN, ACTTABLN
  FROM ITMNUMBR, ITPORDER, PURCHASE,
       ITLOCATN, ACTIVLOG
 WHERE ITMITEMN=ITPITEMN AND ITPPONUM=PURPONUM
       AND ITMITEMN=ITLITEMN
       AND ITMITEMN=ACTITEMN
       AND ITMITEMN<'IT010200MNUMBR'
       AND ITPQREMN<30000 AND ITPPONUM<'P05600'
       AND ITLWKCEN<'WK200' AND ITLTENTR<'2000'
       AND ACTLTIME<' 500' AND ACTVDATE<'10'
```

In Figure 3, each node is a table in the FROM clause, and each edge is a conjunct in the WHERE clause predicate. The local (i.e., nonjoin) predicates are represented by loop edges. This query accesses and joins five tables, some with local predicates on them. The query joins the five tables and outputs a column from each table. We assume that the user is able to absorb the output as fast as it is produced. Hence, the response time is determined solely by the DBMS execution time. For each table, the tuple and page cardinality, and the selectivity of the local predicates are given in Figure 2. Initially, we assume that table scans are used to access the data. We will discuss how the results change if we use indices, and if we change the selectivities of the predicates. The tables are physically partitioned across the I/O devices. Each partition is handled by one disk arm. We assume that there is one partition per table per CPU.

Table	Number of Tuples (M=Million)	Number of 4KB Pages (K=1000)	Local Predicate Selectivity %
ITMNUMBR	7.0M	75K	60%
ITPORDER	1.4M	174K	85%
PURCHASE	5.2M	477K	-
ITLOCATN	104.5M	2377K	18%
ACTIVLOG	209.0M	2349K	8%

Figure 2: Characteristics of the Benchmark Data Base and the 5fanj Query

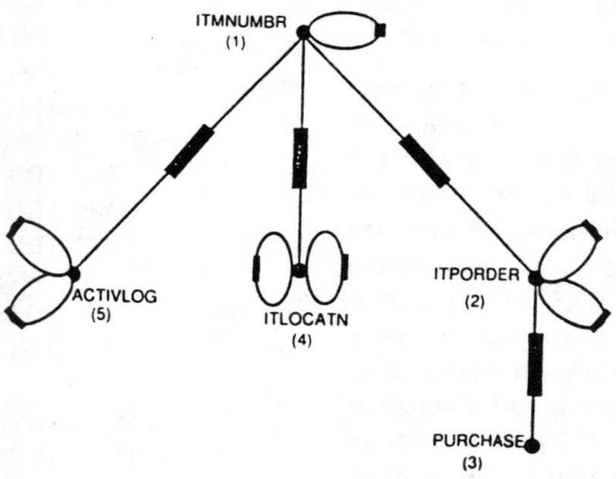

Figure 3: 5fanj Query

The execution plan for this query uses the sort-merge join method, which is usually better than the nested loop method when there is no usable index on the join column of the inner table. The join order we assumed is shown by node numbers in Figure 3 (roughly from the smallest size table to the largest size table). Now, we explain the parallel plan by describing the join between the first two tables. We create one task per partition of ITMNUMBR. Each task accesses its partition, does locking, applies the local predicates, and projects the needed columns of the qualified tuples. This query uses page level locking with cursor stability (level 2 consistency of System R). Then, the task sorts the qualified tuples on the join (with ITPORDER) column and creates the sort runs as temporary workfiles. The same is done for ITPORDER. (During the discussion on scheduling in the section "5.1. Task Scheduling", we will explain the choices for program parallelism.) For example, we have the choice of accessing and sorting the tables ITLOCATN and ACTIVLOG in parallel or one after another.

For performing the merge of the ITMNUMBR and ITPORDER workfiles and doing a merge join, we create 334 parallel tasks. Each task is assigned a portion of the outer table (ITMNUMBR) join column values and performs that part of the join. Assignment of the range of the join column values for these tasks must be done such that their work is balanced. This may be done by collecting statistics during sort (see [LoYo89]). The result of the join done in each task is sorted and put in workfiles as part of the same task. The join of this intermediate result with the rest of the tables follows the same algorithm. Note that the result of the join of (ITMNUMBR, ITPORDER, PURCHASE) and ITLOCATN is sorted on the join column ITMNUMBR, which is the same join column for the following join with ACTIVLOG table. Hence, no further sort of the intermediate result is needed for the last join with ACTIVLOG. Hence, the result of join of the first four tables is directly piped (via a synchronous pipeline) to the join with ACTIVLOG.

Figure 4 shows the pathlength for each operator type used in this query. The aggregate pathlength is about 150 billion instructions.[10] Most of our cost estimates are based on IBM's DB2 [HaJa84]. The cost for Access is separated into two parts. (1)Cost of I/O, page level locking, (2) cost of application of local predicates and extracting the qualified tuples from the pages and projecting out the relevant columns. The cost of I/O and locking is about 10% of the total cost. One reason for such a low cost is that efficient sequential prefetch I/O [TeGu84] was used to access the data. As expected, the cost of sort is dominated by the non-I/O cost. The merge phase, which merges several workfiles, is more I/O intensive because there is little CPU work that needs to be done.

The Access cost is about 38% of the total query cost. 62% of the cost is mainly for sort, merge, and join. In a sense, the Access operators produce the data relevant to the query from the base tables, and the rest of the operators work on that data. Hence, the cost of access may change if the same relevant data must be extracted from a larger data base. We will discuss this variation later in the section "5.4. Further Remarks on Performance". If shared disks (SD) architecture instead of shared nothing architecture (SN) is used for this query, the cost of access goes up slightly because of global

10 It should be mentioned that queries with such a high number of instructions are becoming more and more common, particularly for decision support systems. The pathlength of this query is roughly 5 orders of magnitude higher than TP1 transactions.

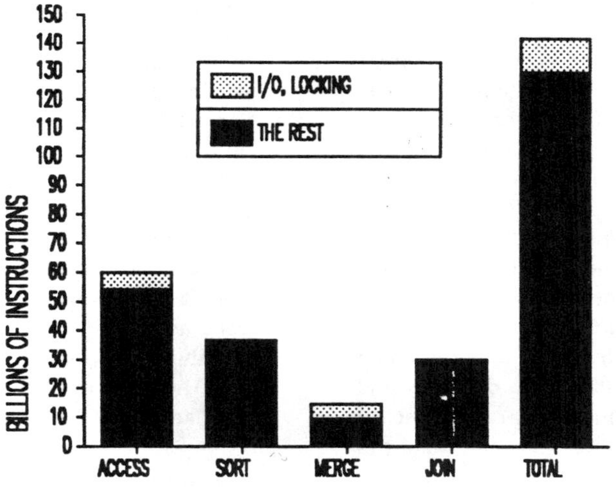

Figure 4: Pathlength for 5fanj Query: per Operator and Aggregate

locking. On the other hand, during the merge phase, no communication is needed to read the data from workfiles, because they are available globally. The difference between the total pathlength on each architecture is insignificant.

5.1. Task Scheduling

Determining the needed I/O and communication bandwidth is more difficult because we have to know at any given time what tasks are running; i.e., we have to know the scheduling of the tasks. Each of the tasks to access and sort ITLOCATN and ACTIVLOG is I/O bound if I/O parallelism is not used. Hence, we would like to run them in parallel for better CPU utilization. This results in higher I/O rate. The scheduler's goal is to minimize the response time by maximizing the efficient usage of resources. The scheduler must consider the dependency between tasks (e.g., join of ITMNUMBR and ITPORDER must be done after completion of the access and the sort of each table when using the sort-merge join method). The scheduler must also consider what resources (e.g., CPU, disk arms, memory, and communication ports) are used by each task in order to decide on the start times of the tasks, control of their speeds (e.g., using priorities), and the proper interleavings of different tasks to avoid contention on the above resources.

The complexity of an algorithm for producing an optimal schedule is NP hard. Hence, a workable scheduler usually needs some heuristics. A complete treatment of the scheduling problem requires further research, and beyond the scope of this paper. For the modeling of our sample problem, we have designed two simplified scheduling algorithms, called *double-stretch*, and *no-stretch*. Neither of these algorithms is the ideal one. We argue that an optimal scheduling algorithm performs somewhere between these two algorithms. Both of these algorithms use, as parameters, the rate that I/O, CPU, and communication resources are consumed by each task to determine the execution schedule. We assume the aggregate CPU MIPS is given. We maximize the usage of CPU resource, and we compute the rate of usage of other resources, such as I/O and communication.

Let's define the following task types for different parts of execution of the 5fanj query. Task type (T_1), (T_2), (T_3), (T_4), (T_5) for access and sort of tables ITMNUMBR, ITPORDER, PURCHASE, ITLOCATN, ACTIVLOG respectively. As explained above, each task type consists of 334 task instances. Task type (T_{12}) for merge and join of output of (T_1) and (T_2) and sort of the result. Task type (T_{123}) for merge and join of (T_{12}) output with the output of (T_3). Task type (T_{12345}) for merge and join of (T_{123}) output with the outputs of (T_4) and (T_5) (as mentioned above, the result of join of the first four tables is directly piped to be merged and joined with the fifth table, hence all of these are part of the task type (T_{12345})).

Each task instance runs on one CPU. We can calculate the total amount of CPU, I/O, and communication resource consumption of each task. Based on these, we can calculate the duration of a task. We can calculate the total CPU time essentially based on the pathlength. Likewise, given the I/O parameters of a task (i.e., how many sequential prefetches, how many random I/Os, how many pages, etc.), we can determine the I/O time. Similarly, the communication time can be calculated. Based on these, we determine the time duration of a task, and the rate that CPU, I/O, and communication resources are used. Figure 5 shows one rectangle per task type, where the width is the duration and the height is the CPU utilization of that task. If CPU bound, the height is 100%; otherwise, the height is less than 100%. This diagram also shows the dependency amongst the different tasks. A similar diagram can be obtained for other resources, such as I/O. The critical path is $((T_4), (T_{12345}))$. If we remove the tasks associated with this critical path, we get the second critical path: $((T_5))$. These two critical paths are numbered 1 and 2 respectively. Likewise, we get $((T_{1,2,3}), (T_3))$, $((T_{1,2}, T_2))$, $((T_1))$ for critical paths 3, 4, and 5 respectively.

The ***no-stretch*** algorithm tries to place these rectangles such that the total height is less than 100% of the aggregate MIPS. This is essentially a bin-packing problem except that the dependency constraints between rectangles must not be violated. Figure 6 shows the result of this scheduling. First, it places the tasks associated with critical path 1, $((T_4),(T_{12345}))$. Then, it places the task associated with critical path 2, $((T_5))$. Since we have enough CPU MIPS left, task (T_5) is placed on top of task (T_4). That is, they are run in parallel. Then, it places tasks associated with critical path 3, $((T_{1,2,3}))$. Note that this task does not fit on top of tasks (T_4) and (T_5). The rest is obvious. The total response time is 23 seconds.

This scheduling algorithm wastes some CPU resource. One way around this is to stretch some of the rectangles, and even break them into pieces and place them in the gaps. We could stretch task (T_{123}) and place it on top of tasks (T_4) and (T_5). This is possible by assigning the left-over CPU resource to task (T_{123}) during this period. This may be done by assigning to this task a lower priority compared with the other two tasks. In a sense, we are slowing down task (T_{123}). This is acceptable because its

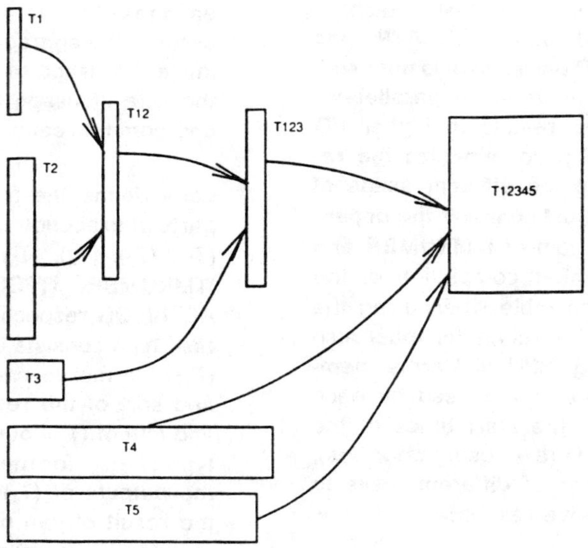

Figure 5: Time-Resource Diagram for Different Task Types

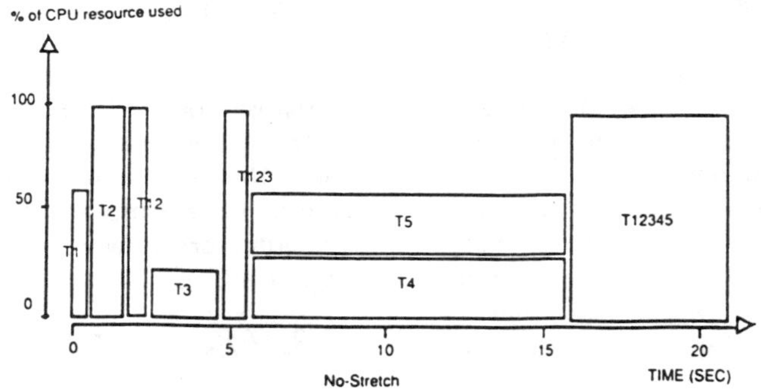

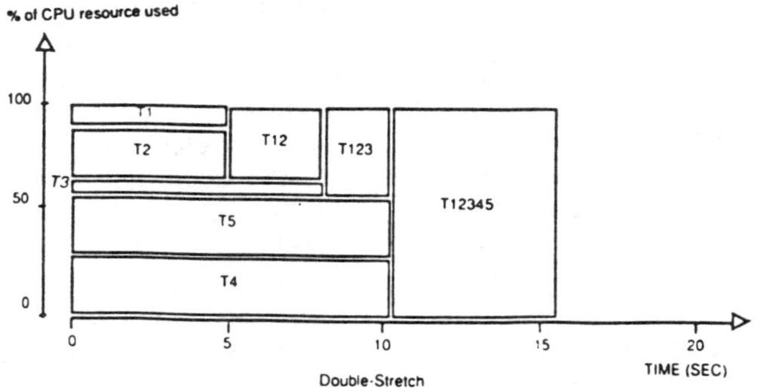

Figure 6: Schedule of Different Tasks for the No-Stretch and Double-Stretch Algorithms.

results are not needed until the start of task (T_{12345}). Note that the area of the rectangle, which is the total amount of CPU resource consumed by this task, does not change. As a result of stretching, the height is reduced. Another way is to break a rectangle into pieces and put pieces in the gaps. For this, we start a task, then we stop it for a while, and then we start it again. Combination of stretching and breaking allows us to place the rectangles such that no CPU resource will be wasted. This leads us to the ***double-stretch*** algorithm. Note that in reality, stretching and breaking may increase the total resource consumption of a task due to some overhead associated with task interference. We expect the design of the scheduler will be such that this cost is not significant.

The result of the double-stretch algorithm is shown in Figure 6. Essentially, this algorithm stretches all the critical paths such that they start at time 0 and finish when their results are needed (note that by definition, any critical path, as defined above, can start at time 0). As a result, it tries to keep as many tasks active as possible at any time, thereby reducing the chances of a CPU being idle. In this algorithm, we place the tasks of critical path 1, ((T_4), (T_{12345})), in sequence. Then, we place the task of critical path 2, (T_5), right above ((T_4)). We stretch this task (hence reducing its height) so that it starts at the same time as task (T_4). Task (T_5) is started at time 0 and finishes when its result is needed. Then, we place tasks associated with critical path 3, (($T_{1,2,3}$), (T_3)) on top of task (T_5). Then, we stretch all the tasks of critical path 3 so that it starts from time 0 and finishes when its results are needed. We do the same for the rest of the critical paths.

At this point, the algorithm calculates the aggregate height (which is a step function). If the aggregate height for any period of time is more than 100% of the aggregate MIPS, then we stretch the rectangles for that period of time, reducing their aggregate height to 100% of the aggregate MIPS. If the aggregate height for any period is less than 100% of the aggregate MIPS, then we increase the degree of parallelism for the tasks active in that period to increase the height. As a result of this, the resource utilization for other resources, such as I/O, may increase.[11] This algorithm does not waste any CPU resource, hence giving the optimum response time under the CPU resource constraint assumption.

One of the major problems with stretching is the increase in memory consumption. A task needs its working set in memory. By stretching, a task uses the resource given to its working memory (set of real memory pages needed for this task) for a longer period of time. This usually results in an increase in the aggregate memory consumption. Another way of looking at this is that as a result of stretching (and breaking) we are increasing the level of multiprogramming, which usually results in greater memory consumption. Hence, we believe that a scheduler must reduce stretching as much as possible.

5.2. Effective I/O Bandwidth

Figure 7 shows the I/O rate as a function of time for the no-stretch and double-stretch scheduling algorithms, respectively. For the no-stretch algorithm, the ratio of MIPS over peak I/O rate is about 7 MIPS/MBPS (million instructions per second over million bytes per second). The ratio for the double-stretch algorithm is about 5. The latter ratio was used to study the I/O versus CPU parallelism in the section "2.5. I/O Versus CPU Versus Communication Parallelism". The peak aggregate effective I/O bandwidth is about 2000MBPS. Each 30 MIPS CPU needs about 6MBPS of effective I/O bandwidth. We discussed this in greater detail in the section "2.5. I/O Versus CPU Versus Communication Parallelism". Observe that the double-stretch algorithm results in higher average effective bandwidth because it has a shorter response time (the same amount of I/O must be done in a shorter period of time). The I/O rate for the no-stretch algorithm has more fluctuation. This is mainly because the double-stretch algorithm keeps more tasks running at the same time, though more slowly, and it introduces a more averaging effect.

5.3. Effective Communication Bandwidth

Figure 8 shows the effective aggregate communication bandwidth between nodes. Again, the double-stretch algorithm has less fluctuation than the no-stretch algorithm. For the no-stretch algorithm, the ratio of MIPS over peak effective communication bandwidth is about 9 MIPS/MBPS. The ratio for the double-stretch algorithm is about 16. For a ratio of 16, the aggregate effective communication bandwidth is about 600MBPS.[12] Each CPU needs about 2MBPS effective communication bandwidth. As expected, the average effective communication bandwidth for the no-stretch algorithm is less than that for the double-stretch algorithm since the response time in the former is higher. However, the peak of the no-stretch algorithm is higher. The reason is that the merge tasks that retrieve data from remote

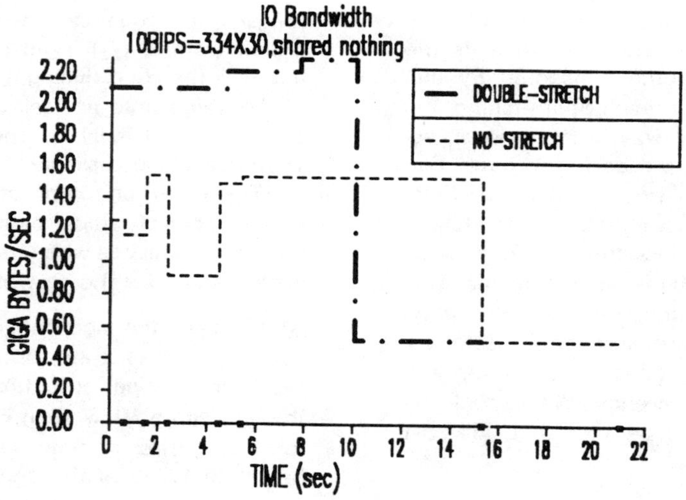

Figure 7: I/O Bandwidth

11 Note that in this example, the algorithm is always feasible because we only put a constraint on the CPU resource type.

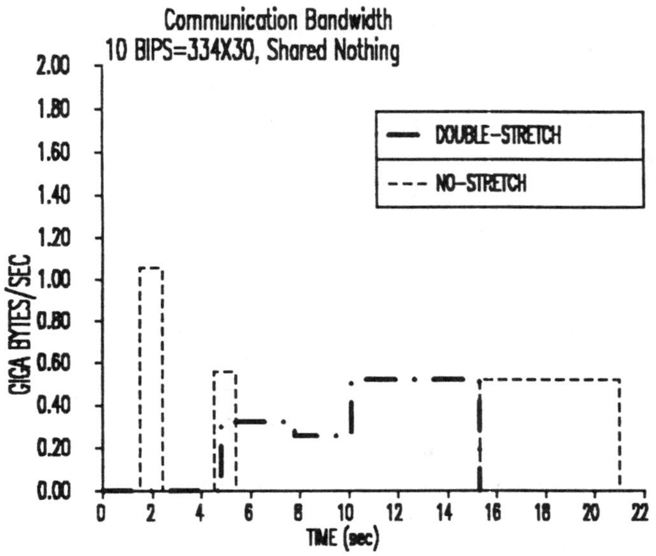

Figure 8: Communication Bandwidth

sort workfiles are not stretched, hence they go at a faster speed, resulting in a higher effective communication bandwidth peak. However, as explained before, the merge operators, which mostly get their inputs from other nodes, pipe their results to the join operators. The join operators (except for one) pipe their results into sort operators. As a result, the speed of the merge operators are controlled (reduced) also by the join and sort operators. Thus, pipelining helps reduce the communication peaks considerably. This is one of the key benefits of pipelining.

5.4. Further Remarks on Performance

In the above query, most of the data accessed from the base tables is used for further processing (sort, join, etc.). This query has low physical selectivity; ratio of relevant data (defined to be the set of tuples that satisfy the local predicates) over the data retrieved from the base tables is low. Now suppose 5fanj query studied above is over a much larger data base (e.g., terabyte), but the relevant data is kept the same. Let's call this the high physical selectivity case, as compared with the low selectivity case studied above.[13] An example of such a situation is physical integration of two existing data bases. The tuples used by queries on each data base may be scattered across much larger set of pages after integration. In the high physical selectivity case, the access part of the plan must filter out much greater amount of irrelevant data compared with the low physical selectivity case. If no indices are available, then a table scan must be used. As a result, the Access cost will be much higher than what is shown in Figure 4, dominating the rest of the costs, because most of the pages accessed contain little or no relevant data. The effective I/O bandwidth is much higher because the ratio L/I is much lower, i.e., the CPU does not need to do much work on each retrieved page. Note that this case argues for architectures where the I/O devices are locally attached to the processors. The reason is that in such an architecture it is much cheaper to provide high bandwidth I/O compared with the shared disks case, where all I/Os must go through a processor to disk switch.

In the high physical selectivity case, if indices are available, then usually index ANDing and/or ORing [MHWC90] is used to restrict access to pages containing relevant data. In this case, the I/O bandwidth is usually higher than the high physical selectivity case. But the change in the I/O bandwidth is not nearly as drastic as in the case with low physical

12 Note that this is at least an order of magnitude higher than what the Ethernet LANs provide currently.

13 Obviously we assume queries are optimized, pushing predicates down for better physical selectivity.

selectivity and no applicable index. The same is true for cost of Access.

If the select list of the query has a large number of fields or large-sized fields, the effective communication bandwidth grows almost proportionately. Techniques similar to semi-join [BeCh81] can be used to reduce the effective communication bandwidth.

6. Summary and Conclusions

In this paper, we discussed some architectural alternatives and design approaches for introducing intra-query parallelism in a relational DBMS. We discussed the pros and cons of the shared nothing (SN) and shared disks (SD) architectures. While scalability might be a problem for SD, it has many advantages with respect to load balancing and data base design. Further research is needed to clarify these points. A possibility is using the SD architecture in the nodes of an SN system. This gives us more powerful nodes which are easier to manage and whose load is easier to balance. Availability in case of failures of some processors within a node is also enhanced with this hybrid approach. We also discussed the increasingly important role that disk arrays will play in improving the I/O subsystem's performance to match the latter with that of the CPUs. We also discussed asynchronous pipelining using table queues and the overheads that they impose compared to synchronous pipelining. Parallel synchronous pipelining was pointed out as the preferred method of accomplishing parallelism, whenever possible.

Finally, we emphasized the need for a comprehensive benchmark for complex queries. We presented a quantitative analysis of the usage of different resource types (CPU, I/O, etc.) for a particular complex query. Based on this, we reemphasized the fact that the I/O bandwidth might be very high, if table scans are used and the predicates have high selectivity. In SN, it is usually easier and cheaper to provide high bandwidth I/O since disks are locally attached. With respect to load balancing, we discussed some of the major issues. We may not foresee the skew problems at compile time due to the absence of knowledge about the values of bindings of host variables, correlations, etc. This requires doing some work at run time. This is a major research problem.

Other major topics that must be considered in the study of a parallel DBMS include system management, utilities (data base reload, unload, reorganization, etc.), performance of transaction workload on large number of small CPUs, and mix of transaction and query workloads. We are continuing work on the research topics that we have identified in this paper.

7. Acknowledgements

We would like to acknowledge a number of our colleagues for their help and insights: Ted Messinger for his efforts to create and maintain a large benchmark data base; Don Haderle for providing extensive technical advice; Akira Shibamiya for helping us understand DB2 execution costs; Jim Brady, John Lindley and Irv Traiger for emphasizing the importance of parallelism; Raymond Lorie, Peter Haas, Bala Iyer, Bruce Lindsay, John McPherson, Inderpal Narang, Kurt Shoens, Irving Traiger for many useful discussions, and Danny Dolev and Barbara Simons for helping us understand the task scheduling techniques.

8. References

ABCGK79 Astrahan, M., Blasgen, M., Chamberlin, D., Gray, J., King, F., Lindsay, B., Lorie, R., Mehl, J., Price, T., Putzolu, F., Schkolnick, M., Selinger, P., Slutz, D., Strong, R., Tiberio, P., Traiger, I., Wade, B., and Yost, R. *System R: A Relational Data Base Management System* **IEEE Computer**, May 1979.

AgSe89 Agrawal, D., Sengupta, S. *Modular Synchronization in Multiversion Databases: Version Control and Concurrency Control*, **Proc. ACM-SIGMOD International Conference on Management of Data**, Portland, May 1989.

AlCo88 Alexander, W., Copeland, G. *Process and Dataflow Control in Distributed Data-Intensive Systems*, **Proc. ACM-SIGMOD International Conference on Management of Data**, Chicago, May 1988.

AnCK89 Andrade, J., Carges, M., Kovach, K. *Building a Transaction Processing System on UNIX Systems*, **Proc. Unix Transaction Processing Workshop**, Pittsburgh, May 1989, USENIX Association.

AnCo88 Anderson, M., Cole, R. *An Integrated Data Base*, In **IBM Application System/400 Technology**, Document Number SA21-9540, IBM, June 1988.

Anon85 Anon, et al. *A Measure of Transaction Processing Power*, **Datamation**, April 1, 1985.

BeCh81 Bernstein, P.A., Chiu, D.W. *Using Semi-Joins to Solve Relational Queries*, **Journal of the ACM**, Vol. 28, No. 1, January 1981.

Bhid88 Bhide, A. *An Analysis of Three Transaction Processing Architectures*, **Proc. 14th International Conference on Very Large Data Bases**, Los Angeles, August 1988.

BoPu88 Borr, A., Putzolu, F. *High Performance SQL Through Low-Level System Integration*, **ACM SIGMOD International Conference on Management of Data**, Chicago, June 1988.

Bora88a Boral, H. *Parallelism and Data Management*, **Technical Report Number ACA-ST-156-88**, MCC, May 1988.

Bora88b Boral, H. *Parallelism in Bubba*, **Proc. International Symposium on Databases for Parallel and Distributed Systems**, Austin, December 1988.

Borr81 Borr, A. *Transaction Monitoring in Encompass: Reliable Distributed Transaction Processing*, **Proc. 7th International Conference on Very Large Data Bases**, Cannes, September 1981.

Borr84 Borr, A. *Robustness to Crash in a Distributed Database: A Non Shared-Memory Multi-Processor Approach*, **Proc. 10th International Conference on Very Large Data Bases**, Singapore, August 1984.

CABK88 Copeland, G., Alexander, W., Boughter, E., Keller, T. *Data Placement in Bubba*, **Proc. ACM-SIGMOD International Conference on Management of Data**, Chicago, May 1988.

CaHS85 Carr, C., Huddleston, R.L., Strickland, J. *Method and Means for the Retention of Locks Across System, Subsystem, and Communication Failures in a Multiprocessing, Multiprogramming, Shared Data Environment*, **U.S. Patent 4,480,304**, IBM, 1985.

ChGY81 Chamberlin, D., Gilbert, A., Yost, R. *A History of System R and SQL/Data System*, **Proc. 7th International Conference on Very Large Data Bases**, Cannes, September 1981.

ChGr85 Chan, A., Gray, R. *Implementing Distributed Read-Only Transactions*, **IEEE Transactions on Software Engineering**, Vol. SE-11, No. 2, 1985.

CHHIM90 Cheng, J., Haderle, D., Hedges, R., Iyer, B., Messinger, T., Mohan, C., Wang, Y. *An Efficient Hybrid Join Algorithm: Design, Prototype, Modelling and Measurement*, **IBM Research Report**, IBM Almaden Research Center, March 1990.

ChMy88 Chang, P.Y., Myre, W.W. *OS/2 EE Database Manager Overview and Technical Highlights*, **IBM Systems Journal**, Vol. 27, No. 2, 1988.

CLSW84 Cheng, J., Loosely, C., Shibamiya, A., Worthington, P. *IBM Database 2 Performance: Design, Implementation, and Tuning*, **IBM Systems Journal**, Vol. 23, No. 2, 1984.

Corn88 Cornelis, R. *Site Autonomy in a Distributed Database Environment*, **Proc. IEEE Compcon Spring '88**, San Francisco, March 1988.

DeGS88 DeWitt, D., Ghandeharizadeh, S., Schneider, D. *A Performance Analysis of the Gamma Database Machine*, **Proc. ACM-SIGMOD International Conference on Management of Data**, Chicago, May 1988.

DeSB87 DeWitt, D., Smith, M., Boral, H. *A Single-User Performance Evaluation of the Teradata Database Machine*, **Proc. 2nd International Workshop on High Performance Transaction Systems**, Asilomar, September 1987. Also in **Lecture Notes in Computer Science Vol. 359**, D. Gawlick, M. Haynie, A. Reuter (Eds.), Springer-Verlag, 1989.

DGRS89 Duppel, N., Gugel, D., Reuter, A., Schiele, G. *Progress Report #6 of PROSPECT*, **University of Stuttgart**, November 1989.

DGRSZ88 Duppel, N., Gugel, D., Reuter, A., Schiele, G., Zeller, H. *Progress Report #4 of PROSPECT*, **University of Stuttgart**, 1988.

DIRY89 Dias, D., Iyer, B., Robinson, J., Yu, P. *Integrated Concurrency-Coherency Controls for Multisystem Data Sharing*, **Proc. IEEE Transactions on Software Engineering**, Vol. 15, No. 4, April 1989.

Duqu87 Duquaine, W. *LU6.2 as a Network Standard for Transaction Processing*, **Proc. 2nd International Workshop on**

High Performance Transaction Systems, Asilomar, September 1987. Also in **Lecture Notes in Computer Science Vol. 359**, D. Gawlick, M. Haynie, A. Reuter (Eds.), Springer-Verlag, 1989.

EGKS89 Englert, S., Gray, J., Kocher, T., Shah, P. *A Benchmark of NonStop SQL Release 2 Demonstrating Near-Linear Speedup and Scaleup on Large Databases*, **Technical Report 89.4**, Tandem Computers, May 1989.

Epst88 Epstein, R. *RDBMS Architecture Boosts Performance, Reliability*, **Mini-Micro Systems**, August 1988.

FTSN89 Serlin O., editor *DEC 9000 to Challenge IBM 3090*, **FT Systems News Letter**, Issue No. 86, Oct. 24 1989.

GaKi85 Gawlick, D., Kinkade, D. *Varieties of Concurrency Control in IMS/VS Fast Path*, **IEEE Database Engineering**, Vol. 8, No. 2, June 1985.

GeDe87 Gerber, R., DeWitt, D. *The Impact of Hardware and Software Alternatives on the Performance of the Gamma Database Machine*, **Computer Sciences Department Technical Report #708**, University of Wisconsin at Madison, July 1987.

Grae90 Graefe, G. *Encapsulation of Parallelism in the Volcano Query Processing System*, **Proc. ACM-SIGMOD International Conference on Management of Data**, Atlantic City, May 1990.

Gray78 Gray, J. *Notes on Data Base Operating Systems*, In **Operating Systems - An Advanced Course**, R. Bayer, R. Graham, and G. Seegmuller (Eds.), Lecture Notes in Computer Science, Volume 60, Springer-Verlag, 1978. Also Available as IBM Research Report RJ2188, IBM San Jose Research Laboratory, February 1978.

Haer88 Haerder, T. *Handling Hot Spot Data in DB-Sharing Systems*, **Information Systems**, Vol. 13, No. 2, p155-166, 1988.

HaJa84 Haderle, D., Jackson, R. *IBM Database 2 Overview*, **IBM Systems Journal**, Vol. 23, No. 2, 1984.

HaSS88 Haerder, T., Schoning, H., Sikeler, A. *Parallelism in Processing Queries on Complex Objects*, **Proc. International Symposium on Databases in Parallel and Distributed Systems**, Austin, p131-143, December 1988. Also Available as Report No. 37/88, University of Kaiserslautern, October 1988.

HaSS89 Haerder, T., Schoning, H., Sikeler, A. *Evaluation of Hardware Architectures for Parallel Execution of Complex Database Operations*, **Proc. 3rd Annual Parallel Processing Symposium**, Fullerton, p564-578, 1989. Also Available as Report No. 23/89, University of Kaiserslautern, April 1989.

HFLP89 Haas L., Freytag J.C., Lohman G., Pirahesh H. *Extensible Query Processing in Starburst*, **Proc. ACM-SIGMOD International Conference on Management of Data**, Portland, May 1989.

Hobs87 Hobson, S. *ALCS - A High-Performance, High-Availability DB/DC Monitor*, **Proc. 2nd International Workshop on High Performance Transaction Systems**, Asilomar, September 1987. Also in **Lecture Notes in Computer Science Vol. 359**, D. Gawlick, M. Haynie, A. Reuter (Eds.), Springer-Verlag, 1989.

HsDe90 Hsiao, H., DeWitt, D. *Chained Declustering: A New Availability Strategy for Multiprocessor Database Machines*, **Proc. 6th IEEE International Conference on Data Engineering**, Los Angeles, February 1990.

IyDi90 Iyer, B., Dias, D. *System Issues in Parallel Sorting for Database Systems*, **Proc. 6th IEEE International Conference on Data Engineering**, Los Angeles, February 1990. Also Available as **IBM Research Report RJ6585**, IBM Almaden Research Center, November 1988.

IyRV89 Iyer, B., Ricard, G., Varman, P. *Percentile Finding Algorithm for Multiple Sorted Runs*, **Proc. 15th International Conference on Very Large Data Bases**, Amsterdam, August 1989.

JoRo89 Joshi, A., Rodwell, K. *A Relational Database Management System for Production Applications*, **Digital Technical Journal**, No. 8, February 1989.

KITM83 Kitsuregawa, M., Tanaka, H., Moto-Oka, T. *Application of Hash to Data Base Machine and Its Arachitecture*, **New Generation Computing**, Vol. 1, pp 63-74, 1983.

KrLS86 Kronenberg, N., Levy, H., Strecker, W. *VAXclusters: A Closely-Coupled Distributed System*, **ACM Transactions on Computer Systems**, Vol. 4, No. 2, May 1986.

LDHSY89 Lorie, R., Daudenarde, J., Hallmark, G., Stamos, J., Young, H. *Adding Intra-Transaction Parallelism to an Existing DBMS: Early Experience*, **Data Engineering**, Vol. 12, No. 1, March 1989. Also Available as IBM Research Report RJ6165, IBM Almaden Research Center, 1988.

LMHDL85 Lohman, G., Mohan, C., Haas, L., Daniels, D., Lindsay, B., Selinger, P., Wilms, P. *Query Processing in R**, In **Query Processing in Database Systems**, W. Kim, D. Reiner, and D. Batory (Eds.), Springer-Verlag, 1985. Also Available as IBM Research Report RJ4272, April 1984.

Loos86 Loosley, C. *Measuring IBM Database 2 Release 2 - The Benchmark Game*, **InfoDB**, Vol. 1, No. 2, 1986.

LoYo89 Lorie, R., Young, H. *A Low Communication Sort Algorithm for a Parallel Database Machine*, **Proc. 15th International Conference on Very Large Data Bases**, Amsterdam, August 1989. Also Available as **IBM Research Report RJ6669**, IBM Almaden Research Center, February 1989.

McGe77 McGee, W.C. *The Information Management System IMS/VS - Part IV: Data Communication Facilities*, **IBM Systems Journal**, Vol. 16, No. 2, 1977.

MHLPS89 Mohan, C., Haderle, D., Lindsay, B., Pirahesh, H., Schwarz, P. *ARIES: A Transaction Recovery Method Supporting Fine-Granularity Locking and Partial Rollbacks Using Write-Ahead Logging*, To Appear in **ACM Transactions on Database Systems**. Also Available as **IBM Research Report RJ6649**, IBM Almaden Research Center, January 1989.

MHWC90 Mohan, C., Haderle, D., Wang, Y., Cheng, J. *Single Table Access Using Multiple Indexes: Optimization, Execution, and Concurrency Control Techniques*, **Proc. International Conference on Extending Data Base Technology**, Venice, March 1990, Springer-Verlag. Also Available as **IBM Research Report RJ7341**, IBM Almaden Research Center, March 1990.

MiSu88 Mikkilineni, K., Su, S. *An Evaluation of Relational Join Algorithms in a Pipelined Query Processing Environment*, **IEEE Transactions on Software Engineering**, Vol. 14, No. 6, June 1988.

Moha89 Mohan, C. *ARIES/KVL: A Key-Value Locking Method for Concurrency Control of Multiaction Transactions Operating on B-Tree Indexes*, **IBM Research Report RJ7008**, IBM Almaden Research Center, September 1989.

Moha90 Mohan, C. *Commit_LSN: A Novel and Simple Method for Reducing Locking and Latching in Transaction Processing Systems*, **IBM Research Report RJ7344**, IBM Almaden Research Center, February 1990.

MoLe89 Mohan, C., Levine, F. *ARIES/IM: An Efficient and High Concurrency Index Management Method Using Write-Ahead Logging*, **IBM Research Report RJ6846**, IBM Almaden Research Center, August 1989.

MoLO86 Mohan, C., Lindsay, B., Obermarck, R. *Transaction Management in the R* Distributed Data Base Management System*, **ACM Transactions on Database Systems**, Vol. 11, No. 4, December 1986. Also Available as IBM Research Report RJ5037, IBM Almaden Research Center, February 1986.

MoNa90 Mohan, C., Narang, I. *ARIES/SD: A Transaction Recovery and Concurrency Control Method for the Shared Disks Environment*, **IBM Research Report**, IBM Almaden Research Center, Forthcoming, 1990.

MoNP90 Mohan, C., Narang, I., Palmer, J. *A Case Study of Problems in Migrating to Distributed Computing: Page Recovery Using Multiple Logs in the Shared Disks Environment*, **IBM Research Report RJ7343**, IBM Almaden Research Center, March 1990.

MoPi90 Mohan, C., Pirahesh, H. *ARIES-RRH: Restricted Repeating of History in the ARIES Transaction Recovery Method*, **IBM Research Report RJ7342**, IBM Almaden Research Center, February 1990.

Nech86 Neches, P. *The Anatomy of a Data Base Computer - Revisited*, **Proc. IEEE**

Compcon Spring '86, San Francisco, March 1986.

ObSW83 Obermarck, R., Strickland, J., Watts, V. *Method and Means for the Sharing of Data Resources in a Multiprocessing, Multiprogramming Environment*, **U.S. Patent 4,399,504**, IBM, August 1983.

OlRo89 Olken, F., Rotem, D. *Random Sampling from B^+ Trees* , **Proc. 15th International Conference on Very Large Data Bases**, Amsterdam, August 1989.

Onei89 O'Neil, P. *Revisiting DBMS Benchmarks*, **Datamation**, p47, 48, 52, 54, September 15, 1989.

PaGK88 Patterson, D., Gibson, G., Katz, R. *A Case for Redundant Arrays of Inexpensive Disks (RAID)*, **Proc. ACM-SIGMOD International Conference on Management of Data**, Chicago, May 1988.

PeSt83 Peterson, R.J., Strickland, J.P. *Log Write-Ahead Protocols and IMS/VS Logging*, **Proc. 2nd ACM SIGACT-SIGMOD Symposium on Principles of Database Systems**, Atlanta, March 1983.

Rahm87 Rahm, E. *Design of Optimistic Methods for Concurrency Control in Database Sharing Systems*, **Proc. 7th International Conference on Distributed Computing Systems**, Berlin, September 1987.

Rahm88 Rahm, E. *Design and Evaluation of Concurrency and Coherency Control Techniques for Database Sharing Systems*, **Internal Report 182/88**, University of Kaiserslautern, 1988.

Rahm89a Rahm, E. *A Framework for Workload Allocation in Distributed Transaction Systems*, **Technical Report**, University of Kaiserslautern, September 1989.

Rahm89b Rahm, E. *Recovery Considerations for Data Sharing Systems*, **Technical Report**, University of Kaiserslautern, October 1989.

Reed78 Reed, D. *Naming and Synchronization in a Decentralized Computer System*, **PhD Thesis**, Technical Report MIT/LCS/TR-205, MIT, September 1978.

ReSW89 Rengarajan, T.K., Spiro, P., Wright, W. *High Availability Mechanisms of VAX DBMS Software*, **Digital Technical Journal**, No. 8, February 1989.

Ross89 Ross, F. *An Overview of FDDI: The Fiber Distributed Data Interface*, **IEEE Transactions on Selected Areas in Communications**, Vol. 7, No. 7, September 1989.

SACL79 Selinger, P., Astrahan, M., Chamberlin, D., Lorie, R., Price, T. *Access Path Selection in a Relational Database Management System*, **Proc. ACM-SIGMOD International Conference on Management of Data**, June 1979.

SaGa86 Salem, K., Garcia-Molina, H. *Disk Striping*, **Proc. 2nd IEEE International Conference on Data Engineering**, Los Angeles, February 1986.

ScDG89 Schneider, D., DeWitt, D., Ghandeharizadeh, S. *An Overview of the Gamma Database Machine*, **Proc. IEEE Compcon Spring '89**, San Francisco, March 1989.

Sche87 Scherr, A.L. *Structures for Networks of Systems*, **IBM Systems Journal**, Vol. 26, No. 1, p4-12, 1987.

Scru87 Scrutchin, T. *TPF: Performance, Capacity, Availability*, **Proc. IEEE Compcon Spring '87**, San Francisco, February 1987.

SeAd80 Selinger, P.G., Adiba, M. *Access Path Selection in Distributed Database Management Systems*, **Proc. International Conference on Databases**, Aberdeen, Scotland, July 1980.

Serl89 Serlin, O. *CICS is Key to IBM's OLTP Success*, **UNIX World**, November 1989.

Shoe86 Shoens, K. *Data Sharing vs. Partitioning for Capacity and Availability*, **Database Engineering**, Vol. 9, No. 1, March 1986.

Siwi77 Siwiec, J.E. *A High-Performance DB/DC System*, **IBM Systems Journal**, Vol. 16, No. 2, 1977.

SKPO88 Stonebraker, M., Katz, R., Patterson, D., Ousterhout, J. *The Design of XPRS*, **Proc. 14th International Conference on Very Large Data Bases**, Los Angeles, August-September 1988.

SMLC86 Su, S., Mikkilineni, K., Liuzzi, R., Chow, Y.C. *A Distributed Query Processing Strategy Using Decomposition, Pipelining and Intermediate Result Sharing Techniques*, **Proc. 2nd**

IEEE International Conference on Data Engineering, Los Angeles, February 1986.

SMMTG84 Sekino, A., Moritani, K., Masai, T., Tasaki, T., Goto, K. *The DCS - A New Approach to Multisystem Data-Sharing*, **Proc. National Computer Conference**, Las Vegas, July 1984.

SNOP85 Shoens, K., Narang, I., Obermarck, R., Palmer, J., Silen, S., Traiger, I., Treiber, K. *Amoeba Project*, **Proc. IEEE Compcon Spring '85**, San Francisco, February 1985.

SQL23 Melton, J. (Ed.) *(ISO-ANSI Working Draft) Database Language SQL2 and SQL3*, **X3H2-90-001 and DBL SEL-3**, ISO/IEC JTC1/SC21/WG3 N986, December 1989.

SSSHD87 Sundstrom, R.J., Staton III, J.B., Schultz, G.D., Hess, M.L., Deaton, Jr., G.A., Cole, L.J., Amy, R.M. *SNA: Current Requirements and Direction*, **IBM Systems Journal**, Vol. 26, No. 1, p13-36, 1987.

StAS89 Stonebraker, M., Aoki, P., Seltzer, M. *Parallelism in XPRS*, **Memorandum No. UCB/ERL M89/16**, University of California, Berkeley, February 1989.

Ston86 Stonebraker, M. *The Case for Shared Nothing*, **IEEE Database Engineering**, Vol. 9, No. 1, 1986.

StUW82 Strickland, J., Uhrowczik, P., Watts, V. *IMS/VS: An Evolving System*, **IBM Systems Journal**, Vol. 21, No. 4, 1982.

Tand87 The Tandem Database Group *NonStop SQL: A Distributed, High-Performance, High-Availability Implementation of SQL*, **Proc. 2nd International Workshop on High Performance Transaction Systems**, Asilomar, September 1987. Also in **Lecture Notes in Computer Science Vol. 359**, D. Gawlick, M. Haynie, A. Reuter (Eds.), Springer-Verlag, 1989.

Tand88 Tandem Performance Group *A Benchmark of Non-Stop SQL on the Debit Credit Transaction*, **ACM-SIGMOD International Conference on Management of Data**, Chicago, June 1988.

TeGu84 Teng, J., Gumaer, R. *Managing IBM Database 2 Buffers to Maximize Performance*, **IBM Systems Journal**, Vol. 23, No. 2, 1984.

Tera88 Teradata *DBC/1012 Data Base Computer Concepts and Facilities - Release 3.1*, **Documber Number C02-0001-05**, Teradata Corp., May 1988.

TPC89 Transaction Processing Performance Council *TPC Benchmark A*, **Draft 6-PR Proposed Standard**, 1989. Available from ITOM International Co., POB 1450, Los Altos, CA 94023.

TuOB89 Turbyfill, C., Orji, C., Bitton, D. *AS^3AP- A Comparative Relational Database Benchmark*, **Proc. IEEE-Compcon Spring '89**, San Francisco, February 1989.

Weih87 Weihl, W. *Distributed Version Management for Read-Only Actions*, **IEEE Transactions on Software Engineering**, Vol. SE-13, No. 1, January 1987.

Wolf88 Wolfson, O. *Sharing the Load of Logic-Program Evaluation*, **Proc. International Symposium on Databases in Parallel and Distributed Systems**, Austin, p46-55, December 1988.

Optimizing SQL Queries for Parallel Execution

Günter von Bültzingsloewen

Forschungszentrum Informatik an der Universität Karlsruhe
Haid-und-Neu-Straße 10–14, D–7500 Karlsruhe 1

Abstract: *The optimization problem discussed in this paper is the translation of an SQL query into an efficient parallel execution plan for a multiprocessor database machine under the performance goal of reduced response times as well as increased throughput in a multiuser environment. We describe and justify the most important research problems which have to be solved to achieve this task, and we explain our approach to solve these problems.*

1 Introduction

Recently, several experimental database machines (e.g. ARBRE [Lori89], BUBBA [AlCo88, CABK88], GAMMA [DeWi86] and KARDAMOM [Bült89]) have been designed which use parallelism to obtain increased performance (both response times and throughput). They are based on a loosely or closely coupled multiprocessor system. A disk can be accessed only by the processor it is attached to (i.e. no disk sharing). Disks may be attached to some or all of the processors. Relations are partitioned and spread over several disks.

Parallelism is exploited at two levels (at least): we have inter-transaction parellelism for increased throughput as well as intra-query (and thus intra-transaction) parallelism on the level of set-oriented algebraic operations for reduced response times. A query execution plan in such a system can be represented by a data flow program, a directed acyclic graph whose nodes represent operations and whose arcs represent the flow of data between operations [Chan76, BoDe82]. Independent operations of a dataflow program can be executed in parallel. Additional potential parallelism can be obtained in the following ways:

- *Change order of operations:* An example of this kind of transformation is the use of flatter and bushier join trees compared to the linear trees often used in today's optimizers (e.g. [Seli79]).
- *Node splitting:* Operations, which access or manipulate base relations, have to be split into suboperations according to data distribution: each partition of a base relation resides on a disk attached to a certain processor and can be accessed only by this processor. Additional node splitting can be performed for operations like join and aggregation which operate on intermediate relations produced by former operations (e.g. parallel join algorithms [DeGe85, KTMo83, RiLM87]).
- *Pipelining:* Consecutive operations can be executed in parallel if they do not require complete operands but can work on tuple packets which are iteratively produced. Pseudo-parallel execution of the operations of such a pipe is already useful in a single processor execution plan: main memory requirements for intermediate results are reduced, hence the swapping of intermediate results to disk may be avoided. For parallel execution, a pipe is decomposed into parts which are assigned to different processors, each part consisting of one operation or several consecutive operations.

In order to express how much of the potential parallelism is actually realized, the dataflow program can be augmented by scheduling information (e.g. assignment of operations to processors, priority of operations).

The optimization problem we are concerned with is: Determine an efficient parallel execution plan for a given query using the above possibilities, which can afterwards be executed several times (i.e. precompilation of queries). In the remainder of this paper, we describe and justify the most important research problems which have to be solved to achieve this task, and we explain our approach to solve these problems.

"Optimizing SQL Queries for Parallel Execution" by G. von Bültzingsloewen from *ACM SIGMOD Record*, Vol. 18, No. 4, Dec. 1989, pp. 17-22. Reprinted by permission of the author.

2 Objective of Optimization

Usual objectives of query optimization are to minimize total processing cost (a weighted sum of CPU-cost, I/O-cost, memory-cost and communication cost) or to minimize execution time. In centralized database systems, these objectives are largely equivalent, and optimizers attempt to minimize total processing cost [JaKo84]. In a multiprocessor database machine, these objectives do not coincide as a higher degree of parallelism usually implies reduced execution times and increased total processing cost because of increased processing, communication and control overhead. Hence we have

Problem 1: *How should the objective of optimization in a multiprocessor database machine be defined?*

Proposed Solution: The overall performance goal of a multiprocessor database machine is to obtain increased throughput as well as reduced response times in a multiuser environment. Throughput is reduced if we increase the parallelism inside single queries because of increased processing overhead; average response time is usually reduced because of reduced execution time. However, in case of high resource utilization (high throughput) it may actually be increased as higher resource requirements (higher total processing cost) may cause longer waiting times until a query can be executed. Hence, the optimization problem involves a tradeoff between execution time and total processing cost. Which combination leads to the desired throughput and response times depends on the load conditions and can only be determined at run time. Therefore, the optimizer should construct several alternative plans under the following objectives:

(1) Minimize total processing cost.

(2) Minimize execution time subject to a maximum x%-increase of total processing cost (for several values of x).

In order to minimize execution time the degree of parallelism (defined as the average number of processors used during the execution of the query) has to be increased starting from a plan with (near) minimal cost. To choose an appropriate plan at runtime, we have to know more about the effects of increased total processing cost and reduced execution time on response time and throughput. In order to obtain this knowledge, simulation experiments or performance measurements should be performed, which examine the performance of a multiprocessor database machine under several load conditions using query execution plans with differing cost and execution time. Related experiments have been performed in Bubba [Smit89], however under a different objective: to determine the impact of node splitting enforced by data distribution on response times.

3 Architecture of the Optimizer

The generation of an optimal query execution plan is a complex (NP-hard) optimization problem. Solution procedures for such problems have been studied extensively in Operations Research and Artificial Intelligence [Pear84]. They can be described using the following basic elements:

- A *code* which can represent each *object of the search space* (solution candidate, set of possible solution candidates).
- A *rule base* containing rules to transform the encoding of one object to that of another object in order to scan the search space.
- A *search strategy*, i.e. an effective method to select the next transformation rule to be applied to an object.
- *Cost functions* which serve to evaluate objects of the search space.

We can distinguish two basic possibilities to organize the search space:

(1) *Stepwise Improvement:* Objects represent complete solution candidates. Starting from an initial solution, transformations are applied in order to obtain improved solutions.

(2) *Split-and-prune:* Objects correspond to subsets which contain all potential solutions which are derivable from a certain partial solution. Transformations split subsets into smaller subsets (extend partial solutions). Subsets which presumably do not contain an optimal solution can be pruned, i.e. excluded from further expansion. If only such subsets which certainly do not contain an optimal solution are pruned, we obtain a *branch-and-bound* algorithm.

Both possibilities have been used in query optimization. Examples of the use of stepwise improvement are [IoWo87, SwGu88, GrDe87], examples of branch-and-bound (or the corresponding dynamic programming algorithm) are [Shan88, LeFL88]. Several search strategies can be used in combination with these possibilities: unsystematic search (e.g. local search, simulated annealing), blind, systematic search (depth-first search, breadth-first search) and informed, systematic search (best-first search, A*-algorithm). Up to now, there is no clear evidence which choice is best. Hence we have

Problem 2: *Should a query optimizer use stepwise improvement or split-and-prune (branch-and-bound, dynamic programming)? If either possibility is chosen, which search strategy should be used?*

Proposed solution: We choose to investigate split-and-prune strategies for one main reason: it leads to a better analysis of the optimization problem, as we have to define precisely the decisions involved in the generation of a parallel execution plan. Thus we can possibly exercise more control on the solution candidates examined during the search; to accomplish this, we have to develop heuristics to prune the search space and to evaluate objects in order to perform a best-first search.

We can organize the search as a number of steps, each of which makes certain decisions and thus reduces the number of plans obtainable from a partial solution:

(1) Generate all reasonable algebraic expressions for a given SQL query. An algebraic expression corresponds to the set of all query execution plans, which perform the algebraic operations in the same order as in the expression.

(2) Generate execution methods for the operations of an algebraic expression. The result of this step is a single processor execution plan.

(3) Generate parallel execution plans using node splitting and pipelining and adding scheduling information. According to the different objectives, several execution plans are generated.

Code, rule base and search strategy used in these steps are discussed in the following sections.

4 Generating Single Processor Execution Plans

In conventional implementations of SQL, queries are executed at least partially tupel-oriented, i.e. by nested iteration (System R, System R*). In contrast to that, we want to generate execution plans that contain only (methods for) set-oriented algebraic operations. All known approaches to translate SQL queries into relational algebra [CeGo85, LeVi85, Daya87, Kim82] are incomplete and some are partially incorrect (see [Bült87]). Furthermore, all approaches except [Daya87] generate very complicated expressions which are no good starting point for further optimization. Hence we have

Problem 3: *How can we generate all reasonable algebraic expression for a given SQL query in a systematic way?*

Proposed solution: The generation of algebraic expressions is performed in three steps:

(1) An SQL query is translated into an expression of an extended relational algebra (extension of [Klug82]). The expression is in a special normal form which defines an order of algebraic operations only as far as absolutely necessary, so that an optimal expression can be reached from this starting point. The translation has been developed starting from [Bült87], however avoiding unnecessarily complicated expressions.

(2) The expression is simplified using transformations which are known to produce better expressions.

(3) Starting from this normal from, algebraic expressions and methods for the execution of algebraic operations are generated using functional rules similar to [LeFL88].

The normal form we use is a union of expressions

$$\pi_{X(Y)}\ \sigma_{p_1}\ E_1 \ldots E_k\ \phi_{X_g\ F}\ \sigma_{p_2}\ E_{k+1} \ldots E_m\ (R_1 \times R_2 \times \ldots R_n).$$

Each E_i is derived from a subquery and essentially an expression of the same form, however with one additional relation parameter $\mathcal{R}$ in the cross product and possibly including difference, division or outer aggregation (see below). $E\ e = E[\mathcal{R}/e]$ denotes the replacement of $\mathcal{R}$ by the algebraic expression e, thus binding the outer references of the subquery.

Projections are extended to retain duplicates ($\pi_{X(Y)}$ denotes a projection on X which retains duplicates according to the number of different Y-values). An extended selection predicate p is a conjunction of simple predicates (without logical connectives). However, in case of a selection on a single relation ($n = 1$), it may also contain disjunctions to avoid unnecessary unions. Furthermore, it may include semijoin conditions ($\exists e\ p$) as we wish to perform several semijoin operations on a relation in a single filter operation.

$\phi_{X_g\,F}\,e$ denotes the aggregation, which groups e by X_g-values and applies the aggregate functions F to each group. In subquery expressions E_i, we also use an outer aggregation $e_1 \bowtie_F e_2$ which attaches aggregate function values to each tuple t of e_1 and is equivalent to an outer join followed by the standard aggregation $\phi_{X_1\,F}$, X_1 being the attributes of e_1. Arithmetic expressions may be used in projections, selection predicates and aggregations.

Transformations performed in the second step include the replacement of an outer aggregate formation by a standard aggregation (without using an outer join); the elimination of unneccesary join predicates; and the replacement of two negative semijoins by a division. All of these transformations are only applicable under certain restricted conditions.

The generation of algebraic expressions starting from this normal form requires the following decisions: In conjunctive expressions, the main decision is the ordering of join operations. Furthermore, we have to decide wether selections are performed before or after a join. Aggregation operations have to be positioned with respect to join operations. We may use the outer aggregation in combination with simple joins or the standard aggregation in combination with outer joins.

Algebraic expressions whose results are combined by a union may be optimized independently, whereupon subexpressions common to several algebraic expressions can be combined. An alternative to this appraoch is the optimization of the complete expression in one step. The advantage of this alternative is that common subexpressions can be produced intentional, possibly yielding a better expression ([Bry89]).

5 Generating Parallel Execution Plans

To generate parallel execution plans we can introduce additional potential parallelism by changing the order of operations, node splitting and pipelining. A change in the order of operations is considered automatically, if we parallelize not only the most cost effective single processor execution plan, but also the second, third, etc (but only such plans, where the order of operations and not only the execution methods differ). Pipelining is enabled by decomposing pipes into parts. Hence the only change in the underlying dataflow program is by node splitting which may be enforced (access of base relations) or optionally chosen (other operations).

In order to evaluate total processing cost of a dataflow program, we have to assign the operations to processors (assuming that an operation is executed completely by one processor), as the cost for local communication on one processor is different from the cost for remote communication. The minimization of total processing cost is thus similar to query optimization in distributed database systems (however, communication is not the most important cost factor).

In order to evaluate execution time, we have to build a schedule as in deterministic scheduling theory [Coff76]. Besides the assignment of operations to processors, it also assigns execution intervals to each operation. Minimization of execution time is thus similar to the problems studied in scheduling theory; it differs mainly in the possibility of pipelining and node splitting, and in a more complicated cost model including CPU-cost, I/O-cost, memory cost and communication.

The scheduling decisions underlying the evaluation of execution time have to be transformed into scheduling information, upon which runtime scheduling can be based. As cost estimates are generally imprecise, it does not make sense to fix execution intervals for each operation. Instead, we need a more abstract description of a parallel execution plan, from which execution intervals can be deduced for cost evaluation and which can be used for runtime scheduling.

Problem 4: *What scheduling information should parallel execution plans contain?*

Proposed solution: We assume that an operation is executed by a process running on a certain processor and can be interrupted only, if it is waiting for a certain event (I/O, operand, pipelining), or if an operation (process) with a higher priority becomes executable. Under these assumptions which are usually fulfilled by a real time operating system, runtime scheduling decisions depend on the following information:

(1) *Assignment of operations to processors.* It has to be fixed only for operations that access base relations. All other operations can be collected into groups which are mapped to processors at runtime, at most one group to one processor. Thus a limited dynamic load balancing at runtime is possible besides the choice of an appropriate execution plan.

(2) *Priority of an operation.* It is assigned to the process which executes the operation and thus influences the scheduling of the underlying operating system.

Execution intervals can be deduced from assignment and priority of operations assuming that always the executable operation (i.e. all operands are at least partially available) with highest priority is scheduled.

The number of possible parallel execution plans is much larger than the number of single processor execution plans due to the possibility of node splitting and pipelining and the scheduling decisions. Hence, while the complete enumeration of all reasonable single processor execution plans may still be feasible, this is certainly impossible for parallel execution plans. Therefore, we need effective heuristics to prune the search space.

Former solutions for the generation of parallel execution plans are not convincing. [CePS85] considers only parallelism between independent operations and an a priori fixed degree of node splitting for each operation. [BaYH87] assumes that node splitting is always possible without additional CPU-cost, and uses pipelining always, if any reduction in execution time is achieved, thereby possibly precluding a better parallelization. Hence we have

Problem 5: *What are effective heuristics for the generation of parallel execution plans?*

Proposed solution: We want to find execution plans which minimize response time subject to a maximum x%-increase in total processing cost. Two basic decisions are involved in this task: adding additional potential parallelism by node splitting and pipe decomposition and realising parallelism by associating processors and priorities with operations. As we can not decide in advance, wether it is better to use pipelining or node splitting, we define potential parallelism on a per pipe basis. Thus the generation of parallel execution plans also involves a number of steps:

(1) Iteratively generate execution plans with increased potential parallelism (number of processors associated with a pipe). The search can be limited, as in each iteration we only have to increase the number of processors for pipes lying on the critical path in order to obtain reduced execution times.

(2) Minimize the execution time of a pipe utilizing the number of processors allowed. We may use node splitting and pipe decompositions and have to assign operations to processors. The execution time is minimized by balancing the load across the participating processors with as less expensive node splitting and communication as possible.

(3) Determine an optimal schedule given the degree of parallelism and execution time of each pipe. The scheduling decisions can be based on a heuristic which has been proven to be useful in deterministic scheduling theory: critical path scheduling.

We expect that both degree of parallelism and processing cost will increase while we proceed increasing potential parallelism, hence we can finally choose an optimal processing plan for each increase in total cost we are interested in.

6 Conclusion

We have described an approach to the optimization of SQL queries for parallel execution in a multiprocessor database machine, which, considering the increasing performance of communication networks, will become relevant for distributed database systems as well. Its implementation will replace the limited optimizer for an SQL subset currently used within the prototype of the KARDAMOM database machine.

Our approach is rather static in that only a limited number of decisions is performed at runtime. Therefore it depends on reliable cost estimates which are not easy to obtain. Thus the next problem to be examined will be

Problem 6: *What is the influence of imprecise cost estimates on the quality of execution plans? In case imprecise estimates have a significant influence, how can we perform dynamic optimization at runtime?*

An approach to solve the first part of this problem is to use our optimizer to produce execution plans under different cost estimates and compare their quality under the different estimates. The design of dynamic optimization at runtime can be based upon an analysis of the differences of the produced execution plans. A possible implementation technique are dynamic query execution plans [GrWa89].

References

[AlCo88] W. Alexander, G. Copeland: Process and Dataflow Control in Distributed Data-Intensive Systems. Proc. ACM SIGMOD, Chicago, June 1988

[BaYH87] T. Baba, S.B. Yao, A.R. Hevner: Design of a Functionally Distributed Multiprocessor Database Machine Using Data Flow Analysis. IEEE Trans. on Computers, C-36,6, June 1987, pp. 650-666

[BoDe82] H. Boral, D.J. DeWitt: Applying Data Flow Techniques to Database Machines. IEEE Computer, August 1982, pp. 57–63

[Bry89] F. Bry: Towards an Efficient Evaluation of General Queries: Quantifier and Disjunction Processing Revisited. Proc. ACM SIGMOD, Portland, June 1989, pp. 193-204

[Bült87] G. v. Bültzingsloewen: Translating and Optimizing SQL Queries Having Aggregates. Proc. 13th Int. Conf. on Very Large Data Bases, Brighton, September 1987, pp. 235-243

[Bült89] G. v. Bültzingsloewen, C. Iochpe, R.-P. Liedtke, R. Kramer, M. Schryro, K. R. Dittrich, P. C. Lockemann: Design and Implementation of KARDAMOM — A Set-oriented Data Flow Database Machine. Proc. 6th Int. Workshop on Database Machines, Springer Lecture Notes, Vol. 368, June 1989, pp. 18-33

[CABK88] G. Copeland, W. Alexander, E. Boughter, T. Keller: Data Placement in Bubba. Proc. ACM SIGMOD, Chicago, June 1988, pp. 99-108

[CeGo85] S. Ceri, G. Gottlob: Translating SQL into Relational Algebra: Optimization, Semantics and Equivalence of SQL Queries. IEEE Trans. S.E., April 1985, pp. 324-345

[CePS85] F. Cesarini, F. Pippolini, G. Soda: A Technique for Analyzing Query Execution in a Multiprocessor Database Machine. Proc. 4th Int. Workshop on Database Machines, Grand Bahama Island, March 1985, pp. 68-90

[Chan76] P.Y. Chang: Parallel Processing and Data Driven Implementation of a Relational Database System. Proc. of the 1976 Conf. of the ACM, pp. 314-318

[Coff76] E.G. Coffmann (ed.): Computer and Job-Shop Scheduling Theory. John Wiley & Sons, 1976

[Daya87] U. Dayal: Of Nests and Trees: A Unified Approach to Processing Queries That Contain Nested Subqueries, Aggregates, and Quantifiers. Proc. 13th Int. Conf. on Very Large Data Bases, Brighton, September 1987, pp. 197-208

[DeGe85] D.J. DeWitt, R. Gerber: Multiprocessor Hash-Based Join Algorithms. Proc. 11th Int. Conf. on Very Large Data Bases, Stockholm, 1985

[DeWi86] D.J. DeWitt et al.: GAMMA - A High Performance Dataflow Database Machine. Proc. 12th Int. Conf. on Very Large Data Bases, Kyoto, August 1986

[GaJo79] M.R Garey, D.S. Johnson: Computers and Intractability — A Guide to the Theory of NP-Completeness. W.H. Freeman and Company, San Francisco, 1979

[GrDe87] G. Graefe, D.J. DeWitt: The Exodus Optimizer Generator. Proc. ACM SIGMOD, San Francisco, May 1987, pp. 160-172

[GrWa89] G. Graefe, K. Ward: Dynamic Query Evaluation Plans. Proc. ACM SIGMOD, Portland, June 1989, pp. 358-366

[IoWo87] Y.E. Ioannidis, E. Wong: Query Optimization by Simulated Annealing. Proc. ACM SIGMOD, San Francisco, May 1987, pp. 9-22

[JaKo84] M. Jarke, J. Koch: Query Optimization in Database Systems. ACM Computing Surveys, June 1984, pp. 111-152

[Kim 82] W. Kim: On Optimizing an SQL-like Nested Query. ACM TODS, Sept. 1982, pp. 443-469

[Klug82] A. Klug: Equivalence of Relational Algebra and Relational Calculus Query Languages Having Aggregate Functions. Journal of the ACM, Vol. 29, No.3, July 1982, pp. 699-717

[KTMo83] M. Kitsuregawa, H. Tanaka, T. Moto-oka: Application of Hash To Data Base Machine and Its Architecture. New Generation Computing, Vol. 1, No. 1, 1983

[LeFL88] M.K. Lee, J.C. Freytag, G.M. Lohman: Implementing an Interpreter for Functional Rules in a Query Optimizer. IBM Research Report RJ 6125, March 1988

[LeVi85] C. Le Viet: Translation and Compatibility of SQL and QUEL Queries. Journ. Inf. Proc., Vol. 8, No. 1, 1985, pp. 1-15

[Lori89] R. Lorie et. al.: Adding Intra-Transaction Parallelism to an Existing DBMS: Early Experience. IEEE Data Engineering, Vol. 12, No. 1, March 1989, pp. 2-8

[Pear84] J. Pearl: Heuristics: Intelligent Search Strategies for Computer Problem Solving. Addison Wesley, 1984

[RiLM87] J.P. Richardson, H. Lu, K. Mikkilineni: Design and Evaluation of Parallel Pipelined Join Algorithms. Proc. ACM SIGMOD, San Francisco, May 1987, pp. 399-409

[Seli79] P.G Selinger et. al.: Access Path Selection in a Relational Database System. Proc. ACM SIGMOD, Boston, May 1979, pp 23-34

[Shan88] M.-C. Shan: Optimal Plan Search in a Rule-Based Query Optimizer. Proc. Int. Conf. on Extending Database Technology, Venedig, March 1988, pp. 92-112

[Smit89] M. Smith et. al.: An Experiment on Response Time Scalability in Bubba. Proc. 6th Int. Workshop on Database Machines, Springer Lecture Notes, Vol. 368, June 1989, pp. 34-57

[SwGu88] A. Swami, A. Gupta: Optimization of Large Join Queries. Proc. ACM SIGMOD, Chicago, June 1988, pp. 8-17

Chapter 2: Architecture of Parallel Database Systems

In this chapter, we give a brief description of the reference architecture of parallel database systems. A detailed study on the architecture of parallel database systems is beyond the scope of this book. It is hoped that the concepts discussed here will provide readers with some common terminologies to aid in understanding the following chapters.

There are three major types of resources in parallel database systems: processor, main memory, and secondary storage (usually disks). Data are stored on disks. During query processing, data are brought to memory from the disks. The results may also be written back to disk. The way in which the processors, memory, and disks interact affects the parallel query processing strategies dramatically. This is one of the features that distinguishes parallel database systems from general parallel computing systems. The major architectural concern of most research work on general parallel computing is the topology in which the processing units (PEs) are connected. For parallel database systems, the connection between the secondary storage and the other two types of resources, the processors and memory, also plays a very important role. Based on this observation, the parallel database system architectures are classified into three basic categories — shared everything, shared nothing, and shared disks — as shown in Figure 2-1.

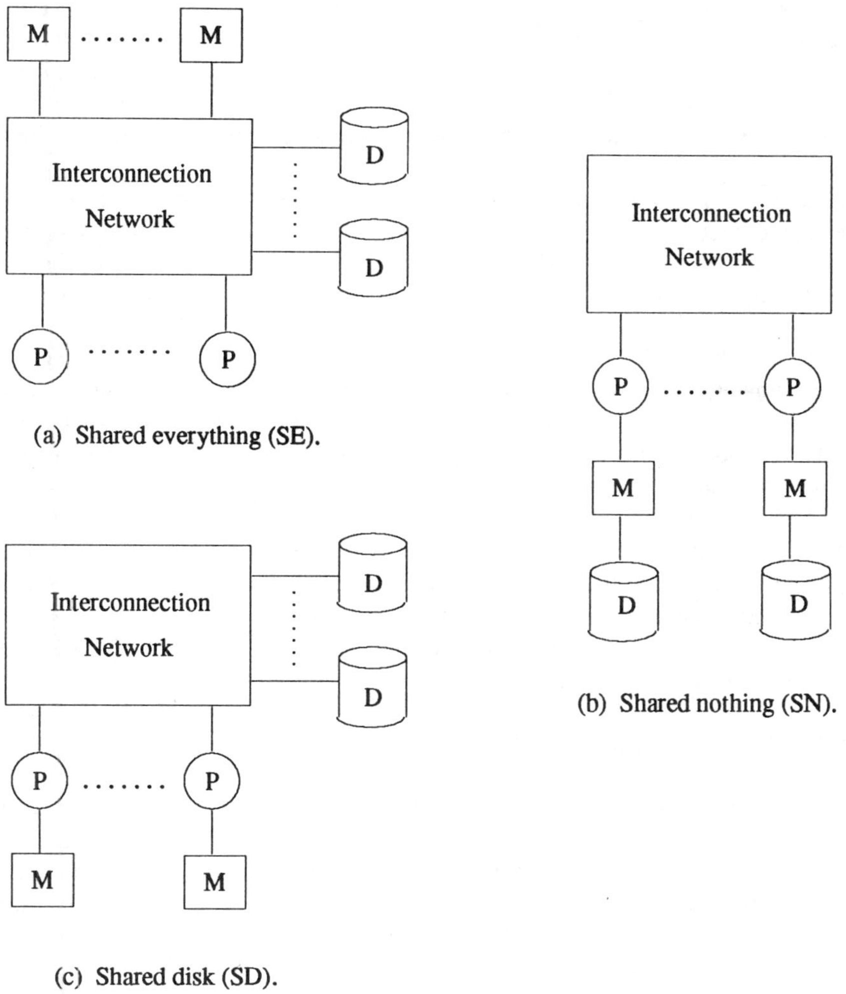

Figure 2-1. Parallel database system architectures.

Shared everything multiprocessors

In shared everything (SE) or shared memory (SM) systems, the disks and the memory are shared among all the processors. The system is composed of fast network interconnecting processor modules, shared memory modules, and disks. The general purpose multiprocessor computers are of such architecture. The SE systems have two major advantages. First, they have no communication cost, as message exchange and data sharing among processors are through the shared memory. The synchronization can also be implemented by cheap and low-level mechanisms. Second, they are suitable for load balancing. One major drawback of the SE architecture is its limited scalability. The interconnection network that allows any processor to access any memory module increases the memory-access latency. In order to reduce its effect on system performance, processors usually have a fast local cache memory. Accessing the cached data is much faster (5 to 50 times) than accessing the noncached data. However, the use of cache requires certain mechanisms to ensure cache coherency and introduces certain overhead. When the number of processors or the number of memory modules increases, this overhead also increases. Thus, it seems impractical to have a shared everything system with hundreds of processors. Examples of shared everything systems include the IBM 3090 series of machines,[1] Berkeley's XPRS,[2] and Colorado's Volcano.[3]

Shared nothing multiprocessors

The shared nothing (SN) architecture is the other extreme: every processor has its own memory and disks. Such a processor-memory-disks group is also called a node. There is no direct access from one processor to the disks and memory of the other processors. The processors can communicate with one another only by sending messages through an interconnection network. Of course, it is not true that nothing is shared: the database is shared so that the same operations can be performed concurrently by a number of processors. Usually, the database is partitioned and stored on disks of different processors. Mass storage in such an architecture is generally distributed among the processors by connecting one or more disks to each processor.

The major advantage of the SN architecture is its potential to be scaled to thousands of processors. This is contrary to the shared everything machines, where scaling beyond 30 to 40 processors may already be difficult to achieve. It is believed that the SN architecture is the only architecture that can scale up to the performance level dictated by the design goals. They also provide better reliability and availability by isolating faults.

SN systems have their own problems. For such systems to perform well, the processing load across the nodes must be approximately the same. Parallelizing an operation, such as sort or join, may not bring any returns when the data is highly skewed. Good algorithmic design that considers load-balancing issues will resolve this problem. As pointed out in Reference 4, shared nothing systems may also have problems in scaling large join operations caused by the O(N*M) numbers of messages needed to redistribute the joined relations (in general each of N nodes routes tuples to M joining nodes), especially as N and M become large. The effect on performance will depend on the relative cost of communication versus other join processing. In spite of this scaling limitation, the overall performance for large joins is expected to be better in shared nothing architecture than in the other two architectures.

The shared nothing architecture is adopted in Tandem's Encompass and NonStop SQL,[5] Teradata's DBC/1012,[6] MCC's Bubba,[7] and Wisconsin's Gamma.[8]

Shared disk multiprocessors

In shared disk (SD) systems, disks are shared. In other words, every processor can directly read from and write to any of the disks in the system. However, processors manage their own memory buffer that stores the data read from disks. A processor cannot access the data in the memory of the other processors. The shared disk approach is adopted in IBM's IMS/VS Data Sharing product,[9,10] TPF product,[11,12] the Amoeba research project,[13,14] DEC's VAX DBMS and VAX Rdb/VMS product,[15,16] and NEC's DECS.[17]

Hybrid architecture

To enjoy the advantages provided by the shared everything architecture and, at the same time, to increase the system's scalability, Richardson, Lu, and Mikkilineni[18] propose a multiprocessor data management architecture that consists of a set of clusters linked by an interconnection network. Each cluster consists of a set of processors, a shared memory bank addressable by all the processors in the cluster, and a set of disk storage units and associated controllers. In other words, each cluster is a shared everything system, while the clusters form a shared nothing architecture. Such a hybrid architecture has also been proposed in References 19 and 20.

Comparison of different architectures

Each of the three major architectures has its own strengths and weaknesses. For each basic architecture, there are indeed quite a number of products or prototype systems, developed by major vendors and research organizations. The debate on the relative merits of the three approaches still goes on.

An early comparison of the above-mentioned architectures is given in Reference 21. Each architecture is assigned a comparative score of 1 (the best), 2 (the second best), or 3 (the third best) for 12 system features including difficulty of concurrency control, cash recovery, database design, load balancing, high availability, number of messages, bandwidth required, ability to scale to a large number of machines and to have large distances between machines, susceptibility to critical sections and hot spots, and number of system images. Among these features, the shared nothing architecture scores the best in high availability, the ability to scale to large numbers of processors, and the ability to have large distances between machines. It also requires the least bandwidth and is the least susceptible to critical sections than the other two alternative architectures. The shared memory architecture, on the other hand, scores the best in crash recovery and ease of load balancing. It requires the least number of messages and only one system image. The author concludes that the shared nothing architecture has no apparent disadvantages in building scalable and tunable database systems, compared to the other alternatives. On the other hand, the shared everything architecture does not scale to a large number of processors, making it less interesting than the other alternatives. The shared disk architecture seems to be a compromise of the other two architectures and will lose to the shared nothing architecture since it is never the best in any features compared.

Boral et al. summarize lessons learned from designing and implementing a shared nothing prototype parallel database system, BUBBA.[7] For high-end systems using SQL (requiring > 400 transactions per second (TPS)), it appears to be the only alternative. For large systems (200 to 400 TPS), it is much more cost-effective than mainframes. For small to medium systems (< 200 TPS), there are many alternatives with similar cost performance; however, the shared nothing architecture is the only architecture that can scale throughout the entire range.

Shoens[22] points out one major advantage that a shared disk system enjoys over a shared nothing system — the system structure does not change when processors or disks are added or fail. In shared nothing systems, whenever a new processor or disk is added a decision must be made as to how the database should be redistributed among the available processors and disks. In contrast, with the shared disk architecture, the disks and processors can be considered separately: should more computing power be needed, additional processors can be added without changing the arrangement of data on the disks. If more disk space is needed, additional disks can be added and the database can be rearranged on them without determining which of the new disk drives should be owned by which processors. Table 2-1 summarizes some of the existing commercial and research systems.

Another architecture-related issue is whether the system is dedicated to database operations. Systems dedicated to database applications are often classified as database machines. A number of parallel database machines or prototypes have been developed. One architectural feature of database machines is that they may consist of a large number of processors, such as 1024 processors. There are general-purpose multiprocessor machines currently available, too. DBMS running on such machines can also explore parallelism among database operations. Major features of general-purpose multiprocessor computer systems for parallel database processing include a relatively small number of processors, no special hardware for database primitive operations, and nonpredictable resource availability.

Table 2-1. Some existing parallel database systems.

System name	Developer	Type	Features	Reference
Gamma V1.0	UW-Madison	SN	17 VAX 11/750 processors, each with 2 Mbytes of memory connected by an 80-Mbit/s token ring. Eight of the processors have a 333-Mbyte Fujitsu disk drive.	23
Gamma V2.0	UW-Madison	SN	Intel 32-processor iPSC/2 hypercube, each with a 386 CPU, 8 Mbytes of memory, and a 333-Mbyte 5¼" disk drive.	8
Bubba	MCC	SN	40-node Flex/32 multicomputer. Each node consists of a 16-MHz Motorola 68020 CPU, 68851 MMU, and 6881 FPU, with 2 Mbytes of on-board SRAM. Each node also has a set of VME peripherals including 4 Mbytes of external DRAM, a 180-Mbyte 5¼" CDC Wren III Winchester disk, and a high-performance disk controller.	7
DBS3	Bull	SE	Multiprocessor Encore Multimax 520 configured with 10 NS32532 processors (8.5 MIPS, each with a 256-KB cache memory), 96 Mbytes of main memory, and 1-Gbyte disk storage. Processors memory and I/O boards are interconnected by one 100-Mb/s bus.	24
Volcano	Colorado	SE	Sequent Symmetry with 12 Intel 16-MHz 80386 CPUs. Each CPU has 64-KB cache and delivers about 4 MIPS.	3
XPRS	UC-Berkeley	SE	Sequent Symmetry with 12 processors, five disks controlled by three disk controllers connected via an 80 Mbyte/s bus.	2

Papers in this chapter

In this chapter, we include four papers, three of which describe the architecture of existing parallel database systems. The last paper is a performance comparison of the three generic parallel architectures.

The first paper, "The Design of XPRS," is by Stonebraker, Katz, Patterson, and Ousterhout. It describes how parallelism is explored in XPRS, which is a shared everything system.

The next paper is "The Gamma Database Machine Project," by DeWitt, Ghandeharizadeh, Schneider, Bricker, Hsiao, and Rasmussen. It describes the design of the shared nothing Gamma database machine. The techniques employed in its implementation to facilitate its scalability are also discussed.

The third paper is "Architecture and Performance of Relational Algebra Machine GRACE" and is by Kitsuregawa, Tanaka, and Moto-Oka. It is one of the earliest works to use hashing techniques to achieve high performance. The paper also introduces the pipeline bucket processing scheme.

Finally, "An Analysis of Three Transaction Processing Architectures" by Bhide examines how the three generic architectures perform relative to one another.

References

1. S.G. Tucker, "The IBM 3090 System: An Overview," *IBM Systems J.,* Vol. 25, No. 1, 1986, pp. 4-19.
2. M. Stonebraker et al., "The Design of XPRS," *Proc. 14th Int'l Conf. Very Large Data Bases,* Morgan Kaufman, San Mateo, Calif., 1988, pp. 318-330.
3. G. Graefe, "Encapsulation of Parallelism in the Volcano Query Processing System," *Proc. ACM Int'l Conf. Management Data,* Assoc. for Computing Machinery, New York, N.Y., 1990, pp. 102-111.
4. M.S. Lakshmi and P.S. Yu, "Effectiveness of Parallel Joins," *IEEE Trans. Knowledge and Data Eng.,* Vol. 2, No. 3, Sept. 1990, pp. 410-424.
5. S. Englert et al., "A Benchmark of Nonstop SQL Release 2 Demonstrating Near-Linear Speedup and Scaleup on Large Databases," Tech. Report 89.4, Tandom Computer Inc., 1989.

6. "DBC/1012 Database Computer Concepts and Facilities," rel. 3.1 edition, Teradata document c02-0001-05. Teradata Corporation, Los Angeles, Calif., 1988.
7. H. Boral et al., "Prototyping Bubba, A Highly Parallel Database System," *IEEE Trans. Knowledge and Data Eng.*, Vol. 2, No. 1, Mar. 1990, pp. 4-24.
8. D.J. DeWitt et al., "The Gamma Database Machine Project," *IEEE Trans. Knowledge and Data Eng,*, Vol. 2, No. 1, Mar. 1990, pp. 44-62.
9. R.J. Peterson and J.P. Strickland, "Log Write-Ahead Protocols and IMS/VMS Logging," *Proc. Second ACM SIGART-SIGMOD Symp. Principles Database Systems,* Assoc. for Computing Machinery, New York, N.Y., 1983.
10. J. Strickland, P. Uhrowczik, and V. Watts, "IMS/VS: An Evolving System," *IBM Systems J.*, Vol. 21, No. 4, 1982.
11. S. Hobson, "ALCS — A High-Performance, High Availability DB/DC Monitor," *Proc. Second Int'l Workshop High Performance Transaction Systems,* 1987.
12. T. Scrutchin, "TPF: Performance, Capacity, Availability," *Proc. IEEE Compcon,* IEEE CS Press, Los Alamitos, Calif., 1987, pp. 158-160.
13. C. Mohan and I. Narang, "Aries/sd: A Transaction Recovery and Concurrency Control Method for Shared Disks Environment," IBM Research Report, IBM Almaden Research Center, 1990.
14. C. Mohan, I. Narang, and J. Palmer, "A Case Study of Problems of Migrating to Distributed Computing: Page Recovery Using Multiple Logs in the Shared Disks Environment," IBM Research Report RJ7343, IBM Almaden Research Center, 1990.
15. N. Kronenberg, H. Levy, and W. Strecker, "Vaxclusters: A Closely-Coupled Distributed System," *ACM Trans. Computer Systems,* Vol. 4, No. 2, 1986.
16. T.K. Rengarajan, P. Spiro, and W. Wright, "High Availability Mechanisms of VAX DBMS Software," *Digital Technical J.*, Feb. 1989.
17. A. Sekino et al., "The DCS — A New Approach to Multisystem Data Sharing," *Proc. Nat'l Computer Conf.*, AFIPS Press, Reston, Va., 1984, pp. 59-68.
18. J.P. Richardson, H. Lu, and K. Mikkilineni, "Design and Evaluation of Parallel Pipelined Join Algorithms," *Proc. ACM Int'l Conf. Management Data,* Assoc. for Computing Machinery, New York, N.Y., 1987, pp. 399-409.
19. K.A. Hua, C. Lee, and J.K. Peir, "A High Performance Hybrid Architecture for Concurrent Query Execution," *Proc. Second IEEE Symp. Parallel and Distributed Processing,* IEEE CS Press, Los Alamitos, Calif., 1990, pp. 348-351.
20. H. Pirahesh et al., "Parallelism in Relational Data Base Systems: Architectural Issues and Design Approaches," *Proc. Second Int'l Symp. Databases Parallel and Distributed Systems,* IEEE CS Press, Los Alamitos, Calif., 1990, pp. 4-29.
21. M. Stonebraker, "The Case for Shared Nothing," *Database Eng.*, Vol. 9, No. 1, 1986, pp. 4-9.
22. K. Shoens, "Data Sharing vs. Partitioning for Capacity and Availability," *Database Eng.*, Vol. 9, No. 1, 1986, pp. 10-16.
23. D.J. DeWitt, S. Ghandeharizadeh, and D. Schneider, "A Performance Analysis of the Gamma Database Machine," *Proc. ACM Int'l Conf. Management Data,* Assoc. for Computing Machinery, New York, N.Y., 1988, pp. 350-360.
24. B. Bergsten, M. Couprie, and P. Valduriez, "Prototyping DBS3, a Shared Memory Parallel Database System," *Proc. First Int'l Conf. Parallel and Distributed Information Systems,* IEEE CS Press, Los Alamitos, Calif., 1991, pp. 226-234.

THE DESIGN OF XPRS

Michael Stonebraker, Randy Katz, David Patterson, and John Ousterhout
EECS Department
University of California, Berkeley

Abstract

This paper presents an overview of the techniques we are using to build a DBMS at Berkeley that will simultaneously provide high performance and high availability in transaction processing environments, in applications with complex ad-hoc queries and in applications with large objects such as images or CAD layouts. We plan to achieve these goals using a general purpose DBMS and operating system and a shared memory multiprocessor. The hardware and software tactics which we are using to accomplish these goals are described in this paper and include a novel "fast path" feature, a special purpose concurrency control scheme, a two-dimensional file system, exploitation of parallelism and a novel method to efficiently mirror disks.

1. INTRODUCTION

At Berkeley we are constructing a high performance data base system with novel software and hardware assists. The basic goals of XPRS (eXtended Postgres on Raid and Sprite) are very high performance from a general purpose DBMS running on a conventional operating system and very high availability. Moreover, we plan to optimize for either a single CPU in a computer system (e.g. a Sun 4) or a shared memory multiprocessor (e.g a SEQUENT Symmetry system). We discuss each goal in turn in the remainder of this introduction and then discuss why we have chosen to exploit shared memory over shared nothing or shared disk.

This research was sponsored by the Defense Advanced Research Projects Agency under contract N00039-84-C-0089, the Army Research Office under contract DAAL03-87-G-0041, and the National Science Foundation under contract MIP-8715235.

1.1. High Performance

We strive for high performance in three different application areas:

1) transaction processing
2) complex ad-hoc queries
3) management of large objects

Previous high transaction rate systems have been built on top of low-level, hard-to-program, underlying data managers such as TPF [BAMB87] and IMS/Fast Path [DATE84]. Recent systems which are optimized for complex ad-hoc queries have been built on top of high-function data managers (e.g. GAMMA [DEWI86] and DBC/1012 [TERA85]); however such systems have used custom low-level operating systems. Lastly, applications requiring support for large objects (such as images or CAD geometries) have tended not to use a general purpose data manager because of performance problems.

The first goal of XPRS is to demonstrate that high performance in each of these areas can be provided by a next generation DBMS running on a general purpose operating system without unduly compromising performance objectives. Clearly, this will be a major advantage as it will bring the benefits of ease of application construction, ease of application migration, data independence and low personnel costs to each of these areas. Specifically, we are using a slightly modified version of POSTGRES [STON86] as the underlying data manager and the Sprite network operating system [OUST87]. Our concrete performance goals for XPRS in each of the three application areas are now described.

We feel that general purpose CPUs will obey Joy's law of:

$$MIPS = 2 ** (year - 1984)$$

at least for the next several years. As such, we are confident that single processor systems of 50-100 MIPS will appear by 1991 and that shared memory multiprocessors of several hundred MIPS will also occur in the same time frame. Consequently, we expect that CPU limitations of current transaction processing engines will become less severe in the future. Therefore we strive only for "good" performance on TP1 [ANON85] which has come to be the standard benchmark by which transaction processing performance is measured, i.e:

100,000 instructions per transaction

or

XACTS/sec = 10 * MIPS

For example, a 100 MIPS system should be capable of 1000 TP1s per second.

Achieving this goal requires system tuning, the removal of critical sections in the code, and avoiding lock contention on so-called **hot spots,** i.e. records or blocks with high traffic. To alleviate this latter problem, it is necessary for the DBMS to hold locks for shorter periods of time, and we are planning to use two tactics to help in this regard. First, we plan to run the various DBMS commands in a transaction in parallel where possible to shorten the amount of time they hold locks. In addition, we are using a special purpose concurrency control algorithm which avoids locking altogether in certain situations. These tactics are described later in this paper.

Some researchers believe that high performance is achieved easily by using a low-function high-performance DBMS such as IMS/Fast Path. Others question the propriety of removing DBMS services such as query optimization and views and suggest utilizing only high level interfaces. Clearly, the elimination of function from the path length of high traffic interactions is a possible optimization strategy. Although we are not enthusiastic about this strategy because we feel that the potential problems outweight the advantages, we are going to allow exploitation of this concept by implementing a novel **fast path** scheme to achieve a **variable speed interface.** We also discuss this tactic later in this paper.

Although transaction processing systems typically perform short tasks such as TP1, there are occasional longer running transactions. Such transactions will be a clear locking bottleneck, unless they can be parallelized. Parallel execution of single commands has been addressed in [DEWI85, DEWI86, RICH87]. In this paper we sketch a slightly different approach that focuses on a multi-user environment, the presence of shared memory and the necessity of carefully exploiting a large amount of main memory. Our performance goal is to outperform recent systems such as GAMMA and the DBC/1012 on ad-hoc queries using comparable amounts of hardware.

Lastly, high performance is necessary in engineering environments where large objects are stored and retrieved with great regularity. A typical image might be several megabytes and an application program that processes images requires retrieval and storage of such objects at high bandwidth. Current commercial systems tend not to store such objects at all, while prototype extendible systems (e.g. POSTGRES [STON86] and EXODUS [CARE86]) have been designed with object management needs in mind. The current design of both systems will limit the speed at which large objects can be retrieved to the sequential reading speed of a single disk (about 1.5 mbytes/sec for current low-end disks). Hence, a 64 mbyte object will require about 43 seconds of access time. Especially if a supercomputer is the one making the request, it is unreasonable to require such delays. Our last goal of XPRS is an order of magnitude improvement in access times to large objects. We plan to achieve this goal with a variable-speed two-dimensional file system which is described below.

1.2. High Availability

A second goal of XPRS is to make data base objects unavailable as infrequently as possible. There are two common causes of data unavailability, errors and locking problems, and we discuss each in turn. Errors have been classified by [GRAY87] into:

hardware errors (e.g. dish crashes)
software errors (e.g. OS or DBMS crashes)
operator errors (e.g. accidental disk erasure)
environment errors (e.g. power failure)

Because we are designing an I/O system, our goal is to make a contribution to improved availability in this area in the presence of hardware errors. Our initial ideas have resulted in an efficient way to mirror disks at much reduced storage costs [PATT88]. On the other hand, in the case of CPU failures, we assume that XPRS would be part of a distributed data base system such as Non-stop SQL [GRAY87A], INGRES/STAR [RTI87] or ORACLE/STAR. Availability in the presence of CPU or memory failures is provided in such systems by traditional distributed DBMS multi-copy techniques. Hence, this area is not discussed further in this paper.

Software errors are soon likely to be the dominant cause of system failures because hardware and operator errors are declining in frequency and environment errors are largely power problems which can be avoided by uninterruptable power supplies [GRAY87]. It should be noted that many current techniques for achieving high availability (such as process-pairs for non-stop operation and mirrored disks) are vulnerable to software errors. Obviously, an errant DBMS will write bad data on each disk in a mirrored pair, and the backup process may write the same bad data that caused its mate to fail. Hence, our assumption in XPRS is to realize that software errors will happen. Therefore, our goal in XPRS is to recover from software crashes in seconds. The tactics which we have in mind are described later in the paper and depend on the characteristics of the storage system built into POSTGRES [STON87].

Operator errors are best avoided by having no operator. Hence, another goal of XPRS is to perform all utility functions automatically, so that an operator-free environment is feasible. Among other things an operator-free environment requires that the system self-adapt to adding and deleting disks, automatically balance the load on disks arms, and create and drop indexes automatically.

In summary our goals for XPRS are improved I/O system availability in the event of hardware errors, ensuring that data is not lost as a result of software errors, instantaneous recovery from software errors, and a system capable of running with no operator.

A second availability goal in XPRS is never to make a data base object unavailable because of locking problems. These result from running large (usually retrieval) commands which set read locks on large numbers of data objects, and from housekeeping chores performed by the data manager. For example, in current systems it is often advisable to reorganize a B-tree index to achieve physical contiguity of index pages after a long period of splits and recombinations of pages. Such a reorganization usually makes the index unavailable for the duration of the reorganization and perhaps the underlying relation as well. In XPRS this and all other housekeeping chores must be done incrementally without locking a relation or taking it off line.

1.3. Shared Memory

In contrast to other recent high performance systems such as NONSTOP SQL [GRAY87A], GAMMA [DEWI86] and the DBC 1012 [TERA85] which have all used a shared-nothing [STON86A] architecture, we are orienting XPRS to a shared memory environment. The reason for making this choice is threefold. First the memory, bus bandwidth and controller technology are at hand for at least a 2000 TP1/sec system. Hence, speed requirements for advanced applications seem achievable with shared memory. Moreover, a 2000 TP1/sec. system will require around 8000 I/Os per second, i.e. about 250 drives. The aggregate bandwidth of the I/Os, assuming 4K pages, is about 32 mbytes/sec. Current large mainframes routinely attach this number of drives and sufficient channels to deal with the bandwidth.

Second, the reason to favor shared memory is that it is 25 to 50 percent faster on TP1 style benchmarks than shared nothing [BHID88] and has the added advantage that main memory and CPUs are automatically shared and thereby load balanced. Hence, we avoid many of the software headaches which are entailed in shared nothing proposals.

Lastly, some people criticize shared memory systems on availability grounds. Specifically, they allege that shared nothing is fundamentally more highly available than shared memory, because failures are contained in a single node in shared nothing system while they corrupt an entire shared memory system. Certainly this is true for hardware errors.

On the other hand, consider software errors. With conventional log-based recovery a shared nothing system will recover the failed node in a matter of minutes by processing the log. A shared memory system will take at least as long to recover the entire system because it will have a larger log, resulting in lower availability. However, suppose the operating system and the data manager can recover instantaneously from a software or operator error (i.e. in a few seconds). In this case, both a shared memory and shared nothing system recover instantly, resulting in the same availability.

In summary, we view a shared memory system as nearly equally available as an equivalent shared nothing system. In addition, we view XPRS as having higher availability than any log-based system because it recovers instantly from software errors. Moreover, a shared memory system is inherently higher performance than shared nothing and easier to load balance.

In the rest of this paper we discuss the solutions that we are adopting in XPRS to achieve these goals. In Section 2 we present our tactics to provide high performance on transaction processing applications. Specifically, we discuss our **fast path** mechanism that is being added to POSTGRES to cut overhead on simple transactions. Moreover, we discuss inter-query parallelism which can cut down on the length of time transactions hold locks. Finally, we consider a specialized concurrency control system which avoids locks entirely in some situations. Section 3 then turns to performance techniques applicable to complex commands. We present our approach to query processing in this section which attempts to achieve intra-query parallelism to improve response time as well as make excellent use of large amounts of main memory. Then, in Section 4 we indicate how to achieve high performance when materializing large objects. We first argue that traditional file systems are inadequate solutions in our environment and suggest a novel two-dimensional file system that can provide a **variable speed** I/O interface.

Section 5 continues with our ideas for achieving high availability in the presence of failures. We briefly discuss hardware reliability and suggest a novel way to achieve ultra-high disk reliability. Then, we turn to software techniques which can improve availability and indicate how we expect to achieve instantaneous recovery. Section 6 then closes with our algorithms to avoid data unavailability because of locking problems.

2. TRANSACTION PROCESSING PERFORMANCE

This section explores three tactics relevant to transaction processing performance.

2.1. Fast Path

It is common knowledge that TP1 consists of 4 commands in a query language such as SQL [DATE84] or POSTQUEL [ROWE87] together with a begin XACT and an end XACT statement. If an application program gives these commands to the data manager one at a time, then the boundary between the data manager and the application must be crossed in both directions 6 times. Moreover, if the application runs on a workstation and the DBMS runs on a host, the messages must go over the network, increasing the cost of the boundary crossing. This overhead contributes 20-30 percent of all CPU cycles consumed by a TP1 transaction. To alleviate this difficulty, several current commercial systems support procedures in the data base and POSTGRES does likewise. Hence, TP1 can be defined as a procedure and stored in a relation, say

COMMANDS (id, code)

and then later executed as follows:

execute (COMMANDS.code with check-amount, teller#) where COMMANDS.id = "TP1"

In this way the TP1 procedure is executed with the user supplied parameters of the check amount and the teller number, and the boundary between POSTGRES and an application will be crossed just once.

To go even faster POSTGRES makes use of user-defined functions. For example, a user can write a function OVERPAID which takes an integer argument and returns a boolean. After registration with the data manager, any user can write a query such as:

retrieve (EMP.name)
where OVERPAID (EMP.salary)

Of course it is also legal to execute a simpler query such as:

retrieve (result = OVERPAID (7))

which will simply evaluate OVERPAID for a constant parameter.

Fast Path is a means of executing such user defined functions with very high performance. Specifically, we have extended the POSTQUEL query language to include:

function-name(parameter-list)

as a legal query. For example,

OVERPAID(7)

could be submitted as a valid POSTGRES query. The run-time system will accept such a command from an application and simply pass the arguments to the code which evaluates the function which is linked into the POSTGRES address space without consuming overhead in type checking, parsing or query optimization. Hence, there will be 200 or fewer instructions of overhead between accepting this command and executing it. Using this facility (essentially a remote procedure call capability) TP1 can be defined as a POSTGRES function and a user would simply type:

TP1(check-amount, teller-name)

The implementation of the TP1 function can be coded in several ways. The normal implementation would be for the function to simply execute preconstructed query plans for the four commands which make up TP1. This will result in a somewhat faster implementation of TP1 than executing a stored procedure because of the reduced overhead in the procedure call.

Alternately, an application designer can more directly control the low level routines in POSTGRES. POSTGRES has user defined access methods, which correspond to a collection of 13 functions described in [WENS88]. These functions can be directly called by a user written procedure. As a result, high performance can be achieved by coding TP1 directly against the access method level of POSTGRES. Although this provides no data independence, no type checking and no integrity control, it does allow the possibility of excellent performance. Moreover, there are also interfaces to the buffer manager as well as higher level interfaces in the query execution system.

Using this technique of user written procedures, POSTGRES can provide a **variable speed interface.** Hence, a transaction can make use of the maximum amount of data base services consistent with its performance requirements. This approach should be contrasted with "toolkit" systems (e.g. EXODUS [CARE86]) which require a data base implementor to build a custom system out of tool-kit modules.

2.2. Inter-query Parallelism

There is no reason why all commands in TP1 cannot be run in parallel. If any of the resulting parallel commands fails, then the transaction can be aborted. In the usual case where all commands succeed, then the net effect will be that locks are held for shorter periods of time and lock contention will be reduced. Since an application program can open multiple **portals** to POSTGRES, each can be executing a parallel command. However, we expect high performance systems to store procedures in the system which are subsequently executed. A mechanism is needed to expedite inter-query parallelism in this situation. Although it is possible to build a semantic analyzer to detect possible parallelism [SELL86], we are following a much simpler path. Specifically, we are extending POSTGRES with a single keyword **parallel** that can be placed between any two POSTGRES commands. This will be a marker to the run-time system that it is acceptable to execute the two commands in parallel. Hence, TP1 can be constructed as four POSTQUEL commands each separated from its neighbor by **parallel.**

The reason for this approach is that it takes, in effect, a theorem prover to determine possible semantic parallelism, and we do not view this as a cost-effective solution.

2.3. Special Purpose Concurrency Control

We make use of a definition of **commutative** transactions in this section. Suppose a transaction is considered as a collection of atomic actions, a1, ..., am; each considered as a read-modify-write of a single object. Two such transactions T1 and T2, with actions a1, ...,am and b1,..., bn will be said to **commute** if any interleaving of the actions of the two transactions for which both transactions commit yields the same final data base state. In the presence of transaction failures we require a somewhat stronger definition of commutativity which is similar to the one in [BADR87]. Two transactions will be said to **failure commute** if they commute and for any initial data base state S and any interleaving of actions for which both T1 and T2 succeed, then the decision by either transaction to voluntarily abort cannot cause the other to abort.

For example, consider two TP1 withdrawals. These transactions commute because both will succeed if there are sufficient funds to cover both checks being written. Moreover, both withdrawals failure commute because when sufficient funds are present either transaction will succeed even if the other decides to abort. On the other hand, consider a $100 deposit and a $75 withdrawal transaction for a bank balance of $50. If the deposit is first, then both transactions succeed. However, if the deposit aborts then the withdrawal would have insufficient funds and be required to abort. Hence, they do not failure commute.

Suppose a data base administrator divides all transactions in XPRS into two classes, C1 and C2. Members of C1 all failure commute, while members of C2 consist of all other transactions. Moreover, he provides an UNDO function to be presently described. Basically, members of C1 will be run by XPRS without locking interference from other members of C1. Members of C2 will be run with standard locking to ensure serializability against other members of C2 and also for members of C1.

To accomplish this POSTGRES must expand the normal read and write locks with two new lock types, C1-read and C1-write. Members of C1 set these new locks on objects that they respectively read and write. Figure 1 shows the conflict table for the four kinds of locks: Obviously, C1 transactions will be run against each other as if there was no locking at all. Hence, they will never wait for locks held by other members of C1. Other transactions are run with normal locks. Moreover, C1-read and C1-write locks function as ordinary locks

	R	W	C1-R	C1-W
R	ok	no	ok	no
W	no	no	no	no
C1-R	ok	no	ok	ok
C1-W	no	no	ok	ok

Compatibility modes for locks.
Figure 1.

with regard to C2 transactions.

Because multiple C1 transactions will be processed in parallel, the storage manager must take care to ensure the correct ultimate value of all data items when one or more C1 transactions aborts. Consider three transactions, T1, T2 and T3 which withdraw respectively $100, $50 and $75 from an account with $175 initially. Because the POSTGRES storage system is designed as a no-overwrite storage manager, the first two transactions will write new records as follows:

initial value: $175
next value: $75 written by T1 which is in progress
next-value: $25 written by T2 which is in progress

The transaction T3 will fail due to insufficient funds and not write a data record.

POSTGRES must be slightly altered to achieve this effect. It currently maintains the "state" of each transaction in a separate data structure as:

committed
aborted
in progress

To these options a fourth state must be added:

C1-in-progress

Moreover, POSTGRES must return data records that are written by either C1-in-progress or committed transactions to higher level software instead of just the latter. The locking system will ensure that these C1-in-progress records are not visible to C2 transactions. Using this technique C1 updates are now immediately visible to other concurrent C1 transactions as desired.

When an ordinary transaction aborts, POSTGRES simply ignores its updates and they are ultimately garbage-collected by an asynchronous vacuum cleaner. However, if a C1 transaction aborts, there may be subsequent C1 transactions that have updated records that the aborted transaction also updated. For example, if T1 aborts, the state of the account will be:

initial value:	$175	
next value:	$75	written by T1 which aborted
next-value:	$25	written by T2 which is in progress

Since all the versions of an individual record are compressed and chained together on a linked list by the storage manager, this situation will occur if the storage manager discovers a record written by an aborted transaction followed by one or more records written by a transaction with status "C1-in-progress" or "commit".

In this case, the storage manager must present the correct data value to the next requesting transaction. Consider the record prior to the aborted transaction as "old-data" and the record written by the aborted transaction as "new data." The run time system simply remembers these values. Then, when it discovers the end of the chain, it finds a third record which we term "current data." The run time system now calls a specific UNDO function:

UNDO (old-data, new-data, current-data)

which returns a modified current record. The run time system writes this revised record with the same transaction and command identifier as the aborted record. In this case, the UNDO function would return $125 and the account state would be changed to:

initial value:	$175	
next value:	$75	written by T1 which aborted
next-value:	$25	written by T2 which is in progress
next-value:	$125	written on behalf of T1 as a correction

Hence, later in the chain of records there will be a specific "undo" record. Of course, if the run time system sees the undo record, it knows not to reapply the UNDO function.

It is possible to generalize this technique to support several classes of C1 transactions each with their own UNDO function. However, we view the result as not worth the effort that would be entailed.

3. INTRA-QUERY PARALLELISM

3.1. Introduction

Intra-query parallelism is desirable for two reasons. First, less lock conflicts are generated if a query finishes quickly, and thereby increased throughput can be achieved. For example, a recent study [BHID88] has shown that substantial gains in throughput are possible using parallel plans if a command accesses more than about 10 pages. Second, one can achieve dramatically reduced response time for individual commands. This section presents a sketch of the optimization algorithm planned for XPRS.

In supporting parallel query plans, it is essential to allocate a single relation to multiple files. We choose to do this by utilizing a **distribution criteria,** e.g:

EMP where age < 20	TO file 1
EMP where age > 40	TO file 2
EMP where age >= 20 and age <= 40	TO file 3

to partition a relation into **fragments.** Such distribution criteria will be arbitrary one-relation predicates and can include used defined functions such as hash functions.

When creating indexes on the EMP relation, say on the salary field, it is equally natural to construct three physical indexes, one for each fragment. This will ensure that parallel plans do not often collide for access to the same disk arm or collection of arms. These indexes would have the form:

index on EMP(salary) where age < 20
index on EMP(salary) where age > 40
index on EMP(salary) where age >= 20 and age <= 40

Such data structures are **partial indexes** and offer a collection of desirable features as discussed in [STON88]. Notice that such indexes are smaller than a current conventional index and should be contrasted with other proposals (e.g join indexes [VALD87], links [ASTR76] and the indexes in IMS [DATE84]) which are larger than a conventional index.

Three issues must be addressed by a parallel optimizer in the XPRS environment. First, we assume that that main memory in a 1991 computer system will approach or exceed 1 gigabyte. Obviously with 900 megabytes or more of buffer pool space, a DBMS will keep large portions of data base objects in main memory. For example, one can join two 450 megabyte objects by reading both into main memory and then performing a main-memory sort-merge.

On the other hand, in a multiuser environment much less buffer space may actually be available. Unfortunately, different query plans for the same query are optimal depending on how much buffer space is available. Consider for example the following query:

retrieve (R1.all) where R1.a = R2.b
and R2.c = R3.d

and assume that R2 and R3 have a clustered index on fields c and d respectively. Further assume that all relations occupy the same number of pages, P, and that the join of R2 to R3 yields a temporary of size .1P while the one between R1 and R2 contains 1 record. Lastly, suppose the optimizer cost function includes only I/O.

In this case one can first join R1 to R2 and then join the result to R3. Alternately, one can first join R2 to R3 and then join the result to R1. If there is a large amount of memory, the first option will read R1 and R2 into main memory, compute the one record join and then read the single page from R3 which is required. On the other hand, the second option will read all three relations in their entirety, resulting in a higher cost. If only minimal main memory is available, the result is somewhat different. The first option will perform a disk-based merge-sort join of R1 and R2, at a cost of 2P * log P + 2P. The resulting one record temporary will reside in main memory where a single extra page fetch will obtain the matching values from R3. The second option will read R1 and R2 through the clustered index at cost 2P producing a temporary which is written to disk at cost .1P. A disk based merge sort must be done between this temporary and R1 at a cost of .1P * log .1P + .1P + P log P + P. The formulas for the two cases are presented below and generally the second option will be cheaper for minimum memory.

query plan	cost with zero memory	cost with large memory
(R1 join R2) join R3	2P*Log P+2P+1	2P+1
R1 join (R2 join R3)	3.2P+P*log P+ .1P*log .1P	3P

In this case the first plan is superior for a large buffer pool while the second wins if little or no space is available. Consequently, even without considering possible parallelism, the XPRS query optimizer should carefully consider available main memory in its decision making.

When parallelism is considered, the optimizer must also face the number of parallel plans into which to decompose a user query. For example, suppose a user requests:

retrieve (R1.all) where R1.a = R2.b and
R2.c = R3.d and R3.e = R4.f

and suppose the best sequential plan is found to be

a) join R1 to R2
b) join R3 to R4
c) join the results of a) and b)

In this case, there may (or may not be) sufficient memory to perform steps a) and b) in parallel. Consequently, the XPRS optimizer must be cognizant of memory allocation when deciding the amount of parallelism to exploit.

Lastly, the XPRS optimizer must be able to decide between two different plans, one of which has greater parallelism while the other consumes less resources.

We feel that optimizers are becoming exceedingly complex, and we have pointed out that main memory and parallelism considerations will necessarily result in additional complexity. Although others [GRAE87, LOHM88] are trying to make optimizers extendible, we are more concerned with making them simpler so that additional optimization, such as that discussed above, can be performed. To accomplish this goal, we plan to restrict the collection of available join tactics. All optimizers must include iterative substitution to process non-equijoins. Moreover, some results must be sorted (those specified by an SQL ORDER BY clause), and therefore merge-sort comes with marginal extra complexity. However, other join tactics (e.g. hash-joins) are inessential, and we plan to not include them in XPRS.

In theory the optimizer search space includes all possible ways to parallelize all sequential plans for all possible buffer pool sizes. This space is hopeless to search exhaustively, and we plan a two step heuristic. In the first step we expect to find good sequential plans for various memory sizes. Then, in the second step we plan to explore parallel versions of only these plans. The final outcome is a collection of plans and a memory range over which each should be run.

At the time of execution, the query executor will make a call on the buffer manager to determine space availability and based on the reply will choose one of the collection of plans. It will then supervise execution of the resulting parallel algorithm. We turn now to constructing this collection of plans.

3.2. Constructing Parallel Query Plans

Our optimizer first finds a collection of good sequential plans as follows. Using a conventional disk-oriented sequential plan optimizer, we expect to produce a plan P(0, Q) for each query Q which is the best plan under the assumption of zero main memory. In addition we expect to produce a plan P (BIG, Q) which assumes as much main memory, BIG, as needed. This plan will typically read each relation accessed into main memory and do all joins in main memory with as much parallelism as possible. BIG is then calculated as the amount of memory needed by all pairs of parallel join operands and their answers. If

$$P (0, Q) = P (BIG, Q)$$

then we will stop constructing plans. If not, we will construct P (BIG/2, Q) and compare it to the previous two plans. If it is the same as either plan or has a cost within (say) 10 percent of either plan, we will assume that the optimized plan at each endpoint is, in fact, optimal for the whole interval. Then, we will subdivide the remaining interval (if any), and repeat the process. The net result is a collection of sequential plans and an interval of memory within which each is optimal.

Next we will explore all possible ways to parallelize this collection of plans. To decide between competing plans, we must use a different cost function from traditional optimizers. Specifically, our initial cost function for a query plan, Q, using X units of buffer space will be:

cost (X , Q) = (RES (X, Q) / MIN_RES (Q)) (1 +
W2 (TIME (X, Q) / MIN_TIME (Q)))

where

RES (X, Q) = Ntuples (X, Q) + W1 * EIO (X, Q) ;
this is the traditional optimizer cost function
Ntuples (X, Q) = number of tuples examined
EIO (X, Q) = expected number of I/O's to evaluate Q with X amount of buffer space
W1 = the traditional fudge factor relating I/O and CPU utilization
MIN_RES (Q) = the minimum cost plan for Q using the traditional function
TIME (X, Q) = expected elapsed time with X amount of buffer space assuming all processors can be allocated to this plan
MIN_TIME (Q) = the time of the fastest plan for the query Q.
W2 = fudge factor relating response time to resource consumption

If W2 = 0, this new cost function reduces to one equivalent to the traditional one. On the other hand, choosing a large value of W2 will make response time a major criteria.

The XPRS optimizer will iterate over most of the ways to parallelize each plan. However, many leaf nodes of any candidate query plan consists of a scan of a data relation or a scan of a secondary index. Each such leaf node will be automatically decomposed into parallel sub-plans, one for each data fragment or partial index involved. This tactic can always be applied because it will lower TIME (X, Q) without altering main memory requirements. Moreover, if any scan is followed by a sort node, this node can also be split into the same number of parallel nodes as the scan node.

The ultimate outcome will be a collection of parallel plans with the memory requirements for each one. We expect to proceed with an optimizer on this sort. Clearly, finding good heuristics to prune the search space will be a major challenge that we plan to explore further.

4. PERFORMANCE ON MATERIALIZING LARGE OBJECTS

4.1. Introduction

We expect XPRS to run on a system with a large number of disks. As noted in [PATT88], we believe that only 3 1/2" and 5 1/4" drives will be attractive in a couple of years. Hence, we expect large capacity storage systems to made up of substantial numbers (say 100 or more) of such drives. Additionally, these drives do not have removable platters, so the concept of a mounted file system is not required, and we can think of the collection of drives as a two-dimensional array.

In keeping with our objective of using a conventional file system, the problem becomes one of designing a Sprite file system for this disk array which simultaneously yields good performance in transaction processing, complex commands, and materializing large objects. To simplify the discussion, we will assume that a storage system has D drives, numbered 1,...,D, the allocation unit is a disk track and the ith disk has Ti tracks. Hence, the storage system is a two dimensional array of tracks, and we will assume that the horizontal dimension is the drive number and the vertical dimension is the track number on a drive.

In many traditional file systems a user can add a new **extent** to a file which is allocated sequentially on a single drive. If necessary, it would be broken into multiple smaller contiguous extents. In our storage system an extent of size E would correspond to a vertical rectangle of width 1 and height E.

Recently, researchers have suggested striping files across a collection of disks [SALE86, LIVN85]. Striping L <= D disks entails allocating the Ith track to the Jth disk determined by:

J = remainder (I/L) + 1

In this way, a large sequential I/O can be processed by reading all disks in parallel, and very high bandwidth on sequential I/O is possible. In our model this corresponds to a rectangle of width L and height of 1 or more.

In the next subsections we argue that both horizontal (striped over all D drives) and vertical (i.e. traditional) allocation schemes are undesirable in our environment and that a **two-dimensional** file system which allocates extents as general M by W rectangles is the best alternative. Then, we close this section with a few comments on the design of **FTD** (Files -- Two Dimensions).

4.2. Horizontal Allocation

Define the **width** W of a rectangle of storage as the number of drives it is striped over. The choice:

W = D

will result in tricky problems in the area of high availability and space management.

In all real environments the number of disks changes over time. Hence, infrequently, the value of D will change, usually to a bigger value. When a disk is added or dropped, one must restripe all remaining disks. This is a bulk reorganization that will result in the file that is restriped being unavailable during the reorganization. Any incremental restriping algorithm must result in two different widths (namely old D and new D) being supported during the reorganization.

In addition, if the various disks have different capacities, then space management will be problematic because there will be no way to use extra space on larger drives.

Lastly, it is unlikely that hot spots will develop in a striped file system. However, in the unlikely event that they do occur, there is absolutely nothing that can be done about them, because the allocation algorithm is fixed.

4.3. Vertical Allocation

One might be led to consider vertical allocations, i.e. W = 1. Unfortunately this solution fails to achieve our performance goal on large objects.

A large object will occur in a single tuple of a single data base object. For example, the following relation might store an image library:

IMAGE (name, description)

Here, the description field would be several megabytes in size. In a system with W = 1, a description would be stored on a single drive, and therefore the bandwidth available to return it to an application program would be limited to the sequential read speed of the drive (about 1.5 mbyes/sec depending on the drive selected). Clearly, XPRS would fail to achieve its performance goal on these applications with vertical allocation.

4.4. The Design of FTD

The clear conclusion is that neither horizontal nor vertical allocation is a desirable solution, and the file system, FTD, of XPRS must be able to support extents which are arbitrary rectangles. Consequently each extent, Ei, of a file is a data structure:

DRi: the drive number on which the extent starts
Wi: the width of the extent in disks
Si: the size of the extent in tracks
{TRj: 1 <= j <= Wi} the track number on the jth disk on which the extent starts

Hence, each extent is allocated to a contiguous collection of disks and contains Si tracks on each disk. However, the starting location of the portion of the extent can be different for each disk, thus easing the space allocation problem. In addition, addressing in an extent is striped. Hence, track 1 is allocated to drive DRi, track 2 to DRi+1, etc.

In the remainder of this section we discuss the choice of Wi. There are at least two considerations that would cause one to increase Wi and at least two that would cause it to be lowered. First, bandwidth on large read operations will be proportional to Wi. Hence, in supercomputer access to a DBMS, one should choose a large Wi. In addition, a larger choice of Wi will tend to minimize the impact of "hot spots" in the disk system, i.e. drives on which there is contention for blocks from multiple transactions. If a single file is spread over a larger number of drives, one would expect contention for blocks in that file to decrease. However, there can also be contention for blocks in different files on the same drive. Reducing such contention is a file placement problem. The amount of such inter-file contention will decrease as the Wi for both files is increased. As a result, concern for hot spots would cause one to increase Wi.

On the other hand, there are two considerations which would cause one to choose lower values for Wi. First, space management will probably be easier with lower values. This will clearly be true if some disks have different capacities from others. We expect to demonstrate this conjecture with a simulation study which has already started.

Second, there are many environments where the extra bandwidth from a large Wi cannot be utilized by the DBMS. As noted earlier, parallelism will be obtained by splitting data relations into multiple files and allocating parallel query plans to process each file. Suppose the CPU processing one of these parallel plans is (say) 15 MIPS. Furthermore, suppose we assume typical records of (say) 100 bytes and a query which requires (say) 500 CPU instructions per record. In this case, we require 5 instructions per byte of data and a 15 MIPS CPU can keep up with at most 2 disks. If the CPU cost per record is cut in half, then four disks can be supported. Hence, the benefit of striping more than a few disks will be lost because of CPU saturation.

In conclusion we expect to design a file system where files can be extended an extent at a time and application software can optionally suggest the value of W that would be appropriate for the extent. Larger values of W may result in higher bandwidth and less problems with hot spots. On the other hand, lower values may result in equal effective bandwidth and less problems with space management.

5. HIGH AVAILABILITY IN THE PRESENCE OF ERRORS

5.1. RAID

The I/O system in XPRS will be based on RAIDs (Redundant Arrays of Inexpensive Disks) [PATT88]. The underlying premise is that small numbers of large expensive disks can be replaced by very large numbers of inexpensive disks to achieve substantially increased transfer bandwidth at a comparable system cost. The major problem with disk arrays is the drastically reduced mean time to failure (MTTF) because of the large numbers of additional system components.

RAIDs are only of interest if they can be made fault tolerant. At one extreme, each data disk can have an associated "mirror" disk, which is comparable to Tandem's mirrored disk approach. However, 50% of the available disk capacity is dedicated to redundant data storage, a rather high price to pay.

We take an alternative approach and assume that each FTD "logical drive" is, in fact, made up of a **group** of N physical disks. On N-1 of these disks normal data blocks are stored, while on the Nth disk, we store the parity bit for the remaining drives. Blocks on different drives can be read independently; however, writes require (up to) four physical I/Os:

(1) read original data block
(2) read its associated parity block
(3) write the updated data block
(4) write the updated parity block

Intelligent buffer management and/or read-modify-write transactions can eliminate one or two of these I/Os in many cases.

To avoid the hot spot on the Nth drive during write operations, parity blocks are actually interleaved across all N disks. Consequently, up to N/2 writes can be serviced simultaneously.

Note that the parity blocks represent much reduced overhead compared to the fully mirrored approach. For N = 8, one in every eight blocks is a parity block. This represents only a 12.5% capacity overhead.

When the controller discovers that a disk has a hard failure, processing continues in a degraded fashion as follows. A **hot spare** is allocated to the group, replacing the failed disk. A read to the failed disk is mapped into parallel reads of the data and parity blocks of the remaining disks, and the lost data is reconstructed on the fly. Writes are processed as above, and are written through to the spare.

Just as in the case of fully mirrored disks, a second failure renders the group unavailable. Thus it is also important to reconstruct the contents of the failed disk onto the spare drive expeditiously. Two strategies are possible: stop and reconstruct, or reconstruct in the background. In the former, access to the group is suspended while the reconstruction software runs flat out to rebuild the lost disk. Sequential access can be used to advantage to keep the reconstruction time to a minimum, but assuming a group of 8 100 Mbyte 3 1/4" disks, this is a computationally intensive task which will take at least

100 mbytes/1.5 mbytes per second = 67 seconds

assuming that the I/O processor doing the reconstruction can keep up. This approach does not satisfy the high availability goals of XPRS.

The alternative is to spread the reconstruction over a longer period, interleaving reconstruction and conventional I/O. We assume the actual elapsed time to reconstruct the disk thereby increases by a factor of 400 to four hours.

The drawback of this approach is that a longer recovery period will adversely affect the MTTF because a second physical failure will cause data loss during the longer reconstruction period. To be specific, assume the average time to a physical disk failure is 30000 hours, and therefore the failure rate, λ, is 1/30000. Assume that the average repair time is 4 hours, and therefore the repair rate, μ, is 1/4. The mean time to failure of a group of N disks is:

$$MTTF = \frac{\mu}{N(N-1)\lambda^2}$$

Thus, MTTF decreases linearly with increasing repair time (decreasing repair rate). For N = 8 and a 4 hour repair interval, the MTTF exceeds 3.5 million hours. Put differently, one can have a disk array of 20 of these groups containing 160 drives, and be assured that the MTTF of the entire system is 175,781 hours, a little over 20 years.

In XPRS we will consequently assume that the disk system is perfectly reliable.

5.2. Software Errors

The POSTGRES storage manager is discussed in [STON87] and has the novel characteristic that it has no log in the conventional sense. Instead of overwriting a data record, it simply adds a new one and relies on an asynchronous vacuum cleaner to move "dead" records to an archive and reclaim space. The POSTGRES log therefore consists of two bits of data per transaction giving its status as

committed
aborted
in progress
C1-in-progress

To commit a transaction in POSTGRES one must:

move data blocks written by the transaction to "stable" memory
set the commit bit

To abort a transaction one need only set the abort bit. To recover from a crash where the disk is intact, one need only abort all transactions alive at the time of the failure, an instantaneous operation. Since RAID has an infinite MTTF for disk errors, there are no crashes which leave disk data unreadable.

To achieve higher reliability one must be able to recover from software errors caused by the DBMS or the OS writing corrupted disk blocks. In this section we sketch our design which has the side benefit of making the buffer pool into "stable" storage. This will make committing POSTGRES transactions extremely fast. We base our design on two assumptions:

Assumption 1: The OS ensures that each main memory page is either GUARDED or FREE. Any guarded page is assumed to be physically unwritable and its contents obtainable after any crash.

We expect to implement GUARDED and FREE by setting the bit in the memory map that controls page writability. With a battery back-up scheme for main memory and the assumption that memory hardware is highly reliable, Assumption 1 seems plausible.

Assumption 2: The DBMS and the OS consider the operation of GUARDING a page as equivalent to "I am well." Hence, issuing a GUARD command is equivalent to the assertion by the appropriate software that it has not written bad data.

Although there is no way to ascertain the validity of Assumption 2, we expect to attempt to code routines near GUARD points as "fail fast."

Our buffering scheme makes use of the fact that the OS has one copy of each block read and the DBMS has a second in its buffer pool. Moreover there are 6 system calls available to the DBMS:

G-READ (X,A)	:Read disk block X into main memory page A leaving A GUARDED
READ (X,A)	:Read disk block X into main memory page A leaving A FREE
G-WRITE (A,X)	:Write main memory page A to disk block X leaving A GUARDED
WRITE (A,X)	:Write main memory page A to disk block X leaving A FREE
GUARD (A)	:GUARD main memory page A
FREE (A)	:FREE main memory page A

The OS implements a G-READ command by allocating a buffer page, B, in its buffer pool and performing the following operations:

FREE (B)
physical read of X into B
GUARD (B)
FREE (A)
copy B into A
GUARD (A)

The READ command is nearly the same, omitting only the last GUARD (A). The OS implements G-WRITE (X,A) by using its version of the page, B, as follows:

GUARD (A)
FREE (B)
copy A into B
GUARD (B)

The WRITE command is the same except it adds a FREE (A) at the end. The OS can write pages from its buffer pool to disk at any time to achieve its space management objectives.

Each time the DBMS modifies a data page, it must perform a WRITE or a G-WRITE command to move the OS copy into synchronization. Moreover, it must assert that it has not written invalid data. According to Assumption 2, it would perform a GUARD command preceding the WRITE or G-WRITE command. For efficiency purposes, we have combined the two calls together; therefore a WRITE or G-WRITE command is equivalent to a "wellness" assertion by the DBMS.

If a crash occurs, then the OS takes the initiative to discard all unguarded pages in its buffer pool as well as in the DBMS buffer pool. All other buffer pool pages are preserved. Moreover, the code segments of the OS and DBMS are automatically guarded, so they are intact.

Lastly, it should be noted that both the DBMS and OS copies of a page are never simultaneously unguarded. Hence, if the DBMS page is discarded, it will be refreshed from the OS page. If the OS page is discarded, it will be rewritten from the DBMS page. Moreover, since the number of unguarded pages at any one time is small, the two copies can be brought into synchronization quickly during recovery time.

It is acceptable for multiple transactions to have the same page simulatancously FREE. In this case, a GUARD operation by one transaction requires the OS to perform the obvious bookkeeping leaving the page FREE. Only when the last transaction GUARDS the page can the actual page be guarded. Of course, a transaction must delay committing until all the pages it has written have become physically guarded. It will be useful to periodically delay transactions which wish to FREE a "hot spot" page so that the current writers of the page can finish and the page can be GUARDED. This is similar in concept to action consistent checkpoints discussed in [GRAY81].

There are additional details that concern how to preserve the data structure which holds the mapping of disk pages to buffer pages. However, space precludes an explanation here. Also, assuming that the I/O system does not write blocks to the wrong place along with Assumptions 1 and 2 above, our scheme does not lose data and recovers essentially instantly.

6. AVOIDING DATA UNAVAILABILITY DUE TO LOCKING

In this section we indicate the approach taken by XPRS to avoid data unavailability on large user reads and on storage reorganizations.

6.1. User Reads

POSTGRES automatically supports access to a relation as of some time in the past. For example, a user can obtain the names of employees as of January 15th as follows:

retrieve (EMP.name)
using EMP@"January 15, 1988"

All retrieve commands can be run as of some time in the past. Because no locks are set for such commands, they cause no data unavailability. In addition, our technique does not require a user to predeclare his transaction to be read-only as required by some other techniques, e.g [CHAN82].

6.2. Storage Reorganization Without Locking

We now illustrate how partial indexes can be used by an automatic demon to achieve incremental index reorganization.

To convert from a B-tree index on a key to either a rebuilt B-tree index or a hash index on the same key, one can proceed as follows. Divide the key range of the index into N intervals of either fixed or varying size. Begin with the first interval. Lock the interval and construct a new index entry for each tuple in the interval. When the process is complete, unlock the interval. The new index is now valid for the interval

key < VALUE-1

where VALUE-1 is the low key on the next index page to be examined. The old index can be considered valid for the whole key range or it can be restricted to:

key >= VALUE-1

In this latter case, the space occupied by the index records of the first interval can be reclaimed. If the intervals are chosen to be the key ranges present in the root level of the old B-tree, then this space reclamation can occur without destroying the B-tree property for the old index.

The query optimizer need only be extended to realize that the two indexes together cover the key range. Hence, if a query must be processed with a qualification of the form:

where VALUE-3 < key < VALUE-4

it is necessary to construct two query plans, one for each index. There is little complexity to this optimizer extension. At one's leisure, the remaining N-1 intervals can be processed to generate the complete index.

All storage reorganizations to achieve alternate access paths or arm balance can be similarly coded as incremental operations using distribution criteria and partial indexes. We expect to embed these techniques into a collection of asynchronous demons that will run in background, thereby relieving the operator of manual (and error prone) operations.

It would also be possible to build an index without setting any locks and then process the log to correct the index afterwards. This would be similar to incremental techniques for dumping relations, so called "fuzzy dumps". Our technique is superior because portions of the index can be utilized as soon as they have been constructed. There is no need to wait for the end of the entire build procedure.

7. CONCLUSIONS

We have described the design of a hardware and software system to support high performance applications. This entails modifying POSTGRES to support fast-path and partial indexes, writing a collection of demons to provide housekeeping services without the presence of a human, building a controller for RAID, and providing parallel query plans.

The hardware platform utilized will either be a large Sun machine or a SEQUENT Symmetry system. The construction of RAID is in progress and we expect an initial prototype by late 1988. The fast-path feature of POSTGRES is nearly operational and we are tuning up the system to achieve our TPS performance goal. During 1989 we will concentrate on partial indexes and parallel plans.

REFERENCES

[ASTR76] Astrahan, M. et. al., "System R: A Relational Approach to Data," ACM-TODS, June 1976.

[ANON85] Anon et. al., "A Measure of Transaction Processing Power," Tandem Computers, Cupertino, CA, Technical Report 85.1, 1985.

[BADR87] Badrinath, B. and Ramamritham, K., "Semantics-Based Concurrency Control: Beyond Commutativity," Proc. 1987 Data Engineering Conference, Los Angeles, CA, February 1987.

[BAMB87] Bamberger, F., "Citicorp's New High Performance Transaction Processing System," Proc. 2nd International Workshop on High Performance Transaction Systems, Asilomar, CA, Sept. 1987.

[BHID88] Bhide, A. and Stonebraker, M., "A Performance Comparison of Two Architectures for Fast Transaction Processing," Proc. 1988 IEEE Data Engineering Conference, Los Angeles, CA, Feb. 1988.

[CARE86] Carey, M. et. al., "The Architecture of the EXODUS Extensible DBMS," Proc. International Workshop on Object-oriented Data Bases, Pacific Grove, CA, Sept. 1986.

[CHAN82] Chan, A. et. al., "The Implementation of an Integrated Concurrency Control and Recovery Scheme," Proc. 1982 ACM-SIGMOD Conference on Management of Data, Orlando, Fl., June 1982.

[DATE84] Date, C., "An Introduction to Database Systems, 3rd Edition" Addison-Wesley, Reading, Mass., 1984.

[DEWI85] Dewitt, D. and Gerber, R., "Multiprocessor Hash-based Join Algorithms," Proc. 1985 VLDB Conference, Stockholm, Sweden, Sept. 1985.

[DEWI86] Dewitt, D. et. al., "GAMMA: A High Performance Dataflow Database Machine," Proc. 1986 VLDB Conference, Kyoto, Japan, Sept. 1986.

[GRAE87] Graefe, G. and Dewitt, D., "The EXODUS Optimizer Generator," Proc. 1987 ACM-SIGMOD Conference on Management of Data, San Francisco, CA, May 1987.

[GRAY81] Gray, J. et. al., "The Recovery Manager of the System R Database Manager," Computing Surveys, June 1981.

[GRAY87] Gray, J., (private communication).

[GRAY87A] Gray, J. et. al., "NON-STOP SQL," Proc. 2nd International Workshop on High Performance Transaction Systems, Asilomar, CA, Sept. 1987.

[LIVN86] Livny, M. et. al., "Multi-disk Management Algorithms," IEEE Database Engineering, March 1986.

[LOHM87] Lohman, G., "Grammar-like Functional Rules for Representing Query Optimization Alternatives," IBM Research, San Jose, CA, RJ5992, Dec. 1987.

[OUST87] Ousterhout, J. et. al., "The Sprite Network Operating System," Computer Science Division, University of California, Berkeley, CA, Report UCB/CSD 87/359, June 1987.

[PATT88] Patterson, D. et. al., "RAID: Redundant Arrays of Inexpensive Disks," Proc. 1988 ACM-SIGMOD Conference on Management of Data, Chicago, Ill., June 1988.

[RICH87] Richardson, J. et. al., "Design and Evaluation of Parallel Pipelined Join Algorithms," Proc. 1987 ACM-SIGMOD Conference on Management of Data, San Francisco, CA, May 1987.

[ROWE87] Rowe, L. and Stonebraker, M., "The POSTGRES Data Model," Proc. 1987 VLDB Conference, Brighton, England, Sept. 1987.

[RTI87] Relational Technology, "INGRES/STAR Reference Manual, Version 5.0" Relational Technology, Inc., Alameda, CA, June 1986.

[SALE86] Salem, K. and Garcia-Molina, H., "Disk Striping," Proc. 1986 IEEE Data Engineering Conference, Los Angeles, CA, February 1986.

[SELL86] Sellis, T., "Global Query Optimization," Proc. 1986 ACM-SIGMOD Conference on Management of Data, Washington, D.C., May 1986.

[SELI79] Selinger, P. et. al., "Access Path Selection in a Relational Data Base System," Proc. 1979 ACM-SIGMOD Conference on Management of Data, Boston, Mass., June 1979.

[STON86] Stonebraker, M. and Rowe, L., "The Design of POSTGRES," Proc. 1986 ACM-SIGMOD Conference on Management of Data, Washington, D.C., May 1986.

[STON86A] Stonebraker, M., "The Case for Shared Nothing," IEEE Database Engineering, March 1986.

[STON87] Stonebraker, M., "The POSTGRES Storage System," Proc. 1987 VLDB Conference, Brighton, England, Sept. 1987.

[STON88] Stonebraker, M., "The Case for Partial Indexes," Electronics Research Laboratory, University of California, Berkeley, CA, Report ERL M88/62, June. 1988.

[TERA85] Teradata Corp., "DBC/1012 Data Base Computer Reference Manual," Teradata Corp., Los Angeles, CA, November 1985.

[VALD87] Valduriez, P., "Join Indices," ACM-TODS, June 1987.

[WENS88] Wensel, S. (ed.), "The POSTGRES Reference Manual," Electronics Research Laboratory, University of California, Berkeley, CA, Report M88/20, March 1988.

The Gamma Database Machine Project

DAVID J. DEWITT, SHAHRAM GHANDEHARIZADEH, DONOVAN A. SCHNEIDER, ALLAN BRICKER, HUI-I HSIAO, AND RICK RASMUSSEN

Abstract—**This paper describes the design of the Gamma database machine and the techniques employed in its implementation. Gamma is a relational database machine currently operating on an Intel iPSC/2 hypercube with 32 processors and 32 disk drives. Gamma employs three key technical ideas which enable the architecture to be scaled to hundreds of processors. First, all relations are horizontally partitioned across multiple disk drives enabling relations to be scanned in parallel. Second, novel parallel algorithms based on hashing are used to implement the complex relational operators such as join and aggregate functions. Third, dataflow scheduling techniques are used to coordinate multioperator queries. By using these techniques it is possible to control the execution of very complex queries with minimal coordination—a necessity for configurations involving a very large number of processors.**

In addition to describing the design of the Gamma software, a thorough performance evaluation of the iPSC/2 hypercube version of Gamma is also presented. In addition to measuring the effect of relation size and indexes on the response time for selection, join, aggregation, and update queries, we also analyze the performance of Gamma relative to the number of processors employed when the sizes of the input relations are kept constant (speedup) and when the sizes of the input relations are increased proportionally to the number of processors (scaleup). The speedup results obtained for both selection and join queries are linear; thus, doubling the number of processors halves the response time for a query. The scaleup results obtained are also quite encouraging. They reveal that a nearly constant response time can be maintained for both selection and join queries as the workload is increased by adding a proportional number of processors and disks.

Index Terms—**Database machines, dataflow query processing, distributed database systems, parallel algorithms, relational database systems.**

I. Introduction

FOR the last 5 years, the Gamma database machine project has focused on issues associated with the design and implementation of highly parallel database machines. In a number of ways, the design of Gamma is based on what we learned from our earlier database machine DIRECT [10]. While DIRECT demonstrated that parallelism could be successfully applied to processing database operations, it had a number of serious design deficiencies that made scaling of the architecture to hundreds of processors impossible, primarily the use of shared memory and centralized control for the execution of its parallel algorithms [3].

As a solution to the problems encountered with DIRECT, Gamma employs what appear today to be relatively straightforward solutions. Architecturally, Gamma is based on a shared-nothing [37] architecture consisting of a number of processors interconnected by a communications network such as a hypercube or a ring, with disks directly connected to the individual processors. It is generally accepted that such architectures can be scaled to incorporate thousands of processors. In fact, Teradata database machines [40] incorporating a shared-nothing architecture with over 200 processors are already in use. The second key idea employed by Gamma is the use of hash-based parallel algorithms. Unlike the algorithms employed by DIRECT, these algorithms require no centralized control and can thus, like the hardware architecture, be scaled almost indefinitely. Finally, to make the best of the limited I/O bandwidth provided by the current generation of disk drives, Gamma employs the concept of *horizontal partitioning* [33] (also termed *declustering* [29]) to distribute the tuples of a relation among multiple disk drives. This design enables large relations to be processed by multiple processors concurrently without incurring any communications overhead.

After the design of the Gamma software was completed in the fall of 1984, work began on the first prototype which was operational by the fall of 1985. This version of Gamma was implemented on top of an existing multicomputer consisting of 20 VAX 11/750 processors [12]. In the period of 1986–1988, the prototype was enhanced through the addition of a number of new operators (e.g., aggregate and update operators), new parallel join methods (Hybrid, Grace, and Sort-Merge [34]), and a complete concurrency control mechanism. In addition, we also conducted a number of performance studies of the system during this period [14], [15], [19], [20]. In the spring of 1989, Gamma was ported to a 32 processor Intel iPSC/2 hypercube and the VAX-based prototype was retired.

Gamma is similar to a number of other active parallel database machine efforts. In addition to Teradata [40], Bubba [8] and Tandem [39] also utilize a shared-nothing architecture and employ the concept of horizontal partitioning. While Teradata and Tandem also rely on hashing to decentralize the execution of their parallel algorithms, both systems tend to rely on relatively conventional join algorithms such as sort-merge for processing the fragments of the relation at each site. Gamma, XPRS [38],

Manuscript received August 15, 1989; revised December 12, 1989. This work was supported in part by the Defense Advanced Research Projects Agency under Contract N00039-86-C-0578, by the National Science Foundation under Grant DCR-8512862, by a DARPA/NASA sponsored Graduate Research Assistantship in Parallel Processing, and by research grants from Intel Scientific Computers, Tandem Computers, and Digital Equipment Corporation.

The authors are with the Department of Computer Sciences, University of Wisconsin, Madison, WI 53705.

IEEE Log Number 8933803.

and Volcano [22] each utilize parallel versions of the Hybrid join algorithm [11].

The remainder of this paper is organized as follows. In Section II, we describe the hardware used by each of the Gamma prototypes and our experiences with each. Section III discusses the organization of the Gamma software and describes how multioperator queries are controlled. The parallel algorithms employed by Gamma are described in Section IV and the techniques we employ for transaction and failure management are contained in Section V. Section VI contains a performance study of the 32 processor Intel hypercube prototype. Our conclusions and future research directions are described in Section VII.

II. Hardware Architecture of Gamma

A. Overview

Gamma is based on the concept of a shared-nothing architecture [37] in which processors do not share disk drives or random access memory and can only communicate with one another by sending messages through an interconnection network. Mass storage in such an architecture is generally distributed among the processors by connecting one or more disk drives to each processor as shown in Fig. 1. There are a number of reasons why the shared-nothing approach has become the architecture of choice. First, there is nothing to prevent the architecture from scaling to thousands of processors unlike shared-memory machines for which scaling beyond 30–40 processors may be impossible. Second, as demonstrated in [15], [8], and [39], by associating a small number of disks with each processor and distributing the tuples of each relation across the disk drives, it is possible to achieve very high aggregate I/O bandwidths without using custom disk controllers [27], [31]. Furthermore, by employing off-the-shelf mass storage technology one can employ the latest technology in small 3 1/2 in. disk drives with embedded disk controllers. Another advantage of the shared nothing approach is that there is no longer any need to "roll your own" hardware. Recently, both Intel and Ncube have added mass storage to their hypercube-based multiprocessor products.

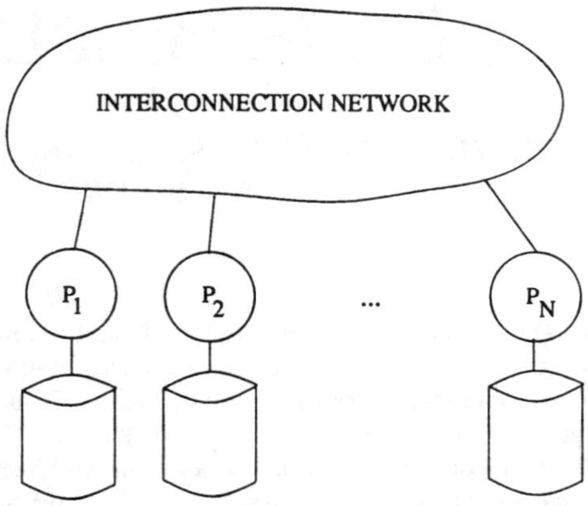

Fig. 1.

B. Gamma Version 1.0

The initial version of Gamma consisted of 17 VAX 11/750 processors, each with 2 megabytes of memory. An 80 Mb/s token ring [32] was used to connect the processors to each other and to another VAX running UNIX. This processor acted as the host machine for Gamma. Attached to eight of the processors were 333 megabyte Fujitsu disk drives that were used for storing the database. The diskless processors were used along with the processors with disks to execute join and aggregate function operators in order to explore whether diskless processors could be exploited effectively.

We encountered a number of problems with this prototype. First, the token ring has a maximum network packet size of 2K bytes. In the first version of the prototype, the size of a disk page was set to 2K bytes in order to be able to transfer an "intact" disk page from one processor to another without a copy. This required, for example, that each disk page also contain space for the protocol header used by the interprocessor communication software. While this initially appeared to be a good idea, we quickly realized that the benefits of a larger disk page size more than offset the cost of having to copy tuples from a disk page into a network packet.

The second problem we encountered was that the network interface and the Unibus on the 11/750 were both bottlenecks [18], [15]. While the bandwidth of the token ring itself was 80 Mb/s, the Unibus on the 11/750 (to which the network interface was attached) has a bandwidth of only 4 Mb/s. When processing a join query without a selection predicate on either of the input relations, the Unibus became a bottleneck because the transfer rate of pages from the disk was higher than the speed of the Unibus [15]. The network interface was a bottleneck because it could only buffer two incoming packets at a time. Until one packet was transferred into the VAX's memory, other incoming packets were rejected and had to be retransmitted by the communications protocol. While we eventually constructed an interface to the token ring that plugged directly into the backplane of the VAX, by the time the board was operational the VAX's were obsolete and we elected not to spend additional funds to upgrade the entire system.

The other serious problem we encountered with this prototype was having only 2 megabytes of memory on each processor. This was especially a problem since the operating system used by Gamma does not provide virtual memory. The problem was exacerbated by the fact that space for join hash tables, stack space for processes, and the buffer pool were managed separately in order to avoid flushing hot pages from the buffer pool. While there are advantages to having these spaces managed separately by the software, in a configuration where memory is already tight, balancing the sizes of these three pools of memory proved difficult.

C. Gamma Version 2.0

In the fall of 1988, we replaced the VAX-based prototype with a 32 processor iPSC/2 hypercube from Intel.

Each processor is configured with a 386 CPU, 8 megabytes of memory, and a 330 megabyte MAXTOR 4380 (5 1/4 in.) disk drive. Each disk drive has an embedded SCSI controller which provides a 45 Kbyte RAM buffer that acts as a disk cache on read operations.

The nodes in the hypercube are interconnected to form a hypercube using custom VLSI routing modules. Each module supports eight[1] full-duplex, serial, reliable communication channels operating at 2.8 megabytes/s. Small messages ($\leq$ 100 bytes) are sent as datagrams. For large messages, the hardware builds a communications circuit between the two nodes over which the entire message is transmitted without any software overhead or copying. After the message has been completely transmitted, the circuit is released. The length of a message is limited only by the size of the physical memory on each processor. Table I summarizes the transmission times from one Gamma process to another (on two different hypercube nodes) for a variety of message sizes.

The conversion of the Gamma software to the hypercube began in early December 1988. Because most users of the Intel hypercube tend to run a single process at a time while crunching numerical data, the operating system provided by Intel supports only a limited number of heavyweight processes. Thus, we began the conversion process by porting Gamma's operating system, NOSE (see Section III-E). In order to simplify the conversion, we elected to run NOSE as a thread package inside a single NX/2 process in order to avoid having to port NOSE to run on the bare hardware directly.

Once NOSE was running, we began converting the Gamma software. This process took 4–6 man months but lasted about 6 months as, in the process of the conversion, we discovered that the interface between the SCSI disk controller and memory was not able to transfer disk blocks larger than 1024 bytes (the pitfall of being a beta test site). For the most part, the conversion of the Gamma software was almost trivial as, by porting NOSE first, the differences between the two systems in initiating disk and message transfers were completely hidden from the Gamma software. In porting the code to the 386, we did discover a number of hidden bugs in the VAX version of the code as the VAX does not trap when a null pointer is dereferenced. The biggest problem we encountered was that nodes on the VAX multicomputer were numbered beginning with 1 while the hypercube uses 0 as the logical address of the first node. While we thought that making the necessary changes would be tedious but straightforward, we were about half way through the port before we realized that we would have to find and change every "for" loop in the system in which the loop index was also used as the address of the machine to which a message was to be sent. While this sounds silly now, it took us several weeks to find all the places that had to be changed. In retrospect, we should have made NOSE mask the differences between the two addressing schemes.

[1]On configurations with a mix of compute and I/O nodes, one of the eight channels is dedicated for communication to the I/O subsystem.

TABLE I

Packet Size (in bytes)	Transmission Time
50	0.74 ms.
500	1.46 ms.
1000	1.57 ms.
4000	2.69 ms.
8000	4.64 ms.

From a database system perspective, however, there are a number of areas in which Intel could improve the design of the iPSC/2. First, a lightweight process mechanism should be provided as an alternative to NX/2. While this would have almost certainly increased the time required to do the port, in the long run we could have avoided maintaining NOSE. A much more serious problem with the current version of the system is that the disk controller does not perform DMA transfers directly into memory. Rather, as a block is read from the disk, the disk controller does a DMA transfer into a 4K byte FIFO. When the FIFO is half full, the CPU is interrupted and the contents of the FIFO are copied into the appropriate location in memory.[2] While a block instruction is used for the copy operation, we have measured that about 10% of the available CPU cycles are being wasted doing the copy operation. In addition, the CPU is interrupted 13 times during the transfer of one 8 Kbyte block partially because a SCSI disk controller is used and partially because of the FIFO between the disk controller and memory.

III. Software Architecture of Gamma

In this section, we present an overview of Gamma's software architecture and describe the techniques that Gamma employs for executing queries in a dataflow fashion. We begin by describing the alternative storage structures provided by the Gamma software. Next, the overall system architecture is described from the top down. After describing the overall process structure, we illustrate the operation of the system by describing the interaction of the processes during the execution of several different queries. A detailed presentation of the techniques used to control the execution of complex queries is presented in Section III-D. This is followed by an example which illustrates the execution of a multioperator query. Finally, we briefly describe WiSS, the storage system used to provide low-level database services, and NOSE, the underlying operating system.

A. Gamma Storage Organizations

Relations in Gamma are *horizontally partitioned* [33] across all disk drives in the system. The key idea behind horizontally partitioning each relation is to enable the database software to exploit all the I/O bandwidth provided by the hardware. By declustering[3] the tuples of a relation,

[2]Intel was forced to use such a design because the I/O system was added after the system had been completed and the only way of doing I/O was by using a empty socket on the board which did not have DMA access to memory.

[3]Declustering is another term for horizontal partitioning that was coined by the Bubba project [29].

the task of parallelizing a selection/scan operator becomes trivial as all that is required is to start a copy of the operator on each processor.

The query language of Gamma provides the user with three alternative declustering strategies: *round robin*, *hashed*, and *range partitioned*. With the first strategy, tuples are distributed in a round-robin fashion among the disk drives. This is the default strategy and is used for all relations created as the result of a query. If the hashed partitioning strategy is selected, a randomizing function is applied to the key attribute of each tuple (as specified in the partition command for the relation) to select a storage unit. In the third strategy, the user specifies a range of key values for each site. For example, with a four disk system, the command *partition employee on emp_id (100, 300, 1000)* would result in the distribution of tuples shown in Table II. The partitioning information for each relation is stored in the database catalog. For range and hash-partitioned relations, the name of the partitioning attribute is also kept and, in the case of range-partitioned relations, the range of values of the partitioning attribute for each site (termed a *range table*).

Once a relation has been partitioned, Gamma provides the normal collection of relational database system access methods including both clustered and nonclustered indexes. When the user requests that an index be created on a relation, the system automatically creates an index on each fragment of the relation. Unlike VSAM [41] and the Tandem file system [17], Gamma does not require the clustered index for a relation to be constructed on the partitioning attribute.

As a query is being optimized, the partitioning information for each source relation in the query is incorporated into the query plan produced by the query optimizer. In the case of hash and range-partitioned relations, this partitioning information is used by the query scheduler (discussed below) to restrict the number of processors involved in the execution of selection queries on the partitioning attribute. For example, if relation X is hash partitioned on attribute y, it is possible to direct selection operations with predicates of the form "$X.y$ = Constant" to a single site; avoiding the participation of any other sites in the execution of the query. In the case of range-partitioned relations, the query scheduler can restrict the execution of the query to only those processors whose ranges overlap the range of the selection predicate (which may be either an equality or range predicate).

In retrospect, we made a serious mistake in choosing to decluster all relations across all nodes with disks. A much better approach, as proposed in [8], is to use the "heat" of a relation to determine the degree to which the relation is declustered. Unfortunately, to add such a capability to the Gamma software at this point in time would require a fairly major effort—one we are not likely to undertake.

B. Gamma Process Structure

The overall structure of the various processes that form the Gamma software is shown in Fig. 2. The role of each process is described briefly below. The operation of the distributed deadlock detection and recovery mechanism are presented in Sections V-A and V-B. At system initialization time, a UNIX daemon process for the catalog manager (CM) is initiated along with a set of scheduler processes, a set of operator processes, the deadlock detection process, and the recovery process.

TABLE II
AN EXAMPLE RANGE TABLE

Distribution Condition	Processor #
emp_id ≤ 100	1
100 < emp_id ≤ 300	2
300 < emp_id ≤ 1000	3
emp_id > 1000	4

Catalog Manager: The function of the catalog manager is to act as a central repository of all conceptual and internal schema information for each database. The schema information is loaded into memory when a database is first opened. Since multiple users may have the same database open at once and since each user may reside on a machine other than the one on which the catalog manager is executing, the catalog manager is responsible for ensuring consistency among the copies cached by each user.

Query Manager: One query manager process is associated with each active Gamma user. The query manager is responsible for caching schema information locally, providing an interface for ad-hoc queries using gdl (our variant of Quel [37]), query parsing, optimization, and compilation.

Scheduler Processes: While executing, each multisite query is controlled by a scheduler process. This process is responsible for activating the operator processes used to execute the nodes of a compiled query tree. Scheduler processes can be run on any processor, ensuring that no processor becomes a bottleneck. In practice, however, scheduler processes consume almost no resources and it is possible to run a large number of them on a single processor. A centralized dispatching process is used to assign scheduler processes to queries. Those queries that the optimizer can detect to be single-site queries are sent directly to the appropriate node for execution, bypassing the scheduling process.

Operator Process: For each operator in a query tree, at least one operator process is employed at each processor participating in the execution of the operator. These operators are primed at system initialization time in order to avoid the overhead of starting processes at query execution time (additional processes can be forked as needed). The structure of an operator process and the mapping of relational operators to operator processes is discussed in more detail below. When a scheduler wishes to start a new operator on a node, it sends a request to a special communications port known as the "new task" port. When a request is received on this port, an idle operator process is assigned to the request and the communications port of this operator process is returned to the requesting scheduler process.

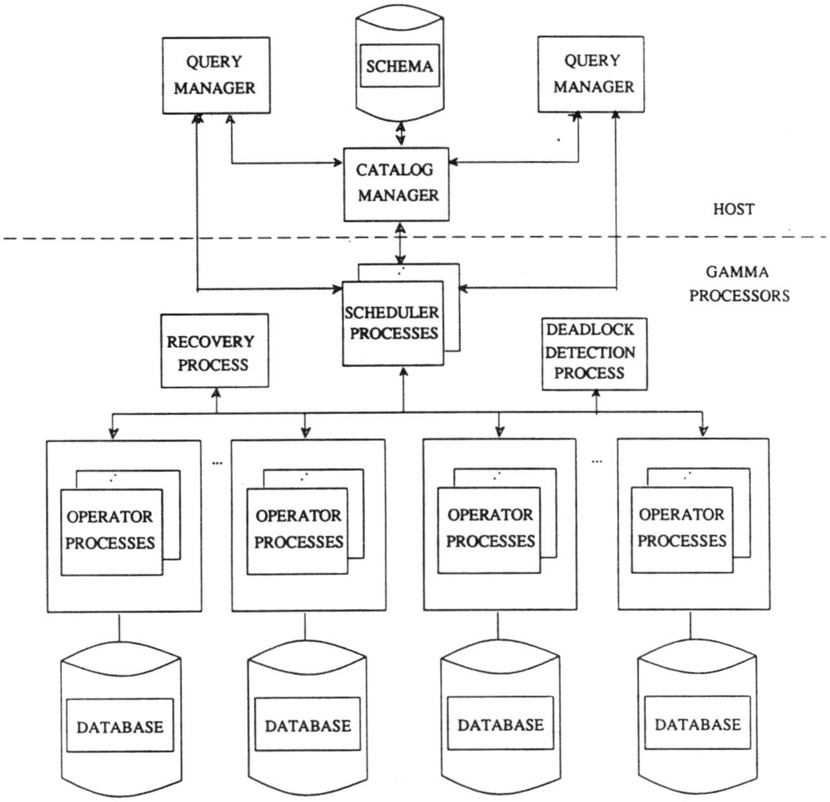

Fig. 2. Gamma process structure.

C. An Overview of Query Execution

Ad-hoc and Embedded Query Interfaces: Two interfaces to Gamma are available: an ad-hoc query language and an embedded query language interface in which queries can be embedded in a C program. When a user invokes the ad-hoc query interface, a query manager (QM) process is started which immediately connects itself to the CM process through the UNIX Internet socket mechanism. When the compiled query interface is used, the preprocessor translates each embedded query into a compiled query plan which is invoked at run-time by the program. A mechanism for passing parameters from the C program to the compiled query plans at run time is also provided.

Query Execution: Gamma uses traditional relational techniques for query parsing, optimization [36], [26], and code generation. The optimization process is somewhat simplified as Gamma only employs hash-based algorithms for joins and other complex operations. Queries are compiled into a left-deep tree of operators. At execution time, each operator is executed by one or more operator processes at each participating site.

In designing the optimizer for the VAX version of Gamma, the set of possible query plans considered by the optimizer was restricted to only left-deep trees because we felt that there was not enough memory to support right-deep or bushy plans. By using a combination of left-deep query trees and hash-based join algorithms, we were able to ensure that no more than two join operations were ever active simultaneously and hence were able to maximize the amount of physical memory which could be allocated to each join operator. Since this memory limitation was really only an artifact of the VAX prototype, we have recently begun to examine the performance implications of right-deep and bushy query plans [35].

As discussed in Section III-A, in the process of optimizing a query, the query optimizer recognizes that certain queries can be directed to only a subset of the nodes in the system. In the case of a single site query, the query is sent directly by the QM to the appropriate processor for execution. In the case of a multiple site query, the optimizer establishes a connection to an idle scheduler process through a centralized dispatcher process. The dispatcher process, by controlling the number of active schedulers, implements a simple load control mechanism. Once it has established a connection with a scheduler process, the QM sends the compiled query to the scheduler process and waits for the query to complete execution. The scheduler process, in turn, activates operator processes at each query processor selected to execute the operator. Finally, the QM reads the results of the query and returns them through the ad-hoc query interface to the user or through the embedded query interface to the program from which the query was initiated.

D. Operator and Process Structure

The algorithms for all the relational operators are written as if they were to be run on a single processor. As shown in Fig. 3, the input to an operator process is a stream of tuples and the output is a stream of tuples that is demultiplexed through a structure we term a *split table*.

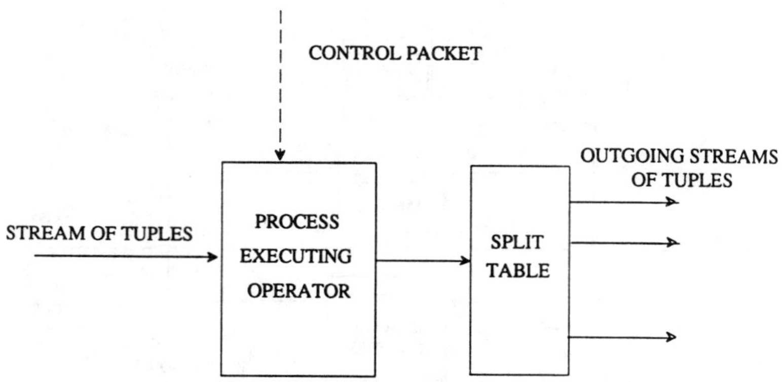

Fig. 3.

Value	Destination Process
0	(Processor #3, Port #5)
1	(Processor #2, Port #13)
2	(Processor #7, Port #6)
3	(Processor #9, Port #15)

Fig. 4. An example split table.

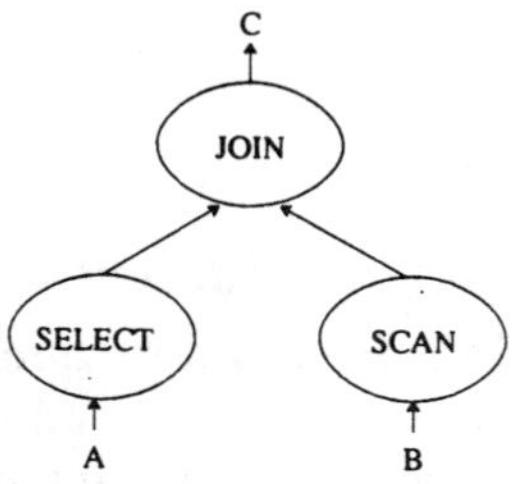

Fig. 5.

Once the process begins execution, it continuously reads tuples from its input stream, operates on each tuple, and uses a split table to route the resulting tuple to the process indicated in the split table.[4] When the process detects the end of its input stream, it first closes the output streams and then sends a control message to its scheduler process indicating that it has completed execution. Closing the output streams has the side effect of sending "end of stream" messages to each of the destination processes.

The split table defines a mapping of values to a set of destination processes. Gamma uses three different types of split tables depending on the type of operation being performed [14]. As an example of one form of split table, consider the use of the split table shown in Fig. 4 in conjunction with the execution of a join operation using four processors. Each process producing tuples for the join will apply a hash function to the join attribute of each output tuple to produce a value between 0 and 3. This value is then used as an index into the split table to obtain the address of the destination process that should receive the tuple.

An Example: As an example of how queries are executed, consider the query shown in Fig. 5. In Fig. 6, the processes used to execute the query are shown along with the flow of data between the various processes for a Gamma configuration consisting of two processors with disks and two processors without disks. Since the two input relations *A* and *B* are partitioned across the disks attached to processors *P*1 and *P*2, selection and scan operators are initiated on both processors *P*1 and *P*2. The split tables for both the select and scan operators each contain two entries since two processors are being used for the join operation. The split tables for each selection and scan are identical—routing tuples whose join attribute values hash to 0 (dashed lines) to *P*3 and those which hash to 1 (solid lines) to *P*4. The join operator executes in two phases. During the first phase, termed the *building phase*, tuples from the inner relation (*A* in this example) are inserted into a memory-resident hash table by hashing on the join attribute value. After the first phase has completed, the *probing* phase of the join is initiated in which tuples from the outer relation are used to probe the hash table for matching tuples.[5] Since the result relation is partitioned across two disks, the split table for each join operator contains two entries and tuples of *C* are distributed in a round-robin fashion among *P*1 and *P*2.

One of the main problems with the DIRECT prototype was that every data page processed required at least one control message to a centralized scheduler. In Gamma, this bottleneck is completely avoided. In fact, the number of control messages required to execute a query is approximately equal to three times the number of operators in the query times the number of processors used to execute each operator. As an example, consider Fig. 7 which depicts the flow of control messages[6] from a scheduler process to the processes on processors *P*1 and *P*3 in Fig. 6 (an identical set of messages would flow from the sched-

[4]Tuples are actually sent as 8K byte batches, except for the last batch.

[5]This is actually a description of the simple hash join algorithm. The operation of the hybrid hash join algorithm is contained in Section IV.

[6]The "Initiate" message is sent to a "new operator" port on each processor. A dispatching process accepts incoming messages on this port and assigns the operator to a process. The process, which is assigned, replies to the scheduler with an "ID" message which indicates the private port number of the operator process. Future communications to the operator by the scheduler use this private port number.

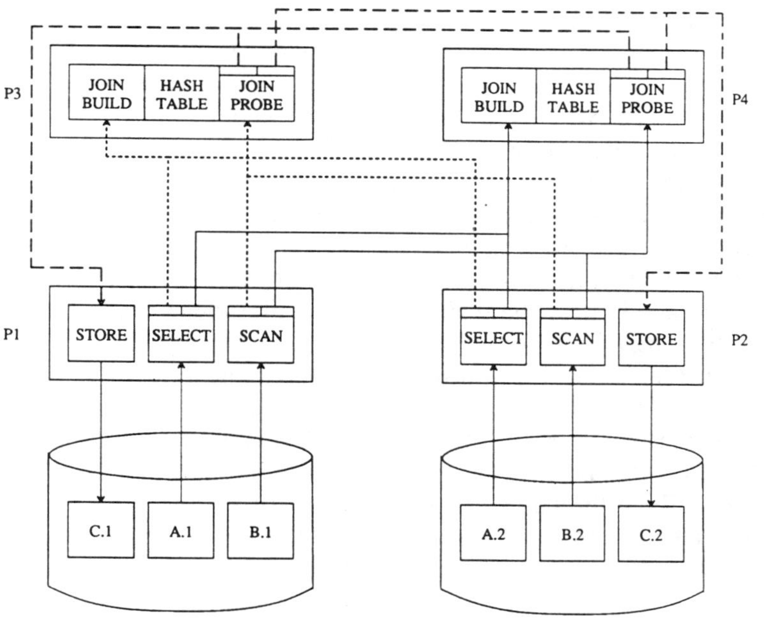

Fig. 6.

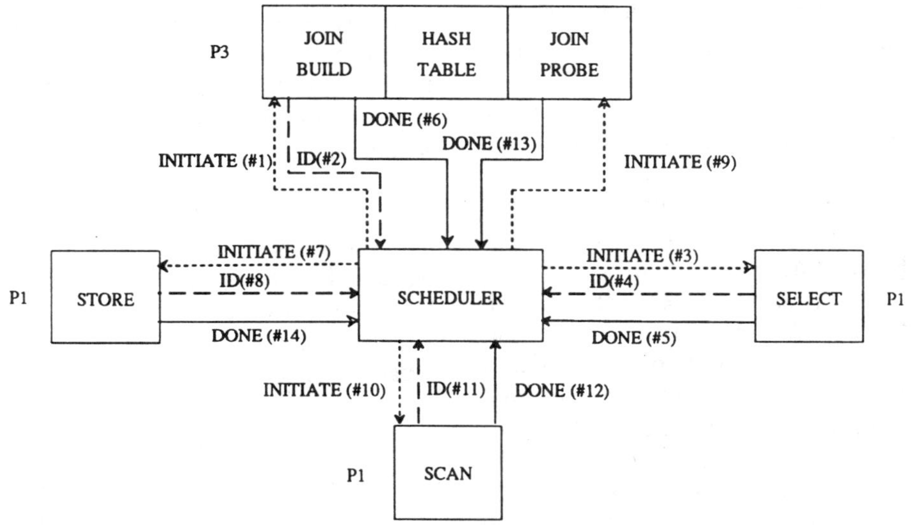

Fig. 7.

uler to P2 and P4). The scheduler begins by initiating the building phase of the join and the selection operator on relation *A*. When both these operators have completed, the scheduler next initiates the store operator, the probing phase of the join, and the scan of relation *B*. When each of these operators has completed, a result message is returned to the user.

E. Operating and Storage System

Gamma is built on top of an operating system designed specifically for supporting database management systems. NOSE provides multiple, lightweight processes with shared memory. A nonpreemptive scheduling policy is used to prevent convoys [4] from occurring. NOSE provides communications between NOSE processes using the reliable message passing hardware of the Intel iPSC/2 hybercube. File services in NOSE are based on the Wisconsin Storage System (WiSS) [7]. Critical sections of WiSS are protected using the semaphore mechanism provided by NOSE.

The file services provided by WiSS include structured sequential files, byte-stream files as in UNIX, B^+ indexes, long data items, a sort utility, and a scan mechanism. A sequential file is a sequence of records. Records may vary in length (up to one page in length), and may be inserted and deleted at arbitrary locations within a sequential file. Optionally, each file may have one or more associated indexes which map key values to the record identifiers of the records in the file that contain a matching value. One indexed attribute may be designated as a clustering attribute for the file. The scan mechanism is similar to that provided by System R's RSS [2] except that the predicates are compiled by the query optimizer into 386 machine language to maximize performance.

IV. Query Processing Algorithms

A. Selection Operator

Since all relations are declustered over multiple disk drives, parallelizing the selection operation involves simply initiating a selection operator on the set of relevant nodes with disks. When the predicate in the selection clause is on the partitioning attribute of the relation and the relation is hash or range partitioned, the scheduler can direct the selection operator to a subset of the nodes. If either the relation is round-robin partitioned or the selection predicate is not on the partitioning attribute, a selection operator must be initiated on all nodes over which the relation is declustered. To enhance performance, Gamma employs a one page read-ahead mechanism when scanning the pages of a file sequentially or through a clustered index. This mechanism enables the processing of one page to be overlapped with the I/O for the subsequent page.

B. Join Operator

The multiprocessor join algorithms provided by Gamma are based on the concept of partitioning the two relations to be joined into disjoint subsets called *buckets* [21], [28], [6] by applying a hash function to the join attribute of each tuple. The partitioned buckets represent disjoint subsets of the original relations and have the important characteristic that all tuples with the same join attribute value are in the same bucket. We have implemented parallel versions of four join algorithms on the Gamma prototype: sort–merge, Grace [28], Simple [11], and Hybrid [11]. While all four algorithms employ this concept of hash-based partitioning, the actual join computation depends on the algorithm. The parallel hybrid join algorithm is described in the following section. Additional information on all four parallel algorithms and their relative performance can be found in [34]. Since this study found that the Hybrid hash join almost always provides the best performance, it is now the default algorithm in Gamma and is described in more detail in the following section. Since these hash-based join algorithms cannot be used to execute nonequijoin operations, such operations are not currently supported. To remedy this situation, we are in the process of designing a parallel nonequijoin algorithm for Gamma.

Hybrid Hash-Join: A *centralized* Hybrid hash–join algorithm [11] operates in three phases. In the first phase, the algorithm uses a hash function to partition the inner (smaller) relation R into N buckets. The tuples of the first bucket are used to build an in-memory hash table while the remaining $N - 1$ buckets are stored in temporary files. A good hash function produces just enough buckets to ensure that each bucket of tuples will be small enough to fit entirely in main memory. During the second phase, relation S is partitioned using the hash function from step 1. Again, the last $N - 1$ buckets are stored in temporary files while the tuples in the first bucket are used to immediately probe the in-memory hash table built during the first phase. During the third phase, the algorithm joins the remaining $N - 1$ buckets from relation R with their respective buckets from relation S. The join is thus broken up into a series of smaller joins; each of which hopefully can be computed without experiencing join overflow. The size of the smaller relation determines the number of buckets; this calculation is independent of the size of the larger relation.

Our parallel version of the Hybrid hash–join algorithm is similar to the centralized algorithm described above. A *partitioning split table* first separates the joining relations into N logical buckets. The number of buckets is chosen such that the tuples corresponding to each logical bucket will fit in the *aggregate* memory of the joining processors. The $N - 1$ buckets intended for temporary storage on disk are each partitioned across all available disk sites. Likewise, a *joining split table* will be used to route tuples to their respective joining processor (these processors do not necessarily have attached disks), thus parallelizing the joining phase. Furthermore, the partitioning of the inner relation R into buckets is overlapped with the insertion of tuples from the first bucket of R into memory-resident hash tables at each of the join nodes. In addition, the partitioning of the outer relation S into buckets is overlapped with the joining of the first bucket of S with the first bucket of R. This requires that the partitioning split table for R and S be enhanced with the joining split table as tuples in the first bucket must be sent to those processors being used to effect the join. Of course, when the remaining $N - 1$ buckets are joined, only the joining split table will be needed. Fig. 8 depicts relation R being partitioned into N buckets across k disk sites where the first bucket is to be joined on m processors (m may be less than, equal to, or greater than k).

C. Aggregate Operations

Gamma implements scalar aggregates by having each processor compute its piece of the result in parallel. The partial results are then sent to a single process which combines these partial results into the final answer. Aggregate functions are computed in two steps. First, each processor computes a piece of the result by calculating a value for each of the partitions. Next, the processors redistribute the partial results by hashing on the "group by" attribute. The result of this step is to collect the partial results for each partition at a single site so that the final result for each partition can be computed.

D. Update Operators

For the most part, the update operators (replace, delete, and append) are implemented using standard techniques. The only exception occurs when a replace operator modifies the partitioning attribute of a tuple. In this case, rather than writing the modified tuple back into the local fragment of the relation, the modified tuple is passed through a split table to determine which site should contain the tuple.

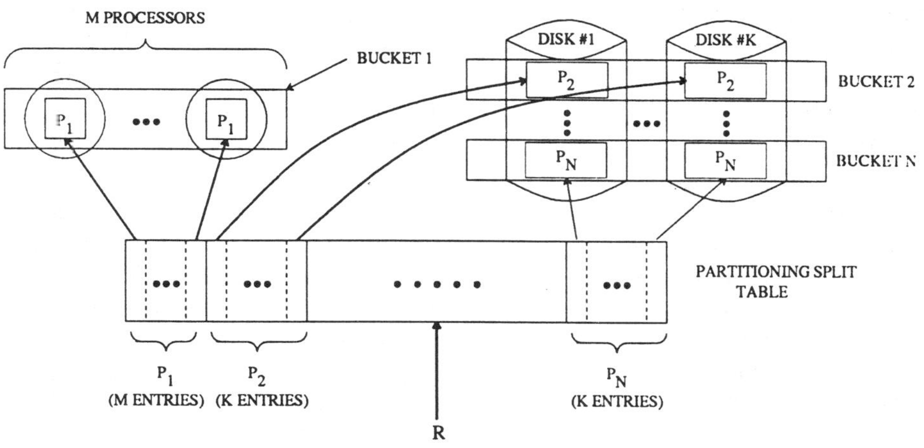

Fig. 8. Partitioning of R into N logical buckets for hybrid hash-join.

V. Transaction and Failure Management

In this section, we describe the mechanisms that Gamma uses for transaction and failure management. While the locking mechanisms are fully operational, the recovery system is currently being implemented. We expect to begin the implementation of the failure management mechanism in early 1990.

A. *Concurrency Control in Gamma*

Concurrency control in Gamma is based on two-phase locking [23]. Currently, two lock granularities, file and page, and five lock modes, *S*, *X*, *IS*, *IX*, and *SIX* are provided. Each site in Gamma has its own local lock manager and deadlock detector. The lock manager maintains a lock table and a transaction wait-for-graph. The cost of setting a lock varies from approximately 100 instructions, if there is no conflict, to 250 instructions if the lock request conflicts with the granted group. In this case, the wait-for-graph must be checked for deadlock and the transaction that requested the lock must be suspended via a semaphore mechanism.

In order to detect multisite deadlocks, Gamma uses a centralized deadlock detection algorithm. Periodically, the centralized deadlock detector sends a message to each node in the configuration, requesting the local transaction wait-for-graph of that node. Initially, the period for running the centralized deadlock detector is set at 1 s. Each time the deadlock detector fails to find a global deadlock, this interval is doubled and each time a deadlock is found the current value of the interval is halved. The upper bound of the interval is limited to 60 s and the lower bound is 1 s. After collecting the wait-for-graph from each site, the centralized deadlock detector creates a global transaction wait-for-graph. Whenever a cycle is detected in the global wait-for-graph, the centralized deadlock manager chooses to abort the transaction holding the fewest number of locks.

B. *Recovery Architecture and Log Manager*

The algorithms currently being implemented for coordinating transaction commit, abort, and rollback operate as follows. When an operator process updates a record, it also generates a log record which records the change of the database state. Associated with every log record is a log sequence number (LSN) which is composed of a node number and a local sequence number. The node number is statically determined at the system configuration time whereas the local sequence number, termed *current LSN*, is a monotonically increasing value.

Log records are sent by the query processors to one or more log managers (each running on a separate processor) which merges the log records it receives to form a single log stream. If M is the number of log processors being used, query processor i will direct its log records to the (i mod M) log processor [1]. Because this algorithm selects the log processor statically and a query processor always sends its log records to the same log processor, the recovery process at a query processing node can easily determine where to request the log records for processing a transaction abort.

When a page of log records is filled, it is written to disk. The log manager maintains a table, called the *flushed log table*, which contains, for each node, the LSN of the last log record from that node that has been flushed to disk. These values are returned to the nodes either upon request or when they can be piggybacked on another message. Query processing nodes save this information in a local variable, termed the *flushed LSN*.

The buffer managers at the query processing nodes observe the WAL protocol [23]. When a dirty page needs to be forced to disk, the buffer manager first compares the page's LSN with the local value of flushed LSN. If the LSN of a page is smaller or equal to the flushed LSN, that page can be safely written to disk. Otherwise, either a different dirty page must be selected, or a message must be sent to the log manager to flush the corresponding log record(s) of the dirty page. Only after the log manager acknowledges that the log record has been written to the log disk will the dirty data page be written back to disk. In order to reduce the time spent waiting for a reply from the log manager, the buffer manager always keeps T (a preselected threshold) clean and unfixed buffer pages available. When buffer manager notices that the number of clean, unfixed buffer pages has fallen below T, a process, termed *local log manager*, is activated. This process sends a message to the log manager to flush one or more log records so that the number of clean and unfixed pages plus the number of dirty pages that can be safely written to disk is greater than T.

The scheduler process for a query is responsible for sending commit or abort records to the appropriate log managers. If a transaction completes successfully, a commit record for the transaction is generated by its scheduler and sent to each relevant log manager which employs a group commit protocol. On the other hand, if a transaction is aborted by either the system or the user, its scheduler will send an abort message to all query processors that participated in its execution. The recovery process at each of the participating nodes responds by requesting the log records generated by the node from its log manager (the LSN of each log record contains the originating node number). As the log records are received, the recovery process undoes the log records in reverse chronological order using the ARIES undo algorithm [30]. The ARIES algorithms are also used as the basis for checkpointing and restart recovery.

C. Failure Management

To help ensure availability of the system in the event of processor and/or disk failures, Gamma employs a new availability technique termed *chained declustering* [25]. Like Tandem's mirrored disk mechanism [5] and Teradata's interleaved declustering mechanism [40], [9], chained declustering employs both a primary and backup copy of each relation. All three systems can sustain the failure of a single processor or disk without suffering any loss in data availability. In [25], we show that chained declustering provides a higher degree of availability than interleaved declustering and, in the event of a processor or disk failure, does a better job of distributing the workload of the broken node. The mirrored disk mechanism, while providing the highest level of availability, does a very poor job of distributing the load of a failed processor.

Data Placement with Chained Declustering: With chained declustering, nodes (a processor with one or more disks) are divided into disjoint groups called *relation clusters* and tuples of each relation are declustered among the drives that form one of the relation clusters. Two physical copies of each relation, termed the *primary copy* and the *backup copy*, are maintained. As an example, consider Fig. 9 where M, the number of disks in the relation cluster, is equal to 8. The tuples in the primary copy of relation R are declustered using one of Gamma's three partitioning strategies with tuples in the ith primary fragment (designated Ri) stored on the $\{i \bmod M\}$th disk drive. The backup copy is declustered using the same partitioning strategy but the ith backup fragment (designated ri) is stored on $\{(i + 1) \bmod M\}$th disk. We term this data replication method *chained declustering* because the disks are linked together, by the fragments of a relation, like a chain.

The difference between the chained and interleaved declustering mechanisms [40], [9] is illustrated by Fig. 10. In Fig. 10, the fragments from the primary copy of R are declustered across all eight disk drives by hashing on a "key" attribute. With the interleaved declustering mechanism the set of disks is divided into units of size N called *clusters*. As illustrated by Fig. 10, where $N = 4$, each backup fragment is subdivided into $N - 1$ subfragments and each subfragment is placed on a different disk within the same cluster other than the disk containing the primary fragment.

Since interleaved and chained declustering can both sustain the failure of a single disk or processor, what then is the difference between the two mechanisms? In the case of a single node (processor or disk) failure, both the chained and interleaved declustering strategies are able to uniformly distribute the workload of the cluster among the remaining operational nodes. For example, with a cluster size of 8, when a processor or disk fails, the load on each remaining node will increase by 1/7th. One might conclude then that the cluster size should be made as large as possible; until, of course, the overhead of the parallelism starts to overshadow the benefits obtained. While this is true for chained declustering, the availability of the interleaved strategy is inversely proportional to the cluster size since the failure of any two processors or disk will render data unavailable. Thus, doubling the cluster size in order to halve (approximately) the increase in the load on the remaining nodes when a failure occurs has the (quite negative) side effect of doubling the probability that data will actually be unavailable. For this reason, Teradata recommends a cluster size of 4–8 processors.

Fig. 11 illustrates how the workload is balanced in the event of a node failure (node 1 in this example) with the chained declustering mechanism. During the normal mode of operation, read requests are directed to the fragments of the primary copy and write operations update both copies. When a failure occurs, pieces of both the primary and backup fragments are used for read operations. For example, with the failure of node 1, primary fragment $R1$ can no longer be accessed and thus its backup fragment $r1$ on node 2 must be used for processing queries that would normally have been directed to $R1$. However, instead of requiring node 2 to process all accesses to both $R2$ and $r1$, chained declustering offloads 6/7ths of the accesses to $R2$ by redirecting them to $r2$ at node 3. In turn, 5/7ths of access to $r3$ at node 3 are sent to $R4$ instead. This dynamic reassignment of the workload results in an increase of 1/7th in the workload of each remaining node in the cluster. Since the cluster size can be increased without penalty, it is possible to make this load increase as small as is desired.

What makes this scheme even more attractive is that the reassignment of active fragments incurs neither disk I/O nor data movement. Only some of the bound values and pointers/indexes in a memory resident control table must

Node	0	1	2	3	4	5	6	7
Primary Copy	R0	R1	R2	R3	R4	R5	R6	R7
Backup Copy	r7	r0	r1	r2	r3	r4	r5	r6

Fig. 9. Chained declustering (relation cluster size = 8).

	Cluster 0				Cluster 1			
Node	0	1	2	3	4	5	6	7
Primary Copy	R0	R1	R2	R3	R4	R5	R6	R7
Backup Copy		r0.0	r0.1	r0.2		r4.0	r4.1	r4.2
	r1.2		r1.0	r1.1	r5.2		r5.0	r5.1
	r2.1	r2.2		r2.0	r6.1	r6.2		r6.0
	r3.0	r3.1	r3.2		r7.0	r7.1	r7.2	

Fig. 10. Interleaved declustering (cluster size = 4).

Node	0	1	2	3	4	5	6	7
Primary Copy	R0	---	$\frac{1}{7}$R2	$\frac{2}{7}$R3	$\frac{3}{7}$R4	$\frac{4}{7}$R5	$\frac{5}{7}$R6	$\frac{6}{7}$R7
Backup Copy	$\frac{1}{7}$r7	---	r1	$\frac{6}{7}$r2	$\frac{5}{7}$r3	$\frac{4}{7}$r4	$\frac{3}{7}$r5	$\frac{2}{7}$r6

Fig. 11. Fragment utilization with chained declustering after the failure of node 1 (relation cluster size = 8).

be changed and these modifications can be done very quickly and efficiently.

The example shown in Fig. 11 provides a very simplified view of how the chained declustering mechanism actually balances the workload in the event of a node failure. In reality, queries cannot simply access an arbitrary fraction of a data fragment, especially given the variety of partitioning and index mechanisms provided by the Gamma software. In [25], we describe how all combinations of query types, access methods, and partitioning mechanisms can be handled.

VI. Performance Studies

A. Introduction and Experiment Overview

To evaluate the performance of the hypercube version of Gamma, three different metrics were used. First, the set of Wisconsin [3] benchmark queries were run on a 30 processor configuration using three different sizes of relations: 100 000, 1 million, and 10 million tuples. While absolute performance is one measure of a database system, speedup and scaleup are also useful metrics for multiprocessor database machines [16]. Speedup is an interesting metric because it indicates whether additional processors and disks result in a corresponding decrease in the response time for a query. For a subset of the Wisconsin benchmark queries, we conducted speedup experiments by varying the number of processors from 1 to 30 while the size of the test relations was fixed at 1 million tuples. For the same set of queries, we also conducted scaleup experiments by varying the number of processors from 5 to 30 while the size of the test relations was increased from 1 to 6 million tuples, respectively. Scaleup is a valuable metric as it indicates whether a constant response time can be maintained as the workload is increased by adding a proportional number of processors and disks. [16] describes a similar set of tests on Release 2 of Tandem's NonStop SQL system.

The benchmark relations used for the experiments were based on the standard Wisconsin Benchmark relations [3]. Each relation consists of tuples that are 208 bytes wide. We constructed 100 000, 1 million, and 10 million tuple versions of the benchmark relations. Two copies of each relation were created and loaded. Except where noted otherwise, tuples were declustered by hash partitioning on the Unique1 attribute. In all cases, the results presented represent the average response time of a number of equivalent queries. Gamma was configured to use a disk page size of 8K bytes and a buffer pool of 2 megabytes.

The results of all queries were stored in the database. We avoided returning data to the host in order to avoid having the speed of the communications link between the host and the database machine or the host processor itself affect the results. By storing the result relations in the database, the impact of these factors was minimized—at the expense of incurring the cost of declustering and storing the result relations.

B. *Selection Queries*

Performance Relative to Relation Size: The first set of selection tests was designed to determine how Gamma would respond as the size of the source relations was increased while the machine configuration was kept at 30 processors with disks. Ideally, the response time of a query should grow as a linear function of the size of input and result relations. For these tests six different selection queries were run on three sets of relations containing, respectively, 100 000, 1 million, and 10 million tuples. The first two queries have a selectivity factor of 1% and 10% and do not employ any indexes. The third and fourth queries have the same selectivity factors but use a clustered index to locate the qualifying tuples. The fifth query has a selectivity factor of 1% and employs a nonclustered index to locate the desired tuples. There is no 10% selection through a nonclustered index query as the Gamma query optimizer chooses to use a sequential scan for this query. The last query uses a clustered index to retrieve a single tuple. Except for the last query, the predicate of each query specifies a range of values and, thus, since the input relations were declustered by hashing, the query must be sent to all the nodes.

The results from these tests are tabulated in Table III. For the most part, the execution time for each query scales as a fairly linear function of the size of the input and output relations. There are, however, several cases where the scaling is not perfectly linear. Consider, first the 1% nonindexed selection. While the increase in response time as the size of the input relation is increased from 1 to 10 million tuples is almost perfectly linear (8.16–81.15 s), the increase from 100 000 tuples to 1 million tuples (0.45–8.16 s) is actually sublinear. The 10% selection using a clustered index is another example where increasing the size of the input relation by a factor of ten results in more than a tenfold increase in the response time for the query. This query takes 5.02 s on the 1 million tuple relation and 61.86 s on the 10 million tuple relation. To understand why this happens one must consider the impact of seek time on the execution time of the query. Since two copies of each relation were loaded, when two one million tuple relations are declustered over 30 disk drives, the fragments occupy approximately 53 cylinders (out of 1224) on each disk drive. Two ten million tuple relations fill about 530 cylinders on each drive. As each page of the result relation is written to disk, the disk heads must be moved from their current position over the input relation to a free block on the disk. Thus, with the 10 million tuple relation, the cost of writing each output page is much higher.

As expected, the use of a cluster *B*-tree index always provides a significant improvement in performance. One observation to be made from Table III is the relative consistency of the execution time of the selection queries through a clustered index. Notice that the execution time for a 10% selection on the 1 million tuple relation is almost identical to the execution time of the 1% selection on the 10 million tuple relation. In both cases, 100 000 tuples are retrieved and stored, resulting in identical I/O and CPU cost.

TABLE III
SELECTION QUERIES. 30 PROCESSORS WITH DISKS (ALL EXECUTION TIMES IN SECONDS)

Query Description	Number of Tuples in Source Relation 100,000	1,000,000	10,000,000
1% nonindexed selection	0.45	8.16	81.15
10% nonindexed selection	0.82	10.82	135.61
1% selection using clustered index	0.35	0.82	5.12
10% selection using clustered index	0.77	5.02	61.86
1% selection using non-clustered index	0.60	8.77	113.37
single tuple select using clustered index	0.08	0.08	0.14

The final row of Table III presents the time required to select a single tuple using a clustered index and return it to the host. Since the selection predicate is on the partitioning attribute, the query is directed to a single node, avoiding the overhead of starting the query on all 30 processors. The response time for this query increases significantly as the relation size is increased from 1 million to 10 million tuples because the height of the *B*-tree increases from two to three levels.

Speedup Experiments: In this section we examine how the response time for both the nonindexed and indexed selection queries on the 1 million tuple relation[7] is affected by the number of processors used to execute the query. Ideally, one would like to see a linear improvement in performance as the number of processors is increased from 1 to 30. Increasing the number of processors increases both the aggregate CPU power and I/O bandwidth available, while reducing the number of tuples that must be processed by each processor.

In Fig. 12, the average response times for the nonindexed 1% and 10% selection queries on the one million tuple relation are presented. As expected, the response time for each query decreases as the number of nodes is increased. The response time is higher for the 10% selection due to the cost of declustering and storing the result relation. While one could always store result tuples locally, by partitioning all result relations in a round-robin (or hashed) fashion one can ensure that the fragments of every result relation each contain approximately the same number of tuples. The speedup curves corresponding to Fig. 12 are presented in Fig. 13.

In Fig. 14, the average response time is presented as a function of the number of processors for the following three queries: a 1% selection through a clustered index, a

[7]The 1 million tuple relation was used for these experiments because the 10 million tuple relation would not fit on 1 disk drive.

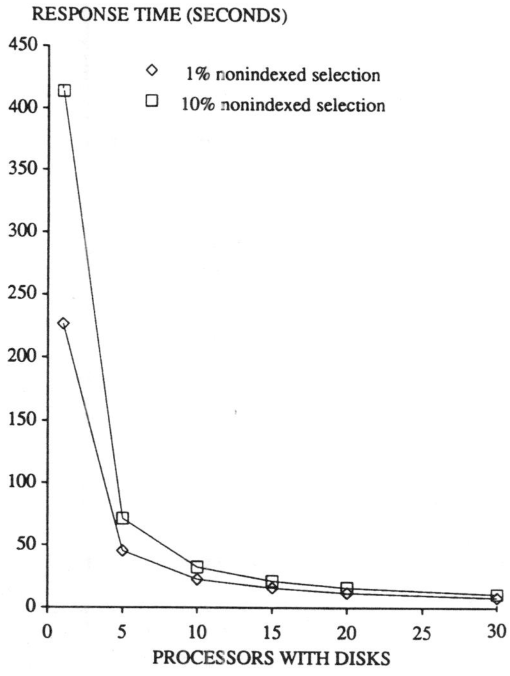

Fig. 12.

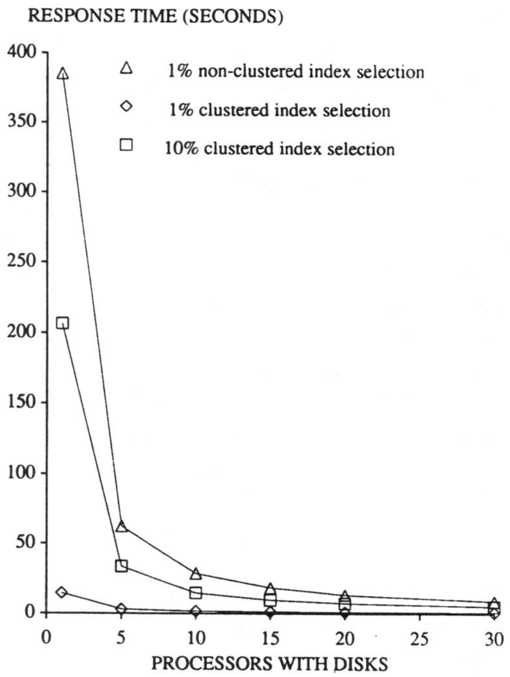

Fig. 14.

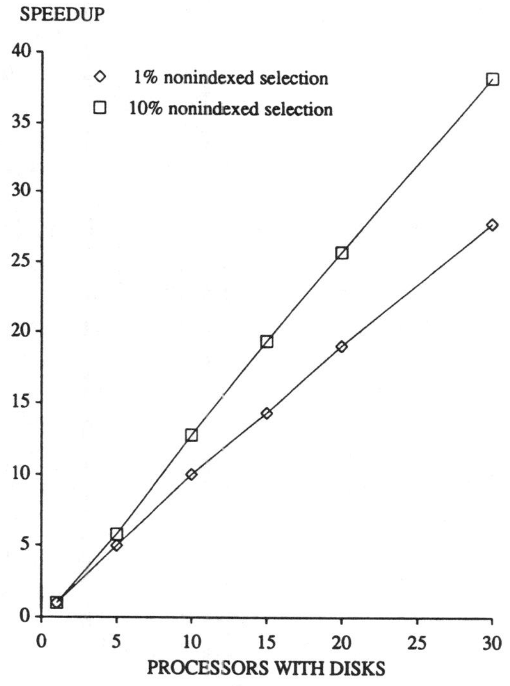

Fig. 13.

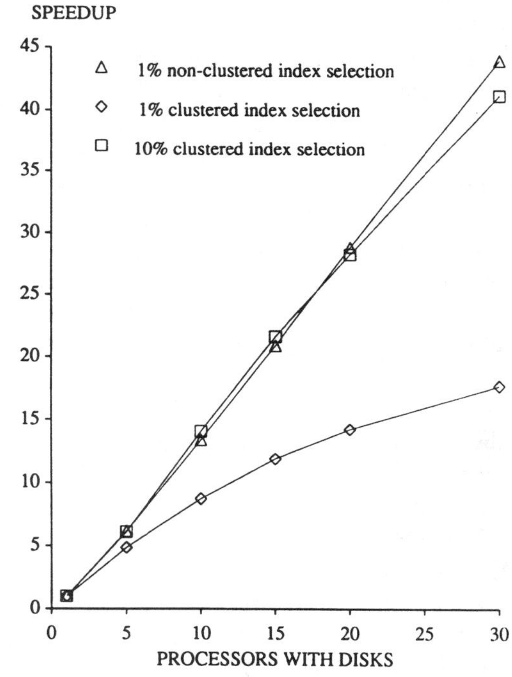

Fig. 15.

10% selection through a clustered index, and a 1% selection through a nonclustered index, all accessing the 1 million tuple relation. The corresponding speedup curves are presented in Fig. 15.

Of the speedup curves presented in Fig. 13 and 15, three queries are superlinear, one is slightly sublinear, and one is significantly sublinear. Consider first the 10% selection via a relation scan, the 1% selection through a nonclustered index, and the 10% selection through a clustered index. As discussed above, the source of the superlinear speedups exhibited by these queries is due to significant differences in the time the various configurations spend seeking. With one processor, the 1 million tuple relation occupies approximately 66% of the disk. When the same relation is declustered over 30 disk drives, it occupies about 2% of each disk. In the case of the 1% nonclustered index selection, each tuple selected requires a random seek. With one processor, the range of each random seek is approximately 800 cylinders while with 30 processors the range of the seek is limited to about 27 cylinders. Since the seek time is proportional to the square root of the distance traveled by the disk head [24], reducing the size of the relation fragment on each disk significantly reduces the amount of time that the query spends seeking.

A similar effect also happens with the 10% clustered index selection. In this case, once the index has been used to locate the tuples satisfying the query, each input page will produce one output page and at some point the buffer pool will be filled with dirty output pages. In order to write an output page, the disk head must be moved from its position over the input relation to the position on the disk where the output pages are to be placed. The relative cost of this seek decreases proportionally as the number of processors increases, resulting in a superlinear speedup for the query. The 10% nonindexed selection shown in Fig. 13 is also superlinear for similar reasons. The reason that this query is not affected to the same degree is that, without an index, the seek time is a smaller fraction of the overall execution time of the query.

The 1% selection through a clustered index exhibits sublinear speedups because the cost of initiating a select and store operator on each processor (a total of 0.24 s for 30 processors) becomes a significant fraction of the total execution as the number of processors is increased.

Scaleup Experiments: In the final set of selection experiments, the number of processors was varied from 5 to 30 while the size of the input relations was increased from 1 million to 6 million tuples, respectively. As shown in Fig. 16, the response time for each of the five selection queries remains almost constant. The slight increase in response time is due to the overhead of initiating a selection and store operator at each site. Since a single process is used to initiate the execution of a query, as the number of processors employed is increased, the load on this process is increased proportionally. Switching to a tree-based query initiation scheme [18] would distribute this overhead among all the processors.

C. Join Queries

Like the selection queries in the previous section, we conducted three sets of join experiments. First, for two different join queries, we varied the size of the input relations while the configuration of processors was kept constant. Next, for one join query a series of speedup and scaleup experiments were conducted. For each of these tests, two different partitionings of the input relations were used. In the first case, the input relations were declustered by hashing on the join attribute. In the second case, the input relations were declustered using a different attribute. The hybrid join algorithm was used for all queries.

Performance Relative to Relation Size: The first join query [3], join*AB*prime, is a simple join of two relations: *A* and *B*prime. The *A* relation contains either 100 000, 1 million, or 10 million tuples. The *B*prime relation contains, respectively, 10 000, 100 000, or 1 million tuples. The result relation has the same number of tuples as the *B*prime relation.[8] The second query, join*A*sel*B*, is composed of one join and one selection. *A* and *B* have the same number of tuples and the selection on *B* reduces the size of *B* to the size of the *B*prime relation in the corresponding join*AB*prime query. The result relation for this query has the same number of tuples as in the corresponding join*AB*prime query. As an example, if *A* has 10 million tuples, then join*AB*prime joins *A* with a *B*prime relation that contains 1 million tuples, while in join*A*sel*B* the selection on *B* restricts *B* from 10 million tuples to 1 million tuples and then joins the result with *A*.

[8]For each join operation, the result relation contains all the fields of both input relations and thus the result tuples are 416 bytes wide.

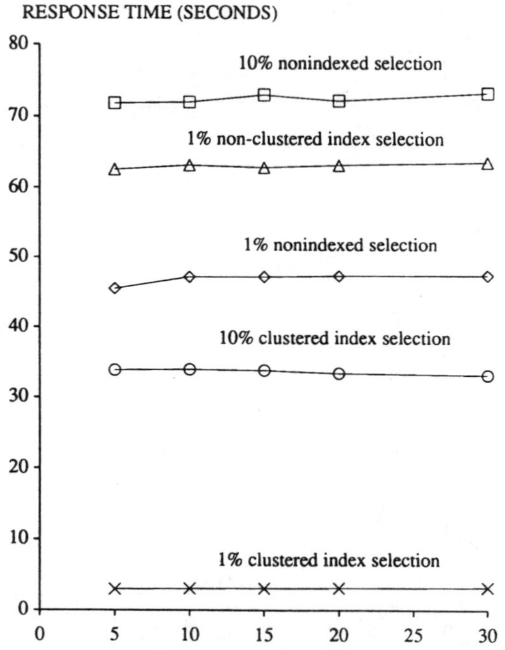

Fig. 16.

The first variation of the join queries tested involved no indexes and used a nonpartitioning attribute for both the join and selection attributes. Thus, before the join can be performed, the two input relations must be redistributed by hashing on the join attribute value of each tuple. The results from these tests are contained in the first 2 rows of Table IV. The second variation of the join queries also did not employ any indexes but, in this case, the relations were hash partitioned on the joining attribute; enabling the redistribution phase of the join to be skipped. The results for these tests are contained in the last 2 rows of Table IV.

The results in Table IV indicate that the execution time of each join query increases in a fairly linear fashion as the size of the input relations are increased. Gamma does not exhibit linearity for the 10 million tuple queries because the size of the inner relation (208 megabytes) is twice as large as the total available space for hash tables. Hence, the Hybrid join algorithm needs two buckets to process these queries. While the tuples in the first bucket can be placed directly into memory-resident hash tables, the second bucket must be written to disk (see Section IV-B).

As expected, the version of each query in which the partitioning attribute was used as the join attribute ran

TABLE IV
JOIN QUERIES. 30 PROCESSORS WITH DISKS (ALL EXECUTION TIMES IN SECONDS)

Query Description	Number of Tuples in Relation A 100,000	1,000,000	10,000,000
JoinABprime with non-partitioning attributes of A and B used as join attributes	3.52	28.69	438.90
JoinAselB with non-partitioning attributes of A and B used as join attributes	2.69	25.13	373.98
JoinABprime with partitioning attributes of A and B used as join attributes	3.34	25.95	426.25
JoinAselB with partitioning attributes of A and B used as join attributes	2.74	23.77	362.89

faster. From these results one can estimate a lower bound on the aggregate rate at which data can be redistributed by the Intel iPSC/2 hypercube. Consider the version of the join*AB*prime query in which a million tuple relation is joined with a 100 000 tuple relation. This query requires 28.69 s when the join is not on the partitioning attribute. During the execution of this query, 1.1 million 208 byte tuples must be redistributed by hashing on the join attribute, yielding an aggregate total transfer rate of 7.9 megabytes/s during the processing of this query. This should not be construed, however, as an accurate estimate of the maximum obtainable interprocessor communications bandwidth as the CPU's may be the limiting factor (the disks are not likely to be the limiting factor as from Table III one can estimate that the aggregate bandwidth of the 30 disks to be about 25 megabytes/s).

Speedup Experiments: For the join speedup experiments, we used the join*AB*prime query with a 1 million tuple *A* relation and a 100 000 tuple *B*prime relation. The number of processors was varied from 5 to 30. Since with fewer than five processors two or more buckets are needed, including the execution time for one processor (which needs five buckets) would have made the response times for five or more processors appear artificially fast; resulting in superlinear speedup curves.

The resulting response times are plotted in Fig. 17 and the corresponding speedup curves are presented in Fig. 18. From the shape of these graphs it is obvious that the execution time for the query is significantly reduced as additional processors are employed. Several factors prevent the system from achieving perfectly linear speedups. First, the cost of starting four operator tasks (two scans, one join, and one store) on each processor increases as a function of the number of processors used. Second, the effect of short-circuiting local messages diminishes as the number of processors is increased. For example, consider a five-processor configuration and the nonpartitioning attribute version of the join*AB*prime query. As each processor repartitions tuples by hashing on the join attribute, 1/5th of the input tuples it processes are destined for itself and will be short-circuited by the communications software. In addition, as the query produces tuples of the result relation (which is partitioned in a round-robin manner), they too will be short-circuited. As the number of processors is increased, the number of short-circuited packets decreases to the point where, with 30 processors, only 1/30th of the packets will be short-circuited. Because these intranode packets are less expensive than their corresponding internode packets, smaller configurations will benefit more from short-circuiting. In the case of a partitioning-attribute join, *all* input tuples will short-circuit the network along with a fraction of the output tuples.

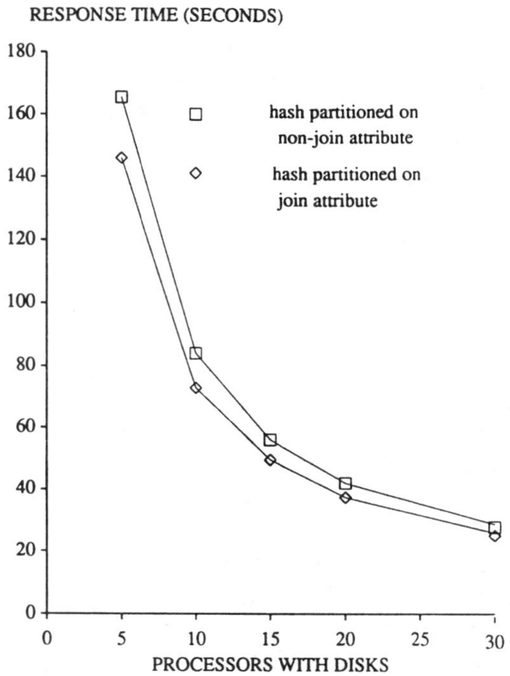

Fig. 17.

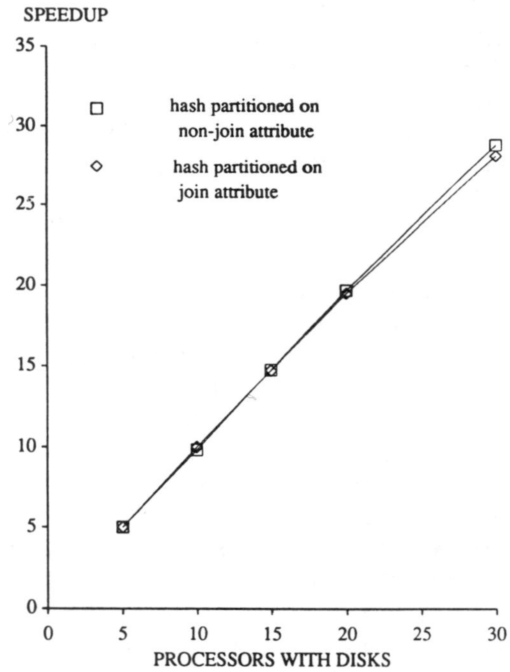

Fig. 18.

Scaleup Experiments: The join*AB*prime query was also used for the join scaleup experiments. For these tests, the number of processors was varied from 5 to 30 while the size of the A relation was varied from 1 million to 6 million tuples in increments of 1 million tuples and the size of Bprime relation was varied from 100 000 to 600 000 tuples in increments of 100 000. For each configuration, only one join bucket was needed. The results of these tests are presented in Fig. 19. Three factors contribute to the slight increase in response times. First, the task of initiating four processes at each site is performed by a single processor. Second, as the number of processors increases, the effects of short-circuiting messages during the execution of these queries diminishes—especially in the case when the join attribute is not the partitioning attribute. Finally, the response time may be being limited by the speed of the communications network.

D. Aggregate Queries

Our aggregate tests included a mix of scalar aggregate and aggregate function queries run on the 30 processor configuration. The first query computes the minimum of a nonindexed attribute. The next two queries compute, respectively, the sum and minimum of an attribute after partitioning the relation into 20 subsets. Three sizes of input relations were used: 100 000, 1 million, and 10 million tuples. The results from these tests are contained in Table V. Since the scalar aggregates and aggregate function operators are executed using algorithms that are similar to those used by the selection and join operators, respectively, no speedup or scaleup experiments were conducted.

E. Update Queries

The next set of tests included a mix of append, delete, and modify queries on three different sizes of relations: 100 000, 1 million, and 10 million tuples. The results of these tests are presented in Table VI. Since Gamma's recovery mechanism is not yet operational, these results should be viewed accordingly.

The first query appends a single tuple to a relation on which no indexes exist. The second appends a tuple to a relation on which one index exists. The third query deletes a single tuple from a relation, using a clustered B-tree index to locate the tuple to be deleted. In the first query, no indexes exist and hence no indexes need to be updated, whereas in the second and third queries, one index needs to be updated.

The fourth through sixth queries test the cost of modifying a tuple in three different ways. In all three tests, a nonclustered index exists on the unique2 attribute, and, in addition, a clustered index exists on the Unique1 attribute. In the first case, the modified attribute is the partitioning attribute, thus requiring that the modified tuple be relocated. Furthermore, since the tuple is relocated, the secondary index must also be updated. The second modify query modifies a nonpartitioning, nonindexed attribute. The third modify query modifies an attribute on which a nonclustered index has been constructed, using the index to locate the tuple to be modified.

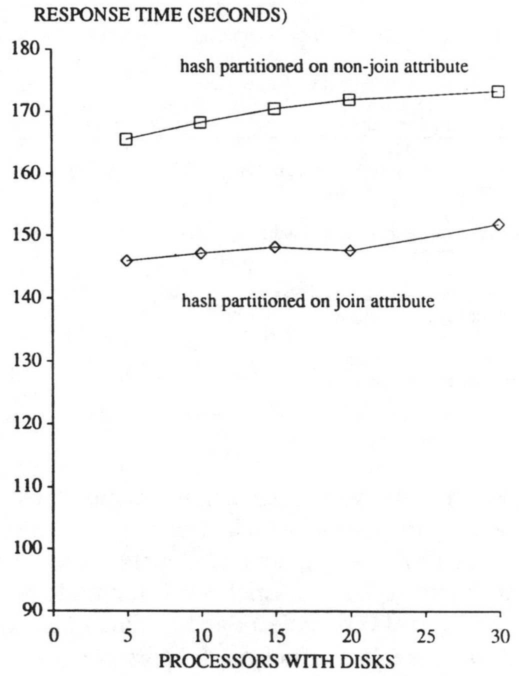

Fig. 19.

TABLE V
AGGREGATE QUERIES. 30 PROCESSORS WITH DISKS (ALL EXECUTION TIMES IN SECONDS)

Query Description	Number of Tuples in Source Relation 100,000	1,000,000	10,000,000
Scalar aggregate	1.10	10.36	106.42
Min aggregate function (20 Partitions)	2.03	12.48	120.03
Sum aggregate function (20 Partitions)	2.03	12.39	120.22

TABLE VI
UPDATE QUERIES. 30 PROCESSORS WITH DISKS (ALL EXECUTION TIMES IN SECONDS)

Query Description	Number of Tuples in Source Relation 100,000	1,000,000	10,000,000
Append 1 Tuple (No indices exist)	0.07	0.08	0.10
Append 1 Tuple (One index exists)	0.18	0.21	0.22
Delete 1 tuple	0.34	0.28	0.49
Modify 1 tuple (#1)	0.72	0.73	0.93
Modify 1 tuple (#2)	0.18	0.20	0.24
Modify 1 tuple (#3)	0.33	0.38	0.52

VII. Conclusions and Future Research Directions

In this paper, we have described the design and implementation of the Gamma database machine. Gamma employs a shared-nothing architecture in which each processor has one or more disks and the processors can communicate with each other only by sending messages via an interconnection network. While a previous version of the Gamma software ran on a collection of VAX 11/750's interconnected via a 80 Mbit/s token ring, currently the system runs on an Intel iPSC/2 hypercube with 32 processors and 32 disk drives.

Gamma employs three key ideas which enable the architecture to be scaled to hundreds of processors. First, all relations are horizontally partitioned across multiple disk drives which are attached to separate processors; enabling relations to be scanned in parallel without any specialized hardware. In addition, in order to enable the database design to be tuned to the needs of the application, three alternative partitioning strategies are provided. The second major contribution of the Gamma software is its extensive use of hash-based parallel algorithms for processing complex relational operators such as joins and aggregate functions. Finally, the system employs unique dataflow scheduling techniques to coordinate the execution of multioperator queries. These techniques make it possible to control the execution of very complex queries with minimal coordination—a necessity for configurations involving a large number of processors.

In addition to describing the design of the Gamma software, we have also presented a thorough performance evaluation of the iPSC/2 hypercube version of Gamma. Three sets of experiments were performed. First, with a constant machine configuration of 30 processors, the response time for the set of Wisconsin benchmark queries was measured for three different sizes of relations. For a subset of these queries we also measured the performance of the system relative to the number of processors employed when the sizes of the input relations are kept constant (speedup) and when the sizes of the input relations are increased proportionally to the number of processors (scaleup). The speedup results obtained for both selection and join queries are almost perfectly linear; thus doubling the number of processors halves the response time for a query. The scaleup results obtained are also quite encouraging. They reveal that a constant response time can be maintained for both selection and join queries as the workload is increased by adding a proportional number of processors and disks.

We currently have a number of new projects underway. First, we plan on implementing the chained declustering mechanism and evaluating its effectiveness. With respect to processing queries, we have designed [35] and are currently evaluating alternative strategies for processing queries involving multiple join operations. For example, consider a query involving ten joins on a machine with 100 processors. Is it better to use all 100 processors for each join (allocating 1/10 of the memory on each processor to each join), or to use ten processors for each join (in which case each join operator will have full use of the memory at each processor)? Finally, we are studying several new partitioning mechanisms that combine the best features of the hash and range partitioning strategies.

Acknowledgment

Like all large systems projects, a large number of people beyond those listed as authors made this paper possible. R. Gerber deserves special recognition for his work on the design of Gamma plus his leadership on the implementation of the first prototype. The query optimizer was implemented by M. Muralikrishna. R. Jauhari implemented the read-ahead mechanism to improve the performance of sequential scans. A. Sharma implemented both the aggregate algorithms and the embedded query interface. G. Graefe and J. Chen implemented a predicate compiler. They deserve special credit for being willing to debug the machine code produced by the compiler.

We would also like to thank J. Gray and S. Englert of Tandem Computers for the use of their Wisconsin benchmark relation generator. Without this generator, the tests we conducted would simply not have been possible as previously we had no way of generating relations larger than 1 million tuples.

References

[1] R. Agrawal and D. J. DeWitt, "Recovery architectures for multiprocessor database machines," in *Proc. 1985 SIGMOD Conf.*, Austin, TX, May 1985.

[2] M. M. Astrahan *et al.*, "System R: A relational approach to database management," *ACM Trans. Database Syst.*, vol. 1, no. 2, June 1976.

[3] D. Bitton, D. J. DeWitt, and C. Turbyfill, "Benchmarking database systems—A systematic approach," in *Proc. 1983 Very Large Database Conf.*, Oct. 1983.

[4] M. W. Blasgen, J. Gray, M. Mitoma, and T. Price, "The convoy phenomenon," *Oper. Syst. Rev.*, vol. 13, no. 2, Apr. 1979.

[5] A. Borr, "Transaction monitoring in encompass [TM]: Reliable distributed transaction processing," in *Proc. VLDB*, 1981.

[6] K. Bratbergsengen, "Hashing methods and relational algebra operations," in *Proc. 1984 Very Large Database Conf.*, Aug. 1984.

[7] H-T. Chou, D. J. DeWitt, R. Katz, and T. Klug, "Design and implementation of the Wisconsin storage system (WiSS)," *Software Practices and Exper.*, vol. 15, no. 10, Oct. 1985.

[8] G. Copeland, W. Alexander, E. Boughter, and T. Keller, "Data placement in Bubba," in *Proc. ACM-SIGMOD INT. Conf. Management Data*, Chicago, IL, May 1988.

[9] G. Copeland and T. Keller, "A comparison of high-availability media recovery techniques," in *Proc. ACM-SIGMOD Int. Conf. Management Data*, Portland, OR, June 1989.

[10] D. J. DeWitt, "DIRECT—A multiprocessor organization for supporting relational database management systems," *IEEE Trans. Comput.*, June 1979.

[11] D. J. DeWitt, R. Katz, F. Olken, D. Shapiro, M. Stonebraker, and D. Wood, "Implementation techniques for main memory database systems," in *Proc. 1984 SIGMOD Conf.*, Boston, MA, June 1984.

[12] D. J. DeWitt, R. Finkel, and M. Solomon, "The Crystal multicomputer: Design and implementation experience," *IEEE Trans. Software Eng.*, vol. SE-13, no. 8, Aug. 1987.

[13] D. DeWitt and R. Gerber, "Multiprocessor hash-based join algorithms," in *Proc. 1985 VLDB Conf.*, Stockholm, Sweden, Aug. 1985.

[14] D. DeWitt, R. Gerber, G. Graefe, M. Heytens, K. Kumar, and M. Muralikrishna, "GAMMA—A high performance dataflow database machine," in *Proc. 1986 VLDB Conf.*, Japan, Aug. 1986.

[15] D. DeWitt, S. Ghandeharizadeh, and D. Schneider, "A performance analysis of the gamma database machine," in *Proc. ACM-SIGMOD Int. Conf. Management Data*, Chicago, IL, May 1988.

[16] S. Englert, J. Gray, T. Kocher, and P. Shah, " A benchmark of NonStop SQL Release 2 demonstrating near-linear speedup and scaleup on large databases," Tandem Computers, Tech. Rep. 89.4, Tandem Part no. 27469, May 1989.

[17] "Enscribe programming manual," Tandem Part 82583-A00, Tandem Computers Inc., Mar. 1985.

[18] R. Gerber and D. DeWitt, "The impact of hardware and software alternatives on the performance of the Gamma database machine," Comput. Sci. Tech. Rep. 708, Univ. of Wisconsin-Madison, July 1987.

[19] S. Ghandeharizadeh and D. J. DeWitt, "A multiuser performance evaluation of selection queries in a single processor database machine," July 1989, submitted for publication.

[20] —— "Performance analysis of alternative declustering strategies," in *Proc. 6th Int. Conf. Data Eng.*, Los Angeles, CA, Feb. 1990.
[21] J. R. Goodman, "An investigation of multiprocessor structures and algorithms for database management," Univ. California at Berkeley, Tech. Rep. UCB/ERL, M81/33, May 1981.
[22] G. Graefe, "Volcano: A compact, extensible, dynamic, and parallel dataflow query evaluation system," Working Paper, Oregon Graduate Center, Portland, OR, Feb. 1989.
[23] J. Gray, "Notes on database operating systems," RJ 2188, IBM Res. Lab., San Jose, CA, Feb. 1978.
[24] J. Gray, H. Sammer, and S. Whitford, "Shortest seek vs shortest service time scheduling of mirrored disks," Tandem Computers, Dec. 1988.
[25] H. I. Hsiao and D. J. DeWitt, "Chained declustering: A new availability strategy for multiprocessor database machines," in *Proc. 6th Int. Conf. Data Eng.*, Los Angeles, CA, Feb. 1990.
[26] M. Jarke and J. Koch, "Query optimization in database system," *ACM Comput. Surveys*, vol. 16, no. 2, June 1984.
[27] M. Kim, "Synchronized disk interleaving," *IEEE Trans. Comput.*, vol. C-35, no. 11, Nov. 1986.
[28] M. Kitsuregawa, H. Tanaka, and T. Moto-oka, "Application of hash to data base machine and its architecture," *New Generation Comput.*, vol. 1, no. 1, 1983.
[29] M. Livny, S. Khoshafian, and H. Boral, "Multi-disk management algorithms," in *Proc. 1987 SIGMETRICS Conf.*, Banff, Alta., Canada, May 1987.
[30] C. Mohan, D. Haderle, B. Linsay, H. Pirahesh, and P. Schwarz, "ARIES: A transaction recovery method supporting fine-granularity locking and partial rollbacks using write-ahead logging," RJ 6649, IBM Almaden Research Center, San Jose, CA, Jan. 1989.
[31] D. A. Patterson, G. Gibson, and R. H. Katz, "A case for redundant arrays of inexpensive disks (RAID)," in *Proc. ACM-SIGMOD Int. Conf. Management Data*, Chicago, May 1988.
[32] Proteon Associates, Operation and Maintenance Manual for the ProNet Model p8000, Waltham, MA, 1985.
[33] D. Ries and R. Epstein, "Evaluation of distribution criteria for distributed database systems," UCB/ERL Tech. Rep. M78/22, UC Berkeley, May 1978.
[34] D. Schneider and D. DeWitt, "A performance evaluation of four parallel join algorithms in a shared-nothing multiprocessor environment," in *Proc. 1989 SIGMOD Conf.*, Portland, OR, June 1989.
[35] ——, "Design tradeoffs of alternative query tree representations for multiprocessor database machines," Comput. Sci. Tech. Rep. 869, Univ. of Wisconsin-Madison, Aug. 1989, submitted for publication.
[36] P. G. Selinger *et al.*, "Access path selection in a relational database management system," in *Proc. 1979 SIGMOD Conf.*, Boston, MA, May 1979.
[37] M. Stonebraker, "The case for shared nothing," *Database Eng.*, vol. 9, no. 1, 1986.
[38] M. Stonebraker, R. Katz, D. Patterson, and J. Ousterhout, "The design of XPRS," in *Proc. Fourteenth Int. Conf. Very Large Data Bases*, Los Angeles, CA, Aug. 1988.
[39] Tandem Performance Group, "A benchmark of Non-Stop SQL on the debit credit transaction," in *Proc. 1988 SIGMOD Conf.*, Chicago, IL, June 1988.
[40] Teradata, "DBC/1012 database computer system manual release 2.0," Document C10-0001-02, Teradata Corp., Nov. 1985.
[41] R. E. Wagner, "Indexing design considerations," *IBM Sys. J.*, vol. 12, no. 4, pp. 351-367, Dec. 1973.

David J. DeWitt received the Ph.D. degree from the University of Michigan, Ann Arbor, in 1976.

He joined the faculty at the University of Wisconsin in 1976 where he presently holds the rank of Professor and Romnes Fellow in the Computer Sciences Department. One of his current research program involves the design and implementation of highly parallel database machines. This research project is studying such issues as the effectiveness of alternative parallel join algorithms, the impact of different declustering algorithms on multiuser transaction rates, and the evaluation of dataflow query processing strategies. To support this research, the project has implemented the Gamma database machine on a 32 node iPSC/2 hypercube with 32 disk drives. The other thrust of his current research program is attempting to address the problems posed by emerging applications of database system technology including GIS, CAD/CAM, and scientific applications. To solve the needs of these applications, he is investigating the design and implementation of an extensible database management system named EXODUS which is designed to enable the rapid implementation of high-performance, application-specific database systems.

Dr. DeWitt served as the Chairman of the ACM Special Interest Group on the Management of Data (SIGMOD) from 1985-1989 and acted as program chair for the 1983 SIGMOD Conference and the 1988 VLDB Conference.

Shahram Ghandeharizadeh is a graduate student in the Department of Computer Sciences at University of Wisconsin-Madison. He received the B.S. and M.S. degrees in computer sciences from the University Wisconsin in 1985 and 1987, respectively and is currently working on his Ph.D. dissertation.

His areas of interest include design and implementation of database machines, parallel algorithms for multiprocessor database machines, and performance evaluation of database management systems.

Donovan A. Schneider received the B.S. degree in computer sciences from the University of Wisconsin, Oshkosh, in 1985, and the M.S. degree in computer sciences from the University of Wisconsin, Madison, in 1987.

He is currently working towards the Ph.D. degree at the University of Wisconsin-Madison. His research interests include database machines, database performance analysis, parallel join strategies, and query size estimation.

Allan Bricker joined the research staff of the Department of Computer Sciences at the University of Wisconsin-Madison in 1983 where he received the M.S. degree in 1986.

His research activities concerned a wide array of distributed operating system issues including the design and implementation of a multithreaded operating system to provide the basis for the development of very high-speed network protocols, as well as the design and implementation of Condor, a system for utilizing otherwise unused workstations in a local area network. He is currently on leave from the University of Wisconsin and is working for Chorus Systemes in France doing development on the Chorus distributed operating system.

Hui-I Hsiao is a Ph.D. candidate in computer science at University of Wisconsin. He received the M.S. degree in computer science from the University of Wisconsin in 1984.

Previously, he worked at Nicolet Instrument Corporation where he was involved in the design and implementation of software for several microprocessor-based medical diagnosis systems. He is the recipient of an Associate Fellowship from Nicolet Instrument Corporation. His major research interests are in the availability and performance of multiprocessor database machines with replicated data. His other interests include parallelism in query execution and distributed concurrency control and recovery mechanism.

Rick Rasmussen received the Bachelor of Science degree from the University of Wisconsin in May 1989.

He is currently an Assistant Researcher at the University of Wisconsin on the Computer Science Department's NSF CER grant. He primarily provides systems support on the Intel iPSC/2 hypercube for the Gamma Database Machine Project. His current projects include the implementation of the GNU project C compiler as a cross-compiler to the hypercube.

ARCHITECTURE AND PERFORMANCE OF RELATIONAL ALGEBRA MACHINE **GRACE**

Masaru Kitsuregawa * Hidehiko Tanaka ** Tohru Moto-oka **

* Institute of Industrial Science
The University of Tokyo

** Faculty of Electrical Engineering
The University of Tokyo

Abstract

In this paper we present the architecture and performance of relational algebra machine GRACE. GRACE adopts an efficient relational algebra processing algorithm based on hash and sort, and can execute join quickly in O((N+M)/K) time, where N and M are the cardinalities of two relations and K is the number of memory banks involved. In GRACE, the relations are partitioned dynamically into several buckets using a hash function and the buckets are processed in pipelined fashion by multiple processors. This efficient parallel processing mechanism and its expected performance are discussed in detail.

GRACE is expected to exhibit high performance even under the join dominant environment.

1. Introduction

Several types of machines have been proposed to improve the performance of data base management systems, especially the relational data base system. The key idea common to them is the 'Logic per Track' concept originated by Slotnick[1], which resolves the bottleneck at the data transfer between the secondary storage device and main memory of a host computer. As long as the relatively light load operations such as selection and update are concerned, this filter processing approach outperforms the conventional system by orders of magnitude. We can expect, however, only a slight improvement for heavy operations such as join and projection including duplicate elimination[2]. Especially for join operation, we have not obtained the desired efficiency. For example, it is true that joinability filter approach in CAFS[3] sieves out many of the tuples that cannot be joined by using hash function, but that is no more than preprocessing, and remaining tasks such as the elimination of spurious tuples and tuple concatenation in explicit join must be done on the host machine. Although multiprocessor machine DIRECT[4] and associative machine RELACS[5] have high processing power, they adopt ordinary exhaustive matching algorithms and may not be efficient enough for large relations.

We have developed the relational algebra machine GRACE[6,7,8,17], which exhibits high performance even under a join dominant environment. GRACE adopts the efficient relational algebraic processing strategy based on hash and sort, and executes join efficiently in O((N+M)/K) time, where N and M are the cardinalities of two relations and K the number of memory banks to be involved in the processing.

In this paper, we focus on the architecture and performance of GRACE. Several design problems in parallel processing algorithm utilizing the clustering feature of hash function are discussed in previous papers[6,7,8].

2. Relational Algebra Processing Algorithm based on Hash and Sort

2.1 Hash based relational algebra processing

The clustering feature of the hash function is fully utilized to achieve efficient join processing in GRACE. Unlike the joinability filter approach, this does not reduce the cardinality of the relations, but the processing performance of heavy operations such as equi-join, projection, division, and set operations can be dramatically improved.

An ordinary join algorithm such as nested-loop join takes time proportional to the product of cardinalities of two relations to be joined. If the tuples of these relations are partitioned into several buckets according to the hashed values of the join attributes, the join operation itself is reduced into 'small' joins among the tuples in each bucket, because the tuples of the i-th bucket in one relation cannot be joined with those

0-8186-5452-X/94 $3.00

of the j-th bucket($j \neq i$) in the other relation. Let

$$N=\sum_{i=1}^{s} n_i, \qquad M=\sum_{i=1}^{s} m_i$$

where N and M are the cardinalities of two relations, n_i and m_i be the sizes of the i-th bucket of each clustered relation, and s be the number of buckets. Thus the total processing time of join can be expressed as follows.

$$T \propto \sum_{i=1}^{s} n_i \times m_i$$

We call this effect the hash clustering feature. Fig.1 graphically represents the expression above, where the two axes denote two relations which are divided into s intervals by clustering. Shaded cross sections reveal the join load of n x m. It is clear that this clustering approach can dramatically reduce the processing load in comparison with the non-clustered one. This approach has been utilized in some software based data base management system. While many of the data base machines so far adopts the nested loop join or sort merge join algorithm, few machines take clustering approach[6,9,10].

2.2 Parallel relational algebra processing based on hash and sort

Through the preprocessing of the relation by the hash function, we can expect drastic reduction of processing load of join and projection operation. Since the buckets are independent of each other, the relational algebraic operation could be executed even faster by processing buckets in parallel using multiple processors instead of using only one processor. Once the tuples of each bucket are appropriately distributed, that is, every processor gets the tuples of his allocated bucket, there need be no inter-processor communication during bucket processing. Buckets can be processed in parallel. A tuple needs to move from original location to the certain processor which is allocated the bucket of that tuple.

Suppose the relation stored over multiple source memory banks are to be hashed and transferred to the same number of destination banks. The most natural approach is to make the number of buckets equal to the number of destination memory banks and to assign each band a bucket. A tuple in some bank is distributed to the bank whose id is the value of hashed code. While this approach is simple, we encounter several problems. One of them is a bank overflow problem which is caused by nonuniformity of hash function. Since the data distribution can not be uniform and a bank capacity is limited, a situation would occur where some banks need to accept tuples beyond its capacity. At least we have to prepare the larger space than the actual size of the relation. As the number of banks increases, this problem becomes apparent. The determination of load factor is difficult. This is also related to the memory utilization efficiency. In addition, conflict during the data distribution degrades the performance. These problems are crucial in this approach, which

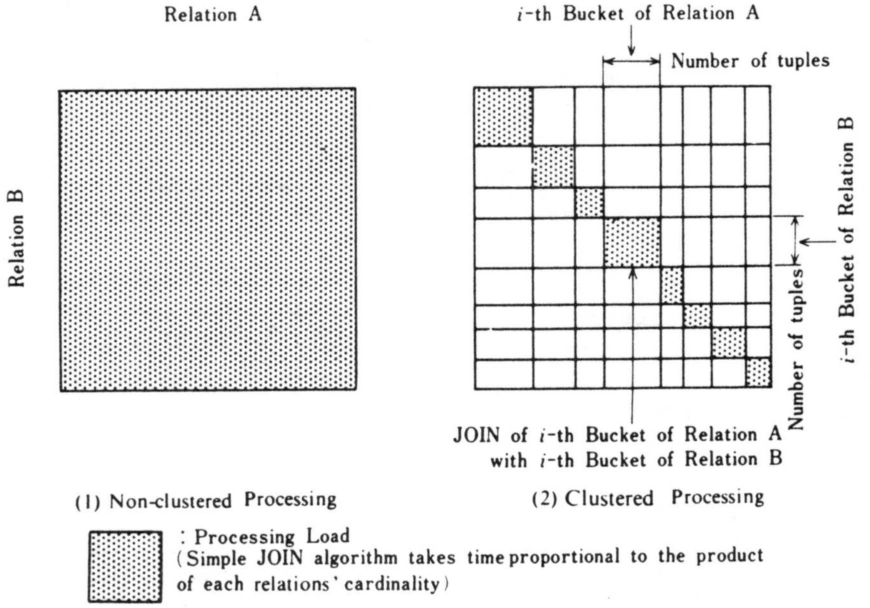

Fig.1 Illustration of the Load Reduction Effect by Hashing in a Join Operation

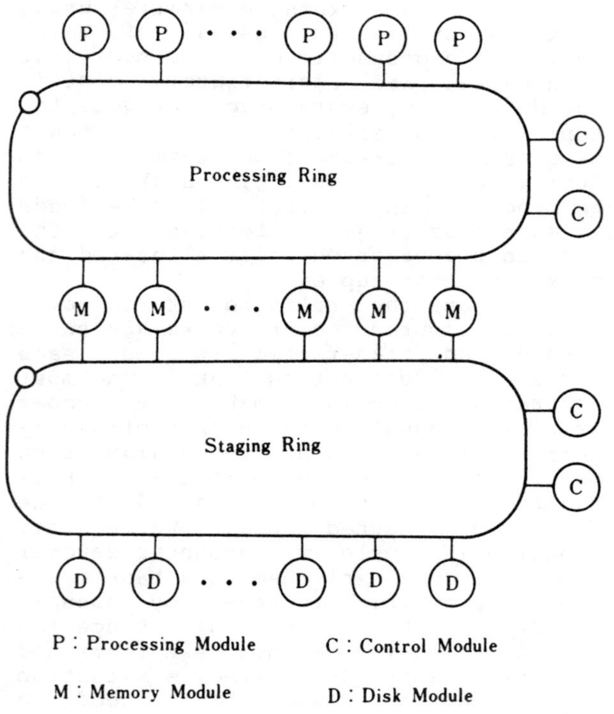

Fig.2 Architecture of GRACE

we named bucket converging approach in [8]. Data base processing on X-tree[9] follows the bucket converging scheme. We have investigated several architectures based on the parallel algorithm based on the hash function and another design problems are discussed in [6,8].

Thus we need the efficient bucket allocation and processing mechanism in parallel execution of hash based join. GRACE is classified into the pipelined bucket processing architecture[8]. The buckets are processed in pipelined fashion. The tuples of each bucket are almost equally spread over multiple memory banks(bucket spreading scheme rather than bucket converging scheme), through which bank overflow can be avoided. The number of banks is not necessarily equal to that of buckets. Since the number of buckets could be very large in general, it is difficult to prepare same number of processors physically. In GRACE, buckets are processed serially beyond the physically available parallelism.

Here we present a rough sketch of processing strategy in GRACE. After the description of the hardware architecture of GRACE, the actual query processing view is presented in section 4. The memory banks generate the data streams bucket-serially flowing through processors. A bucket is allocated to a processor dynamically. The tuples of a bucket are gathered by a processor in pipelined fashion. They are processed using an O(N) time hardware sorter therein without distubing the incoming data stream. The result tuples emerging from processors are hashed over the next join attribute and returned to another memory banks. In this architecture, the bucket-serial data streams generated by memory banks are regarded as the main processing objects and must be controlled so as to be disturbed as little as possible. All the necessary processing is performed along the streams flowing through the system.

3. Architecture of GRACE

3.1 Global Architecture

Here we present the hardware architecture of GRACE. As shown in Fig.2, GRACE consists of four kinds of fundamental modules: processing module(PM), memory module(MM), disk module(DM) and control module(CM). These modules are connected with two inter-module networks. The processing modules and memory modules are connected by a processing network while memory modules and disk modules are connected by a staging network. The relations stored in disk modules are staged into memory modules through the staging network and then the data streams generated by memory modules flow into processing modules through the processing network. The system was designed using a multi-channel ring bus as the network. Here we look at the organization of the individual modules.

3.2 Processing Module

Fig.3 shows the block diagram of the processing module. Its role is to process a bucket efficiently.

The control unit activates the other units in the module appropriately, by interpreting the commands given by

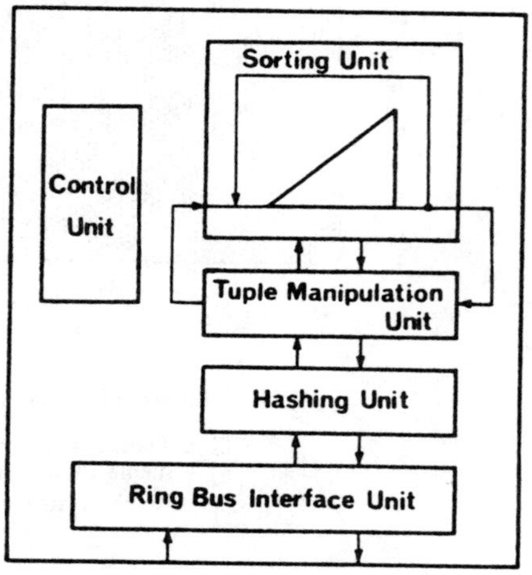

Fig.3 Organization of Processing Module

the control module, which contain information such as the module identifiers of both source and result relations and, hash attributes.

The sorting unit sorts the incoming tuple stream of the allocated bucket, where the pipeline merge sort algorithm[11] is used. This sorter uses $\log_k N$ processing elements to sort the N records in O(N) time. The input data stream is supplied byte serially in the pilot system. Each byte of the data stream is processed with two micro-instructions. A processing rate of 3MB/sec has been achieved, which is comparable to the data transfer rate of IBM 3380 disk. Several parameters such as record length are initialized by the control unit. VLSI implementation of the sorter is now in progress. The detailed design of the sorter is described in [12].

The tuple manipulation unit performs relational algebraic operation to the sorted data stream emerging from the sorting unit. Qualification over the joined tuple is processed and the attributes are rearranged to appropriate form.

The hashing unit hashes the result tuples over the attributes to be involved in the next operation.

The network interface unit performs data transmission control.

3.3 Memory module

The role of the memory module is to generate the bucket-serial data stream and also to provide the large intermediate storage space in which clustered relations are produced. Magnetic bubble memory and semiconductor RAM are candidates for the storage medium. At present, advanced semiconductor technology can provide relatively large random access space at reasonable cost and seems to surpass the bubble technology. Contiguous disk bubble memory, however, is expected to attain the capacity of 4 ~ 16 Mbit per chip. The Bloch line memory seems to be promising because of its very large capacity (1 Gbits per chip) and much higher data transfer rate. Since these storage domain rotating devices are considered to employ Major/minor organization and the organization with RAM is relatively straightforward, the pilot module is implemented with bubble memory. Instead of the ordinary bubble chip, the improved one with on-chip hierarchy is employed: the minor loop is segmented into short(buffer) and long(main) loops connected by swap gate[19]. Fig.4 shows the block diagram of the memory module.

The bubble control unit controls this device so that a continuous data stream could be formed.

All the accesses to the bubble memory are performed based on the hashed values of the tuples. The tuples are not accessed by their physical locations. Instead we provide a record descriptor memory(RDM) constructed of RAM which contains hashed values of the tuples and memory management tags. Synchronized with the magnetic field rotation, this memory is used to access the bubble memory associatively. On staging, the arbitrary empty block denoted by the entry of RDM is dynamically allocated. For data stream generation, the tuples with the same hashed value which belong to a bucket are taken into the buffer loops dynamically to produce the continuous bucket-serial data stream with little inter-record gap time. The pilot bubble memory system has been developed to have sixteen 1 Mbit chips with 4096 bit main loop and 128 bit buffer loop. This control unit consists of the gate control block, generator control block, major line delay control block, and defect loop control block. The design details are to appear in [13].

The tuple control unit sets the

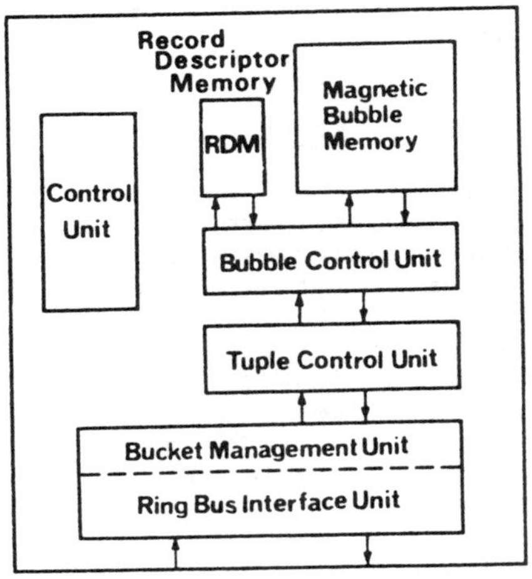

Fig.4 Organization of Memory Module

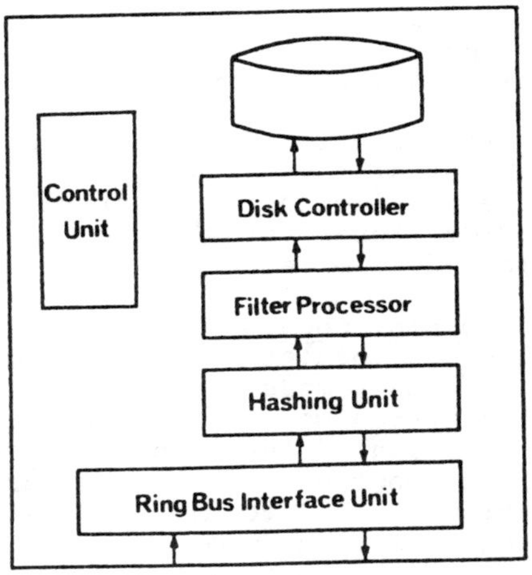

Fig.5 Organization of Disk Module

operational modes of the bubble control unit and supplies it with the bucket identifiers to be output. Look ahead buffering control is employed so that the tuples of the next bucket is brought up in buffer loops while those of the current bucket are being output. The data from the bubble control unit is rearranged to the appropriate format therein.

The bucket management unit maintains the number of tuples of each bucket and schedules their output sequence.

3.4 Disk module

The relations are stored in disk modules. Only the necessary portions of these are staged onto the memory modules. Fig.5 shows the block diagram of the disk module.

The filter processor performs the simple predicate qualification on-the-fly, removes the unnecessary records, and arranges the attributes of the qualified tuples. These functions can be found in several types of filter hardware such as RAP[2], TIP of DBC[14], CASSM[15] and CAFS[3] proposed so far. This lightens the data transfer load of the staging network.

The hashing unit hashes the qualified tuple from the filter processor over the join attributes. The processing module, described before, also has the hashing unit. In the disk module some statistical information could be utilized for the base relation instead of the pure hash function. For the intermediate relation, such information is unavailable, since the hashing is performed at the same time the result tuple is produced. Thus a randomizing function is employed in processing modules.

As for the physical representation of the relation in the disk, most of the previous machines have no auxiliary structure and handle the flat files. GRACE reveals a great performance improvement over the conventional machines under such environment. But in order to accelerate the processing time of simple selection for large relations with the usual moving head disks instead of the expensive logic per track disks, multi-dimensional clustering organization is under implementation[16].

3.5 Control module

Control modules activate and control the other modules appropriately so that the system works efficiently. At the beginning of the staging phase (see Sec.4) a control module sends the activation command to disk modules which have the relations the current query refers to. The memory modules are also given a message about the data stream to input. Thus modules are linked each other. The disk modules are informed of the relation id, qualification predicates for the filter processors, and attribute name to be hashed. The length of a tuple and its hashed value are given to memory modules, which is used for bubble memory control. In the processing phase, memory modules for both source and result relations and processing modules are activated. The operational information, such as qualification predicates, attributes rearrangement format, together with the hashed attributes for the next operation are delivered to processing modules. The memory modules for the result relation are informed of the length of a tuple and hashed value. Thus all the necessary information is given by a control module.

In general a query consists of several relational algebraic operators. GRACE executes such operators serially from leaf to root in the query tree, or in parallel if possible. Each operator is an object of control. That is, assignment of necessary resources is dynamically performed on an operator-by-operator basis. The number of necessary modules depends on the nature of the query, the sizes of operand relations, and the required parallelism. A set of such resources is the unit of object to be controlled, which we call a process.

In GRACE the status of each process is represented by the number of resources allocated to it. On creation of a certain process for the relational algebraic operator, control module recruits an adequate number of processing modules by broadcasting the message. The processing modules which are idle or are working on a process vith lower priority come together. The identifiers of these modules are not maintained in the control module. All that is necessary for resource management is the volume of the processing power allocated to each process.

4. Relational Algebra Processing on GRACE

In this section we describe the overview of query execution in GRACE architecture. Query execution consists of two phases: staging phase and processing phase. In the staging phase, the necessary portions of the relations in disk modules are staged onto the memory modules. Thereafter the tuples in the memory modules are processed by processing modules in parallel in the processing phase.

4.1 Staging Phase

Fig.6 shows the conceptual view of

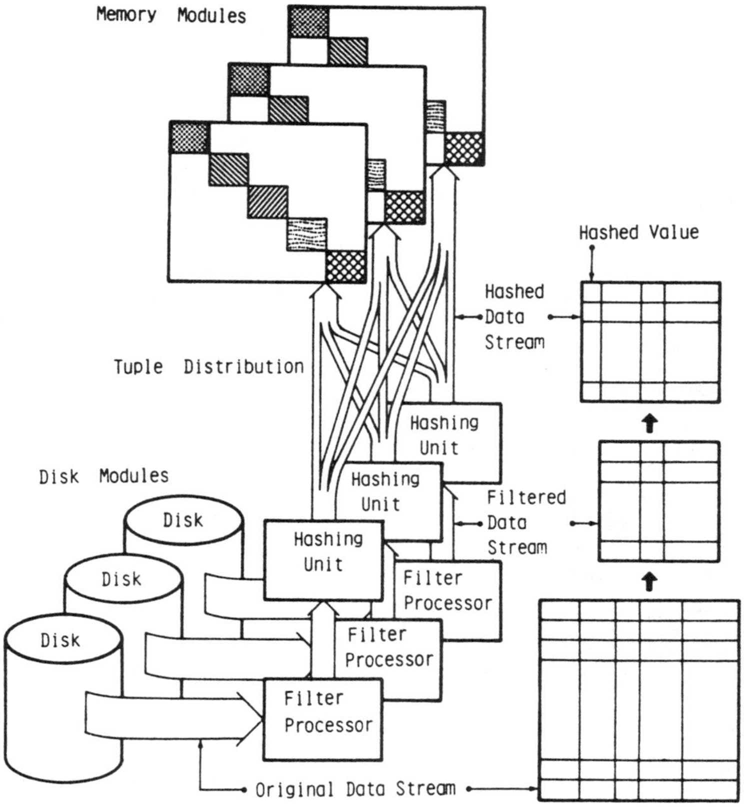

Fig.6 Conceptual View of Staging Phase

the staging phase. The base relation is staged in parallel from the several disk modules as the data stream. In the disk module, unnecessary records are filtered out and the irrelevant attributes are removed at first on-the-fly by the filter processor. The shrunken tuple stream is then led into the hashing unit and the hashed value of the concerned attributes is added to the tuple dynamically. These hashed data streams are distributed to memory modules through the staging network. In memory modules, the tuples are stored in magnetic bubble memory, and tags of hashed values are stored in RDM. Data streams are controlled so that tuples of a bucket are evenly distributed over the memory modules. This flat distribution mechanism of tuples affects the performance of the bucket processing pipeline considerably in the processing phase. When the data transfer completes, the hashed relation is conceptually generated in memory modules. Thus the tuples are hashed on the fly during the staging operation. The hash operaion is overlapped with the data transfer in staging operaton.

4.2 Processing phase

In this phase, actual relational algebra processing of the buckets is performed by processing modules. Fig.7 and Fig.8 show the schematic diagram of this phase. Memory modules generate bucket-serial data streams to processing modules. In each memory module, the tuples are selected by examining the hashed values stored in RDM and output to processing modules bucket after bucket. The magnetic bubble device with the on-chip hierarchy described in section 3.3 can efficiently generate the continuous bucket-serial data stream. One processing module is allocated to one bucket. Since tuples in the bucket are distributed over memory modules, each processing module must visit all the memory modules to get the tuples in the bucket allocated to it. This bucket-gathering process proceeds in pipelined fashion, which is shown in Fig.7. In the processing module, the input tuple stream is first led to the O(N) hardware sorter where bucket input is overlapped with the sorting. The actual relational algebra processing is applied to the data stream emerging from the sorter. The result tuples are hashed over the attribute to be involved in the next operation and sent back to

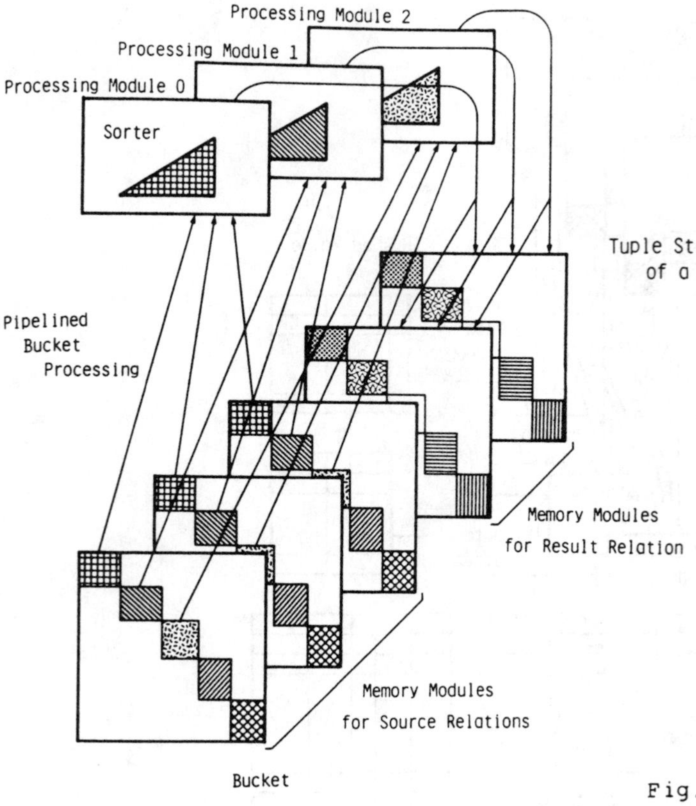

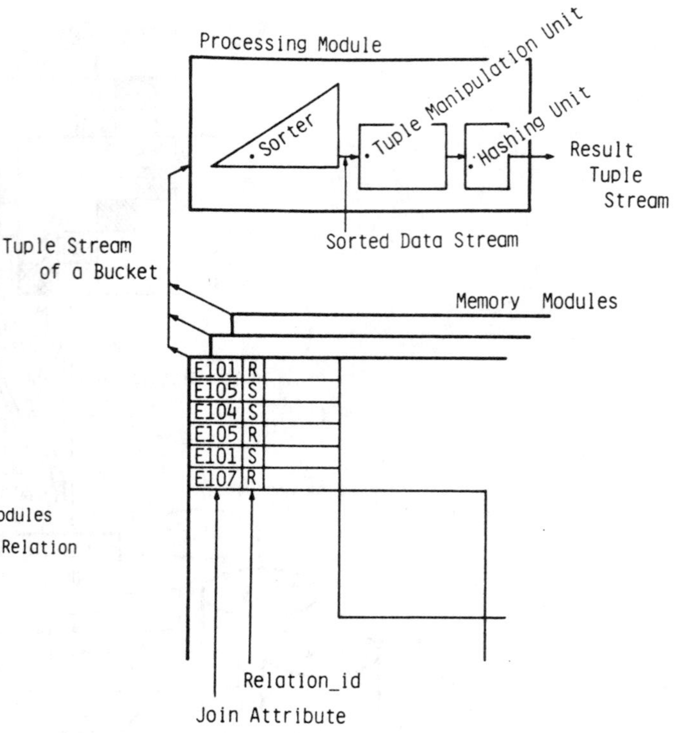

Fig.8 Conceptual View of Bucket Processing in Processing Module

Fig.7 Conceptual View of Processing Phase (Pipelined Bucket Processing)

the memory modules. The hashing operation is performed on the fly in the same fashion with the staging phase. As soon as the processing module has finished with the current bucket, it begins on the next bucket. This bucket processing pipeline continues until all the buckets are consumed.

5. Performance of Pipelined Bucket Processing

5.1 Pipeline disturbance in one memory module system and scheduled pipeline

As described in the previous section, the buckets are processed in pipelined fashion during the processing phase. It takes 2n unit of time for a processor to process a bucket of n tuples: n unit time to input and sort the bucket and another n unit of time to perform relational algebraic operation on the sorted tuples. Let D_{ij}, called subbucket, be the set of tuples of the j-th bucket stored in the i-th memory module. Fig.9 shows the pipeline processing overview, where there are four processing modules and two memory modules. It is assumed here that D_{ij} is equal for any i and j.

In general, pipeline processing works well when each segment time is equal. If some segment takes a longer time, it causes a bottle neck. We cannot expect such an ideal situation as in Fig.9. In our machine, segment time corresponds to the size of subbucket.

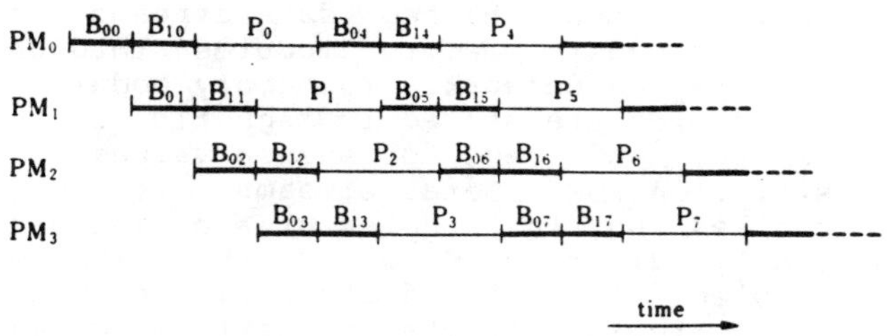

PM_i : i-th Processing Module
P_j : Processing of j-th Bucket
B_{ij} : Input & Sort of j-th Bucket in i-th Memory Module

Fig.9 Overview of Pipelined Bucket Processing

The volumes of buckets may differ and, what is worse, the sizes of subbuckets in each bucket also may differ considerably. That is, the segment time of the pipeline varies dynamically. This causes the pipeline disturbance and results in performance degradation. Here we consider this problem. The simplest case is shown in Fig.10, where the relation is stored in only one memory module. Two processing modules are activated in turn. Since subbuckets are buckets themselves in this case, we can concentrate only on the effect due to the bucket size fluctuation. Since the sizes of the buckets vary considerably, the pipeline does not work well. There will be a lot of idle time. One processor is idle, while the memory module is devoted to the other processor. The memory module is idle while both of the processors are busy. Such idle time induces performance degradation. In order to complete the processing, it is clear that at least enough time for the memory module to output all the tuples is required. The overhead due to the pipeline disturbance increases the processing time. Our major concern is how the overhead can be reduced. Form the view point of the total processing time, is is the memory idle time that should be shortened as much as possible. To keep high utilization efficiency of the processors is the second objective.

Here we define normalized processing time E as follows.

$$E = \frac{\text{Actual Processing Time}}{\text{Time for memory module to output all the tuples}}$$

The numerator is the sum of the denominator and the overhead time caused by pipeline disturbance. The bucket processing pipeline needs to be controlled so that E is as close to one as possible.

We should remember that information on the bucket size is available in our hash-based approach. At the beginning of the processing phase, the number of tuples in the bucket is already known. We can reduce the overhead time by scheduling the bucket processing using this information. Fig.11 shows the scheduled bucket processing, where each bucket size is equal to that of Fig.10. Clearly we can avoid the pipeline disturbance by arranging the output sequence of buckets in ascending order of their sizes. Since the previous bucket is smaller than the current one, the processing module allocated to the previous bucket is ready to input the next bucket when the other module pumps up all the tuples in the current bucket and leaves the memory module. The data stream from the memory module is not

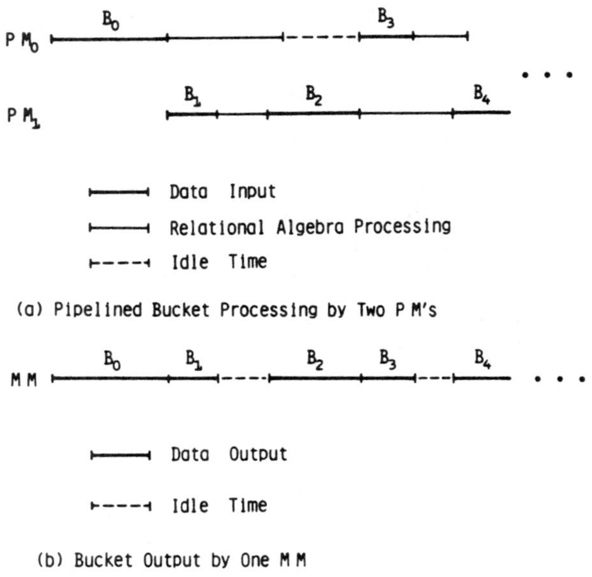

Fig.10 Bucket Processing Pipeline with One Memory Module (Pipeline Disturbance Due to Bucket Size Fluctuation)

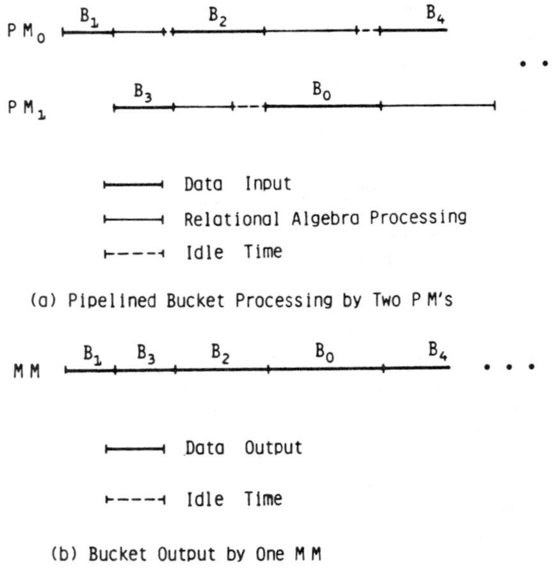

Fig.11 Scheduled Bucket Processing Pipeline for the Data Stream in Fig.10

disturbed at all. Thus the fairly efficient performance is obtained with a simple scheduling policy.

5.2 Bucket Processing Pipeline in Multiple Memory Module System and Its Performance

We have examined the simple case where there is only one memory module in the system. The actual system consists of multiple memory modules. The processor visits the memory banks sequentially to gather the tuples in the bucket. There arises another problem caused by subbucket size fluctuation, which also disturbs the pipeline. A bucket is nonuniformly distributed over memory modules, that is, for a certain j, D_{ij} has a different size for every i. Under multiple memory module environment with subbucket size fluctuation, it is difficult to obtain sufficient performance. This is similar to the multiprocessor job scheduling problem.

We would line to extend our previous bucket scheduling approach to the multiple memory module system. It is believed that if the tuples of a bucket are equally spread over the memory modules, the same scheduling policy as in the single memory module system would also be effective in this case. To clarify this claim we assume the condition that the sizes of subbuckets of a bucket are equal, which can be realized as discussed later. We call it bucket flat distribution. The size of each bucket itself might vary. Fig.12 shows the performance of bucket processing pipeline under the assumption of the bucket flat distribution, where the longitudinal axis denotes E and the horizontal axis the bucket size fluctuation. Eight memory modules are activated. The bucket sizes are generated uniformly with random numbers which fall between Bmin and Bmax. Bucket size fluctuation is defined as the ratio of Bmax to Bmin. When all the D_{ij} are equal, this value becomes 1. Two evaluations are performed: without scheduling and with scheduling. The performance of the pipeline without scheduling deteriorates considerably as the fluctuation increases, while much higher performance can be achieved through the scheduling by bucket size sorting. The overhead decreases to only 1 ~ 3 percent. In multiple memory organization it is not possible to completely avoid memory module overhead time. Thus it is shown that we can attain good performance in bucket flat distribution by introducing the scheduling based on the sorting of subbucket sizes.

Here complete connection among modules is assumed. Since the connection pattern is fairly restricted in this case, however, the indirect n-cube network using NlogN switches for the connection of N modules exhibits sufficient performance. The effect of the blocking inherent in the network is slight. The details of such problems are presented in [18].

As described above, bucket flat distribution is fully utilized in the bucket processing pipeline. Here we consider this flat distribution itself. Before the bucket processing pipeline is activated, distribution of tuples into memory modules must be completed. This implies that flat distribution must be realized during the data transfer time: from disk modules to memory modules in the staging phase and from processing modules to memory modules in the processing phase. The tuples of the relation are hashed over the attributes for the next operation and distributed to the destination modules. During this tuple distribution process, a tuple of the j-th bucket emitted by a source module is controlled to fall into the i-th destination module, where the size of D_{ij} is minimum among the modules at that time. Thus the tuples of a certain bucket can be almost equally spread over the memory modules. Due to the limited space here, the details of the control mechanism are to be reported elsewhere.

It should be noticed that the sizes of buckets themselves are not equal. We cannot avoid the bucket size fluctuation, because of the inherent features of the hash function. But this does not affect the performance so mush.

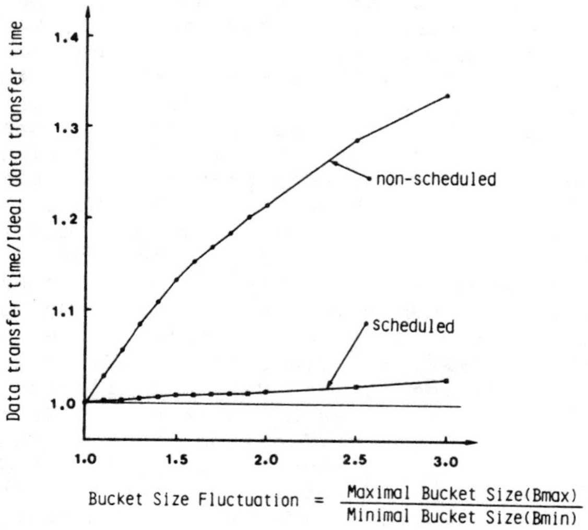

Fig.12 Performance Degradation of Due to Bucket Size Fluctuation and Performance Improvement in Scheduled Bucket Processing Pipeline (Eight Memory Modules are Activated)

6. Conclusion

In this paper, we have presented the architecture and performance of a relational algebra machine.

Our approach has several distinct aspects. First, the clustering feature of hash function is fully utilized. Second the pipelined bucket processing scheme is introduced, where a bucket is spread over several memory banks and multiple buckets are processed simultaneously in pipelined fashion. The processing time is accelerated by the parallel execution of the generated buckets using multiple processors. Third there is no overhead time of hash, since the actual relational algebraic processing of the current operation is overlapped with hashing the result tuple for the next operation. The first clustering processing is overlapped with the staging operation.

Besides the above features, processing strategies of GRACE are quite different from those of conventional machines. Unlike the previous cellular logic type data base machine such as RAP, the data is not fixed in a certain bank but flows through the system as a stream. In GRACE a bucket serial data stream is regarded as a processing object. All the processing is performed on the stream, where the stream is controlled so that the flow should not be disturbed.

The effect of bucket size fluctuation on the performance of pipelined bucket processing is examined in detail. The simulation results of the scheduled pipeline indicates efficient performance.

GRACE exhibits much higher performance even under the join dominant environment of a heavy load in comparison with the previous machines emploing the nested loop approach, we believe.

There remains many important features of GRACE we cannot present in this paper, such as transmission control details on ring bus and efficient staging mechanism for large relations whose sizes exceed the capacity of the memory modules. These features and the query execution examples are presented in the future paper.

References

[1]. D.L. Slotnick, Logic per Track Devices, Advances in Computers, Vol.10, Academic Press, New York, 291-296, 1970.

[2]. E.A. Ozkarahan, et al., Performance Evaluation of a Relational Associative Processor, ACM Trans.Database Syst., Vol 2, No.2, 175-195 1977.

[3]. E. Babb, Implementing a Relational Database by Means of Specialized Hardware, ACM TODS, Vol.4, No.1, 1-29, 1979.

[4]. D.J. DeWitt, DIRECT-A Multiprocessor Organization for Supporting Relational Database Management Systems, IEEE Trans.Comput., Vol.C-28, No.6, 395-406, 1979.

[5]. E.J. Oliver, et al., RELACS A Relational Associative Computer System, Proc.of the Fifth Workshop on Computer Architecture for Non-Numeric Processing, 106-114, 1980.

[6]. M.Kitsuregawa, S.Suzuki, H.Tanaka, T.Moto-oka, Relational Algebra Machine Based on Hash and Sort, IECE Japan Technical Group Meeting, EC81-35, 1981.

[7]. M. Kitsuregawa, H.Tanaka, T. Moto-oka, Relational Algebra Machine GRACE, RIMS Symposia on Software Science and Engineering, 1982, Lecture Note in Computer Science, Springer-Verlag, 1983

[8]. M.Kitsuregawa, H.Tanaka, and T.Moto-oka, Application of Hash to Data Base Machine and Its Architecture, New Generation Computing, Vol.1, No.1, pp.63-74, 1983.

[9] J.R.Goodman, An Investigation of Multiprocessor Structure and Algorithms for Data Base Management, UCB ERL M81/33 Univ. of California, Berkeley, 1981.

[10] Oda,Y. Database Machine Architecture Using Data Partitioning Network, IECE Japan Technical Group Meeting, EC80-72, 1980

[11]. S. Todd, Algorithm and Hardware for a Merge Sort Using Multiple Processors, IBM J.RES.DEV., Vol.22, pp.509-517, 1978.

[12]. M. Kitsuregawa, S. Fushimi, K. Kuwabara, H. Tanaka, T. Moto-oka, The Organization of Pipeline Merge Sorter, Trans. IECE Japan, J66-D, pp.332-339, 1983.

[13]. M.Kitsuregawa, T.Ogino, H.Tanaka, and T.Moto-oka, Control Mechanism for Magnetic Bubble Devices with On-chip Memory Hierarchy And Its Implementation, to be appeared.

[14]. J.Banerjee, R.I.Baum, D.K.Hsiao, The Concepts and Capabilites of a Database Computer, ACM Trans.Database Syst., Vol.3, No.4, pp.347-384, 1978.

[15]. S.Y.W.Su, L.H.Nguyen, A.Eme, G.J.Lipovski, The Architectual Features and Implementation Techniques of the Multicell CASSM, IEEE Trans. on Comput. Vol.28, No.6, pp.430-445, 1979.

[16]. S.Fushimi, Research on the secondary memory system of a data base machine based on multi-dimentional clustering, Master Thesis, The University of Tokyo, 1983.

[17]. T.Moto-oka, and K.Fuchi, The Architectures in Fifth Generation Computers, IFIP 83, pp.589-0602, 1983.

[18]. S.Sakai, Inter-module network for highly parallel data base machine, Master Thesis, The University of Tokyo, 1983.

[19]. H. Kohara, et al., Novel megabit bubble memory chip organization and its characteristics, Proc.of ICMB-4, D-3, 1980.

An Analysis of Three Transaction Processing Architectures

Anupam Bhide
Computer Science Division
University of California, Berkeley
Berkeley, CA 94720.

Abstract

In this paper, we investigate the issues involved in using multiprocessors for high performance transaction processing applications. We use a simulation model to compare the performance of three different architectures, namely, Shared Everything, Shared Nothing and Shared Disks. In Shared Everything, any processor can access any disk and all memory is shared. In Shared Nothing, neither disks nor memory is shared. In Shared Disks, any processor can access any disk, but each has its own private main memory. We first study four different variations of the Shared Disks architecture which attempt to minimize lock request messages. We will then compare the best Shared Disks variation with Shared Nothing and Shared Everything. In addition, we study how intra-query parallelism affects the performance of the architectures.

1. Introduction

Applying multiple processors to database problems has been an active area of research. In the database machine area, several research prototypes as well as a few commercial products have been built. However, most of these systems have attempted to accelerate long running queries such as joins. Less attention has been directed by researchers to efficient transaction processing on multiprocessors. The design of multiprocessors for high speed transaction processing is the main focus of our research. There has been a lot of debate in the transaction processing industry about the suitabaility of various architectures for transaction processing. This debate has focussed on issues such as reliability and performance. We attempt to provide answers about the performance of these architectures by comparing them with uniform assumptions.

This research was sponsored by the Defense Advanced Research Projects Agency under contract N00039-84-C-0089, the Army Research Office under contract DAAL03-87-G-0041, and the National Science Foundation under contract MIP-8715235.

In this paper, we will concentrate on three issues:

(1) The main aim of this paper is to compare the performance of three different architectures, namely, Shared Everything(SE), Shared Nothing(SN) and Shared Disks(SD) with uniform assumptions. In a SE system, all disks are directly accessible from all processors with the same access times and all memory is shared. Examples of this architecture include the Sequent Symmetry system[SEQU 86], the Firefly, the IBM 3090 series of machines and SPUR[HILL 86]. In an SN architecture, each disk is connected to a single processor and each processor has its own private memory. A collection of SUNs on an Ethernet exemplifies this architecture. Additionally, a TANDEM TXP system is essentially an SN architecture[BART 81] with extra hardware for high availability. In a SD architecture any processor can access any disk but each processor has its own private memory. IBM provides the "multi-system data sharing facility" [STRI 82] as a feature of its IMS database system which is the ability to couple different systems running IMS in a SD configuration.

(2) In a brute force implementation of a SD architecture almost every lock request needs two messages. Since messages are expensive, the SD architecture is unattractive unless this can be avoided. We will study different variations of SD which try to reduce the number of messages and compare their performance. We will then compare the best SD architecture with SN and SE.

(3) We also study the effect of intra-query parallelism for SE, SN and SD. In a SN system parallelism in a query is structural in nature. Each processor must run the portion of the query plan relevant to the database on its disks. Therefore,

"An Analysis of Three Transaction Processing Architectures" by A. Bhide from *Proc. 14th VLDB Conf.,* 1988, pp. 339-350. Copyright © 1988 by VLDB Endowment, Inc., reprinted with permission.

the degree of parallelism in a query plan is determined by the distribution of data. The optimal distribution of data is a very hard problem since one needs to balance the load on all the processors and yet not cause too many messages. However, in a SE system, a query can be split into n pieces, for any n > 1 and any processor can run each of the n pieces. There is no cost for switching jobs between processors and the only cost paid for parallelism is the cost of starting up a new process. However, the extensibility of the SE architecture is limited by the bandwidth offered by the latest bus and memory technology. The SD architecture offers an intermediate range of flexibility between SE and SN. Unlike SN, any portion of the query plan can be executed by any processor. However, once a portion of the query plan is assigned to a processor, reassigning it for load balancing reasons involves sending messages. Therefore, we will not consider reassignment for SD. Also, like SN, transmission of query pieces to processors involves sending messages. One of the most interesting design decisions in each of the architectures is the degree of intra-query parallelism one should aim for. For SE and SD, this decision can be made at query optimization time. For SN, the decision must be made at data distribution time.

In [BHID 87] and [BHID 88] we have studied SE and SN under various workload conditions and compared their performance. In [BHID 88], we studied how SN and SE performed as lock contention was varied. In [BHID 87], [BHID 88] we studied different types of workloads and reported that results for both the above issues were substantially different for two different classes of workloads:

(a) either high lock contention or strict response constraints present

(b) low lock contention and no response constraints

The main observation we made was that high lock contention or strict response constraints magnify both the performance gap between SE and SN and the performance gains due to parallelism. In addition, we compared the effect of load imbalances on both architectures and studied alternative file organizations. We showed that a sequential file system creates disk hot spots when intra-query parallelism is present and a parallel file system is necessary. In this paper, we will first compare the performance of different variations of the SD architecture and then compare the best one with SN and SE.

We have built discrete event simulators for all the architectures. In section 2, we will discuss the different variations of the SD architecture. The simulators and the input workloads that we have used are discussed in the section 3. In section 4, we then present a variety of simulation results.

2. The SD Architectures

In this section, we will describe the different variations of the SD architecture which attempt to minimize the cost of lock request messages. The SD architecture bears a distinct resemblance to a fully replicated database system as far as the design of a locking protocol. Locking schemes for SD architectures may be classified based on two criteria: (1) centralized or distributed (2) synchronous or asynchronous.

Another issue for SD architectures is how to keep buffers consistent. Each processor in an SD system has its own buffer pool. Consistency must be maintained between the different buffer pools, and between the buffer pools and the database version on disk. One easy solution is to purge the updates of a transaction from the buffer pool after commit: the transaction is committed when the log is written out, but locks are not released until all the updated pages are written out on disk. Thus the database always contains the latest copy. Pages are always read from disk and there are no buffer hits. We call this the *buffer purge* method. Another alternative would be to design a *buffer invalidation* protocol which marks as invalid all buffer pages on a processor updated by another processor. The problem is that a buffer invalidation protocol can result in a large number of messages, unless it is well-designed.

One method to reduce messages would be to route transactions to processors such that locality of reference is maximized. However, a study of IMS traces [REUT 84] has shown that there is a portion of data (10-15%) which is referenced in 80% of all update lock requests. Updates to such high-traffic data would result in notifications to almost all the processors. Thus it is not clear whether an invalidation protocol would do better than a purge protocol and any such invalidation protocol must be carefully designed.

Buffer invalidation protocols are:

(1) hard to optimize
(2) sensitive to hot spots

Therefore, for the purpose of this paper, we have chosen to use the simpler buffer purge protocol only. We will study the design of buffer invalidation protocols and the tradeoffs between them and buffer purge in a future paper. In this paper, we have considered a database size which is fairly large: 8 Gigabytes (2,000,000 pages of 4Kbytes each). Even with a 80-20 access pattern and 160 Mbytes (40,000 buffers of 4 Kbytes each, 4000 on each processor) of total buffer space the best buffer hit ratio we can hope for is of the order of 0.08. Therefore, the effect of no buffer hits in the SD architecture variations should have small performance effects.

We will now describe the four SD variations that we intend to study.

(1) Disk Controller Locking (**DIS**): In this distributed scheme, each disk controller maintains a lock table for all the data on the disks connected to it. An example is the Limited Lock Facility for the 3830 IBM disk controller. Locking is performed with the Lock and Proceed channel command word. If the lock is available, the I/O program can continue to read or write the disk. If the lock is not available, the I/O program terminates early. When the lock is released, an interrupt is generated so that the I/O program can be issued again. Other channel command words are supported to release a lock and read the lock table. A spare control unit is needed to recover from a locking unit failure. In this architecture no messages are needed for lock requests. The only extra price is that of communicating with the disk controller for a lock even in the case of a buffer hit. However, specialized hardware in the form of sophisticated disk controllers is needed.

(2) Central Lock Manager (**CLM**): In this centralized scheme, one processor is designated to be the lock manager. Other processors send all lock request messages to this processor. In our simulations, we have used a 10 processor system for all the architectures. In CLM, we designate one of these as the lock manager and use the other 9 as transaction processors. This will ensure a fair comparison with the other architectures. Since sending messages is expensive in terms of CPU instructions, we will attempt to optimize on the number of messages sent by batching many lock requests into one message.

(3) Primary Copy Method: (**PRI**): In this distributed scheme, the database is divided into partitions and each processor is given authority over one partition. This method gets its name from the analogy with the method of the same name proposed for replicated databases. A lock request can be handled locally if it lies in the processor's partition. Otherwise, a message must be sent to the processor which controls the partition. The choice of database partitions and assignment of primary authority need not be static and could be made by global load balancing software on the basis of current load and reference pattern. However, our simulation model does not consider changes in primary copy authority in order to maintain simplicity. In this scheme, one can save on lock messages by routing transactions to processors such that most of the lock requests are local. In section 4.1, we will study how lock request locality affects performance.

(4) Asynchronous Primary Copy Method: (**APRI**): In the PRI scheme, one cannot batch messages because the time interval between a processor sending two messages to another processor is too large and thus there is a degradation in response time. In PRI, lock requests are synchronous. However, if the lock requests are asynchronous, batching would be possible. In the APRI scheme, a processor sends a message containing a lock request and continues processing assuming that it will get the lock. If a negative response is received, then the transaction must be aborted. At commit time, the transaction waits until it gets all responses to its lock requests. It commits successfully if it gets all its locks, otherwise, it is aborted. This is similar to optimistic concurrency control, except that the serializability check is not postponed till commit time; as soon as any negative response is received to a lock request the transaction is aborted.

2.1. Previous Work

[YU 85a], [YU 85b] have studied the performance of SD architectures. [YU 85b] concentrates on a distributed pass-the-buck locking protocol that is used by IMS to synchronize locking in a SD environment. They have shown that this protocol does not work beyond 8 processors, because of increase in contention due to increase in buck cycle time. Our distributed protocols, PRI and APRI are limited only by the bus bandwidth and have no such inherent limitation. [YU 85a] studies a model similar to our CLM, but there is no study of message batching to improve performance. [REUT 84] proposes a range of SD architectures, but there is no performance study. The main contribution of this paper is to compare SE, SN and SD architectures with uniform assumptions. We are not aware of any paper in existing literature which does that.

3. The Simulation Model

In turn, we discuss the architecture, the file system, the workload, the concurrency control algorithm and the buffer cache and logging aspects of our simulation model. In the last sub-section, we will describe the queueing model we used.

3.1. The Machine Architectures

To make a fair comparison between SD, SE and SN, we have used the same system parameters in both environments whenever this assumption is realistic. The parameters are summarized in Table 1. The default value shown in the table has been used in the simulation runs, however, for particular runs, we have used different values from those in Table 1. These will be noted wherever they occur.

The choice of parameter values has been influenced by the fact that the ultimate goal of our project is to study the viability of using the SPUR architecture (a SE type architecture) being developed here at Berkeley[HILL 86] as a transaction processor. We assume that *page_size* is 4 Kbytes. *Cpu_speed* has been set to 4 MIPs for every processor. We use a uniform distribution for *disk_random-access-time* with a mean of 20 ms. Log pages are written onto the log disks in a sequential manner. The parameters for sequential log writes are *disk_rot_time*, the rotation time for a disk, *disk_page-access-time*, the time required to read/write a page.

Table 1: System Parameters	
Machine Parameters	
Parameters	Default Value
page_size	4 Kbytes
cpu_speed	4 MIPs
disk_random_access_time	20 ms mean, uniform distribution
disk_rot_time	16 ms mean, uniform distribution
disk_page_access_time	1.333 ms
network_speed	10 Mb/sec / 30 Mbyte/sec
inst_per_message	5000 inst/message (mean)
number_of_cpus	10
number_of_disks	80
number_of_buffers	40000
System Parameters	
Parameters	Default Value
file_system_type	random/sensibly split
batch_size	1
lock_request_locality	0.1
par_degree	1
Workload Parameters	
Parameters	Default Value
access_pattern	random, 80-20 rule
no_of_pages	10 (mean)
write_access_ratio	0.5
no_of_terminals	4000
think_time	20 sec mean, exp distribution
Dbase_Size	2,000,000 granules
inst_per_page	12,500 (mean)
Concurrency Control Parameters	
Parameters	Default Value
timeout_interval	10 sec
delay	0 sec
mult_degree	400

For the SN system, we have used 10 Mb/sec as the speed of the local area network. For the SD system, we have used 30 Mbyte/sec as the speed of the network which connects all the disks and all the processors. The higher speed is necessary, since all the pages accessed by transactions must be read across the network. We assume that messages are exponentially distributed with a mean size of 1000 bits. Hence, the time each message requires for transmission on the network will be distributed exponentially with mean 1000/*network_speed*. In our simulations, we have observed network utilizations of only 5 - 30% with these parameters. Therefore, the network related parameters are not critical in determining system performance. The number of CPU instructions required to process a message is assumed to be exponentially distributed with mean *inst_per_message*, and this parameter has been set to 5000 instructions/message. Our simulation results are sensitive to this parameter and it is one of the main factors which determines the difference in performance between the SN/SD architectures and SE. We will study the sensitivity to message cost of SD results in section 4.3. We have already studied this for SN and SE in [BHID 88]. We have used a 10 processor system for each of the architectures as the basic configuration in which to run our experiments because SPUR[HILL 86] currently runs out of memory bandwidth with 10 four MIP processors. By limiting the size of the SE system, we avoid having to explicitly model memory and bus contention. For the CLM variation of the SD architecture, we designate one processor out of 10 as the lock manager and use the other 9 to process transactions. Also, we have used a total of 80 database disks. In both the SE and SD architectures these are all attached to the bus and can be accessed from any processor. In SN, 8 are attached to each of the 10 processors. In addition to the database disks, we use 4 to 6 dedicated disks for the SE and SD logs, and one disk per processor for the SN log. The number of SE/SD log disks is chosen based on workload parameters, so that the log disks will not become a bottleneck.

3.2. The Software System Model

For both the SD and SE architecture we used a random file model, in which consecutive disk blocks of a file are distributed randomly over all the disks. This choice is motivated by our desire to explore intra-query parallelism. We wish to maximize the probability that multiple sub-plans can be processed in parallel without bottlenecking on accessing a single disk drive. For the SN architecture we have a "sensibly split" file model where a file is split between the disks of some number of processors (this number would depend on how many files a query accesses, the pattern of access etc.) such that the degree of parallelism achieved for a query is n. It should be noted that achieving a parallelism of exactly n depends on knowing a lot about the application and the set of pages accessed by a query. The portion of a file on one single processor has disk blocks allocated randomly on all disks attached to it. Note, that if the random file model were to be used for SN a single file would be distributed over all the nodes. Thus a single query would very likely be executed on all nodes and would result in poor performance. For CLM and APRI, the default message batch size used is 1. For PRI and APRI, the default lock request locality used is 0.1. This value represents the case where lock requests are randomly scattered over the entire database. *Par_degree* is the degree of parallelism which is to be used in executing each query and indicates the number of parallel sub-queries into which each query is decomposed. We have varied *Par_degree* in section 4.4, elsewhere we use a value of 1.

3.3. The Workload Model

We have assumed that transactions access pages according to Zipf's Law with 80% of the accesses going to 20% of the database. The 20% frequently accessed pages are distributed uniformly over all the disks and also over all the processors for SN. Table 1 also describes the other workload parameters. *No_of_pages* is the total no of pages that each transaction accesses which we assume to have an exponential distribution with mean 10. This makes our transactions about the same size as the TP1 benchmark[GRAY 84] which does 5 to 10 I/Os. The number of instructions spent in processing a page is exponentially distributed with a mean of *inst_per_page*, which is set to 12,500. *Write/access ratio* is the ratio of number of pages updated to total number of pages accessed. Consequently, each page is updated with this probability. *No_of_terminals* is the number of terminals which are attached to the system from which users enter queries. *Think_Time* is the time a user thinks before submitting a new query after he gets a reply to his previous query. This is assumed to have an exponential distribution with mean 20 sec. *Dbase_Size* is the size of the database in terms of the number of lockable objects. We have set *Dbase_Size* to 2,000,000 granules. This leads to a low lock contention probability. Elsewhere ([BHID 88], [BHID 87]), we have studied workloads with high lock contention. Our results indicate that in high lock contention environments, performance is similar to environments where response constraints are present.

If response time constraints are specified for a particular workload, then the *No_of_terminals* parameter is varied until the maximum number of terminals that can be supported with the given response time constraints is found. Thus getting one data point for a given workload with response time constraints can involve a number of simulation runs.

3.4. The Concurrency Control Model

We use dynamic 2-phase locking as the concurrency control method. We chose to implement timeouts instead of deadlock detection since global deadlock detection is difficult to model in SN. The timeout mechanism seemed to work very well and the number of restarts was negligible. If timeout occurs, all locks are released and the transaction is restarted after a time equal to *delay*. In APRI we use asynchronous locking. This means that transactions do not wait for lock requests to complete and continue processing. If the lock is busy, the transaction must be aborted.

Mult_degree is the number of active transactions in the system at any time.

3.5. The Buffer Cache and Logging Model

For SD, we have used the *buffer purge* scheme described in section 2. For SN and SE, we have implemented a database cache scheme[ELHA 84]. We have assumed a database cache large enough to contain all the updated pages of a transaction. This cache is used to hold all pages that are (1)currently "pinned" for reading by an active transaction (2)"dirty" pages that have been updated by an active transaction and (3) frequently accessed pages which are not in categories (1) and (2). When a transaction commits, its updates are not written to the database. Instead, the buffers are marked as "updated" and the actual database update is deferred until the buffer replacement policy needs to reclaim an "updated" buffer. A list of available buffers (those not in categories (1) and (2) above) is maintained as a FIFO queue. Every time a buffer is accessed it goes to the tail of the FIFO queue. At commit time updated pages are written to the log. This use of page level logging corresponds to the tactic used by some commercial systems, and we plan to experiment with record level logging in the future. In our model of SE/SD we have to multiplex the log among 4 to 6 dedicated disks to prevent the log from becoming a bottleneck. In SN, we keep one log disk per processor. In case of a timeout, the transaction is aborted. In this scheme, aborting a transaction is simple; all its updates are discarded. We have not modelled the recovery from system or media failure. The default cache size is 40000 buffers.

3.6. The Simulation Queueing Model

In this section, we describe the queueing simulation model for both the SE, SN and SD architectures. Figure 1 shows the queueing model for the SE architecture. A transaction waits at the Ready Queue until the number of active transactions in the system falls below the degree of multiprogramming that has been chosen. Then it enters the system and is split into a number of sub-queries equal to the degree of parallelism. Each sub-query is modelled as a list of pages to be processed.

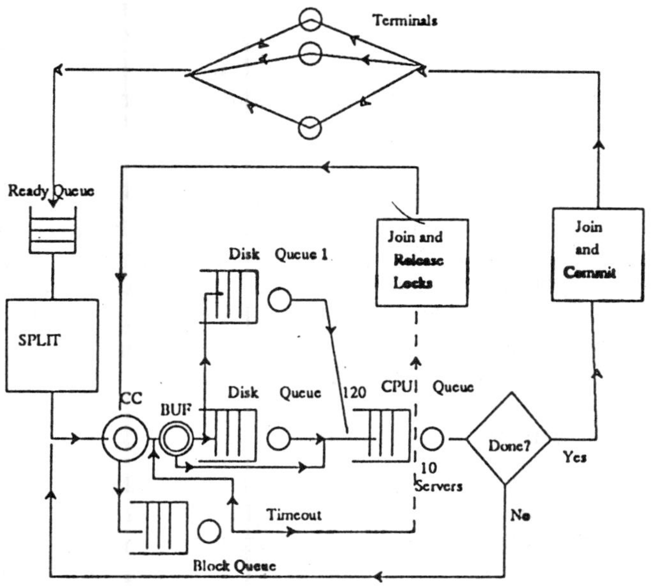

Fig. 1

Shared Everything Queueing Model

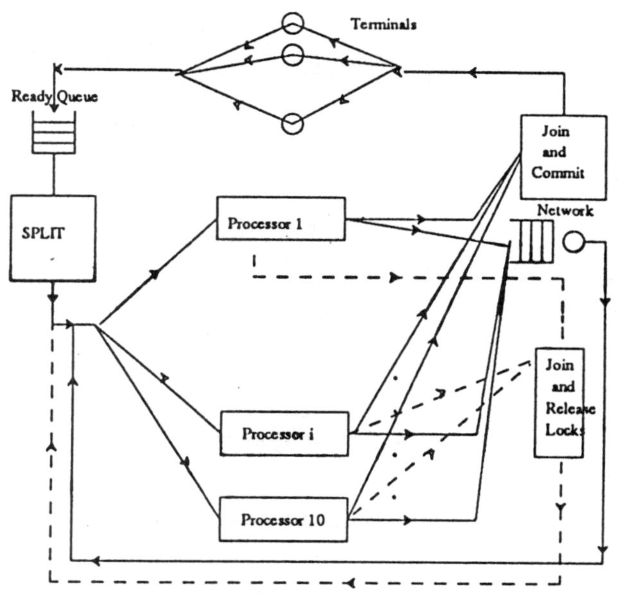

Fig. 2 a
Shared Nothing Queueing Model

The number of pages assigned to each sub-query is exponentially distributed with a mean equal to the average number of pages read by the transaction divided by the degree of parallelism. Each sub-query is an independent job in the queueing network and cycles between the disk queue, using the disk, the CPU queue, using the CPU and the blocked queues until all its pages have been processed. There is a single queue for all CPUs since the scheduler assigns a job to the next available CPU. CC is the node where a sub-query generates concurrency control requests. The blocked queue holds sub-queries which are waiting for locks. For each page in its read or write set, a sub-query first goes to CC node to get a lock and then to the BUF node to get a buffer. If the particular page is already in the cache, the sub-query goes directly to the CPU queue. Otherwise, it goes to the disk queue for a particular disk, then it goes to the CPU queue to process that page. After all its pages have been processed a sub-query job goes to the Join node and waits until all its sibling sub-queries arrive. Then all locks are released, the log record containing all the updated pages is written, and the transaction job goes back to the terminal queue. If a sub-query times out while waiting for a lock, it goes to the *Join and Release Locks* node where it waits for its sibling sub-queries. Each sibling is located and forced to this node. Then, they release all locks and the transaction is restarted after a time *delay*. However, the read and write lists of the transaction are preserved so that the same access pattern is repeated on restart.

Figure 2a shows the queueing model for the SN architecture and a detailed view is shown for one of the 10 identical processors in Figure 2b. The Ready Queue and the SPLIT node have the same functions as in SE. In this case, however, there are 10 separate processors which communicate over a network. Each transaction has a home node which is the node at which it entered the system and the splitting of a transaction into sub-queries takes place at the home node. For each sub-query, a message is sent to its execution site to start up the sub-query. This corresponds to a model of the file-system where files are split such that each query is executed on n processors, where n is the degree of parallelism for that simulation run. Each sub-query joins the CPU queue at the Net Out node and consumes the CPU time needed to send a message. On arriving at its destination, the sub-query joins the CPU queue at the Net In node and consumes the CPU time spent in processing the arriving message. For each page, the order of access is CC, BUF, disk and CPU as in the previous architecture. When all its pages have been processed, a sub-query moves to the Join and Commit node, where it waits for all its siblings to complete. The log record for the query is then written and all locks are released. There are a total of 3 rounds of messages exchanged: (1) a message is sent from the home node to each execution site containing the subquery to be executed (2) a message is sent from each execution site to the home node indicating that subquery processing is done and it is ready to commit (3) after the home node gets a "done" messages from all sites a "commit" message is sent to each of them. Thus, if degree of parallelism is n, the number of messages

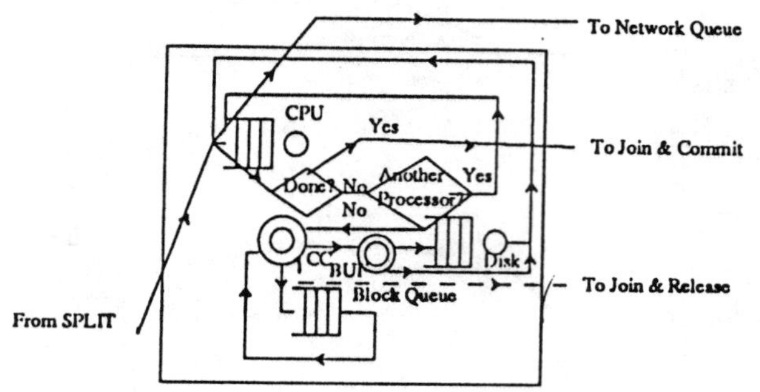

Fig. 2b
A Shared NothiProcesssor

exchanged is 3*n. This protocol is appropriate when only one query is performed at each site. If multiple queries were simulated, we would need a general 2-phase commit protocol with additional messages. In case a timeout occurs at any of the execution sites while waiting for locks, an "abort" message is sent to the home node, which in turn sends an "abort" message to each of the other execution sites. Jobs which timeout go to the Join and Release Locks node, where they wait for their siblings, and once all their siblings have been forced to this node, their locks are released and they are restarted after time *delay*.

The SD simulation model resembles the SN model except for lock requests and the fact that disks are shared. In CLM, a job wanting to make a lock request waits at a *batch* node until *batch_size* other jobs collect. Then these jobs are bundled up and the CPU message cost for sending the message is paid. The message goes out over the network and is received by the lock manager processor. The cost of receiving the message is paid and each lock request is processed. The lock manager processor maintains 9 separate *batch* nodes, one for each transaction processor. After waiting at the right *batch* node for *batch_size* other responses, they are packed into a message, the CPU cost of sending is paid and the message goes to the network queue. The lock response is received by the requesting processor after paying the CPU cost of receiving a message. After a transaction commits, a lock release message is sent to the lock manager. PRI and APRI have similar simulation models except that the lock requests go to appropriate transaction processors, instead of a lock manager processor. In APRI, another difference is that a job spins off a lock request and continues processing. If the response received is negative, the transaction gets aborted. Each job waits for all its lock responses to come back after it has finished all its processing and just before it gets to the *Join and Commit* node. After a transaction commits a lock release message is sent to the all processors from which locks were requested. These release messages are batched along with the lock request messages. In DIS, the lock requests go to the disk controller. In all the SD architectures, we route transactions to the processor with the least number of active transactions. This helps in balancing processor loads.

The simulator is written is C and is about 10,000 lines of code. Each data point is obtained by a simulation run lasting for 1,000,000 events. A transition from one queue to another is counted as an event. Results were observed to very stable at this point. Each run lasts 90 minutes on a Sequent Balance machine and simulates 60 - 75 minutes of system time.

4. Simulation Results

Our main emphasis is on transaction throughput in the three architectures. As mentioned in section 2, the two main techniques we will study for improving SD performance are batching of messages and increasing lock request locality. In section 4.1 we will study the effect of lock request locality on PRI and APRI. In section 4.2 we will show the effects of batching lock request messages for CLM and APRI.. In section 4.3 we will compare the four SD variations, namely, DIS, CLM, PRI and APRI for different message costs. We will choose the best SD architecture from section 4.3 and compare it with SN and SE for different degrees of intra-query parallelism in section 4.4. The simulations in sections 4.1, 4.2 and 4.3 were performed without response time constraints. In section 4.4, we will use response time constraints to compare SE, SN and SD.

4.1. Effect of Locality

In a SD architecture, a transaction can be executed on any processor unlike SN. An optimal processor allocation policy for transactions must reconcile two sometimes conflicting objectives: (1)In both PRI and APRI, efforts can be made to route transactions to that processor which holds the lock authority for most of the granules accessed by the transaction (assuming that accesses can be predicted with some degree of accuracy). This saves two messages for each local lock request. (2)The second objective is to try to balance the load on all the processors.

In this experiment, we will try to estimate the pay-off from trying to maximize lock request locality. This will help a designer in making the correct trade-off between balancing processor loads and maximizing lock locality. Also, if a designer knows roughly how much locality can be obtained from his workload, he can judge whether APRI/PRI is better than CLM which has no concept of locality. Changing the access pattern enables us to change the locality ratio.

Figures 3 and 4 show the throughput and response time respectively against the locality ratio (fraction of

Figure 3
PRI: Effect of Primary Copy Locality

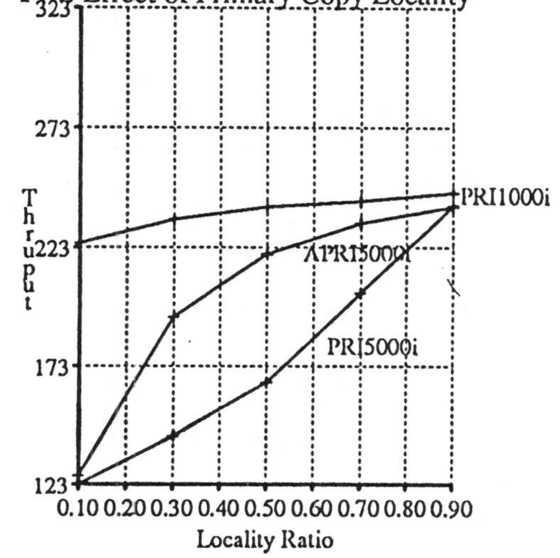

Figure 4
PRI: Effect of Primary Copy Locality

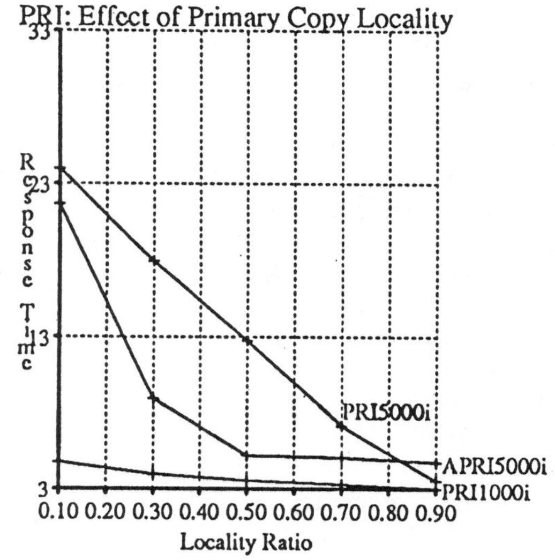

Figure 5
CLM: Effect of Message Batching

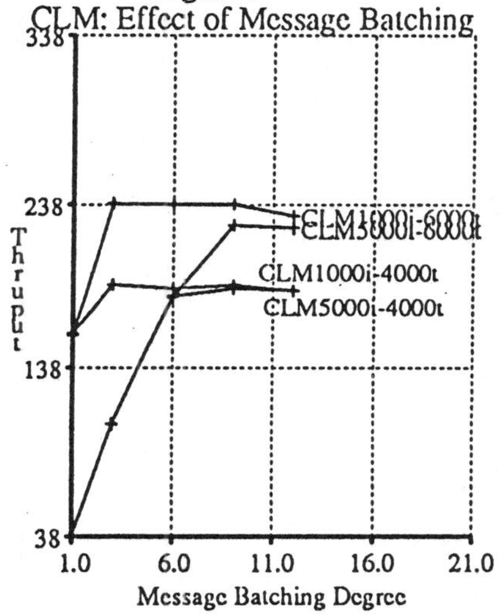

Figure 6
CLM: Effect of Message Batching

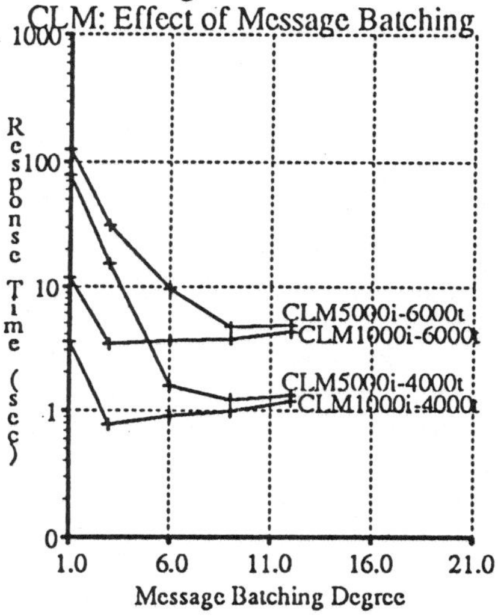

Figure 7
APRI: Effect of Message Batching

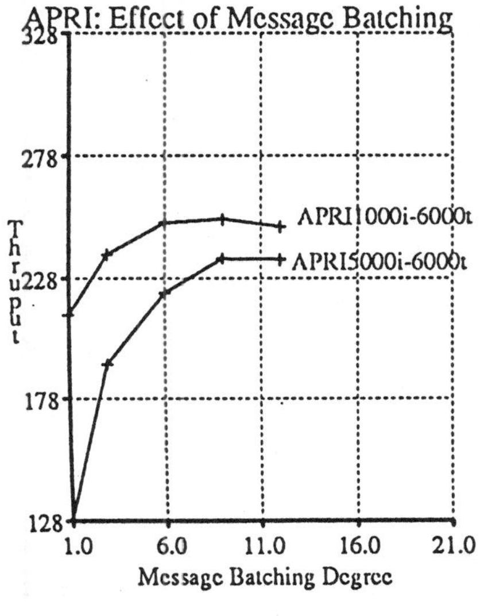

Figure 8
APRI: Effect of Message Batching

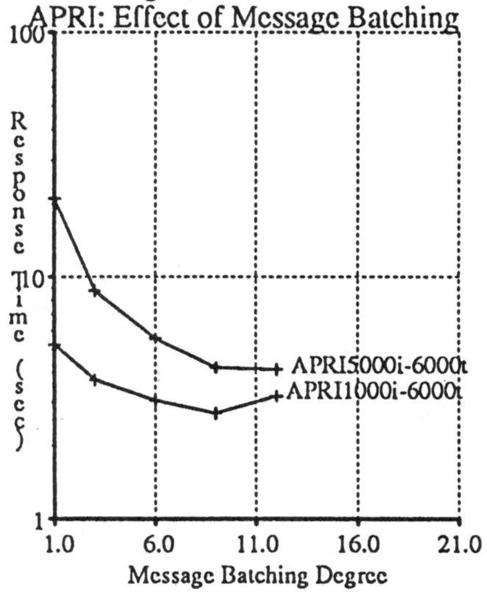

local lock requests) for PRI and APRI. The number of terminals is held constant at 6000. PRI1000i stands for the PRI architecture with a message cost of 1000 instructions and PRI5000i stands for PRI with message cost of 5000; similarly for APRI5000i. The gain for the PRI1000i curve is small because 1000 is too small a message cost to cause a substantial overhead. However, the gain for the PRI5000i curve is substantial(almost 100%) as the locality is increased from 0.1 to 0.9. Notice, however, that the PRI5000i curve is concave upwards, which means that most of the gain is between localities 0.5 and 0.9. It might be hard to achieve such high localities. Figure 4 shows that the response time for PRI5000i improves with better locality. The gains for APRI are approximately the same as for PRI. However, the APRI curve is convex upwards which means that most of the gains are in the 0.1 to 0.5 locality region. This degree of locality is easier to achieve and thus APRI shows better locality gains than PRI.

4.2. Effect of Batching

In this experiment, we will study the effects of batching lock messages, for CLM and APRI. Message batching would be a loser for PRI since the interval between lock requests from a processor A to a processor B is of the order of 50 ms. Since lock requests are synchronous, and each transaction makes 10 requests, for a degree of batching of 4 this will add about 750 ms to the response time. This kind of overhead would make it impossible to keep the subsecond response time constraints that are necessary for most transaction systems. In APRI the lock requests are asynchronous and the batching overheads are lower. In CLM, all lock requests go to the central lock manager; therefore, the period between requests is only 5 ms.

Figures 5 and 6 show throughput and response time as a function of degree of batching for four variations of CLM. In the curve labels, 1000i stands for a CLM with message cost of 1000 instructions and 5000i stands for a message cost of 5000 instructions. 6000t and 4000t stand for 6000 and 4000 terminals respectively. As the degree of batching increases all the four curves in Figure 5 show large throughput gains and then flatten out. After batching degree 9 the curves fall slightly showing that the advantage of reduced message costs are overcome by the disadvantage of waiting for more lock requests. At higher batching degrees, the message costs become insignificant, therefore, the curves for 1000i and 5000i merge together. For lower number of terminals, the throughput is smaller but the response time is better.

Figures 7 and 8 show throughput and response time as a function of degree of batching for two variations of APRI. Comparing figures 5 and 7, APRI performs about the same as CLM at higher batching degrees, but performs much better than CLM at lower batching degrees.

Batching has two effects: (1) reducing the message cost for lock requests by a factor equal to the batching degree. (2) increasing the response time due to waiting for a batch to form. We performed an experiment to isolate and observe the effect of (2). In figure 9 CLM1 stands for CLM with degree of batching 1. CLM9 stands for CLM with degree of batching 9. However, the CLM1 curve represents an architecture where the message costs are 1/9th of those of CLM9. For example, the CLM1 point at X coordinate = 2000 was taken by using a message cost of 2000/9 = 222 instructions. Thus, both CLM1 and CLM9 have the same message costs; however, CLM9 has to pay the penalty for batch waiting times. Thus CLM9 has a throughput about 20 transactions/sec below CLM1 and a response time which is about 2 seconds higher.

4.3. Effect of Message Cost

In this section, we compare the effect of CPU message cost on the different SD architectures. Figures 10, 11 and 12 show the throughput, response time and the CPU utilization for various SD variations against the CPU cost of sending a message. This is the number of instructions it takes a processor to send a message. We assume that it takes the same number of instructions for the receiving processor to receive a message. For DIS, however, the "CPU cost of messages" represents the extra number of CPU instructions needed to communicate lock requests to the disk controller. This is the only extra overhead in DIS, since, all the architectures need to communicate with the disk controller to read/write pages. This number is typically small. That is why the DIS curve is plotted only between 500 and 2500. CLM9 stands for the CLM variation with a batch size = 9 and CLM1 stands for batch size = 1. Similarly for APRI1 and 9. In Figure 12, the CPU utilizations of the central lock manager and those of the other processors are different; for example, CLM1-clm curve shows the lock manager utilization of the CLM1 architecture and similarly the CLM1-all curve shows the utilization of the other processors. Figure 10 shows that CLM1 is very sensitive to message cost. Figure 12 explains why: since the lock manager processor spends most of its time processing messages, the CLM1-clm curve rises very fast and is very near saturation. Thus the central lock manager becomes the bottleneck in this system. This shows that it is worthwhile to keep the CPU utilization of the central lock processor low, perhaps by using a faster processor. For CLM9, the CLM9-all curve rises very fast also, but is farther away from saturation, so CLM9 shows very good performance. If the workload is heterogenous, with few infrequently running transactions which make many lock requests and most transactions which make few, the presence of the lock intensive transactions will degrade the rsponse time of the short

Figure 9
CLM: Batching vs Reduced Message Costs

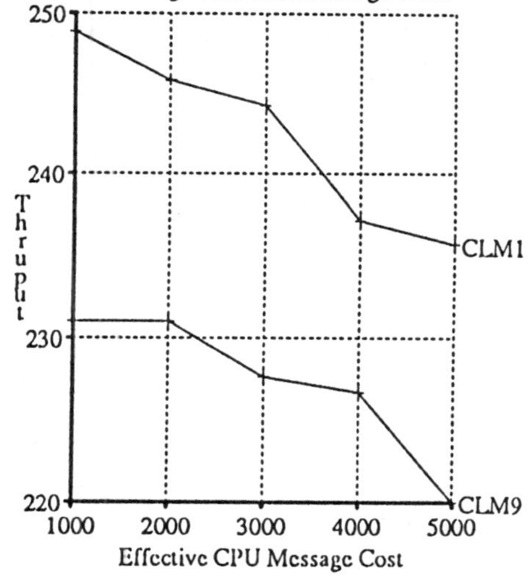

Figure 10
Effect of Message Cost

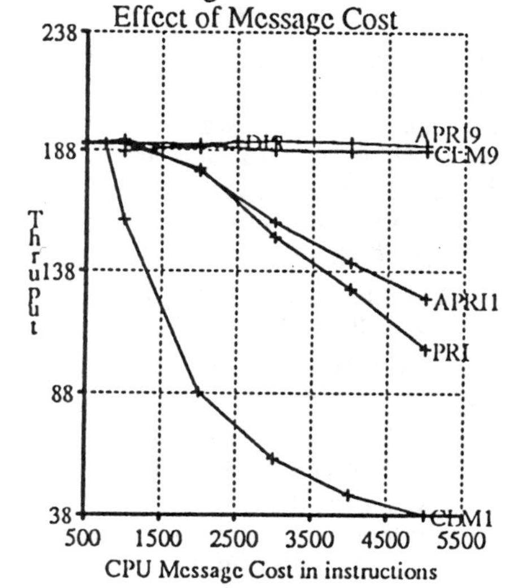

Figure 11
Effect of Message Cost

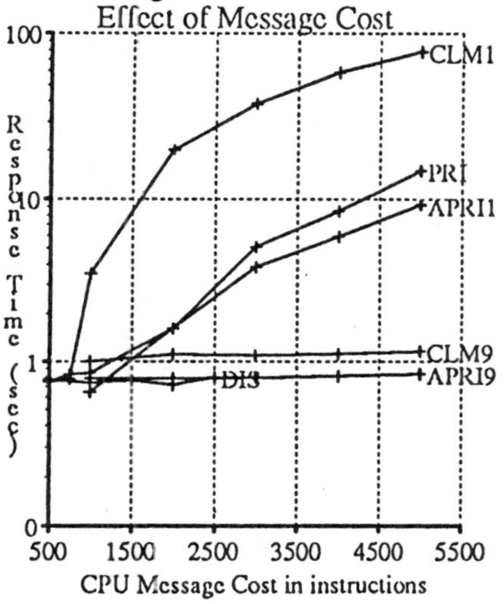

Figure 12
Effect of Message Cost

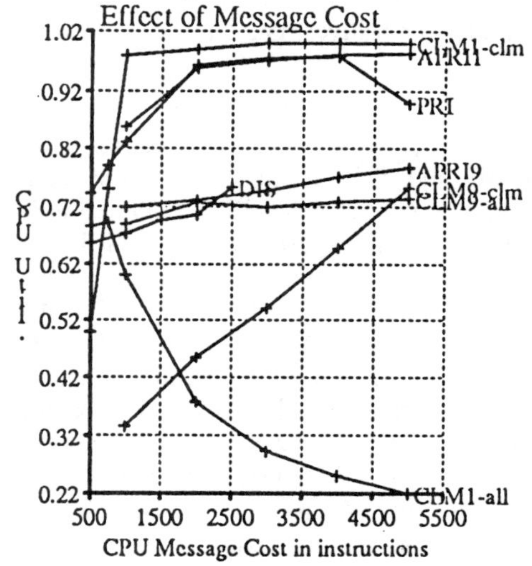

Figure 13
Effect of Degree of Parallelism with Response Constraints

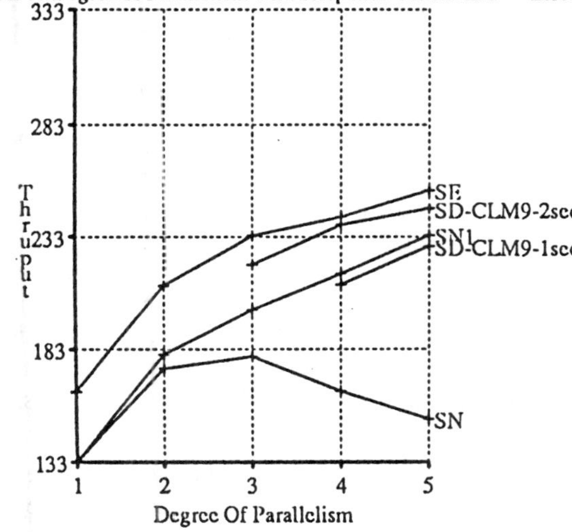

Figure 14
Effect of Degree of Parallelism with Response Constraints

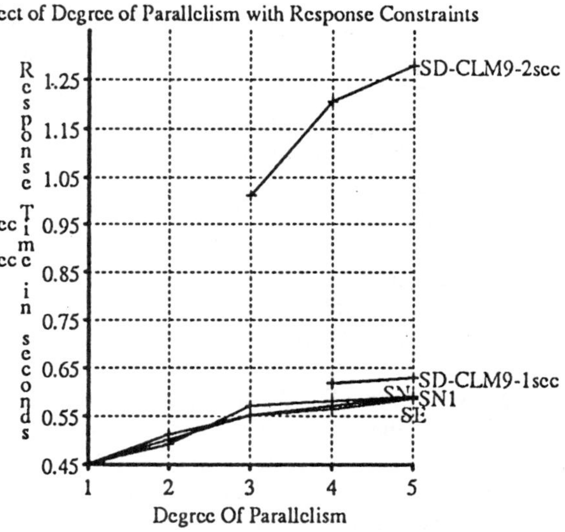

transactions. CLM thus is an unstable design because of the presence of a potential hot spot.

The best performers are DIS, APRI9 and CLM9. The good performance of DIS is intuitively expected. However, DIS requires extra hardware in the form of a disk controller which is able to keep track of locks. Therefore, it is reassuring to know that both CLM9 and APRI9 can match the performance of DIS very closely. APRI9 is better than CLM9 in terms of response time and almost the same in terms of throughput. PRI does worse than both APRI9 and CLM9 but better than CLM1. As explained before, the lock messages in PRI cannot be batched because the degradation in response time would be too high. Also notice that APRI1 does better than PRI specially at higher message costs. The gap between APRI1 and PRI is the gain of asynchronous locking over synchronous locking at low lock contentions (The probability of conflict on making a lock request is approximately 0.0007 with these parameters). For higher lock contention workloads, APRI should perform worse; we have not investigated this effect yet.

4.4. Comparison of SE, SN and SD

In this section, we compare the effect of parallelism on SD, SE and SN. From the previous section (figures 10 and 11), we see that DIS, CLM9 and APRI9 have approximately similar performance. Both DIS and APRI9 have the same throughputs as CLM9 but the response times are about 20% better. Since DIS needs special hardware it would be unfair to use it to compare SD against SN and SE. The APRI architecture has an additional locality parameter which is hard to estimate. Therefore we chose the CLM9 variation (central lock manager with message cost of 5000 and batching degree 9) for this experiment. We asssume the same message cost for SN: 5000 instructions. The default parameters from Table 1 were used for this set of simulations. Figures 13 and 14 show throughput and response time against the degree of parallelism for the different architectures in a response time constrained environment. The response time constraint is that 90 % of the transactions must have a response time of less than 1 second. This is a fairly tight constraint since the average total stand-alone execution time of a single transaction is 0.233 seconds. For SD, we have also plotted another curve with the response constraint changed to 90% transactions respond within 2 seconds. This curve is labelled as SD-CLM9-2sec and the one with the 1 second constraint is labelled as SD-CLM9-1sec. SN and SE curves are plotted with a 1 second constraint only and are labelled SN, SN1 and SE. We have plotted two variations of SN. For the curve labelled SN, sub-queries belonging to the same transaction were executed on different processors and hence had to pay a message cost for 3*n messages if n is the degree of parallelism. For the curve labelled SN1, all the subqueries belonging to a transaction were executed on one processor and thus no message cost had to be paid. To obtain each data point in figures 13 and 14, a number of simulation runs were required. Each simulation run was taken with a given number of terminals and depending on whether the constraint is achieved or not the number of terminals is increased or decreased for the next run. A binary search type technique was used to find the maximum number of terminals that can be supported with the given constraint.

At low degrees of parallelism, SD-CLM9 has response times of the order of 2 seconds. Therefore, almost no transactions can meet the 1 and 2 second deadlines. The points not shown for the SD curves should be taken to be almost 0. Thus intra-query parallelism is necessary for good SD performance when tight response constraints are present. Note that the SD curves lie in between the curves for SN and SE. In fact if the response constraint is relaxed to 2 seconds, SD (the SD-CLM9-2sec curve) performs almost as well as SE for high degrees of parallelism.

In Figure 13, the SN curve goes up initially as parallelism helps to increase the number of transactions making the response time constraint. After parallelism degree 3, however, the cost of messages starts to drive the curve down. SN1 does much better than SN at higher degrees of parallelism because no message cost has to be paid. However, in a real SN architecture, it would be hard to achieve SN1, since it involves localizing the data of every transaction on one processor. Therefore the performance of SN would lie somewhere between SN and SN1. Note that SE beats both SN and SD. In Figure 16, SE and SN are about 30 transactions/sec apart at a degree of parallelism of 1 and this gap increases at higher degrees of parallelism. Both SE and SD (with 1 second response time) achieve their best performances of 253 transactions/sec and 228 transactions/sec at a degree of parallelism of 5, while SN achieves its best performance of 179 transactions/sec at a parallelism degree of 3. Thus, there is a 41 % performance gap between SE and SN and a 22% gap between SN and SD. SN1 and SE are about 30 transactions/sec apart at all the degrees of parallelism.

From Figure 13 it is clear that parallelism improves performance substantially for all three architectures. For SE, the performance jumps 55 % between parallelism degrees 1 and 5. For SN, the jump is smaller, about 35 % between degrees 1 and 3 and then throughput falls between degrees 3 and 5. Parallelism reduces the response time and hence more transactions satisfy the response time constraint of 1 second. It also helps to balance the loads on the CPUs and the disks, and to achieve higher utilizations.

Figure 14 shows the average transaction response time. Response times increase as the degree of parallelism is increased, because, at higher degrees of parallelism more terminals are supported and throughput increases. The fact that the throughput increases shows that even though average response time increases, the variation in response time decreases (more transactions make the 1 second deadline) for higher degrees of intra-query parallelism.

5. Conclusions

We have described a study of the performance of three multiprocessor architectures, namely, Shared Nothing(SN), Shared Everything(SE) and Shared Disks(SD), in transaction processing. We first studied four different variations of SD which attempted to optimize on the number of lock request messages sent. We studied the performance effects of two mechanisms for doing this: batching for CLM and APRI and increasing lock request locality for PRI and APRI. We observed that DIS, APRI with batch size 9 and CLM with batch size 9 had roughly comparable performance and were better than the other variations. We used CLM with batch size 9 to compare SD against SN and SE and to study the effect of the degree of intra-transaction parallelism. We observed that SD performs as well as the optimistic SN version (which assumes that each transaction is local to a single processor) and much better than a reasonably pessimistic version. Thus SD is a viable architecture in cases where it is not possible to partition the database so that the data for most transactions is local to one processor. However, we also observed that CLM with batch size 9 needs high degrees of parallelism to meet response time constraints.

We observed that SE outperformed SN and SD by a fairly wide margin. However, SE has two disadvantages:

(1) It is limited by bus and memory bandwidths.
(2) It has a potential single point of failure:
the shared memory.

Therefore, SE is the architecture of choice for environments where the transaction throughput requirements are within the bus/memory technological barrier and failures can be handled in other ways. One way to do this would be to connect up SE nodes in a SN configuration. SD would be the architecture of choice if throughput requirements were too large to use SE. Designing a SD transaction processing system is easier than designing a SN system because the database partitioning problem does not arise. SD, of course, has its own technological limitations, namely bus bandwidth. However, this bus is less loaded as compared to an SE bus, since, the SE bus must handle memory traffic in addition to disk traffic. Thus, the choice of an architecture for a transaction processing system depends on throughput requirements, availability requirements, workload considerations and hardware technologies available.

References.

[BART 81] Bartlett, J.F., "A Non-Stop Kernel," Proc. 8th Symposium on Operating Systems Principles, 1981.

[BHID 87] Bhide, A., and Stonebraker, M., "Performance Issues in High Performance Transaction Processing Architectures" Proc. 2nd International Workshop on High Performance Transaction Processing, Oct 1987.

[BHID 88] Bhide, A., and Stonebraker, M., "A Performance Comparison of Two Architectures for Transaction Processing" Proc. 4th Intl. Conference on Data Engineering, Feb 1988.

[ELHA 84] Elhard, K. and Bayer, R., "A Database Cache for High Performance and Fast Restart in Database Systems," ACM Trans. on Database Systems, Dec 1984.

[GRAY 84] Gray, J., et. al. " A Measure of Transaction Processing Power," Datamation 1984.

[HILL 86] Hill, M., et. al., "Design Decisions in SPUR," IEEE Computer, Nov. 1986.

[REUT 84] Reuter, A. and Shoens, K., "Synchronization in a Data Sharing Environment," unpublished manuscript.

[SEQU 86] Sequent Computers, "Balance Guide to Parallel Programming," June. 1986.

[STRI 82] Strickland, J., et. al., "IMS/VS: An Evolving System", IBM Systems Journal 21, 4(1982).

[YU 85a] Yu, P., et. al., "Modelling of Centralized Concurrency Control in a Multi-System Environment," Proceedings of the 1985 SIGMETRICS Conference on Measurement and Modelling of Computer Systems, Aug 1985.

[YU 85b] Yu, P., et. al., "Distributed Concurrency Control Analysis for Data Sharing," Proceedings of the Intl. Conference on Management and Performance Evaluation of Computer Systems, 1985.

Chapter 3: Parallel External Sorting

Sorting is the process of rearranging a sequence of values in ascending or descending order. In database systems, it is not uncommon to produce a sorted report. Moreover, sorting has also been widely used to facilitate other operations such as merge join, duplicate elimination, division, and aggregate functions. For example, to remove duplicate records, a relation is sorted to group all the duplicate records together, followed by a scan to remove all but one of the duplicates. Because of its impact on operations that it supports, any improvement in the performance of a sorting algorithm will benefit the system drastically. As such, we have devoted this chapter to look at the basic sorting algorithms in parallel database systems.

In database systems, data files tend to be much larger than the main memory and hence, internal sorting is not possible. In the context of shared-memory parallel systems, it is assumed that the size of the relation to be sorted is larger than the shared memory. For shared disk or shared nothing systems, the total amount of local memory from all the processors is not large enough to hold the records. External peripheral devices (tapes, disks, and so forth.) are needed to provide the space required. Such sorting schemes are called external sorting algorithms as opposed to those internal ones where the sort values can be stored in main memory. External sorting is different from internal sorting in that input/output accounts for most of the execution time in external sorting. Data structures provided by the algorithms must be arranged in such a way that slow peripheral devices can efficiently accommodate the algorithms.

External sorting algorithms, both serial and parallel versions, have been extensively studied.[1] Most of the algorithms that parallelize the external sort fall under two categories — merge-based and partition-based. The merge-based sorting techniques first partition the relation (file) into subrelations (subfile), usually a set of physical pages, that can be contained in memory. These subrelations are internally sorted and then iteratively merged. For approaches that employ partitioning, the data are range-partitioned and distributed across the processors so that each processor can independently perform the sort of the range allocated to it using any known fast uniprocessor sorting algorithm. Although merge-based techniques do not need to determine how the data are to be partitioned, the partition-based approaches are simpler.

Merge-based parallel sorting

Merge-based parallel sorting algorithms can be further classified into two groups. The first group, k-way merge-sort, assumes that the set of processors is logically connected into a tree. Each processor at the leaf level of the tree sorts one portion of the original relation (file) assigned to it first and generates so-called sorted runs. Sorted runs from the leaves are merged by the processors at a higher level, generating longer runs (k times longer). This merging process continues with merged runs being sent to another higher level until finally, a single sorted run is obtained. Algorithms that come under this category include the 2-way merge-sort[2] and the *k-way* merge-sort.[3–5] The major advantage of these algorithms is that their output is a single sorted relation. However, the number of active processors decreases as the level gets higher. Eventually, at the final level, merging becomes sequential. As such, the parallelism of algorithms in this group is limited.

The other group was proposed by Menon.[6] The algorithms are based on sorting algorithms that use sorting networks. However, the comparison and exchange operator used in the sorting networks is replaced by a *k-way* merge. Several such algorithms presented include the Odd-Even External Sort and the Block Bitonic External Sort algorithms.[7] Unlike algorithms in the former group, the final sorted result is de-clustered across all disks (as in partition-based sorting).

Partition-based parallel sorting

The major idea of partition-based parallel sorting algorithms is to first split the relation to be sorted into disjoint partitions so that each of these partitions can be sorted by a processor concurrently and independently. Since the data are usually distributed among the processors and are typically sorted locally before the final sorting, the major task of a partition-based sorting algorithm is to solve the following problem:

> Given p processors and p sorted subfiles, partition each sorted file into p ranges such that (1) all elements in range i are less than range j for $i < j$ and $1 \le i, j \le p$ and (2) the number of elements for each range is the same.

Here, the set of values that defines the range is called the split vector.

Based on the use of exact or approximate split vectors, we can classify partition-based parallel sorting algorithms into two groups. Approaches that employ an exact split vector can be found in References 8 and 9. The split vector derived from exact methods distributes the data (approximately) evenly across the processors by employing the idea of selecting the kth smallest element in the sorted list. With this element, one would have split the set of subruns into two partitions, one with elements less than or equal to the kth element and the other with elements greater than the kth element. Next, within each partition, we may find the ith and j^{th} smallest elements, respectively. This process of finding some smallest element is repeated for each of the (sub) partitions formed until we have the $p - 1$ partitioning keys. One straightforward approach is to first find the $\frac{1}{p}^{th}$ smallest element, then find the $\frac{1}{p}^{th}$ smallest element within the larger partition, and the process repeats.

Most of the work on finding splitting vectors employs approximate methods. The easiest way to compute the partitioning keys is to partition the domain evenly into the required number of partitions. For example, if the domain is in the range 1–1,000, then to have 10 partitions, the required partitioning keys are 100, 200, …, 900. This approach may be simple, but it is effective only when the data are uniformly distributed. When the data are skewed, some partitions may have (much) more data than the others. Another approximation technique, proposed by Quinn,[10] obtains the splitting vector from only one sorted run (the first run). The splitting vector is given by the $p - 1$ evenly spaced keys of the run. These keys are then used as the partitioning keys to split each of the remaining sorted runs into p subruns. As pointed out by Quinn, the speedup may be severely compromised in some situations, such as when all the elements in the first run are always less than all elements in some other runs.

Sampling has also been widely used to compute the partitioning keys.[11,12,13] The sampling approach works as follows: To partition a relation R of size N, a random sample of size $p \times l - 1$ is taken for some l. This sample is then sorted in ascending order so that we have, say, the following order:

$$r_1, r_2, \ldots, r_l, \ldots, r_{2l}, \ldots, r_{pl-1}$$

We can then use the $p - 1$ points $r_l, r_{2l}, \ldots, r_{(p-1)l}$ as the splitting vector to achieve the required p partitions:

$$p_1 = r : r < r_l$$
$$p_i = r : r_{(i-1)l} \le r < r_{il} \quad \text{for } 2 \le i \le p - 1$$
$$P_p = r : r_{(p-1)l} \le r$$

It is hoped that the splitting vector obtained could split a relation into partitions of approximately equal numbers of records. Now, the accuracy of sampling techniques depends on the size of the sample. The larger the sample size, the higher its probability in reflecting the distribution of the data in the actual relation. However, a larger sample implies a higher cost. Since approximation approaches are not exact, the risk is always that the splitting vector obtained is far from ideal. Reference 11 provides a good comparison of the exact and approximate approaches.

It is unfortunate that most of the sorting algorithms proposed in the literature are not isolated on their own. Instead, they are incorporated to sort-merge join algorithms and published as join processing papers.[14, 15]

Comments

To the best of our knowledge, no work has been done in comparing the relative performance of merge-based and partition-based sorting methods. For the merge-based sorting algorithms, the degree of parallelism decreases as sorted runs are merged. On the other hand, the partition-based sorting algorithms require a preprocessing phase to ensure that the processing load across each processor is the same. In addition, the final merging is also serialized, since the processor with the first range will be sent to the user first, followed by that of the second, and so on.

The merge-based sorting algorithms are more suitable for shared memory systems, followed by shared disk, and finally shared nothing systems. In the latter systems, as the sorted runs are merged, communication overhead is incurred. Moreover, unlike shared memory and shared disk systems, the merged runs are stored in the local disks of the nodes only. In shared memory and shared disk systems, the merged runs may be declustered across several disks.

The partition-based sorting algorithms seem to be suitable for all environments, though most research has been performed on shared nothing environments.

Papers in this chapter

The first paper "A Study of Sort Algorithms for Multiprocessor Database Machines," by Menon, describes several merge-based external sort algorithms that should provide the reader with a comfortable understanding of merge-based algorithms.

The second paper "Parallel Sorting on a Shared Nothing Architecture Using Probabilistic Splitting," by DeWitt, Naughton, and Schneider, studies the partition-based sorting algorithms. Both the sampling and exact methods are used to compute the split vector.

The last paper "A Low Communication Sort Algorithm for a Parallel Database Machine," by Lorie and Young, studies how communication costs may be reduced by moving keys rather than entire records. Developing algorithms that minimize communication costs is crucial, especially when the trend of parallel database systems is moving toward shared nothing architectures.

References

1. D.E. Knuth, *The Art of Programming, Vol. 3: Sorting and Searching.* Addison-Wesley, Reading, Mass., 1973.
2. D. Bitton, "Parallel Algorithms for the Execution of Relational Database Operations," *ACM Trans. Database Systems,* Vol. 8, No. 3, Sept. 1983, pp. 324-353.
3. M. Beck, D. Bitton, and W.K. Wilkinson, "Sorting Large Files on a Backend Multiprocessor," *IEEE Trans. Computers,* Vol. 37, No. 7, July 1988, pp. 769-778.
4. B. Salzberg et al., "Fastsort: A Distributed Single-Input Single-Output External Sort," *Proc. 1990 ACM SIGMOD Int'l Conf. Management Data,* Assoc. for Computing Machinery, New York, N.Y., 1990, pp. 94-101.
5. P. Valduriez and G. Gardarin, "Join and Semijoin Algorithms for a Multiprocessor Database Machine," *ACM Trans. Database Systems,* Vol. 9, No. 1, Mar. 1984, pp. 133-161.
6. J. Menon, "A Study of Sort Algorithms for Multiprocessor Database Machines," *Proc. 12th Int'l Conf. Very Large Data Bases,* Morgan Kaufman, San Mateo, Calif., 1986, pp. 197-207.
7. D. Bitton et al., "A Taxonomy of Parallel Sorting," *ACM Computing Surveys,* Vol. 16, No. 3, Sept. 1984, pp. 287-318.
8. Y. Yamane and R Take, "Parallel Partition Sort for Database Machines," in *Database Machines and Knowledge Base Machines,* Kluwer Academic Publishers, Norwell, Mass., 1988, pp. 117-130.
9. B.R. Iyer, G.R. Ricard, and P.J. Varman, "Percentile Finding Algorithm for Multiple Sorted Runs," *Proc. 15th Int'l Conf. Very Large Data Bases,* Morgan Kaufman, San Mateo, Calif., 1989, pp. 135-144.
10. M.J. Quinn, "Parallel Sorting Algorithms for Tightly Coupled Multiprocessors," *Parallel Computing,* Vol. 6, 1988, pp. 349-367
11. D.J. DeWitt, J. Naughton, and D. Schneider, "Parallel Sorting on a Shared-Nothing Architecture Using Probabilistic Splitting," *Proc. First Int'l Conf. Parallel and Distributed Information Systems (PDIS),* IEEE CS Press, Los Alamitos, Calif., 1991, pp. 280-291.
12. G. Graefe, "Parallel External Sorting in Volcano," Tech. Report CU-CS-459-90, Univ. of Colorado, Boulder, Co., Mar. 1990.
13. J.S. Huang and Y.C. Chow, "Parallel Sorting and Data Partitioning by Sampling," *Proc. Seventh Int'l Computer Software and Applications Conf.,* IEEE CS Press, Los Alamitos, Calif., 1983, pp. 627-631.

14. J.P. Richardson, H. Lu, and K. Mikkilineni, "Design and Evaluation of Parallel Pipelined Join Algorithms," *Proc. ACM Int'l Conf. Management Data,* Assoc. for Computing Machinery, New York, N.Y., 1987, pp. 399-409.
15. J.L. Wolf et al., "An Effective Algorithm for Parallelizing Sort Merge Joins in the Presence of Data Skew," *Proc. Second Int'l Symp. Databases Parallel and Distributed Systems,* IEEE CS Press, Los Alamitos, Calif., 1990, pp. 103-115.

A Study of Sort Algorithms for Multiprocessor Database Machines

Jai Menon

IBM Almaden Research Center
San Jose, California 95120-6099

Abstract

This paper presents and analyzes algorithms for parallel execution of sort operations in a general multiprocessor architecture. We consider both internal and external sorting algorithms. For the latter, we study the performance of sorting algorithms that are derived from sorting algorithms that only do comparison and exchange by replacing each comparison-exchange with a B-way merge. In particular, we propose a new algorithm called the modified block bitonic sort. We then present the results of analyzing the performance of these different parallel external sorting algorithms. We show that the modified block bitonic sort is the fastest of the algorithms over a wide range of values of interest to us.

Introduction

Several multiprocessor database machines [GARDA81] [BABBE79] [DEWIT79]. have been or are currently being developed. Two of the most demanding operations that must be performed by such multiprocessor database machines are sorting and join. This paper presents a study of various algorithms for performing the first of these two operations on a general model of a multiprocessor database machine.

We will begin by considering ways to use parallel processors to sort files stored in random access memory (***parallel internal sorting***). In particular, we will show how to use the bitonic merge in order to do parallel internal sorting ([HSIAO80], [BITTO84]). We have presented the ***bitonic merge*** principle before, but the particular algorithm described here, and its analysis are presented for the first time.

Due to memory limitations, sorting of large files cannot be done in memory, and ***external sorting algorithms*** need to be used. The study of the external sorting algorithms is the main focus of this paper.

For external sorting algorithms, we study the performance of sorting algorithms that are derived from sorting networks that only do comparison and exchange by replacing each comparison-exchange with a B-way merge. We are interested in this class of algorithms because of the result of [BITTO83] where a sorting algorithm that is derived by replacing each comparison-exchange with a 2-way merge was presented and shown to be superior to all other algorithms presented in that paper. In this study, we are interested in the use of B-way merges, where B is significantly larger than 2. This is important because of the continuing drop in the costs of semiconductor memory, making it feasible to build multiprocessors with large amounts of semiconductor memory. For this class of external sorting algorithms, we investigate the impact of larger amounts of memory. While [BRATS84] analyzed the impact of large amounts of main memory on uniprocessor sorting algorithms, we believe our work is the first such investigation for multiprocessors.

For the class of external sorting algorithms that are derived as described above, we also consider several general techniques for further improving their performance. We feel that there are three techniques that have general applicability. We give examples of use of two of these three techniques to improve the performance of algorithms in the class of interest to us. The two techniques we consider are the use of ***pipelining*** and the use of ***parallel internal sorting***. The application of these techniques leads us to the discovery of an algorithm we call the ***modified block bitonic sort***.

We then present the results of analyzing the performance of these different parallel external sorting algorithms. We show that the modified block bitonic sort is the fastest of the algorithms over a wide range of values of interest to us and that it makes the best use of additional main memory buffer space.

The Architectural Model

In this paper, we are concerned with the parallel execution of sorting algorithms on multiprocessor database machines that do not have any special-purpose hardware for execution of the sorting operation [BITTO83] [VALDU84]. Such machines will have several general-purpose processors linked through a contention-free interconnection network of some sort. Each processor will have its own local memory, and all the processors also share some amount of global memory. The processors exchange data via this shared global memory which may be accessed simultaneously by several processors.

The database machines also use conventional disk drives for secondary storage. Relations (files) to be sorted are stored on these disk drives as fixed-size pages. The shared global memory is assumed to be the cache for accesses to secondary store. Then, any page stored in secondary store may be transferred and stored in any page frame in the cache. The local memory of the processors is also assumed to be page-oriented.

In general, our algorithms assume that each processor has B pages of memory associated with it. We may think of this as B pages of local memory, making a total of BP pages of local memory spread across the P processors, or we may think of it as B pages of global memory, making a total of BP pages of global memory shared by the P processors.

"A Study of Sort Algorithms for Multiprocessor Database Machines" by J. Menon from *Proc. 12th Int'l Conf. on Very Large Data Bases,* 1986, pp. 197-206. Copyright © 1986 by VLDB Endowment, Inc., reprinted with permission.

The general organization of our multiprocessor database machine is shown in Figure 1. The local memories of each processor are not shown in the figure.

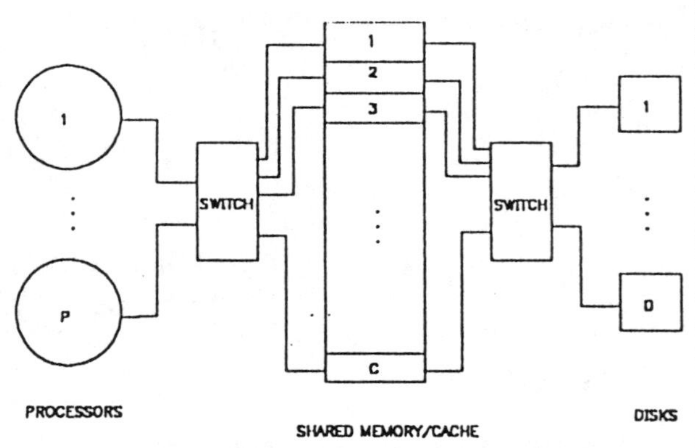

Figure 1: General Organization of a Multiprocessor Database Machine

Parallel Internal Sorting Algorithms Using Bitonic Merge

Most of the work on sorting using parallel processors [VALIA75] [PREPA78] [MULLE75] [HIRSC78] [THOMP77] [NASSI78] assume that P processors will be used to sort P records. We are more interested in considering methods which can use P processors to sort MP records, where M, which is very large, is the number of records that will fit in the local memory of each one of the P processors (alternatively, the space for MP records may be in the shared global memory).

[BAUDE78] was the first paper to consider this problem and present algorithms for sorting MP records using P processors. The class of algorithms presented in their paper was obtained by replacing every comparison-exchange step (in a sorting algorithm consisting of comparison-exchange steps) by a two-way merge. The merged sequence is split two ways, with the "lower" half sent to one destination processor, and the "upper" half sent to another destination processor.

The problem with the approach taken by [BAUDE78], is that their algorithms require each processor to have 4M memory. Thus, in order to sort MP records using P processors, they use 4MP memory. We present, below, a class of algorithms that can sort MP records using P processors, with (M+1)P memory [HSIAO80].

Our class of algorithms is also obtained from sorting algorithms that do comparison-exchanges. However, rather than replace each comparison-exchange with a two-way merge, we propose that we replace each comparison-exchange with a ***bitonic merge***. We have presented the ***bitonic merge*** principle before [BITTO84], but the particular algorithm described here, and its analysis are presented here for the first time.

An example of a bitonic merge is shown in Figure 2, where we show 2 processors, each with enough local memory to hold five records. The smallest record in P1 is compared with the largest record in P2, the smaller of the two is placed in P1's memory, the larger of the two is placed in P2's memory. Next, the second smallest record in P1's memory is compared with the second largest record in P2's memory. Once again, the smaller record is placed in P1's memory, and the larger record is placed in P2's memory. The process continues until no more exchanging is needed. At the end of these exchanges, the smallest 5 records are in P1 and the largest 5 records are in P2. The bitonic merge is complete, if P1 does a local sort of its memory and P2 does a local sort of its memory in parallel. The fact that the smallest records will be in P1 was proved by Alekseyev [KNUTH73]. He also showed that at the end of the exchanging, the M smallest records in P1 and the M largest records in P2 each form a bitonic sequence (a bitonic sequence is the concatenation of two sorted sequences, one sorted in ascending order, and one sorted in descending order). Clearly, such a bitonic sequence may be sorted by merging the two sorted subsequences from opposite ends.

Several reasons make the bitonic merge superior to the two-way merge of [BAUDE78]. First, we only require that each processor have enough memory to hold M+1 records, whereas the two-way merge requires each processor to have enough memory to hold 4M records. Second, the bitonic merge is more suitable for implementation on parallel computers that require a high degree of synchronization between their processors. Third, the two-way merge requires an entire block of data to be transferred to a processor's memory before the merge operation is initiated, whereas the bitonic merge only requires the first record to be transferred before the merge operation is initiated.

Parallel Internal Shuffle Sort

A fast parallel internal sort can be derived from Stone's algorithm [STONE71] to sort P elements using P processors in $\log_2 P$ steps, where P must be a power of two. To describe the algorithm, we use the following notation. Let EXCHANGE(i,j) represent the procedure adopted to exchange records between processor i and processor j, so that the smallest M records are in processor i's memory and the largest M records are in processor j's memory. Also, let us give each processor a binary index - with four processors, processor 0 is '00', processor 1 is '01', ... , processor three is '11'. Then, we define the ***shuffle processor*** for processor k as processor l, if l is k left-circularly shifted. Finally, we say that during a ***perfect shuffle***, each processor sends the records in its memory to the memory of its shuffle processor.

The parallel internal shuffle sort is described below for the case of P=4. In general, the algorithm consists of $\log_2 P$ stages, and each stage has $\log_2 P$ steps.

- STAGE I
  1. Perform the perfect shuffle.
  2. Perform the perfect shuffle. EXCHANGE(0,1),EXCHANGE(3,2) in parallel.
- STAGE II
  1. Perform the perfect shuffle. EXCHANGE(0,1),EXCHANGE(2,3) in parallel.
  2. Perform the perfect shuffle. EXCHANGE(0,1),EXCHANGE(3,2) in parallel.
- FINAL STEP - Do localized sorts.

Analysis of Parallel Internal Shuffle Sort

Let us use the following notation for the analysis.

P	Number of processors
M	Number of records per processor

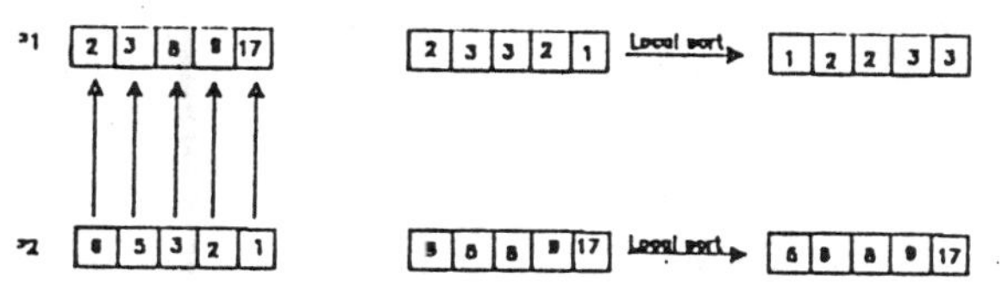

Figure 2: An Example of the Bitonic Merge

B	Number of pages per processor local memory
k	Number of records per page, M=Bk
C	Time to do a compare of two keys
V	Time to move a record in memory (or time for a complex move)

We note that the algorithm consists of one exchange step in the first stage, two exchange steps in the second stage, etc., and log P exchange steps in the final stage. Thus, there are a total of $(\frac{1}{2})(\log P)(1 + \log P)$ exchange steps. We also note that there is one final localized sort step.

For our analysis, we will assume that the k tuples inside a page are in sorted order to begin with. Then, for the first exchange, each local processor may sort the Bk records into sorted order by performing a B-way merge of the B sorted pages. The time for the B-way merge is $BkV + Bk(\log_2 B)C$. In order to complete the first exchange, processors must compare and move Bk corresponding records requiring Bk(C+V) time. Therefore, the total time for the first exchange is $BkV + Bk(\log_2 B)C + Bk(C + V)$. For each of the remaining

$$(\frac{\log_2 P}{2} + \frac{\log_2^2 P}{2} - 1)$$

exchanges, the sort step is simpler, since the sequence to be sorted is bitonic and may be sorted by merging from the two ends. The time for each of these exchanges is 2Bk(C+V). The time for the final sort step is also Bk(C+V). So, the total time for the execution of the algorithm is

$$Bk(C + V)\left[\log_2 P + \log_2^2 P\right] + BkV + Bk(\log_2 B)C$$

Parallel External Sorting Algorithms

Let us now turn our attention to parallel external sorting algorithms. These are algorithms which use P processors, each with B pages of memory (and an additional page for holding output tuples), to sort N pages, where N is much greater than B (not necessarily much greater than BP). Just as parallel internal sorting algorithms can be derived from sorting algorithms that only do compare and exchange, so also can parallel external algorithms. This fact was pointed out in [BITTO83]. In that paper, a parallel external sorting algorithm called a ***block bitonic sort*** is derived from Batcher's bitonic sort [BATCH68] by replacing each comparison-exchange with a two-way external merge of two runs of size $\frac{N}{2P}$.

Using this same idea for generating parallel external algorithms, we first present an external sorting algorithm based on the odd-even transposition sort [KNUTH73]. For the odd-even external sort, we will show how to use pipelining to arrive at a ***pipelined odd-even external sort*** which is superior in performance to the odd-even external sort. We will then examine the block bitonic sort ([BITTO83]). Using the technique of pipelining on the block bitonic sort, we will derive a ***pipelined block bitonic sort*** which, unfortunately, has inferior performance to the block bitonic sort. From that, we will draw some conclusions about the efficacy of pipelining as a general technique for performance enhancement.

In order to improve the performance of the block bitonic sort, we will the examine the idea of using parallel internal sorts.

The Parallel Odd-Even External Sort

Execution of the odd-even external sort for two processors (P = 2) and eight pages (N = 8) is illustrated in Figure 3. The class of algorithms suggested in [BITTO83] can process at most 2P runs with P processors. Therefore, a preprocessing stage is necessary when the number of pages to be sorted exceeds 2P. The function of this preprocessing stage is to produce 2P sorted runs of size $\frac{N}{2P}$ each. Since our external odd-even sort is an algorithm in the class of algorithms suggested in [BITTO83], it will also have a preprocessing stage. In our example, the preprocessing stage will produce four sorted runs of two pages each. Following this preprocessing stage, the odd-even external sort will have 2P more stages (this follows from the odd-even transposition sort), in each stage of which, the processors, in parallel, merge two runs of size $\frac{N}{2P}$.

Analysis of Parallel Odd-Even External Sort

We use the following notation, in addition to those developed for the analysis of the parallel internal sorting algorithms.

Cr	Time to read an external page
Cw	Time to write an external page
Cm	Time to merge two pages = 2k(C+V)
C_P^2	Time to read, merge and write two pages. This is equal to $2Cr + 2Cw + 2k(C + V)$.
C_P^B	Time to read, merge and write B pages. This is equal to $BCr + BCw + BkV + B(\log_2 B)kC$.

As described and analyzed in [BITTO83], the preprocessing stage consists of processors, in parallel, successively merging longer and longer pairs of runs, until the number of runs is twice the number of processors. It is the job of each processor to produce two runs of size $\frac{N}{2P}$. This will take

$$(\frac{N}{2P})\log_2(\frac{N}{2P})C_P^2$$

Then, each of the 2P steps of the odd-even external sort requires $(\frac{N}{2P})C_P^2$ steps. Therefore, the total time for the odd-even external sort is

$$((\frac{N}{2P})\log_2(\frac{N}{2P}) + N)C_P^2$$

Parallel B-ary Odd-Even External Sort

We now consider the following refinement. Until now, we had assumed that each processor had enough memory to hold 3 pages, where one page was for output, and the other two pages was to hold the input during a two-way merge. Now, let us assume that

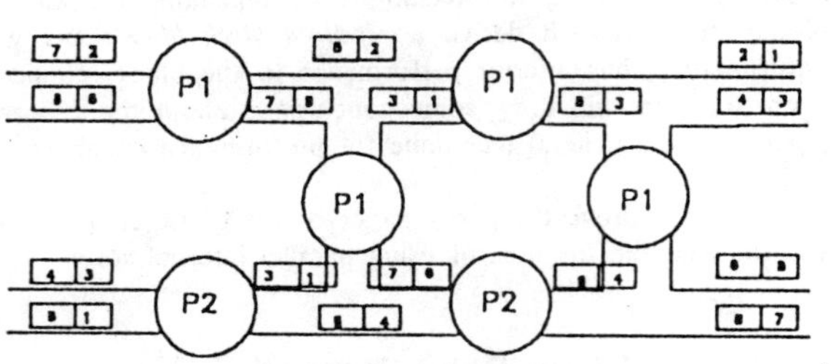

Figure 3: Illustration of the External Odd-Even Sort

each of the processors has more than 3 pages of buffer. Let each processor have B+1 pages of buffer, so that it may do a B-way merge, rather than a two-way merge. In other words, we are proposing a class of external parallel sorting algorithms that are derived by replacement of each comparison-exchange with a B-way external merge of B runs of size $\frac{N}{BP}$.

The preprocessing stage must now produce BP runs of size $\frac{N}{BP}$. Then, each of the 2P steps of the odd-even external sort requires $(\frac{N}{BP})C_P^B$ steps. Therefore, the total time for the odd-even external sort is

$$((\frac{N}{BP})\log_B(\frac{N}{BP}) + (\frac{2N}{B}))C_P^B$$

Consider the following example.

Example 1. Let N = 4096, P = 16, Cr = 6.4 msecs, Cw = 14.4 msecs, k = 40, C = .01 msecs, V = .20 msecs. Then, C_P^2 is 58.4 msecs and C_P^4 is 118.4 msecs. With these values, the time for the two-way odd-even sort is 291.5 seconds and the time for the four-way odd-even sort is 265.2 seconds. Therefore, it is attractive to do a four-way odd-even sort.

The values chosen for Cr, Cw, C and V above are those used in [BITTO83]. In general, increasing B helps to a point. Beyond that critical point, increasing B will actually hurt the performance of the odd-even external sort. The faster the CPU, and the slower the mass storage devices used, the higher the optimal value of B.

Pipelined B-ary Odd-Even External Sort

We wish to reduce the time taken to execute the 2P merge steps in the odd-even sort that follow the preprocessing stage. As it currently stands, the second merge step cannot be executed until the first step completes, the third step cannot be completed until the second step completes, and so on. However, if we had several more processors, then we could assign these extra processors to execute all the 2P steps in a pipelined fashion. Looking back at Figure 3, we see that two processors are used in the first step, one processor is used in the second step, two processors are used in the third step and one processor is used in the final step. Therefore, if we had six processors to do the odd-even sort, we could *pipeline* between the stages. As soon as the first pages of all the input runs to step 2 were available, step 2 would be started. Then, as soon as the first pages of all the input runs to step 3 were available, it would be started, and so on. This would speed up the algorithm, at the cost of additional processors.

Let us illustrate the difference between the odd-even sort and the pipelined odd-even sort by means of an example. Let P = 6 and B = 2. In the odd-even sort, we will have a preprocessing stage in which we will create 2P or 12 runs of size $\frac{N}{12}$. Then, we will execute 2P or 12 merge steps in a non-pipelined fashion. In the pipelined odd-even sort, we will have a preprocessing stage in which we will create four runs of size $\frac{N}{4}$. We will then organize the six processors in four steps (two in step 1, one in step 2, two in step 3, one in step 4). Then, we will execute four merge steps in a pipelined fashion.

Clearly, the pipelined odd-even sort takes longer during the preprocessing stage, because it needs to create longer runs. However, it makes up for the longer preprocessing stage by virtue of the fact that it only needs fewer merge steps and because these fewer merge steps can be executed in a pipelined fashion.

Analysis of Pipelined Odd-even Sort

We will do the analysis for B = 2. It is easy to show that with P processors, the pipelined odd-even sort executes the same number of merge steps as a normal odd-even sort with $K = (\frac{1+\sqrt{(1+8P)}}{4})$ processors. Thus, for example, with P = 6, the pipelined odd-even sort has the same number of merge steps as a normal odd-even sort with K = 2 processors.

In the first step of the pipelined odd-even sort, we will need to create 2K runs of size $\frac{N}{2K}$, using 2K out of the P processors. It is easy to see that $P \geq 2K$ as long as $P \geq 3$. So, if we only consider P to be three or greater, we can do this first step in

$$(\frac{N}{4K})\log_2(\frac{N}{2K})C_P^2$$

Now, we need to wait until the first pages reach the last step (there are 2K steps) of merging. This takes $(2K-1)C_P^2$ time units.

Finally, in the last step, all processors will merge two runs of size $\frac{N}{2K}$, in $(\frac{N}{2K})C_P^2$ steps.

Consider the following example.

Example 2. Let N = 24, P = 6, K = 2, and Cr, Cw, k, C and V are as in example 1. Then, the time for the odd-even sort is 26 time units, whereas the time for the pipelined odd-even sort is 3 log 6 + 9, which is 16.75 time units, and hence, better.

External Block Bitonic Sort

Next, let us consider the Block Bitonic Sort which had been described in [BITTO83]. It is derived from Batcher's bitonic sorter in the same manner as we derived the odd-even external sort from the odd-even transposition sort. The algorithm is illustrated in Figure 4, for P = 2 and N = 8. The preprocessing step is identical to that for the odd-even external sort. However, instead of 2P merge steps, the algorithm only needs $(\frac{1}{2})(\log_2 2P)(1+\log_2 2P)$ merge steps, so that its total execution time, as analyzed in [BITTO83] is

$$\left[\log_2 N + \frac{\log_2^2 2P}{2} - \frac{\log_2 2P}{2}\right](\frac{N}{2P})C_P^2$$

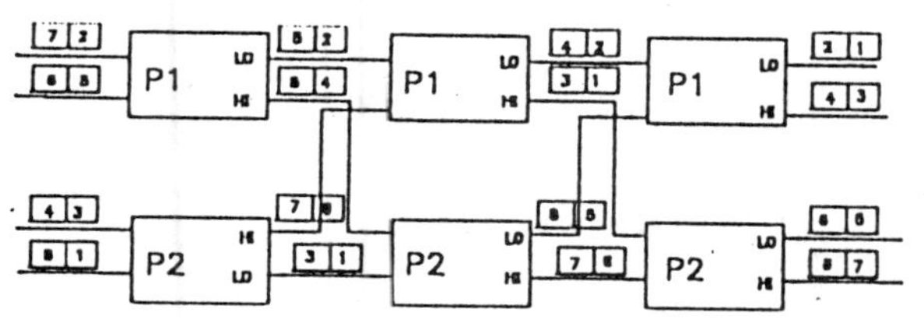

Figure 4: Illustration of the Block Bitonic Sort ([BITTO83])

We begin by improving the performance of this algorithm using B buffers, so that the total execution time now is

$$\left[\log_B\left(\frac{N}{BP}\right) + \frac{\log_2^2 2P}{2} + \frac{\log_2 2P}{2}\right]\left(\frac{N}{BP}\right)C_P^B$$

Consider the following example.

Example 3. Let N = 512, P = 8, Cr, Cw, k, C and V as in Example 1. Then, the time for the block bitonic sort with B = 2 is 28.8 seconds, whereas the time with B = 8 is 21.12 seconds.

Improving the Performance of the Block Bitonic Sort

Once again, our first avenue of exploration in the search for a better sorting algorithm is to consider the idea of pipelining. We will do the analysis for the case of B=2. The pipelined block bitonic sort will have a preprocessing stage in which 2K runs of size $\frac{N}{2K}$ are created. Subsequently, the pipelined block bitonic sort will do the merge steps in a pipelined fashion, using K processors at each stage of the pipeline. It is not difficult to see that K can be calculated by solving the equation

$$\left(\frac{K}{2}\right)(\log_2 2K)(1 + \log_2 2K) = P$$

To take an example, consider P=6, K=2. In this example, processors 3 and 4 will wait a single time unit (C_P^2) before they begin merging, and processors 5 and 6 will wait two time units before they begin merging. In general, the last processors must wait $(\frac{1}{2})(\log_2 2K)(1 + \log_2 2K) - 1$ time units before beginning merging.

To complete the analysis, let us assume that we are interested only in cases where P, the number of processors, is 6 or greater. Then, it is easy to see, from the formula for K above, that 2K is less than or equal to P. In the first step of the pipelined block bitonic sort, we will need to create 2K runs of size $\frac{N}{2K}$, using 2K out of the P processors. This will take

$$\left(\frac{N}{4K}\right)\log_2\left(\frac{N}{2K}\right)C_P^2$$

Then, we must wait

$$\left(\left(\frac{1}{2}\right)(\log_2 2K)(1 + \log_2 2K) - 1\right)C_P^2$$

time units until the last processors get pages to start merging. Finally, in the last step, all processors will merge two runs of size $\frac{N}{2K}$, in $(\frac{N}{2K})C_P^2$ steps.

Consider the following example.

Example 4. Let N = 1920, P = 80, K = 8, and Cr, Cw, K, C and V as in example 1. Then, the time for the block bitonic sort is 444 time units, whereas the time for the pipelined block bitonic sort is 609 time units.

We see that the pipelined block bitonic sort is worse than the block bitonic sort. Pipelining, as a general technique, is clearly not always rewarding - it helped the odd-even sort, but not the block bitonic sort. We have explored the idea of pipelining on other algorithms and have come to the conclusion that it is only useful when the number of merge steps in the original algorithm is high.

There are two other possible avenues of attack that may now be explored in order to improve the performance of the Block bitonic sort further. We may either improve the performance of the preprocessing stage without changing the number of merge steps needed, or we may try to decrease the number of merge steps needed without hurting the performance of the preprocessing stage. In the following sections, we will discuss the former. Details of the latter technique may be found in [MENON86].

Improving the Performance of the Preprocessing Stage

In order to improve the performance of the preprocessing stage, we suggest the use of the parallel internal sort that we developed in the section titled "Parallel Internal Shuffle Sort". Consider the case when N is very large and when $\frac{N}{BP}$ is equal to BP. Then, we may make one pass over the file, bring in BP records at a time, and sort these BP records using the parallel internal sort developed previously. After BP such internal sorts, we have completed the preprocessing stage and created BP runs of size $\frac{N}{BP}$.

Consider the following example.

Example 5. Let N = 4096, P = 16, B = 4, k = 40, Cr = 17 msecs, Cw = 17 msecs, C = 0.01 msecs and V = 0.1 msecs. In this case BP is equal to $\frac{N}{BP}$. Using the method of iterated merging, the preprocessing stage will take 35.33 seconds. This consists of approximately 26.12 seconds of I/O time and 9.21 seconds of CPU time. On the other hand, if we use the parallel internal sorts, we can accomplish the preprocessing in 34.3 seconds (25.6 CPU and 8.7 I/O). In other words, the parallel internal sort can be used to improve the performance of the preprocessing stage. The improvement is achieved by trading off CPU time for I/O time.

If the CPU is any faster or the disks are any slower than in the example, the use of the internal parallel sort for the preprocessing stage is recommended. On the other hand, if the CPU is any slower, or the disks are any faster, the method of iterated merging remains superior.

We conclude that it is possible to improve the performance of the preprocessing stage by using parallel internal sorts rather than iterated merging, as long as our processors are fairly powerful. The example shown above considered the case when the file to be sorted was larger than BP. We may also consider the case when the file to be sorted is smaller than BP. In that case, the modified bitonic sort would simply read the file into local memory, do a parallel internal sort, and then write the sorted file back to disk. On the other hand, the unmodified block bitonic sort would need to perform $(\frac{1}{2})(\log_2 2P)(1 + \log_2 2P)$ merge steps.

Consider the following example.

Example 6. Let N = 64, P = 16, B = 4, k = 40, and Cr, Cw, k, C and V as in Example 1. In this case, BP is equal to N. Using the unmodified block bitonic sort, requires 7.6032 seconds for the execution to complete. Using the modified block bitonic sort, we would need only .52 seconds. Therefore, the modified block bitonic sort can be an order of magnitude faster than the unmodified block bitonic sort. We conclude that there are situations where, even with a slow CPU and fast disks, the modified bitonic sort is still the preferred algorithm.

Analyzing the Resultant Modified Block Bitonic Sort

The algorithm consists of a preprocessing stage in which we create BP runs of size $\frac{N}{BP}$. This is followed by the merge steps which we have analyzed before. We need to analyze the time to execute the preprocessing stage, since we have modified the technique for preprocessing. We recall that the purpose of the preprocessing stage is to create BP runs of size $\frac{N}{BP}$. Let us consider three cases, and analyze the preprocessing time for each of the three cases.

The first case is when N (the number of elements to be sorted) is less than BP (the number of elements that can be sorted internally). Using the formula developed in "Parallel Internal Shuffle Sort", it is easy to see that the internal sorting time is:

$$(\frac{N}{P})k(C+V)\left[\log_2 P + \log_2^2 P\right] + (\frac{N}{P})kV + (\frac{N}{P})k(\log_2 B)C$$

In addition, we must add the time to read and write the N pages to be sorted (each processor reads and writes $\frac{N}{P}$ pages) which is $(\frac{N}{P})(Cr + Cw)$. So, the total time for the preprocessing stage for the case when N is less than BP is

$$(\frac{N}{P})k(C+V)\left[\log_2 P + \log_2^2 P\right] +$$

$$(\frac{N}{P})kV + (\frac{N}{P})k(\log_2 B)C + (\frac{N}{P})(Cr + Cw)$$

In this case, there is no need for a subsequent merge stage. Therefore, the total time for sorting is as above.

Next, let us consider the case when N is greater than BP, but it is less than or equal to B^2P^2. In this case, the preprocessing stage will consist of BP passes, and each pass will consist of a parallel internal sort of $\frac{N}{BP}$ elements. At the end of these BP passes, we will have the required BP runs of size $\frac{N}{BP}$. Since N is less than or equal to B^2P^2, so $\frac{N}{BP}$ is less than or equal to BP. Assume $\frac{N}{BP}$ is equal to XP. Then, the time for each pass is

$$Xk(C+V)\left[\log_2 P + \log_2^2 P\right] +$$

$$XkV + Xk(\log_2 B)C + X(Cr + Cw)$$

The total sort has BP passes and must include the time for merging and is

$$(\frac{N}{P})k(C+V)\left[\log_2 P + \log_2^2 P\right] +$$

$$(\frac{N}{P})kV + (\frac{N}{P})k(\log_2 B)C + (\frac{N}{P})(Cr + Cw)$$

$$+(\frac{1}{2})(\log_2 2P)(1 + \log_2 2P)C_P^B$$

Finally, we consider the case when N is greater than B^2P^2 or $\frac{N}{BP}$ is greater than BP. In this case, we will begin by creating $\frac{N}{BP}$ runs of size BP each. This is done by making $\frac{N}{BP}$ internal sorts, each internal sort creating runs of size. BP. Now, each processor can take runs of size BP and create runs of size B^2P, then take runs of size B^2P and create runs of size B^3P, and so on until runs of size $\frac{N}{BP}$ are created. It can be shown that the total time, including merging is

$$(\frac{N}{P})k(C+V)\left[\log_2 P + \log_2^2 P\right] +$$

$$(\frac{N}{P})kV + (\frac{N}{P})k(\log_2 B)C + (\frac{N}{P})(Cr + Cw)$$

$$+(\log_B(\frac{(\frac{N}{BP})}{BP}))(\frac{N}{BP})(C_B^P) + (\frac{1}{2})(\log_2 2P)(1 + \log_2 2P)C_P^B$$

Comparative Analysis of External Sorting Algorithms

In this section, we present the results of a comparative analysis of the different algorithms that we have presented. The numerical results for the execution times of the different sorting algorithms are obtained from APL programs that were written to calculate them based on the equations derived in the previous sections. For all the results presented in the following sections, we assumed that Cr and Cw, the times to read and write a page from the disk was 17 msecs, that k the number of tuples (records) per page was 40, that C, the time to compare two keys was .01 msecs, and that V, the time to move a record in memory was .1 msecs.

First, we compare the pipelined odd-even sort, the block bitonic sort, and the modified block bitonic sort. Since the pipelined odd-even sort was only analyzed with B the number of buffers equal to two, we only present results for B=2.

Comparing the Pipelined Odd-Even Sort With the Bitonic Sorts

The results of our comparison are shown in Figures 5, 6, 7, and 8. In these graphs, 1 is the block bitonic sort, 2 is the modified block bitonic sort and 3 is the pipelined odd-even sort.

From the first two graphs, we see that the sorting time for all three methods increases with the size of the relation being plotted. These graphs also tell us that the pipelined odd-even sort is inferior to the two block bitonic sorts except for very low number of processors when all the three methods are approximately equivalent in performance.

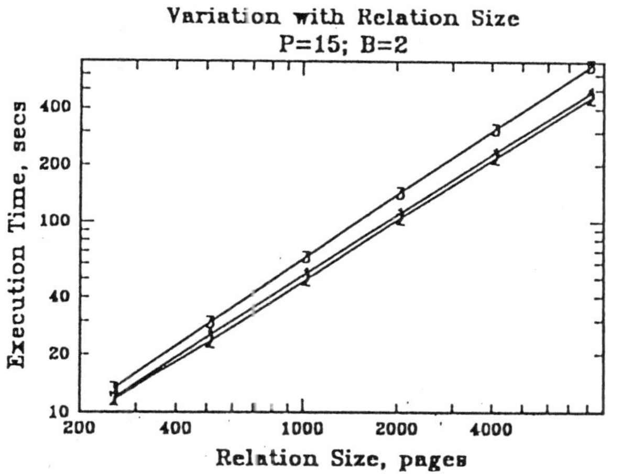

Figure 5: Execution Time Versus Relation Size for Sorting Methods

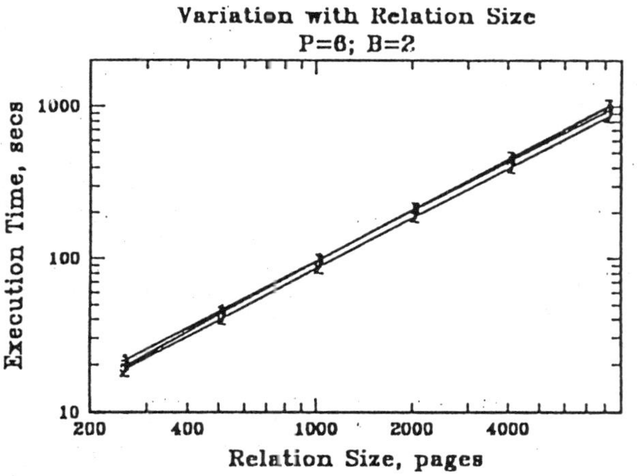

Figure 6: Execution Time Versus Relation Size for Sorting Methods

Looking at the latter two graphs, we see that all the sorting algorithms improve in performance when they can use more processors. Once again, it is clear that the pipelined odd-even sort is inferior to the other two sorting methods, except for very low number of processors when it actually outperforms the block bitonic sort.

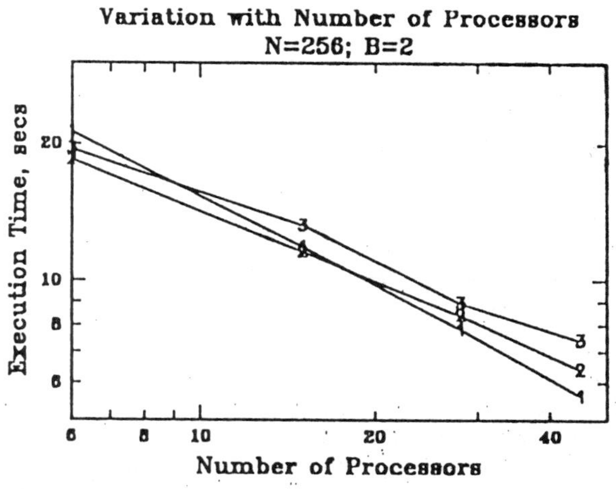

Figure 7: Execution Time Versus Number of Processors

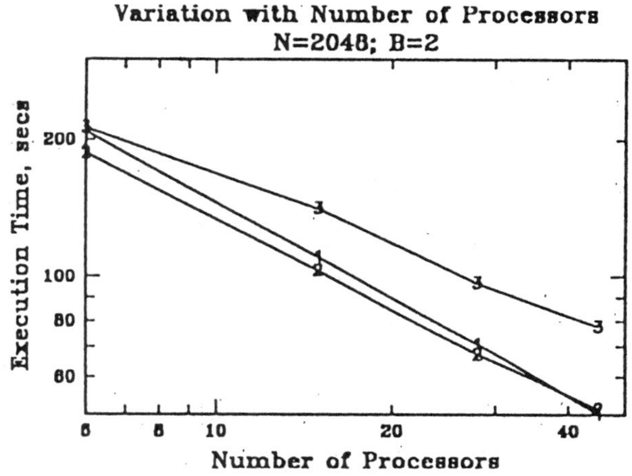

Figure 8: Execution Time Versus Number of Processors

For the chosen values of the parameters, there does not appear to be much difference in performance between the block bitonic sort and the modified block bitonic sort. The modified block bitonic sort is slightly better for small number of processors (less than 20 when the relation size is small (256 pages) and less than 40 when the relation size is large (2048 pages). It also appears better when the relation sizes to be sorted are large. The block bitonic sort appears to be slightly better for large number of processors and small relation sizes.

Comparing the Odd-Even Sort With the Block Bitonic Sorts

In this section, we show the odd-even sort, rather than the pipelined odd-even sort, for a couple of reasons. First, we were able to analyze the pipelined odd-even sort only for B=2, whereas the other sorting methods were analyzed for all values of B. Secondly, we found that while the pipelined odd-even sort was better than the odd-even sort, when compared against the performance of the block bitonic sorts, it looked as bad as the odd-even sort.

In Figures 9, 10 and 11, we show the variation in execution time with the size of the relation being sorted. In these graphs, 1 is the block bitonic sort, 2 is the odd-even sort, and 3 is the modified block bitonic sort. The odd-even sort is clearly the most inferior of the three algorithms. The relative performance of the bitonic sorts is more interesting. In Figure 9, we see that the modified block bitonic sort outperforms the block bitonic sort when the size of the relation to be sorted is less than about 1000 pages, and in Figure 10, we see that the modified block bitonic sort outperforms the block bitonic sort when the size of the relation to be sorted is less than about 8000 pages. For other values of the relation size, the two methods are approximately equal in performance. In general, it is seen that the modified block bitonic sort outperforms the other methods when the size of the relation to be sorted is smaller than, equal to, or slightly greater than the product of the number of processors P and the number of buffers B. For other values of the various parameters, the performance of the modified block bitonic sort is almost equal to that of the unmodified block bitonic sort. In summary, the modified block bitonic sort is superior for very large values of P and B, or very small values of N. From the previous section, we are also aware that the modified block bitonic sort is superior for very large values of N, and very small values of P.

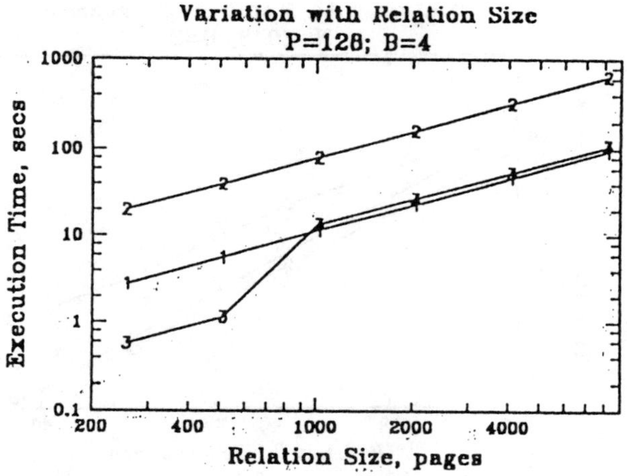

Figure 9: Execution Time Versus Relation Size for Sorting Methods

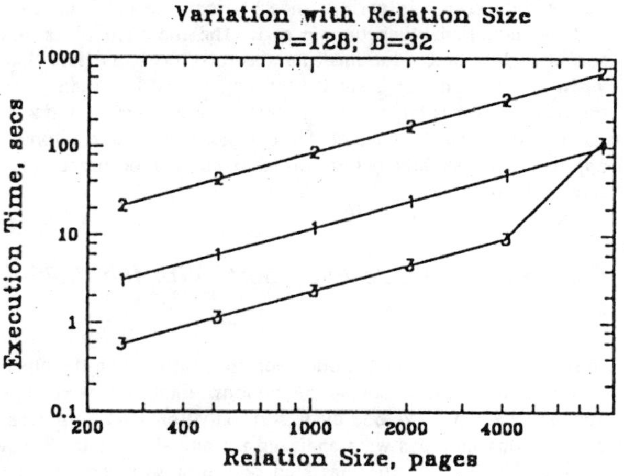

Figure 10: Execution Time Versus Relation Size for Sorting Methods

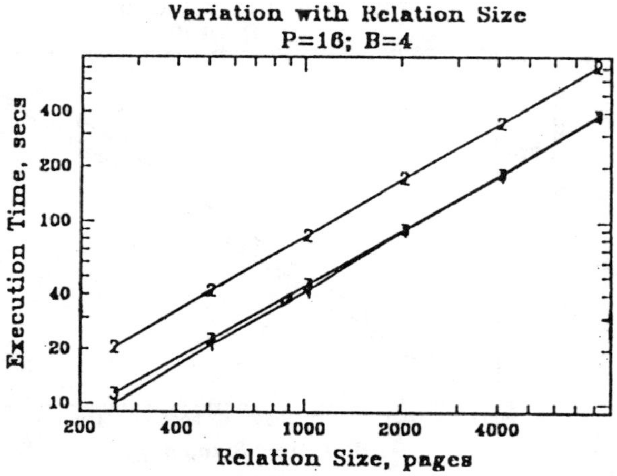

Figure 11: Execution Time Versus Relation Size for Sorting Methods

In Figure 12, we show the variation in execution time with the number of processors involved in the sorting. Once again, it may be seen that the modified block bitonic sort and the unmodified block bitonic sort are almost equal in performance until a threshold number of processors is reached. Beyond this threshold number of processors, the modified block bitonic sort is the best performer. The threshold is reached when there are enough processors so that the total size of the records to be sorted only slightly exceeds the total capacity of the combined memories in the multiprocessor given by B times P. The performance of the modified block bitonic sort is seen to improve even when the number of processors is increased beyond the threshold number of processors we described above.

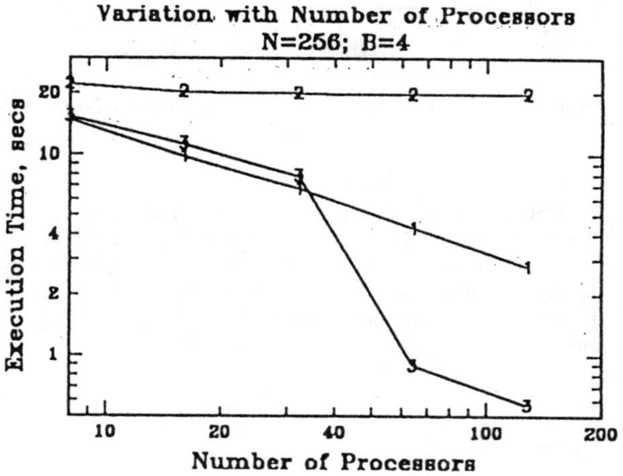

Figure 12: Execution Time Versus Number of Processors

Finally, in Figures 13 and 14, we show the variation in execution time with the number of buffers available per processor. It is seen that the odd-even sort and the unmodified block bitonic sorts exhibit a very mild bowl-shaped behavior - that is, increasing the number of buffers helps to a point. Increasing the number of buffers beyond that point actually hurts the performance of these algorithms.

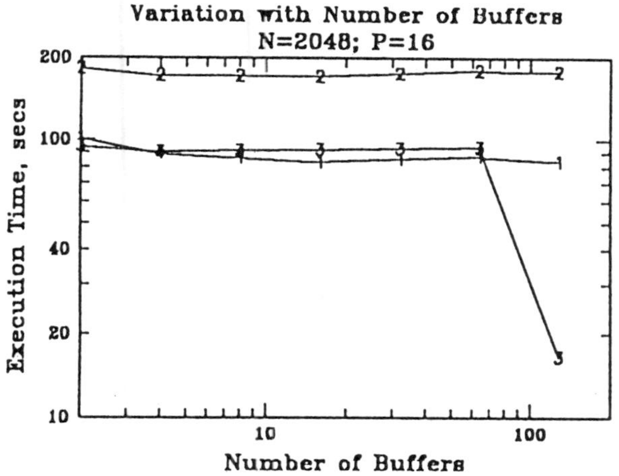

Figure 13: Execution Time Versus Number of Buffers

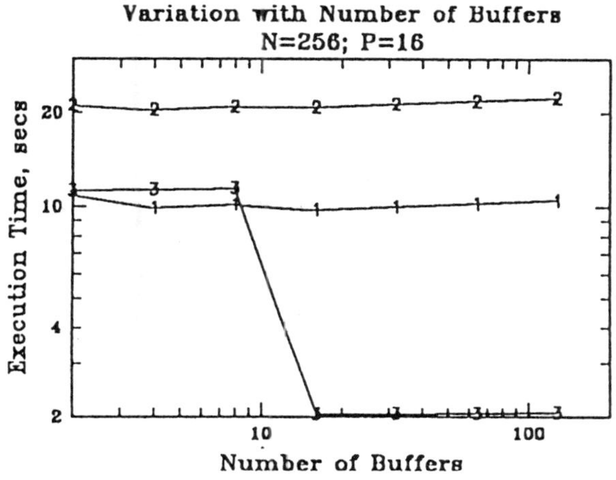

Figure 14: Execution Time Versus Number of Buffers

The modified block bitonic sort exhibits a very different kind of behavior. It begins with the same bowl-shaped behavior. However, beyond a certain buffer size, its performance improves dramatically. Once again, this buffer size beyond which the dramatic performance improvement takes place is when the total size of the records to be sorted only slightly exceeds the total capacity of the combined memories in the multiprocessor given by B times P.

Finally, we note that the modified block bitonic sort is the only algorithm that can make use of buffer sizes in excess of about 8 or 16 pages (for example 64 pages in Figure 13).

Conclusions and Summary

In this paper, we have studied the problem of sorting using multiple processors. Both internal sorting and external sorting have been considered. For internal sorting, we presented an algorithm that uses the idea of ***bitonic merging***.

For external sorting algorithms, we have studied the class of sorting algorithms that are derived from sorting algorithms that only do comparison and exchange, by replacing each comparison-exchange with a B-way merge. For this class of algorithms, we have suggested three and studied two techniques for improving performance - the use of ***pipelining*** and the use of ***parallel internal sorting***. These are general techniques that may be used to improve the performance of any of the algorithms in the class of algorithms of interest to us.

For pipelining, we concluded that it may be used to improve the performance of those algorithms that have a large number of merge steps, but is less useful for those algorithms where the number of merge steps is not very large.

We have also shown how to improve the block bitonic sort by using parallel internal sorting, and called our new algorithm the ***modified block bitonic sort***.

We have analyzed and studied the performance of several sorting algorithms under various conditions. We believe that our work represents the first attempt to study the variation in performance of multiprocessor sorting algorithms with changing buffer size. This study is important given that memory costs are dropping, making it quite feasible to build multiprocessors with large buffers. We showed that the odd-even and the unmodified block bitonic sorts exhibit a very mild bowl-shaped behavior - that is, increasing the number of buffers helps to a point. Increasing the number of buffers beyond that point actually hurts the performance of these algorithms. The modified block bitonic sort, on the other hand, behaves differently. It initially exhibits the same, mild, bowl-shaped behavior. However, beyond a certain buffer size, its performance improves dramatically. This buffer size beyond which the dramatic performance improvement takes place is when the total size of the records to be sorted only slightly exceeds the total capacity of the combined memories in the multiprocessor.

We saw that the modified block bitonic sort is much better than all the other methods for very large values of P (the number of processors) and B (the number of buffers per processor minus 1), or very small values of N (the size of the relation being sorted). We also saw that the modified block bitonic sort is slightly better than the other methods for very large values of N, and very small values of P (less than 20 to 40). For other values of N, B, and P, the modified block bitonic sort is slightly worse in performance than the block bitonic sort which is the best sorting algorithm under those conditions.

Our results show that the modified block bitonic sort is the fastest or close to the fastest algorithm over a wide range of values among the class of algorithms of interest to us. Furthermore, of all the algorithms we considered in this paper, the modified block bitonic sort made the best use of additional main memory buffers.

Bibliography

[BABBE79] Babb, E., Implementing a Relational Database by Means of Specialized Hardware, *ACM Transactions on Database Systems* **4**, **No.1** (March 1979) pp. 1-29.

[BATCH68] Batcher, K. E., Sorting Networks and their Applications, *Proceedings of the 1968 Spring Joint Computer Conference* **32** (Atlantic City, N. J., May 1968) pp. 307-314.

[BAUDE78] Baudet, G. and Stevenson, D., Optimal Sorting Algorithms for Parallel Computers, *IEEE-TC* C-27, No.1 (Jan. 1978).

[BITTO83] Bitton, D., Boral, H., Dewitt, D. J., and Wilkinson, W. K., Parallel Algorithms for the Execution of Relational Database Operations, *ACM Transactions on Database Systems* **8, No. 3** (Sept 1983).

[BITTO84] Bitton, D., Dewitt, D. J., Hsiao, D. K., and Menon, M. J., A Taxonomy of Parallel Sorting, *Computing Surveys* **16, No.3** (Sep. 1984).

[BRATS84] Bratsbergsengen, K., Hashing Methods and Relational Algebra Operations, *Proceedings of Tenth International Conference on VLDB* (Singapore, August 1984).

[DEWIT79] Dewitt, D. J., Query Execution in DIRECT, *Proceedings of ACM SIGMOD Conference* (New York, May 1979).

[GARDA81] Gardarin, G., An Introduction to SABRE: a multimicroprocessor database machine, *Sixth Workshop on Computer Architecture for Non-numeric Processing* (Hyeres, France, June 1981).

[HIRSC78] Hirschberg, D. S., Fast Parallel Sorting Algorithms, *Communications of the ACM* **21, No.8** (Aug. 1978).

[HSIAO80] Hsiao, D. K., and Menon, M. J., Parallel Record Sorting Methods for Hardware Realization, Technical Report, OSU-CISRC-TR-80-7, Computer and Information Science Department, Ohio State University, Columbus, Ohio (July 1980).

[KNUTH73] Knuth, D. E., *The Art of Computer Programming*, Addison Wesley (Reading, 1973).

[MENON86] Menon, M. J., A Study of Sort Algorithms for Multiprocessor Database Machines, IBM Research report RJ-5047 (Feb. 1986).

[MULLE75] Muller, D. E., and Preparata, F. P., Bounds to Complexities of Networks for Sorting and for Switching, *Journal of the ACM* **22, No. 2** (Apr. 1975).

[NASSI78] Nassimi, D., and Sahni, S., Bitonic Sort on a Mesh Connected Parallel Computer, *IEEE Transactions on Computers* **C-27, No. 1** (Jan. 1978).

[PREPA78] Preparata, F. P., New Parallel Sorting Schemes, *IEEE Transactions on Computers* **C-27, No. 7** (July 1978).

[STONE71] Stone, H. S., Parallel Processing with the Perfect Shuffle, *IEEE Transactions on Computers* **C-20,2** (Feb. 1971).

[THOMP77] Thompson, C. D., and Kung, H. T., Sorting on a Mesh-Connected Parallel Computer, *Communications of the ACM* **20, 4** (Apr. 1977).

[VALDU84] Valduriez, P. and Gardarin, G., Join and Semi-Join Algorithms for a Multiprocessor Database Machine, *ACM Transactions on Database Systems* **9, No. 1** (March 1984).

[VALIA75] Valiant, L. G., Parallelism in Comparison Problems, *SIAM Journal of Computing* **3, No. 4** (Sept. 1975).

Parallel Sorting on a Shared-Nothing Architecture using Probabilistic Splitting

David J. DeWitt* Jeffrey F. Naughton* Donovan A. Schneider†

Abstract

We consider the problem of external sorting in a shared-nothing multiprocessor. A critical step in the algorithms we consider is to determine the range of sort keys to be handled by each processor. We consider two techniques for determining these ranges of sort keys: *exact splitting*, using a parallel version of the algorithm proposed by Iyer, Ricard, and Varman; and *probabilistic splitting*, which uses sampling to estimate quantiles. We present analytic results showing that probabilistic splitting performs better than exact splitting. Finally, we present experimental results from an implementation of sorting via probabilistic splitting in the Gamma parallel database machine.

1 Introduction

In this paper we consider the problem of external sorting in a shared-nothing parallel database system. "Shared-nothing" means that the database system is implemented on top of a multiprocessor in which each processor has its own local memory and disk, and all communication between processors must take place through an interconnection network. The specific sorting problem we address is "multiple-input multiple-output" sorting. In this sorting problem, initially the data in the file to be sorted is on disk, distributed throughout the multiprocessor, and unsorted. At the termination of the sorting algorithm, the file must again be on disk, but partitioned into approximately equal sized non-overlapping sorted runs, one at each processor.

At the top level, an algorithm for this problem is: (1) Determine a "splitting vector" that would partition the sorted file into approximately equal-sized subfiles, one subfile per processor. (2) Based upon this splitting vector, redistribute the records in the file so that each record is at the appropriate processor. (3) After this redistribution, locally sort the records on each processor to produce the final result. In this paper we consider two different approaches to determining the splitting vector. The first approach, which we call "exact splitting," is due to Iyer, Ricard, and Varman [IRV89]. (An earlier paper due to Yamane and Take [YT88] proposes a similar algorithm with the same asymptotic running time as the algorithm of Iyer, Ricard, and Varman. However, since the description in Yamane and Take is not sufficiently detailed to estimate anything other than rough asymptotic running times, we chose the algorithm due to Iyer et al. for this study.) "Exact splitting" deterministically computes a splitting vector such that each processor is allocated the same number of records (plus or minus one). The second approach, which we call "probabilistic splitting," computes an approximate splitting vector by sampling the unsorted file. As we discuss below, probabilistic splitting and similar techniques have apparently been discovered and rediscovered many times in the sorting literature, but to our knowledge have never been carefully studied in the context of external parallel sorting.

We show, using an analytical model, that on shared-nothing parallel systems, probabilistic splitting beats exact splitting. Furthermore, we present scaleup, speedup, and sizeup experimental data from an implementation of sorting using probabilistic splitting on the Gamma database machine.

In related work on parallel external sorting, Salzberg et al. [STG+90] present a parallel sort-merge algorithm for single-input single-output sorting. A parallel sort-merge has the benefit that it is not necessary to compute a splitting vector; however, sort-merge is probably not appropriate in a multiple-input multiple-output sort, since the final merge cannot be accomplished faster than a sequential pass through the entire file. Beck et al. [BBW88] describes a similar sort. Other earlier algorithms that also used a final sequential merge phase include Bitton et al. [BBDW83], and Valduriez and Gar-

*Computer Sciences Department, University of Wisconsin at Madison

†Hewlett Packard Labs, Palo Alto, CA

Reprinted from *Proceedings First Int'l Conf. Parallel and Distributed Information Systems*, 1991, pp. 280-291.

0-8186-5452-X/94 $3.00 © 1991 IEEE

darin [VG84].

Graefe [Gra90] presents a thorough description of the implementation and evaluation of a multiple-input, multiple-output sorting algorithm for a shared-memory multiprocessor. This algorithm uses a splitting vector. Graefe suggests that this splitting vector might be computable by sampling, but he does not investigate this alternative. His experimental results assume that the splitting vector is known exactly before the algorithm is run.

As noted previously, the idea of sorting using an approximate splitting vector obtained by sampling has been invented and re-invented many times in the sorting literature. Frazer and McKellar [FM70] proposed a uniprocessor internal sort based upon sampling. They showed that asymptotically, given some restrictions on the distribution of the data being sorted, their algorithm runs in linear time. Distributive Sorting, a recursive bucket sort based upon sampling, has some similarities with sorting via probabilistic splitting as well. Dobosiewicz [Dob78] originally proposed the algorithm and proved that if the data is uniformly distributed, it runs in time $O(n)$. Later, Janus and Lamagna [JL85] proposed a fix to distributive sorting that uses sampling to provide better performance for non-uniform data distributions. They did not investigate a parallel implementation of the algorithm. Quinn [Qui88] has suggested implementing a parallel quicksort as follows: to sort on k processors, choose $k-1$ pivot elements at random, and run the recursive quicksorts in parallel. His experiments showed zero speedup beyond 10 processors, because of the skew in the sizes of the arguments to the recursive quicksorts.

Huang and Chow [HC83] consider parallel external sorting using approximate partitioning based upon sampling. Using combinatorial analysis they present analytic formulas showing good asymptotic performance, but did not implement their approach or compare it to any other. Baugstø and Greipsland [BG89] also consider parallel external sorting using approximate partitioning based upon synchronized sampling of sorted subfiles. In more detail, in their algorithm, they implement sampling as follows: first, each processor sorts its local file fragment. Next, each processor samples some fraction of the fragment by looking at every kth record for some predetermined k. The resulting set of samples is then sorted and a partitioning vector is formed. Baugstø and Greipsland do not discuss how to analyze the quality of the resulting partitioning vector or how to determine what fraction of the file should be sampled. Lorie and Young [LY89] describe an algorithm for multiple-input, single-output sorting. Their algorithm uses a splitting vector, which they suggest might be computable by some statistical technique. In an example they appear to be using a technique virtually identical to that of Baugstø and Greipsland, but the technique is not further described. In the analytic data presented, Lorie and Young assume that the splitting vector is known exactly before the algorithm begins.

Most recently, in work done concurrently with and independently from the work presented in this paper, Blelloch et al. [BLM+91] investigated internal sorting algorithms for a 2048 processor CM-2. They concluded (through experimental and analytic comparisons) that probabilistic splitting followed by local radix sorts provided the highest performance, beating a parallel bitonic sort and a parallel radix sort.

The remainder of this paper is organized as follows. Sections 2 and 3 describes the probabilistic and exact partitioning algorithms, and gives a cost model for each. Section 4 uses these cost models to compare the performance of the two. Section 5 describes our implementation of probabilistic splitting in the Gamma parallel database machine, and Section 6 presents the results of experiments on that implementation.

2 Probabilistic Splitting

Algorithm Description

Probabilistic splitting is based upon a simple idea: to find an approximate splitting vector for the file, compute a random subset of the file; find an exact splitting vector for the random subset; finally, use this exact splitting vector for the subset as an approximate splitting vector for the whole file. While this idea is simple, some care must be taken in evaluating the quality of this approximate splitting vector. Let s, for skew, denote the ratio of the maximum number of records at any site to the average number of records at a site. If we have k processors, and N records in the file to be sorted, then the average number of records per processor is N/k. Then by definition of s, the maximum number of records at any site is sN/k. By Theorem 7.1 from Seshadri and Naughton [SN91], if we take a total of kn samples, then the probability p that any processor contains more than sN/k keys is at most $p = ke^{-(1-1/s)^2 sn/2}$. Solving this for n gives

$$n = \frac{2\ln(k/p)}{(1-1/s)^2 s} \qquad (1)$$

as the number of samples required to guarantee a skew of at most s with probability $1-p$.

Trading Samples for Skew

To complete the description of probabilistic splitting, we need to describe how to find the optimal value of the skew s. Setting s too small will result in poor performance due to the cost of too many samples in the sampling phase; setting s too large will result in poor performance due to the uneven sizes of the subproblems sent to the processors in later phases of the algorithm.

Finding this optimal s is an optimization problem, and to set up and solve this optimization problem, we need cost estimates for the various phases of the algorithm. The cost model developed below is extremely simple, and as such should not be interpreted as an attempt to predict absolute numbers for running times for the algorithm. Our intent is that although the model is not sufficiently precise to yield accurate absolute running times, it will be good enough to predict which choice among a set of alternatives can be expected to give the best performance. This is analogous to the situation with query optimizers, where optimizers are often successful in choosing a good evaluation plan even though their cost estimates are not accurate in an absolute sense.

The main simplifying assumptions we make are that there is no overlap between I/O operations, CPU operations, or network traffic, that there is no contention in the network, and that the work of the individual nodes of the machine (including I/O, CPU, and network) is done completely in parallel with the other nodes of the machine. These assumptions allow us to consider that the time for a single node to perform its segment of the computation is the total time for the multiprocessor to perform the full computation.

COMP	0.012	ms. to compare keys
KS	0.036	ms. to exchange two keys
MOVE	0.053	ms. to move a record
IO_S	44.000	ms. to do a sequential IO
IO_R	50.000	ms. to do a random IO
MSG	1.000	ms. to send and receive msg
SAMPLE	120.000	ms. to take a random sample

Table 1: Parameters for the cost model.

We used the set of parameters in Table 1 in the cost model. These parameters are based upon measurements from the Gamma parallel database machine. Many of these times are higher than we had guessed before measuring them in the system. The COMP time is high because for comparisons we used the general purpose Gamma `compare_key()` routine, which works for keys of arbitrary type at arbitrary positions within a tuple. The MOVE times are measurements for moving a tuple from one slotted page to another slotted page, which incurs additional overhead when compared to a simple Unix `bcopy()`. The I/O times were for 32K byte pages. Finally, in general each sample involved two random IOs: one for the index page to locate the data page for the randomly selected tuple, and another for the data page itself.

Furthermore, we use the following notation:

B	num. records per page
P	num. bytes per page (mem and disk)
M	num. pages main memory
N	num. records in the file
k	num. of processors

The most interesting case to consider here is the case where the multiprocessor can sort the file in two passes. This requires only that each processor's buffer space exceeds the square root of the number of file pages it is allocated, which allows very large files. For example, if each processor has 100 pages available for sorting, then each processor can sort a 10000 page subfile. With 32 processors, and 8K byte pages, the multiprocessor can sort a two gigabyte file in two passes. The table on page 95 in [STG+90] gives more examples of how large a file can be sorted in two passes for various memory sizes.

In this case (the two-pass case), at the top level the algorithm works as follows:

1. In parallel, the processors sample their fragment of the disk-resident file.

2. In parallel, the processors sort their samples, then send the samples to a single processor, where the sorted sets of samples are merged. Then an approximate splitting vector is computed from the total sorted set of samples, and this splitting vector is broadcasted to the other processors.

3. In parallel, the processors read their fragment of the file, and using the splitting vector, redistribute the records to the appropriate processor.

4. When a processor's memory has filled with incoming records, the processor sorts these records, writes a sorted run to disk, then continues reading incoming records.

5. In parallel, the processors merge the sorted runs from the disk and back onto the disk.

We now consider the cost for each step in turn. For concreteness, we use $n = \frac{2\ln(k/0.99)}{(1-1/s)^2 s}$, which is the expected number of samples required per processor to guarantee a skew of s with 99% certainty. Then

Step 1: Sampling takes time $n * \text{SAMPLE}$.

Step 2: Sorting each local set of sampled keys, assuming that we use an in-memory heapsort to do so, takes

$$n * \log_2(n) * (\text{KS} + \text{COMP})$$

CPU time. Next, these local sets of sampled keys must be gathered at a single node and sorted there. The simplest way to do this is to have each processor send a message to the designated processor, then to have this processor do a total sort. A more efficient way is to embed a binary tree in the hypercube. Then initially the leaves send their sorted samples to their parents, where the two sets of samples are merged. Next, the parents send these sets of samples to their parents, and so on, until the root of the tree has the complete sorted set of samples. The total time from the initiation of the sort at the leaves until the completion of the final merge at the root of the tree is given by $n \log_2(n) * (\text{KS} + \text{COMP})$ to sort the initial sets of samples at each processor, plus $2n(k-1) * (\text{COMP} + \text{MOVE})$ to do the merges up the tree. The time for the merges is computed as follows. The parents of the leaves merge two files of size n, at a cost of $2n * (\text{COMP} + \text{MOVE})$; the grandparents of the leaves merge two files of size $2n$, and so on, until the root merges two files of size $2^{\log_2(k)-1}n$. The sum of these quantities is $2n(k-1) * (\text{COMP} + \text{MOVE})$. Also, the network cost to gather the samples is $\log_2(k) * \text{MSG}$ seconds, and the network cost to broadcast the resulting splitting vector to all k processors will take another $\log_2(k) * \text{MSG}$ seconds.

Step 3: While actually partitioning the source file, we will assume that, for each record r, a processor does a binary search of the splitting vector to determine to which processor r belongs, then copies r to a buffer page for tuples bound for that processor. The cost for this step is

$$\frac{N}{kB} * \text{IO}_\text{S} + (N/k) * (\log_2(k-1) * \text{COMP} + \text{MOVE})$$

Finally, to ship the data will take time $\frac{N}{kB} * \text{MSG}$.

Step 4: For the sort of incoming records, note that each processor can hold MB records in its memory, and it must sort this many records $s\frac{N}{kBM}$ times, where the extra factor of s comes from the skew. Assuming that the sort is done by heapsorting (key,ptr) pairs, then copying records to their final position, the cost is

$$s\frac{N}{kBM}((MB) * (\log_2(MB)) * (\text{KS} + \text{COMP}))$$

to sort the keys and

$$s\frac{N}{kBM}((MB) * \text{MOVE} + M * \text{IO}_\text{S})$$

to move the records to the output buffers and write them to disk.

Step 5: In the final merge, the processor with the heaviest load will have $s\frac{N}{kBM}$ runs of MB records each, so the time spent will be

$$s\frac{N}{kBM}M * \text{IO}_\text{R}$$

to read in the runs and

$$s\frac{N}{kBM}((MB) * \log_2(s\frac{N}{kMB})(\text{KS} + \text{COMP}))$$

to do the compares during the merge and finally

$$s\frac{N}{kBM}((MB) * \text{MOVE} + M * \text{IO}_\text{S})$$

to copy the records to the output pages and then write them to disk.

Gathering together all the terms that depend on the skew s, we get an equation for the cost as a function of the skew. This expression involves terms in s, $1/s$, $1/s^2$, and $\log_2(s)$. To determine an optimal skew (and hence an optimal number of samples) we could use a numeric method to find roots of the derivative of this equation; however, it is simpler to just compute $c(s)$ for a reasonable range of skews (say $s = 1.0$ to 2.0 by increments of 0.01) and return the value of s that gave the smallest $c(s)$. This value of s can then be used to determine the appropriate number of samples to take. We implemented this approach of searching for the best value of s, and found that over a wide range of numbers of processors and a wide range of problem sizes, taking 100 samples per processor was close to optimal. This result is supported by our experiments with the implementation, reported in Section 6.

Although our goal was not to predict absolute performance numbers, a comparison of the predicted numbers and the measured numbers in our implementation show that the two are in fairly good agreement — the analytic model underestimates the experimental results by about 10%.

3 Exact Splitting

In this section we consider the algorithm proposed by Iyer et al. for finding an exact splitting vector. The complete algorithm is rather complex; see Iyer [IRV89] for details. We have adapted some of the steps for a shared-nothing multiprocessor, since the original algorithm was designed with shared memory in mind. Our goal in this section is to present enough of the algorithm to give the intuition behind it and also to justify our model of its cost.

As in the probabilistic splitting section, assume that we have k processors and that the file has N records. The first step of the exact splitting algorithm is that each processor fully sorts its fragment of the file, producing k sorted runs, one per processor. Recall that our overall goal is to compute a $k-1$-element splitting vector that divides the entire file into k equally sized segments.

The algorithm can perhaps best be explained in terms of how it computes a single splitting element. Suppose that we wish to find the sort-key value that partitions the entire file into two segments, one containing the initial fN records of the entire sorted file, the other containing the last $(1-f)N$ records of the entire sorted file. Furthermore, assume that $f \leq 0.5$ (the case $f > 0.5$ is symmetric.) Then the algorithm proceeds as follows:

1. Each processor selects $(1-f)/f$ equally spaced elements from its sorted run. (Note that these are not randomly chosen elements; they are chosen at equal intervals from the sorted run.)

2. Each of the processors sends its $(1-f)/f$ elements to a single processor, which merges the elements and then computes the exact f splitting value for these $k(1-f)/f$ elements.

3. This exact f splitting value is broadcasted to all k processors.

4. Each processor determines the pair of elements from the $(1-f)/f$ elements chosen in Step 1 that bracket the broadcasted splitting value.

5. The processors do a form of coordinated binary search on the records in the intervals between these "bracketing" elements to determine the exact splitting value for the whole file. In more detail, suppose that on the previous iteration, the splitting value was determined to be v, and that for $1 \leq i \leq k$, processor p_i has determined that records u_i and l_i in sorted order bracket this value v. On the current iteration, for $1 \leq i \leq k$, each processor reads element $(u_i + l_i)/2$ in the sorted order, and sends this element to one coordinating processor, which then determines a new splitting value v'. This process continues until $u_i = l_i$ for $1 \leq i \leq k$, at which point the current v is guaranteed to be an exact f splitting value for the entire file.

The last step of this description is actually greatly simplified — it is not guaranteed that at any time in the algorithm, the true final splitting value will indeed be bracketed by the current u_i and l_i. In general, the algorithm must search forward or backward outside of this interval. However, what we have given, the case in which the exact splitting value is always bracketed by u_i and l_i, is the best case in that it results in the fewest number of records read. (In terms of the description in Iyer et al. [IRV89], we are assuming the cases 2 and 3 on pages 138–139 never occur.)

Recall that this just describes how to find a single element of the splitting vector $v[i]$. To compute the full vector, the previous algorithm is repeated for $f = 1/k, 2/k, \ldots, (k-1)/k$. These k iterations make the work per processor in exact splitting proportional to the number of processors in the system.

We now develop a simple analytic model for the performance of a sorting algorithm that uses exact splitting. As was the case in the model for probabilistic splitting, our goal is not to predict absolute numbers. Rather, we want to make a relative comparison between probabilistic and exact splitting, and also to identify the key parameters that determine how the two algorithms relate.

Again, as in the case for probabilistic splitting, we assume that the file can be sorted in two passes. In this case, the algorithm at the top level looks like:

1. Each processor sorts its local segment of the file.

2. The processors cooperate to determine an exact splitting vector.

3. The processors redistribute the data and write sorted incoming runs to disk.

4. Each processor merges the runs from disk.

We now consider the cost of each step in turn.

Step 1: The initial sort of the file takes IO time $\frac{N}{kB} * \mathrm{IO_S}$ to read the local segment of the file in order to form the initial sorted runs, and also $\frac{N}{kB} * \mathrm{IO_S}$ to write these runs to disk. The cpu to form these initial sorted runs is just $(MB) * (\log_2(MB)) * \mathrm{KS} + \mathrm{MOVE})$ per run, and there will be $\frac{N}{BkM}$ such runs. The IO to merge these runs is $\frac{N}{kB} * (\mathrm{IO_S} + \mathrm{IO_R})$ since the reads are sequential while the writes are random. The CPU for the merge will be $\frac{N}{k} * (\log_2(\frac{N}{BkM}) * \mathrm{KS} + \mathrm{MOVE})$.

Step 2: Analyzing the cost of determining the splitting vector is again more complicated. We will divide the cost into two parts, one for the initialization, one for the iterations. Furthermore, recall that this process must determine $k-1$ splitting elements; we first consider the cost of finding the single splitting element at quantile $i/(k-1)$ (the whole set consists of the quantiles $i/(k-1)$ for $i = 1, \ldots, k-1$.)

- **Basis:** Initially, we need to read $(1-\frac{i}{k})/\frac{i}{k} = \frac{k}{i} - 1$ pages from disk. This will cost $(\frac{k}{i} - 1) * (\mathrm{IO_R})$. Next, each processor must send these initial keys to some processor to be sorted. As we did for probabilistic splitting, we assume that the keys are gathered by being passed up a binary tree of processors, sorting them as they go. The initial sort will take $(\frac{k}{i} - 1)\log(\frac{k}{i} - 1) * (\mathrm{KS} + \mathrm{COMP})$, while the merges up the tree will take a total of $2(\frac{k}{i} - 1)(k-1) * (\mathrm{KS} + \mathrm{COMP})$, while the network cost is $\log_2(k) * \mathrm{MSG}$ to gather the keys, and another $\log_2(k) * \mathrm{MSG}$ to distribute the splitting constant afterwards. The cost for the sum of the basis operations for all the quantiles will be the sum of the preceding quantities, from $i = 1$ to $k-1$.

- **Iterations:** Now consider the cost of the iterations for the quantile i/k. First, as explained above, the number of iterations is just $\log_2(\frac{N}{k}/(\frac{k}{i}-1))$. Each iteration consists of reading the "midpoint" between two consecutive elements (for a cost of IO_R), sending it to a designated processor ($\log_2(k) * MSG$, assuming we pass the elements up a binary tree of processors), then sorting these k elements ($k(\log_2(k) * (KS+COMP))$), and finally sending a message back to each processor ($log_2(k) * MSG$). Again, the total cost is the sum of this quantity for $i = 1$ to $k-1$.

This completes the cost for the quantile determination. **Step 3:** After the quantiles have been computed, the computation proceeds as in the case for probabilistic splitting. To redistribute the data, we again assume that, for each record r, a processor does a binary search of the splitting vector to determine on which processor r belongs, then copies r to a buffer page for tuples bound for that processor. The cpu cost for this step is $(N/k)*(\log_2(k-1)*COMP+MOVE)$ while the IO cost is just $\frac{N}{kB} * IO_S$. The network cost to redistribute the data is $\frac{N}{kB} * MSG$. Next, each processor must write the incoming tuples to disk, which will cost $\frac{N}{kB} * IO_S$.
Step 4: Finally, the processor must merge these runs, which will entail IO cost $\frac{N}{kB} * IO_S + \frac{N}{kB} * IO_R$ and cpu cost $(N/k) * (\log_2(\frac{N}{kB}/M) * KS + MOVE)$. Note that there is no skew here.

4 Analytic Results

It is perhaps most clear to consider probabilistic splitting and exact splitting in terms of what they both add over an ideal (and usually unrealistic) situation where a perfect splitting vector is known a priori at zero cost. Probabilistic splitting adds the explicit cost of sampling and the implicit cost due to skew in the later phases of the algorithm. Exact splitting adds the explicit costs of each processor sorting its original segment of the file and of the iterative algorithm to compute the exact splitting vector. In broad terms, our analytic model predicts that in a shared-nothing multiprocessor, it is better to sample and tolerate some skew than to compute an exact splitting vector. Furthermore, the relative difference in the performance of the two algorithms increases as the number of processors applied to the sort grows.

Figure 1 shows the performance predicted for the two algorithms on sorting one million 100 byte tuples. Each processor was allocated 25 buffer pages (32K bytes each) for a total of 800K bytes. This sounds like a small number of pages, and it is, but as we discuss in Section 5, we found that as long as there was enough memory to sort the file in two passes, the performance of the sorting algorithm was relatively insensitive to the amount of memory allocated. At 25 pages, and 320 tuples per page, each processor can sort $25 * 25 * 320 = 200000$ tuples in two passes. Even with just five processors (the smallest number of processors in the plot in Figure 1), the multiprocessor can sort up to a one million tuple relation in two passes.

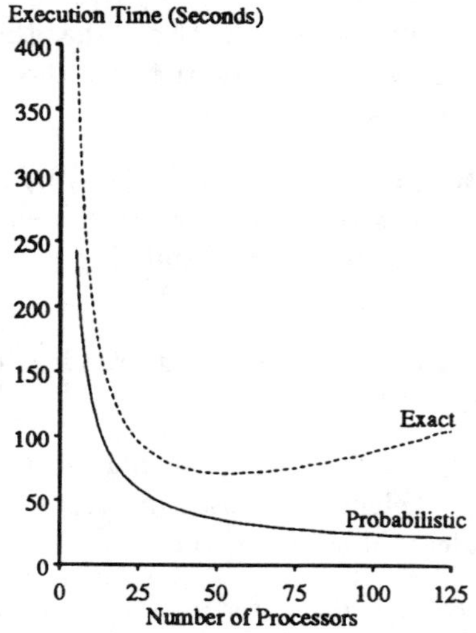

Figure 1: Analytic model predictions for sorting 1M tuples.

Over the complete range of processors considered, probabilistic splitting is faster than exact splitting. For large numbers of processors, the execution time for exact partitioning actually begins to increase as more processors are added. This is due to the fact that if there are k processors in the system, the algorithm to find an individual partitioning element must be repeated $k-1$ times. As mentioned in the sections that developed these models, we regard the relative positions of the two curves and their shapes as more important than the absolute numbers. For this reason, in the remainder of this section we will present graphs of the ratios of the execution times of these two algorithms instead of the execution times themselves. Specifically, we show the ratio of the time for exact splitting over the time for probabilistic splitting. Hence, the line $y = 2$ on the the graph corresponds to probabilistic splitting being twice as fast as exact splitting.

The next factor we investigated was the dependence of performance of the two algorithms on the record size. Sampling is more expensive as tuple sizes decrease, since each random sample must pull in a complete page. As tuple sizes decrease, each random sample represents a larger percentage of the time to scan the whole file. Figure 2 relative performances of the two algorithms in sorting one million 50 byte tuples, one million 100 byte tuples, and one million 200 byte tuples. The graph indicates that the relative performance of the two algorithms remains approximately constant for all three tuple sizes. This is that exact splitting is also adversely impacted by small record sizes, since in much of the binary search phase of the algorithm, each probe of the relation must pull in a complete page in order to examine a single tuple. The curve for 50 byte tuples stops at 60 processors because with one million 50 byte tuples, and 25 memory pages of 32K bytes each per processor, if there are more than 60 processors the entire relation fits into the aggregate memory of the multiprocessor.

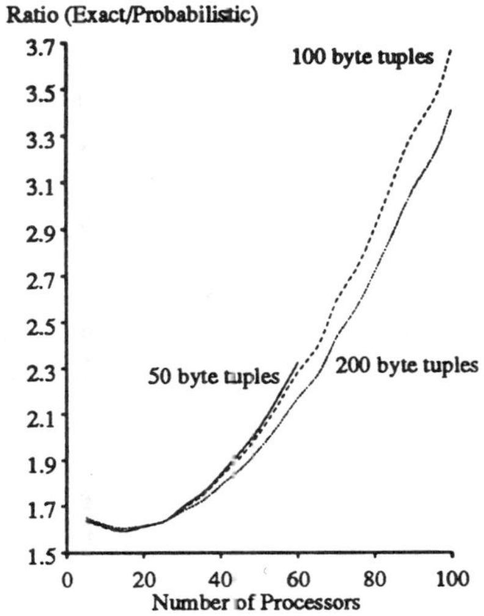

Figure 2: Analytic model predictions for sorting, 50, 100, and 200 byte tuples.

Figure 3 shows the predicted relative performances of the algorithm on files of 1M, 10M, and 100M 100 byte tuples. To produce the curves in the figure, we scaled the memory per processor with the problem size: 25 pages for 1M tuples, 66 pages for 10M tuples, and finally 180 pages for 100M tuples. Also, we started at 10 processors rather than 5. This ensured that at every data point, the sort could be completed in two passes. These curves can be explained by noting that, roughly, the number of page reads per processor in the sampling portion of probabilistic splitting is 100 to 200 (the precise number depends upon the hit ratio for index pages in the buffer pool during the sampling.) The number of page reads per processor in the percentile determination phase of exact splitting is $O(k^2)$, where k is the number of processors. As k grows, these k^2 I/O's become a significant factor in the running time of exact splitting, so the ratio of the running time of exact splitting to that of probabilistic splitting grows. However, as n grows, the fraction of the total running time represented by these k^2 I/Os is hidden by the running time for the sorting portion of the algorithm.

Finally, we anticipated that as the size of the file grows, probabilistic splitting becomes more attractive

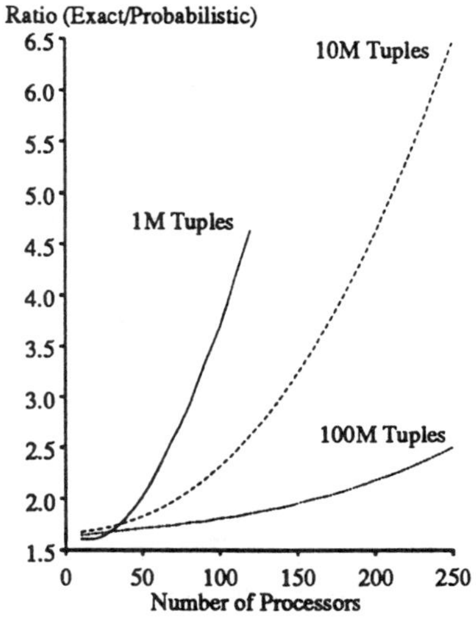

Figure 3: Analytic predictions for ratios of algorithms on 1M, 10M, and 100M tuple files.

in an absolute sense (not just in comparison with exact splitting.) Figure 4 shows the speedups for probabilistic partitioning for various file sizes. In the figure, the basis point is 10 processors, so speedups are ratios with respect to the 10 processor time. This implies that perfect speedup is 10, not 100. (We used 10 processors instead of 1 as the basis because with only a single processor, the files cannot be sorted in two passes.) Figure 4 implies that the larger the file size, the more processors probabilistic splitting can apply effectively to the sorting problem. Intuitively, the reason for this is that as we add more processors, the amount of sorting work per processor decreases, but the amount of sampling work per processor remains constant. For large file sizes, even at 100 processors the sampling time is a tiny fraction of the total execution time (e.g., 12 seconds out of 1400 seconds at 100M tuples.) However, for smaller files the sampling time at 100 processors becomes a significant fraction of the total execution time (e.g., 12 seconds out of 25 seconds for 1M tuples.)

5 Implementation

To investigate the performance of parallel sorting algorithm based on probabilistic splitting, we implemented the algorithm using the Gamma Database Machine [DGS+90] as our experimental vehicle. Gamma is a *shared-nothing* [Sto86] database machine. The hardware consists of a 32 processor Intel iPSC/2 hypercube. Each processor is configured with a 80386 CPU, 8 megabytes of memory, and a 330 megabyte MAXTOR 4380 (5 1/4 in.) disk drive. Each disk drive has an embedded SCSI controller which provides a 45 Kbyte RAM buffer that acts as a disk cache on sequential read

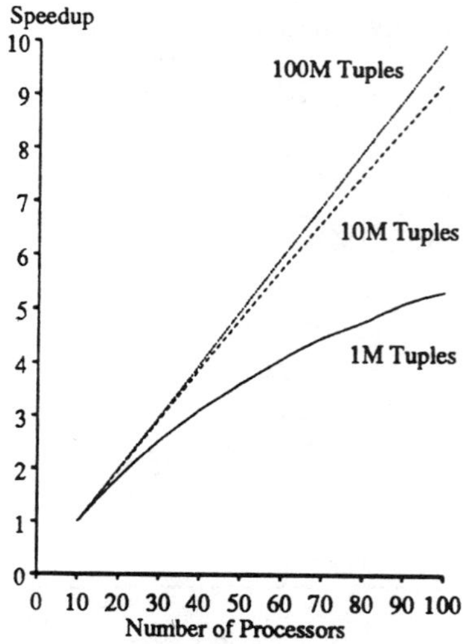

Figure 4: Analytic model predictions of speedup for 1M, 10M, and 100M tuple files.

operations. The nodes in the hypercube are interconnected to form a hypercube using custom VLSI routing modules. Each module supports eight full-duplex, serial, reliable communication channels operating at 2.8 megabytes/sec.

Gamma is built on top of an operating system designed specifically for supporting database management systems. NOSE provides multiple, lightweight processes with shared memory. A non-preemptive scheduling policy is used to help prevent convoys [BGMP79] from occurring. NOSE provides communications between NOSE processes using the reliable message passing hardware of the Intel iPSC/2 hypercube. File services in NOSE are based on the Wisconsin Storage System (WiSS) [CDKK85]. The services provided by WiSS include sequential files, B^+ tree indices, long data items, and a scan mechanism. A sequential file is a sequence of records that may vary in length (up to one page) and that may be inserted and deleted at arbitrary locations within a file. Optionally, each file may have one or more associated indices that map key values to the record identifiers of the records in the file that contain a matching value. One indexed attribute may be designated to be a clustering attribute for the file.

In the Gamma database machine, relations are *horizontally partitioned* [RE78] across all disk drives in order to increase the aggregate I/O bandwidth provided by the hardware. (This is also known as declustering [LKB87].) The query language of Gamma provides the user with several alternative declustering methods. For the experiments described below, the user determined which tuples reside on each site based on a range predicate applied to the partitioning attribute of each tuple of the relation. A collection of tuples stored on a processor is referred to as a *fragment* of the relation.

Our parallel sorting algorithm based on probabilistic splitting operates as follows. First, each processor randomly samples its local fragment of the relation to be sorted and sends the sort attribute values of the sampled tuples to a central coordinator. The coordinator sorts all the sampled values and determines the partitioning elements such that the relation will be divided into as many partitions as there are processors. The coordinator then sends a vector of these partitioning elements to each processor whose disk contains a fragment of the relation.

During the second phase of the algorithm the relation is redistributed according to the elements of the splitting vector. This phase begins by initiating scan, sort, and I/O processes on each processor. After being initiated, each scan process reads its local fragment of the relation and re-distributes it over the network using the elements of the partitioning vector (in Gamma terminology, a split table) to determine to which processor each tuple should be routed to. Tuples are redistributed using 8K byte network packets.

As each packet of tuples arrives at a processor, the sort process adds the packet to a memory resident sort buffer (without incurring a copy). Each time this sort buffer fills, an array of pointers to the tuples is sorted using the WiSS quicksort algorithm. Finally, the sorted run is given to the I/O process, which materializes the sorted run (by copying each tuple from its network packet to an output page) and writes it to disk.

In the final phase of the algorithm, each of the sort processes merges its sorted runs into a single run, which is then written back to disk. As currently implemented, the algorithm terminates with the sorted relation partitioned across all the disks in the system. That is, in a configuration with k processors, the first $1/k$th (approximately) of the relation is stored on the disk attached to processor 1, the next $1/k$th on processor 2, etc. Modifying the implementation so that the entire relation is materialized in sorted order on the host processor or in an application program would be straightforward.

In order to minimize the number of random seeks performed, pages of sorted runs are read and written in blocks composed of two 32K byte pages. Such random seeks occur in both phases of the algorithm. During the first phase of the algorithm, while the scan process at a node is reading blocks of the unsorted relation for redistribution, the I/O process on the same node is concurrently writing sorted runs to disk. Since these two processes read/write from/to different regions of the disk, each I/O operation involves a random seek. The same problem occurs during the merge phase of the sort as each page that is read from an input run or written to an output run almost always incurs a random seek.

While performing I/O operations in blocks of pages does provide some improvement, since the I/O system of the iPSC-2 hypercube does not support IBM-style channel programs, the improvement is not dramatic. In particular, once a process has issued an I/O request, the operating system determines whether another process is runnable. If so, a context switch is performed. If the process selected to run next immediately performs an I/O operation then by the time the first process is allowed to run again, the disk heads will have been moved, negating any benefits provided by blocking I/O operations.

Our initial implementation used 8K byte pages. Since this configuration did not provide "adequate" performance, we added the multi-block I/O feature described above. This change did not, however, improve performance as much as we had expected. For example, doing I/O four pages at a time improved performance by only 5-10% over a single page. On the other hand, switching to a single 32K byte page improved performance by almost 30%. In general (for database system operations other than sorting), using such large pages can actually decrease performance; for example, with index operations. Instead of long pages, a much better long-term solution would be to modify Gamma's operating system to accept vector's of I/O operations that would always be executed in order.

One interesting thing that we observed while running some preliminary experiments was that using the maximum buffer space available did not generally minimize the execution time for a sort. When memory was a scarce resource, obtaining long runs was important in order to minimize the number of passes through the file. However, as long as the amount of memory available is between the square root of the data file size and the size of the entire data file, the file can always be sorted into two passes. Since the CPU cost of the sort is independent of the size of each run, producing longer runs tends to reduce the I/O cost while making the sort CPU bound. (Graefe made a similar observation in [Gra90].) Since all our tests required two passes through the file, through experimentation we found that using a buffer size of about 100 pages balanced the CPU and I/O time and tended to minimize the overall execution time of the sort operation. We also implemented a second version of the algorithm in which the sorted runs were produced using a tournament sort. Despite the fact that the runs produced were twice as long as the ones produced using quicksort, this version actually ran slower.

6 Results

In this section we present the results of scaleup, speedup, and sizeup experiments we conducted with our implementation.For every configuration for which results are reported in this section, each relation to be sorted was evenly distributed during relation creation amongst all the processors by applying a range predicate to the `unique1` attribute (whose values range from 0 to the relation cardinality minus 1). The sort was performed on the unique2 attribute of each relation. The values of this attribute also range from 0 to the relational cardinality minus 1. However, since the values of the `unique1` and `unique2` attributes for a tuple are not correlated with one another, sorting a relation on its `unique2` attribute on k processors results in $(k-1)/k$th of the tuples in the relation being redistributed during the repartitioning phase of the algorithm.

Randomness and Sample Size

We will return to scaleup, speedup, and sizeup later in this section; initially, we present results illustrating the dependence of the execution time on the sample size. Briefly, up to a certain point, taking more samples significantly reduces skew and hence the total execution time; however, beyond a certain point, the time spent in the sampling itself outweighs the savings due to reducing the skew. Another aspect of the dependence between execution time and the number of samples taken has to do with the probabilistic nature of probabilistic splitting. If we take two different sets of samples of the same size, the quality of the splitting vector generated from the two samples will in general not be the same, since some random samples are more representative of the actual population than others. This means that if we run the sorting algorithm using two different random samples of the same size, the running time of the sort using the two sets of samples will also differ. The more samples taken, the lower the variance in the running time between different sets of samples.

Figure 5 illustrates these two aspects of the relationship between the number of samples and the execution time. The graph presents data from a sort of one million 100 byte tuples on 30 processors using varying sample sizes. For each sample size, we ran 30 trials, initializing the random number generator with a different seed each time. There are four lines in the graph. For a point (x, y) on the lowest line, labeled "sampling," y is the average elapsed time (over thirty trials) to take x samples. For a point (x, y) on the middle of the upper three lines, y is the average total execution time for the sort (over the thirty trials) using x samples. For a point (x, y) on the uppermost of the upper three lines, y is the average

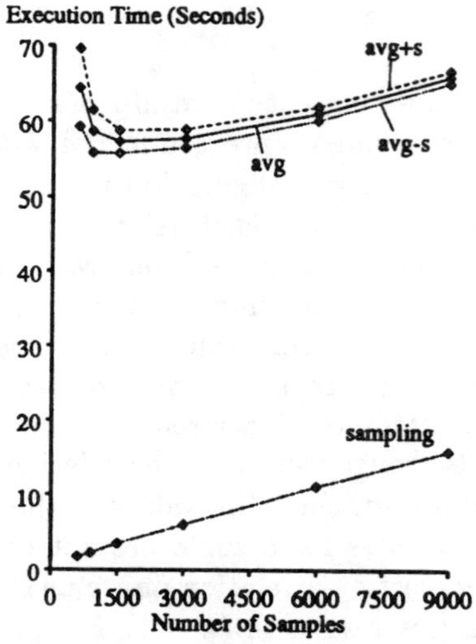

Figure 5: Sorting time as a function of sample size.

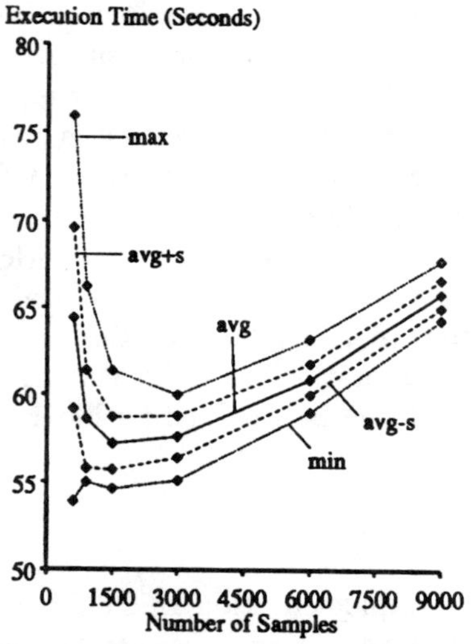

Figure 6: The variance of sorting time as a function of sample size.

total execution time for the sort plus one standard deviation s, using x samples, where the standard deviation is computed over the same thirty trials. Similarly, for a point (x, y) on the lowest of the upper three lines, y is the average total execution time for the sort minus one standard deviation, using x samples, where the standard deviation is computed over the same thirty trials.

The graph in Figure 6 expands the scale for the top three lines of the graph in Figure 5. Also, two additional lines have been added, one showing the maximum execution time observed over all 30 trials at a given number of samples, the other showing the minimum.

The final point we wish to emphasize is that the performance of probabilistic splitting does not depend on the distribution of the data in the sort attribute. To demonstrate this experimentally, we generated an instance of the relation to be sorted in which the sort attribute was drawn from a highly skewed normal distribution (one million values drawn from a normal distribution with mean 500,000 and variance 10,000.) Table 2 shows the performance of the sorting algorithm for both the skewed and the uniformly distributed sort attribute. Both lines of that table refer to sorting one million 100 byte tuples using 30 processors and 3000 samples; the average, min, max, and variance reported are over 30 trials, each trial with a different random seed.

dist.	avg time	max	min	std. dev.
uniform	57.6	60.6	54.3	1.34
skewed	57.0	60.0	55.1	1.22

Table 2: Performance of sorting on skew vs. uniform distribution.

Scaleup

For the scaleup experiments, we varied the number of processors with disks from 5 to 30, in steps of 5, sorting an average of 160K, 100 byte tuples per processor. Thus, with 5 processors, a 0.8 million, 100 byte tuple relation was sorted. At 30 processors, the size of the relation sorted was 4.8 million tuples. As described in Section 2, in our implementation for k processors we took a total of $100k$ samples. This means that with 5 processors, we took 500 samples; with 30 processors, 3000. All timings presented are averages over 5 trials, where each trial used a different random seed.

Table 3 presents the scaleup results we obtained. Ideally the algorithm should exhibit a constant response time as the relation size and hardware configuration is scaled. Three factors contribute to the slight increase in response times. First, as additional processors are added, the skew in the sizes of the portions of the file allocated to each processor grows. Second, the task of initiating four processes at each site (a sampling operator, a relation scan, a sort operator, and a store operator) is performed by a single processor. Finally, as the number of processors increase, the effects of short-circuiting [DGS+90] messages during the execution of the query diminishes.

Speedup

For the speedup experiments, we fixed the size of the relation being sorted at one million tuples while varying the number of processors from 5 to 30. We again held constant (at 100 samples per processor) the number of samples used to determine the partitioning elements. The **unique2** attribute was again used as the sort at-

no. of proc.	rel size (tuples)	time	actual/ideal
5	0.8M	217	1.00
10	1.6M	227	1.05
15	2.4M	235	1.08
20	3.2M	244	1.12
25	4.0M	249	1.15
30	4.8M	257	1.18

Table 3: Scaleup results.

tribute. Again, all timings presented are averages over 5 trials, where each trial used a different random seed.

no. of proc.	time	speedup	% efficiency
5	270.7	1.0	100
10	143.5	1.9	95
15	103.2	2.6	87
20	80.4	3.4	85
25	67.2	4.0	80
30	58.3	4.6	77

Table 4: Speedup results.

The response time and speedup for the one million tuple relation sort are shown in Table 4. It is obvious that adding additional processors significantly reduces the execution time of the query. Several factors prevent the system from achieving perfectly linear speedups. (It is important to note that since the base case was 5 processors a perfect speedup factor for 30 processors would be 6.0 and not 30.0!) As was the case in the scaleup experiments, performance is limited by the overhead of scheduling the operators of the query tree, the effects of short-circuiting, and the effects of skew in the size of the sort tasks allocated to each processor.

Sizeup

For the sizeup experiments, we fixed the number of processors at 30, and sorted relations of various sizes ranging from 1.2M tuples to 4.8M tuples. In all cases, the number of samples was fixed at 3000 (100 per processor), and the times presented are averages over 5 trials.

Table 5 shows the somewhat surprising result that our implementation achieved sublinear sizeup. That is, sorting 4.8M tuples took less than four times as long as sorting 1.2M tuples. The reason this occurs is that the portion of the running time due to sampling takes an amount of time that is independent of the size of the problem. Hence, for smaller problem sizes, the sampling overhead is a more significant component of the running time than it is for larger problem sizes. Table 6 presents the same data as Table 5 except that the sampling overhead is subtracted from each of the running times. This table shows that if we ignore the sampling component, the speedup is approximately linear. This highlights an important point: the larger the problem size, the more effective is probabilistic splitting.

rel. size (tuples)	execution time	ratio
1.2M	70.4	1.0
2.4M	133.0	1.89
3.6M	196.1	2.79
4.8M	257.0	3.65

Table 5: Sizeup results.

rel. size (tuples)	total time - sample time	ratio
1.2M	58.4	1.00
2.4M	121.0	2.07
3.6M	184.1	3.15
4.8M	245.0	4.20

Table 6: Sizeup results exclusive of sampling time.

7 Conclusion

Partitioning the file being sorted is a critical step in multiple-input multiple-output external sorting. Our analytic results suggest that for this problem, probabilistic splitting dominates a previously proposed deterministic method; our experimental results prove that for up to thirty processors (the maximum we could test), probabilistic splitting achieves good speedup and scaleup performance.

This speedup and scaleup will not continue indefinitely. In order to maintain constant expected skew in the sizes of the subfiles produced by probabilistic splitting, the number of samples taken must grow with the number of processors. This means that as the number of processors scales, eventually one must choose between large skews or large numbers of samples, neither of which will give good performance in general. However, it is important to note that the speedup achieved by probabilistic splitting improves as the size of the file to be sorted grows (recall Figure 4.) For sorting one million record files on systems with tens of processors, our implementation proves that probabilistic splitting is a highly effective technique. Although we are unable to prove it on our current hardware, we expect that for files of one billion records and beyond, probabilistic splitting will be effective even on systems with a few hundreds of processors.

Acknowledgements

This research was supported by donations from DEC, IBM, NCR, and Tandem. We would also like to thank Rick Rasmussen for his assistance in dealing with the Gamma hardware and software.

References

[BBDW83] D. Bitton, H. Boral, D. Dewitt, and W. K. Wilkinson. Parallel algorithms for the execution of relational database operations. *ACM TODS*, 8(3):324–353, September 1983.

[BBW88] M. Beck, D. Bitton, and W. K. Wilkinson. Sorting large files on a backend multiprocessor. *IEEE Trans. on Computers*, 37(7):769 – 778, 1988.

[BG89] B. Baugstø and J. Greipsland. Parallel sorting methods for large data on a hypercube database computer. In *Proc. of the Sixth Int'l Workshop on Database Machines*, pages 127 – 141, 1989. Springer-Verlag.

[BGMP79] M. W. Blasgen, J. Gray, M. Mitoma, and T. Price. The convoy phenomenon. *OS Review*, 13(2), 1979.

[BLM+91] G. E. Blelloch, C. E. Leiserson, B. M. Maggs, C. G. Plaxton, S. J. Smith, and M. Zagha. A comparison of sorting algorithms for the Connection Machine CM-2. In *Proc. of the 3rd Annual ACM SPAA*, 1991.

[CDKK85] H-T. Chou, David J. Dewitt, Randy H. Katz, and Anthony C. Klug. Design and implementation of the Wisconsin Storage System. *Software—Practice and Experience*, 15(10):943–962, October 1985.

[DGS+90] D. DeWitt, S. Ghandeharizadeh, D. Schneider, A. Bricker, H.-I Hsiao, and R. Rasmussen. The Gamma database machine project. *IEEE TKDE*, 2(1), March 1990.

[Dob78] W. Dobosiewicz. Sorting by distributive partitioning. *IPL*, 7(1):1–6, 1978.

[FM70] W. D. Frazer and A. C. McKellar. Samplesort: A sampling approach to minimal storage tree sorting. *JACM*, 17(3):496 – 507, 1970.

[Gra90] Goetz Graefe. Parallel external sorting in volcano. TR CU-CS-459-90, University of Colorado - Boulder, March 1990.

[HC83] J. S. Huang and Y. C. Chow. Parallel sorting and data partitioning by sampling. In *Proc. of the Seventh COMSAC*, pages 627 – 631, 1983.

[IRV89] Balakrishna R. Iyer, Gary R. Ricard, and Peter J. Varman. Percentile finding algorithm for multiple sorted runs. In *Proceedings of the Fifteenth VLDB*, pages 135 – 144, 1989.

[JL85] Philip J. Janus and Edmund A. Lamagna. An adaptive method for unknown distributions in distributive partitioned sorting. *IEEE Trans. on Computers*, C-34(4):367–372, April 1985.

[LKB87] M. Livny, S. Khoshafian, and H. Boral. Multi-disk management algorithms. In *Proc. of 1987 SIGMETRICS Conf.*, May 1987.

[LY89] Raymond A. Lorie and Honesty C. Young. A low communication sort algorithm for a parallel database machine. In *Proc. of the Fifteenth VLDB*, 1989.

[Qui88] M. J. Quinn. Parallel sorting algorithms for tightly coupled multiprocessors. *Parallel Computing*, 6:349 – 367, 1988.

[RE78] D. Ries and R. Epstein. Evaluation of distribution criteria for distributed database systems. UCB/ERL Tech. Rep. M78/22, UC-Berkeley, May 1978.

[SN91] S. Seshadri and Jeffrey F. Naughton. Sampling issues in parallel database systems. Submitted for publication, June 1991.

[STG+90] Betty Salzberg, Alex Tsukerman, Jim Gray, Susan Uern, and Bonnie Vaughan. FastSort: A distributed single-input single-output external sort. In *Proc. of the ACM-SIGMOD Conf.*, 1990.

[Sto86] M. Stonebraker. The case for shared nothing. *Database Engineering*, 9(1), 1986.

[VG84] Patric Valduriez and Georges Gardarin. Join and semijoin algorithms for a multiprocessor database machine. *ACM TODS*, 9(1):133–161, March 1984.

[YT88] Y. Yamane and R. Take. Parallel partition sort for database machines. In Masaru Kitsuregawa and Hidehiko Tanaka, editors, *Database Machines and Knowledge Base Machines*, pages 117 – 130. Kluwer Academic Publishers, 1988.

A Low Communication Sort Algorithm for a Parallel Database Machine

Raymond A. Lorie and Honesty C. Young

IBM Almaden Research Center
San Jose, CA 95120-6099, USA

Abstract

The paper considers the problem of sorting a file in a distributed system. The file is originally distributed on many sites, and the result of the sort is needed at another site called the "host". The particular environment that we assume is a backend parallel database machine, but the work is applicable to distributed database systems as well.

After discussing the drawbacks of several existing algorithms, we propose a novel algorithm that exhibits complete parallelism during the sort, merge, and return-to-host phases. In addition, this algorithm decreases the amount of inter-processor communication compared to existing parallel sort algorithms. We describe an implementation of the algorithm, present performance measurements, and use a validated model to demonstrate its scalability. We also discuss the effect of an uneven distribution of data among the various processors.

1 Introduction

A database machine based on multiple nodes that share nothing is one way to provide the functionality of a conventional relational database system, with performance that goes far beyond what can be achieved with a single node. In particular, we consider a multiple node backend database machine that is connected to one or more host nodes. The interface to the database machine is SQL-like. This means that a complex query can be executed completely in the backend, and that only the request and the results are exchanged on the host–backend connection. For the sorting problem, however, we assume the host gathers sorted records in such a way that does not require sort key comparison. In other words, we do not carry out any comparison-based global sort or global merge at the host site. We also assume that the host extracts tuples from the communication messages and returns them to the application program.

The backend itself is a collection of n loosely-coupled nodes communicating by message passing on a network. Each node has its own processor(s), memory, channels, disks, and operating system. We assume that the hardware is symmetric in the sense that every node is equivalent to every other node. Besides the network which supports the n-to-n communication between the nodes, each node has a communication channel that it can use to receive a request from the host or send data back to the host. We refer to these communication channels as the n-to-1 network (see Fig. 1). We also assume that n-to-n communication shares the same media where each of the n-to-1 communication has its own media. One or more instances of the DBMS software may run on a single node, and each instance is called a *site*. The scheme of running multiple sites on a single node is called "virtualization" in [9].

We call data sites the sites where the records are originally stored and merge sites the sites where the merge operation is performed. In addition, there is a host site and a coordinator site. To simplify the discussion, we assume a site consists of a data site and a merge site, unless specified otherwise. P_i denotes the i-th site and P_{di} and P_{mi} denote the i-th data, and merge site, respectively. Depending on the algorithm, the sort operation may be performed on either the data sites or the merge sites.

Given a table T, with columns C1, C2, ... Ck, the sorting problem consists of returning to the host, the desired fields of the records that satisfy a predicate, ordered on the value of an expression computed on one or several columns. In order to simplify the analysis, we

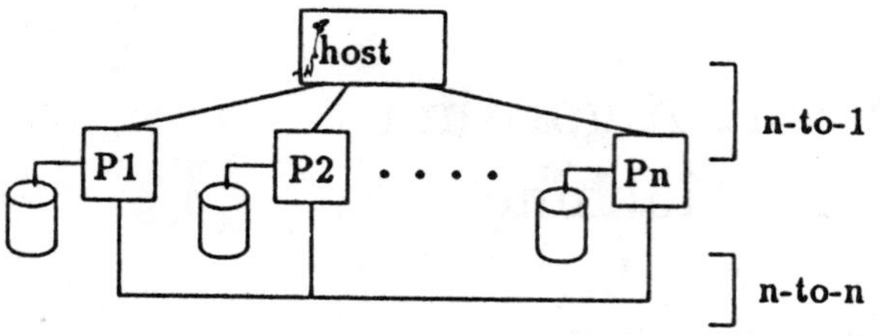

Figure 1: A Generic Backend Database Machine.

assume that the predicate is always true, that all fields are returned, and that the order is defined on a single column, as in the following SQL statement.

```
SELECT * FROM T ORDER BY C1
```

Barring data skew, the performance of a sort depends on the amount of CPU used at each site, the amount of disk I/O done at each site, the amount of n-to-1 communication, and the amount of n-to-n communication, and of course, the degree of parallelism. The cost complexity of n-to-n communication is typically superlinear: n^2 for a full crossbar switch or $n \log n$ for a multistage interconnection network. The cost complexity of n-to-1 communication in contrast is proportional to n^1. So, a good sort algorithm for a distributed configuration is one that minimizes the amount of n-to-n communication, and exploits high degree of parallelism without substantially increasing the CPU and disk activity.

Section 2 discusses some related work. Section 3 proposes a novel, fully parallel algorithm (FPA) that decreases the amount of communication substantially. Section 4 describes briefly the ARBRE prototype built at the IBM Almaden Research Center, and provides some overall performance for a benchmark sort. Section 5 outlines a model to evaluate the new sort algorithm for a variety of parameter ranges. In section 6, we discuss the effect of an uneven distribution of data on the overall performance of the algorithm. In the conclusion, we summarize the benefits and applicability of the proposed sort algorithm.

2 Related Work

Researchers have studied the parallel sorting problem extensively (see the surveys in [2,8]). Most of the assumptions and results, however, are of theoretical interest (*e.g.*, the number of processors required is a function of the number of records to be sorted). Moreover, practical issues such as the times to read the source records from their data site(s) and to deliver the sorted records to a single host site are often ignored.

The sorting algorithms that are related to our current discussion are sometimes called "limited parallelism sorting algorithms" [2]. Four variations of such algorithms are worth mentioning.

Algorithm A: data sites send all records to a sort site S. S does the sort, then returns the sorted file to the host site. Although the scans are done in parallel, the sort itself is done serially.

Algorithm B: sort the data locally at each data site and merge the sorted file at a single merge site. This is similar to Tandem's FASTSORT [5] except that, in FASTSORT, the input data constitute a single file and a preliminary phase distributes the data before the local sorts take place.

Algorithm C: sort the data locally in each data site, organize the merge sites into a binary tree, and merge the sorted files in a pipelined fashion. This is a variation of the *parallel binary merge algorithm* in [3], which is itself an improved version of an algorithm described in [4] in that it pipelines the merge phase. The sort used in DBC/1012 [11] is similar to algorithm C in that each AMP does a local sort and sends the sorted stream through the Y-net, which carries out the merge operation in hardware.

Algorithm D: data sites use key-range partitioning to redistribute the data to sort sites; sort sites sort the redistributed data locally, and the host site concatenates the sorted file. This is a parallel version of the distributive partitioned sorting proposed in [7]. This algorithm computes, by some method, a partitioning of the key range R into subranges R1, R2, ..., Rn such that a roughly equal number of records falls in each subrange. Any well-known distributed random sampling algorithms may be used here. Each subrange Ri is assigned to one sort site in a one-to-one fashion; for example, Ri is assigned to P_{mi}. Then, each data site sends each of its records to the appropriate sort site that handles the range containing the record's sort key. When all records have been sent, all records with keys in the first range are all in P_{m1}. All records with keys in the second range are in P_{m2}, etc. Each site can then sort the records that it received. When done, P_{m1} returns its sorted records to the host. When it finishes, P_{m2} does the same, etc., until P_{mn}.

Each of the above algorithms has at least one phase where parallelism is not exploited. Algorithm A has a serial sort phase. Algorithm B has a serial (non-pipelined) merge phase. Algorithm C also has a serial (pipelined) merge phase. Algorithm D has the most parallelism, but it sends entire records on the n-to-n communication network, imposing a load of (number_of_records * record_length).

In algorithms B, C, and D, the return of the results

[1] n is the number of nodes in the system

to the host is serialized. There is a single site that sends the sorted records to the host in algorithms B and C. In algorithm D, the sorted records are sent first from P_1, then from P_2, etc. In our experiments, this is responsible for most of the response time.

In the next section, we propose a novel algorithm, similar to algorithm D, that eliminates the drawbacks mentioned above. The technique used to decrease the n-to-n communication is similar to the one used in a semi-join. To our knowledge, the only other research work that sends only the sort keys during an intermediate step of a sorting algorithm is the "key broadcasting" algorithm described in [10], where a parallel sort is executed in a common-bus local network environment.

3 A Fully Parallel Algorithm

Our sort algorithm has parallel sort, merge, and return-to-host phases. Thus, it is called a fully parallel algorithm (FPA). We will exploit the size difference between the sort key and the entire record by sending only sort keys from the data sites to the merge sites. The data sites send sorted files directly to the host which efficiently "merges" them without doing sort key comparisons. As explained below, the host's merge algorithm uses information computed during the merge sites' processing of the sort keys. The merge sites send only this information to the host; the sort keys are discarded as they are merged.

Before presenting the details of our sort algorithm, we describe it at a high level. Each data site sorts locally the portion of the file that it owns; in doing so, it computes the distribution of the keys that it encounters, and sends the distribution to a global coordinator. Based on such information from all data sites, the coordinator assigns each merge site a range of keys for which it is responsible. Each data site sends each of its record keys (in sorted order) to a certain merge site. For each record, the merge site is chosen as the site responsible for the key of that record. Each merge site merges the keys that it receives from all data sites, determining the order that the data sites deliver the next record to the host site.

3.1 Detailed Description

There are four kinds of tasks involved in the sort (see Fig. 2): the host task (always executed on the host machine), the coordinator (executed on any site), the scan tasks (one on each data site), and the merge tasks (one on each merge site). The tasks enclosed by the dotted line box are running on each site. The sort and the scan operations can be done by the same scan task because their operations do not overlap in time. In order to distinguish the work between merging the sort

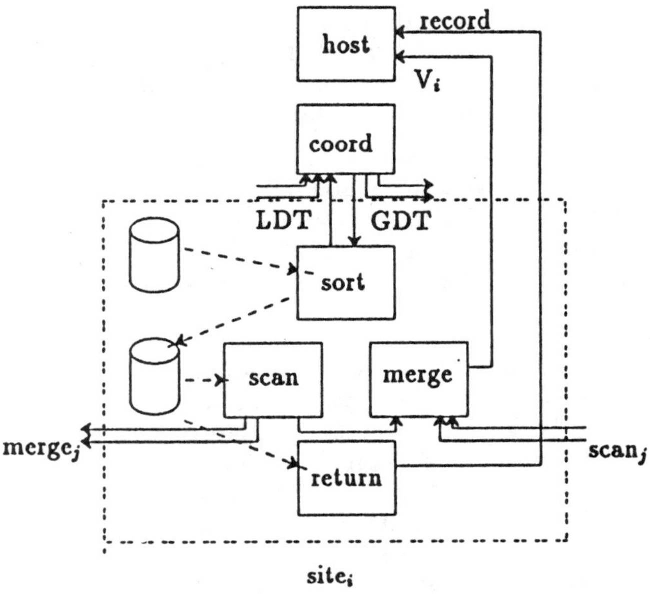

Figure 2: The Dataflow among Tasks.

keys and returning the sorted records to the host, the data sites do not send sorted records to the host site until all the sort keys have been sent to the merge sites. Therefore, the scan task is also responsible for returning the sorted records to the host site.

The host task sends the sort request to the coordinator and waits until it starts receiving a stream of site Ids V_1 from the P_{m1}, etc. At that time, the host considers successively each value in V_1. A value i indicates that it needs to read the next record from the stream of records coming from data site P_{di}.

The coordinator waits for a request from the host. When it receives the request for a sort, it sends the request to all data sites and merge sites. It then waits for all data sites to send their distribution tables. Based on these distribution tables the coordinator constructs the GDT (Global Distribution Table). The GDT is then sent to all data sites. The coordinator needs to be involved no longer.

The sort itself has four phases–local sort, synchronization, merge, and return-to-host.

Phase 1: Local Sort

Phase 1 starts on any P_{di} as soon as it receives its sort request from the coordinator. P_{di} scans its local records and sorts the records using any algorithm. The result of the sort is a file S_i of sorted records. Each record in S_i contains a key and a record body. While the sort is taking place, two objects are being built besides the sorted output: (1) A list that contains the lowest key stored in a single page of S_i and a descriptor for that page. This list is called the *index list*, because it is used to determine the page that contains the first record of a key range. (2) A small table, called distribution table, containing information on the key distribution; it is derived from the index list mentioned above.

This sorting algorithm and the data structures it uses are best illustrated by an example. Consider a system with three sites. Each record has two fields and the first (single byte) field is the sort key field. Let the contents of the sorted files S1, S2 and S3 be, respectively:

S1	S2	S3
A Alice	C Carl	A Adam
B Barbara	D Debbie	B Brian
G Greg	F Frances	C Christine
H Helen	F Frank	D Dan
H Henry	G Gloria	E Elizabeth
K Kevin	M Mary	E Eric
L Linda	N Nancy	J Jane
M Mark	P Peggy	J John
N Norman	R Ron	K Kathy
S Steve	S Sue	L Larry
	T Teresa	P Peter
	W Walter	R Ruth
		T Tom
		W Wendy

(a)

A particular sampling algorithm may generate the following distribution tables:

B	D	B
H	F	D
K	M	E
M	P	J
S	S	L
	W	R
		W

(b)

Phase 2: Synchronization

As soon as Phase 1 is completed on a P_{di}, this P_{di} sends its distribution table to the coordinator and waits for the GDT from the coordinator. Once the coordinator has received the distribution tables from all sites, it combines their contents and builds a single GDT. The GDT contains the boundaries of n subranges, such that the numbers of records with keys falling in each range are roughly equal. Each range is assigned to a merge site on a one-to-one basis (for example range R1 to site P_{m1}, etc). The coordinator then sends the GDT to all sites.

Let's use the previous example to show how the coordinator computes the GDT. The coordinator receives the data in (b), merges the distribution tables, and partitions the results into 3 roughly equal size groups, to obtain the range definitions that constitute the GDT:

```
B B D D E F   H J K L M M   P R S S W W

----------- F ----------- M -----------
lowest                           highest
```

Phase 3: Merge

During this phase, there are two tasks at each site, working concurrently: a producing scan task and a consuming merge task. Once a data site receives the GDT its producing scan task reads sequentially the records from its sorted file. For each record in the sorted file, the key is extracted and sent to the merge site P_j, where j is such that the key falls in the j-th range defined by GDT. It is received by the consuming merge task of P_j for merging.

A strictly sequential processing of file S_i is not optimal as the following scenario illustrates. Assume all sites start sending only records that fall in the first range. Therefore all traffic is destined for the merge site in charge of the first range, which becomes overloaded. When records in the second range are sent, another merge site becomes overloaded, and the process continues. Our solution to the problem consists of processing only a small portion of the records in the first range (for which the target is P_{m1}). The small portion may be a single page from each data site. While P_{m1} handles the corresponding merge, all producing tasks jump to the beginning of the second range, etc. After the first batch of Rn has been processed, each producing task sends its second batch of R1 and so on, in a round-robin fashion. Clearly, if one looks at a sufficiently large period of time, all data sites produce records that are sent to the appropriate merge sites. So all sites are kept busy, sending, receiving and merging records.

In the following example, we denote a key sent by data site P_{di} to merge site P_{mj} by <key, i>→ P_j[2] for illustrative purpose. P_i starts producing records, sending them to the indicated merge sites. If each data site sends 2 records in a batch, the following communication pattern occurs:

batch1:

<A,1> → P1	<C,2> → P1	<A,3> → P1
<B,1> → P1	<D,2> → P1	<B,3> → P1
<G,1> → P2	<G,2> → P2	<J,3> → P2
<H,1> → P2	<M,2> → P2	<J,3> → P2
<N,1> → P3	<N,2> → P3	<P,3> → P3
<S,1> → P3	<P,2> → P3	<R,3> → P3

[2] The sender's site identifier can be decoded easily from a message and is not included in the message body.

batch2:

<H,1> → P2 <F,2> → P1 <C,3> → P1
<K,1> → P2 <F,2> → P1 <D,3> → P1
...

Since the data sites are not synchronized, the actual communication pattern will differ from the lock-step pattern shown here.

P_1 receives from all sites (including itself):

<A,1>	<C,2>	<A,3>
<B,1>	<D,2>	<B,3>
EOS	...	...
	EOS	EOS

Since the keys are sent to a different consuming merge task in each round, all merge tasks may start at about the same time. Clearly, the merge task of Pmk receives records that have keys that fall into the range for which the site P_{dk} is responsible, and all records received from a single site arrive in order. These ordered streams of keys can thus be merged to produce a single output stream. Each entry in the output stream contains only the identifier of the data site.

For example, consider the first merge site. It merges its records to obtain the following order:

<A,1> <A,3> <B,1> <B,3> <C,2> <C,3> ...

and produces the following V_1 stream:

```
V1        1 3 1 3 2 3 2 3 2 2 3 3
```

The other two merge sites produce their output streams in a similar fashion:

```
V2        1 2 1 1 3 3 1 3 1 3 1 2
V3        1 2 2 3 2 3 1 2 2 3 2 3
```

Phase 4: Returning Records to the Host
When Phase 3 is finished at site P_i, the corresponding stream V_i and sorted file S_i are sent as streams to the host. If the next entry in V is k, the host knows that it needs to get the next record from S_k sent by data site P_k.

In the example, the host receives a stream of site identifiers (V), which is the concatenation of V_1, V_2 and V_3. It also receives the sorted S's (a) from each site. Following the site id order of V, it retrieves records in that order:

A Alice	from P1
A Adam	from P3
B Barbara	from P1
B Brian	from P3
C Carl	from P2
C Christine	from P3
...	

3.2 Alternative Implementations

The algorithm as explained above is the one that we implemented and evaluated (see section 5 below). Some variations are worth discussing.

1. In the above description, the entire file S is read twice–once to send the keys to the merge tasks, and once to return the records to the host. It may be preferable to have the local sort write two files: S with the entire records and a much smaller file K with keys only. In phase 3, the smaller file K is read, instead of S.
2. When multiple merge sites are running on a single node (because of site virtualization), the merge phase can be divided into several sub-phases. The host site cannot start receiving records in the R2 ranges until it has received all records in R1, which cannot finish before P_{m1} finishes. If the merge phase has several sub-phases, the host can start receiving records in the ranges for which the corresponding merge operations have completed. That is, the host site receiving operation is pipelined with the merge site merging operation. The most important advantage of the pipelined scheduling is that the time to receive the records is expanded, thus, the resource requirements on the host can be smoothed out. Consequently, the same host can accommodate more nodes without incurring response time penalty.
3. Finally, other sampling algorithms may be used to compute the GDT.

4 Prototype

At IBM Almaden Research Center, we have built a prototype of a backend database machine, called ARBRE (Almaden Research Backend Relational Engine), in order to explore the use of parallelism within complex relational queries, and across many independent transactions [9].

A prototype of the database machine is now operational. It runs on three dyadic 4381 nodes providing 6 processors for the backend database machine; a fourth 4381 is used as a host. Each processor is approximately 3.5 MIPS (million instructions per second). The operating system is MVS and a 3088 is used for channel-to-channel communication. The database system is organized as follows: on each of the 4381's, four virtual sites are emulated by running four DBMS's in four address spaces, providing 12 sites in total. Each relation is split horizontally into partitions; each partition is stored in a different DBMS. The access method is borrowed from SQL/DS (DBSS) [6].

Since we have not implemented a query compiler, we

hand-code programs that specify the strategy that would normally be chosen by the optimizer. A strategy is expressed as a series of routines which are generally duplicated at each site. These routines produce or consume streams of data that are passed between disks, nodes, and the host. The execution is controlled by data flow and stream communication is controlled by a pacing mechanism.

We exercised the prototype for various sets of parameters. Here we report the results for one particular set of parameters which we use later to validate our model:

- number of sites : 12 (2 site per processor of 3.5 MIPS, 21 MIPS aggregate)
- number of records: 12 * 16000 records = 192,000 records
- record length : 64 bytes
- key length : 8 bytes (included in the 64)

For each of the four phases, we measured the CPU time, the number of I/O's, the number of messages, and the response time. Results on each site are shown below.

	sort	sync	merge	return	total
CPU (sec)	12.0	-	10.2	6.2	28.4
I/O	-	-	-	-	2884
Comm	2	2	159	509	672
Resp (sec)	44.7	1.6	22.4	23.6	92.3

Note that the CPU for the synchronization is too small to be measured and that we only show the total I/O because some pages logically modified in one phase are written later, due to the buffer page replacement algorithm, blurring the boundaries between phases.

5 Model

In this section, we model every phase separately, and immediately apply the model to the experiment just described.

Let's define the path length of various operations by the following symbols (approximate values from the prototype are given in parentheses):

- to extract a record from a list: Ex (= 950)
- to enqueue a record to a stream: Eq (= 150)
- to dequeue a record from a stream: Dq (= 150)
- to send or receive a message: Cm (= 4000)
- to perform an I/O: Io (= 8000)
- to carry out a key comparison: Cp (= 150)

The system parameters and their values are:

- the page size: P (= 4086[3])
- the message size: M (= 2048)
- the record length: Rl (= 64)
- the key field length: Kl (= 8)
- the number of sites: S (= 12)

The following symbols are also used, and all refer to one site only:

- the number of records: Ni
- the number of disk I/O's: Nio
- number of pages in the base table: Nb
- number of pages in the index list: Nl
- the number of communication messages: Nc

When two sites are sharing the same physical processor, we model the response time to be either the sum of the CPU and I/O times (when it is not CPU bound) or twice the CPU time (when it is CPU bound). Let us analyze what happens at one site.

Phase 1: Local Sort
We developed a model for the CPU and I/O times of local sorts and validated the model by running multiple experiments on our prototype. The detailed description of the local sort model is not relevant to this paper; thus, it will not be explained further. For the chosen parameters, the CPU time is 12 sec and the I/O time is 33 sec. Based on our response time model, the response time for 2 simultaneous sorts is (12 + 33) = 45 sec.

Phase 2: Synchronization
A message is sent from each site to the coordinator and from the coordinator to each site. This is a small linear overhead. Each site has an equal number of records to sort; so all sorts can be expected to terminate roughly at the same time; therefore we will neglect the time required for this phase but will return to the skew problem in a later section.

Phase 3: Merge
Using the symbols defined above, the first order[4] approximation gives us:

- $Nb = \text{ceiling}(Ni/\text{floor}(P/Rl))$
- $Nl = \text{ceiling}(Nb/\text{floor}(P/Kl + 4^5))$
- $Nio = Nb + Nl$
- $Nc = \text{ceiling}(Ni/\text{floor}(M/Kl))$

Consequently, we have

- $Nb = \text{ceiling}(16000/\text{floor}(4086/64)) = 254$
- $Nl = \text{ceiling}(254/\text{floor}(4086/12)) = 1$
- $Nio = 254 + 1 = 255$
- $Nc = \text{ceiling}(16000/\text{floor}(2048/8)) = 63$

The total path length and its breakdown are shown below:

[3] 4096 bytes less 10 bytes page header

[4] In particular, we ignore the path length related to the site identifier manipulation since each site identifier is very small (one to two bytes).

[5] The page descriptor has 4 bytes.

operation	formula	path length (M)
I/O	Nio * Io = 255 * 8000	2.04
Key Extraction	Ni * (Ex + Cp)) = 16000 * (950 + 150)	17.60
Enqueue	Ni * Eq = 16000 * 150	2.40
Send	Nc * Cm = 63 * 4000	0.25
Receive	Nc * Cm = 63 * 4000	0.25
Dequeue	Ni * Dq = 16000 * 150	2.40
Merge	Ni * (ceiling(log_2(S)*Cp) = 16000 * (4*150)	9.60
Total		34.5

The order of the operations shown above reflects the sequence for a "typical" record. The Cp term in the formula for key extraction is the path length associated with the partition range check. The CPU time on a 3.5 MIPS processor for 34.5 M instructions is 9.9 sec. Assuming each I/O takes 20 ms, the elapsed time for I/O is $255 * 0.020 = 5.1$ sec. The phase is strongly CPU bound. Therefore running simultaneously two such phases on one processor will yield an elapsed time of $(2 * 9.9) = 19.8$ sec.

These 19.8 sec are somewhat less than the measured 22.4 sec. Part of the difference is due to the fact that the merge needs always a record from a specific incoming stream in order to proceed. Therefore, some waiting time can be expected. A simulation has shown that the relative response time increase due to the deterministic merge varies very little with the increase in the number of sites: 3% for 4 sites to roughly 11% for 64 or 128 sites.

Phase 4: Return
For the return phase, we obtain the following path length:

operation	formula	path length (M)
I/O	Nio * Io = 254 * 8000	2.03
Record Extraction	Ni * Ex = 16000 * 950	15.20
Enqueue	Ni * Eq = 16000 * 150	2.40
Send	Nc * Cm = 500 * 4000	2.00
Total		21.6

The CPU time on a 3.5 MIPS processor for 21.6 M instructions is 6.2 sec. The I/O time is $254 * 0.020 = 5.1$ sec. Again, since the phase is CPU bound, the elapsed time for two such phases executed simultaneously is $2 * 6.2 = 12.4$ sec. This is true only if the host and the communication network are infinitely fast. In fact one can show that the host CPU requirement is 15.5 sec.

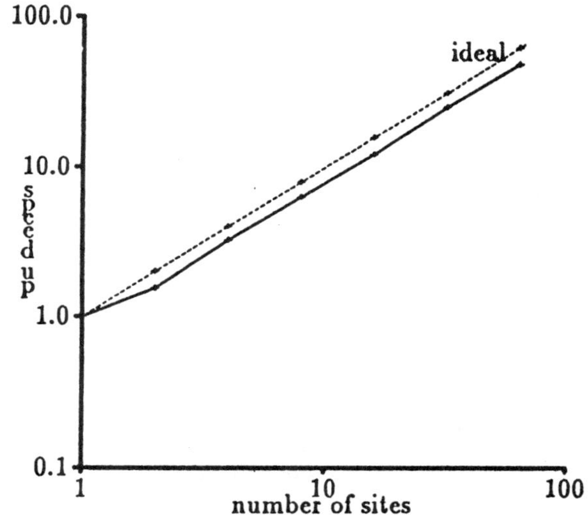

Figure 3: Response Time Reduction.

To summarize, let us compare the results of the model and the actual measurements:

		sort	merge	return
CPU		12.0	10.2	6.2
	(mod)	12.0	9.9	6.2
Resp.		44.7	22.4	23.6
	(mod)	45.0	19.8	>15.5

The response time of the return phase is longer than estimated because the channel-to-channel used in the prototype to implement the n-to-1 communication network becomes the bottleneck.

5.1 Exercising the Model

After having validated the model with actual measurements, we exercised it at will to examine response time reduction and horizontal growth. We adjusted some parameters to values that are more appropriate for high-performance relational DBMS, but difficult to change in our current prototype implementation. We assume that I/O streams read sixteen 4096 byte pages at a time with a latency of $(20 + 15 * 16) = 44$ ms, and message size of 4KB instead of 2KB. To eliminate the site virtualization effect, we run one site on a processor. We also consider 4 MIPS backend processors, and a 32 MIPS host processor.

We studied the response time reduction by sorting a total of 1 million 64 byte records that are evenly distributed among all sites. We also assume here that the GDT gives the exact partition. For the single site case, the synchronization, and merge phases are not executed. Fig. 3 shows the speed up with respect to the single site case for various configurations.

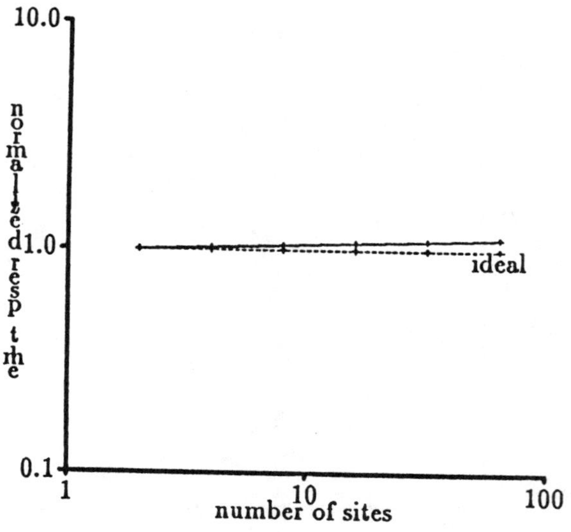

Figure 4: Horizontal Growth.

As the figure indicates, one pays for the distribution overhead when the number of sites goes from 1 to 2; afterwards the speed up is quasi-linear. This is true under the assumptions that the records are evenly distributed initially, and that the GDT ensures a pretty accurate partition. In Section 6, we will address the problem of uneven distribution of initial records.

We also studied horizontal growth by increasing the number of sites and the total number of records to be sorted, in the same proportion. That is, the number of records on each site remains unchanged. In particular, we sort 16K records per site. Since we are interested in multiple site cases, the response time in Fig. 4 is normalized to that of two sites. As expected, when the number of sites in the system increases, the response time increases slightly as well. (Remember that the number of key comparisons needed to produce a record in the merge phase varies with the logarithm of the number of sites.) For the chosen parameters, the response time is increased by about 2.4% when the number of sites doubles.

5.2 Comparison with Other Sort Algorithms

Let's use our model to compare the proposed fully parallel algorithm (FPA) with a variation of FPA (called FPA') without employing the "semi-sort" communication reduction technique and with the algorithms described in Section 2. The work load is to sort 1M 64 byte records using 64 4 MIPS processors. The communication CPU time is added wherever appropriate. The total CPU time is computed as the sum of all non-overlapped CPU times, and the total time is computed as the sum of the total CPU time and the I/O time.

For all methods, the n-to-1 communication is 64 MB and is not discussed any further. In the table 5.2, two CPU times are shown for the return phases of both FPA and FPA': the smaller one is the CPU time on a backend processor while the larger one is that on the host processor. These two numbers are carried on in the subtotal and total. The real elapsed time should lie between the total CPU time and the total time.

The major reason for algorithm D performing much worse than FPA is that the sorted results are sent to the host in a serialized fashion. For algorithms B, C, and D, the scan time is not much smaller than the sort time because the particular database system used in the prototype has the property that reading a record for the internal sort is much cheaper (in terms of path length) than returning a record via the record-at-a-time interface. Algorithm C performs better than algorithm B because the merge fan-in of the former is much smaller.

Unless the n-to-n communication has a very high effective bandwidth, algorithms A, C, and D may experience a slow down because the n-to-n communication becomes a bottleneck when all sites exchange records among themselves. The bottleneck is caused by high aggregate communication, bursty communication or both, depending on the sort algorithm. For algorithm C, the amount of n-to-n communication is 64B $*$ 1M $*$ $\log_2$ (S), where S is the number of sites. For a system with 64 sites, the total n-to-n communication is 384 MB. For all algorithms A, B, and D, the amount of n-to-n communication is 64B $*$ 1M = 64 MB. On the other hand, the amount of n-to-n communication for FPA is 8B $*$ 1M = 8 MB. Comparing FPA with FPA', we demonstrate that the "semi-sort" technique not only reduces the n-to-n communication but also decreases the total CPU path length.

For algorithms A and D, the n-to-n communication happens in bursts, even though the total response time is much longer than that of FPA. The n-to-n communication in algorithms B and C can be spread over the entire merge phase. However, the entire record is sent $\log_2$ (S) (6 under the chosen parameters) times for algorithm C.

In fact, the sorting algorithm reported in [1] (on which algorithms C is based) is limited by the network data transfer. Also, algorithms B and C were compared in [10], which concluded that algorithm B performs better than algorithm C in the common-bus local network for the same reason.

6 Sensitivity to Data Skews

The FPA automatically balances the load for both the merge and return phases, independently of the initial distribution of data. The local sort phase, however, depends upon this initial distribution: if one site has

algorithm		FPA	FPA'	A	B	C	D
CPU (sec)	scan			4.8	4.8	4.8	4.8
	sort	5.1	5.1	436.0	5.1	5.1	6.0
	merge	9.5	10.5		370.3	173.7	
	return	0.4/7.0	0.4/7.0	22.9			22.9
subtotal		15.0/21.6	16.0/22.6	464	380	184	32.7
I/O (sec)	scan			0.7	0.7	0.7	0.7
	sort	1.8	1.8	160.1	1.8	1.8	1.8
	merge	0.8	0.8				
	return	0.7	0.7	45.1			45.1
subtotal		3.3	3.3	206	2.5	2.5	47.6
CPU+I/O (sec)		18.3/24.9	19.3/25.9	670	383	187	80
n-to-n comm (MB)		8	64	64	64	384	64

Table 1: Algorithm Comparisons

more data than another, the local sort phase will take more time. The total elapsed time is thus a function of the maximum local sort time.

We propose the following technique to reduce the effect of skew. Suppose each data site periodically informs the other data sites where it is in the scan (in particular, if it has finished or not). Then, an overloaded site can send pages to other sites that have finished. The overloaded site still needs to read the pages and send them on the communication network; the receiving sites need to receive and extract the data from the page. If records are short, then scanning a page is time consuming; if records are long the path length for communication becomes more important and this load balancing technique is not as efficient. Of course having several sites being able to access the same disk would help in this case.

In order to study the effect of an uneven distribution of the data, let us consider one site that has A records while all other sites have B records. Assuming A > B, we define the skew as Z= A/B. It is easy to calculate the response time degradation of the initial scan as a function of Z. The corresponding curve is plotted as a dotted line in Fig. 5. The figure also shows how the proposed technique may improve the situation for different record lengths. Note again that the degradation applies only the pre-scan phase; its effect should be amortized over the whole duration of the global sort.

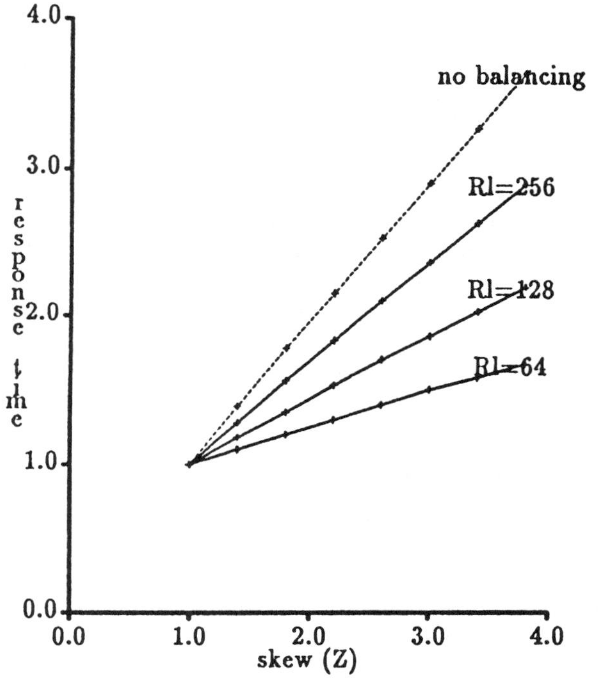

Figure 5: Effect of Redistributing Excess Records.

7 Conclusions

There is increased interest in using multiple nodes to improve the throughput and response time of database operations. Sort is just one of these operations; but it may be the most important one since it also plays a role in other operations such as duplicate elimination, grouping, joining, etc.

We have proposed an efficient parallel sort algorithm that assumes only a "shared nothing" architecture. In such an architecture, the nodes do not share main memory; nor do they share disks. Instead, they communicate among themselves, and with the host, by message passing.

The algorithm, evaluated by exercising a model validated by an actual prototype, exhibits the following nice properties:

1. All sites (except for very short intervals) are performed simultaneously, yielding high utilization of resources.
2. It scales very well. It decreases response time practically linearly when more processors are working on the same problem; it also supports horizontal growth, where 2n processors sort 2N records in roughly the same time that n processors sort N records. The primary reason for such good performance is that the sorted records are returned from all sites to the host site concurrently.
3. It reduces the amount of n-to-n communication and the path length to send/receive communication messages by using a "semi-sort" algorithm, where only keys have to be sent on the n-to-n communication network.

The efficiency of the algorithm is affected by the amount of skew in the data (the uneven distribution of data on the sites). Since skew only affects the initial scan of the data, and not the other phases of the sort, adverse effect is diluted. In any case, we discuss a load-balancing technique that can often be used to reduce the effect of skew on the initial scan itself. This technique is very efficient if the work needed to process a page is significantly larger than the work required to read and send/receive it. If this is not the case, the same technique can be used if several processors are connected to the same disk (which is generally needed in some small amount for availability, anyway); then the data can be read through the I/O channel with large prefetch rather than through communication.

Acknowledgements

We acknowledge the important contribution of Jean-Jacques Daudenarde, Gary Hallmark, and Jim Stamos to the development of the ARBRE prototype. We also thank Jim for useful discussions on the performance analysis, and for many valuable comments on the draft, which improved the presentation of this paper very substantially.

References

[1] M. Beck, D. Bitton, and W. K. Wilkinson. Sorting large files on a backend multiprocessor. *IEEE Transactions on Computers*, C-37(7):769–778, July 1988.

[2] D. Bitton, D. J. DeWitt, D. K. Hsiao, and J. Menon. A taxonomy of parallel sorting. *ACM Computing Surveys*, 16(3):287–318, September 1984.

[3] D. Bitton-Friedland. *Design, Analysis and Implementation of Parallel External Sorting Algorithms.* PhD thesis, Computer Sciences Department, University of Wisconsin—Madison, January 1982.

[4] S. Even. Parallelism in tape-sorting. *Commun. ACM*, 17(4):202–204, April 1974.

[5] J. Gray, M. Stewart, A. Tsukerman, S. Uren, and B. Vaughan. FASTSORT: an external sort using parallel processing. *Tandem Systems Review*, 2(3):40–47, December 1986.

[6] IBM Corporation. *SQL/Data System General Information.* IBM Form No. GH24-5012.

[7] P. J. Janus and E. A. Lamagna. An adaptive method for unknown distributions in distributive partitioned sorting. *IEEE Transactions on Computers*, C-34(4):367–372, April 1985.

[8] S. Lakshmivarahan, S. K. Dhall, and L. L. Miller. Parallel sorting algorithms. *Advances in Computers*, 23:295–354, 1984.

[9] R. Lorie, J. Daudenarde, G. Hallmark, J. Stamos, and H. Young. Adding intra-transaction parallelism to an existing dbms: early experience. *IEEE Data Engineering Bulletin*, 12(1):2–8, March 1989.

[10] K. P. Mikkilinent and S. Y. W. Su. An evaluation of sorting algorithms for common-bus local networks. *Journal of Parallel and Distributed Computing*, 5(1):59–81, February 1988.

[11] P. M. Neches. The anatomy of a data base computer system. In *Proceedings of the 2nd International Conference on Supercomputing*, pages 102–104, 1987.

Chapter 4: Parallel Processing of Join

Join is an expensive and frequently used operation. Therefore, a great deal of effort has been expended in the development of efficient join algorithms. Although parallel database systems could greatly increase processing power, designing efficient join processing methods is still one of the main focuses of research, for two main reasons. First, even in a parallel system, processing of a join of two very large relations is still very costly. Second, new problems are introduced by parallelism; hence, join algorithms must be redesigned to fully exploit the processing capability of parallel processors and at the same time overcome problems inherent in parallel processing. Nevertheless, most parallel join algorithms are based on uniprocessor algorithms. In this chapter, the join algorithms for uniprocessor systems are briefly reviewed before we look at the parallel join algorithms.

Join in uniprocessor database systems

The *equijoin* operation is the most frequently used join operation in relational database systems. The result of an equijoin between two relations R and S on join attributes $R.A$ and $S.B$ consists of tuples that are concatenations of tuples from R (R-tuples) and tuples from S (S-tuples) with $R.A = S.B$. Our discussion will first focus on such equijoins. We denote the two base relations as R and S. The numbers of pages and tuples in R (S) are denoted as $|R|$ ($|S|$) and $||R||$ ($||S||$), respectively. The join condition is $R.A = S.B$.

Conceptually, the join operation needs to compare every R-tuple with every S-tuple to check whether they match; that is, have the same join attribute values. If a system has enough memory to accommodate both relations, or even one of them, join operation would not be so costly, and algorithm design becomes much easier. However, in most systems, it is reasonable to assume that the relations to be joined are much larger than the size of memory available. With this assumption, quite a large number of join algorithms have been developed for uniprocessor systems, which can be categorized into three major paradigms: (1) nested-loops, (2) sort-merge, and (3) hash-based.

Uniprocessor nested-loops join

The nested-loops join method is a straightforward implementation based on the definition of join. As the name implies, the join operation is accomplished by two nested loops. The outer loop scans the tuples in one of the two base relations, designated as the outer relation. For each outer relation tuple scanned, the inner loop scans the other base relation, the inner relation, to find the matches. The basic nested-loops join method works as follows:

```
Algorithm BasicNestedLoopsJoin
for each tuple r in R do
        for each tuple s in S do
                if r.A = s.B
                then output (r, s);
```

When the nested-loops join method is implemented, tuples from both relations R and S are read in from the disks in pages. In order to reduce the number of disk I/Os incurred, with M pages of available memory, the nested-loops join are implemented as follows:

```
Algorithm BasicBlockNestedLoopsJoin
repeat
        read (M – 1) pages of R into memory
        repeat
                read one page of S
                for each R-tuple r in memory do
                        for each S-tuple s in memory do
                        if  r.A = s.B
```

then output (r, s);
until no more unscanned pages of *S*
until no more unprocessed pages of *R*

When the relations involved are large, the nested-loops join method tends to be very expensive. The whole of relation *S* needs to be scanned a number of times, depending on the size of the outer relation, *R*, and the memory size, *M*. Thus, the number of page I/Os required to complete the join is

$$|R| + \lceil |R| / (M-1) \rceil \cdot |S|$$

The first term is required for reading *R*, and the second is for reading *S* multiple times.

Kim[1] proposed a technique to reduce this cost. Instead of always scanning the inner relation from the start to the end, for each block of *R*, the inner relation is first forward scanned and then backward scanned, rocking the relation through the buffer. In this way, the number of I/Os is decreased by *M* in all except the first iterations.

In the above algorithms, with a given *R*-tuple, the whole of relation *S* is sequentially scanned to find the matching tuples. If there is an index on the join attributes of the inner relation, the matching *S*-tuple can be retrieved using the index, which could be much more efficient than a sequential scan. With the index, the nested loops join works as follows:

```
Algorithm IndexedNestedLoopsJoin
repeat
        read one page of R into memory
        for each R-tuple r in memory do
                search the index on s.B for value r.A
                        for each S-tuple found do
                                retrieve the corresponding data page;
                                output (r, s);
until no more unprocessed pages of R
```

It is obvious that, with the help of an index, the join cost may be reduced, especially when the join selectivity is low, as only those pages containing the matching tuples are read into memory. Join selectivity is defined as $\frac{\|R \bowtie S\|}{\|R\| \times \|S\|}$ Furthermore, since the number of scans on *S* does not depend on the number of *R* blocks in memory, *R* can be read in page by page. The major portion of memory can be used to contain the index and to buffer the data pages to further reduce disk I/Os.

Note that the impact of indexing on the join performance depends on whether the index on *S* is clustered or not. For a clustered index, the tuples with the same value $s.B = r.A$ are clustered together so that for each *R*-tuple, the number of *S* pages retrieved is equal to the number of matching *S*-tuples divided by the number of tuples per *S* page. On the other hand, with a nonclustered index, the number of *S* pages retrieved could be as high as the number of matching *S*-tuples. There is indeed another optimization opportunity in the above IndexedNestedLoopsJoin algorithm when the index on *S* is a clustered index: to sort the outer relation on the join attributes. When the outer relation is sorted on the join attributes and the inner relation has a clustered index on the join attributes, the number of pages accessed for both the data and index of the *S* relation will be proportional to the distinct *r.A* values rather than the number of *R*-tuples. In other words, *S*-tuples are scanned in sorted order so that the data pages containing the matching tuples are only read once. Rereading of index pages can also be avoided.

Uniprocessor sort-merge join

Sort-merge join algorithms first sort the two base relations on the join attributes and then merge matching tuples of the two sorted relations. Of course, if any relation has already been sorted on its join attributes, the sorting step for the relation can be skipped. The merging process starts from the first pair of tuples from the two relations. Each tuple pair is examined to find matches. Unlike the nested-loops join, only a single scan (with possible backward moves to earlier portions of the relation because of duplicate attribute values) over the two relations is necessary. The basic sort-merge join algorithm works as follows:

```
Algorithm BasicSortMergeJoin
sort R on R.A and S on S.B in ascending order
set r, r_cur to be the first tuple in R
set s, s_cur to be the first tuple in S
while not (eof(R) or eof(S)) do
        while not (eof(R) or eof(S) or r.A = s.B) do
                if (r.A < s.B)
                        set r, r_cur to be the next tuple in R
                else
                        set s, s_cur to be the next tuple in R
        if not (eof(R) or eof(S))
                while r.A = r_cur.A and not eof(R) do
                        while s.B = r.A and not eof(S)
                                output tuple (r_cur, s_cur)
                                set s to be the next tuple in S
                        endwhile
                        set r to be the next tuple in R
                        if r.A = s_cur.B
                                reset s to s_cur
                endwhile
endwhile
```

The above algorithm seems lengthy because it considers the case where *R.A* and *S.B* are not the keys of the relation. In such a case, a number of *R* (*S*)-tuples may have the same value of *R.A* (*S.B*) and the merge process has to scan both relations in a back-and-forth fashion to generate all results. If the join attributes are the keys, sort-merge join needs to scan the two sorted relations only once.

Uniprocessor hash-based join

The reader may recall that the nested-loops join compares each tuple of the outer relation with every tuple in the inner relation. Therefore, the number of tuple comparisons will be $\|R\| \times \|S\|$. However, only those *R*-tuples and *S*-tuples with $R.A = S.B$ are joinable, that is, can produce the results. When the join selectivity is low, most of the comparisons are unnecessary. Hash-based join is motivated by this fact. The basic hash-based join method partitions two relations into n disjoint pairs of buckets, $R_1, R_2, \ldots, R_n$ and $S_1, S_2, \ldots, S_n$, in such a way that for any two tuples, r and s, where $r \in R_i$ and $s \in S_j$, if $i \neq j$ then $r.A \neq s.B$. In this way, as can be seen in Figure 4-1, R_i needs to be joined with S_i only. Thus,

$$R \bowtie S = \bigcup_{i=1}^{i=n} R_i \bowtie S_i \qquad (4.1)$$

To further reduce the costs of hash-based join methods, the buckets can be generated in such a way that they can fit into the available memory. As a result, the I/O cost in repeated scanning of the relations can be avoided or reduced. The following basic hash-based join algorithm, known as the GRACE algorithm[2], is a straightforward implementation of the above idea:

Algorithm *BasicHashJoin*

```
partition R into n buckets using hashing on R.A
partition S into n buckets using the same hash function on S.B
for each bucket i do
        for each tuple r in R_i do
                hashing on r.A and insert into a hash table
        for each tuple in s in S_i do
                hashing on s.B and probe the hash table
                if s.B = r.A, output tuple (r, s)
```

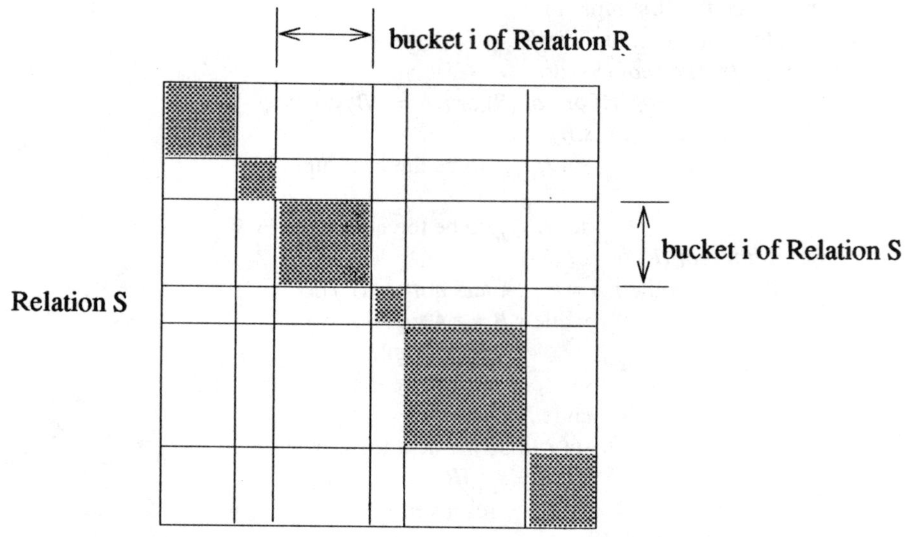

Figure 4-1. Hash-based algorithm.

The GRACE join algorithm comprises two phases: the partition phase, which partitions two relations into buckets and writes them back to disk, and the join phase, which builds hash tables for buckets from one relation and probes the hash table using tuples of the corresponding buckets from the other relation. It should be pointed out that the hash function that is used to partition the relations into buckets during the partitioning phase may also be used for building and probing the hash tables during the joining phase. However, using two different hash functions would minimize collisions during the joining phase.

One of the major design considerations of the hash-based algorithm is the size of the buckets, or the number of buckets to be generated. As hash tables should be constructed for each bucket in the join phase, the bucket size is limited by the available memory space. That is, the following constraint must hold:

$$|R_i| \leq M - 2 \text{ for } 1 \leq i \leq n \tag{4.2}$$

where M is the size of the available memory in pages, with one page being used as an input buffer of S_i and another page as an output buffer of the join results. As it is very difficult to predict the distribution of attribute values, the hash tables of some buckets may be much larger than the available memory. Therefore, a second major consideration in the design of hash-based join algorithms is the treatment of such overflown buckets. One common technique is to repartition buckets that are too large.

Since the hash-based join algorithm was first proposed, a large number of variations have been studied. One major variant is the Hybrid hash join algorithm.[3] Instead of writing all buckets back to disk during the partition phase, the Hybrid hash algorithm retains tuples that belong to the first bucket of R, R_0, in memory to make full use of available memory to reduce the number of disk I/Os. After completing the partitioning phase, the hash table for R_0 is already constructed. The major saving is the number of I/Os needed to write R_0 back to and reread it from the disk. The algorithm can be outlined as follows:

```
Algorithm HybridHashJoin
for each tuple r in R, hashing on r.A to determine bucket number i
        if i = 0 insert r into the hash table for R0
        else write r into bucket Ri
endfor
for each tuple in s in S, hashing on s.B to determine bucket number i
        if i = 0 probe the hash table for R0 in memory
                if found some r with s.B = r.A, output the join result
        else write s into bucket Si
endfor
for each bucket Ri do
        // build a hash table
        for each tuple ri read in, hashing on r.A and insert into the hash table for Ri
        for each tuple si read in from Si do
                hashing on si.B and probe the hash table
                if found some tuple ri with si.B = ri.A, output the join result
        endfor
endfor
```

Both the BasicHashJoin algorithm and HybridHashJoin algorithm partition relations and write the obtained buckets back to the disk that incurs random I/Os. The following algorithm is another variation known as the SimpleHashJoin algorithm:

```
Algorithm SimpleHashJoin
for each bucket i do
        for each unprocessed R-tuple r do
                hashing on r.A to determine bucket number j
                if j = i, insert r into the hash table
                else write r back to disk
                endif
        endfor
        for each unprocessed S-tuple s do
                hashing on s.B to determine bucket number j
                if j ≠ i, write s back to disk
                else    hashing on s.B and probe the hash table
                        if s.B = r.A, output tuple (r, s)
                                endif
                        endfor
                endfor
```

In this SimpleHashJoin, tuples that belong to the current bucket are processed, while tuples that fall outside of the current bucket are not processed, but are written back to disk. This process is repeated with the unprocessed tuples until all the tuples are processed. To avoid writing back to disk, the SimpleHashJoin algorithm can also be modified so that tuples not belonging to the current bucket are simply tossed away. The rationale is to avoid random disk I/Os with the price of incurring more rehashing and sequential I/Os, which is less expensive than random I/Os. In this case, the whole of relations R and S are read n times, where n is the number of buckets, but no tuples are written back.[4,5]

If partitioning the relations using hashing is one feature of the hash-based join, another important feature is to build the hash tables for one relation and to probe the hash tables using tuples from the other relation. This technique can indeed be used in the nested-loops join: Hash tables are built for the outer relation pages. In this case, the outer relation is not partitioned based on join attribute values but according to physical pages:

Algorithm *HashBasedNestedLoopsJoin*
repeat
    read $M - 2$ pages of R and build the hash table on $r.A$
    for each S-tuple s do
        hashing on $s.B$ and probing the hash table
        if $s.B$ is found to be equal to some r in the hash table
            output tuple (r, s)
    endfor
until all R pages are processed

It is obvious that there are more variations of the hash-based join than those join methods described above. In fact, the hash-based join algorithms proposed so far use one of the following ways to partition one of the relations, say R, whose tuples are used to build the hash tables:

1. **To partition the relation prior to the join process**. All tuples in the relation are read, hashed on the join attributes, and written back to disk as partitions according to the hash values.

2. **To partition the relation on-the-fly.** The relation is partitioned on-the-fly with the join. That is, tuples are read from unprocessed portions of the relation and hashed. According to the predetermined hash values, the qualified tuples are used to build the hash table; that is, those tuples that belong to the current partition are retained in memory and inserted into the hash table. There are three ways to deal with the tuples that belong to other buckets:

- *tossed away*: the tuples are tossed away without writing back to disks.
- *written back as a sequential file*: the unprocessed tuples are written back to disk in a single file.
- *written back as bucket files*: the unprocessed tuples are written back to disk according to their hash values; that is, tuples belonging to the same partition are stored together.

Among the three alternatives, the first is the simplest to implement, but it incurs repeated reading and hashing of the whole relation. The third alternative requires one scan over the relation and no rehashing on the tuples. However, both the writes and reads will be random, which is more expensive than the sequential I/Os required if the second alternative is adopted.

3. **To partition the relation without hashing**. The simplest way to partition a relation is to read in pages sequentially until memory is fully occupied by the hash table.

Relation S, which is used to probe the hash tables, can be treated in similar ways. The benefit of prior partitioning of S is that only those tuples from the corresponding batches need to be compared to form the join results. Otherwise, all tuples from relation S have to be used to probe the hash table during each batch. Based on this viewpoint, the hash-based join algorithms can be categorized as shown in Table 4-2.

Table 4-2. Categorization of hash-based join algorithms.

			Partition S				
				on-the-fly			
			prior join	toss	sequential write back	random write back	no hashing
R	prior join		GRACE				
	on-the-fly	toss seq. write back random write back		Simple	Hybrid		
	no hashing						Hash-based nested-loops

Parallel join algorithms

Although many algorithms have been proposed to process the join operation as efficiently as possible, the join operation remains an expensive operation in relational systems. One way to achieve significant improvements in the response time of a join operation is to parallelize the join processing; that is, use p ($p > 1$) processors to join two relations concurrently. Similar to other parallel processing algorithms, the parallel processing of join involves three steps:

- decompose the join into n *tasks*,
- assign those tasks to p processors, and
- assemble the results as the join result.

Here, tasks themselves are joins of subrelations of two base relations. The subrelations are obtained from the decomposition process, and they have the property that the final result could be correctly assembled from the results of joining them concurrently by p processors. As such, different join methods lead to different ways of generating the tasks.

Parallel nested-loops join

The nested-loops join method is particularly suitable for parallel execution since a high degree of parallelism can easily be achieved. The parallel nested-loops join method was briefly mentioned in References 6 and 7 without further study. Recently, DeWitt et al.[8] reported their analytical and experimental study on parallel nested-loops join algorithms.

In shared memory or disk systems, the nested-loops join is rather easy to be parallelized since the inner relation is accessible by all the processors. Each processor processes a portion of the outer relation and joins it with the whole inner relation. The only design consideration may be to reduce the disk access contention and repeated loading of the inner relation from disk. In shared-nothing systems, as tuples from the outer relation must be compared with every inner tuple, the inner relation must be replicated at every node of the system, such as by broadcasting. The straightforward parallel version of the nested-loops join algorithms[6, 7] works as follows:

Algorithm *ParallelNestedLoopsJoin*
each node with S fragment broadcasting the fragment to all processors
redistribute R among all processors
each processor P_i joins its local fragment R_i with the entire S relation

The second step of the algorithm is optional if only those nodes with R segment are chosen to process the join. The reasons for distributing R to as many processors as possible are to increase the parallelism and to balance the load. The resulting relation of the join is also fragmented, and each participating node stores one fragment. The third step of the algorithm, which performs the local join of the R fragments with S, can employ any join methods.

If one of the relations, say S, is indexed on the join attributes at its storage site, the index may be used in the join. However, in this case, the outer relation R should be replicated at all processors. The indexed version is shown below:

Algorithm *ParallelIndexedNestedLoopsJoin*
each node with R fragment broadcasting the fragment to all processors
each processor P_i joins R with its local S_i fragment
    using IndexedNestedLoopsJoin

In the above parallel nested-loops join algorithms, one relation is simply replicated at all processors as no information is available on the distribution of the join attribute values of the other relation. It is quite common that fragments of relations stored in different sites are partitioned according to certain attribute values. This can then be used to limit the replication of the relation. DeWitt, Naughton, and Burger[8] propose an algorithm that uses an additional relation, *MapS* with schema *MapS (P, B)* to determine the sites where an *R*-tuple should be sent (replicated). As only the subsets of the relation are replicated, the algorithm was named subsetting parallel nested loops. *MapS* is constructed as follows: For each tuple *s* of *S*, there is a tuple *m* in *MapS* such that $m.B = s.B$, and $m.P$ is the surrogate of *s*, on which relation *S* is partitioned and stored at different sites. With the help of *MapS*, given a tuple *r* of relation *R*, the value of $r.A$ is used to find an *m*-tuple such that $m.B = r.A$. Once the *m*-tuple is found, the *r*-tuple is sent to the site determined from the value of $m.P$ as *S* is partitioned according to $S.P = m.P$. When relation *S* is large, so is *MapS*. *MapS* itself can also be partitioned on $m.B$ and stored in different sites. In this case, a tuple of *R* will first be sent to the site containing the partition of *MapS* with $m.B = r.A$ and then sent to the sites containing *S* tuples with $s.P = m.P$. The algorithm can be summarized as follows:

Algorithm *SubsettingParallelNestedLoopsJoin*
assume *S* is partitioned on $S.P$ and partition S_k is stored at p_k
for each tuple *s* in *S*
    maintain a tuple *m* in *MapS* with $m.P = s.P$ and $m.B = s.B$
partition *MapS* on $m.B$ and store $MapS_i$ at site p_i
for each tuple *r* in *R*
    find p_i containing $MapS_i$ with $m.B = r.A$
    find p_j containing S_i with $s.P = m.P$
    send *r* to all sites p_j
endfor
perform NestedLoopsJoin at each site p_i

Parallel sort-merge join

Recall that the sort-merge join method consists of two steps:

1. sort both relations on the join attributes;
2. scan the sorted relations in parallel and merge the matching tuples.

Because of the sequential nature of the second step, the merge join operation, initial work on parallel sort-merge join algorithms[6,7] parallelizes only the first phase of the sort-merge join algorithm — sorting the base relations. After two base relations are sorted, most simple parallel sort-merge join algorithms use only one processor to merge-join two relations to generate the join result. This becomes the performance bottleneck of parallel sort-merge join algorithms.

To increase the parallelism in the merge phase, the fragment-and-replicate method can be used in the merge join step.[9] Two base relations are partitioned to generate a set of sorted runs as in the *M*-way merge-sort algorithms. Instead of merging those runs for each relation into an entire sorted relation and then merge-joining the two sorted relations, the merge-join is directly applied to runs generated from sorting each partition. This can be accomplished in two ways:

1. Each sorted run of *R* is merge-joined with each run of *S*. That is, both *R* and *S* are fully fragmented. If there are *m* sorted runs of *R* and *n* sorted runs of *S*, $m \times n$ merge-joins are performed by all processors in the system concurrently; or

2. Sorted runs of the smaller relation, say *R*, are merged first to obtain the sorted *R*, and each run of *S* is merge-joined with *R* concurrently. That is, *R* is replicated and *S* is fragmented.

The above strategies can improve the parallelism of the sort-merge join. However, it suffers from the increased total processing time as the merge-join becomes nested-loops in nature. Furthermore, the data transmission among the processors will become the bottleneck when the communication cost is high.

Another algorithm to parallelize the merge-join step is to use *k* processors to concurrently partition the sorted relations *R* and *S* into *k* partitions, R_1, R_2, ... R_k and S_1, S_2, ... S_k where

1. all tuples in R_i and S_i have join attribute values smaller than the the join attribute values of all elements in R_{i+1} and S_{i+1}, respectively, for $1 \le i \le k-1$;

2. the sum of the number of elements of a partition of R_i and the corresponding partition of S_i is approximately the same for all partitions; that is, $\|R_i\| + \|S_i\| = \|R_{i+1}\| + \|S_{i+1}\|$ for $1 \le i \le k-1$.

After this partitioning process, each of the k processors merge-joins one pair of R and S partitions.[10]

The above algorithm provides a solution to partition a sorted run into a set of runs with the specified property so that the merge-join can be carried out in parallel by k processors. However, it requires the merging of the m sorted runs into one sorted run first, which still limits the parallelism. A more ideal solution is to obtain the k partitions directly from an arbitrary number of runs generated by k processors using internal sort. To achieve this goal, sampling techniques were used to find the boundary value for each partition. Iyer, Richard, and Varman[11] proposed such an algorithm. It divides the m arbitrary-sized sorted runs into two partitions such that one partition contains any given arbitrary fraction f of the total number of elements in the runs, and all elements in that partition are no greater than the elements in the other. By employing the algorithm repeatedly, the m sorted runs can be partitioned into k partitions. As a result, the parallel sort-merge join algorithm comprises the following three phases.

1. m sorted runs are generated for each relation using certain sort algorithm.

2. The elements in the m runs are sampled to determine k key ranges. Based on the k ranges, each of the m runs is then partitioned into k sublists such that the total number of elements in any key range is approximately equal to the total number of elements in any other key range.

3. Each of the k processors is assigned a key range and access to the tuples from all the runs that fall in the key range. That is, processor 1 will access all the tuples whose join attribute values are within the first key range, processor 2 the second, and so on. Each processor will then merge the m sublists of R and S that are allocated to it. The merged sublists of R and S are then merge-joined to produce the result.

One of the advantages of the sort-merge-based algorithms is that they produce the join result in a certain order. Furthermore, if the base relations are already sorted on the join attributes, the join can be accomplished by simply merging the two relations, which is quite efficient.

Parallel hash-based join

Hash-based join is probably the most suitable technique for parallelization, as hash-based join methods partition the base relations into collections of disjoint subsets that can be processed independently and in parallel. Both the two phases of the basic hash-based join methods, the partition phase and the join phase, can be parallelized. One of the basic issues is how to effectively use the processors in both the partition and join phases. In shared everything systems, all the disks are accessible by all the processors. During the partition phase, each processor will read pages of R and hash the tuples into different partitions. During the join phase, as every processor can access the shared memory, all processors can cooperate to build a global hash table in parallel by reading pages of an R-bucket. After the hash table is built, all processors read different pages of the corresponding S-bucket and probe the table concurrently for matching tuples. All uniprocessor hash-based join algorithms, such as the GRACE algorithm, the Hybrid-hash join algorithm, and the hash-based nested-loops join, can be parallelized in this fashion.[12]

In a shared-nothing system, a processor can access only the local disk and memory. The base relations are usually partitioned in some way, and the fragments are stored at different sites (processors). Generally, there is no correlation between the sites (processors), where a tuple is stored, and the values of its join attributes. Therefore, data transfer is usually involved in parallel hash-based join, as processors have to exchange tuples so that each processor will have all the tuples belonging to the buckets assigned to it. The basic parallel hash-based join algorithm in such a system works as follows: During the partition phase, each processor reads tuples from the local fragment of the relation and applies the hash function. A predetermined split table is used to route a tuple to the processor, where the bucket to which the tuple belongs is to be joined. The relation S is partitioned and redistributed in the same way, if necessary. That is, after the partition phase, each processor will have all the buckets to be processed by it stored in its local disks. The joining phase is in fact a uniprocessor processing at each site.[13]

There are cases where some processors in the shared-nothing system do not have local disks — a different set of (diskless) processors may be assigned for the partitioning and joining phase.[4] In such cases, each processor with a disk partitions the smaller relation, R, into buckets that are then sent to the processors without disks. These diskless processors build hash tables for the arriving tuples that belong to the bucket. When all the hash tables are built, the larger relation, S, is partitioned, and the tuples are sent to the diskless processors where the hash table for the corresponding R-bucket has been built. These tuples are used by the diskless processors to probe for matches in the hash tables. If the number of buckets exceeds the number of diskless processors, several phases are necessary, and unused buckets need to be written to disks first.

Though hash-based algorithms seem to outperform the other two types of join algorithms in most cases because of the reduced work load, there are two major issues in implementation that hinder their applications. First, the choice of a suitable hashing function is not easily guaranteed. To ensure a perfect partitioning of relations is almost impossible. Second, it is not easy to determine the size of each bucket. Ideally, each bucket should be as large as possible to make full use of the available memory. However, the bucket should not be too large to fit in the memory; that is, the partition overflow problem should be avoided.

Partition overflow in the parallel hash-based join algorithms is basically the same as in the uniprocessor systems. In general, partition overflow can be detected and resolved either during the partitioning or building phases of the algorithm.[5] In Reference 2, bucket size tuning is employed to prevent partition overflow. This approach is based on the intuition that the size of the partitions is inversely proportional to the number of partitions. Hence, by creating a large number of partitions, the probability that the partition can be staged in the memory is high. During the building phase, some of the smaller partitions may then be integrated to form a large one that is close to, but not exceeding, the size of the available memory. Another preventive measure is to choose and use several effective hashing functions to randomize the distribution of records across partitions. The effectiveness of these hashing functions for specific attributes may be determined through sampling and monitoring their use at run time.

Should the preventive measures fail, the overflow partitions or even the entire relation may be repartitioned using another hashing function. When a partition is further split, new hashing functions used must also be applied to the corresponding partition of the probing relation.

Unfortunately, it is still possible for repartitioning to fail. For example, when most of the records have identical join attribute values, repartitioning or preventive measures are not effective. In such cases, full or partial replication of the relations is the only solution.

Comments

Despite the large number of join algorithms proposed in the literature, a comparative study on the nested-loops, sort-merged, and hash-based algorithms is still lacking. Furthermore, most of these works assume uniform distribution of data. In Reference 6, it is shown that nested-loops can outperform sort-merge due to its higher degree of parallelism. The relative performance of a nested-block join, hash-based join, and sort-merge join have also been studied.[7] The work verified the result in Reference 6. Moreover, it shows that the nested-block join performs best when the ratio between the two relation sizes is different from 1. However, hash-based techniques are shown to perform best in general, while the sort-merge is superior when both relations are about the same size.

Among all the hash-based algorithms, the hybrid hash join performs best.[13] In Reference 8, analytical and experimental results show that hash-based join outperforms the nested loops join in most cases. However, there are cases where indexed nested-loops joins are efficient enough that systems could benefit from implementing both algorithms. Furthermore, the SubsettingParallelNestedLoopsJoin algorithm, with optimization of sorting the outer relation, performs better than many other nested loops algorithms.

As mentioned, a major disadvantage of hash-based join algorithms is that their performances degrade when the data are skewed (see Chapter 5). On the other hand, nested-loops algorithms are not affected by data skew. Sort-merge join, however, has the advantage that the join result is in sorted order.

Papers in this chapter

A large number of papers on parallel join processing have appeared recently. These papers can be roughly divided into two groups. One group of papers deals with the basic parallel join methods and their performance; the other emphasizes the handling of data skewness in join operation in order to further improve the performance. As data skew and load balancing is a very important issue in parallel processing, it will be discussed in a separate chapter of this book (Chapter 5). In this chapter, we include four papers that discuss the join algorithms designed for parallel systems with different architecture.

The first paper, "Join and Semijoin Algorithms for a Multiprocessor Database Machine," by Valduriez and Gardarin, is one of the earliest papers to address parallel processing of join. It presents analytical results on the relative performance of nested-block, sort-merge, and hash-based join algorithms.

The second paper, "A Performance Evaluation of Four Parallel Join Algorithms in a Shared Nothing Multiprocessor Environment," by Schneider and DeWitt, compares the performance of hash-based join algorithms with sort-merge join algorithms on the Gamma shared-nothing database system.

The analysis of a large number of join algorithms for shared-memory systems is presented in the third paper, "The Join Algorithms on a Shared Memory Multiprocessor Database Machine" by Qadah and Irani.

The fourth paper, "Design and Evaluation Parallel Pipelined Join Algorithm," by Richardson, Lu, and Mikkilineni,. discusses join processing in a highly parallel hybrid environment. Several sort-based and hash-based join algorithms that explore pipeline parallelism are proposed and studied.

References

1. W. Kim, "A New Way to Compute the Product and Join of Relations," *Proc. ACM SIGMOD 1980 Conf.,* Assoc. for Computing Machinery, New York, N.Y., 1980, pp. 179-187.
2. M. Kitsuregawa, H. Tanaka, and T. Moto-oka, "Application of Hash to Data Base Machine and Its Architecture," *New Generation Computing,* Vol. 1, No. 1, 1983.
3. D. DeWitt et al., "Implementation Techniques for Main Memory Database Systems," *Proc. ACM SIGMOD 1984 Conf.,* Assoc. for Computing Machinery, New York, N.Y., 1984, pp. 1-8.
4. D.J. DeWitt and R. Gerber, "Multiprocessor Hashed-Based Join Algorithms," *Proc. 11th Int'l Conf. Very Large Data Bases*, Morgan Kaufman, San Mateo, Calif., 1985, pp. 151-164.
5. R.H. Gerber, "Dataflow Query Processing Using Multiprocessor Hash Partitioned Algorithms," Tech. Report No. 672, Univ. of Wisconsin, Madison, Wisc., Oct. 1986.
6. D. Bitton, "Parallel Algorithms for the Execution of Relational Database Operations," *ACM Trans. Database Systems*, Vol. 8, No. 3, Sept. 1983, pp. 324-353.
7. P. Valduriez and G. Gardarin, "Join and Semijoin Algorithms for a Multiprocessor Database Machine," *ACM Trans. Database Systems,* Vol. 9, No. 1, Mar. 1984, pp. 133-161.
8. D. DeWitt, J. Naughton, and J. Burger, "Nested Loops Revisited," *Proc. Second Parallel and Distributed Information Systems Conf.,* IEEE CS Press, Los Alamitos, Calif., 1993, pp. 230-242.
9. J.P. Richardson, H. Lu, and K. Mikkilineni, "Design and Evaluation of Parallel Pipelined Join Algorithms," *Proc. ACM Int'l Conf. Management Data,* Assoc. for Computing Machinery, New York, N.Y., 1987, pp. 399-409.
10. S.G. Akl and N. Santroo, "Optimal Parallel Merging and Sorting Without Memory Conflicts," *IEEE Trans. Computers,* Vol. 36, No. 11, Nov. 1987, pp. 1367-1369.
11. B.R. Iyer, G.R. Ricard, and P.J. Varman, "Percentile Finding Algorithm for Multiple Sorted Runs," *Proc. 15th Int'l Conf Very Large Data Bases,* Morgan Kaufman, San Mateo, Calif., 1989, pp. 135-144.
12. H. Lu, K.L. Tan, and M.C. Shan, "Hash-Based Join Algorithms for Multiprocessor Computers with Shared Memory," *Proc. 16th Int'l Conf. Very Large Data Bases,* Morgan Kaufman, San Mateo, Calif., 1990, pp. 198-209.
13. D.A. Schneider and D.J. DeWitt, "A Performance Evaluation of Four Parallel Join Algorithms in a Shared-Nothing Multiprocessor Environment," *Proc. ACM Int'l Conf. Management Data,* Assoc. for Computing Machinery, New York, N.Y., 1989, pp. 110-121.

Join and Semijoin Algorithms for a Multiprocessor Database Machine

PATRICK VALDURIEZ and GEORGES GARDARIN
SABRE Project, INRIA and University of Paris VI

This paper presents and analyzes algorithms for computing joins and semijoins of relations in a multiprocessor database machine. First, a model of the multiprocessor architecture is described, incorporating parameters defining I/O, CPU, and message transmission times that permit calculation of the execution times of these algorithms. Then, three join algorithms are presented and compared. It is shown that, for a given configuration, each algorithm has an application domain defined by the characteristics of the operand and result relations. Since a semijoin operator is useful for decreasing I/O and transmission times in a multiprocessor system, we present and compare two equi-semijoin algorithms and one non-equi-semijoin algorithm. The execution times of these algorithms are generally linearly proportional to the size of the operand and result relations, and inversely proportional to the number of processors. We then compare a method which consists of joining two relations to a method whereby one joins their semijoins. Finally, it is shown that the latter method, using semijoins, is generally better. The various algorithms presented are implemented in the SABRE database system; an evaluation model selects the best algorithm for performing a join according to the results presented here. A first version of the SABRE system is currently operational at INRIA.

Categories and Subject Descriptors: H.2.6 **[Database Management]**: Database Machines; H.2.3 **[Database Management]**: Languages—*data manipulation languages* (*DML*); C.1.2 **[Processor Architectures]**: Multiple Data Stream Architectures

General Terms: Algorithms, Performance

Keywords and Phrases: Relational algebra, join, semijoin

1. INTRODUCTION

Several relational database machines are currently being developed [1, 4, 14, 30]. The main objective of these projects is to answer complex queries, expressed in a nonprocedural language on a very large database, with better performance than conventional database systems [11, 28]. These machines are generally equipped with a set of processors executing requests in parallel. They are examples of a design approach which tends to distribute the processing power in close proximity to the data storage units. This relieves the main computer of the data processing functions.

Authors' address: SABRE Project, INRIA and University of Paris VI, BP 105, 78150 Le Chesnay, France.

"Join and Semijoin Algorithms for a Multiprocessor Database Machine" by P. Valduriez and G. Gardarin from *ACM Trans. Database Systems*, Vol. 9, No. 1, Mar. 1984, pp. 133-161. Copyright 1984, Association for Computing Machinery, Inc., reprinted with permission.

One factor limiting the performance of relational systems is the join operation. The θ-join [13] (or simply join) of two operand relations R and S on attributes A from R, and B from S is the result relation T, obtained by concatenating each tuple in R with each tuple in S, such as, for example, $A \theta B$, where θ is one of the operators $=, <, \leq, \geq, >, \neq$. Join is an important operation generally needed to answer multirelation queries, but it can be very time consuming. A semijoin is a special case of join, in which the attributes of the result relation belong to only one operand relation.

Several uniprocessor algorithms have been presented and discussed [8, 19, 29]. In such a context, and without indexing, the obvious method of computing joins by nested loops has an execution time proportional to n**2 for relations of cardinality n. A better method, based on sorting, can reduce this time to $a \cdot n \log n$, where a is a constant [8]. A still better method, based on hashing [2], can further reduce the time to $b \cdot n$, where b is also a constant. However, this last method allows the performance of semijoins only.

A large collection of parallel algorithms can be derived from monoprocessor algorithms for performing join. We explore here a class of algorithms based on "divide and conquer" principles; this means that data are divided into equal parts, and a similar algorithm is then applied by each processor to join the parts. A first study of this class of algorithms has been done in [9]. In this paper we extend their results to the SABRE database machine architecture, using a larger class of algorithms; we also show the value of performing semijoins before joins in a multiprocessor system.

In summary, this paper presents three implementations of parallel join algorithms—the nested loops, the sort-merge, and the hashing algorithms—in the SABRE multiprocessor system [18], and it more precisely analyzes the algorithms' performance. In Section 2, the architecture model that enables us to study the algorithms is precisely described; it is derived from the SABRE database machine project. The SABRE database machine components involved in computing joins or semijoins are a set of filtering processors associated with the disk units, a cache memory, and a set of join processors. The processors own a local memory which stores data during processing, and are linked together by an interconnection network. In Section 3, the analysis criteria are introduced, including the performance parameters needed for the evaluation of the execution times (I/O, CPU, and message transmission) of the algorithms. The basic assumption is that the operand relations are too large to fit into the cache memory or into the join processors' local memories. In Section 4, three multiprocessor join algorithms are presented: the nested loop join algorithm [15], the sort-merge-join algorithm, and the hashing join algorithm. The execution times of these algorithms are then compared. The results depend mainly on the number of processors, the size of the operand relations, and the proportion of matching tuples in a relation. It turns out that, for a given configuration, each algorithm has an application domain defined by the characteristics of the operand and result relations.

Recent results have shown the value of semijoins for optimizing query execution [5–7, 12]. The length of time for this operation is substantially less than that for a join, and is linearly proportional to the size of the operand and result relations.

The semijoin is useful in distributed relational databases [23, 26] for reducing the time for processing queries involving binary operations, by means of initially selecting relevant data and thereby reducing the size of the operand relations. We show in this paper that it is also very useful for optimizing join processing in a multiprocessor database machine. In Section 5, two equi-semijoin algorithms are presented and compared. A third non-equi-semijoin algorithm is also proposed. Their execution time is generally proportional to the size of the operand and result relations, and inversely proportional to the number of processors. In a uniprocessor environment, a semijoin can be used efficiently to replace the join of relations by the join of their semijoins [29]. Thus comparisons of two join methods, one based directly on the nested loop algorithm [9] and the other performing semijoins before the join, are developed. These comparisons indicate the general advantage of performing joins by using semijoins.

2. ARCHITECTURAL MODEL

The environment in which join and semijoin algorithms are studied is the SABRE database machine [18], composed of a set of processors linked through an interconnection network. The processors exchange commands directly and exchange data via a cache memory. We now give a simplified model which describes the main architectural components of SABRE, focusing on those components useful in implementing joins and semijoins.

The first layer of the architecture is arranged as a set of data filtering processors [3, 16, 27]. These processors, called filters, perform selections (restriction and projection) on data coming from disks. It has been shown in [10] that, if parallel readout disks are employed, the usage of processor-per-disk together with an efficient placement strategy gives the best results, since channel contention is thereby avoided. Furthermore, this usage provides cheap filtering power. Thus, in SABRE, we implement a filter-per-disk device. Filters are very simple processors, close to the general form of automata. They permit realization of asynchronous processing "on the fly"— in other words, filters perform a selection at disk rotation speed on a secondary memory page, which generally corresponds to a track. A selection expression is composed of a set of references that specify the projection attributes and the selection condition. A selection condition is a logical combination of predicates of the form (Ai op C), expressed in normal conjunctive form, where Ai is an attribute of an operand relation, op an operator chosen among $<$, $\leq$, $=$, $\neq$, $\geq$, $>$, and C, a value. The number of predicates which can be taken into account by a filter depends on characteristics of the automata only, and not on the data flow or on the tested expressions. In [16] evaluations show that, for an average memory size of 64K bits, a filter can accept up to 200 predicates.

The second layer of the architecture is a cache memory. The filters are connected to the cache memory through a special bus [17]. We assume that this bus does not provide any contention. Selected data are moved via the bus to the cache memory, divided in pages. In SABRE the basic processing and moving unit is the page. The cache manager should anticipate page reading and use a replacement algorithm to swap the useless pages to the disk. A filter can be

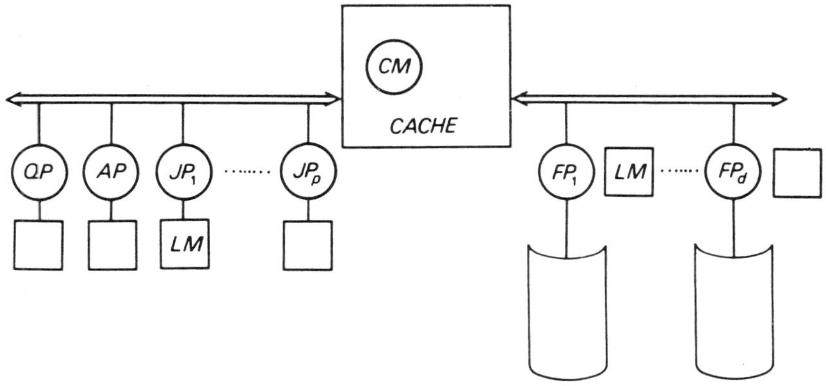

QP: Query Processor *CM:* Cache Manager
AP: Access Processor *FP:* Filtering Processor
JP: Join Processor *LM:* Local Memory

Fig. 1. Simplified architecture model.

associated to the cache memory in order to carry out the necessary selection among pages already in the cache.

The third layer of the architecture is a set of join processors devoted to computing joins of relations. Join processors send reading and writing requests to the cache in order to get pages of relations and to write back result pages. Pages are stored in the local memories of the processors during processing. The join processors are connected with the cache memory by a specific interconnection network. The requirements for this network are the ability to carry out parallel transfers between the cache and any join processor, and the capability to broadcast a page from the cache to several join processors. This kind of interconnection network is feasible [14], and different alternatives have been studied. The current developments of SABRE are based on a French multimicroprocessor called the SM90 [17]. Although this machine has a very fast common bus (eight megabytes per second), we try to be independent of the interconnection network, as it would affect the performance of the whole system. For our purposes, we assume an ideal interconnection network, which would provide the two needed services and introduce no contention.

Finally, the complete architecture of SABRE includes two more processor types (i.e., the access path management processor and the query decomposition processor [18]). These processors are connected to the join processor bus, and share with the join processors the task of executing external requests. The architectural components of SABRE are depicted in Figure 1, where, for simplicity, the interconnetion networks are reduced to buses. Thus, SABRE allows a high degree of intra- and interrequest parallelism by means of a set of specialized processors. In the following, we are going to more precisely focus on intrarequest parallelism for performing joins.

3. ANALYSIS CRITERIA

In the following, we assume that a semijoin or join operation is performed on relations R and S, producing the result relation T. We recall that the semijoin of R by S is the set of tuples of R participating in the join of R and S. The following notation is needed to evaluate the proposed algorithms:

- m, n: number of pages in R and S, respectively;
- $b + 1$: size of local memory (in number of pages) of each join processor (JP);
- p: number of join processors (JP) assigned to the operation;
- c: cache memory size allocated to the join operation (in number of pages);
- d: number of filters assigned to the operation;
- t: number of tuples in a page, assumed to be the same for both R and S;
- JS: join selectivity factor, defined by size (R join S)/$(m \cdot n)$;
- SR: semijoin of (R by S) selectivity factor which is defined by size(semijoin (R by S))/m;
- SS: semijoin of (S by R) selectivity factor which is defined by size(semijoin (S by R))/n;
- j: average number of distinct join attribute values in a page. Thus, mj and nj are the total numbers of distinct join attribute values in R and S, respectively;
- Nc: number of predicates accepted by a filter;
- Ct: occupation factor of join attributes in a tuple, defined by the size of the join attribute divided by the size of the tuple. Thus, the number of pages of the relation obtained after projecting relation S on join attributes without duplicate elimination is defined by $na = n \cdot Ct$.

The presented algorithms will be compared according to their execution times. The basic performance parameters necessary for the evaluation of the execution times are those detailed above. These parameters allow one to measure the I/O time, the CPU time, and the interprocessor communication time when executing a multiprocessor algorithm. The identified parameters depend on hardware capabilities, and will be fixed for purposes of comparison only.

3.1 I/O Time

In a multiprocessor architecture, two kinds of transfers are considered as I/O operations: page transfers from a mass storage unit and transfers from the cache memory to a processor's local memory. The page transfer time from disk to cache is denoted Tdc, and includes the selection time due to filtering on the fly. The page transfer time from cache to processor is denoted Tcp. The average time of a read by a join processor is now defined by introducing the probability that the requested page is already in the cache memory [9]. The cache manager should maximize this probability by anticipating page reading, which is made easier by the fact that a referenced relation will be read in its entirety. This probability is equivalent to the cache hit ratio, denoted by F. Thus the average time of a read, defined as CR, is

$$\mathrm{CR} = F \cdot T\mathrm{cp} + (1 - F) \cdot (T\mathrm{cp} + T\mathrm{dc}).$$

The average time of a write by a join processor can be evaluated in the same fashion by introducing F′—the probability that there is an available page frame in the cache during the write operation. This probability is supposed to be relatively low and constant. The cache manager uses an algorithm different than LRU, since the main difference with a classical cache memory is that the entire operation is known in advance. Therefore, the cache manager can swap out pages in order to keep F' constant. Thus the average time of a write, defined by CW, is

$$\mathrm{CW} = F' \cdot T\mathrm{cp} + (1 - F') \cdot (T\mathrm{cp} + T\mathrm{dc}).$$

3.2 Communication Time

Page moves are regarded as I/O operations. Therefore, the only communication time which needs be taken into account is from page request and reply messages. This message time, denoted as M, is then added to the I/O time. Thus CR is replaced by CR + M(request) + M(reply), and CW is replaced by CW + M(request) + M(reply). Control messages, such as those used for processor allocation, are few in number and small in size, relative to the page request and reply messages. Therefore they will be ignored.

3.3 CPU Time

Two basic operation times are defined. 0 denotes the time of a simple operation, such as comparing two attributes or computing a hashing function. The time for moving a tuple in a page of local memory is denoted by I. With these two basic operation times, we can compute all other times as follows.

Join time. The pages to be joined may or may not be sorted. If they are unsorted, two methods for joining are possible. The first consists in internally sorting the pages, followed by a merge-type join operation. The second method, which is simpler, compares each tuple in a page with each tuple in another page; it is better than the first method, since it only requires comparison operations, which are cheaper than the tuple movement that internal sorting requires. Thus, the time for joining two unsorted pages, denoted as CJ0, is CJ0 = $0 \cdot t$**2. The time for joining two sorted pages by a merge-type operation is defined as CJ1 = $2t \cdot 0$.

One page sort time. The average time for internally sorting a page of t tuples requires $t \cdot \log_2 t$ comparisons and move operations [22]. It is defined as

$$\mathrm{Cs} = (0 + I) t \cdot \log_2 t.$$

q page merge time. The merging of q sorted pages needs $q(q-1)t$ comparison operations and $q \cdot t$ move operations. By adding the q page reading and writing times, the q page merge time is defined by

$$\mathrm{CM}q = (q(q-1)t \cdot 0) + (q \cdot t \cdot I) + (q(\mathrm{CR} + \mathrm{CW})).$$

4. JOIN ALGORITHMS

4.1 The Nested Loop Join Algorithm

This algorithm is a parallel version of the most inefficient uniprocessor join algorithm, since it composes the Cartesian product of the relations. This simple algorithm is particularly well suited to parallel execution. The method is to join each page of one relation with the entire other relation. The algorithm has been described and evaluated in [9] for processors having three pages of local memory, where two buffers are used to input pages and one buffer to output pages. The method is now generalized to support execution with more than three pages of local memory. The execution of this algorithm by p processors, each having $(b + 1)$ pages of local memory proceeds as follows. The smaller relation is chosen as the external one and is sequentially distributed among p join processors in blocks of $(b - 1)$ pages. Next, the second (internal) relation is broadcast page by page to the p processors. Then, each processor joins each $(b - 1)$ page block of the external relation with the entire internal relation. For each page of the internal relation, each processor computes an internal join with $(b - 1)$ pages of the external relation, using a result buffer of one page. If the external relation does not fit into the processors' local memories, then the same process must be repeated for the remaining pages of the external relation.

We should point out that, since each tuple of one relation will be compared to each tuple of the other one, this algorithm also supports non-equijoin. Finally, the execution time of the nested loop join algorithm is derived in Appendix A. The final result is

$$\text{TIME(NL)} = m \cdot \text{CR}/p + m \cdot n(\text{CR}/(p(b - 1)) + (\text{CJ0} + \text{JS}(t \cdot I + \text{CW}))/p).$$

The formula shows that this time is proportional to $m/p + a \cdot mn/p$. Therefore, the smaller relation must be chosen as external in order to decrease the first term. This equation also shows that the degree of parallelism is constant (i.e., the amount of work each processor performs is constant) during the entire execution of the algorithm. It should be noted, however, that the last pass of the algorithm can use a fewer number of processors if the ratio $m/(p(b - 1))$ does not give an integer result.

4.2 The Sort-Merge-Join Algorithm

This algorithm employs a parallel sort of the operand relations on join attributes, followed by a uniprocessor merge-type operation of the two sorted relations to complete the join. For simplicity, we consider the equijoin. The sorting algorithm is a parallel version of the uniprocessor ascending (or merge sort) algorithm (described in [22], p. 247). In [9] a join algorithm is presented using a parallel binary merge sort, where the processors are organized in the form of binary trees [25]. Performance analysis of this join algorithm shows that it is generally less efficient than the multiprocessor nested loop join algorithm, if the number of processors is high. This is mainly because, after a certain stage, the degree of parallelism is divided by two at each merge pass, so that, at the last pass, one processor merges the entire relation. We propose a parallel b-way merge sorting, which is more efficient in a multiprocessor environment. Moreover, if the number of processors p is less than or equal to b, the last stage only needs one pass.

We briefly review the b-way merge sort algorithm. Let us suppose that there are n elements to be sorted. A run is defined as an ordered sequence of elements, thus the set to be sorted contains n runs of one element. The method consists of iteratively merging b runs of K elements into a sorted run of $K \cdot b$ elements, starting with $K = 1$. For pass i, each set of b runs of $b^{**}(i-1)$ elements is merged into a sorted run of $b^{**}i$ elements. Starting from $i = 1$, the number of passes necessary to sort n elements is $\log_b n$ [22].

We now describe the application of this method in a multiprocessor database machine. Let us suppose we have to sort a relation of n pages that is too large to fit into the cache memory.

Recall that each of the p processors has a local memory of $b + 1$ pages, where b pages are used as input pages and 1 is used as an output page. At each pass, each processor merges a set of b runs of $b^{**}(i-1)$ pages into a sorted run of $b^{**}i$ pages. The merge of b runs is done by successively reading one necessary page of each run into b input buffers and then moving ordered tuples into the output buffer, writing in the cache memory when full. When read at the first pass, pages are internally sorted. To clarify the analysis, we assume that modulo $(n, p) = 0$ (i.e., that p processors divide the relation into equal parts and share exactly the same amount of work). At each merge pass the number of runs is divided by b, while the size of each run is multiplied by b, and the whole relation is read and written. For the first pass, let N be the number of runs to be merged; if N is greater than $p \cdot b$, one step is necessary for each of the p processors to merge b runs, and this step is repeated $N/(p \cdot b)$ times until all the runs have been read. When N is equal to $p \cdot b$, only one step is necessary, and each processor merges exactly b runs of $n/(p \cdot b)$ pages. This pass is called the optimal stage [9]. The optimal stage then generates p runs of n/p pages and, if p equals b, one processor can merge them in a single pass. But, in certain configurations, p can be very much greater than b, in which case the solution is to arrange the processors as a tree of order b during the last stage, called the postoptimal stage. The number of necessary processors is divided by b at each pass. At the last pass, one processor merges the entire relation. The number of passes for the postoptimal stage is $\log_b p$. This stage degrades the degree of parallelism. However, the result relation is sorted on the join attributes, which can be very useful if such a sort is required in the query.

Joining two sorted relations is done by a uniprocessor merge-type operation, where each relation is read one page at a time. The adaptation of this algorithm to the non-equijoin modifies the merge-type operation into a more complex and time consuming one.

In Appendix B, we evaluate the execution time for sorting a relation for n pages. We then derive the execution time of the sort-merge-join algorithm, which is

$$\text{TIME(SM)} = n/p[\text{C}s + \text{CM}b\cdot\log_b(n/p)/b + \text{CM}b\cdot(1 - b^{**}\log_b p)/(1 - b)] + m/p[\text{C}s + \text{CM}b\cdot\log_b(m/p)/b + \text{CM}b\cdot(1 - b^{**}\log_b p)/(1 - b)] + (m + n)\text{CR} + \max(m, n)\cdot\text{CJ1} + m\cdot n\cdot\text{JS}\cdot\text{CW}.$$

This formula is rather complex, and will be interpreted later with the given parameters.

4.3 The Hashing Join Algorithm

The proposed method uses hashing techniques and Boolean arrays. The use of Boolean arrays for implementing the semijoin operation has been described by Babb [2]. The idea is to hash the join attribute and to then use the result as an address into the Boolean array. The presence of a marked bit in the array means that matching tuples exist. The value of the Boolean arrays is to eliminate most of the data not needed in the result. In order to support join as well as semijoin operations, the method is improved and adapted to a multiprocessor context. For simplicity, we describe the equijoin. The method proceeds in two stages, prior to which a Boolean array B is initialized in the cache memory. In the first stage, the smaller relation is read into the cache memory and hashed on the join attribute by the cache processor so that each tuple is written in a bucket of a hashed file. The hashed file is composed of buckets having a variable number of linked pages. For each bucket, a page frame is maintained in cache memory. This avoids the need to manage an overflow area. Simultaneously, for each join attribute value v, $B(h(v))$ is marked (set to 1), where h is a hashing function applied to the join attribute. The first stage is completed when the entire relation has been hashed. In the second stage, the Boolean array is broadcast to p processors, and the larger relation is sequentially distributed among p processors. Each processor uses two buffers as input pages, one buffer as the output page and one buffer to store the Boolean array. Thus, each processor receives one page of the larger relation and performs the following processing. For each tuple of the page such that the join attribute value v' satisfies $B(h(v')) = 1$, one bucket of the hashed file is accessed by specifying the key v' to find the matching tuple(s). Since a bucket of the hashed file may contain more than one page, the bucket is read page by page. The tuples of each page are then compared with v' to complete the join.

This method makes extensive use of hashing. In order for it to be applicable, the number of distinct join attribute values in the hashed relation must be significantly greater than the number of buckets. At the first stage, the choice of hashing the smaller relation is made to minimize the creation and storage times of the hashed file.

The classical problem with hashing is collisions. If $v1$ and $v2$ are different join attribute values, we can have $h(v1) = h(v2)$. Since the Boolean array is accessed by hashing, collisions can lead to useless access to the hashed file during the second stage. In order to reduce collisions, several hashing functions $h1, h2, \ldots, hq$ can be used, each associated with a Boolean array $B1, B2, \ldots, Bq$. Then, for each value v, all of the corresponding bits in each Bi must be set (i.e., $B1(h1(v)) = 1, B2(h2(v)) = 1, \ldots Bq(hq(v)) = 1$). In [2] it is shown that increasing q causes the probability of collisions to approach 0.

If the hashing function for the hashed file has the property of maintaining order (i.e., given two attribute values $v1$ and $v2$, if $v1 < v2$, then $h(v1) < h(v2)$, and the algorithm can then support non-equijoin).

In Appendix C, we derive the execution time of the algorithm, which is

$$\text{TIME(H)} = m[(1 - F)T\text{dc} + t(0 + I)] + (m - C)(1 - F')T\text{dc} + (n/p)[\text{CR} + t \cdot 0 + t \cdot \text{SS} \cdot (m/c) \cdot \text{CR} + m \cdot \text{JS} \cdot \text{CW}].$$

It is of the form $a1 \cdot m + a2 \cdot n/p + a3 \cdot mn/p$, where $a3$ is proportional to the join and semijoin selectivities. It already appears therefore that the algorithm will be almost linear for join with a very small selectivity; thus, it is a very efficient algorithm for such a case.

4.4 Comparisons

For purposes of comparison, we fix the values of the parameters discussed in Section 3. The chosen values according to our current implementation are the following:

- 0: the time to compare two attributes is equal to 10 microseconds;
- I: the time to move a tuple in a page is equal to 250 microseconds, based on a page size of 4K bytes and a tuple length of 40 bytes;
- t: the number of tuples in a page is equal to 100 microseconds;
- F, F': cache hit ratios, $F = 0.8$ and $F' = 0.3$;
- *Tdc:* the time of a disk-cache page transfer is equal to 30 milliseconds;
- *Tcp:* the time of a cache-processor page transfer is equal to 4 milliseconds, based on an average bus bandwidth of 1 megabyte per second;
- M: the time to process a message which includes sending, transfer, and receiving times and is assumed to be 10 milliseconds;
- *Ct:* occupation factor of a join attribute is equal to 0.2, so semijoin attribute length is 8 bytes.

Using these fixed values and the previous equations, the three join algorithms are compared. Other comparisons have been done with different values of F and F,' showing that their influence is weak (since the differences between the execution times remain approximately constant). However, decreasing F' increases somewhat the execution time of the sorting join algorithm relative to the other algorithms, since the final merges are done by a unique processor. For simplicity, we denote the nested loop join algorithm as the NL algorithm, the sort-merge-join algorithm as the SM algorithm, and the hashing join algorithm as the H algorithm.

4.4.1 *Execution Times versus Relation Sizes.* Figure 2 illustrates the behavior of the algorithms versus relation sizes. The sizes of the two relations are assumed

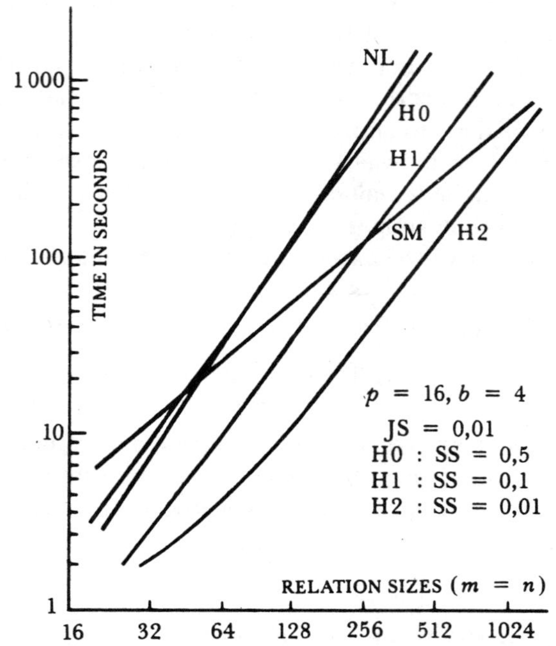

Fig. 2. Execution times of the algorithms versus relation sizes.

to be the same ($m = n$). The configuration comprises 16 processors, each having a local memory of 5 pages with a cache memory size (allocated to the join) of 16 pages. Three curves describe the performances of the H algorithm for three different semijoin selectivity factors (0.5, 0.1, 0.01). The join selectivity factor is assumed to be 0.01. It appears that the SM algorithm is better than both the NL algorithm and the H algorithm (with SS $\geq$ 0.1), when the operand relations are large. The behavior of the H algorithm depends essentially on SS, the semijoin selectivity factor, which yields the number of matching tuples from the distributed relation with the hashed file. When SS is small (SS < 0.01), the number of accesses to the hashed file is low, and the H algorithm is superior. For the given configuration, when SS is less than 0.5, the H algorithm always performs better than the NL algorithm. Beyond SS $\simeq$ 0.5, the H algorithm does not perform well (curve H0). The size of the cache memory allocated to the join (denoted by C) significantly influences the execution time of the H algorithm, because, if C is high enough, the hashed file can fit into the cache without swapping out to the disk.

The previous comparisons show that, for the given configuration, each algorithm has a domain of application where it performs better than the others. Figure 3 illustrates the domains of the NL algorithm in comparison with the SM algorithm, for various sizes of relations. Similarly, Figure 4 depicts the domains of the SM algorithm in comparison with the H algorithm for SS = 0.1, which is a realistic coefficient.

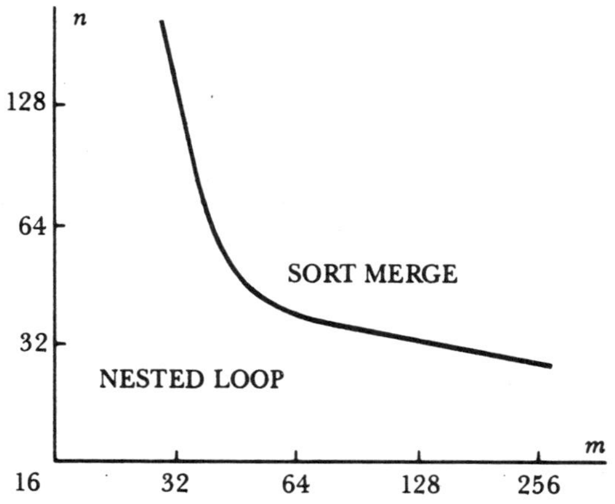

Fig. 3. Limit of the NL algorithm in comparison with the SM algorithm. ($p = 16$, $b = 4$, JS = 0.01)

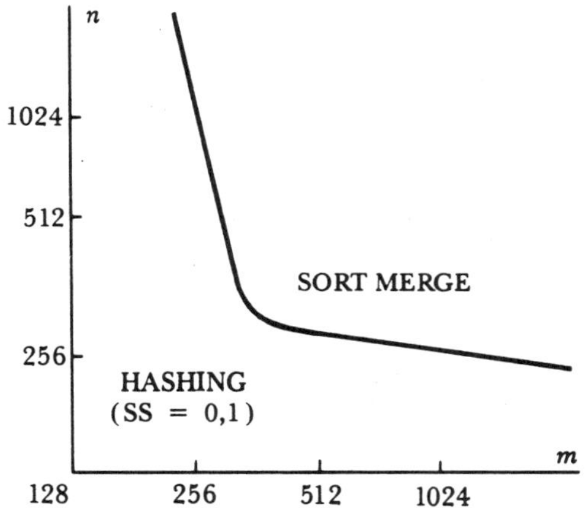

Fig. 4. Limit of the H algorithm in comparison with the SM algorithm.

In conclusion, one of the important results of this first comparison is that no algorithm is predominant. Therefore, a well-designed database machine should implement all the algorithms and select the best one to perform a join, according to the estimated time in utilizing the previous formulas. That is the way the SABRE system performs joins.

4.4.2 *Comparisons with Respect to the Number of Processors.* The configuration is essentially characterized by the number of join processors and the size of the cache memory. Figures 5 and 6 show the behavior of the algorithms for various numbers of processors for small relations (Figure 5) and larger relations (Figure 6). The complexity of the NL algorithm is $1/p$, while that of the SM algorithm is $1/\log_b p$. Thus, when the number of processors increases, the NL

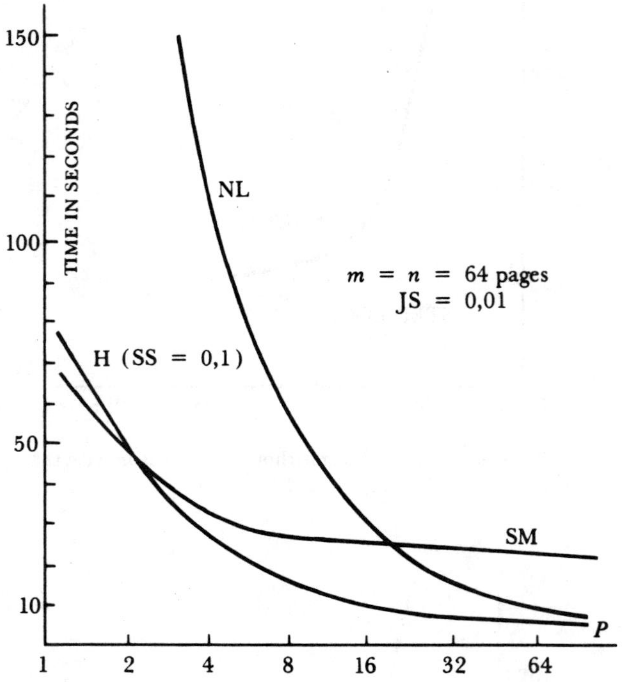

Fig. 5. Execution times of the algorithms versus the number of processors.

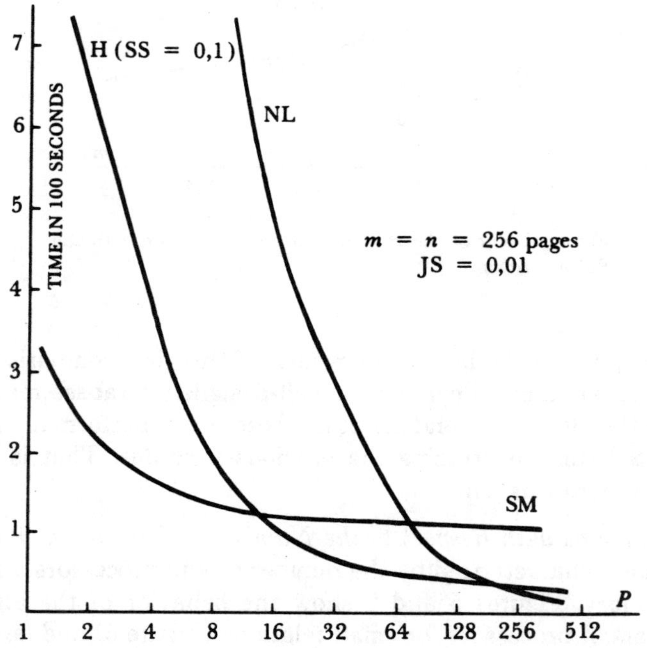

Fig. 6. Execution times of the algorithms versus the number of processors (p).

algorithm performs better than the SM algorithm. The curve of the H algorithm for SS = 0.5 would be approximately the same as that of the NL algorithm. With a favorable semijoin selectivity factor (0.1), the H algorithm gives good results when the number of processors is high. This is because the time of the second stage of the H algorithm is of complexity $1/p$. Generally, the semijoin selectivity factor will be low, and, in that case, the H algorithm seems very attractive. It is notable that, for the SM algorithm, after a certain number of processors, duplicating the number of processors causes very little decrease in the execution time. This is owing to the increasing number of passes of the postoptimal stage, proportional to the number of processors. In fact, the SM algorithm is better for configurations in which $p = b$, when only one postoptimal pass is needed. When p becomes greater than b, the postoptimal stage degrades the degree of parallelism.

5. SEMIJOIN ALGORITHMS

If the comparison operator θ, in the join definition of Section 1, is equal, and if the result attributes belong to a single relation, the operation is called an equi-semijoin. In this section we will mainly discuss and evaluate two equi-semijoin algorithms, one using bit arrays and the other using the selection operation performed by the filtering processors. Finally, we will consider non-equi-semijoins, where the comparison operator θ is not equal.

5.1 Equi-Semijoin with Bit Arrays

The proposed method is an extension of the uniprocessor method for performing semijoins, as described in [2]. The basic version uses a bit array to aid the operation. In our parallel version this array is replicated in the join processors' local memories. The operation in a multiprocessor environment proceeds in two stages. First, semijoin source attributes are retrieved in parallel by d filtering processors, moved to the cache memory, and finally compacted in pages. These pages are then distributed among p join processors. Thus each processor reads na/p pages of the source relation S after projection—called relation S'— and places source attribute values in a local memory resident data structure W, in ascending order, if the value is not already in W. Simultaneously, one bit in the bit array M is marked for each source attribute value v. The bit address is calculated by a hashing function h, where $M(h(v))$ is set to 1. At the end of this first stage, the bit array in each processor represents a part of the attribute values of the source relation, while the union of all the bit arrays represents all the distinct attribute values. The logical union of the p arrays is then computed by one processor, which broadcasts the result to the $p - 1$ other processors. The intermediate lists (W) of each processor are merged to form a single list containing all the distinct source attribute values. This step is performed by one processor in one b-way merge pass if $p \leq b$, or in $\log_b p$ passes if $p > b$, where the number of processors is divided by b at each pass. The resultant merged list does not contain any duplicates and is broadcast to the remaining $p - 1$ processors. The main assumption of this method is that a processor's local memory can contain both the bit array and the list W. This assumption holds in most cases. If, however, the list does not fit into the local memory, the problem is treated in the same way as the join problem analyzed in Section 4.

The second stage of the algorithm is to distribute the target relation R (after selection by filters) among p processors. Each processor gets a page of R, and each tuple, whose join attribute value v' satisfies $M(h(v')) = 1$, is projected into the result relation if v' is in W. The latter check is necessary because of possible collisions during hashing. (Note that more than one bit array can be used to decrease the probability of collisions.)

The total time of the semijoin algorithm using bit arrays is derived in Appendix D. It includes the I/O time, which is

$$\text{I/O(SJH)} = (n/d)\cdot T\text{dc} + (na/p)\cdot \text{CR} + [p + 1 + (\log_b p)\cdot (b/2)\cdot T\,\text{cp} + (m/p)\cdot(\text{CR} + \text{SR}\cdot\text{CW}).$$

and the CPU time, which is

$$\text{CPU(SJH)} = (na/p)\cdot(t/Ct)\cdot(0 + Iw) + Cm + p\cdot 0 + (m/p)\cdot[0\cdot(t + t\cdot\text{SR}\cdot\log_2 nj) + \text{SR}\cdot I].$$

5.2 Equi-Semijoin Using Selection

This method depends entirely on the selection devices offered by the filtering processors [16] to compute the equi-semijoin. The operation proceeds in two stages. The first stage is similar to that of the previous algorithm; bit arrays are, however, not used. The second stage realizes the semijoin by restricting the target relation to the tuples whose semijoin attribute value is in the list W. Only one processor is needed to initiate the operation. From the merged list, W, this processor constructs selection conditions in the target relation by constructing a restriction predicate. This predicate is a disjunction of clauses of the form $(A = Bi)$, where A is the semijoin attribute of R, and Bi are the distinct attribute values in W. If the number of Bis is greater than Nc, which is the number of predicates accepted by a filter, several selection operations are involved. The number of operations is then $\text{Sup}(nj/Nc)$. Since every selection operation requires reading R in its entirety, the performance of this algorithm depends on the filter processing capabilities. One should keep in mind that a simple filter could accept a high number of predicates.

The total time of the semijoin algorithm using selection is derived in Appendix E. It includes the I/O time, which is

$$\text{I/O(SJS)} = (n/d)\cdot T\text{dc} + (na/p)\cdot\text{CR} + \log_b p\cdot(b/2)\cdot T\text{cp} + (nj/Nc)\cdot(m/d)\cdot T\text{dc}.$$

and the CPU time, which is

$$\text{CPU(SJS)} = (na/p)\cdot(t/Ct)\cdot Iw + Cm + nj\cdot 0.$$

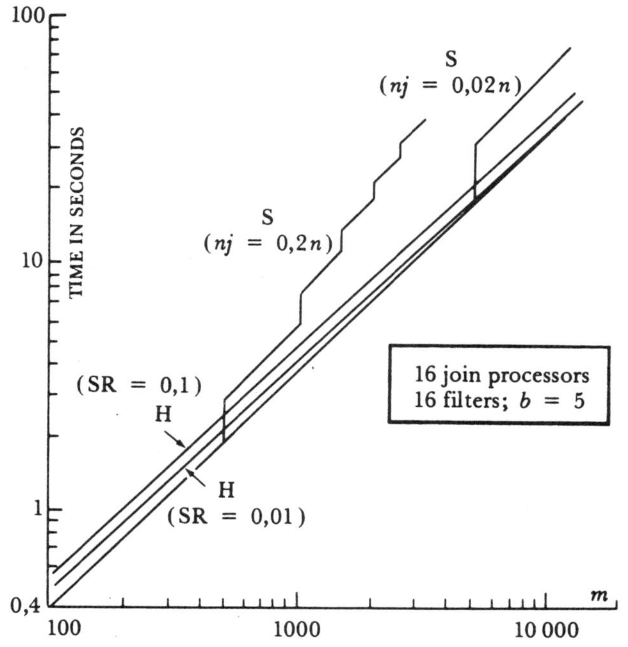

Fig. 7. Execution times versus relation sizes.

5.3 Comparisons

This section presents performance comparisons of the two equi-semijoin algorithms, using the time formulas developed in the previous sections. Results are shown in Figures 7 and 8. Assumptions concerning the processor capabilities, as parametrized by the times defined in Section 3, are the same as those of Section 4.

Figure 7 illustrates the behavior of the algorithms with varying relation sizes. The sizes of both the source and target relations are assumed to be the same ($m = n$). The configuration chosen to represent a multiprocessor architecture is composed of 16 filters and 16 join processors, each owning five pages of local memory. A filter is assumed to accept up to 100 predicates. The stage which consists of reading the projected relation S' and merging the lists W is the same for both algorithms, therefore parameters Ct, Cm, and Iw do not influence the performance. Figure 7 consists of four curves. The two curves representing the time for the algorithm using bit arrays (SJH) vary linearly according to the size of relations (n), and depend on two different semijoin selectivity factors. The selectivity factor slightly affects the write time of the result. The two time curves of the algorithm using selection (SJS) depend on two distinct nj values, and show that this algorithm is heavily influenced by the ratio Sup (nj/Nc), which is the number of needed selection operations. This can be seen by the stair shape of the curves. This algorithm is better when there are a few distinct attribute values. More generally, the algorithm by selection is better than the algorithm using bit

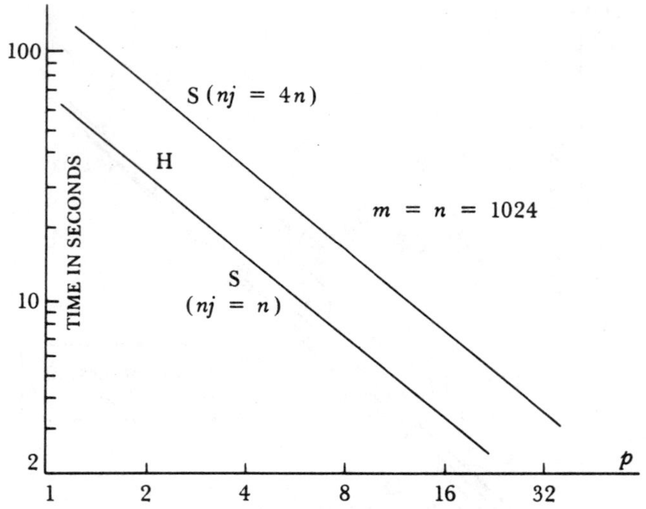

Fig. 8. Execution times versus the number of processors.

arrays when the approximate expression

$$(m/p)\cdot(\mathrm{CW} + \mathrm{SR}\cdot\mathrm{CW}) - \mathrm{Sup}(nj/Nc)\cdot(m/d)\cdot T\mathrm{dc}$$

is strictly positive.

The presence of p join processors cuts the time of the bit arrays algorithm by a factor of p, just as the presence of d filters cuts time off the selection algorithm.

Figure 8 represents execution times as a function of the number of processors, assuming that $p = d$. Performances of these algorithms are proportional to the number of processors, and the difference between the two curves is also due to the ratio (nj/Nc). Two curves depict the performances of the algorithm by selection ($nj = n$, $nj = 4n$). The curve for the selection algorithm for $nj = n$ is the same as the curve for the algorithm using bit arrays. For greater values of nj, the algorithm by selection is worse. The performance of the algorithm by selection depends on the number of filters and their capabilities.

5.4 Non-Equi-Semijoin Algorithms

The non-equi-semijoin represents the case when the comparison operator represents the forms $<$, $\leq$, $\geq$, $>$. In this section we propose a simple algorithm to perform non-equi-semijoin in a multiprocessor database machine. The method is based upon the following observation: the non-equi-semijoin consists of selecting those tuples r of the target relation whose semijoin attributes satisfy "$r\cdot A$ op X," where X is either the minimum attribute value in the source relation, if op is $>$ or $\geq$, or the maximum value, if op is $<$ or $\leq$. The search for a maximum or minimum value in a data set is an easily performed function supported by the filtering processors. Each read attribute value is compared by the filter to a maximum or minimum current value in its local memory, and replaces the current value if the comparison holds. Then, d filters get partial results which will be integrated into one result by a processor, which can be the filter controller. The non-equi-semijoin is finally performed by restricting the tuples in the target through d filters which require tuples to satisfy A op X. Furthermore, this algorithm has the advantage of not using the cache.

The CPU time of this algorithm is negligible, since it only consists of two function calls. The I/O time is the reading time of the source relation (of size n) necessary to calculate the minimum or maximum in parallel by d filters, plus the reading time of the target relation (of size m) to apply the selection. The result relation is written directly in cache, thus the write time is included in the selection time. The execution time of this algorithm is

$$\text{TIME(ISJ)} = ((n/d) + (m/d)) \cdot T\text{dc}.$$

It is assumed that the cache manager always keeps track of available pages during the operation, in order not to slow down the filters by waiting.

6. JOIN USING SEMIJOIN

The previously proposed semijoin algorithms are computed in a time linearly proportional to the size of the operands. The main advantage of the semijoin operator is to reduce the operand relation to just those tuples that participate in the join. Therefore, it may sometimes be advantageous to replace the join of two relations by the join of two semijoins. In order to compare the two alternatives (join or semijoin), we have chosen the multiprocessor nested loop join algorithm presented in Section 4.1, since it is simple and generally satisfactory, with a high degree of real parallelism.

The nested loop join of the initial relations is denoted by NL and is then compared to the nested loop of the semijoins of each relation by the other, denoted NLSJ. The semijoin algorithm using bit arrays is chosen for comparisons, since it is more general than the semijoin algorithm using selection, and more frequently used than the non-equi-semijoin algorithm. The condition that has to be satisfied in order to apply this method is that the entire list of distinct join attribute values fit into local memory. When this condition cannot be satisfied, the semijoin is solved like a join. Therefore, it is assumed that the condition is true in the remainder of this section.

Comparisons of the two methods, NL and NLSJ, are illustrated in Figures 9, 10, 11, and 12. The basic configuration is the same as in Section 4.4. Figure 9 presents the performance of the two methods according to the ratio JS′ = size (R join S)/($m' \cdot n'$), where m' and n' are the sizes of the semijoins of R by S and of S by R, respectively. For each method, three join selectivity factors are considered (JS = 0.16, 0.016, 0.5), while the relation sizes are kept large ($m = n$ = 1024 pages). The parameter JS′ significantly influences the algorithm using semijoins. As JS′ approaches 0, the size of the join result approaches the size of the biggest semijoin result; as JS′ approaches 1, the size of the join result approaches the size of the Cartesian product of the semijoin results. In the latter case, the semijoin reduces the size of the initial relations significantly. The method using semijoin is generally better than the nested loop method, and

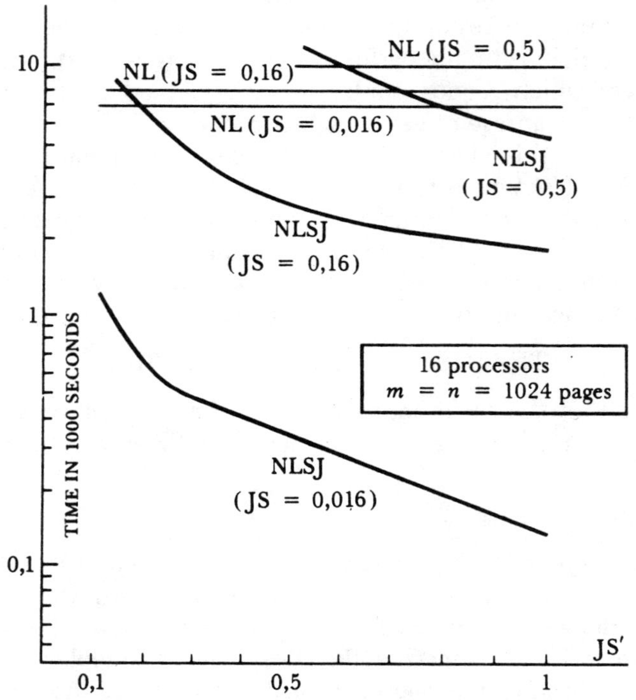

Fig. 9. Comparisons of the time of the nested loop join method (NL) and the join method using semijoin (NLSJ) versus JS′. JS′ = size (*R* join *S*)/[size (*R* semijoin *S*)·size (*S* semijoin *R*)].

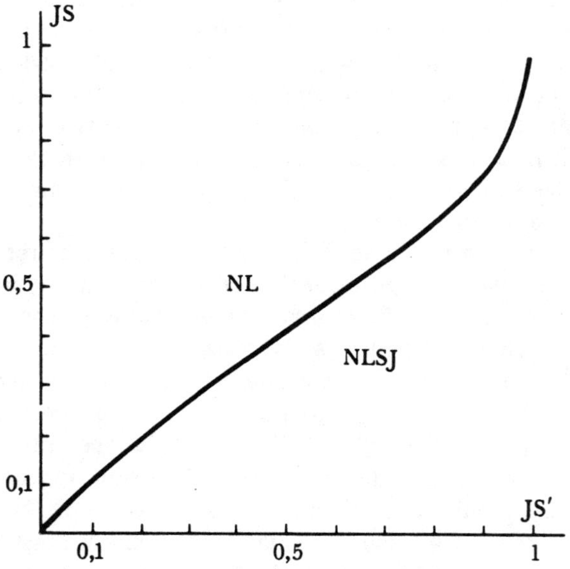

Fig. 10. Limit of the methods for varying JS and JS′. ($p = 16$, $b = 4$, $m = n = 1024$)

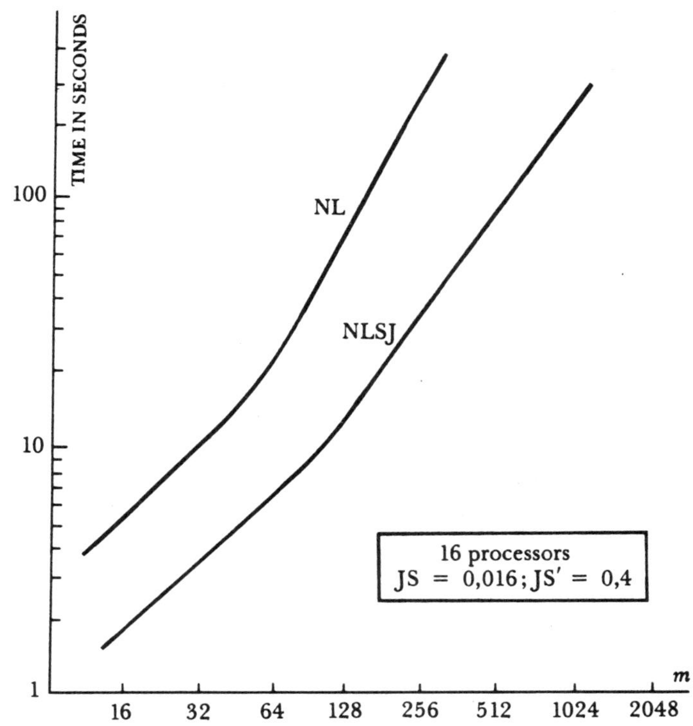

Fig. 11. Comparisons of the algorithms' times versus relation sizes.

becomes quite superior when the join selectivity factor decreases. Figure 10 illustrates the domains of the two methods for various JS and JS′ and shows that the NL method is only competitive when the ratio (JS/JS′) approaches 1. In that case, performing semijoin does not reduce the size of the operand relations.

Figure 11 illustrates the performance of the two methods according to the size of the relations (assumed to be equal) for a join selectivity factor of 0.016 and the ratio JS′ equal to 0.4. The curves show the obvious superiority of the method using semijoins. This is because semijoin time is negligible compared to join time, and the operand relations to be joined are smaller with the semijoin method than with the join method.

The performance of the algorithms with an increasing number of processors, as depicted in Figure 12, still indicates that the performance of the semijoin method is preferable for a typical join selectivity factor of 0.016. The difference between the two methods may be reduced somewhat by increasing that factor.

The comparisons show that if a semijoin of the operand relations precedes the application of the nested loop join algorithm, the total time of the join is generally decreased, which confirms the value of the semijoin operator. Similar comparisons were made, based on the sort-merge-join algorithm and the hashing join algorithm, and similar results were found.

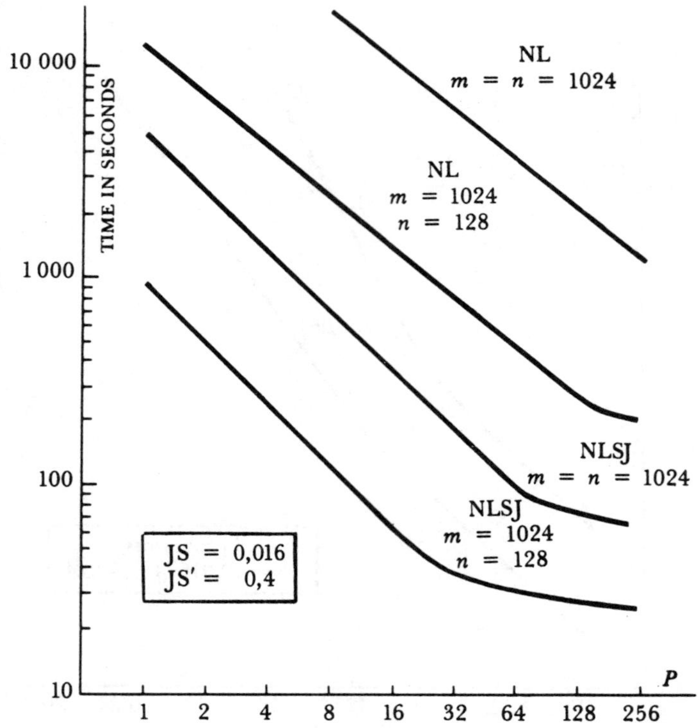

Fig. 12. Comparisons of the algorithms' times versus the number processors.

7. CONCLUSION

In this paper we have presented and analyzed several algorithms for computing joins and semijoins in a multiprocessor database machine. First, we described the architectural components useful for computing joins in the SABRE database machine, and the time parameters, including I/O, CPU, and communication times, were also described. We then presented and compared three join algorithms according to their execution times. The nested loop join algorithm turns out to be the simplest, and its execution time was found to be inversely proportional to the number of processors. It works best when the number of processors is very high. Furthermore, since each tuple is compared to every other tuple, the nested loop join algorithm easily supports non-equijoin. The sort-merge-join algorithm is more complex and performs better as the operand relations become large. For a certain configuration, the addition of new processors causes very little improvement in performance. But the sort-merge-join algorithm has the merit of utilizing another useful operator (sorting), and yields a result relation which is sorted on the join attributes. The hashing join algorithm is better when the number of matching tuples in the larger relation is small. In that case, using bit arrays results in avoiding much useless access to the hashed file. It is shown that, for a given configuration, each of the algorithms can excel, according to the characteristics of the operand and result relations. Since the join operation is very important in relational systems, a well-designed database machine would implement various algorithms and, for each join, choose the best one by computing their execution times.

Focusing on the interprocessor transfers in a multiprocessor database machine and considering that semijoin reduces the transmission times, we have presented parallel algorithms for semijoin operations.

Two multiprocessor equi-semijoin algorithms were analyzed. The algorithm using bit arrays gives good results; its execution time is proportional to $na/p + m/p + r/p$, where m is the number of pages of the target relation, na the number of pages containing the projected source semijoin attributes, r the number of pages of the result relation, and p the number of processors. But the main assumption in the application of the algorithm using bit arrays is that the list of distinct semijoin attribute values should fit into the processor's local memory. A second equi-semijoin algorithm using selection was proposed. This algorithm depens upon the parallel filtering power offered by the selection processors assigned to the disks. It is superior to the first algorithm when the semijoin can be computed in a single pass; that is, when the number of distinct semijoin attribute values is less than the number of admitted predicates in a filter. Otherwise, the algorithm using bit arrays is better.

A non-equi-semijoin algorithm was also proposed. It uses the maximum and minimum functions provided by the filter processors and does not need any room in the cache during execution, except for writing the final result. This algorithm has an execution time proportional to $m/d + n/d$, where m and n are the size of the operand relations and d the number of filters associated with the operation.

Comparisons were then performed between the two join strategies. The method of joining two operand relations and the method of joining the result relations of semijoins were comparerd using the nested loop join algorithm. Finally, it was shown that the semijoin method is generally better, which indicates the value of implementing this operator in a database machine.

The results can be extended in several directions. First, the algorithms can be optimized. For example, the postoptimal stage of the multiprocessor b-way merge, which degrades the degree of parallelism, can be improved by using another, more complex, method. Second, other methods, based on index or pre-evaluated joins, can be found. These indices would be organized in such a fashion as to facilitate parallel execution. The performances of the methods would essentially depend on the placement strategies of relations on disk units. An original multiattribute clustering technique [21] will be used in SABRE, and will improve join executions.

APPENDIX A

Analysis of the Nested Loop Algorithm

The algorithm can be divided into several steps, such that each step corresponds to one pass of reading the internal relation. First, let us determine the execution time of one step.

During one step, each processor starts reading $(b - 1)$ pages of R. Thus, $p(b - 1)$ pages of R are read in parallel. The time necessary for reading these pages is

$$t1 = (b - 1)\mathrm{CR}.$$

Then, each page of S is broadcast and joined with $(b - 1)$ pages of R by each processor. The time to read a page of S is

$$t2 = \mathrm{CR}.$$

The time to join $(b - 1)$ unsorted pages of R with one unsorted page of S is

$$t3 = (b - 1)\mathrm{CJ0}.$$

This join generates a result of size $(b - 1)$JS pages. The resulting tuples must be moved to an output buffer; that cost in time is

$$t4 = (b - 1)\mathrm{JS} \cdot t \cdot I.$$

The output buffer, when filled, must be written in cache memory (or on disks). This write requires an average time of

$$t5 = (b - 1)\mathrm{JS} \cdot \mathrm{CW}.$$

Finally, the total time for one step of the algorithm is

$$T1 = t1 + n(t2 + t3 + t4 + t5),$$

which turns out to be

$$T1 = (b - 1)\mathrm{CR} + n(\mathrm{CR} + (b - 1)\mathrm{CJ0} + (b - 1)\mathrm{JS} \cdot t \cdot I + (b - 1)\mathrm{JS} \cdot \mathrm{CW})$$

or, equivalently,

$$T1 = (b - 1)\mathrm{CR} + n(\mathrm{CR} + (b - 1)(\mathrm{CJ0} + \mathrm{JS}(t \cdot I + \mathrm{CW}))).$$

At each step, $p(b - 1)$ pages of R are read. Therefore, the number of steps is

$$k = m/(p(b - 1)).$$

Consequently, the total execution time of the algorithm is

$$\mathrm{TIME(NL)} = k \cdot T1,$$

which turns out to be

$$\boxed{\mathrm{TIME(NL)} = m \cdot \mathrm{CR}/p + m \cdot n(\mathrm{CR}/(p(b - 1)) + (\mathrm{CJ0} + \mathrm{JS}(t \cdot I + \mathrm{CW}))/p).}$$

APPENDIX B

Analysis of the Sort-Merge-Join Algorithm

First, let us evaluate the execution time to sort a relation of n pages. As they are read during the first pass, pages are internally sorted. Each processor internally sorts n/p pages. Thus, the time to internally sort n pages is approximately.

$$t1 = n \cdot Cs/p.$$

During all the passes preceding the optimal stage, each processor is fully utilized. At each pass of the relation a processor performs $n/(p \cdot b)$ merge operations of b pages. The cost of merging b sorted pages is CMb. Thus, the additional cost of each pass before the optimal stage is

$$t2 = n \cdot \mathrm{CM}b/(p \cdot b).$$

At the optimal stage corresponding to the pass K, each processor produces a sorted run of $b^{**}K$ pages. Since each of the p processors has merged exactly n/p pages, the following equation is satisfied:

$$b^{**}K = n/p,$$

and so we have

$$K = \log_b(n/p).$$

Finally, the time necessary to reach the optimal stage is

$$T1 = t1 + K \cdot t2,$$

which turns out to be

$$T1 = n \cdot Cs/p + (N \cdot \mathrm{CM}b \cdot \log_b(n/p))/(b \cdot p).$$

Let us now derive the time necessary after the optimal stage. The optimal stage generates p runs of n/p pages. The number of passes to merge p runs in $\log_b p$. At each pass of the postoptimal stage, the number of processors needed is divided by b, while the work of each is multiplied by b. At the first postoptimal pass, p/b processors perform n/p merge operations of b pages at a cost in time of

$$m1 = \mathrm{CM}b \cdot n/p.$$

More generally, at the ith postoptimal pass, $p/b^{**}i$ processors perform $b^{**}(i-1) \cdot n/p$ merge operations at a cost in time of

$$mi = \mathrm{CM}b \cdot b^{**}(i-1) \cdot n/p.$$

Finally, the total cost of the postoptimal stage is

$$T2 = m1 + m2 + \cdots + mi + \cdots + m \log_b p,$$

which turns out to be

$$T2 = \mathrm{CM}b \cdot (n/p) \cdot (1 + b + b^{**}2 + \cdots + b^{**}((\log_b p) - 1)).$$

Then, applying the well-known formula:

$$1 + b + b^{**}2 + \cdots + b^{**}(k-1) = (1 - b^{**}k)/(1 - b),$$

we obtain

$$T2 = \mathrm{CM}b \cdot (n/p) \cdot (1 - b^{**}\log_b p)/(1 - b).$$

The execution time required to sort a relation of n pages is then:

$$\mathrm{SORT}(n) = T1 + T2,$$

that is,

$$\mathrm{SORT}(n) = n/p[Cs + \mathrm{CM}b\cdot\log_b(n/p) + \mathrm{CM}b(1 - b^{**}\log_b p)/(b - 1)].$$

The execution cost of the algorithm is the cost of sorting the relation R, plus the cost of sorting the relation S, plus the cost of joining the sorted relations by a merge. The uniprocessor merge-type operation consists in reading the sorted relations, joining them, and writing the result relation. The cost of merging m and n pages is then

$$\mathrm{MERGE}(m, n) = (m + n)\mathrm{CR} + \max(m, n)\cdot\mathrm{CJ1} + m\cdot n\cdot\mathrm{JS}\cdot\mathrm{CW}.$$

Finally, the execution time of the sort-merge-join algorithm is

$$\mathrm{TIME(SM)} = \mathrm{SORT}(n) + \mathrm{SORT}(m) + \mathrm{MERGE}(m, n),$$

which turns out to be

$$\begin{aligned}\mathrm{TIME(SM)} = {} & n/p[Cs + \mathrm{CM}b\cdot\log_b(n/p)/b + \mathrm{CM}b\cdot(1 - b^{**}\log_b p)/(1 - b)] \\ & + m/p[Cs + \mathrm{CM}b\cdot\log_b(m/p)/b + \mathrm{CM}b \\ & \cdot(1 - b^{**}\log_b p)/(1 - b)] \\ & + (m + n)\mathrm{CR} + \max(m, n)\cdot\mathrm{CJ1} + m\cdot n\cdot\mathrm{JS}\cdot\mathrm{CW}.\end{aligned}$$

APPENDIX C

Analysis of the Hashing Join Algorithm

The execution time of the algorithm comprises time $T1$ for hashing the smaller relation by the cache processor, time $T2$ for distributing the larger relation among p processors, time $T3$ for accessing the hashed file, and, finally, time $T4$ for writing the result. The time for broadcasting the Boolean arrays is negligible and, thus, is ignored. We remind the reader that c page frames are available in the cache for the join operation. Thus the creation of the hashed file consists of creating m buckets if $c > m$, or c buckets, otherwise. In the first case, the hashed file could be maintained in cache memory during the entire execution of the join operation. In the latter case, the pages of the same bucket would be linked and written on disk, and retrieved using a table of physical addresses. The time for reading a page for R, taking into account the ratio F, is

$$t1 = (1 - F)T\mathrm{dc}.$$

The time for hashing a page of t tuples is

$$t2 = t(0 + I).$$

The time for writing the hashed file is the time for writing $(m - c)$ pages, since c pages are reserved in cache memory during the join execution. Furthermore, page frames may be available in the cache with the probability F'. Thus the time for writing $(m - c)$ pages from cache to disk is

$$t3 = (m - c)(1 - F')T\mathrm{dc}.$$

Then, the execution time for hashing a relation for m pages is

$$T1 = m(t1 + t2) + t3,$$

which turns out to be

$$T1 = m[(1 - F)T\text{dc} + t(0 + I)] + (m - c)(1 - F')T\text{dc}.$$

The execution time for the second stage is the time for reading the relation S by p processors in parallel, the time for accessing the hashed file, and the time for writing the result relation. Each processor reads n/p pages of the relation S, and, for each of the t tuples of a page, accesses the Boolean array. This leads to a time of

$$T2 = (\text{CR} + t \cdot 0)n/p.$$

An access to the hashed file is needed for each matching tuple of S. The number of matching tuples is defined by the semijoin selectivity factor SS, and each bucket of the hashed file contains (m/c) pages. Thus, for each page of S, the number of pages read from the hashed file is $t \cdot \text{SS} \cdot (m/c) \cdot \text{CR}$, and this occurs (n/p) times for the entire relation S. Therefore, we obtain

$$T3 = (n/p)(m/c)\text{CR} \cdot t \cdot \text{SS}.$$

The time for writing the result relation of size $m \cdot n \cdot \text{JS}$ in parallel by p processors is

$$T4 = m \cdot n \cdot \text{JS} \cdot \text{CW}/p.$$

Finally, the execution time of the multiprocessor hashing join algorithm (H) is

$$\text{TIME(H)} = T1 + T2 + T3 + T4,$$

which turns out to be

$$\text{TIME(H)} = [(1 - F)T\text{dc} + t(0 + I)] + (m - C)(1 - F')T\text{dc} + (\text{n/p})[\text{CR} + t \cdot 0 + t \cdot \text{SS} \cdot (m/c) \cdot \text{CR} + m \cdot \text{JS} \cdot \text{CW}.$$

APPENDIX D

Analysis of the Semijoin Algorithm Using Bit Arrays

The total time of the semijoin algorithm using bit arrays is the sum of the I/O time and the CPU time, which can be represented as

$$\text{TIME (SJH)} = \text{I/O (SJH)} + \text{CPU (SJH)}.$$

(1) *I/O time.* The I/O time consists of the interprocessor page move time, incurred by reading the operand relation, performing the union and merge operations, and finally writing the result relation. First, relation S is projected over the semijoin attributes to relation S'. This operation requires reading S entirely from disk to cache by d filters. The time required for this operation is $t1 = (n/d) \cdot T\text{dc}$. The relation S' has na pages and is read in parallel by p processors for a time $t2 = (na/p) \cdot \text{CR}$.

We suppose that the q bit arrays in a processor's memory are contained in a page, thus the union operation needs p interprocessor moves plus one more to broadcast the result. This operation takes time $t3 = (p + 1) \cdot T\text{cp}$. The merging of p attribute lists is done in $\log_b p$ passes by a b-way merge and, assuming an average list size of $b/2$ pages, the merge I/O time is $t4 = \log_b p \cdot (b/2) \cdot T\text{cp}$.

The time for the second stage of the algorithm consists of reading relation R, of size m, which is $t5 = (m/p) \cdot \text{CR}$, and writing the result relation T, whose size depends on the semijoin selectivity factor SR, for a time $t6 = (m/p) \cdot \text{SR} \cdot \text{CW}$.

Finally, the I/O time is

$$\text{I/O (SJH)} = t1 + t2 + t3 + t4 + t5 + t6,$$

which may be written as

$$\text{I/O(SJH)} = (n/d) \cdot T\text{dc} + (na/p) \cdot \text{CR} + [p + 1 + (\log_b p) \cdot (b/2)] \cdot T\text{cp} + (m/p) \cdot (\text{CR} + \text{SR} \cdot \text{CW}).$$

(2) *CPU time.* The CPU time of the semijoin algorithm using bit arrays is now calculated. During the first stage, for each read page of the relation S' (containing t/Ct attribute values), a hashing function is applied to each value, which is then inserted into list W. We define the time of inserting an element in W by Iw. Then, the CPU time for this stage is

$$c1 = (na/p) \cdot (t/Ct) \cdot (0 + Iw).$$

The merge time of the p lists is denoted by Cm. The union of the p arrays needs p comparisons (i.e., $p \cdot 0$ time units). This requires a time

$$c2 = Cm + p \cdot 0.$$

During the second stage, for each read page of R, a hashing function is applied to the t attribute values. Furthermore, for the $t \cdot \text{SR}$ tuples held in a page, W is accessed in order to confirm the absence of collision. The list W contains nj attribute values in sorted order. Thus, binary search [22, p. 406] can be applied to W, with a time of $(\log_2 nj) \cdot 0$ per tuple. The move time of the tuples in the result page is $\text{SR} \cdot I$ for each read page of R. The time of the second page is therefore,

$$c3 = (m/p) \cdot [0 \cdot (t + t \cdot \text{SR} \cdot \log_2 nj) + \text{SR} \cdot I].$$

Thus, the total CPU of this algorithm is $c1 + c2 + c3$, that is,

$$\text{CPU(SJH)} = (na/p) \cdot (t/Ct) \cdot (0 + Iw) + Cm + p \cdot 0 + (m/p) \cdot [0 \cdot (t + t \cdot \text{SR} + \log_2 nj) + \text{SR} \cdot I].$$

APPENDIX E

Analysis of the Semijoin Algorithm by Selection

The time of this algorithm also consists of the I/O and the CPU times.

(1) *I/O time.* The algorithm proceeds in two stages. The first stage, similar to

the previous algorithm, projects relation S over the semijoin attributes into relation S', which demands a time

$$t1 = (n/d) \cdot Tdc,$$

and reads the relation S' in parallel by p processors, requiring a time

$$t2 = (na/p) \cdot CR.$$

The merge operation requires the same time as the merge in the previous algorithm, that is,

$$t3 = Tcp \cdot \log_b p \cdot (b/2).$$

The task of the second stage is to perform selection in parallel by d filters on relation R (of size m). One selection on the entire relation requires a time $(m/d) \cdot Tdc$, and may have to be repeated nj/Nc times if nj is greater than Nc. It should be noted that the selection time includes the write time of the result relation in cache. Thus, the time for this second stage is

$$t4 = (nj/Nc) \cdot (m/d) \cdot Tdc.$$

Finally, the I/O time of the algorithm is

$$\text{I/O(SJS)} = t1 + t2 + t3 + t4,$$

which turns out to be

$$\text{I/O(SJS)} = (n/d) \cdot Tdc + (na/p) \cdot CR + \log_b p \cdot (b/2) \cdot Tcp + (nj/Nc) \cdot (m/d) \cdot Tdc.$$

(2) *CPU time.* The CPU time is incurred by the insertions in the list W containing the semijoin source attribute values. This time is the same as in the previous algorithm, namely $(na/p) \cdot (t/Ct) \cdot Iw$. The merge time of p lists is denoted Cm.

The CPU time for the second stage is due to the initialization of the selection operations. The time of constructing selection predicates with nj attributes in list W is $nj \cdot 0$. The CPU time of the algorithm is then,

$$\text{CPU(SJS)} = (na/p) \cdot (t/Ct) \cdot Iw + Cm + nj \cdot 0.$$

ACKNOWLEDGMENTS

The authors wish to thank P. Bernadat, P. Faudemay, K. Karlsson, Y. Viemont, and the other members of the SABRE project, for their helpful discussions. The authors also wish to acknowledge the many valuable comments of T. Ozsu.

REFERENCES

1. AUER, H. ET AL. R.D.B.M.: a relational database machine. Internal Rep. nr8005, Technisch Univ. Braunchweig, June 1980.
2. BABB, E. Implementing a relational database by means of specialized hardware. *ACM Trans. Database Syst. 4*, 1 (March 1979), 1–29.
3. BANCILHON, F.; AND SCHOLL, M. Design of a back-end processor for a database machine. In *Proc. ACM-SIGMOD* (Santa Monica, Calif., May 1980), ACM, New York, 1980.

4. BANERJEE, J.; HSIAO, D.K.; AND BAUM, R.I. Concepts and capabilities of a database computer. *ACM Trans. Database Syst. 3*, 4 (Dec. 1978), 347–384.
5. BERNSTEIN, P.A.; AND CHIU, D.M. Using semijoins to solve relational queries.
6. BERNSTEIN, P.A.; AND GOODMAN, N. Full reducers for relational queries using multiattribute semijoins. In *Proc. 1979 NBS Symposium on Computer Networks* (Dec. 1979), NBS, Washington, D.C.
7. BERNSTEIN, P.A.; AND GOODMAN, N. Inequality semijoins. Tech. Rep. CCA-79-28, Computer Corp. of America, Cambridge, Mass., Dec. 1979.
8. BLASGEN, M.W.; AND ESWARAN, K.P. Storage and access in relational databases. *IBM Syst. J. 16*, 4 (1977), 363–378.
9. BORAL, H.; DEWITT, D.J.; FRIEDLAND, D.; AND WILKINSON, W.K. Parallel algorithms for the execution of relational operations. Tech. Rep. 402, Computer Science Dept., Univ. of Wisconsin, Madison, Jan. 1980.
10. BORAL, H.; DEWITT, D.J.; AND WILKINSON, W.K. Performances evaluation of associative disk designs. In *6th Workshop on Computer Architecture for Nonnumeric Processing* (Hyeres, France, June 1981), ACM, New York, 1981.
11. CHAMBERLIN, D.D.; GILBERT, A.M.; AND YOST, R.A. A history of System-R and SQL/data system. In *7th International Conference on Very Large Data Bases* (Cannes, France, Sept. 1981).
12. CHIU, D.M.; AND HO, Y.C. A methodology for interpreting tree queries into optimal semijoin expressions. *ACM Trans. Database Syst. 5*, 4 (Dec. 1980), 169–178.
13. CODD, E.F. A relational model of data for large shared data banks. *Commun. ACM 13*, 6 (June 1970), 377–387.
14. DEWITT, D.J. Query execution in DIRECT. In *Proc. of the ACM-SIGMOD 1979 International Conference on Management of Data* (May 1979), ACM, New York, 1979, pp 13–22.
15. BORAL, H.; AND DEWITT, D.J. Design considerations for data-flow database machines. In *Proc. of the ACM-SIGMOD Conference on Management of Data* (Los Angeles, Calif., 1980), ACM, New York, 1980, pp 94–104.
16. FAUDEMAY, P. Sur une nouvelle classe de filtres multiexpressions. *J. Machines Bases de Donnees* (Sophia Antipolis, Sept. 1980), INRIA.
17. FINGER, U.; AND MEDIGUE, G. Architectures multimicroprocesseurs et disponibilité: la SM90. *L'echo des Recherches 105* (July 1981).
18. GARDARIN, G. An introduction to SABRE: a multimicroprocessor database machine. In *6th Workshop on Computer Architecture for Nonnumeric Processing* (Hyeres, France, June 1981).
19. GOTLIEB, L.R. Computing joins of relations. In *Proc. of the ACM-SIGMOD Conference on Management of Data* (San Jose, Calif., May 1975), ACM, New York, 1975, pp 55–63.
20. INTEL. Les concepts systemes d'intel: le multibus et ses signaux. E.A.I.263, A. Sabatier, Intel-France, Feb. 1979.
21. KARLSSON, K. Reduced cover-trees and their application in the SABRE access path model. In *7th International Conference on Very Large Data Bases* (Cannes, France, Sept. 1981).
22. KNUTH, D.E. *The Art of Computers Programming; vol. 3: Sorting and Searching*, Addison-Wesley, Reading, Mass., 1973.
23. LEBIHAN, J., ET AL. SIRIUS: a French nationwide project on distributed databases. In *6th International Conference on Very Large Databases* (Montreal, 1980).
24. OZKARAHAN, E.A.; SCHUSTER, S.A.; AND SEVCIK, K.C. Performance evaluation of a relational associative processor. *ACM Trans. Database Syst. 2*, 2 (June 1977), 175–196.
25. PREPARATA, F.P. New parallel-sorting schemes. *IEEE Trans. Comput. C-27* (July 1978).
26. ROTHNIE, J.B., ET AL. SDD1: a system for distributed databases. *ACM Trans. Database Syst. 5*, 1 (March 1980), 1–17.
27. ROHMER, J. Machines et langages pour traiter les ensembles de donnees (textes, tableaux, fichiers). These d'Etat, Grenoble, Dec. 1980.
28. STONEBRAKER, M.; WONG, E.; AND KREPS, P. The design and implementation of INGRES. *ACM Trans. Database Syst. 1*, 3 (Sept. 1976).
29. VALDURIEZ, P. Algorithmes de jointures de relations. *Colloque Les Bases de Donnees* (Tunis, April 1981), AFCET.
30. WAH, B.W.; AND YAO, S.B. DIALOGUE: a distributed-processor organization for a database machine. In *1980 National Computer Conference*, pp 243–253.

Received March 1982; revised February 1983; Accepted May 1983.

A Performance Evaluation of Four Parallel Join Algorithms in a Shared-Nothing Multiprocessor Environment

Donovan A. Schneider
David J. DeWitt

Computer Sciences Department
University of Wisconsin
Madison, WI 53706

ABSTRACT — In this paper we analyze and compare four parallel join algorithms. Grace and Hybrid hash represent the class of hash-based join methods, Simple hash represents a looping algorithm with hashing, and our last algorithm is the more traditional sort-merge. The performance of each of the algorithms with different tuple distribution policies, the addition of bit vector filters, varying amounts of main-memory for joining, and non-uniformly distributed join attribute values is studied. The Hybrid hash-join algorithm is found to be superior except when the join attribute values of the inner relation are non-uniformly distributed and memory is limited. In this case, a more conservative algorithm such as the sort-merge algorithm should be used. The Gamma database machine serves as the host for the performance comparison.

1. Introduction

During the last 10 years, a significant amount of effort has been focused on developing efficient join algorithms. Initially, nested loops and sort-merge were the algorithms of choice. However, work by [KITS83, BRAT84, DEWI84] demonstrated the potential of hash-based join methods. Besides being faster under most conditions these hash-based join algorithms have the property of being easy to parallelize. Thus, with the trend towards multiprocessor database machines, these algorithms have received a lot of attention. In fact, several researchers, including [BRAT87, DEWI88, KITS88], have presented performance timings for a variety of parallel join algorithms. However, the more popular parallel join algorithms have never been compared in a common hardware/software environment. In this paper we present a performance evaluation of parallel versions of the sort-merge, Grace [KITS83], Simple [DEWI84], and Hybrid [DEWI84] join algorithms within the context of the Gamma database machine [DEWI86, DEWI88]. These algorithms cover the spectrum from hashing, to looping with hashing, and finally to sorting.

This research was partially supported by the Defense Advanced Research Projects Agency under contract N00039-86-C-0578, by the National Science Foundation under grants DCR-8512862, MCS82-01870, and MCS81-05904, and by a Digital Equipment Corporation External Research Grant.

We feel that Gamma is a good choice for the experimental vehicle because it incorporates a shared-nothing architecture with commercially available components. This basic design is becoming increasingly popular, both in research, for example, Bubba at MCC [BORA88] and ARBRE at IBM [LORI88] and in the commercial arena, with products from Teradata [TERA83] and Tandem [TAND88].

The experiments were designed to test the performance of each of the join algorithms under several different conditions. First, we compare the algorithms when the join attributes are also the attributes used to distribute the relations during loading. In certain circumstances it is possible to exploit this situation and drastically reduce inter-processor communications. Next, the performance of each of the join algorithms is analyzed when the size of the relations being joined exceeds the amount of available memory. Our goal was to show how the performance of each algorithm is affected as the amount of available memory is reduced.[1] The join algorithms were also analyzed in the presence of non-uniform join attribute values. We also considered how effectively the different join algorithms could utilize processors without disks. Finally, bit vector filtering techniques [BABB79, VALD84] were evaluated for each of the parallel join algorithms.

The remainder of this paper is organized as follows. First, in Section 2, an overview of the Gamma database machine is presented. The four parallel join algorithms that we tested are described in Section 3. Section 4 contains the results of the experiments that we conducted. Our conclusions appear in Section 5.

2. Overview of the Gamma Database Machine

In this section we present a brief overview of the Gamma database machine. For a complete description of Gamma see [DEWI86].

2.1. Hardware Configuration

Currently[2], Gamma consists of 17 VAX 11/750 processors, each with two megabytes of memory. An 80 megabit/second token ring connects the processors to each other and to another

[1] This set of experiments can also be viewed as predicting the relative performance of the various algorithms when the size of memory is constant and the algorithms are required to process relations larger than the the size of available memory.

[2] We are currently in the process of porting the Gamma software to an Intel iPSC-II Hypercube with 32 386 processors and 32 disk drives.

VAX 11/750 running Berkeley UNIX. This processor acts as the host machine for Gamma. 333 megabyte Fujitsu disk drives (8") provide database storage at eight of the processors.

2.2. Software Overview

Physical Database Design

In Gamma, all relations are **horizontally partitioned** [RIES78] across all disk drives in the system. Four alternative ways of distributing the tuples of a relation are provided: round-robin, hashed, range partitioned with user-specified placement by key value, and range partitioned with uniform distribution. As implied by its name, in the first strategy when tuples are loaded into a relation, they are distributed in a round-robin fashion among all disk drives. If the hashed strategy is selected, a randomizing function is applied to the "key" attribute of each tuple to select a storage unit. In the third strategy the user specifies a range of key values for each site. In the last partitioning strategy the user specifies the partitioning attribute and the system distributes the tuples uniformly across all sites.

Query Execution

Gamma uses traditional relational techniques for query parsing, optimization [SELI79], and code generation. Queries are compiled into a tree of operators with predicates compiled into machine language. After being parsed, optimized, and compiled, the query is sent by the host software to an idle scheduler process through a dispatcher process. The scheduler process, in turn, starts operator processes at each processor selected to execute the operator. The task of assigning operators to processors is performed in part by the optimizer and in part by the scheduler assigned to control the execution of the query. For example, the operators at the leaves of a query tree reference only permanent relations. Using the query and schema information, the optimizer is able to determine the best way of assigning these operators to processors.

Operating and Storage System

The operating system on which Gamma is constructed provides lightweight processes with shared memory and reliable, datagram communication services. Messages between two processes on the same processor are *short-circuited* by the communications software.

File services in Gamma are based on the Wisconsin Storage System (WiSS) [CHOU85]. These services include structured sequential files, B^+ indices, byte-stream files as in UNIX, long data items, a sort utility, and a scan mechanism. A one page readahead mechanism is utilized when scanning a file sequentially.

3. Parallel Join Algorithms

We implemented parallel versions of four join algorithms: sort-merge, Grace [KITS83], Simple hash [DEWI84], and Hybrid hash-join [DEWI84]. A common feature of the parallel versions of each of these algorithms is the use of a hash function to partition each relation being joined into a collection of disjoint subsets that can be processed independently and in parallel. This partitioning is performed by applying a hash function to the join attribute of each tuple. The actual join computation depends on the algorithm: building and probing of hash tables is used for the Simple, Grace, and Hybrid algorithms whereas sorting and merging is used for the sort-merge algorithm. As part of the partitioning process, the Grace and Hybrid algorithms first partition the two relations being joined into additional fragments when the inner relation is larger than the amount of available main memory. This is referred to as the **bucket-forming phase** [KITS83]. More details on each algorithm are presented in the following sections.

In the following discussion, R and S refer to the relations being joined. R is the smaller of the two relations and is always the inner joining relation.

3.1. Sort-Merge

Our parallel version of the sort-merge join algorithm is a straightforward adaptation of the traditional single processor version of the algorithm and is essentially identical to the algorithm employed by the Teradata machine [TERA83]. The smaller of the two joining relations, R, is first partitioned through a split table that contains an entry for each processor with an attached disk. A hash function is applied to the join attribute of each tuple to determine the appropriate disk site. As the tuples arrive at a site they are stored in a temporary file. When the entire R relation has been redistributed, each of the local files is sorted in parallel. As an example, Figure 1 depicts R being partitioned across K disk nodes into relation R′.

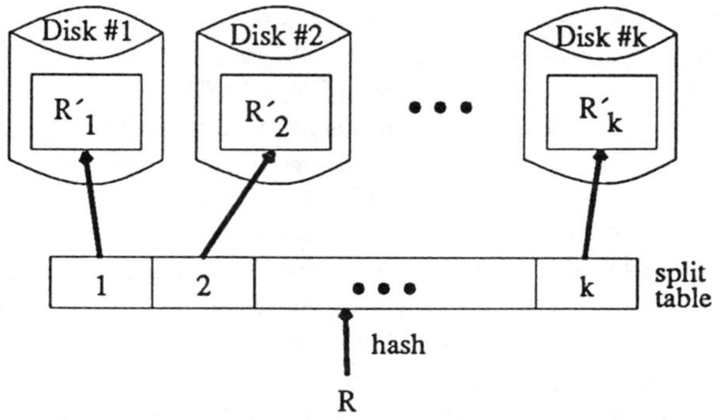

Partitioning of relation R across K disk drives for sort-merge.
Figure 1

Notice that each relation fragment of R on each disk will be passed through the same split table for redistribution. Relation S is then processed in the same manner. Since the same hash function is used to redistribute both relations, only tuples within fragments at a particular site have the possibility of joining [KITS83]. Thus, a local merge join performed in parallel across the disk sites will fully compute the join.

Although it is possible to send tuples to remote, diskless processors for merging, we felt the difficulties involved (especially when the outer relation contains tuples with duplicate attribute values and hence the scan on the inner relation is required to backup) outweighed the potential benefits of offloading CPU cycles from the sites with disks. Thus, the join processors will always correspond exactly to the processors with disks.

To increase intra-query parallelism, it would be possible to partition (or sort) both relations concurrently. However, this could cause performance problems due to disk head and network interface contention. The other problem is that since bit filters must be created from the complete inner relation before they can be applied to the outer relation, we chose to partition the relations serially.

3.2. Simple Hash

A centralized version of the Simple hash-join [DEWI84] operates as follows. First, the smaller joining relation, R, is read from disk and staged in an in-memory hash table (which is formed by hashing on the join attribute of each tuple of R). Next, the larger joining relation, S, is read from disk and its tuples probe the hash table for matches. When the number of tuples in R exceeds the size of the hash table, memory overflow occurs.

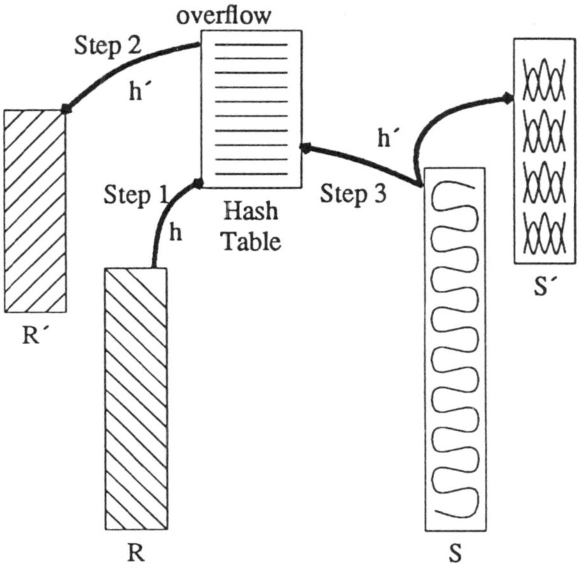

Simple hash-join overflow processing.
Figure 2

Figure 2 depicts the steps taken in order to handle this overflow. In step 1, relation R is used to build the hash table. When the hash table space is exceeded, the join operator creates a new file R´ and streams tuples to this file based on a new function, h´, until the tuples in R are distributed between R´ and the hash table (step 2). The query scheduler then passes the function h´ to the operator producing the tuples of S, the outer relation. In step 3, tuples from S corresponding to tuples in the overflow partition (R´) are spooled directly to a temporary file, S´. All other tuples probe the hash table to affect the join. We are now left with the task of joining the overflow partitions R´ and S´. Since R´ may also exceed the capacity of the hash table, the same process continues until no new overflow partitions are created; at which time the join will have been fully computed.

To parallelize this algorithm we inserted a split table in step 1 which routes tuples (via hashing) to their appropriate joining site. Of course, hash table overflow is now possible at **any** (or all) of these join sites. Overflow processing is still done, though, as described in steps 2 and 3 of the centralized algorithm. In fact, each join site that overflows has its own locally defined h´ and its own associated overflow file R´. Although each overflow file is stored entirely on a single disk (i.e., not horizontally partitioned), different overflow files are assigned to different disks. Although it would have been possible to horizontally partition each overflow file across all nodes with disks, if one assumes that the R tuples are uniformly distributed across the join nodes, all nodes should overflow to approximately the same degree. Hence, the final result will be as if the aggregate overflow partition was horizontally partitioned across the disk sites. It should be noted that the processors used for executing the join operation are not constrained to having disks as was the case for the sort-merge algorithm.

Until very recently, Simple hash was the only join algorithm employed by Gamma and is currently used as the overflow resolution method for our parallel implementations of the Grace and Hybrid algorithms.

3.3. Grace Hash-Join

A centralized Grace join algorithm [KITS83] works in three phases. In the first phase, the algorithm partitions relation R into N disk buckets by hashing on the join attribute of each tuple in R. In phase 2, relation S is partitioned into N buckets using the same hash function. In the final phase, the algorithm joins the respective matching buckets from relations R and S.

The number of buckets, N, is chosen to be very large. This reduces the chance that any bucket will exceed the memory capacity of the processor used to actually effect the join of two buckets. In the event that the buckets are much smaller than main memory, several will be combined during the third phase to form more optimal size join buckets (referred to as bucket tuning in [KITS83]).

The Grace algorithm differs fundamentally from the sort-merge and simple-hash join algorithms in that data partitioning occurs at two different stages - during bucket-forming and during bucket-joining. Parallelizing the algorithm thus must address both these data partitioning stages. To insure maximum utilization of available I/O bandwidth during the bucket-joining stage, each bucket is partitioned across all available disk drives. A **partitioning split table**, as shown in Figure 3, is used for this task. When it is time to join the ith bucket of R with the ith bucket of S, the tuples from the ith bucket in R are distributed to the available joining processors using a **joining split table** (which will contain one entry for each processor used to effect the join). As

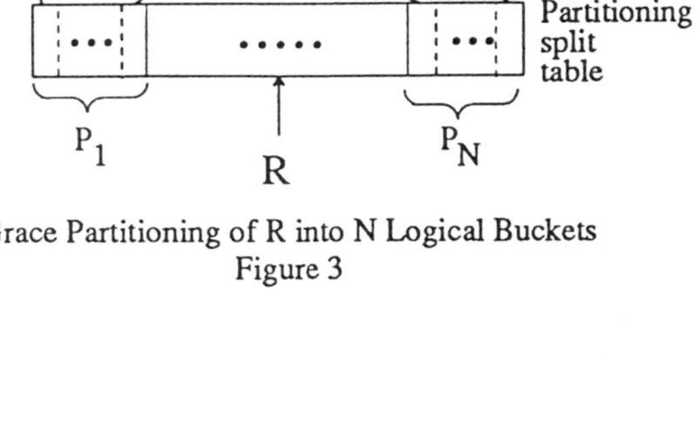

Grace Partitioning of R into N Logical Buckets
Figure 3

tuples arrive at a site they are stored in in-memory hash tables. Tuples from bucket i of relation S are then distributed using the same joining split table and as tuples arrive at a processor they probe the hash table for matches.

The bucket-forming phase is completely separate from the joining phase under the Grace join algorithm. This separation of phases forces the Grace algorithm to write both the joining relations back to disk before beginning the join stage of the algorithm.

Currently, our parallel implementation of the Grace join algorithm does not use bucket tuning. Instead, the number of buckets is determined by the query optimizer in order to ensure that the size of each bucket is just less than the aggregate amount of main-memory of the joining processors.

3.4. Hybrid Hash-Join

A centralized Hybrid hash-join algorithm [DEWI84] also operates in three phases. In the first phase, the algorithm uses a hash function to partition the inner relation, R, into N buckets. The tuples of the first bucket are used to build an in-memory hash table while the remaining N-1 buckets are stored in temporary files. A good hash function produces just enough buckets to ensure that each bucket of tuples will be small enough to fit entirely in main memory. During the second phase, relation S is partitioned using the hash function from step 1. Again, the last N-1 buckets are stored in temporary files while the tuples in the first bucket are used to immediately probe the in-memory hash table built during the first phase. During the third phase, the algorithm joins the remaining N-1 buckets from relation R with their respective buckets from relation S. The join is thus broken up into a series of smaller joins; each of which hopefully can be computed without experiencing join overflow. As with the Grace join algorithm, the size of the smaller relation determines the number of buckets; this calculation is independent of the size of the larger relation. Whereas the Grace join algorithm uses additional memory during the bucket-forming phase in order to produce extra buckets, Hybrid exploits this additional memory to immediately begin joining the first two buckets.

Our parallel version of the Hybrid hash join algorithm is similar to the centralized algorithm described above. A **partitioning split table** first separates the joining relations into N logical buckets. The number of buckets is chosen such that the tuples corresponding to each logical bucket will fit in the **aggregate** memory of the joining processors. The N-1 buckets intended for temporary storage on disk are each partitioned across all available disk sites as with the Grace algorithm. Likewise, a **joining split table** will be used to route tuples to their respective joining processor (these processors do not necessarily have attached disks), thus parallelizing the joining phase. Furthermore, the partitioning of the inner relation, R, into buckets is overlapped with the insertion of tuples from the first bucket of R into memory-resident hash tables at each of the join nodes. In addition, the partitioning of the outer relation, S, into buckets is overlapped with the joining of the first bucket of S with the first bucket of R. This requires that the partitioning split table for R and S be enhanced with the joining split table as tuples in the first bucket must be sent to those processors being used to effect the join. Of course, when the remaining N-1 buckets are joined, only the joining split table will be needed. Figure 4 depicts relation R being partitioned into N buckets across k disk sites where the first bucket is to be joined on m diskless processors.

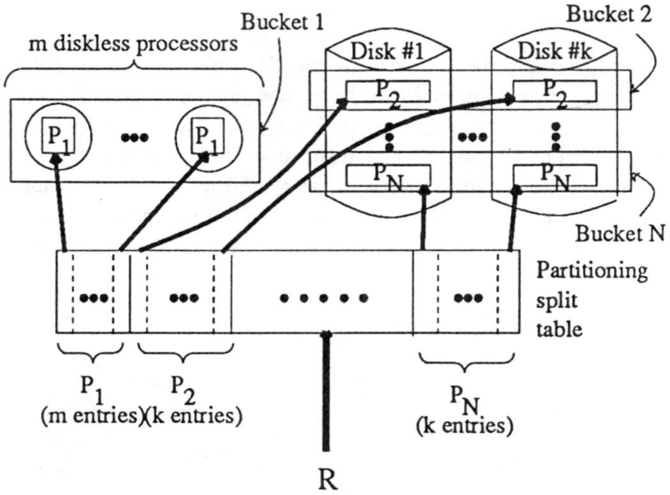

Partitioning of R into N logical buckets for Hybrid hash-join.
Figure 4

4. Experimental Results

We tested the various parallel algorithms under several conditions. First, the performance of the algorithms are studied when the attributes used to partition the joining relations at load time are also used as the joining attributes. Next, we wanted to compare the effects of bit vector filtering on the different algorithms. Third, the use of diskless processors by each of the hash-based algorithms is explored. Finally, the impact of non-uniformly distributed join attribute values on the performance of each of the algorithms is studied.

The benchmark relations are based on the standard Wisconsin Benchmark [BITT83]. Each relation consists of thirteen 4-byte integer values and three 52-byte string attributes. Except where noted otherwise, hashing on the unique1 attribute (an integer field) was used to determine each tuple's destination site during loading of the database. The benchmark join query is joinABprime, which joins a 100,000 tuple relation (approximately 20 megabytes in size) with a 10,000 tuple relation (approximately 2 megabytes in size) and produces a 10,000 tuple result relation (over 4 megabytes in size). We ran the experiments with the other benchmark join queries, joinAselB and joinCselAselB, but the trends were the same so those results are not presented. 8 kilobyte disk pages were used in all experiments. The **default** hardware environment consists of eight processors with disks and a single diskless processor reserved for query scheduling and global deadlock detection. We refer to this configuration as **local** because joins will be performed on the sites with attached disks. In Section 4.3, we explore the performance of the Simple, Grace, and Hybrid algorithms when 8 diskless processors are added. This configuration is termed **remote**.

Join performance (for each of these parallel join algorithms) is very sensitive to the amount of available memory relative to the size of the joining relations. In designing the set of experiments described below, one of the first decisions we had to make was how to capture this aspect of the performance of the different algorithms. One approach would have been to keep the amount of available memory constant while varying the size of the two relations being joined. The other choice was to keep the size of the joining relations constant while (artificially) varying the amount of memory available. We rejected the first choice because increasing the size of the joining relations has the side-effect of increasing the number of I/O's needed to execute the query.

Our experiments analyze join performance over a wide range of memory availability. All results are graphed with the x-axis representing the ratio of available memory to the size of the smaller relation. Note that available memory is the sum of the memory on the joining processors that is available for use to effect the join. In the case of the hash-based join algorithms, this memory is used to construct an in-memory hash table. For the sort-merge join algorithm, this memory is used for both sorting and merging. In the case of the sort-merge join algorithm, we simply reduced the amount of sort/merge space and for the Simple-hash join algorithm we reduced the amount of hash table space, accordingly. For the Grace and Hybrid algorithms, however, a data point at 0.5 relative memory availability, for instance, equates to a two-bucket join. Likewise, a data point at 0.20 was computed using 5 buckets. Thus, neither Grace or Hybrid joins experienced hash table overflow.

4.1. HPJA vs. Non-HPJA Joins: Local configuration

In Gamma and Teradata, when a relation is created, the database administrator is required to specify a partitioning or "key" attribute and, in the case of Gamma, a partitioning strategy: round-robin, hashed, or range (see Section 2 for more details). If the two relations being joined are both hash-partitioned on their joining attributes (termed a HPJA join), the partitioning phase of each of the parallel algorithms described in the previous section is no longer necessary and can be eliminated. Rather than special-case the system to handle a join operation on the partitioning attribute, Gamma relies on its operating system to "short-circuit" packets between two processes on the same machine and the design of the partitioning split table to maximize the extent to which tuples are mapped to hash-join buckets at the same processor.

Figures 5 and 6 display the execution times of the joinABprime query as a function of the amount of memory available relative to the size of the inner relation when the join attributes are the partitioning attributes (Figure 5) and when they are not (termed a non-HPJA join, see Figure 6). These tests were conducted using the "local" configuration of processors in which the joins are executed only on the 8 processors with disks. Several points should be made about these graphs. First, when the smaller relation fits entirely in memory (at 1.0), Hybrid and Simple algorithms have, as expected, identical execution times.

As expected, Grace joins are relatively insensitive to decreasing the amount of available memory but Hybrid is very sensitive, especially when the percentage of available memory relative to the size of the joining relations is large. This occurs because the Grace algorithm is not using the extra memory for joining and hence decreasing memory simply increases the number of buckets, each of which incurs a small scheduling overhead. However,

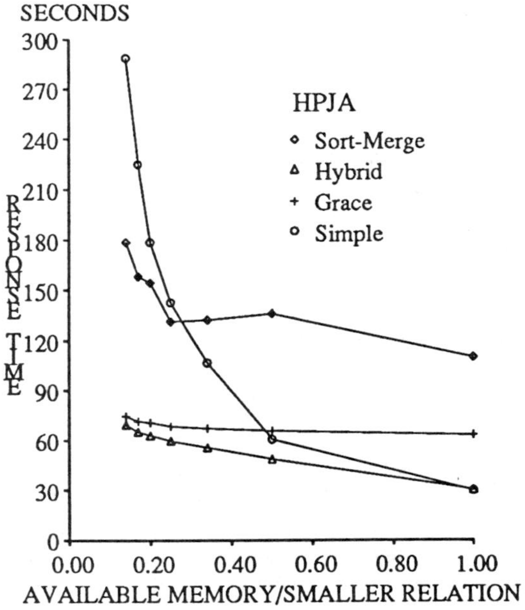

Figure 5
Partitioning Attributes Used as Join Attributes
8 Processors with Disks

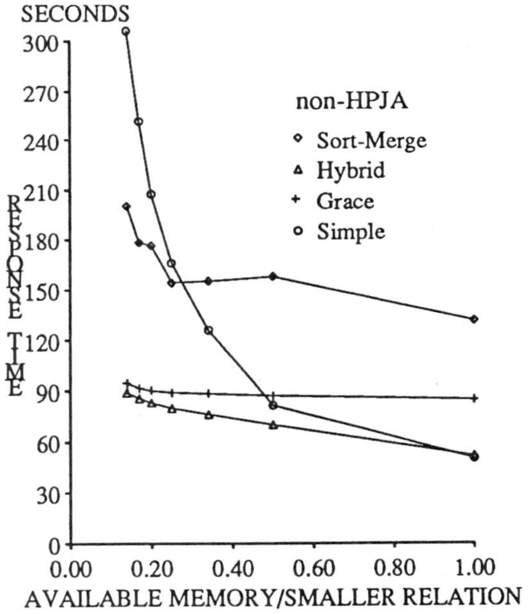

Figure 6
Partitioning Attributes Not Used as Join Attributes
8 Processors with Disks

for Hybrid, decreasing the amount of memory available from a ratio of 1.0 to 0.5 forces the algorithm to stage half of each joining relation back to disk. Furthermore, note that the response time for the Hybrid algorithm approaches that of the Grace algorithm as memory is reduced. Hybrid derives its benefits from exploiting extra memory and, when this memory is reduced, the relative performance of the algorithm degrades.

For both Figures 5 and 6, the Hybrid algorithm dominates over the entire available memory range. Between the memory ratios of 0.5 and 1.0, Simple hash outperforms Grace and sort-merge because a decreasing fraction of the larger joining relation is written back to disk. However, as memory availability decreases, Simple hash degrades rapidly because it repeatedly reads and writes the same data. While the performance of the Sort-merge algorithm is relatively stable, it is dominated by Hybrid and Grace algorithms over the entire memory range. The upward steps in the response time curves for sort-merge result from the cost of the additional merging passes that are required to sort the larger source relation. An interesting feature of the sort-merge curves is the drop in response time as the memory ratio is decreased from 0.5 to 0.25. Although we are entirely not sure why this phenomenon occurs (about a 3% difference), we hypothesize that, while the number of merge passes required for sorting the larger joining relation is constant over this memory range, adding additional sort buffers really just adds processing overhead.

It is important to point out that the trends observed in these graphs and their general shape are almost identical to the analytical results reported in [DEWI84] and the experimental results in [DEWI85] for **single-processor** versions of the same algorithms. There are several reasons why we find this similarity encouraging. First, it demonstrates that each of the algorithms parallelizes well. Second, it serves to verify that our parallel implementation of each algorithm was done in a fair and consistent fashion.

It is interesting to note that the corresponding curves in Figures 5 and 6 differ by a constant factor over all memory availabilities tested. With sort-merge, since the join attributes of the two relations have the same range of values, regardless of whether they are partitioning attributes or not, the time to sort and merge will be constant. However, when relations R and S are partitioned across the joining sites, HPJA joins will shortcircuit all tuples in both R and S. Non-HPJA joins, however, will only shortcircuit 1/8th of the tuples. This shortcircuiting difference accounts for the response time difference.

Simple hash will experience the same effects as the set of joining processors is the same as with sort-merge. However, one might have expected that HPJA joins would increasingly reap the benefits of shortcircuiting when processing join overflows. These savings never materialize because the hash function is changed after each overflow, thus converting HPJA joins into non-HPJA joins. This hash function modification is necessary in order to efficiently process non-uniform data distributions. Consider the case where only a subset of the joining sites overflow. If the same joining hash function is used when the tuples from the overflow partition are read from disk and re-split, all the overflow tuples will re-map to the same overflowing processors. Unfortunately, this will leave the non-overflowing processors idle and perhaps more importantly, their associated local memories unused.

The explanation for Grace joins is slightly more complicated. Independent of the amount of memory available, partitioning of R and S into buckets will be completely shortcircuited for HPJA joins while only 1/8th of the tuples will be shortcircuited for non-HPJA joins. Since this accounts for the total response time difference between HPJA and non-HPJA joins, this implies that the joining phases for the HPJA and non-HPJA attribute joins must be identical, and furthermore that all joining tuples will shortcircuit the network. Why is this the case? We can argue intuitively that this should be the case in a good implementation. The important feature of using hashing in a parallel join algorithm is that the join is broken into buckets, each of which can be processed independently of one another. Obviously, this is what Grace joins do; tuples in bucket j of R are only compared with tuples in bucket j of S. But this technique can be applied to a finer level than buckets. In Figure 3, one saw that each logical bucket is composed of a number of physical fragments. Since these fragments are created by hashing (via the partitioning split table), we are only required to join tuples in fragment i of bucket j of R with tuples from fragment i of bucket j of S, where i ranges from 1 to the number of disk sites and j ranges from 1 to N. Since the corresponding fragments of buckets j of R and S reside on the same disk (since the same partitioning split table is used for R and S), there is no need to redistribute these tuples during a join when only processors with disks are used to perform the join operation. Thus, with the Grace join algorithm, non-HPJA joins become HPJA joins after the initial bucket-forming partitioning phase has been completed.

The performance difference between HPJA and non-HPJA Hybrid joins is easy to explain given their similarity to Grace joins. With the "Local" configuration, a N-bucket Hybrid join will have a partitioning split table identical to that of a N-bucket Grace join with the exception that tuples in the first bucket will be joined immediately instead of being stored in temporary files. Since the joining split table is identical for both algorithms, all tuples will shortcircuit the network during the processing of all N buckets (as was the case with Grace joins). Thus, the difference in execution time between HPJA and non-HPJA Hybrid joins is due to the cost of partitioning R and S into buckets when the join attributes are the HPJA and when they are not.

4.2. Multiprocessor Bit Vector Filtering

In the next set of experiments we ran the joinABprime tests using bit filters [BABB79, VALD84]. With the sort-merge algorithm, a bit filter is built at each disk site as the inner (smaller) relation is partitioned across the network and stored in temporary files. With the hash-based algorithms, a bit filter is built at each of the join sites as tuples from the inner relation are being inserted into the hash tables. This filter is then used to eliminate non-joining tuples from the outer relation.

In our implementation, bit filtering of tuples is only applied during the joining phase. With the Simple hash-join algorithm this means that as the number of overflows increases, the opportunities for filtering out non-joining tuples increases (because each overflow is treated as a separate join). With Grace and Hybrid joins, each bucket is treated as a separate join. Thus, separate bit filters will be built as a part of processing each bucket. Since each join uses the same size bit filter, increasing the number of buckets (or overflows) increases the effective size of the aggregate bit filter across the entire join operation.

Figure 7 shows the results for HPJA joins with bit filtering applied. (Non-HPJA join results are not shown because, as was the case with non-HPJA joins in Figure 6, the trends are the same.) Again, these tests were conducted using only the 8 CPUs with disks. Notice that the relative positions of the algorithms have not changed, only the execution times have dropped in comparison to the results shown in Figure 5. The performance improvements from bit filtering for each individual algorithm are

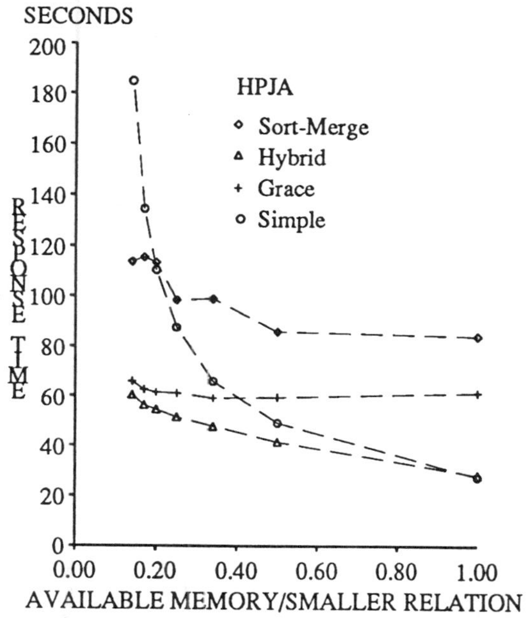

Figure 7
Bit Vector Filtering
8 Processors with Disks

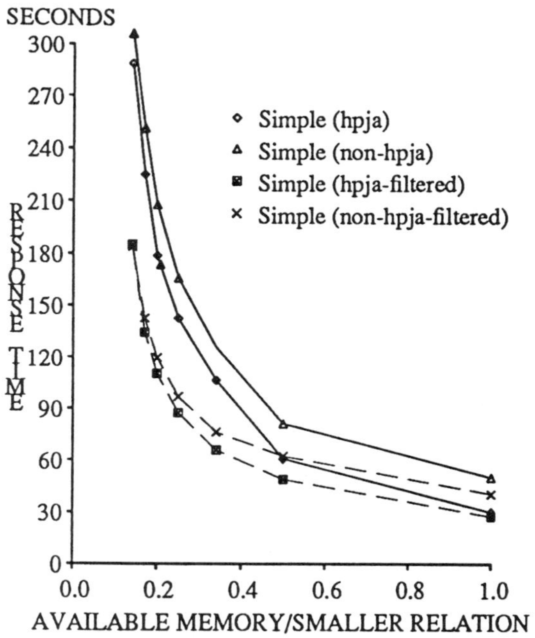

Figure 9

shown in Figures 8 through 11. An interesting effect to note is the shape of the curves for the Grace join algorithm as memory is reduced. Execution time actually **falls** until the available memory ratio reaches 25% (4 buckets) and then begins to rise. This is explained by our implementation of bit filtering. With 100% available memory, all 10,000 tuples (approximately 1,250 at each site) will attempt to set a bit in the filter. Since, Gamma currently uses only a single 2Kbyte packet for a filter (which is shared across all 8 joining sites - yielding 1,973 bits/site after overhead), most bits are set and hence the effectiveness of the filter is low. Thus, only a small percentage of the probing tuples are eliminated by the filter. However, as memory is decreased and the number of buckets increases a separate 2K filter is used for the join of each bucket. With two buckets, the gains from eliminating additional probing tuples exceeds the cost of scheduling the extra bucket and response time drops. This effect keeps occurring until four buckets are used and all non-joining tuples have been eliminated by filtering.

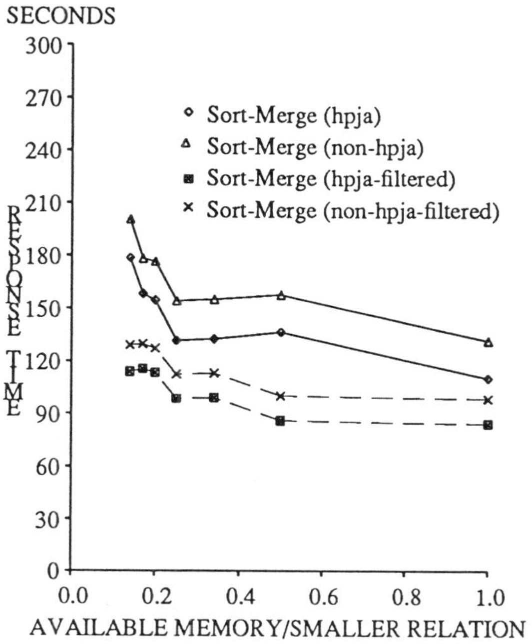

Figure 8

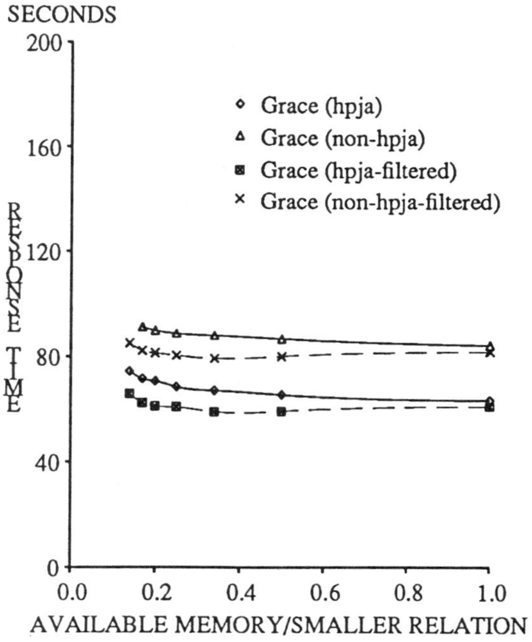

Figure 10

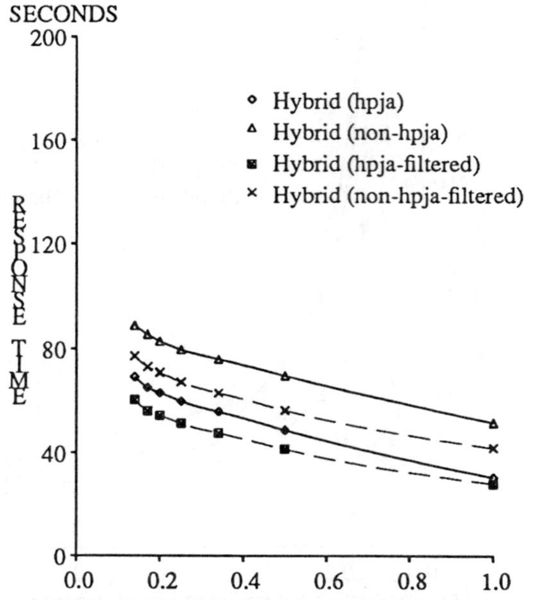

Figure 11

The Hybrid join algorithm experiences the same bit filtering effects but the result is not as obvious because as the amount of available memory is reduced the amount of disk I/O increases. Thus it is harder to isolate the effects of bit filtering than with the Grace algorithm.

A similar effect occurs for Simple hash-join. As memory is reduced (and overflows occur more frequently) more tuples are eliminated by the bit filters. As you can see, large bit filters are necessary for low response times for Simple hash-join. Eliminating non-joining tuples early will avoid writing these tuples to disk and later reading them multiple times.

The performance of the sort-merge join algorithm also benefits significantly from the use of bit filters, even though only a single 2K filter is used. Tuples of the outer relation that are eliminated by the filter do not need to be written to disk, sorted, and later read during merging. Obviously using a larger bit filter would further improve the performance of each of these join algorithms. It should also be noted that extending filtering techniques to the bucket-forming phases of the Grace and Hybrid join algorithms would also improve performance.

4.3. Remote Joins: HPJA vs. Non-HPJA

Since Gamma can use diskless processors for performing join and aggregate operations, the goal of the tests described in this section was to explore the effect of using diskless processors on the performance of the different join algorithms. The sort-merge algorithm has been excluded from this section because our current implementation of this algorithm cannot utilize diskless processors.

Although Gamma is capable of executing a join operation on a mix of processors with and without disks, earlier tests for the Simple hash-join algorithm [DEWI88] indicated the performance of such a configuration was almost always 1/2 way between that of the "local" and "remote" configurations. Thus, for the following experiments, 8 processors with disks were used for storing the relations and 8 diskless processors performed the actual join computation. The Hybrid, Simple, and Grace algorithms were tested using this "remote" configuration and the results for the joinABprime query are displayed in Figure 12.

For the Grace algorithm, the difference in execution time between HPJA and non-HPJA joins is constant over the entire range of memory availability. This occurs because the execution time of the bucket-forming phase is constant regardless of the number of buckets, i.e., both source relations are completely written back to disk. The response time difference between the HPJA and non-HPJA joins reflects the savings gained by shortcircuiting the network during the bucket-forming phases for the HPJA joins. Shortcircuiting also explains the spreading difference shown for Hybrid joins. With 100% available memory, all tuples will be shipped remotely during the processing of the join, for both types of joins. However, when only half the required memory is available, HPJA joins will write half the building and probing tuples to disk **locally** during the bucket-forming phase of the algorithm, thus shortcircuiting the network. Non-HPJA joins will write only 1/16th of these same tuples locally. Table 1 presents the difference in the percentage of local writes for HPJA and non-HPJA joins.

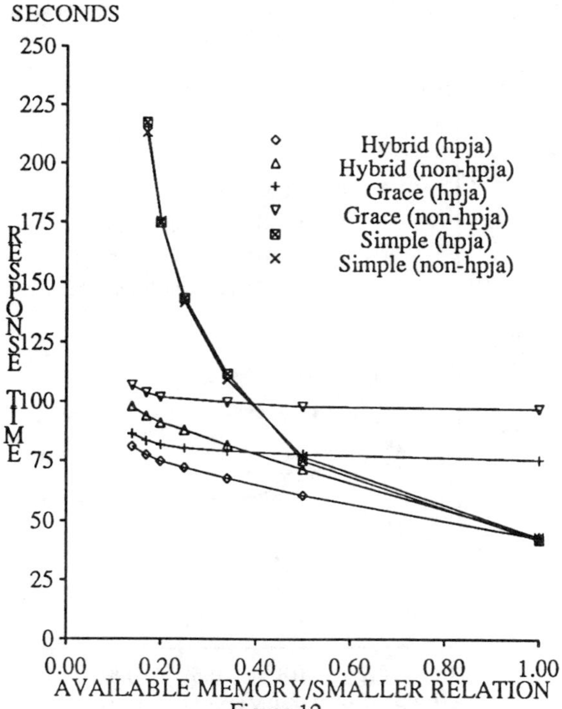

Figure 12

Joins Executed on 8 Diskless Processors

Join Type	Number of Buckets					
	1	2	3	4	5	6
HPJA	0	1/2	2/3	3/4	4/5	5/6
Non-HPJA	0	1/16	2/24	3/32	4/40	5/56
Difference	0	.438	.583	.656	.717	.744

Fraction of local writes during redistribution for HPJA and non-HPJA Hybrid joins.
Table 1

Analyzing this table shows that as the number of buckets increases (ie. memory is reduced), the relative savings of local writes for HPJA joins increases over that for non-HPJA joins.

The fact that non-HPJA joins perform the same as HPJA joins for Simple hash-join may seem puzzling at first. As memory is reduced the curves do not spread as with Hybrid because the hash function is changed after the first overflow, hence turning all joins into non-HPJA joins[3].

Local vs. Remote Joins: HPJA

A comparison of the performance of "local" and "remote" joins for HPJA joins is shown in Figure 13. With Grace joins, the cost of bucket-forming is constant regardless of where the join processing is performed and, since these are HPJA joins, bucket-forming will shortcircuit all tuples. However, during the joining phase, tuples will be distributed to the join processors for building and probing. When joins are done locally, all these tuples will shortcircuit the network (in addition to 1/8th of the result tuples). With remote-join processing, none of these shortcircuiting benefits will be realized during the joining phase. The same explanation describes the observed Hybrid join performance. Please refer to [DEWI88] for an explanation for the observed crossover in the graphs for the Simple hash-join algorithm.

Local vs. Remote Joins: Non-HPJA

With non-HPJA joins, the results presented in the previous sub-section no longer hold. Figure 14 shows the performance of the three hash-join algorithms on non-partitioning attributes for both the "local" and "remote" configurations. We consider Grace joins first. As Figure 14 demonstrates, local joins have superior performance to remote joins by a constant margin over the entire range of available memory. Since the bucket-forming phase of the Grace algorithm involves only the processors with disks, the execution time of this phase is constant regardless of what processors are used for the actual join operation. At a memory ratio of 1.0, one would then expect the join phase of the Grace algorithm to behave exactly like that of a one-bucket Hybrid join. But, as you can see, Hybrid executes joins on diskless processors faster at this memory ratio. What is the cause of this inconsistency? Recall from Section 4.1 that with the Grace algorithm non-HPJA joins effectively become HPJA joins after the bucket-forming phase. Thus, the results obtained for HPJA joins that

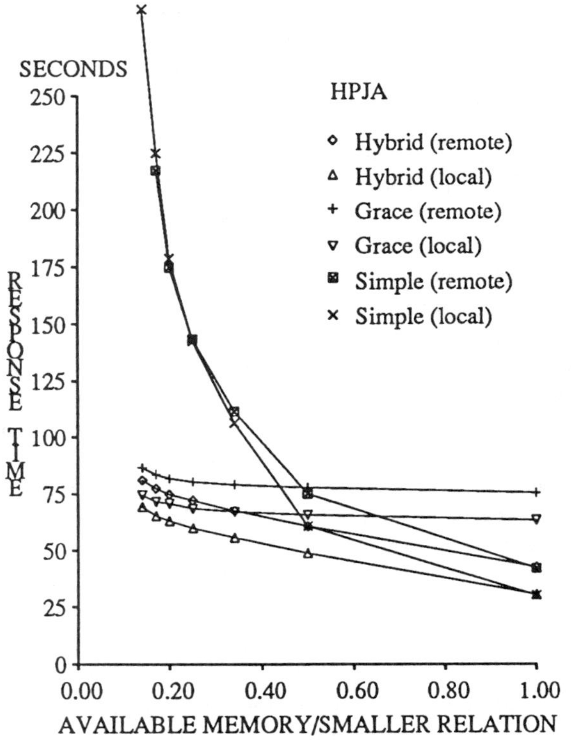

Figure 13
Partitioning Attributes Used as Join Attributes

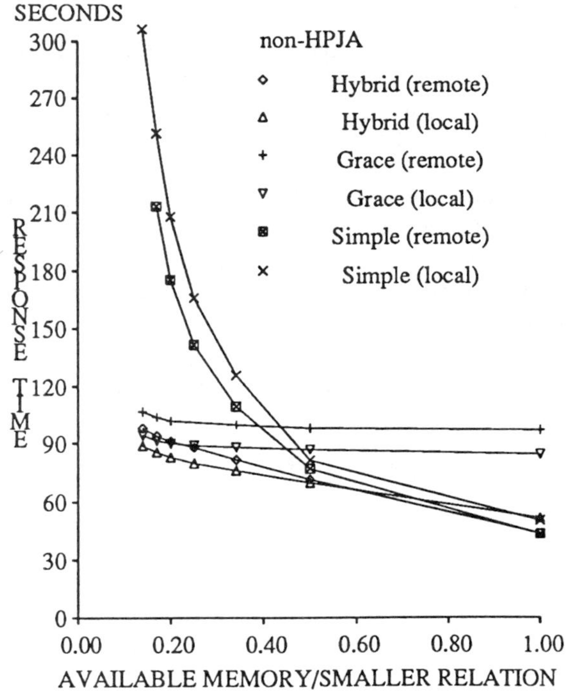

Figure 14
Partitioning Attributes Not Used as Join Attributes

were described in the previous section and displayed in Figure 13 can be directly applied in this case. As one can see, the same difference between local and remote response time exists, although the non-HPJA join times are slower than the HPJA join

[3]See Section 4.1 for the motivation behind this change in hash functions.

times because of the increased costs of bucket-forming.

The discussion contained in Section 4.1 also explains the performance of the Hybrid algorithm. At 100% memory availability, bucket-forming and joining are completely overlapped. Since these experiments involve non-HPJA joins, tuples will be distributed across all the joining processors resulting in substantial network traffic. Remote processing wins in this case because, since the joining relations tuples need to be distributed across the processors anyway, the CPU cycles necessary for building and probing the hash tables can be successfully offloaded to the diskless processors. But, as memory is reduced "Local" joins become better and better. The partitioning phenomena discussed for Hybrid joins in Section 4.1 explains this shift in performance. At a memory availability of 50%, half of the tuples being joined will be written to disk. When this disk bucket is subsequently joined it will effectively become a HPJA join. As memory is further reduced a larger fraction of the join becomes like a HPJA join and, as illustrated by Figure 13, HPJA joins can be executed faster locally than remotely. This explains why the curves crossover and the difference widens as memory is reduced.

Performance of the Simple hash-join algorithm is easy to explain. It is fastest with remote processors at 100% memory availability for the same reasons given for Hybrid. However, it doesn't crossover like Hybrid because its writing and subsequent reading of overflow files never benefits from shortcircuiting as the modification of the hash function after each hash table overflow eliminates the possibility of ever achieving the performance observed with HPJA joins.

4.4. Non-Uniform Data Distributions

In this set of experiments we wanted to analyze the performance of the four parallel join algorithms in the presence of non-uniformly distributed join attribute values. In order to isolate the effects of the non-uniform data distributions we varied the distribution of the two join attribute values independently. Figure 15 shows these four possible combinations that comprised our experimental design space. The key we are using in this figure is XY, where X (Y) represents the attribute value distribution of the inner (outer) relation. U = Uniform distribution and N = Non-uniform distribution.

Inner Relation \ Outer Relation	uniform	non-uniform
uniform	UU	UN
non-uniform	NU	NN

Figure 15

The response time of the joinABprime query is again used as the performance metric for this set of experiments. Recall that this query joins a 100,000 tuple relation (20 megabytes) with a 10,000 tuple relation (2 megabytes). The 10,000 tuple relation is the inner (building) relation and the 100,000 tuple relation is the outer (probing) relation. For the non-uniform distribution we chose the **normal** distribution with a mean of 50,000 and a standard deviation of 750. These parameters resulted in a highly skewed distribution of values over the domain 0-99,999. In fact, 12,500 tuples had join attribute values in the range 50,000 to 50,243. However, no single attribute value occurred in more than 77 tuples. The 10,000 tuple relation was created by randomly selecting 10,000 tuples from the 100,000 tuple relation. Thus the 10,000 tuple relation's primary key had values uniformly distributed from 0 to 99,999. Also, the normally distributed attribute had the same characteristics for its distribution for the 10,000 tuple relation as it did for the 100,000 tuple relation.

To ensure that each processor did the same amount of work during the initial scan of the two relations being joined, we distributed each of the relations on their join attribute by using the range partitioning strategy provided by Gamma. This resulted in an equal number of tuples on each of the eight disks.

As in the previous experiments we used the amount of memory relative to the size of the smaller joining relation as a basis for comparing the join algorithms. Remember, though, that the amount of memory at each joining processor is sufficient to hold its share of tuples from the inner relation **only** if the tuples are distributed evenly across the processors. Eight processors with disks were used for these experiments.

Table 2 presents the results for each of the parallel join algorithms for the cases of 100% and 17% memory availability. The UU joins produced a result relation of 10,000 tuples as did the NU joins. The UN joins produced 10,036 result tuples. Results for the NN joins are not presented as the result cardinality for this query was 368,474 tuples. We could find no way of normalizing these NN results to meaningfully compare them with the results from the other three join types. We analyze the performance of each of the join algorithms with the addition of bit vector filters in the next subsection.

Algorithm	**100% memory**			**17% memory**		
	UU	NU	UN	UU	NU	UN
Hybrid	51.48	57.27	51.37	85.74	111.36	88.87
w/filter	36.84	30.04	37.74	73.60	89.39	78.20
Grace	84.13	84.53	84.83	92.90	97.89	95.66
w/filter	79.37	76.07	79.93	83.20	87.89	87.28
Sort-Merge	167.44	149.45	163.81	210.91	195.78	209.37
w/filter	101.27	66.24	99.03	125.06	70.91	124.88
Simple	51.13	57.76	51.63	251.37	259.30	246.84
w/filter	36.57	30.53	38.00	167.08	121.65	164.41

Join results with non-uniform join attribute value distributions.
(All response times are in seconds)
Table 2

We begin by analyzing the effects of using non-uniformly distributed join attribute values for the inner (building) relation by comparing the NU results with the UU results. For the hash-join algorithms two major factors result from "building" with a non-uniformly distributed attribute. First, tuples will not generally be distributed equally among the physical bucket fragments. Second, chains of tuples will form in the hash tables due to duplicate attribute values. The first factor is significant because some processors will have more work than others and because the aggregate memory allocated for the join was sufficient to hold the building relation's tuples **only** if the tuples were uniformly spread across the joining processors. With the normally distributed join attribute values used in our experiments, the hash function could not distribute the relation uniformly and memory overflow resulted. However, the hash function did not perform that poorly and only one pass of the overflow mechanism was necessary to resolve the overflow of each join bucket. The second factor, chains of tuples forming in the hash tables, also occurred with normally distributed join attribute values. In fact, chains of 3.3 tuples were found on the average, with a maximum hash chain length of 16.

Table 2 shows that NU is indeed slower than UU for these hash-based join algorithms. Since the philosophy behind the Grace join algorithm is to use many small buckets to prevent buckets from overflowing, we executed this algorithm using one additional bucket so that memory overflow would not occur. At 100% memory availability, the Hybrid algorithm processes the overflow fairly efficiently. However, as memory is reduced, each bucket-join in the Hybrid algorithm experiences overflow. As shown by the results at 17% memory availability, the cost of overflow resolution becomes significant.

Why, though, does the sort-merge join algorithm run NU faster than UU and UN? The hashing function will distribute tuples unevenly across the joining processors exactly as it did for the other algorithms, thereby requiring a subset of the sites to store to disk, sort, and subsequently merge more tuples than others. This will surely have a negative impact on response time. The explanation has to do with recognizing how the merge phase of the join works. Since the join attribute of the inner relation is highly skewed (the maximum join attribute value is only 53,071) the merge phase does not need to read all of the outer (100K) relation. In this case, the semantic knowledge inherent in the sort-order of the attributes allowed the merge process to determine the join was fully computed **before** all the joining tuples were read. A similar effect occurs for UN but it is not as significant because only part of the inner (10K) relation can be skipped from reading; all the 100K outer relation must still be read.

The effects of a non-uniform distribution of join attribute values in the outer relation can be determined by comparing the UN results with the UU results. The first effect is that an unequal numbers of tuples are distributed to the joining processors. At 100% memory availability no noticeable effects are shown (except for sort-merge as discussed above). However, as memory is reduced small differences appear for both the Hybrid and Grace algorithms. This occurs because as memory is reduced the joining relations are first divided up into buckets. Because the outer join attribute is non-uniformly distributed, the outer relation will not be uniformly divided among the buckets. The result is that some of the disk sites require additional disk I/Os during the bucket forming **and** bucket joining phases. Thus, as the number of buckets increases the effects of having non-uniformly distributed join attribute values become more significant.

We feel these UN results are very encouraging for the Hybrid join algorithm. One can argue that many joins are done to re-establish relationships. These relationships are generally one-to-many and hence one join attribute will be a key. Since the relation on the "one" side is probably smaller it will be the building relation in a hash-join algorithm. Thus, this case will result in a UN type of join which we have shown can be efficiently processed.

Bit Vector Filtering

As expected, Table 2 shows that the application of bit vector filters improves the performance of each of the parallel join algorithms. Table 3 presents the percentage improvement provided by using bit filters for each of the join algorithms.

Algorithm	100% memory			17% memory		
	UU	NU	UN	UU	NU	UN
Hybrid	28.4%	47.6%	26.5%	14.2%	19.7%	12.0%
Grace	5.7%	10.0%	5.8%	10.4%	10.2%	8.8%
Sort-Merge	39.5%	55.7%	39.5%	40.7%	63.8%	40.4%
Simple	28.5%	47.1%	26.4%	33.5%	53.1%	33.4%

Percentage improvement using bit vector filters.
Table 3

As shown, the sort-merge and Simple join algorithms experience the greatest improvement from bit filtering. This occurs because filtering tuples eliminates a large number of disk I/Os. The performance of the Grace join algorithm is improved the least because filtering is only applied during bucket-joining and not during bucket-forming. Thus, no disk I/O is eliminated by using bit filters with this algorithm. As stated in Section 4.2, extending bit filtering to the bucket-forming phases of the Grace and Hybrid algorithms would significantly increase the performance of these algorithms.

Within each join algorithm the NU join type experienced the greatest improvements from filtering because the normally distributed attribute values resulted in more collisions when setting bits in the bit filter. Thus, fewer bits were set in the filter. This has the effect of screening out more outer (probing) tuples. Sort-merge has the best filtering improvement for NU because the better filtering enabled the outer relation to be sorted in one less pass.

5. Conclusions and Future Work

Several conclusions can be drawn from these experiments. First, for uniformly distributed join attribute values the parallel Hybrid algorithm appears to be the algorithm of choice because it dominates each of the other algorithms at all degrees of memory availability. Second, bit filtering should be used because it is cheap and can significantly reduce response times.

However, non-uniformly distributed join attribute values alter the relative performance of the parallel join algorithms. The performance of the hash-based join algorithms, Hybrid, Grace and Simple, degrades when the join attribute values of the inner relation are non-uniformly distributed. In the case where the join attribute values are highly skewed and the available memory relative to the size of the smaller relation is limited, the optimizer should choose a non-hash-based algorithm such as sort-merge. We find it very encouraging, though, that the Hybrid join algorithm still performs best when the joining attribute of the outer relation is non-uniformly distributed. We expect this type of join to be very common in the case of re-establishing one-to-many relationships.

From the results presented, one might be tempted to conclude that using remote processors for executing join operators is not a good idea except when the Hybrid algorithm is used with sufficient available memory and the join is a non-HPJA join. This may not be as restrictive as it seems as a relation can only have one partitioning attribute. Hence, non-HPJA joins may be fairly likely. In addition, when Gamma processes joins "locally", the processors are at 100% CPU utilization. However, when the "remote" configuration is used, CPU utilization at the processors with disk drops to approximately 60%. Thus, in a multiuser environment, offloading joins to remote processors may permit higher throughput by reducing the load at the processors with disks. We intend on studying the multiuser tradeoffs in the near future.

Several opportunities exist for expanding on the work done. For instance, currently only a single join process operates on a processor at a time. We would like to look at increasing the amount of intra-query parallelism. Dynamically adjusting the number of join processes depending on load information would also be very interesting.

6. References

[BABB79] Babb, E., "Implementing a Relational Database by Means of Specialized Hardware" ACM Transactions on Database Systems, Vol. 4, No. 1, March, 1979.

[BITT83] Bitton, D., D.J. DeWitt, and C. Turbyfill, "Benchmarking Database Systems - A Systematic Approach," Proceedings of the 1983 Very Large Database Conference, October, 1983.

[BORA88] Boral, H. "Parallelism in Bubba," Proceedings of the International Symposium on Databases in Parallel and Distributed Systems, Austin, TX, December, 1988.

[BRAT84] Bratbergsengen, Kjell, "Hashing Methods and Relational Algebra Operations" Proceedings of the 1984 Very Large Database Conference, August, 1984.

[BRAT87] Bratbergsengen, Kjell, "Algebra Operations on a Parallel Computer -- Performance Evaluation", **Database Machines and Knowledge Base Machines**, M. Kitsuregawa and H. Tanaka (eds), Kluwer Academic Publishers, 1987.

[CHOU85] Chou, H-T, DeWitt, D. J., Katz, R., and T. Klug, "Design and Implementation of the Wisconsin Storage System (WiSS)" Software Practices and Experience, Vol. 15, No. 10, October, 1985.

[DEWI84] DeWitt, D. J., et. al., "Implementation Techniques for Main Memory Database Systems," Proceedings of the 1984 SIGMOD Conference, Boston, MA, June, 1984.

[DEWI85] DeWitt, D., and R. Gerber, "Multiprocessor Hash-Based Join Algorithms," Proceedings of the 1985 VLDB Conference, Stockholm, Sweden, August, 1985.

[DEWI86] DeWitt, D., Gerber, B., Graefe, G., Heytens, M., Kumar, K. and M. Muralikrishna, "GAMMA - A High Performance Dataflow Database Machine," Proceedings of the 1986 VLDB Conference, Japan, August 1986.

[DEWI88] DeWitt, D., Ghandeharizadeh, S., and D. Schneider, "A Performance Analysis of the Gamma Database Machine", Proceedings of the 1988 SIGMOD Conference, Chicago, IL, June 1988.

[KITS83] Kitsuregawa, M., Tanaka, H., and T. Moto-oka, "Application of Hash to Data Base Machine and Its Architecture," New Generation Computing, Vol. 1, No. 1, 1983.

[KITS88] Kitsuregawa, M., Nakano, M., and M. Takagi, "Query Execution for Large Relations On Functional Disk System," to appear, 1989 Data Engineering Conference.

[LORI88] Lorie, R., et. al., "Adding Intra-Transaction Parallelism to an Exisiting DBMS: Early Experience", RJ 6165, IBM Almaden Research Center, March 1988.

[RIES78] Ries, D. and R. Epstein, "Evaluation of Distribution Criteria for Distributed Database Systems," UCB/ERL Technical Report M78/22, UC Berkeley, May, 1978.

[SELI79] Selinger,P. G., et. al., "Access Path Selection in a Relational Database Management System," Proceedings of the 1979 SIGMOD Conference, Boston, MA., May 1979.

[TAND88] Tandem Performance Group, *A Benchmark of Non-Stop SQL on the Debit Credit Transaction,* Proceedings of the 1988 SIGMOD Conference, Chicago, IL, June 1988.

[TERA83] Teradata Corp., *DBC/1012 Data Base Computer Concepts & Facilities,* Teradata Corp. Document No. C02-0001-00, 1983.

[VALD84] Valduriez, P., and G. Gardarin, "Join and Semi-Join Algorithms for a Multiprocessor Database Machine" ACM Transactions on Database Systems, Vol. 9, No. 1, March, 1984.

The Join Algorithms on a Shared-Memory Multiprocessor Database Machine

GHASSAN Z. QADAH, MEMBER, IEEE, AND KEKI B. IRANI, SENIOR MEMBER, IEEE

Abstract—**This paper develops and presents a large set of parallel algorithms for implementing the join operation on a shared-memory multiprocessor database machine. The development of these algorithms follows a structured approach. First, the major steps involved in the processing of the join operation by the machine are identified. Second, alternative join algorithms are constructed by concatenating the different ways of performing these steps. Furthermore, a study of the performance of the proposed algorithms is presented. This study shows, among other things, that for a given hardware configuration there is not just one overall best-performing join algorithm, but different algorithms score the best performance, depending on the characteristics of the data participating in the join operation.**

Index Terms—**Computer architecture, database machines, join operation, multiprocessors, parallel algorithms, parallel processing, relational model.**

I. Introduction

DURING the past decade, several conventional relational database systems have been designed [1], [2]. These systems are large complex software systems running on a conventional general-purpose von Neumann computer. The low reliability of these systems, their poor performance in supporting a large class of database operations, and the advancement in processor-memory technology inspired a new approach to support relational databases. This approach replaces the general-purpose von Neumann computer with a dedicated machine, the database machine (DBM), tailored for the data processing environment and, in most cases, utilizing parallel processing to support some or all of the functions of the database system. The new approach claims to overcome the drawbacks of the conventional approach.

Many DBM's have been designed, and some of these designs have also been implemented [3]–[15]. Most of these designs organize the DBM as a back-end machine to one or more general-purpose computers, called the hosts. Although the host is responsible for interfacing the users to the DBM, the DBM itself is responsible for the database access and control. An important class of DBM's is multiprocessor machines. In this class, a DBM is organized as a set of microprocessors intercommunicating through a shared memory [8], [9], [14], [15] or an interconnection network [13].

Manuscript received July 30, 1985; revised October 17, 1986.

G. Z. Qadah is with the Department of Electrical Engineering and Computer Science, Northwestern University, Evanston, IL 60208.

K. B. Irani is with the Department of Electrical Engineering and Computer Science, The University of Michigan, Ann Arbor, MI 48109.

IEEE Log Number 8823669.

One of the most important operations of the relational systems and probably the most important limiting factor on their performance is the Θ-join operation. The Θ-join [16] of a source relation S and a target relation T on attributes A from S, and B from T, is the relation R, obtained by concatenating each tuple $s \in S$ and each tuple $t \in T$ whenever $(s[A]\ \Theta t[B])$ is true. Θ is one of the operators "$=$, $\neq$, $<$, $\leq$, $\geq$, or $>$." The Θ-join operation is generally needed for formulating queries which reference more than one relation. The most frequently used type of Θ-join operation is the equijoin, or simply join, where "Θ" is the operator "$=$."

In this paper, a large set of parallel algorithms to carry out the join operation on a shared-memory multiprocessor DBM [15], [22] is developed and presented. The development of these algorithms follows a structured approach. First, the major steps involved in the processing of the join operation by the machine are identified. Second, alternative join algorithms are constructed by concatenating the different ways of performing these steps. A study of the performance of the developed algorithms is also presented. The outcome of this study suggests that, for a given hardware configuration, there is not just one best-performing parallel join algorithm, but different algorithms score the best performance based on, among other things, the characteristics of the two relations participating in the operation.

From the point of view of the join operation, the shared-memory multiprocessor DBM [15], as shown in Fig. 1, consists of one or more processing clusters, the mass memory, the parallel buffer (pbuffer), and the interconnection network. The mass memory is organized as a set of moving-head disks. Each disk is provided with the capability of reading (writing) from (to) more than one track in parallel. Tracks which can be read (written) from (to) one disk in parallel form the so-called minimum access unit (MACU). The MACU is the smallest accessible unit of data as well as the unit of data transfer between the mass memory, the pbuffer, and the processing clusters. The mass memory stores the database. The database, a set of time-varying relations, is horizontally partitioned into a set of units, each unit having the size of one MACU. Only the tuples of one relation can reside in the same unit.

The pbuffer is organized as a set of blocks, each block having the size of one MACU. A block is further partitioned into a set of subblocks. Each subblock can buffer one track of a mass memory disk. The parallel buffer is

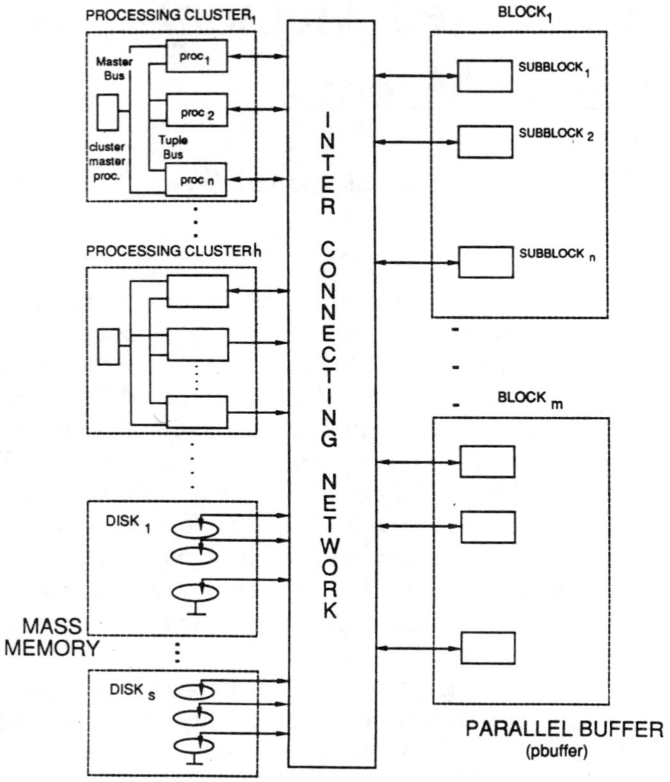

Fig. 1. The organization of the multiprocessor DBM.

implemented using the semiconductor random access memory technology.

A (processing) cluster, as shown in Fig. 1, consists of a set of triplets, each consisting of a processor, a local random access memory (lmemory) and a direct memory access (DMA) controller. An lmemory has the capacity of several disk tracks. The number of processors (triplets) within one cluster is equal to the number of subblocks within one block of the pbuffer. The processors within a cluster are controlled and managed by the cluster master processor. The latter accesses its processors through a broadcast bus, the master bus. Within a cluster, the data are moved between processors via another bus, the tuple bus. This bus is provided with both point-to-point and broadcast capabilities.

The (interconnection) network subsystem interconnects the mass memory disks, the pbuffer blocks, and the processing clusters (refer to Fig. 1). The network is provided with two capabilities, namely, that to enable any number of processing clusters to read the same pbuffer block and that to enable any number of processing clusters or disks to read (write) different blocks of the pbuffer, simultaneously. More details on such a network can be found in [15], [22].

In summary, Section II develops and presents a large set of parallel algorithms for implementing the join operation on the multiprocessor structure presented above. Section III presents a probabilistic average-value framework for modeling the execution of the proposed algorithms. In addition, Section III presents the set of models developed within such a framework for the execution of one class of the proposed algorithms. The models for the other classes of the proposed algorithms are presented in [22]. In Section IV, the models developed within such a framework are used to study and determine the overall best-performing join algorithm(s). In addition, Section IV presents an investigation of the effectiveness of performing some architectural tuning on the presented multiprocessor. Section V reviews some of the join algorithms developed within the context of other DBM's and compares them to those developed in this paper. Finally, Section VI presents some concluding remarks.

II. Performing the Join Operation

The multiprocessor of Fig. 1 permits the implementation of a large set of algorithms for the join operation. These algorithms can be grouped into four categories, namely, "basic," "target relation partial filtering" (TPF), "source–target relations partial filtering" (STPF), and "source–target relations complete filtering" (STCF). In the following subsections, the algorithms within each of these categories are presented.

A. The Basic Join Algorithms

In general, the execution of a "basic" join algorithm by the multiprocessor of Fig. 1 can be decomposed into a number of phases. A typical phase is carried out by one (processing) cluster and involves the joining of some source and target tuples. The different phases of a basic algorithm are independent of each other and can be carried out serially by one cluster or in parallel by a number of clusters.

The basic algorithmic category consists of 12 different algorithms. Each of these algorithms can be viewed as a result of a series of decisions, and the decision space forms a four-level tree (Fig. 2). An individual basic algorithm corresponds to a path that links the root of the tree to one of its leaf nodes. At the root of the tree is the decision representing the choice of a method to be used by an algorithm to assign tuples from the source and target relations to the phases (clusters). This decision is called the "global tuple distribution" decision. Below the root are decisions representing the choice of a method by which an algorithm distributes a phase assignment from the source and target tuples among the processors of one cluster for joining and a method by which a target tuple is joined with a set of source tuples within one processor of a cluster. These decisions are called the "local tuple distribution" and "intratriplet join processing," respectively.

Two methods exist for assigning tuples from the source and target relations to phases. These two methods are as follow.

1) The Global Broadcast Method: In this method, a different MACU of the source relation and all of the MACU's of the target relation are assigned to every phase (therefore, the number of phases in one of the algorithms of the "global broadcast" basic algorithmic group is equal

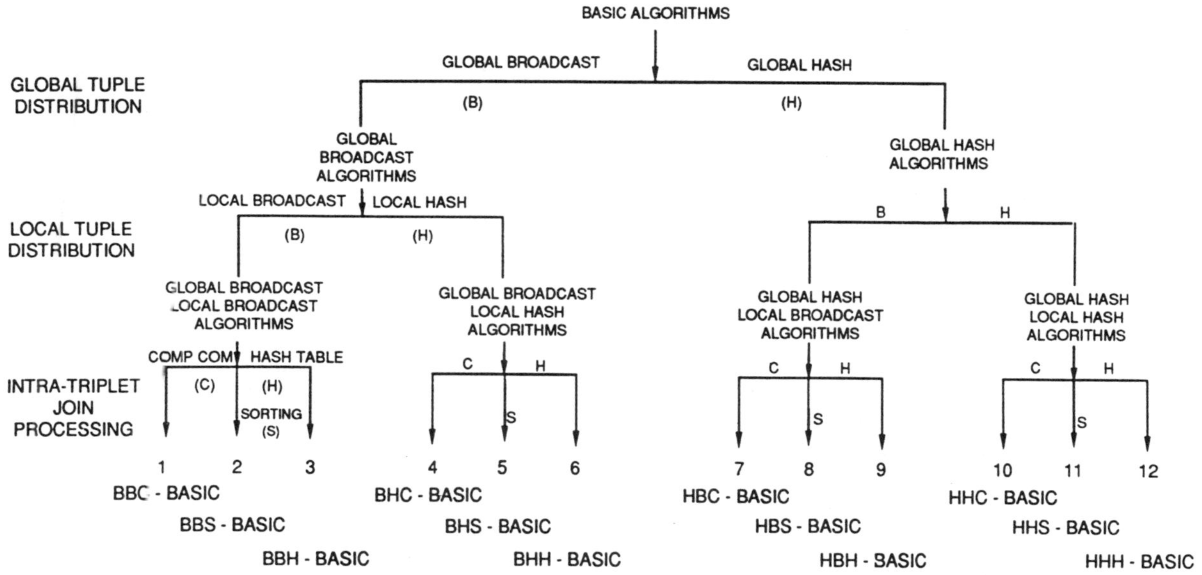

Fig. 2. The basic equijoin algorithms.

to the number of MACU's which store the source relation). This means that a cluster carrying out a typical phase needs to read from the pbuffer and process a source MACU and all of the target MACU's.

2) The Global Hash Method: In this method, a hashing function partitions the domain which underlies the join attributes of both the source and target relations into disjoint subsets (global buckets) such that the expected number of tuples from the source relation per subset fits in the local memory units of the processors within a cluster. The set of source and target tuples which hash to one global bucket constitutes the tuples which are assigned to one phase for joining (i.e., the number of phases in one of the algorithms of the "global hash" basic algorithmic group is equal to the number of global buckets). Selecting the tuples of phase i of a global hash algorithm requires a cluster to read from the pbuffer into its processors all of the source and target MACU's, one MACU at a time. As one MACU is read into the processors' lmemories, the processors themselves, in parallel, compute a hashing function over the join attribute value of every tuple of the MACU and collect those tuples that hash to phase i (global bucket i).

The tuples read (collected) by a particular cluster during the execution of one phase of a basic algorithm can be distributed among the cluster's processors for joining using one of two methods, namely, the following.

1) The Local Broadcast Method: With this method, the source tuples read (collected) by each processor during the initial execution of a phase are left in the processors. However, the target tuples of that phase, temporarily buffered in the processors (and the pbuffer and the mass memory in the case of the global broadcast algorithms), are broadcast, one tuple at a time, over the tuple bus of the cluster. Then, the processors, in parallel, join the broadcast tuples with their share of the source tuples.

2) The Local Hash Method: With this method, the source and target tuples of a phase are hashed based on their join attribute values to the processors of the cluster that executes the phase. The hashing function, statistically independent of the global one, in the case of global hash algorithms, is computed by the processors for every tuple of that phase. Using the tuple bus, the hashed tuples are moved to their destination processors for joining.

Three methods are available to a processor for joining a target tuple with the processor's assignment from the source tuples of one phase. These methods are as follow.

1) The Complete Comparison Method: With this method, the join attribute value of the target tuple is compared to that of every source tuple in the processor. The target tuple is concatenated with a copy of every source tuple having the same join attribute value.

2) The Sorting Method: With this method, the source tuples assigned to a processor are first sorted based on their join attribute value. The joining is performed by using the binary search method [21] to locate those source tuples whose join attribute values are the same as that of the target one. The concatenation of copies from the matching source tuples (if any) and the target tuple follows. In a processor, the sorting of the source tuples is implemented by actually sorting a table of pointers through which the source tuples are referenced.

3) The Hash Table Method: With this method, the source tuples assigned to a processor are first hashed, based on their join attribute values, to a hash table using a suitable hashing function. The join is then performed by hashing the target tuple, based on its join attribute value, using the same hashing function, to the hash table. A scan of the join attribute values of all the source tuples within a bucket of the hash table is needed to locate those source tuples whose join attribute values are the same as that of the target tuple.

The different basic algorithms are named by using the proceeding scheme. An algorithm name can be thought of as the ordered quadruple < nam_1, nam_2, nam_3, basic > where nam_1, nam_2, and nam_3 are the results of the three decisions taken by the named algorithm and the word "basic" indicates that the algorithm belongs to the basic algorithmic category. For example, algorithm 1 of Fig. 2 is called the "global *b*roadcast–local *b*roadcast–*c*omplete comparison–*basic*" algorithm. For simplicity, this name is abbreviated "BBC-BASIC." Fig. 2 contains the abbreviated names of all the join algorithms within the basic category.

From the point of view of a cluster, the execution of one phase of a basic algorithm involves six subphases. During the first subphase, a set of source tuples (the tuples of a source MACU for the global broadcast algorithms or the tuples of the source relation which hash to a global bucket for the global hash algorithms) are read/collected by the processors of the cluster. During the second subphase, the selected tuples of the first subphase are (left in processors)/(hashed to the cluster's processors). During the third subphase, all processors within the cluster (do nothing with)/sort/(store in a hash table) their shares of the source tuples.

The processors within a cluster execute the first, second, and third subphases in a pipeline fashion with the source tuple as the unit of the pipeline. This means that as soon as the tuple is read/collected by a processor in the first subphase, the execution of the second subphase is triggered, which in turn triggers the execution of the third one. When all the tuples of the source relation read/collected in the first subphase are processed through the second and third ones, then the execution of the fourth subphase is triggered.

During the fourth subphase, a set of target tuples (all of the tuples within the target relation for the global broadcast algorithms or the target tuples which hash to a global bucket for the global hash algorithms) is read/collected by the cluster's processors. During the fifth subphase, the target tuples of the fourth subphase are broadcast/hashed to the cluster's processors. During the sixth subphase, every processor within the cluster joins its share from the source and target tuples. Just as in the first three subphases, the cluster's processors execute the fourth, fifth, and sixth subphases in a pipeline fashion, with the target tuple as the unit of the pipeline.

B. *The Other Join Algorithmic Categories*

The algorithms within the TPF, STPF, and STCF categories can be obtained from the basic algorithms by slightly modifying their execution. The modification involves the use of one or more "Boolean arrays" [6] to speed up the execution of the basic algorithms. Because each algorithm in the TPF, STPF, or STCF category is a "speeded up" version of a basic algorithm, the naming convention adopted for the basic algorithms can also be used, after a minor modification, for the naming of the various algorithms in the TPF, STPF, and STCF categories. The word "basic" in the name of a basic algorithm must be replaced by the word "TPF," "STPF," or "STCF," respectively, to arrive at the name of the corresponding algorithm in the TPF, STPF, or STCF category. Adopting this naming convention, the TPF algorithm which corresponds to basic algorithm 1 of Fig. 2, for example, is the "global *b*roadcast-local *b*roadcast-*c*omplete comparison–*TPF*". For simplicity, this name is abbreviated "BBC-TPF." In the following, the TPF, STPF, and STCF algorithmic categories are presented.

1) The TPF Join Algorithms: The algorithmic category TPF is composed of 12 different algorithms. Each algorithm is an extension of a basic one and has the same number of phases. Processing the source and target tuples of one phase of a TPF algorithm is similar to processing the corresponding basic algorithm except that it includes the use of one Boolean array BA-*S*. The Boolean array of a suitable number of bits is initialized (at the beginning of each phase), maintained, and updated by the cluster master processor. The Boolean array and a hashing function are used to encode the join attribute values of the set of source tuples which belong to one phase (say, phase i) of a TPF algorithm. The join attribute value of a source tuple read/collected by a cluster's processor during the execution of the first subphase of phase i is hashed, based on the tuple's join attribute value, to the Boolean array. The hashing function is computed by the processor itself during the execution of the second subphase. The processor then passes the result of the hashing function to the cluster master processor, which in turn sets the corresponding bit in the Boolean arary to "1."

After setting the Boolean array of the cluster according to the source tuples of phase i, a typical target tuple of the same phase is processed during the fifth subphase by checking its join attribute value against the encoded set of the tuples' join attribute values. This is done by transforming, using the hashing function of the second subphase, the join attribute value of the target tuple into an index to the Boolean array The processor which performs the transformation forwards the resulting index to its cluster master processor, which in turn checks the corresponding bit in the Boolean array. If the bit is set to 1, then the target tuple is processed through the rest of the fifth and sixth subphases; otherwise, the target tuple is ignored.

2) The STPF and STCF Join Algorithms: The algorithmic category STPF is composed of six different algorithms. Each algorithm within this category is an extension of one of the global hash basic algorithms. Processing the source and target tuples of one phase of a STPF algorithm is similar to processing the tuples within the corresponding phase of a global hash basic algorithm, except that it includes the use of an additional hashing function and the two Boolean arrays BA-*S* and BA-*T*. These arrays, respectively, are used to encode the sets of join attribute values of both the source and target tuples which belong to one phase of a STPF algorithm. The Boolean arrays are initialized to zero (at the beginning of each phase), maintained, and updated by the cluster master processor. The hashing function computations are performed by the processors of the cluster which execute the current phase of the STPF algorithm. After setting the BA-T (BA-S) according to the target (source) tuples of the phase, this Boolean array is used to filter out some of the source (target) tuples of the current phase which will not contribute to the resulting relation.

The algorithmic category STCF is composed of 12 different algorithms. An STCF algorithm is composed of two major steps, namely, the global filtering step and the join step. The global filtering step, common to all of the STCF algorithms, is carried out by one cluster. During this phase, two Boolean arrays BA-S and BA-T of suitable sizes are created, initialized, and maintained by the cluster master processor. The BA-S, the BA-T, and a hashing function are used to encode the join attribute values of all the tuples which belong to the source and target relations, respectively. The BA-S and the BA-T are then used to filter out some of the tuples from the target and source relations, respectively. The source and target tuples which survive the filtering phase are then processed through the join phase. During this phase, one or more clusters are used to execute the physical joining of the surviving tuples, which is carried out by using one of the basic join algorithms.

III. Models for the Join Algorithms

One of the most important objectives of this research is to study the performance of the proposed parallel algorithms in carrying out the join operation. In such a study, one of the performance measures to be used is the algorithm's total execution time (TTIME). The TTIME of a join algorithm is the total time required by the multiprocessor to execute the algorithm, assuming that there is no overlapping between the activities of its different hardware units. There are two exceptions to the previous assumption. The activities of the different processors within a cluster overlap each other, and the activity of moving (broadcasting) tuples over the tuple bus of a processing cluster completely overlaps the activities performed by the cluster master processor [updating and checking the Boolean array(s)]. To compute TTIME for the different join algorithms, we present a probabilistic average-value modeling framework. Such a framework combines several techniques that are used to study analytically some of the performance issues encountered in the design of databases and DBM's [17], [23]. The execution of every join algorithm is modeled within such a framework. These models are referred to as the join execution models and are used in the next section to study the performance of the join algorithms. In addition, the execution models are used to evaluate the cost-effectiveness (from the join point of view) of performing some architectural tuning to the multiprocessor structure under investigation.

In general, the set of parameters which characterize the join execution models can be grouped into two categories: the input and output. The latter category includes only the performance measure TTIME. The input category includes three groups of parameters, namely, the data, hardware algorithms, and hardware. The parameters within these groups, together with their meanings and the values that some of these parameters assume in this performance study, are presented in Tables I–III, respectively. The assignment of values to the different parameters is discussed in the next section.

TABLE I
The Data Parameters

Name	Meaning	Value(s)
NTy	Cardinality of the relation y, where $y \in \{S, T\}$	10^3–10^5 tuples
LTy	Tuple length of relation y, where $y \in \{S, T\}$	100 bytes
LJ	Join attribute length	10 bytes
ND	Cardinality of the domain underlying the join attribute	

TABLE II
The Hardware Algorithm Parameters

Name	Meaning	Value(s)
NBP	Number of buckets in a hash table of a processor	
NBIT	Number of bits in a Boolean array	

TABLE III
The Hardware Parameters

Name	Meaning	Value(s)
NP	Number of processors within one cluster (or the number of tracks within one cylinder of the moving-head disk)	15
MACUC	Capacity of an MACU	$0.71 \times 10^{+6}$ bytes
TC	Time to compare the join attribute value of a source tuple to that of a target one	0.02 ms
TH	Time to calculate a hashing function with the tuple's join attribute value as the input argument	0.102 ms
TEP	Time to swap two pointers within a processor's memory	0.007 ms
Ty	Time to move a tuple of relation y across the tuple bus of a cluster, where $y \in \{S, T\}$	0.1 ms
TDAC	Average access time of the system disk	16 ms
TSK	Time to move the disk head one track	3 ms
TDT	Time to transfer an MACU between the system disk and the parallel buffer block	16.7 ms
TBT	Time to transfer an MACU between the parallel buffer block and the processors of a cluster	16.7 ms

In developing the join execution models, the following basic assumptions are made.

1) The multiprocessor hardware consists of only one processing cluster, one parallel buffer block, and one disk.

2) The MACU is a cylinder of the moving-head disk. The disk is modified for the parallel read out (write in) from (to) all of the tracks within one cylinder, simultaneously.

3) A tuple of the source or target relation is equally likely to carry in its join attribute any value from the attribute's underlying domain.

4) All of the hashing functions used by a join algorithm are ideal and statistically independent of one another. A hashing function is ideal if it is equally likely to map a value from its domain to any value of its range.

In the following, the relationships representing the different join execution models of the algorithms within the "target partial filtering" category are derived. For the derivation of the models of the other algorithmic categories, the interested reader is referred to [22]. Throughout the derivation process, the notation presented in Appendix A as well as in Tables I–III is used.

The TTIME spent in executing one of the TPF join algorithms can be expressed as follows:

$$\text{TTIME} = \text{TTO} + \sum_{x=1}^{K} [\text{TTI}(x) + \text{TTP}(x) + \text{TTB}(x)].$$

Because TTI(x), TTP(x), and TTB(x) for all $x \in \{1, 2, \cdots, K\}$ are, on the average, equal to TTI(1), TTP(1), and TTB(1), respectively, therefore,

$$\text{TTIME} = \text{TTO} + K \cdot [\text{TTI}(1) + \text{TTP}(1) + \text{TTB}(1)].$$

The total output time TTO for each of the TPF algorithms can be computed by using the following formula:

$$\text{TTO} = \text{NMO} \cdot (\text{TBT} + 2 \cdot \text{TDAC} + \text{TDT})$$

The above formula states that for every MACU of the resulting (output) relation, it takes TBT to move the MACU to the parallel buffer block, TDAC to locate randomly an empty cylinder on the disk, and TDT to move the MACU to the empty cylinder of the disk. In addition, it takes another TDAC to move the disk arm back to resume moving the target relation to the cluster. The formula that relates NMO to the models' input parameters is derived and presented in Appendix B1).

For a global broadcast TPF algorithm, K has the value of NMS, the number of MACU's (cylinders) that store the tuples of the source relation. On the other hand, for a global hash TPF algorithm, K has the value of NGB, the number of global buckets associated with the algorithm. NGB is chosen such that the set of source tuples which hash to one global bucket fits in the local memories of the processors within the cluster. The number of source tuples per global bucket due to an ideal hash function that uniformly distributes a set of tuples with cardinality NTS over a set of NGB buckets is a normally distributed random variable with an expected value of (NTS/NGB). Therefore,

$$\frac{\text{NTS}}{\text{NGB}} \cdot \text{LTS} = \text{MACUC}$$

and

$$K = \text{NGB} = \left\lceil \frac{\text{NTS} \cdot \text{LTS}}{\text{MACUC}} \right\rceil.$$

Two expressions exist for TTI(1), one for a global broadcast TPF algorithm and the other for a global hash TPF algorithm. In deriving these two expressions, it is assumed that the tuples of the source relation are stored on adjacent cylinders of the disk. The same assumption also applies to the tuples of the target relation.

During one phase of a global broadcast (GB) TPF algorithm, one source MACU and all the MACU's of the target relation are read by the processing cluster. Therefore,

$$\begin{aligned}\text{TTI}(1)|_{\text{GB}} &= (\text{TDAC} + \text{TDT} + \text{TBT}) \\ &\quad + (\text{TDAC} + \text{TDT} + \text{TBT}) \\ &\quad + (\text{NMT} - 1)(\text{TSK} + \text{TDT} + \text{TBT}).\end{aligned}$$

The above formula states that moving the first target (source) MACU from the disk to the processors needs, on the average, TDAC to locate the cylinder on the disk that stores the MACU, TDT to transfer the cylinder content to the parallel buffer block, and TBT to transfer the MACU to the processors. In addition, for every remaining target MACU, it takes TSK to move the disk heads to the next cylinder, TDT to transfer the cylinder content to the parallel buffer block, and TBT to transfer the content of the parallel buffer block to the processors.

The number of cylinders that store the tuples of the target relations, NMT, can be computed from the following formula:

$$\text{NMT} = \left\lceil \frac{\text{NTT} \cdot \text{LTT}}{\text{MACUC}} \right\rceil.$$

During the execution of one phase of a global hash (GH) TPF algorithm, all of the MACU's which store the tuples of the source and target relations are read by the processing cluster. This is needed to collect the source and target tuples which hash to one global bucket. Therefore,

$$\begin{aligned}\text{TTI}(1)|_{\text{GH}} &= (\text{TDAC} + \text{TDT} + \text{TBT}) \\ &\quad + (\text{NMS} - 1)(\text{TSK} + \text{TDT} + \text{TBT}) \\ &\quad + (\text{TDAC} + \text{TDT} + \text{TBT}) \\ &\quad + (\text{NMT} - 1)(\text{TSK} + \text{TDT} + \text{TBT}).\end{aligned}$$

The derivation of formulas for the quantities TTB(1) and TTP(1) of the TPF algorithms are presented next.

A. Derivation of Formulas for TTB (1)

During the execution of one phase of a global broadcast TPF algorithm, the tuples of a source MACU are joined with the tuples of the target relation. In doing so, a "global broadcast–local broadcast" (GBLB) TPF algorithm broadcasts to the processors only those target tuples which survive the Boolean array checking. Therefore,

$$\text{TTB}(1)|_{\text{GBLB-TPF}} = \text{LTB} \cdot \text{NTT} \cdot \text{TT}$$

where LTB is the fraction of the target relation tuples that survives the checking of the Boolean array BA-S during the execution of one phase of a global broadcast TPF algorithm. A formula that relates LTB to the models' input parameters is derived and presented in Appendix B2).

To join one source MACU with all of the MACU's of the target relation, a "global broadcast-local hash" (GBLH) TPF algorithm will first redistribute among the processors within the cluster the tuples of a source MACU and those tuples of the target relation which survive the Boolean array checking. The tuple redistribution is performed using a hashing function, and, on the average, only $(1 - 1/\mathrm{NP})$ of both the tuples of the source MACU and the surviving tuples of the target relation need to be moved to the other processors in the cluster. Therefore,

$$\mathrm{TTB}(1)\big|_{\mathrm{GBLH\text{-}TPF}} = \left[\frac{\mathrm{NTS}\cdot\mathrm{TS}}{\mathrm{NMS}} + \mathrm{LTB}\cdot\mathrm{NTT}\cdot\mathrm{TT}\right]\left(1-\frac{1}{\mathrm{NP}}\right)$$

where [NTS/NMS] of the above equation is the average number of tuples in a source MACU.

During the execution of one phase of a global hash TPF algorithm, the tuples of one global bucket are joined. In joining them, a "global hash-local broadcast" (GHLB) TPF algorithm broadcasts to the processors of the cluster those target tuples which hash to the global bucket (phase) and survive the Boolean array checking. Therefore,

$$\mathrm{TTB}(1)\big|_{\mathrm{GHLB\text{-}TPF}} = \mathrm{LTG}\cdot\mathrm{NTT}\cdot\mathrm{TT}$$

where LTG is the fraction of the target relation tuples which hash to a global bucket and survive the checking of the Boolean array BA-S during the execution of one phase of a global hash TPF algorithm. A formula that relates LTG to the models' input parameters is derived and presented in Appendix B3).

To join the tuples of a global bucket, a "global hash-local hash" (GHLH) TPF algorithm redistributes, using a hashing function, the source tuples of the global bucket and those target tuples of the same bucket that survive the checking of the Boolean array BA-S among the cluster's processors. Therefore,

$$\mathrm{TTB}(1)\big|_{\mathrm{GHLH\text{-}TPF}} = \left[\frac{\mathrm{NTS}}{\mathrm{NGB}}\mathrm{TS} + \mathrm{LTG}\cdot\mathrm{NTT}\cdot\mathrm{TT}\right]\cdot\left(1-\frac{1}{\mathrm{NP}}\right)$$

B. Derivation of Formulas for TTP (1)

In general, the TTP(1) for a TPF join algorithm can be expressed as follows:

$$\mathrm{TTP}(1) = \mathrm{TTPH}(1) + \mathrm{TTPS}(1) + \mathrm{TTPC}(1).$$

The formulas which relate the quantities on the right-hand side of the above formula to the model's input parameters are derived next for each of the TPF algorithms.

1) Derivation of Formulas for TTPH (1): When executing one phase of a BBC-TPF, BBS-TPF, or BBH-TPF algorithm, the Boolean array hash function is used. This function is computed by every processor for its share from both the tuples of a source MACU and all of the tuples of the target relation. In addition, The BBH-TPF algorithm uses the hash table function. This function is computed in each phase by every processor for its share from the tuples of a source MACU and those tuples of the target relation which survive the Boolean array BA-S checking. Therefore,

$$\mathrm{TTPH}(1)\big|_{\substack{\mathrm{BBC\text{-}TPF}\\ \mathrm{or\,BBS\text{-}TPF}}} = \left[\frac{\mathrm{NTS}}{\mathrm{NMS}\cdot\mathrm{NP}} + \frac{\mathrm{NTT}}{\mathrm{NP}}\right]\cdot\mathrm{TH}$$

and

$$\mathrm{TTPH}(1)\big|_{\mathrm{BBH\text{-}TPF}} = \mathrm{TTPH}(1)\big|_{\mathrm{BBC\text{-}TPF}} + \left[\frac{\mathrm{NTS}}{\mathrm{NMS}\cdot\mathrm{NP}} + \mathrm{LTB}\cdot\mathrm{NTT}\right]\cdot\mathrm{TH}.$$

In addition to the Boolean array hash function, a processor executing one phase of the BHC-TPF, BHS-TPF, or BHH-TPF computes the local hash function for its share from both the tuples of a source MACU and those tuples of the target relation which survive the Boolean array checking. Furthermore, the processor executing one phase of the BHH-TPF uses another hash function, the hash table function. The latter is computed by every processor for its share from the tuples of a source MACU and those target tuples that survive the Boolean array checking and hash to the processor itself. Therefore,

$$\mathrm{TTPH}(1)\big|_{\substack{\mathrm{BHC\text{-}TPF}\\ \mathrm{BHS\text{-}TPF}}} = \left[\frac{\mathrm{NTS}}{\mathrm{NMS}\cdot\mathrm{NP}} + \frac{\mathrm{NTT}}{\mathrm{NP}}\right]\cdot\mathrm{TH} + \left[\frac{\mathrm{NTS}}{\mathrm{NMS}\cdot\mathrm{NP}} + \frac{\mathrm{LTB}\cdot\mathrm{NTT}}{\mathrm{NP}}\right]\cdot\mathrm{TH}$$

and

$$\mathrm{TTPH}(1)\big|_{\mathrm{BHH\text{-}TPF}} = \mathrm{TTPH}(1)\big|_{\mathrm{BHC\text{-}TPF}} + \left[\frac{\mathrm{NTS}}{\mathrm{NMS}\cdot\mathrm{NP}} + \frac{\mathrm{LTB}\cdot\mathrm{NTT}}{\mathrm{NP}}\right]\cdot\mathrm{TH}.$$

When executing a global hash algorithm, a hash function, the global hash function, is used to partition tuples between phases. This function is computed in each phase by every processor for its share from all of the tuples of the source and target relations. In addition, a processor executing one phase of the HBC-TPF, HBS-TPF, or HBH-TPF computes the Boolean array hashing function for its share from those source and target tuples which hash to one global bucket. Furthermore, a processor executing one phase of the HBH-TPF computes the hash table hashing function for its share from the source tuples which hash to one global bucket and for all of the target tuples which hash to one global bucket and survive the Boolean array filtering. That is,

$$\mathrm{TTPH}(1)\big|_{\substack{\mathrm{HBC\text{-}TPF} \\ \mathrm{or\ HBS\text{-}TPF}}} = \mathrm{CH} \cdot \left[\frac{\mathrm{NTS}}{\mathrm{NP}} + \frac{\mathrm{NTT}}{\mathrm{NP}}\right] \cdot \mathrm{TH} + \left[\frac{\mathrm{NTS}}{\mathrm{NGB} \cdot \mathrm{NP}} + \frac{\mathrm{NTT}}{\mathrm{NGB} \cdot \mathrm{NP}}\right] \cdot \mathrm{TH}$$

and

$$\mathrm{TTPH}(1)\big|_{\mathrm{HBH\text{-}TPF}} = \mathrm{TTPH}(1)\big|_{\mathrm{HBC\text{-}TPF}} + \left[\frac{\mathrm{NTS}}{\mathrm{NGB} \cdot \mathrm{NP}} + \mathrm{LTG} \cdot \mathrm{NTT}\right] \cdot \mathrm{TH}$$

where CH is zero if NGB = 1; otherwise, CH = 1.

In addition to the global hash function, a processor executing the HHC-TPF, HHS-TPF, or HHH-TPF algorithm uses another hash function, the local hash function. The latter function is computed in each phase by every processor for its share from those source and target tuples that hash to one global bucket. In addition, the processor uses the Boolean array hash function. The latter function is computed, in each phase, by every processor for its share from those source and target tuples that hash to one global bucket. Furthermore, the HHH-TPF algorithm uses another hash function, the hash table function. The latter function is computed in each phase by every processor for the source tuples which hash to one global bucket and one processor and for those target tuples which hash to one global bucket, survive the Boolean array BA-*S*, and hash to one processor. Therefore,

$$\mathrm{TTPH}(1)\big|_{\substack{\mathrm{HHC\text{-}TPF} \\ \mathrm{or\ HHS\text{-}TPF}}} = \mathrm{CH} \cdot \left[\frac{\mathrm{NTS}}{\mathrm{NP}} + \frac{\mathrm{NTT}}{\mathrm{NP}}\right] \cdot \mathrm{TH} + 2 \cdot \left[\frac{\mathrm{NTS}}{\mathrm{NGB} \cdot \mathrm{NP}} + \frac{\mathrm{NTT}}{\mathrm{NGB} \cdot \mathrm{NP}}\right] \cdot \mathrm{TH}$$

and

$$\mathrm{TTPH}(1)\big|_{\mathrm{HHH\text{-}TPF}} = \mathrm{TTPH}(1)\big|_{\mathrm{HHC\text{-}TPF}} + \left[\frac{\mathrm{NTS}}{\mathrm{NGB} \cdot \mathrm{NP}} + \frac{\mathrm{LTG} \cdot \mathrm{NTT}}{\mathrm{NP}}\right] \cdot \mathrm{TH}.$$

2) Derivation of Formulas for TTPS(1): The quantity TTPS(1) has a nonzero value for only those algorithms that use the sorting technique to perform the joining of tuples within a processor. In general, a processor sorts a table of pointers on a set of M tuples in, on the average, $(M \log_2 M)$ comparisons and pointer swaps [21]. Thus, a general formula for TTPS(1) is

$$\mathrm{TTPS}(1) = (\mathrm{TC} + \mathrm{TEP}) M \log_2 M$$

where M in this formula is the average number of source tuples to be sorted by a processor during the execution of one phase of a TPF algorithm.

When executing one phase of a BBS-TPF algorithm, the processor sorts its source MACU, and M in this case is $[\mathrm{NTS}/(\mathrm{NMS} \cdot \mathrm{NP})]$. On the other hand, when executing one phase of BHS-TPF algorithm, a processor sorts the source tuples which locally hash to a processor. In this case, M is equal to the expected number of source tuples which hash to one processor during one phase, and this is also equal to $[\mathrm{NTS}/(\mathrm{NMS} \cdot \mathrm{NP})]$.

When executing one phase of the HBS-TPF or HHS-TPF algorithm, the processor sorts its share from the source tuples which hash to one global bucket, and M in this case is $[\mathrm{NTS}/(\mathrm{NGB} \cdot \mathrm{NP})]$.

3) Derivation of Formulas for TTPC(1): In general, the quantity TTPC(1) of a TPF join algorithm can be computed using the following equation:

$$\mathrm{TTPC}(1) = \mathrm{ENC}(1) \cdot \mathrm{TC}$$

where ENC(1) is the expected number of join attribute value comparisons performed by a processor during the execution of one phase of one of the above algorithms and TC is the time to compare the join attribute value of a source tuple to that of a target one.

Let M and N be the average (expected) number of source and target tuples, respectively, assigned to one processor during the execution of one phase of a TPF algorithm. For the subset of the latter algorithms that use the complete comparison method to perform the join within a processor, ENC(1) can be expressed as follows:

$$\mathrm{ENC}(1) = N \cdot M.$$

A processor using the sorting method for joining a target tuple with M source tuples uses the binary search method [21] to locate the pointer to the linked list that stores those tuples whose join attribute values match those of the target tuples. In the worst case, the number of comparisons which the processor must perform is $\log_2 M$. Therefore, for those TPF algorithms which use the sorting method, ENC(1) can be expressed as

$$\mathrm{ENC}(1) = N \log_2 M.$$

It is easy to show that, for the global broadcast TPF algorithms which use the "complete comparison" or the "sorting" method, M has the value of $[\mathrm{NTS}/(\mathrm{NMS} \cdot \mathrm{NP})]$. On the other hand, for the global hash TPF algorithms which use the complete comparison or the sorting method, M has the value of $[\mathrm{NTS}/(\mathrm{NGB} \cdot \mathrm{NP})]$.

It is also easy to show [22] that, for the algorithms BBC-TPF (BBS-TPF), BHC-TPF (BHS-TPF), HBC-TPF (HBS-TPF), or HHC-TPF (HHS-TPF), N has the value of $(\mathrm{LTB} \cdot \mathrm{NTT})$, $(\mathrm{LTB} \cdot \mathrm{NTT}/\mathrm{NP})$, $(\mathrm{LTG} \cdot \mathrm{NTT})$, or $(\mathrm{LTG} \cdot \mathrm{NTT}/\mathrm{NP})$, respectively.

The derivations of formulas for ENC(1) of those TPF algorithms that use the hash table method for a join within a processor are very lengthy and take a large amount of space. Therefore, these derivations are not presented in this paper, however, the interested reader can refer to [22].

IV. Performance Studies

A. The Determination of the Best-Performing Join Algorithm(s)

In this section, the best-performing parallel join algorithm(s) is determined. Throughout this process, the hardware input parameters of all of the models are kept constant at some assigned values; however, the rest of the input parameters are varied to study their effect on the algorithms under investigation. The measures TTIME and the number of hashing functions are used to evaluate the performance of the different join algorithms. In general, the best-performing algorithm among a set containing others over a range of a parameter value is the one with the smallest values to TTIME over that range. However, if several join algorithms have close TTIME values over that range, then the best-performing algorithm is the one with the minimum number of hash functions. The last criterion is adopted to compensate for the fact that in this study the average behavior of the hash functions is considered and not their worst case behavior and, moreover, to compensate for the fact that the overhead involved in handling the overflow phenomena associated with the hashing functions is not considered either.

The values assigned to the hardware parameters (refer to Table III) have been chosen to reflect the current state of the art in hardware technology. The values of those hardware parameters that characterize the moving-head disk (NP, MACUC, TDAC, TSK, and TDT) are those of an IBM 3380 moving-head disk [24]. The disk is assumed to be modified for parallel reading (writing) from (to) a whole cylinder. It is also assumed that this modification does not affect the disk transfer rate. The time to read (write) one track of the disk is assumed to be the value of reading (writing) the whole cylinder (TDT). It is also assumed that TBT has the same value as that of TDT.

In calculating the values of the hardware parameters that characterize a processor (TC, TH, TMS, TMT, TMO, and TEP), it is assumed that the processor is an off-the-shelf microprocessor. The details of such calculations are presented in [22]. The values of the parameters that characterize the tuple bus of a cluster (TS and TT) are calculated assuming that the bus has an effective bandwidth of 1 Mbyte.

To reduce the number of variable[1] input parameters, we assume that both NTS and NTT have the same values. ND changes indirectly by changing the ratio (NTS/ND). In [22], it is shown that throughout the ranges of NTS and [NTS/ND] one can assign values to the parameters NBP and NBIT using formulas that relate such parameters to some of the models' basic parameters and the parameters FNBP and FNBIT. FNBP is the ratio of the number of buckets in a processor's hash table and the processor's expected number of source tuples per one phase of a TPF join algorithm, and FNBIT is the ratio of the number of bits in the Boolean array(s) and the number of tuples in both the source and target relations, respectively. Both FNBP and FNBIT are related to the amount of storage allocated to a hash table and to the Boolean array(s), respectively.

The process of determining the best-performing join algorithm comprises two steps. In the first step, the performance of the algorithms within each category are analyzed and studied under the variable input parameters, using the corresponding execution models. As a result of this step, the best-performing algorithm within each category is selected. In the second step, the best-performing algorithms within the various algorithmic categories are compared to one another, and the overall best-performing one is determined.

The set of computer programs developed to implement the join models are run for NTS (=NTT) $\in \{10^3–10^5\}$, NTS/ND $\in \{1, 0.1, 0.01\}$, and for many values for the parameters FNBP and FNBIT. The behavior of the TTIME for the algorithms within each join algorithmic category is plotted against the parameter NTS (=NTT) for different values of the parameters NTS/ND, FNBP, and FNBIT, in [22]. Based on these figures, some interesting conclusions have been reached. First, beyond the value of 1, increasing the value of FNPB produces almost no improvement in the TTIME of those join algorithms that use the hash table technique at the processor level. Second, at small values of NTS/ND $\in$ (0.1–0.01), the TTIME for the algorithms in the TPF, STPF, and STCF categories decreases exponentially with increasing value of the parameter FNBIT. However, as FNBIT increases beyond the value of 10, the relative improvement in TTIME decreases rapidly to zero. When the value of NTS/ND is relatively large (~ 1), the performance measure TTIME for the algorithms in the TPF, STPF, and STCF categories becomes independent of FNBIT. Third is the fact that "which join algorithm is the best-performing one within its individual category" is a function of the parameters NTS/ND, NTS, FNBT, and FNBIT.[2] It is important to note that the parameter NTS/ND is directly related to the join probability between the tuples of the source and target relations. The source (target) join probability is defined as the probability that a tuple from the source (target) relation joins with at least one tuple from the target (source) relation. In this study, the source and target join probabilities have the same values.

Figs. 3–5 display the performance measure TTIME of the best-performing algorithms within each algorithmic category versus the parameter NTS (=NTT). The three figures correspond to the values 1, 0.1, and 0.01 of the parameter [NTS/ND]. In all of these figures, the parameters FNBP and FNBIT are fixed at the values of 1 and

[1]That is, they are variable with respect to this performance study.

[2]The best-performing algorithm within the basic category is a function of only the first three parameters.

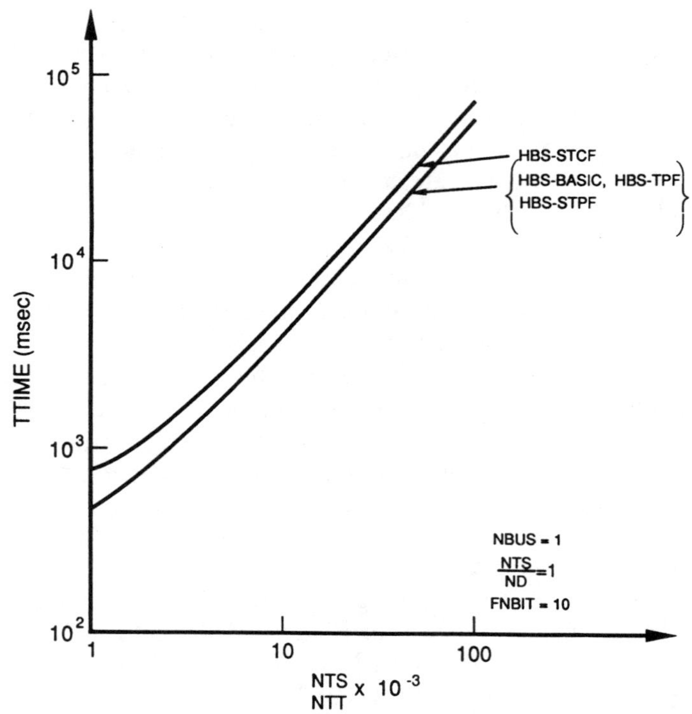

Fig. 3. The best-performing equijoin algorithms within each algorithmic category for NTS/ND = 1.

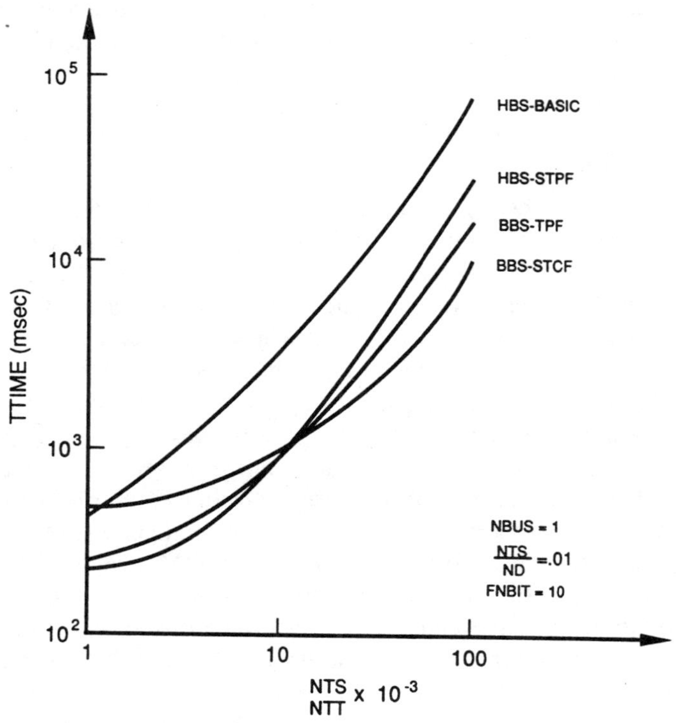

Fig. 5. The best-performing equijoin algorithms within each algorithmic category for NTS/ND = 0.01.

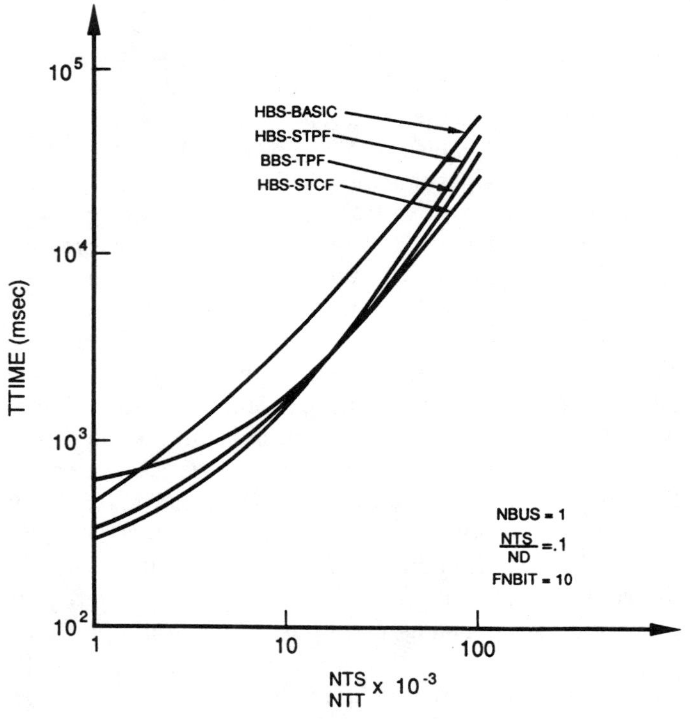

Fig. 4. The best-performing equijoin algorithms within each algorithmic category for NTS/ND = 0.1.

10, respectively. Referring to these figures, one can make the following observations.

1) For large values of the parameter NTS/ND (= ~1, i.e., the join is popular), the algorithm HBS-BASIC is the overall best-performing one (see Fig. 3). Any other algorithm either has an inferior performance (HBS-STCF) or has an equal performance but requires more overhead and storage (HBS-TPF and HBS-STPF).

2) For moderate values of the parameter NTS/ND (= ~0.1, i.e., the join is moderate), the overall best-performing algorithm the BBS-TPF algorithm (see Fig. 4). Any other algorithm either has an inferior performance (HBS-BASIC, HBS-STPF when joining relations with large cardinalities, and HBS-STCF when joining relations with small cardinalities) or has little performance advantage, which does not justify the extra overhead incurred by these algorithms (HBS-STCF when joining relations with small cardinalities and HBS-STCF when joining relations with large cardinalities).

3) For small values of the parameter NTS/ND (= ~0.01, i.e., the join is scarce), the overall best-performing algorithm is a function of the number of tuples participating in the operation (see Fig. 5). For relations with small cardinalities (NTS (=NTT) < 15 000 tuples), the overall best-performing algorithm is BBS-TPF. On the other hand, the overall best-performing algorithm for relations with large cardinalities (> 15 000 tuples) is BBS-STCF.

Based on the above observations, one can conclude that there is not just one overall best-performing join algorithm. Each of the algorithms HBS-BASIC, BBS-TPF, and BBS-STCF scores the best performance over a different range of the parameters NTS and NTS/ND (refer to Fig. 6). These parameters characterize the relations which participate in the join operation. By providing the DBM with a simple optimizer to estimate the values of NTS and NTS/ND, the optimal algorithm to perform a given join can be chosen from those presented in Fig. 6, and thus,

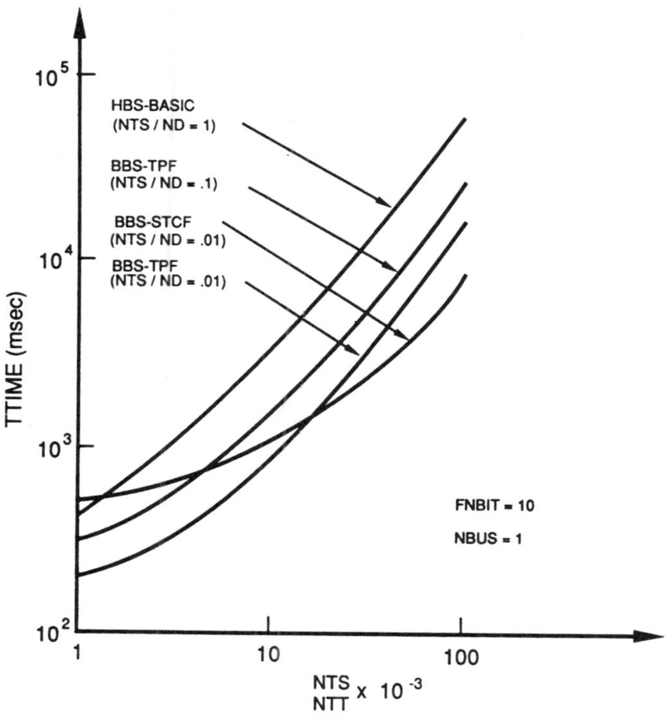

Fig. 6. The selected equijoin algorithms.

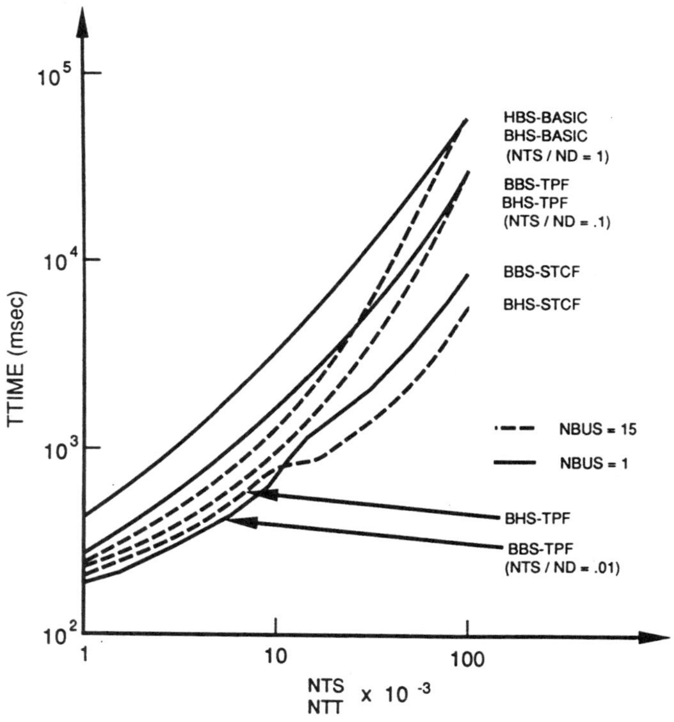

Fig. 7. The comparison between the best-performing algorithms on the two architectures.

the operation can be performed in the most cost-effective way.

Another important conclusion is that all of the best-performing algorithms use the sorting method to perform the tuple join within each individual processor. The fact that the sorting method is superior to the complete comparison one is obvious. However, its superiority over the hash table method is less obvious. As a group of algorithms[3] approaches best performance, the algorithm of such a group that uses the hash table method offers a slight speedup advantage over the algorithm of the same group which uses the sorting method. However, such improvement does not justify the larger overhead incurred in such algorithm due to the usage of another hash function and the maintenance of a hash table. The sorting-based algorithm, therefore, scores the best performance within each individual group.

A third important conclusion is the fact that both the global hash and the Boolean array techniques can be used individually to speed up the execution of the join operation. However, the combination of both techniques to speed up the join execution is not good since not much gain in speedup would result over that from the proper use of one of them.

B. The Effectiveness of Some Architectural Tuning of the Processing Clusters

In this section, the effectiveness of providing the processors within a processing cluster with a multipath intercommunication structure is investigated. In particular, the addition of more buses, each similar in architecture, bandwidth, and function to the tuple bus, is evaluated.

[3]Each three join algorithms that have the same global and local tuple distribution and filtering techniques form one such group.

The addition of one or more buses to the processing cluster does not affect the performance measure TTIME of those algorithms that use the local broadcast method. On the other hand, it affects the performance of those algorithms that use the local hash method. TTIME for the latter algorithms can be calculated by using a slightly modified version of the corresponding models already developed for the one-bus organization. The modification of these models involves the updating of the equations which compute TTB, the time needed to communicate tuples between the processors during the execution of a join algorithm, to account for the new multiple-bus organization of the cluster. This means that the TTB of a local hash algorithm must be divided by NBUS, the number of the tuple buses in the new organization.

In Fig. 7, the performance parameter TTIME of the best-performing join algorithms is plotted for the case when NBUS = 1. The same figure displays the TTIME of the local hash best-performing algorithms for the case when NBUS = NP (the maximum possible number of tuple-bus-like buses). The values of the other model parameters have been kept the same as in Section IV-A. By referring to Fig. 7, the following observations can be made.

1) For large values of the parameter NTS/ND $(= \sim 1)$, or in the absence of a Boolean array, the adoption of the multiple-bus organization together with the BHS-BASIC algorithm improves substantially the performance of the join over that executed on a single-bus organization. However, this improvement becomes insignificant when joining relations with large cardinalities.

2) For moderate to small values of the parameter NTS/ND (<0.1), the adoption of the multiple-bus organization and the best-performing local hash algorithm results in only a slight improvement in the join performance or none at all.

The above observations, coupled with the fact that most join operations tend to have small values for the parameter NTS/ND (a small number of tuples respond to the join operation) suggests that the single-bus organization coupled with a Boolean array filter is more cost-effective in executing the join operation, especially in the very large database environment.

V. Comparison to Other Join Algorithms

Several parallel algorithms have been proposed to implement the join operation on the various multiprocessor DBM's [8], [12]–[14], [17]–[19]. Most of these algorithms are parallel versions of known sequential join algorithms. Dewitt *et al.* [8] proposed the use of a parallel version of the nested-loops algorithm to perform the join operation on the DBM DIRECT. The algorithm assumes that both of the relations S and T are stored in page units on the system disk. The parallel nested-loops algorithm begins by having each of the processors read a different page from relation S. Next, all the pages of relation T are broadcast, one by one, to all of the processors. Upon receiving a page of T, each processor joins its page of S with the incoming page of T, using the nested-loops algorithm [8].[4] These steps are repeated until all of the S pages are joined. The parallel nested-loops algorithm has been extended in [18] to allow a number of pages from relation S to be read into a processor before the broadcast of pages of relation T would begin. This extension improves the speed of the parallel nested-loops algorithm by reducing the number of times the relation T has to be broadcast to the processors during the execution of such an algorithm.

Bitton *et al.* [17] proposed the use of the uniprocessor two-way sort–merge algorithm (described in [21, p. 247]) as a basis for a parallel join algorithm. The algorithm, the sort–merge–join algorithm, proceeds in two steps. First, the processors are used to sort relations S and T on the join attribute, using a parallel version of the uniprocessor two-way merge-sort algorithm. Second, one processor is used to merge the two sorted relations. During this step, the tuples of the two relations with equal join attribute values are joined. An extension to the sort–merge–join algorithm has been presented in [18]. This extension involves the use of the parallel version of the uniprocessor P-way merge-sort algorithm, where $P > 2$, to perform the sorting in the first step of the sort–merge–join algorithm.

Kistsurgawa *et al.* [14] proposed a parallel join algorithm for the GRACE multiprocessor machine. Such an algorithm joins the S and T relations by first distributing their tuples between a number of buckets based on the tuples' join attribute values using a hashing function. The joining of the tuples within the buckets is performed by processors that use a sort-based algorithm. The processors in GRACE are specially designed as hardware sorters with the capability of sorting N tuples in linear time. Dewitt [19] has extended such an algorithm to a distributed memory multiprocessor environment.

Goodman [13] proposed a parallel join algorithm for the HYPERTREE multiprocessor DBM. We refer to such an algorithm as GOOD1. GOOD1 assumes that the tuples of both relations S and T are initially distributed among all of the processors in a uniform fashion. The algorithm begins with each processor applying the same hashing function to the join attribute of its own tuples. The hashing function uses the join attribute value of a tuple to compute a processor number. The tuple is then sent to the processor having such a number. During the second phase of the algorithm, each processor joins the tuples it receives as a result of the execution of the first phase.

Babb [6] proposed a uniprocessor algorithm for the semijoin operation.[5] This algorithm begins by initializing a Boolean array in the uniprocessor memory. The Boolean array is a vector of bits of suitable length. The proposed algorithm proceeds in two phases. In the first phase, the processor reads all the tuples of relation S. As one tuple is read, the processor computes a hashing function on its join attribute value. The result of this computation is an index. The bit in the Boolean array that corresponds to this index is set to 1. During the second phase, the processor reads all the tuples of relation T. As one tuple is read in, the hashing function of the first phase is used to compute an index based on the tuple's join attribute value. The bit of the Boolean array that corresponds to this index is then checked. The tuple is part of the result relation if the bit has the value of 1. Goodman [13] adapted this algorithm to the HYPERTREE multiprocessor environment. We refer to the extended algorithm of Goodman as GOOD2.

Assuming that the number of pages storing the source relation is the same as that of the target relation and that the number is equal to N, it is easy to show that the parallel nested-loops algorithm has a time complexity $O(N^2)$. (Actually, it is N^2 divided by a constant p where p is the number of processors executing such an algorithm. The constant p is absorbed in O.) Bitton and Dewitt's algorithm, the parallel sort–merge–join, has the time complexity $O(N \log N)$, an improvement over the parallel nested-loops algorithm. Because of this improvement, the parallel sort–merge–join algorithm has replaced the parallel nested-loops in executing the join operation on DIRECT. The GRACE algorithm has the time complexity

[4]By using this algorithm, a processor joins the tuples of an S page with those of a T page by comparing the join attribute value of every tuple in the former S page to all the tuples in the T page. Throughout this process, the tuples with matching join attribute values are concatenated together.

[5]The semijoin of a source relation S and a target relation T on attributes A from S and B from T is a relation R. R is formed from each tuple $t \in T$ such that $s[A] = t[B]$ and $s \in S$.

$O(N)$. That is, it is linear with respect to the number of pages that store the source or the target relation.

Although the basic algorithm proposed by Goodman, GOOD1 [13], is a linear algorithm, it is nevertheless restricted to the join of small relations. GOOD1 assumes that the tuples of the source and target relations to be joined must fit in the local memory units of the processors which participate in the execution of the join operation. GOOD2 is also a linear algorithm, but it can be suited to join larger relations since it assumes that only the tuples of the source and target relations that survive the bit array filtering must fit in the local memories of the processors which execute the join operation [13].

At a certain level of abstraction, one can see that for both the GRACE and the GOOD2 algorithms there exists a corresponding algorithm among those presented in this paper. They are the HHS-BASIC and the BHS-STCF (or HHS-STCF) algorithms, respectively. In fact, our BHS-STCF (or HHS-STCF) algorithm is more general than GOOD2 since it can join relations of any size. From the figures presented in [22], one can see that the algorithms HHS-BASIC and HHS-STCF behave similarly to the algorithms HBS-BASIC and HBS-STCF, respectively. From this observation, one can conclude that adopting a GRACE-like or GOOD2-like algorithm alone does not guarantee that the join operation on a given machine will have the best performance. To remedy this shortcoming, we have proposed in this paper three different algorithms that are chosen from a much larger set of suitable ones. The first, HBS-BASIC, is linear and behaves similarly to the GRACE algorithm (actually it was developed independently of GRACE) for joins where the probability of joining is high. The BBS-STCF behaves as GOOD2 does, but is more general and good for joins where the probability of joining is low. A third algorithm, the BBS-TPF, is proposed for those joins that have moderate joining probability. The use of a simple optimizer to choose one of these algorithms for a given join operation is straightforward and guarantees that such an operation will in fact be carried out with high performance.

VI. Conclusion

The join is one of the most important operations of relational database systems. In this paper, we have developed and presented a large set of parallel algorithms to execute the join operation on a shared memory multiprocessor DBM. The development of these algorithms has followed a structured approach. First, the major steps involved in processing the join operation as well as the various ways of carrying out these steps have been identified. Second, different join algorithms have been constructed by concatenating the different ways of performing these major steps. Although the developed algorithms appear to be specialized for the multiprocessor structure presented in this paper, we believe nevertheless that these algorithms can easily be adapted to other multiprocessor DBM's such as DBC [8], RDBM [12], and HYPERTREE [13]. In addition, the "synthesis" approach followed is quite general and can be used to design algorithms for different architectures and operations.

In this paper, we have also presented a probabilistic average-value framework for modeling the performance of the proposed join algorithms. Using the models developed within such a framework, a study of the performance of the proposed join algorithms has been carried out. Such a study reveals that for fixed hardware parameters there is not just one best-performing join algorithm, but different algorithms score the best performance depending on the characteristics of the relations participating in the join operation. We believe that such results will hold for the other multiprocessor DBM's.

Finally, we have used the join models developed in this paper to access the effectiveness of tuning the multiprocessor structure which executes the join operation. Such an investigation has demonstrated the effectiveness of using the Boolean array filtering techniques to speed up such an execution without substantially increasing the hardware cost.

Appendix A
Notation

The following terms used in this paper have the following respective meanings.

K	Number of phases in the execution of a TPF join algorithm.
x	Phase index, where $x \in \{1, 2, \cdots, K\}$.
y	Relation index, where $y \in \{S$ (source relation), T (target relation)$\}$.
TTO	Total output time, time to move the MACU's of the output relation from the cluster's processors to the system disk during the execution of a join operation.
TTI	Total input time, time to move the tuples of the source and target relations from the system disk to the cluster's processors during the execution of a join operation.
TTI(x)	Input time of phase x.
TTP	Total processor time, time spent by a processor to execute a join algorithm.
TTP(x)	Time for a processor to execute phase x.
TTPH(x)	Time spent by a processor in hashing tuples during phase x.
TTPC(x)	Time spent by a processor in comparing the tuples' join attribute values during phase x.
TTPS(x)	Time spent by a processor in sorting source tuples during phase x.
TTB	Total bus transmission time, time to move tuples over the tuple bus of a cluster during the execution of a join operation.
TTB(x)	Bus transmission time of phase x.
NMy	Number of MACU's (cylinders) which store the tuples of the relation y.
NMO	Expected number of MACU's (cylinders) which store the output relation.

NGB Number of global buckets in a global hash TPF algorithm.

LTB Fraction of the target relation tuples which survive the checking of the Boolean array BA-*S* during the execution of one phase of a global broadcast TPF algorithm.

LTG Fraction of the tuples from the relation *T* which hash to a global bucket and survive the checking of the Boolean array BA-*S* during the execution of one phase of a global hash TPF algorithm.

ND*y* Number of distinguished values in the join attribute of the tuples of the relation *y*.

NTS_M Number of tuples in a source MACU.

NDS_M Expected number of distinguished values in the join attribute of the tuples in a source MACU.

NDy_G Expected number of distinguished values in the join attribute of the tuples from relation *y* that belong to one global bucket.

FNBP Ratio of the number of buckets in a processor's hash table and the processor's expected number of source tuples per one phase of a TPF algorithm.

FNBIT Ratio of the number of bits in the Boolean array(s) and the number of tuples in both the source and target relations.

Appendix B
Derivation of Formulas for the Join Execution Models

The derivation of formulas for the join execution models rests on two important propositions. These propositions are stated and proven below.

Proposition B.1: Given a collection of keys (possibly not distinct) with cardinality NK defined on a domain with cardinality ND, if a key is equally likely to have any value of the domain, then the expected number of distinguished values NDK in the collection of keys is

$$\mathrm{NDK} = \mathrm{ND}[1 - e^{-\mathrm{NK}/\mathrm{ND}}] \qquad \text{for NK, ND} \gg 1.$$

Proof: This problem is similar to the classical occupancy problem treated by Feller [25]. The occupancy problem deals with finding the number of empty cells m after throwing r balls to n cells. A ball is assumed to go to any cell with equal probability, and the capacity of each cell is assumed to be infinite.

Feller showed that m has the following mass probability function:

$$p_m(r, m) = \binom{n}{m} \sum_{\nu=1}^{n-m} (-1)^{\nu} \binom{n-m}{\nu} \left[1 - \frac{m+\nu}{n}\right]^r$$

and E_{n-m} = the expected number of occupied cells:

$$= n - \sum_{m=1}^{r} m P_m(r, n). \qquad \text{(B1)}$$

He also showed that as $r, n \to \infty$, $p_m(r, n)$ can be computed from the following approximate formula:

$$p_m(r, n) = e^{-\lambda} \frac{\lambda^m}{m}$$

where $\lambda = ne^{-r/n}$ and the expected number of empty cells E_m is equal to λ. Thus,

$$E_{n-m} = n - E_m = n - ne^{-r/n} = n(1 - e^{-r/n}).$$

Replacing r with NK and n with ND in the above equation yields the following formula:

$$\mathrm{NDK} = \mathrm{ND}[1 - e^{-\mathrm{NK}/\mathrm{ND}}] \qquad \text{for NK, ND} \gg 1. \qquad \text{(B2)}$$

Proposition B.2: Given a collection of keys (distinct) with cardinality NK, if a key hashes to a Boolean array of size NBIT with equal probability, then the expected number of bits set (NBS) in the array is

$$\mathrm{NBS} = \mathrm{NBIT}[1 - e^{-\mathrm{NK}/\mathrm{NBIT}}] \qquad \text{for NK, NBIT} \gg 1.$$

Proof: The proof follows that of Proposition B.1. By replacing ND and NDK of (B2) with NBIT and NBS, respectively, the above formula will result.

1) Derivation of a Formula for NMO: Let NTS_V = the expected number of source tuples with the same value. Then, the expected number of tuples in the output relation NTO is NTT $\cdot$ NTS_V $\cdot$ P (a tuple of the target relation carries, in its join attribute, a value which exists in the join attribute of the source tuples). NTS_V can be expressed as NTS/NDS. Therefore,

$$\mathrm{NTO} = \mathrm{NTT} \cdot \frac{\mathrm{NTS}}{\mathrm{NDS}} \cdot \frac{\mathrm{NDS}}{\mathrm{ND}}$$

and

$$\mathrm{NMO} = \frac{\mathrm{NTT} \cdot \mathrm{NTS}(\mathrm{LTS} + \mathrm{LTT})}{\mathrm{ND} \cdot \mathrm{MACUC}}.$$

2) Derivation of a Formula for LTB: Let B be the event that a target tuple will hash to a set bit in the Boolean array BA-*S* and E be the event that a join attribute value of a target tuple has a match among those of the tuples in a source MACU.

$$\begin{aligned} \mathrm{LTB} = P(B) &= P(B, E) + P(B, \bar{E}) \\ &= P(B|E)\,P(E) + P(B|\bar{E})\,P(\bar{E}). \end{aligned} \qquad \text{(B3)}$$

Therefore,

$$P(B) = 1 \cdot \frac{\mathrm{NDS_M}}{\mathrm{ND}} + \frac{\mathrm{NBS}}{\mathrm{NBIT}} \left[1 - \frac{\mathrm{NDS_M}}{\mathrm{ND}}\right] \qquad \text{(B4)}$$

where NBS is the number of bits set in a Boolean array due to NDS_M.

In Proposition B.2, it is shown that

$$\mathrm{NBS} = \mathrm{NBIT}[1 - e^{-\mathrm{NDS_M}/\mathrm{NBIT}}]. \qquad \text{(B5)}$$

Also, using Proposition B.1, it is easy to show that

$$\mathrm{NDS_M} = \mathrm{ND}[1 - e^{-\mathrm{NTS_M}/\mathrm{ND}}] \tag{B6}$$

where $\mathrm{NTS_M}$ is the number of tuples in a source MACU. This is equal to NTS/NMS.

By combining (B4)-(B6), the following equation for LTB will result:

$$\mathrm{LTB} = [1 - e^{-\mathrm{NTS/NMS \cdot ND}} e^{-\mathrm{NDS_M/NBIT}}].$$

3) Derivation of a Formula for LTG: Let B be defined as before, C be the event that a target tuple will hash to the current global bucket, and E be the event that the join attribute value of a target tuple has a match among those of the tuples of the source relation. Then,

$$\mathrm{LTG} = P(B, C) = P(B, C, E) + P(B, C, \bar{E})$$

$$P(B, C, E) = P(B|C, E)\, P(C|E)\, P(E) = 1 \cdot \frac{\mathrm{NDS_G}}{\mathrm{NDS}} \cdot \frac{\mathrm{NDS}}{\mathrm{ND}} = \frac{\mathrm{NDS_G}}{\mathrm{ND}} \tag{B7}$$

$$P(B, C, E) = P(B|C, \bar{E})\, P(C|\bar{E})\, P(\bar{E}) = \frac{\mathrm{NBS}}{\mathrm{NBIT}} \cdot \frac{1}{\mathrm{NGB}} \cdot \left[1 - \frac{\mathrm{NDS}}{\mathrm{ND}}\right] \tag{B8}$$

where NBS is the number of bits set in the Boolean array due to $\mathrm{NDS_G}$.

By combining (B7) and (B8), the following formula for LTG will result:

$$\mathrm{LTG} = \frac{1}{\mathrm{NGB}}\left[\mathrm{NGB} \cdot \frac{\mathrm{NDS_G}}{\mathrm{ND}} + \frac{\mathrm{NBS}}{\mathrm{NBIT}}\left[1 - \frac{\mathrm{NDS}}{\mathrm{ND}}\right]\right]. \tag{B9}$$

Since the global hash hashing function is assumed to be ideal, it is easy to show that

$$\mathrm{NDS} = \mathrm{NGB} \cdot \mathrm{NDS_G}. \tag{B10}$$

Also, from Propositions B.1 and B.2,

$$\mathrm{NBS} = \mathrm{NBIT}[1 - e^{-\mathrm{NDS_G/NBIT}}]. \tag{B11}$$

Therefore,

$$\mathrm{NDS} = \mathrm{ND}[1 - e^{-\mathrm{NTS/ND}}]. \tag{B12}$$

By combining (B9)-(B12), the following equation for LTG will result:

$$\mathrm{LTG} = \frac{1}{\mathrm{NGB}}[1 - e^{-\mathrm{NTS/ND}} e^{-\mathrm{NDS_G/NBIT}}]$$

where

$$\mathrm{NDS_G} = \frac{\mathrm{ND}}{\mathrm{NGB}}[1 - e^{-\mathrm{NTS/ND}}].$$

References

[1] D. D. Chamberlin, A. M. Gilbert, and R. A. Yost, "A history of system-*R* and SQL/data system," presented at the 7th Int. Conf. Very Large Data Bases, Cannes, France, Sept. 1981.

[2] M. Stonebraker, E. Wong, and P. Kreps, "The design and implementation of INGRES," *ACM Trans. Database Syst.*, vol. 1, no. 3, Sept. 1976.

[3] G. Z. Qadah, "Database machines: A survey," in *Proc. Nat. Comput. Conf.*, 1985, pp. 211–223.

[4] E. A. Ozkarahan, S. A. Schuster, and K. C. Smith, "RAP—An associative processor for database management," *AFIPS Proc.*, vol. 45, pp. 379–387, 1975.

[5] J. Banerjee, D. Hsiao, and K. Kannan, "DBC—A Database computer for very large databases," *IEEE Trans. Comput.*, vol. C-28, pp. 414–429, June 1979.

[6] E. Babb, "Implementing a relational database by means of specialized hardware," *ACM Trans. Database Syst.*, vol. 4, no. 1, pp. 1–29, Mar. 1979.

[7] G. J. Lipovski, "Architectural feature of CASSM: A context segment sequential memory," in *Proc. Fifth Annu. Symp. Comput. Architecture*, Palo Alto, CA, Apr. 1978, pp. 31–38.

[8] D. J. Dewitt, "DIRECT—A multiprocessor organization for supporting relational database management systems," *IEEE Trans. Comput.*, vol. C-28, pp. 395–408, June 1979.

[9] G. Gardarin, "An introduction to SABRE: A multi-microprocessor database machine," presented at the 6th Workshop Comput. Architecture Non-Numeric Processing, Hyeres, France, June 1981.

[10] D. K. Hsiao and M. J. Menon, "Design and analysis of a multibackend database system for performance improvements, functionality expansion and capacity growth, Parts I and II," The Ohio State University, Columbus, OH, Tech. Reps. OSU-CISRC-TR-81-81-7 and OSU-DISRC-TR81-8, 1981.

[11] R. Epstein and P. Hawthorn, "Design decisions for the intelligent database machine," in *Proc. Nat. Comput. Conf.*, 1980, pp. 237–241.

[12] H. Schweppe, H. Zeidler, W. Hell, H. Leilich, G. Stiege, and W. Teich, "RDBM—A dedicated multiprocessor system for database management," in *Advanced Database Architecture.* Englewood Cliffs, NJ: Prentice-Hall, 1983, pp. 36–86.

[13] J. R. Goodman, "An investigation of multiprocessor structures and algorithms for database management," Electron. Res. Lab., College Eng., Univ. Calif., Berkeley, CA, Memo No. UCB/ERLM81, May 1981.

[14] M. Kisuregawa *et al.*, "Architecture and performance of relational algebra machine GRACE," in *Proc. Int. Conf. Parallel Processing*, 1984, pp. 241–250.

[15] G. Z. Qadah and K. B. Irani, "A database machine for very large relational databases," *IEEE Trans. Comput.*, vol. C-34, pp. 1015–1025, Nov. 1985.

[16] E. F. Codd, "A relational model of data for large shared databanks," *Commun. ACM*, vol. 13, no. 1, pp. 377–387, June 1970.

[17] D. Bitton *et al.*, "Parallel algorithms for the execution of relational database operation," *ACM Trans. Database Syst.*, vol. 8, no. 3, pp. 324–353, Sept. 1983.

[18] P. Valduriez and G. Gardarin, "Join and semijoin algorithms for a multi-microprocessor database machine," *ACM Trans. Database Syst.*, vol. 9, no. 1, pp. 133–161, Mar. 1984.

[19] D. J. Dewitt and R. Gerber, "Multiprocessor hash-based join algorithms," in *Proc. 11th Int. Conf. VLDB*, 1985, pp. 151–164.

[20] D. B. Friedland, "Design, analysis, and implementation of parallel external sorting algorithms," Univ. Wisconsin, Madison, WI, Comput. Sci. Tech. Rep. #464, Jan. 1982.

[21] D. E. Knuth, *The Art of Computer Programming, Vol. 3, Sorting and Searching.* Reading, MA: Addison-Wesley, 1973.

[22] G. Z. Qadah, "A relational databases machine: Analysis and design," Ph.D. dissertation, Dep. Elec. Comput. Eng., Univ. Michigan, Ann Arbor, MI, 1983.

[23] S. Christodoulakis, "Implication of certain assumptions in database performance evaluation," *ACM Trans. Database Syst.*, vol. 9, no. 2, pp. 163–186, June 1984.

[24] *IBM 3380 DIRECT Access Storage Description and User's Guide*, IBM Corp., IBM Doc. GA26-1664-0, File No. 51370-07, 1980.

[25] W. Feller, *An Introduction to Probability and Its Application, Vol. 1.* New York: Wiley, 1967.

Ghassan Z. Qadah (S'78–M'84) received the B.Sc. degree in electrical engineering from Ain-Shams University, Cairo, Egypt, in 1974 and the M.S. and Ph.D. degrees in electrical engineering from The University of Michigan, Ann Arbor, in 1977 and 1983, respectively.

From 1975 to 1976 he was a Research Assistant in the Electron Physics Laboratory of The University of Michigan. From 1977 to 1983 he was a Teaching and Research Assistant in the Department of Electrical Engineering at The University of Michigan. He is now with Northwestern University, Evanston, IL, where he is an Assistant Professor in the Department of Electrical Engineering and Computer Science. His current research interests are in computer architecture; database, logic-base, and artificial intelligence machines; parallel algorithms for nonnumeric computations; and database and knowledge-base management.

Dr. Qadah is a member of the Association for Computing Machinery and the IEEE Computer Society.

Keki B. Irani (SM'60) received the B.S. degree in mechanical engineering and the B.S. degree in electrical engineering from the University of Bombay, Bombay, India, in 1946 and 1947, respectively, and the M.S.E. degree in electrical engineering and the Ph.D. degree from The University of Michigan, Ann Arbor, in 1949 and 1953, respectively.

From 1950 to 1957 he was a Research and Design Engineer for Philips Telecommunication Industries, The Netherlands, where he worked on coaxial telephone systems. He joined the faculty of the Department of Electrical Engineering, The University of Kansas, Lawrence, in 1956 and The University of Michigan faculty in 1961. He is now with The University of Michigan, where he is a Professor in the Department of Electrical Engineering and Computer Science. He has worked in the areas of electrical power systems, electrical networks, communications, control, and computers. His current research interests are in computer architecture, distributed computer systems, databases, and artificial intelligence.

Dr. Irani is a member of the Association for Computing Machinery, Sigma Xi, and Tau Beta Pi.

Design and Evaluation of Parallel Pipelined Join Algorithms

James P. Richardson
Hongjun Lu
Krishna Mikkilineni

Honeywell Inc.
Corporate Systems Development Division
Golden Valley, Minnesota

ABSTRACT

The join operation is the most costly operation in relational database management systems. Distributed and parallel processing can effectively speed up the join operation. In this paper, we describe a number of highly parallel and pipelined multiprocessor join algorithms using sort-merge and hashing techniques. Among them, two algorithms are parallel and pipelined versions of traditional sort-merge join methods, two algorithms use both hashing and sort-merge techniques, and another two are variations of the hybrid hash join algorithms. The performance of those algorithms is evaluated analytically against a generic database machine architecture. The methodology used in the design and evaluation of these algorithms is also discussed.

The results of the analysis indicate that using a hashing technique to partition the source relations can dramatically reduce the elapsed time: hash-based algorithms outperform sort-merge algorithms in almost all cases because of their high parallelism. Hash-based sort-merge and hybrid hash methods provide similar performance in most cases. With large source relations, the algorithms which replicate the smaller relation usually give better elapsed time. Sharing memory among processors also improves performance somewhat.

This research was sponsored in part by Rome Air Development Center contract F30602-85-C-0215

1. Introduction

As enterprises use database management systems to manage more of their information, the size of existing databases is increasing rapidly. Databases of over 100 gigabytes now exist; terabyte databases, if they do not exist now, will appear in the next few years. Managing these large databases will require more powerful architectures than are in common use today. Technology now permits the construction of multiprocessor database management architectures with tens or hundreds of processors, a gigabyte or more of main memory, and disk capacity in the terabyte range. The Teradata DBC/1012 is an example of such an architecture [Tera83].

The join operation is an important operation for relational database systems and a large amount of work has been done to develop efficient algorithms to perform the join operation. It will become even more important as logic-based inference capabilities are added to these systems. In this paper, we describe a number of multiprocessor join algorithms. The algorithms use sort-merge and hashing techniques, and are highly parallel and pipelined. The algorithms are designed to execute on a multiprocessor architecture that is parameterized in the degree of memory sharing, so that tightly-coupled, loosely-coupled, and intermediate architectures can be modeled. Other architectural parameters include the number of processors, number of disks, amount of main memory, and interconnection network bandwidth. We model analytically the performance of the algorithms to determine elapsed time, resource utilization, and other quantities as functions of the workload and architectural parameters. The join algorithms overlap computation, disk transfers, and interconnection network transfers. An important feature of our analysis is that this overlap of different system resources is modeled in the analysis of the elapsed time. This analysis also identifies bottlenecks that limit the algorithms' performance. We do not model multiple simultaneous join operations and therefore do not compute system throughput.

Based on this analysis, we will answer the following questions:

- How do the algorithms compare in performance?

"Design and Evaluation of Parallel Pipelined Join Algorithms" by J.P. Richardson, H. Lu, and K. Mikkilineni from *Proc. ACM SIGMOD*, 1987, pp. 399-409. Copyright 1987, Association for Computing Machinery, Inc., reprinted with permission.

When does one outperform another?

- How does elapsed time vary as a function of the architectural parameters?
- How does elapsed time vary with the workload?
- Does shared memory help algorithm performance? To what extent?
- What are the architectural bottlenecks? How could they be alleviated?

In the following sections, we describe the multiprocessor hardware architecture and the join algorithms, develop cost formulas for the algorithms, compare the algorithms' performance under various workloads and hardware configurations, and summarize the results of our investigation.

2. Multiprocessor Data Management Architecture

Many specialized architectures have been proposed for high performance relational database management. These architectures include logic-on-disk machines [Schu79, Su79], VLSI-based special purpose processors [Kits83, Shib84], and loosely- and tightly-coupled multiprocessor architectures [DeWi79, Tera83, DeWi86]. We believe that commercially viable database machines must be constructed principally from the commodity components such as general purpose microprocessors and conventional disk storage devices. This belief is based on the superior price/performance and reliability of commodity components compared to custom components. Therefore, we consider in this study a multiprocessor architecture with the following characteristics:

- The architecture uses a large number (tens to hundreds, at least) of processors to obtain the necessary performance. This assumes that the processors can be used effectively. The Teradata DBC/1012 appears to have demonstrated that this is possible.
- The architecture can use large amounts (hundreds of megabytes to hundreds of gigabytes) of semiconductor memory. In the next few years, this amount of memory will be feasible as well as cost-effective.
- The architecture can support an aggregate disk capacity of a terabyte or more; only a small fraction of the total database can be accommodated in main memory. We assume further that many of the individual database relations will typically not fit in main memory.

Figure 1 shows a block diagram of our architecture. The architecture consists of a set of *clusters* linked by an intercluster bus or ring. Each cluster consists of a set of processors, a shared memory bank addressable by all the processors in the cluster, and a set of disk storage units and associated controllers. Processors read and write the shared memory in units of a few bytes, with little contention. The processors may have local caches to reduce memory contention, but this is invisible to the data management software except possibly for the need to flush the cache occasionally.

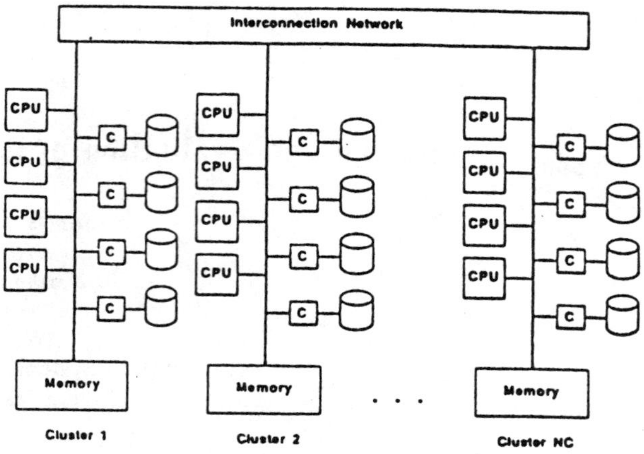

Figure 1: Multiprocessor Data Management Architecture.

Transfers between disk and memory, and between cluster memories over the bus are a page at a time, where a page is a few kilobytes or more in size. A specific configuration of this architecture is determined by the following parameters:

NC	number of clusters
NP	number of processors *per cluster*
ND	number of disks *per cluster*
M	pages of main memory available *per cluster*
PG	page size in bytes

These parameters can be varied to determine the effect of architectural changes. For instance, if the CPU is a bottleneck, more CPUs can be added per cluster or each CPU can be made faster. (CPU speed is defined in terms of execution times for basic operations associated with the join algorithms, such as tuple move.) If the disk is a bottleneck, the page size can be increased, the disk transfer rate can be increased, or more disks can be added per cluster. We have assumed that the network is a single bus, so the only architectural cure for a network bottleneck is to increase the network transmission rate.

3. Join Algorithm Descriptions

The problem that each join algorithm solves is the following: Given relations R and S, compute their natural join on a specified pair of attributes, giving output relation O. R and S are assumed to be uniformly partitioned across all disks on all clusters according to attributes that are often used for selections or joins of these relations. However, to make the join difficult, we assume that the join attributes for R and S are not the partitioning attributes. This forces tuples to be transmitted between clusters to perform the join. The partition is not determined by the values of the join attributes, so that tuples must be transmitted between clusters to perform the join. Let R_i and S_i denote the fragments of R and S, respectively, stored on the disks at cluster C_i. The result of the join can be partitioned across the clusters; it need not be collected on one cluster. No projection is performed on the result except to remove the redundant copy of the join attribute, so no duplicate tuples are produced.

Assume without loss of generality that S is larger (in bytes) than R. Some of the algorithms transmit only one of the relations over the interconnection network, in these cases, they transmit R, the smaller relation.

Each algorithm consists of one or more *phases*. The phases are executed one after another; the activity in one phase completes before the next phase starts. Within each phase, a fixed set of processes execute in parallel, passing data to each other (possibly over the network) and reading from and writing to disk in pipelined fashion. Each cluster has dedicated send and receive processes to act as intermediaries between communicating processes on different clusters.

Processes communicate with each other via streams of data pages. Each process may have several input and output streams. We chose this granularity of communication to minimize the interprocess communication and synchronization overhead. The cost of passing a page of data between processes on the same cluster is assumed to be negligible in comparison to the cost of producing or consuming it. In some algorithms, processes on the same cluster read concurrently from the same page buffer or other memory area; concurrent reading and writing is not used because it would require a high synchronization overhead. The interprocess communication system uses flow control to match the speeds of the producing and consuming processes and to prevent buffer overflow. Enough buffers are allocated to allow all processes to execute concurrently.

In this section we present six algorithms with the above assumptions. The algorithms come in pairs: the first of each pair transmits tuples from both R and S over the network, while the second transmits only tuples from R, reducing communications cost while increasing computation. The two algorithms comprising the first pair are parallel versions of the the basic sort merge join; they are most similar to algorithms described in [Bitt83] [Vald84]. The other four use hashing to decompose R and S into buckets, and then use either a sort-merge or a hashing technique to join each pair of buckets. They are similar to algorithms described in [DeWi84] [Kits83].

3.1. Parallel Sort Merge Algorithms

3.1.1. Parallel Sort-Merge Join Type 1 (SMJ1)

In the basic sort-merge join, each relation is first sorted on its join attribute. Then, the two sorted relations are merge-joined. The merge-join operation matches tuples in the two relations by their join attributes and generates the result tuples. It is pipelined much like a merge operation, except that a tuple in either input relation can be used to construct multiple output tuples.

Previously published algorithms have presented parallel algorithms for the sort phase. Bitton *et al.* describe join algorithms employing a parallel binary merge sort and a block bitonic sort [Bitt83]. The former can be improved, memory permitting, by using a general multi-way merge [Vald84]. Both algorithms start by generating a set of sorted runs from the original unsorted relation. These runs are generated using a main-memory sorting algorithm or a priority queue. The latter is preferable because it generates runs that are on average twice the size of the main memory dedicated to the priority queue, and hence twice the size of the runs generated by a main-memory sorting algorithm [Knut73]. In addition, run generation by priority queue is inherently a pipelined operation, permitting better overlap between CPU and I/O than run generation by main memory sorting. Once the runs are generated, the final sorted output is generated either by merging the runs or by using a block bitonic algorithm.

The sort-merge join algorithm just described parallelizes the sort operations, but the final merge-join operation is still performed sequentially over the entire length of both relations. In the algorithm described below, the final merge-join is partitioned into multiple parallel processes so that no single process must pass over all of either relation. This is accomplished by generating $NFRUN_R$ final runs of relation R and $NFRUN_S$ final runs of relation S, and merge-joining each of the final runs of R with each of the final runs of S, all in parallel. One of these merge-joins is executed at each cluster, leaving the joined relation O partitioned across the clusters. There is an obvious constraint

$$NFRUN_R \cdot NFRUN_S = NC$$

For convenience in describing the algorithm, let the clusters be named C_{ij} for $1 \leq i \leq NFRUN_R$ and $i \leq j \leq NFRUN_S$. The clusters are logically arranged as a two-dimensional array with $NFRUN_R$ rows and $NFRUN_S$ columns, though their physical interconnection is unchanged. (Assume for now that there are at least two rows and two columns. The degenerate case is discussed below.) The portion of R stored on C_{ij} is called R_{ij}. The algorithm has three major phases.

Phase 1: At each cluster C_{ij}, NP processes generate initial runs of R_{ij} and write them back to disk. Each process has its own priority queue for generating the runs.

Phase 2: Each cluster C_{ij} generates initial runs of S_{ij} in the same way.

Phase 3: Merge the initial runs of R into $NFRUN_R$ final runs, and the initial runs of S into $NFRUN_S$ final runs. Also, merge-join each final run of R with each final run of S to produce the result. The merging and merge-joining form a five-stage pipeline. The final runs of R are produced in two stages. The first stage of the merge occurs at each cluster C_{ij}, where a merge process merges all initial runs of R_{ij} into a single sorted version of R_{ij}. One of the clusters in each row, the *row pivot cluster*, executes the second stage, merging the sorted R_{ij}'s into a final sorted run for the row. The final runs of S are generated in the same way except that a *column pivot cluster* executes the second merge stage for clusters in its column. The row (column) pivot clusters send their final runs to the other clusters in the row (column); each cluster merge-joins the final run of R for row i with the final run of S for column j to produce O_{ij}, a fragment of the final result. By choosing C_{ii} as the row pivot cluster for row i and C_{j+1j} as the column pivot cluster of column j, no cluster is both a row and a column pivot.

3.1.2. Parallel Sort-Merge Join Type 2 (SMJ2)

It may be wasteful to sort both relations completely before merge-joining them, especially if the join selectivity is low. At each stage of the merging process, tuples are being processed that may not participate in the final join. The following algorithm makes only one pass over the larger relation (S). In the description, we revert to single subscripts on clusters and relation fragments. The algorithm has three phases.

Phase 1: Generate local runs of R_i at each cluster C_i, as in algorithm SMJ1.

Phase 2: Merge these runs into a single sorted version of R. This is done with a two-stage merge. Each cluster executes the first stage, merging the local runs into a sorted version of R_i. The results from each cluster are sent to C_1, which executes the second stage of the merge and broadcasts the resulting sorted R to all clusters. Each cluster writes this run to disk.

Phase 3: Generate runs of S at each cluster using a priority queue. However, instead of writing these runs to disk, merge-join them immediately with R to produce the output tuples. Let there be NP processes at each cluster executing the run generation stage, paired with an equal number of processes executing the merge-join stage.

The advantage of this algorithm is that it produces the join results with one pass over the S relation. When S is large, this presumably saves much of the I/O and processing that would otherwise be required to produce the final runs of S. The disadvantage is that R must be read repeatedly from disk to be joined against the runs of S. (If R fits entirely in main memory, this is unnecessary. However, hash-based algorithms are probably superior in this case. We do not attempt to fit all of R in main memory.)

3.2. Hash Partitioning Join Algorithms

These algorithms all use a hash partitioning technique described in [DeWi84] to decompose a join of two large relations into a sequence of smaller joins. They partition tuples of R and S into *batches* $RB_0, \ldots, RB_{NBATCH}$ and $SB_0, \ldots, SB_{NBATCH}$ and join the respective batches. The partitioning is based on the value of a hash function applied to the join attribute, so that joining the respective batches generates all required result tuples. The batches are sized so that each batch join can be performed in main memory. Batches $1, \ldots, NBATCH$ of each relation are written to disk during partitioning. Batches RB_0 and SB_0 are joined during or immediately after partitioning, depending on the particular algorithm. If sufficient memory is available, $NBATCH=0$ and no batches must be written to disk. Otherwise, batches $1, \ldots, NBATCH$ are read from disk and joined one after the other. The number of batches can be computed from the size of the relations and available memory; see Section 4. This partitioning technique minimizes the amount of intermediate data that must be written to disk.

All of the algorithms further partition the batches into *buckets* and join the buckets within each batch in parallel. Two of the algorithms, HSM1 and HH1, join respective buckets using a sort-merge technique similar to the GRACE algorithm [Kits83]. The other two, HH1 and HH2, use the in-memory hash table technique described in [DeWi84] [Brat84]. The type 1 algorithms, HSM1 and HSM2, transmit both R and S over the network; the type 2 algorithms, HSM2 and HH2, transmit only R, the smaller relation.

3.2.1. Hash-Based Sort-Merge Join Type 1 (HSM1)

This algorithm partitions each batch of R and S further into $NC \cdot NP_{join}$ buckets that are joined in parallel by NP_{join} processes on each of the NC clusters. A hash function applied to the join attribute of each tuple determines the batch, cluster, and process in which it will be joined. Each pair of buckets is joined using a sort-merge join.

Let RB_{ij} denote the subset of RB_j derived from R_i, the subset of R stored at C_i. Define SB_{ij} similarly. The algorithm has three phases.

Phase 1: At each cluster C_i, NP_{join} processes read R_i from disk a page at a time. The assignment of pages to processes is arbitrary. The processes hash each tuple in a page to determine the batch, cluster, and process in which it will be joined. If the tuple is in batch $j \neq 0$, it is placed in a buffer to be written to a disk file for RB_{ij}. If the tuple belongs to batch 0 but is to be joined on a different cluster, it is placed in a buffer to be sent to that cluster. If the tuple is to be joined by a different process on the same cluster, it is placed in a buffer to be sent to the correct process. When a process fills one of these buffers, it writes it to disk or sends it to another cluster or process as appropriate. When a page is sent to another cluster, it is received by an arbitrary process on that cluster; the tuples in the page are rehashed and sent to another process in the cluster if necessary. Once the tuple arrives at the correct process, it is inserted into a binary search tree. The search tree will be traversed inorder in the next phase to produce a sorted version of the bucket. When all of R_i has been read, S_i is processed in the same way.

Phase 2: This phase is repeated for j ranging from 1 to $NBATCH$. If $NBATCH=0$, this phase is omitted. At each cluster C_i, each process performs an inorder traversal of its R and S search trees to produce a sorted stream of tuples for each bucket. It merge-joins these tuples to produce the join results. As tuples are consumed, the space they occupied is freed. As the memory is freed, the processes read the file for batch RB_{ij}, hash each tuple, send the tuples to the appropriate cluster and process, and insert them into search trees occupying the newly freed space. When all of RB_{ij} has been read, SB_{ij} is processed in the same way.

Phase 3: In this phase, the buckets in batch *NBATCH* are joined as described for phase 2. No data remains to be read from disk and partitioned.

3.2.2. Hash-Based Sort-Merge Join Type 2 (HSM2)

This algorithm differs from Algorithm HSM1 in that relation S is not sent over the network. Instead, each cluster C_i joins all of R with its portion S_i of relation S. A hash function on the join attribute of each tuple determines the batch to which the tuple belongs, and the process on each cluster (in the case of R) or the process on cluster C_i (in the case of S_i) that will do the joining.

The algorithm has three phases. Only the first phase will be described; the other phases should be clear from the description of phase 1 and Algorithm HSM1.

Phase 1: At each cluster C_i, NP_{hash} processes read R_i. They hash each tuple to determine the batch and process number. Each tuple is buffered either to be written to disk or to be broadcast to the correct process on each cluster. Each process constructs a binary search tree of tuples belonging to its own bucket. When all of R_i has been read, S_i is processed in the same way, except that tuples from S_i are not transmitted to other clusters, only to other processes on the same cluster.

3.2.3. Multiprocessor Hybrid Hash Join Type 1 (HH1)

Algorithm HH1 partitions R and S into batches and buckets in the same ways that Algorithm HSM1 does. However, it uses a hash-based algorithm to join each pair of buckets. An in-memory hash table is constructed for each bucket of R. This table is then probed using tuples from the corresponding bucket of S to produce the join results. The concurrent processing of consecutive batches performed in phase 2 of Algorithm HSM1 is not possible here because the hash table for a bucket of R cannot be deallocated until it has been probed by all the tuples in the corresponding S bucket. On the other hand, Algorithm HSM1 requires memory to hold S buckets, while this algorithm does not. The algorithm has four phases.

Phase 1: At each cluster C_i, NP_{join} processes read R_i from disk. They hash each tuple and copy it to the appropriate buffer if it must be written back to disk or sent to another cluster or process, as in Algorithm HSM1. Each process constructs a hash table of tuples belonging to its own bucket.

Phase 2: At each cluster C_i, the NP_{join} processes read S_i from disk. They hash each tuple and buffer it to be written to disk or sent to another cluster if necessary. It is not necessary to send a tuple from one process to another on the same cluster, however. Once a tuple is at the correct cluster, any process can probe the appropriate hash table to generate the join results.

Phases 3 and 4 are repeated for j ranging from 1 to *NBATCH*. If $NBATCH=0$, these phases are omitted.

Phase 3: This is similar to phase 1 except that each cluster C_i reads RB_{ij} from disk instead of R_i, and performs no disk writes.

Phase 4: This is similar to phase 2 except that each cluster C_i reads SB_{ij} from disk instead of S_i, and performs no disk writes.

3.2.4. Multiprocessor Hybrid Hash Join Type 2 (HH2)

This algorithm is to Algorithm HH1 as Algorithm HSM2 is to Algorithm HSM1. It has four phases similar to those of Algorithm HH1. However, tuples of S are not transmitted over the network. In fact, they are not even transmitted between processes on the same cluster since any process can probe a hash table on the same cluster.

3.3. Discussion

The algorithms described above represent the latest versions in a sequence of algorithms. These versions provide better overlap in the usage of different resources than earlier versions. For example, in all four hash partitioning algorithms, the communications load is spread as evenly as possible over the duration of the algorithm execution. Tuples are sent across the network only when they are about to participate in a join. One of our earlier versions transmitted all tuples to the joining cluster when the relations were being partitioned, as in DeWitt and Gerber's algorithm [DeWi85]. We found that this could cause a network bottleneck during partitioning; the disks and CPUs were not well utilized. Spreading the communications load over the duration of the algorithms reduced their execution time.

The overlapping among disk I/O, CPU processing and data transfer over the network gives algorithm designers opportunities to tune the algorithms to obtain the trade-off between the elapsed time, total processing cost and memory usage that is best for their system. Another example regarding this is the way the hash-based algorithms store tuples in batches 1 — *NBATCH*. One possibility is to use one file per batch at each cluster; we chose to use one file per remote cluster at each cluster. In the former case, no repartitioning is needed in the later phases, but more buffer pages have to be allocated in the partitioning phase. In the latter case, the tuples in the same batch have to be rehashed to determine its bucket number, but far fewer buffer pages are needed to hold the tuples rewritten to disks.

4. Performance Comparisons

This section presents performance comparisons of the join algorithms described in Section 3. The main purpose of the performance comparison is to get some insight into the behavior of different algorithms. The novelty of this performance analysis lies in two facts. First, there are few comprehensive performance studies of join algorithms in the multiprocessor-multidisk architectures [DeWi85]. Second, most studies do not model overlap among computation, disk transfers and interconnection network transfers. Unless this overlap is modeled, total processing time and elapsed time are equivalent performance metrics. We do model this overlap so that we can locate bottlenecks in the algorithms. One of the goals of parallel join algorithm design should be to overlap the usage of various system resources as much as possible, thus reducing elapsed time while holding total resource usage constant.

The tests conducted can be categorized into three groups that investigate (1) the effects of communication speed; (2) the effects of system configurations; and (3) the effects of data sizes. In this section, we first describe the methodology used in the analysis. Then the details of the tests, including the parameter settings and test results, are discussed.

4.1. Analysis Methodology

For each algorithm, we will compute the following quantities:

T	elapsed time
T_{cpu}	total CPU time
T_{disk}	total disk transfer time
T_{net}	total network transfer time

Each of these is the sum over all phases i of the corresponding per-phase quantities T^i, T^i_{cpu}, T^i_{disk}, and T^i_{net}. Resource utilization percentages are easily derived from these basic measures. The analysis uses the following times for basic operations:

t_{comp}	CPU time to compare two attributes
t_{hash}	CPU time to compute hash function of a key
t_{move}	CPU time to move a tuple in memory
t_{swapp}	CPU time to swap two pointers in memory
$t_{build-tuple}$	CPU time to build a join result tuple
t_{send}	CPU time to send a page over network
t_{recv}	CPU time to receive a page over network
t_{net}	network hardware page transfer time
t_{disk}	disk page transfer time

We first compute the following basic quantities for each phase i:

P^i_{disk}	the number of disk transfer pages
P^i_{send}	the number of pages sent over the network
P^i_{recv}	the number of pages received over the network
T^i_{join}	CPU time unrelated to disk or net transfers

P^i_{recv} can be greater than P^i_{send} due to broadcasting. Then,

$$T^i_{cpu} = T^i_{join} + P^i_{send} \cdot t_{send} + P^i_{recv} \cdot t_{recv}$$

$$T^i_{disk} = P^i_{disk} \cdot t_{disk}$$

$$T^i_{net} = P^i_{send} \cdot t_{net}$$

We assume that the CPU time attributable to disk transfers is negligible. For network communication, we consider both the CPU time and the hardware transfer time; either is a potential bottleneck.

The elapsed time T^i for phase i will in general be significantly less than $T^i_{cpu}+T^i_{disk}+T^i_{net}$ due to overlap. In our analysis, we assume that sufficient buffering is provided to permit all processes to execute in parallel with each other and with disk and network transfers:

- One buffer is allocated for each input and output stream for each process.
- One buffer is allocated for each disk to contain the data being read or written.
- One buffer is allocated for the network send process at each cluster to hold the next page to be transmitted and one buffer for the network receive process to hold the next incoming page.

We also assume that the time for data to flow from the beginning of a pipeline of processes to the end is negligible compared to the total elapsed time for the phase, so that the pipeline is in steady state for most of the phase. Under these assumptions, the elpased time T^i can be approximated by the maximum of:

- The total disk transfer time of any disk. If I/O is spread evenly over all disks, this quantity is $T^i_{disk}/(NC \cdot ND)$.
- The total network transfer time T^i_{net} for the phase.
- The total CPU time for any single process, including network send and receive processes.
- The total CPU time for any cluster, divided by NP, the number of processors per cluster. If processing is spread evenly over all clusters, this quantity is $T^i_{cpu}/(NC \cdot NP)$. This quantity models processor sharing among the processes at a cluster.

The detailed formulas derived in the analysis are not here. They can be found in another version of this paper [Rich87].

4.2. Parameter Settings

Three types of parameters are used in the comparisons: architectural parameters, timing parameters, and workload parameters. The parameter values used are listed in Table 1.

4.3. Tests and Results

Now we describe the tests conducted in the performance comparisons. Since our results showed that the sort-merge algorithms were generally much slower than the hash-based algorithms, only curves for the the hash-based join algorithms are shown in the figures in this section except for Figure 3, where we include the results of sort-merge algorithms as an example showing the performance difference between sort-

Parameter	Range	Typical Value
Architectural Parameters		
NC	2 - 64	16
ND	2 - 20	8
NP	2 - 64	8
M	16 - 512	128
PG	32K bytes	
Timing Parameters		
t_{comp}	5 μs	
t_{hash}	3 μs	
t_{move}	10 μs	
t_{swapp}	1μs	
$t_{build-tuple}$	20 μs	
t_{send}	0.1 - 3 ms	1 ms
t_{recv}	0.1 - 3 ms	1 ms
t_{net}	0.4 - 2.56 ms (100 - 600 Mbps)	2.56 ms (100 Mbps)
t_{disk}	10 - 30 ms	15 ms
Workload Parameters		
$\|R\|$	50 - 400K pages	100K pages
$\|S\|$	$\|R\|$ - $10 \cdot \|R\|$	$\|R\|$
JS	10^{-8}	

Table 1: Parameter Settings.

merge and hash-based algorithms.

4.3.1. Communication versus Performance

In this test, the bandwidth of the communications line was varied from 100 Mbps to 600 Mbps to study the effects of the data transfer rate on the performance of the algorithms. The results are shown in Figure 2. The elapsed times of type 1 algorithms drop dramatically when the bandwidth increases from 100 Mbps to 300 Mbps. This is because the system is network bound with our typical parameter settings for these algorithms. In other words, the data transfer was the bottleneck and the bandwidth of the communications line determined their elapsed times. In contrast, the elapsed times of type 2 algorithms did not change at all when the bandwidth was varied in the range. In these two algorithms, the amount of data transferred equals the size of the small relation R. It is not a bottleneck when the bandwidth is greater than 200 Mbps.

4.3.2. System Configuration versus Performance

The first group of tests that investigated the effects of system configurations on performance consists of the following five tests.

- The total hardware resources, that is, the total number of disks ($NC \cdot ND$), processors ($NC \cdot NP$), and memory size ($NC \cdot M$) are kept constant. The number of clusters in the system (NC) is varied.
- The configuration of each cluster is kept the same (i. e., fix *NP* and *ND*), but the number of clusters in the system varies.
- The number of disks at each cluster, *ND*, is varied, and other parameters are kept constant.

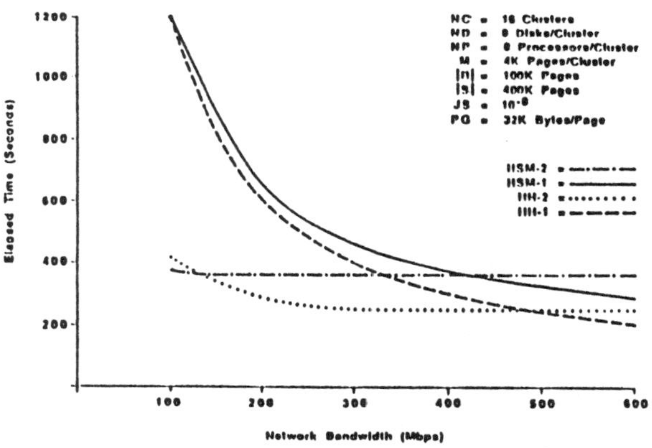

Figure 2: Elapsed Time vs. Network Bandwidth.

- The number of processors at each cluster, *NP*, is varied, and other parameters are kept constant.
- Memory size *M* at each cluster is varied, while other parameters were kept constant.

We will describe these tests in more detail.

(1) *The elapsed time versus different configurations under the same total hardware resources.* One extreme of the spectrum is that all resources form a single large cluster. Another extreme is a system such as Gamma [DeWi86], where each cluster has only one processor and one disk. The results are shown in Figure 3. The later case is not shown in the figure since the trend is already shown when the system consists of 64 clusters having two disks and two processors each. That is the case when each cluster has two disks and two processors. When the system consists of 128 clusters with one processor and one disk, the elapsed time for HSM2 is almost doubled compared to the 64-cluster case. The other three curves remained flat (not shown in the figure).

From Figure 3, it can be seen that a huge single cluster provides the best performance since the communications cost is eliminated. The curves of HH1 and HSM1 are flat since the system is network-bound. This will be seen more clearly later. The total amount of data transferred in the

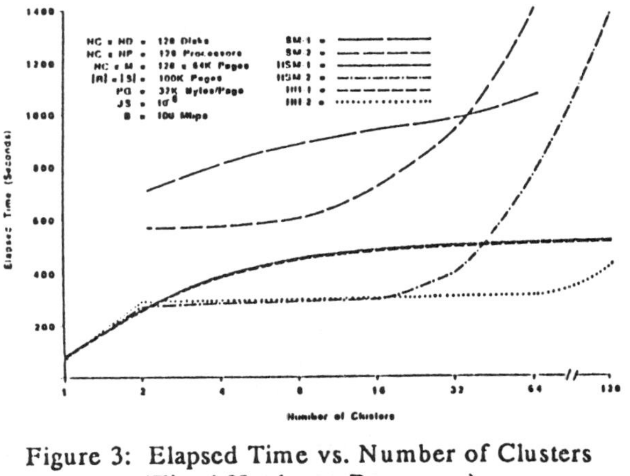

Figure 3: Elapsed Time vs. Number of Clusters (Fixed Hardware Resources).

type 2 algorithms equals the size of relation R, which is a constant when the system configuration is changed. With the large number of clusters (> 32), HSM2 performs poorly since replicating relation R increases the total processing cost. The increasing CPU cost makes the system CPU bound. When the number of clusters is doubled, the elapsed time is also doubled. For the type 1 algorithms, increasing the number of clusters increases the number of pages sent over the network, $\frac{NC-1}{NC} \cdot (|R| + |S|)$. When the number of clusters in the system increases from 2 to 4, this amount increases one third. This is reflected in the increase of the elapsed time. We ignore the memory contention and the cost of synchronizing the concurrent access of disks in our analysis. The huge single cluster case is just an indication of the lower bound of the elapsed time. It is impractical to put a large number of disks and processors with shared memory in one cluster.

Figure 3 was obtained with a 100 Mbps network. With 600 Mbps, the performance is a little different. In this case, the type 1 algorithms performed better than their counterparts. Figure 4 shows the results. As in Figure 3, the type 2 algorithms performed very poorly when the number of clusters exceeded 64.

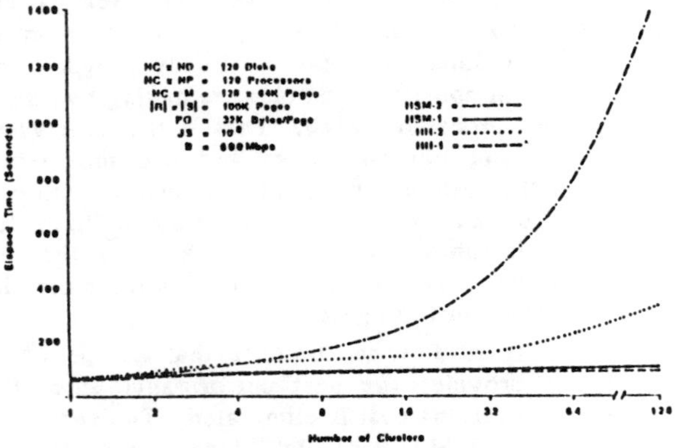

Figure 4: Elapsed Time vs. Number of Clusters (Fixed Cluster Configuration).

(2) *The elapsed time versus the number of clusters.* In this test, the configuration of each cluster was kept the same and the number of clusters in the system was varied. The result of this variation is to increase the parallel processing power of the system and also introduce more data transfer for some algorithms since we assume that the original data is scattered around the system. The result of this test is shown in Figure 5.

(3) *The elapsed time versus the number of disks at each cluster.* In these tests, the number of disks are varied and other parameters is kept as constant. Figure 6 shows the result. It can be seen from the figure that it is unnecessary to attach more disks to a cluster when the bottleneck is not disk I/O. When the number of disks was more than eight in the tested case, increasing the number of

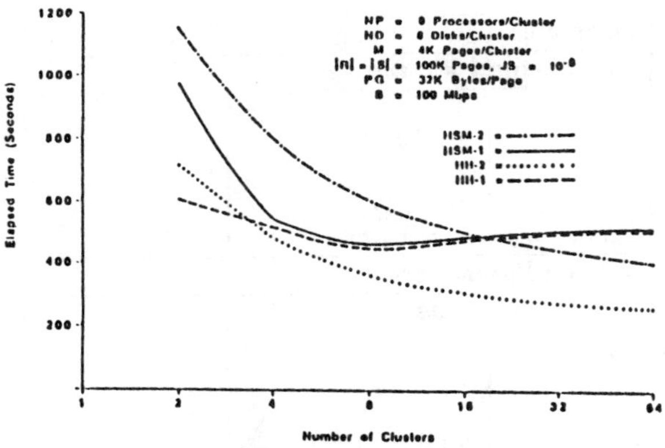

Figure 5: Elapsed Time vs. Number of Clusters (Fixed NP, ND, and M).

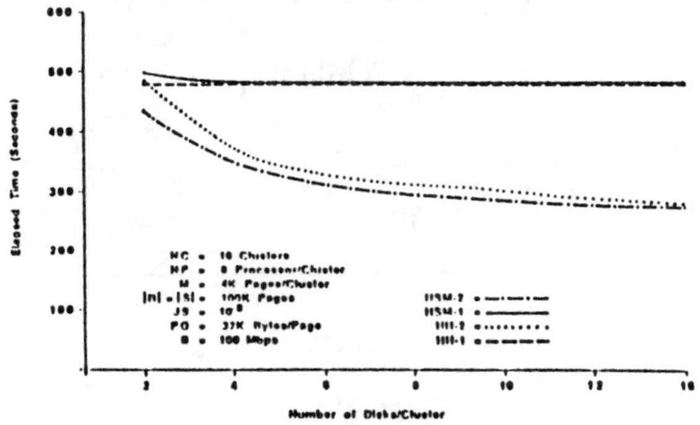

Figure 6: Elapsed Time vs. Number of Disks.

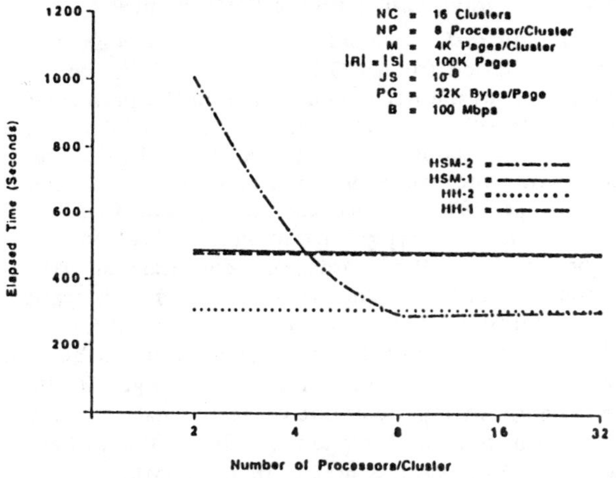

Figure 7: Elapsed Time vs. Number of Processors.

disks did not bring real performance benefit.

(4) *The elapsed time versus the number of processors at each cluster.* In these tests, the number of processors at each cluster was varied and the results are shown in Figure 7. It can be seen from the figure that CPU processing was not the bottleneck even with two processors at each cluster. The only exception was the HSM2 algorithm, which is the most CPU-intensive CPU of these algorithms. However, with more than eight processors per cluster, the elapsed time did not decrease further when more processors were added to the clusters. Another observation is that, in our buffer alloca-

tion scheme, the number of buffers needed increases proportionally to the square of the number of processors, (not linearly). The large number of processors may cause insufficient memory for executing the algorithms.

(5) *The elapsed time versus the amount of memory at each cluster.* In this group of tests, the amount of memory at each cluster was varied. From the results, shown in Figure 8, it can be seen that the type 2 algorithms required more memory space for buffers. That is, the minimum memory requirement is more strict for them. However, as long as the memory was big enough to start the algorithm, there was not a big difference in the elapsed time with different memory sizes. This can be explained as follows. The only benefit a large size memory provide is to save the disk I/O and related rehashing of buckets of 1 — *NBATCH*. The processing of the remaining buckets will not be affected by the bucket sizes, which are determined by memory size. If the processing cost of the first batch is not the dominant factor of the total processing, or disk I/O is not the bottleneck in the first phase, the memory size will not significantly affect the elapsed time, as seen from the figure.

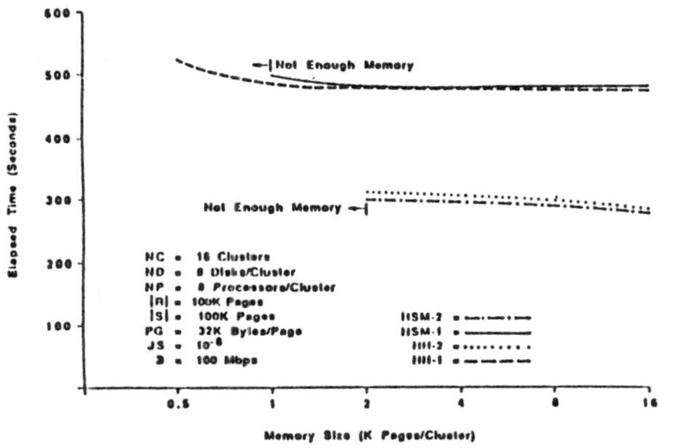

Figure 8: Elapsed Time vs. Memory Size.

4.3.3. Data Sizes versus Performance

The third group of tests studied the effects of the data size on performance of the algorithms. The size of relation R ranged from $1.75 \cdot 10^9$ bytes to $25 \cdot 10^9$. $||S||$ ranged from $||R||$ to $10 \cdot ||R||$. Figure 9 depicts the relationship between the elapsed time and the relation size. Along with the increase of the size of the two relations, the elapsed time of all algorithms also increased. However, the type 1 algorithms were more sensitive to this increase. The elapsed time increased linearly with the size of the relations. The reason for this is that the bottleneck in these tests is the network. The amount of data transferred increases when the relation sizes increases. Figure 10 shows the same system and relation sizes with a high bandwidth network (600 Mbps). The first observation is that the type 1 algorithms outperform the type 2 algorithms when the relations were small. Second, the elapsed time of all algorithms increases to some extent when the relations become larger. The type 1 algorithms were still more sensitive to the relation sizes. When the relation sizes become larger, their performance become worse than the type 2 algorithms.

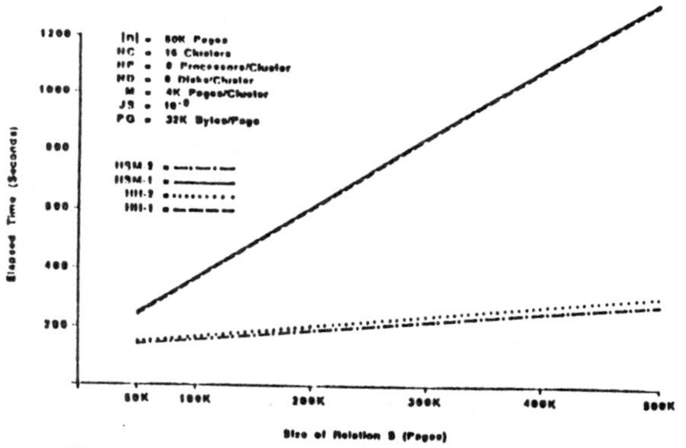

Figure 9: Elapsed Time vs. Relation Sizes.

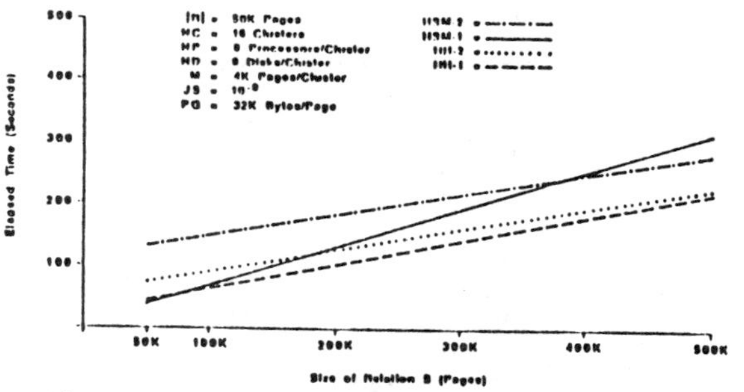

Figure 10: Elapsed Time vs. Relation Sizes (Faster Network).

5. Conclusions

In this paper, we have described six different parallel and pipelined join algorithms. Some results from our analysis are also presented to compare those algorithms. The results of our performance evaluation reiterate the relative performance superiority of the hash-based algorithms compared to sort-based algorithms. Our results also show how the effects of overlaps among the different steps of an algorithm effect its relative performance. We calculate the bottlenecks in the alternative join algorithms and show that the performance of an algorithm improves by distributing the tasks across the various non-overlapping stages of the algorithm so that maximum overlap and equitable resource utilization are achieved. Our results show that intercluster communication bandwidth is typically a bottleneck, and thus, the algorithm or system configuration that reduces intercluster data transfer is preferred. The replicated versions of the algorithms typically perform better than their non-replicated counterparts because of the reduced intercluster data transfer.

From this study, we can state some basic conclusions about parallel processing of join operations in the multiprocessor environment.

(1) The different performance shown by the algorithms studied indicates that it is important to choose appropriate algorithms for a particular join operation with a given system configuration. Furthermore, with a given system and relations to be joined, the query optimizer has to carefully determine the number of clusters, the number of disks and the number of processors that will be used in the join. Generally speaking, the hash-based algorithms outperform the sort-merge algorithms if the output tuples are not required in the sorted order. However, in the case that the source relations are already sorted, or the applications require the output tuples be sorted on the join attributes, the sort-merge algorithms may be advantageous. One possibility not mentioned is that of using an order-preserving hash function in the hash-based sort-merge algorithms. The sorted order is maintained between different buckets, and the final output tuples can thus be in the desired sorted order. The use of an order-preserving hash function should not introduce heavy extra cost.

(2) In multiprocessor-multidisk systems, high parallelism can be achieved by dividing the total processing task among processors and disks and executing the subtasks concurrently. However, in some algorithms, such as the sort-merge algorithms evaluated in this study, the parallel processing becomes difficult for some steps (final merge, for example). Increasing of the number of processes cannot speed up the processing. On the other hand, the hash-based algorithms are naturally parallelizable. Both the partitioning and joining phase can be concurrently executed by all participating processors. This is the main factro that explains why the hash-based algorithms outperform the sort-merge algorithms with regard to the elapsed time.

(3) Among the three major system resources, CPU, disk and communication network, CPU seems to not be the bottleneck of the processing pipeline in general (only in some steps of the sort-merge joins as mentioned above). For hash-based algorithms a small number of processors at each cluster is enough to provide the necessary processing power. On the other hand, disk I/O can be the bottleneck of the pipeline, although we intentionally used large page size (32K) and very high disk-memory transfer rate in our study. One possible approach is to increase the number of disks at each clusters. This multi-disk system can efficiently remove the bottleneck caused by slow disk I/O. However, the number of disks that can be attached to one cluster must be limited by the complexity of control.

For joins with small or moderate size relations, communications cost should not be a dominant factor in local area networks [Lu85], there is, however, still the possibility that the communications line becomes a bottleneck when a large amount of data has to be transferred in a very large system through the communications line. This is especially true for the algorithms where a large amount of data transfer is required (such as HSM1 and HH1).

(4) One key point in the design of a parallel processing algorithm is to achieve maximum overlap among operations requiring different resources in order to increase the parallelism and reduce the effect of the resource that is the bottleneck of the pipeline. For example, in the hash-based algorithms, the remotely processed tuples can be transferred either during partitioning or right before their use in the joining phase. The total communication cost is the same in these two schemes, while their overlapping with disk I/O is different. In the first scheme, all communication occurs while the relations are partitioned. The second scheme distributes the communications cost; each relatively small amount of data transfer overlaps with disk I/O and CPU processing in the joining phases. Which scheme is better will depend on the relative speed of the disk I/O and data transfer over the network. This example reminds us that parallelism between different type of resources can be further increased by tuning the processing steps carefully for each algorithm. Furthermore, the precise analysis of such a parallel processing algorithm is very difficult. Some simulation or tests in real systems would be useful.

Since the system configuration, that is, the number of clusters, the number of processors, the number of disks, and the size of memory used in a join operation, affects the performance along with the relation size and selectivities, query optimization in this multiprocessor environment could be more complicated, and also more important. It might be a useful exercise to more thoroughly investigate the relative behavior of different algorithms with regard to the parameters and derive some heuristics to use in the query processing process for such a data flow database machine.

References

[Bitt83] Bitton, D, *et al.*, "Parallel Algorithms for the Execution of Relational Database Operations," *ACM TODS*, vol. 8, no. 3, Sept. 1983, pp. 324-353.

[Brat84] Bratsbergsengen, K., "Hashing Methods and Relational Algebra Operations," *Proc. Tenth Int'l. Conf. on Very Large Data Bases*, Singapore, Aug. 1984, pp. 323-333.

[DeWi79] DeWitt, D. J., "DIRECT - A Multiprocessor Organization for Supporting Relational Database Managment Systems," *IEEE Trans. Computers*, vol. C-28, no. 6, 1979.

[DeWi84] DeWitt, D. J., *et al.*, "Implementation

Techniques for Main Memory Database Systems," *Proc. SIGMOD '84*, June 1984, pp. 1-8.

[DeWi85] DeWitt, D. J., and Gerber, R., "Multiprocessor Hash-Based Join Algorithms," *Proc. VLDB 85*, Stockholm, Aug. 1985, pp. 151-164.

[DeWi86] DeWitt, D. J., *et al.*, "GAMMA - A High Performance Dataflow Database Machine," *Proc. VLDB 86*, Kyoto, Japan, Aug. 1986, pp. 228-237.

[Kits83] Kitsuregawa, M., Tanaka, H., and Motooka, T., "Application of Hash to Data Base Machine and its Architecture," *New Generation Computing*, vol. 1, no. 1, 1983, pp. 63-74.

[Knut73] Knuth, D. E., *The Art of Computer Programming, Volume 3 (Sorting and Searching)*, Addison-Wesley, Reading, MA, 1973.

[Lu85] Lu, H., and Carey, M. J., "Some Experimental Results on Distributed Join Algorithms in a Local Network," *Proc. VLDB 85*, Stockholm, Aug. 1985.

[Rich87] Richardson, J. P., Lu, H., and Mikkilineni, K., *Design and Evaluation of Parallel Pipelined Join Algorithms*, Honeywell Corporate Systems Development Division Technical Report (to appear).

[Schu79] Schuster, S. A., *et al.*, "RAP.2 - An Associative Processor for Databases and its Applications," *IEEE Trans. Computersl, vol. C-28, no. 6, 1979.*

[Shib84] Shibayama, S., *et al.*, "A Relational Database Machine with Large Semiconductor Disk and Hardware Relational Algebra Processor," *New Generation Computing*, vol. 2, no. 2, 1984.

[Su79] Su, S. Y. W., *et al.*, "The Architectural Features and Implementation Techniques of the Multicell CASSM," *IEEE Trans. Computers*, vol. C-28, no. 6, 1979.

[Tera83] Teradata Corporation, *DBC/1012 Data Base Computer Concepts and Facilities*, Inglewood, CA, Apr. 1983.

[Vald84] Valduriez, P., and Gardarin, G., "Join and Semijoin Algorithms for a Multiprocessor Database Machine," *ACM TODS*, vol. 9, no. 1, March 1984, pp. 133-161.

Chapter 5: Data Skew and Load Balancing

The effectiveness of parallel join processing depends on the ability to equally divide the load among the processors while minimizing the coordination and synchronization overhead. A factor that can impair the ability to parallelize relational operations, especially sort and join, is the amount of skew present in the data to be processed. In real databases, it is often found that certain values for a given attribute occur more frequently than other values.[1-3] This is inherent in the data and is not dependent on the access pattern. Lakshmi found that in the presence of skewed data, the speedup from conventional join algorithms may be severely limited because some processors may be overutilized and others are underutilized.[4] Even a single large-skewed element can cause the processor to which it is assigned to become overloaded. The problem is exacerbated for join operations because correlation in the data skew of each relation results in a join output that is quadratic in nature.

The load imbalance problem may not be so severe or may be easy to overcome in shared-everything systems as every processor can access any portion of data so that the balancing of load can be achieved with less cost. However, in shared-nothing systems, since a processor at one node has no direct access to the memory or disks of other nodes, load balancing among the processing nodes becomes more important and more difficult as well. Most of the recent work on parallel join algorithms indeed concentrated on handling data skew or balancing the join load across the processors in the system.[5-10] In principle, most of these algorithms adopt the three phase task-oriented approach: (1) task generation, (2) task allocation, and (3) task execution. However, the actual implementation of these phases may be interleaved, especially when load balancing is incorporated. Various kinds of optimization can be performed at each phase. In this chapter, we review the optimization issues and solutions that form the basis of design and implementation of load-balanced parallel join algorithms.

Issues and solutions

The issues and possible solutions involved in the design of load-balanced parallel join algorithms are summarized in Figure 5-1, which shows the framework of load-balanced parallel join algorithms.

Task generation

In the task generation phase, a join operation is split into a set of tasks. Each task is essentially a join of subrelations of the base relations. The union of the results of all the tasks should be the same as that from the operation without decomposition. Four basic issues in this phase are

- the decomposition of the base relations into subrelations,
- the number of tasks to be generated,
- the formation of tasks after decomposition, and
- the kind of statistics to be collected and maintained

Decomposition of the base relations. The basic criterion of decomposition is that the union of the results obtained from joining the subrelations (tasks) should be the same as the results of joining the original base relations. There are several ways to decompose the base relations, form tasks, and ensure accuracy:

- *Full fragmentation.* In this category, each tuple participates in only one task. Tasks are generated by partitioning the relations into buckets. Thus, only corresponding buckets from both relations need to be joined. Two techniques employed to partition a relation are range partitioning and hash partitioning. For the former, the range of possible values of the joining attribute is divided into several sub-ranges, one for each bucket. The latter employs a hashing function such that tuples hashed to the same value are grouped into the same partition. The full fragmentation technique is the most commonly used approach. Hybrid hash join, GRACE hash join, and their variants[5-7, 11] are examples that employ this method.

Fragmentation and replication. Although there is no replication in the full fragmentation decomposition technique, the fragmentation and replication decomposition technique allows partial replication of data. It employs the fragment-and-replicate strategy to generate tasks. For a join of two relations, the larger relation is split into buckets while the smaller relation is entirely replicated for each bucket. Each task comprises a bucket of the larger relation and the entire smaller relation. This approach is effective when the smaller relation fits in the memory. The nested-block join[12] is such an example.

Full replication. In full replication, both relations are replicated. The base relation is split into m buckets and the target relation into n buckets, and each of the m buckets will be joined with each of the n buckets, resulting in $m \times n$ tasks. Join algorithms that employ this method have been reported in References 13, 14, 15.

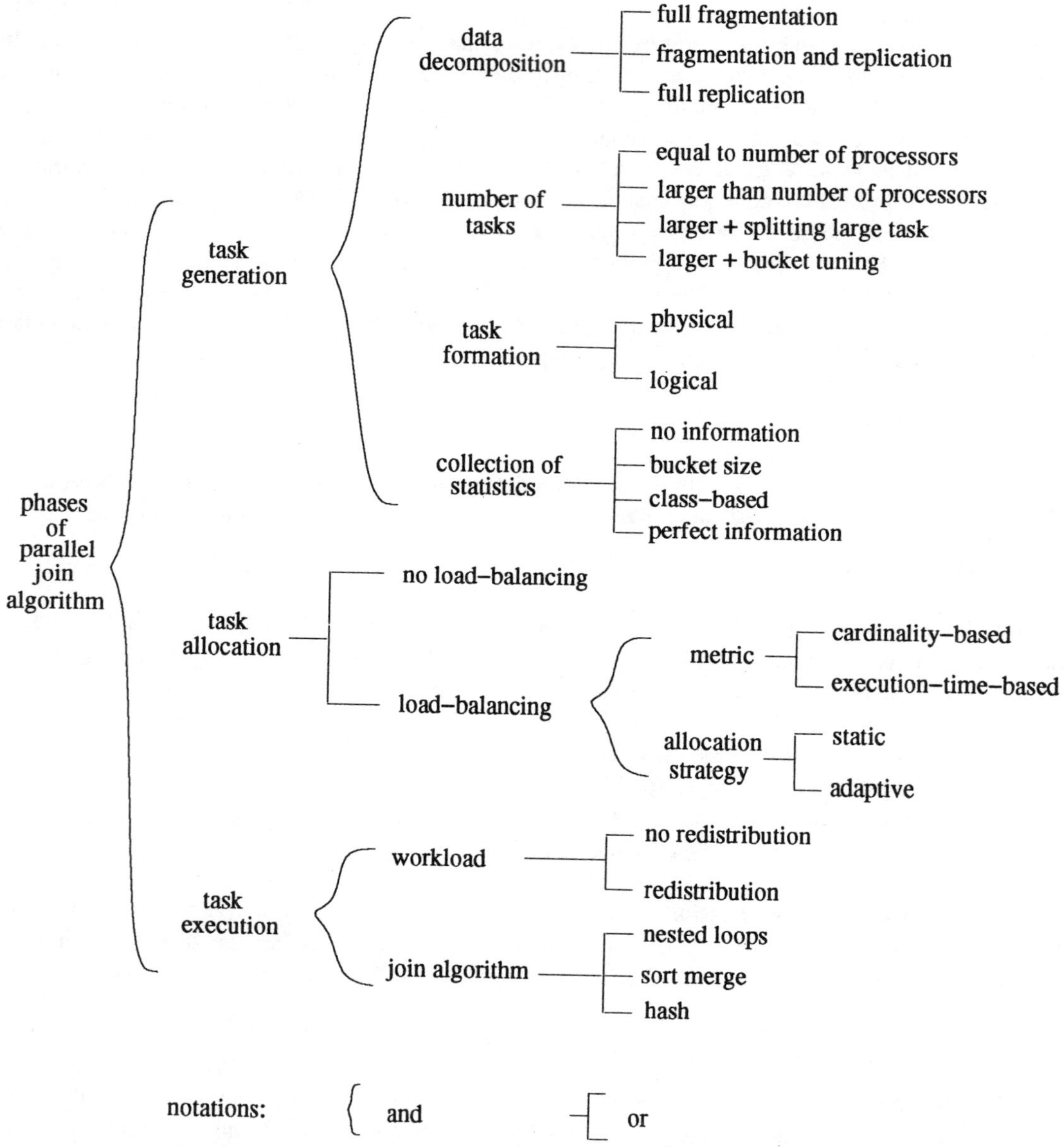

Figure 5-1. Issues and solutions in load-balanced parallel join algorithms.

The full fragmentation strategy seems to be most commonly used, but it is not effective when the data are highly skewed. In such cases, the other two approaches come in handy.

Number of tasks to be generated. The second issue in task generation is to find the optimal number of tasks. The number of tasks to be generated is limited by the decomposability of the tasks. It is also limited by the amount of memory at each processor since space is needed to store the information about the tasks. The optimal number of tasks to be generated is closely associated with the size of the data upon which an operation functions. A large number of tasks may be generated such that an operation works on only a few tuples of data. This may result in poor performance because of the overhead incurred in splitting the data and duplicating the operation, and the additional I/Os as a result of fragmented pages. On the other hand, a small number of tasks may not be favorable since this will limit the flexibility of allocating tasks to the processors and result in uneven load among the processors.

The four basic approaches to task generation that have been adopted in the literature for a system of p nodes are as follows.

1. Generate a task for each node; that is, p tasks will be generated. The GRACE hash join, hybrid hash join, and simple hash join[11] algorithms are examples that employ this strategy.

2. Generate more than p tasks and allocate these tasks to the nodes to satisfy some balancing criterion (to be discussed in the next section). The algorithms in Reference 6 use this approach.

3. Generate more than p tasks and increase the number of tasks prior to allocating these tasks. One approach to achieve this is by splitting large buckets (which exceed the size of the memory) into smaller ones that fit in the memory.[8-10,16]

4. Generate more than p tasks and reduce the number of buckets prior to allocating them to the nodes. The number of buckets may be reduced by "tuning the bucket size" so that several small buckets are combined to form a larger bucket (as long as the larger bucket fits in the memory). GRACE hash join[17] is such an example.

Task formation. The third issue in task generation is whether the tasks generated are physically or logically formed. By physically-formed tasks, we mean that the data associated with the two buckets for each task are located at a single node. On the other hand, the data that correspond to a task may be declustered across several nodes and form a logical task. While a physical task may be processed at the node where it resides, data associated with a logical task must be assembled before it can be processed. However, logical tasks are more useful for load balancing. Both approaches have been explored in the literature and can be found in References 6 and 11 and References 6, 9, and 10, respectively.

Statistics collection. The last related issue in task generation is the statistics to be collected and kept during task generation. These statistics can then be used by the task allocation/load-balancing phase to determine how the tasks are to be allocated. In one extreme, we do not need any information and "blindly" allocate the tasks. In the other extreme, we have perfect information with a prior knowledge of the bucket sizes and result sizes. In Reference 6, only the bucket size is maintained. Alternatively, we can organize the number of distinct values into "equivalence" classes; the data maintained are (1) the number of distinct classes (e), (2) for each class i, the number of distinct attributes (d_i) (if all classes have the same number, then one value is kept), and (3) for each class i, the number of tuples from both the base relations (r_i/s_i). (The ideal case, [perfect information]: the number of distinct attributes per class should be 1; that is, $d_i = 1$ $\forall\, i$, so that the number of distinct attributes is exactly the same as the number of classes. In this case, the statistics will provide an exact result size and therefore allow a good estimate of the processing cost of the bucket at a node. In Reference 19, this case is assumed; however, such detailed information consumes memory and is feasible only for large amounts of memory.) Thus, we can estimate the result size as follows:

$$\sum_{i=1}^{e} \frac{r_i \cdot s_i}{d_i} \tag{5.1}$$

With the bucket and result size information, the execution time of a join may be estimated.[9, 10]

Task allocation/Load balancing phase

After the base relations have been partitioned, we have a pool of tasks (logical or physical) that can be allocated to the nodes for concurrent processing. There are basically two strategies to allocate these tasks to different nodes in the system:

1. *Allocate tasks without load balancing.* The straightforward way to allocate the tasks is to preassign tasks to nodes. When the tasks are generated, they are sent to the appropriate nodes. Earlier work that adopted this approach shows that it is effective when the loads across the nodes are approximately the same[11]. However, the performance could be very poor when the loads are unequally distributed as a result of factors such as data skew.[4,18]

2. *Allocate tasks with load balancing.* With a large number of tasks, tasks can be allocated to the nodes such that the load across the system nodes is approximately the same. The most commonly used heuristics to allocate the tasks are the best-fit-like and first-fit-like strategies that generally work in two phases: (1) the tasks are sorted according to some criterion, and (2) the tasks are allocated in descending order in a "greedy manner" (the next task to be allocated is sent to the node that is expected to finish first). This leads to several issues that concern the load metrics and allocation strategies.

Load metrics. The first issue is the notion of a "balanced system." What criterion should we use to ensure a balanced system? Two commonly used criteria, or load metrics, are the cardinality of the buckets and the estimated execution time:

- *Cardinality.* With this criterion, the objective is to balance the nodes based on the size of the partition so that each node processes approximately the same number of tuples.[6,7] The inherent assumption is that the processing time is proportional to the number of tuples processed.

- *Estimated execution time.* The time to process each task is first estimated using some cost models. The tasks are then allocated so that each node will complete them at about the same time.[9,10] This approach will perform well if statistics that provide an accurate estimation of the execution time of each task are available.

Allocation strategy. The second issue concerns the allocation strategy; that is, how each task is to be allocated. These may be categorized as static and adaptive methods:

- *Static.* In static approaches, all the tasks generated are allocated prior to the execution of the tasks. Thus, each node knows exactly what tasks to process. Most of the published works on load-balanced join algorithms are static.[6,7,9,10]

- *Adaptive.* The main feature of the adaptive approach is that task allocation is demand-driven. Each node will process a task and will acquire the next task only when the current task is processed. In this way, each node knows only the task that it is processing and has no idea what will be the next task. To the best of our knowledge, this approach has not been studied in shared-nothing systems. However, it was adopted in a shared disk environment.[16]

Task execution

In the task execution phase, each node will independently perform the join of the tasks allocated to it. The main issues here concern the redistribution of workload and the choice of join algorithms for each task at each node.

Workload. There are two ways to handle the existing workload:

- *No redistribution of workload.* In this case, once the execution phase begins, there is no redistribution of workload allocated to a node. If the system is unbalanced, it will remain so. Most of the static load-balanced join algorithms fall in this category.

- *Redistribution of workload.* In this case, to avoid an unbalanced system, workload may be redistributed. Tasks may migrate during the execution phase from an overloaded node to an underloaded node. This may be achieved by introducing a task redistribution strategy to redistribute the workload. For example, x overloaded nodes may redistribute their load to y underloaded nodes. The granularity of the workload to be redistributed may be restricted to a whole task as originally generated during the task generation phase or may be a subtask generated from a task for the purpose of distribution. Reference 16 introduces this strategy but restricts the redistribution to only two nodes — a donor and an idle node. More recently, workload redistribution has been employed in shared nothing systems.[20]

Table 5-1. Summary of some existing load-balanced join algorithms.

Algorithm	Task generation	Load balancing	Task execution
Simple hash (Reference 11) (SN)	full fragmentation, # of processors, physical, no information	no load balancing	no workload redistribution, hash
GRACE hash (Reference 11) (SN)		same as Simple hash join	
Hybrid hash (Reference 11) (SN)		same as Simple hash join	
ABJ (Reference 6) (SN)	full fragmention, large, physical, bucket size	load balancing, cardinality, static	no workload redistribution, hash
ABJ+ (Reference 6) (SN)	full fragmention, large, logical, bucket size	load balancing, cardinality, static	no workload redistribution, hash
Scheduling hash (10) (SN)	full fragmention, large+split, logical, class-based	load balancing, execution time, static	no workload redistribution, hash
SVMHHJ (Reference 20) (SN)	full fragmentation, # of processors, physical, no information	no load balancing	workload redistribution, hash
DLPJ (Reference 16) (SD)	full fragmention, large, logical, class-based	load balancing, execution time, adaptive	workload redistribution, hash
Balanced hash (Reference 8) (SE)	full fragmention, large+split, physical, bucket size	load balancing, cardinality, static	workload redistribution, hash

Local join methods. Any uniprocessor join method may be used for each local join. Most of the uniprocessor algorithms can be categorized into

- nested-loops join,
- sort-merge join, and
- hash join.

Studies have shown that none of the methods are superior in all cases. In general, nested-loops join performs well when one of the relations is small and fits in the memory or when an index exists on the inner relation; sort-merge is superior when both relations are already sorted; and hash join performs best when enough main memory is available and when the join attribute values are uniformly distributed.

Load-balanced parallel join algorithms

In the above sections, we have discussed the basic issues that must be addressed when designing a load-balanced parallel join algorithm. Based on the various methods used to process each phase of the algorithm, we can derive a large set of load-balanced join algorithms from the product of a number of methods in each phase. Table 5-1 summarizes some of the existing join algorithms based on the issues discussed above.

Static and dynamic load balancing

Load balancing strategies fall into two categories: static load balancing and dynamic load balancing. In this section, we give a further discussion on these two types of strategies.

Static load balancing

Static load-balanced join algorithms balance the load of processors when the tasks are allocated to the processors. Once a task is initiated for execution, it will not migrate from one processor to another. The following is an example of such an algorithm.

1. The number of tasks generated is usually larger than the number of processors in the system. Each task, obtained from partitioning the two base relations, *R* and *S*, is the join of two corresponding buckets of *R* and *S* in the fully fragmented case, or one bucket of *R* and all of *S* in the fragment-and-replicate case. To generate buckets of a relation, each processor *i*, where $1 \leq i \leq p$ and *p* is the number of processors in the system, allocates one output buffer for each of the *B* buckets, where *B* is the number of desired buckets (limited by the amount of memory available at each node). Each processor then independently scans the portion of the relation stored in its local disks. Tuples read are hashed and moved to the corresponding output buffers based on the hash results. When a buffer is full, the tuples are sent to the processors to which they are assigned through the interconnection network.

2. When each relation is being partitioned, each processor also collects statistics for the buckets that it produces based on the fragments of the relation that reside at the node. Once both relations are partitioned, each node will collect the statistics of the tasks allocated to it and estimate the time to process each of the tasks. At the same time, one processor, which is designated as coordinator, computes the average completion time and broadcasts this information to all the nodes.

3. Based on the estimated average completion time, each processor will find the smallest number of tasks such that the completion time of these tasks will not exceed the average completion time. In essence, we want to find *k* tasks, where *k* is the smallest number of tasks that satisfy the condition:

$$\sum_{j=1}^{k} Cost_j \leq Cost_{avg} \text{ and } \sum_{j=1}^{k+1} Cost_j > Cost_{avg}$$

   where $Cost_j$ and $Cost_{avg}$ are the time to process the jth task and the average completion time, respectively. A processor is considered as overloaded if *k* is less than the number of tasks assigned to it; otherwise, it is underloaded. Each processor reports to the coordinator the difference between its load and the average load. The excess tasks from the overloaded processors are reassigned to the underloaded ones so that each processor has its load close to the average load.

4. After the load redistribution, each processor performs a local join on each of the tasks assigned to it. There is no redistribution of workload once execution begins.

One shortcoming of the above balancing strategy is that the granularity of load balancing is an entire task as produced from the task generation phase. If the join attributes in the base relations are highly skewed, it is very likely that a processor will be overloaded with one or two large tasks, causing a performance bottleneck in the whole system. Furthermore, to reallocate the tasks will incur unnecessary overhead of data transfer. Two possible solutions are

1. to form logical tasks rather than physical tasks and transfer the data only to the final execution processor or

2. to split expensive tasks into smaller (and less expensive) tasks.

To form logical tasks, each processor partitions the relations and writes the partitions back to local disks instead of sending them to the predetermined processors. The so-called expensive tasks are split into subtasks using the fragment-and-replicate algorithm by dividing the bucket from one relation into approximately k equal-sized buckets and duplicating the corresponding bucket from the other relation. In this way, the set of tasks is increased by $k - 1$ tasks after each splitting of a task. Note that the splitting is logical since the actual buckets for the task are still stored at different processors. Finally, the tasks are assigned to processors using some algorithms, to minimize the estimated completion time. One such algorithm is the greedy LPT algorithm[21] that iteratively allocates the most expensive of the remaining tasks to the processors with the least (estimated) processing time until no more tasks are left in the system. The physical task formation is then done by transferring the buckets across the network.

Dynamic load balancing

Dynamic load-balancing algorithms distinguish themselves from the static ones by redistributing tasks, which may be partially executed from one processor to another processor. The task generation phase and the allocation phase of a dynamic load-balanced join algorithm are similar to those of static ones. However, the task execution phase is different.

1. During task execution, each node maintains certain information about the task that is being processed, including the size of data remaining (in pages) and the size of the result generated so far. Such information is necessary in order to make correct decisions regarding transferring loads across nodes during task execution.

2. When a node finishes the processing of all its allocated tasks, it will request a load from a node that has not completed the execution of its allocated tasks. The overloaded node(s) and the amount of load to be transferred are then determined. The task transfer is realized by shipping data buckets from the donor to the idle nodes.

Different strategies can be used to determine the donor and the amount of data to be transferred. Also, the overhead incurred for this transfer can be carried by different processors. The process of transferring load during the execution phase can be summarized as follows:

1. The idle node sends a load-request message to the coordinator to ask for more work.

2. At the coordinator site, requests are queued in a first come-first-served basis. The coordinator will then broadcast a load-information message to all nodes.

3. Upon receiving the load-information message, each node computes its current load and sends it to the coordinator.

4. The coordinator determines the donor and sends a transfer-load message to the donor, after which the coordinator will proceed to serve the next request. Or, if there are multiple requests in the queue, the coordinator could select k busy nodes as the donors of the first k requests in the queue.

5. The donor determines the load to be transferred and sends the load to the idle node. Once the load is determined, the donor proceeds to compute its new processing load for another request.

This process of transferring loads between a busy node and an idle node is repeated until the minimum completion time has been achieved.

As in all load-balancing algorithms, there are a number of important issues involved in this process:

- What information to what accuracy should each processor maintain to facilitate load balancing? Large amounts of information and frequent updates will incur heavy overhead. Less and outdated information may lead to ineffective load-balancing decisions.
- Which processors, the donor or the task receiver, should initiate the load-balancing process?
- Which processors should be chosen as task donors when some processors become idle?
- What is the amount of load that should be transferred?

In the above description, the number of processed pages and the number of pages generated from these processed pages are the major information maintained at each processor that is to be used to estimate the completion time. The load transfer process will be initiated by the idle processors. While these solutions are more or less independent of the system and the join methods, the determination of donor and the amount of load to be transferred are related to the join methods used.

When an idle node requests work, any busy node can be a donor. Intuitively, the donor should be the most heavily loaded processor since it will determine the completion time of the full join. If the estimated completion time (ECT) is used as the measure of the load of a processor, then the processor with the maximum ECT will be chosen by the coordinator as the donor with ties being arbitrarily broken. In short, node i is the donor when (assuming p nodes in the system)

$$ECT_i = max_{j=1}^{p} \ (ECT_j)$$

When there are k unprocessed tasks at node i, ECT_i at node i is given by

$$ECT_i = \sum_{j=1}^{k} EET_{ij} + EFT_i$$

The first component, $\sum_{j=1}^{k} EET_{ij}$, is the total estimated execution time of the tasks at node i that are yet to be processed. EET is estimated based on the statistics collected and is determined by the cost formula of the local join; that is,

$$EET = JoinCost\ (|R|, |S|, |Result|)$$

where $|R|$, $|S|$ are the sizes (in pages) of the source and target buckets of the task and the estimated result size, $|Result|$.

The second component, EFT_i, is the estimated finished time of the task that is currently being processed at node i, the time needed to complete the processing of the currently executed task. Given a task with bucket sizes $|R|$ and $|S|$ respectively, EFT is determined using the following expression:

$$JoinCost(|R|, |S|, |Result|) = JoinCost(r, s, res) - EFT$$

where r and s are respectively the number of pages (including the page that is currently being processed) of R and S already processed, and res is the number of result tuples produced using these tuples. Recall that r, s, and res can be derived from the processing information maintained.

To determine the amount of load that should be transferred from the overloaded processor to the idle processor, the following heuristics seem reasonable:

1. *Unprocessed task first.* If there are unprocessed tasks at the donor processor, an unprocessed task is to be transferred.

2. *The amount of load transferred should be large enough to provide a gain in the completion time of the join operation.* As the transfer of load involves some overhead, this heuristic ensures that the reduction of expected completion time of the donor gained from the load transfer should be larger than the incurred overhead.

3. *The amount of load transferred should not be too large so that the expected completion time of the receiver will not exceed that of its donor.* This heuristic will avoid transferring tasks between two processors back and forth, or transferring a task among a number of processors.

Note that the first heuristic tries to transfer unprocessed tasks if possible. Transferring the unprocessed task is quite often less complicated and more effective than transferring a task that is in execution. If a task has not been processed yet, the load transfer simply sends the related buckets from the donor to the receiver. It is the only overhead involved. If a task is in execution, it would not be as simple and there might be some repeated work. Assume that the hash-based nested-loops join method is used for the joining of the local buckets. There are two possible cases

1. Among the two corresponding buckets, the hash table for the small one, say the R-bucket, can be staged in memory.

2. Neither bucket is small enough to fit in the available memory.

Assume that the load transfer happens after the task starts its execution; for example, a hash table has been built in the memory. In the first case, the whole R-bucket and a portion of the unprocessed S-bucket should be transferred. Therefore, the hash table of R-buckets is built twice, once at the donor site and again at the receiver site. In the second case, a portion of the unprocessed R-buckets and the entire S-bucket should be transferred. In this case, the computation determining the amount of R-tuples to be transferred is a bit more complicated.

Comments

Performance studies on static load-balanced join algorithms were conducted in References 5 and 6. We briefly summarize their findings here. When the data are uniformly distributed or lowly skewed, algorithms that do not attempt to balance the system load perform best. However, the performance of such algorithms degrade as the data skew becomes more serious. Static load-balanced algorithms that introduce some form of preprocessing generally do not perform well for low data skew because of the additional preprocessing cost. However, they perform well at high data skew. On the other hand, dynamic algorithms seem to perform well in most cases. However, because of the overhead incurred during join computation to redistribute data, their performance is expected to be slightly worse than that of static approaches (with good estimates) at high data skew.

For applications that do not modify their databases frequently, static load-balanced join algorithms are the suitable choice. In such an environment, the preprocessing phase can be bypassed by keeping such information in the system catalogue. However, when modifications are common, the lack of accurate statistics and the preprocessing cost to be incurred make static algorithms unattractive. In this case, dynamic algorithms are preferred.

Papers in this chapter

The first paper, "Effectiveness of Parallel Joins," is by Lakshmi and Yu. The paper identifies two major factors that may affect the exploitation of parallelism: the skew in the distribution of join attribute values and the stochastic nature of the task processing time. The results clearly indicate the need for efficient load-balanced join algorithms.

The next two papers present static load-balanced join algorithms. "Performance Analysis of a Load Balancing Relational Hash-Join Algorithm for a Shared-Memory Multiprocessor" by Omiecinski, proposes a hash-based join algorithm that has the following features: (1) Several tasks may be processed each time and (2) Tasks are allocated different numbers of processors depending on the join load. The other paper, by Hua and Lee, is "Handling Data Skew in Multicomputer Database Systems Using Partition Tuning." The study is based upon a shared-nothing environment. Three static load-balancing algorithms are proposed; two attempt to avoid data skew before it occurs and the third tries to resolve skew when it occurs.

The last paper is "Dynamic and Load-Balanced Task-Oriented Database Query Processing in Parallel Systems," by Lu and Tan. It proposes a dynamic load-balanced query processing technique for shared disk environments. In particular, the data structures of an algorithm for processing join are described.

References

1. S. Christodoulakis, "Estimating Record Selectivities," *Information Systems,* Vol. 8, No. 2, 1983, pp. 105-115.
2. C.A. Lynch, "Selectivity Estimation and Query Optimization in Large Databases with Highly Skewed Distribution of Column Values," *Proc. 14th Int'l Conf. Very Large Data Bases,* Morgan Kaufman, San Mateo, Calif., 1988.
3. A.Y. Montgomery, D.J. D'Souza, and S.B. Lee, "The Cost of Relational Algebraic Operations on Skewed Data: Estimates and Experiments," *Information Processing 83,* 1983.
4. M.S. Lakshmi and P.S. Yu, "Effectiveness of Parallel Joins," *IEEE Trans. Knowledge and Data Eng.,* Vol. 2, No. 3, Sept. 1990, pp. 410-424.
5. D.J. DeWitt et al., "Practical Skew Handling in Parallel Joins," *Proc. 18th Int'l Conf. Very Large Data Bases,* Morgan Kaufman, San Mateo, Calif., 1992.
6. K.A. Hua and C. Lee, "Handling Data Skew in Multiprocessor Database Computers Using Partition Tuning," *Proc. 17th Int'l Conf. Very Large Data Bases,* Morgan Kaufman, San Mateo, Calif., 1991, pp. 525-535.
7. M. Kitsuregawa and Y. Ogawa, "Bucket Spreading Parallel Hash: A New, Robust, Parallel Hash Join Method for Data Skew in the Super Database Computer (SDC)," *Proc. 16th Int'l Conf. Very Large Data Bases,* Morgan Kaufman, San Mateo, Calif., 1990, pp. 210-221.
8. E. Omiecinski, "Performance Analysis of a Load-Balancing Relational Hash Join Algorithm for a Shared-Memory Multiprocessor," *Proc. 17th Int'l Conf. Very Large Data Bases,* Morgan Kaufman, San Mateo, Calif., 1991, pp. 375-385.
9. J.L. Wolf et al., "An Effective Algorithm for Parallelizing Sort Merge Joins in the Presence of Data Skew," *Proc. Second Int'l Symp. Databases in Parallel and Distributed Systems,* IEEE CS Press, Los Alamitos, Calif., 1990, pp. 103-115.
10. J.L. Wolf et al., "An Effective Algorithm for Parallelizing Hash Joins in the Presence of Data Skew," *Proc. Seventh Int'l Conf. Data Eng.,* IEEE CS Press, Los Alamitos, Calif., 1991, pp. 200-209.
11. D.A. Schneider and D.J. DeWitt, "A Performance Evaluation of Four Parallel Join Algorithms in a Shared-Nothing Multiprocessor Environment," *Proc ACM Int'l Conf. Management of Data,* Assoc. for Computing Machinery, New York, N.Y., 1989, pp. 110-121.
12. P. Valduriez and G. Gardarin, "Join and Semijoin Algorithms for a Multiprocessor Database Machine," *ACM Trans. Database Systems,* Vol. 9, No. 1, Mar. 1984, pp. 133-161.
13. A.M. Keller and S. Roy, "Adaptive Parallel Hash Join in Main-Memory Databases," *Proc. First Int'l Conf. Parallel and Distributed Information Systems,* IEEE CS Press, Los Alamitos, Calif., 1991, pp. 58-67.
14. J.P. Richardson, H. Lu, and K. Mikkilineni, "Design and Evaluation of Parallel Pipelined Join Algorithms," *Proc. ACM Int'l Conf. Management of Data,* Assoc. for Computing Machinery, New York, N.Y., 1987, pp. 399-409.
15. J.W. Stamos and H.C. Young, "A Symmetric Fragment and Replicate Algorithm for Distributed Joins," Tech. Report RJ 7188, IBM Almaden Research Center, 1989.
16. H. Lu and K.L. Tan, "Dynamic and Load-Balanced Task-Oriented Database Query Processing in Parallel Systems," *Proc. Third Int'l Conf. Extending Data Base Technology,* 1992, pp. 357-372.
17. M. Kitsuregawa, H. Tanaka, and T. Moto-oka, "Application of Hash to Data Base Machine and its Architecture," *New Generation Computing,* Vol. 1, No. 1, 1983.
18. C.B. Walton, A.G. Dale, and R.M. Jenevein, "A Taxonomy and Performance Model of Data Skew Effects in Parallel Joins," *Proc. 17th Int'l Conf. on Very Large Data Bases,* Morgan Kaufman, San Mateo, Calif., 1991, pp. 536-548.
19. A. Swami and H.C. Young, "Online Algorithms for Handling Skew in Parallel Joins," Tech. Report RJ 8363, IBM Almaden Research Center, Sept. 1991.
20. A. Shatdal and J.F. Naughton, "Using Shared Virtual Memory for Parallel Join Processing," *Proc. ACM Int'l Conf. Management Data,* Assoc. for Computing Machinery, New York, N.Y., 1993, pp. 119-128.
21. R. Graham, "Bounds on Multiprocessing Timing Anomalies," *SIAM J. Computing,* Vol. 1, No. 7, 1969, pp. 416-429.

Effectiveness of Parallel Joins

M. Seetha Lakshmi and Philip S. Yu, *Senior Member, IEEE*

***Abstract*— This paper examines the effectiveness of parallel processing of relational join operations. The skew in the distribution of join attribute values and the stochastic nature of the task processing times are identified as the major factors that can affect the effective exploitation of parallelism. Expressions for the execution time of parallel hash join and semijoin are derived and their effectiveness analyzed. When many small processors are used in the parallel architecture, the skew can result in some processors becoming sources of bottleneck while other processors are being underutilized. Even in the absence of skew, the variations in the processing times of the parallel tasks belonging to a query can lead to high task synchronization delay and impact the maximum speedup achievable through parallel execution. For example, when the task processing time on each processor is exponential with the same mean, the speedup is proportional to $P/\ln(P)$ where P is the number of processors. Other factors such as memory size, communication bandwidth, etc., can lead to even lower speedup. These are quantified using analytical models.**

***Index Terms*—Data skew, database machine, parallel join, performance analysis, relational database, task time distribution.**

I. Introduction

As QUERIES become more complex and relations grow larger, performance becomes an increasingly critical issue in database applications running on uniprocessor configurations. Parallel processing of database operations is an attractive alternative which is expected to improve the response time. Parallel architectures which exploit a large number of processors is an area of active research. In recent years, there have been several proposals, prototypes, and commercial systems making use of parallel processor based architectures for database applications [6], [7], [28], [34]. All these systems distribute the data across several storage units and deploy the available processing power near each of the storage units. The processing power is mostly derived from relatively inexpensive microprocessors. The rationale behind a distributed approach is that data can be accessed in parallel from all the storage units, and further, the data can be processed in parallel by all the processors. The parallel architecture is also expected to offer incremental and horizontal growth potential along with linear improvements in performance.

To exploit parallelism, queries have to be divided into multiple tasks which can run on all the processors in parallel. The effectiveness of parallel execution depends upon our ability to equally divide the load among the processors while simultaneously minimizing the coordination and synchronization overhead. A factor that can impair our ability to parallelize join queries in a straightforward fashion is the amount of skew present in the data to be joined. In real databases, it is often found that certain values for a given attribute occur more frequently than other values [5], [24], [27]. Lynch [24] notes, for example, that for many textual databases, the data distribution follows a variant of Zipf's law [36]. This nonuniformity is referred to as data skew. It is an inherent characteristic of the data and does not depend on the access pattern. When the parallel architecture employs many small processors, the data skew can result in some processors having too many tuples to process while other processors are being underutilized. Another aspect that can lead to load imbalance is the processing time characteristics. Even when the tuples to be joined are equally distributed across all the processors, the actual processing time on each processor can vary widely due to the stochastic nature of the execution time in each processor. Factors such as the random accesses to memory/disk, the join selectivity, the predicate selectivity, the number of predicates processed, etc., can contribute to the variations in task processing time in different processors. In this paper, we study the performance of relational join operations on a message passing parallel architecture. We identify the different parameters that can affect the performance and examine the robustness of the parallel architecture with respect to these parameters, using analytic models.

To our knowledge, there is no prior work dealing with skew or variations in task processing time in parallel database architectures. [2], [10], [31], [29], and [34] have evaluated the performance of different database machines. Most of these studies have focused on determining the execution time of a single query on a particular database machine architecture. [11] evaluated the tradeoffs in coupling small and large processors for transaction processing, while [14] presents a study of the tradeoffs between a multimicroprocessor database machine and a large conventional mainframe-based database management system for simple queries in a transaction processing environment. They both considered parallelism in a limited sense—only sequential execution of simple queries by each processor and concurrent execution of several simple queries by the system were studied. They did not consider parallel execution of complex queries such as join queries. A detailed study of join query performance is presented in this paper.

In Section II, a brief description of a loosely coupled message passing parallel architecture is given. The parallel join algorithms modeled in this paper are described in Section III. Both hash join and the use of semijoin in conjunction with hash join are being considered. Discussions of data skew appear in Section IV and discussions of task time distributions appear in Section V. The assumptions and the various parameters used in the analysis are introduced in Section VI. The analytical expressions for the execution time of a join query are derived in Section VII. The performance results from the analysis are examined in Section VIII. The conclusions and future directions are discussed in Section IX.

II. Architectural Model

Examples of parallel architectures for database applications can be found in [15], [6], [9], [28], and [34]. In general, they consist of several processors linked through an interconnection network. The processors communicate with each other by exchanging messages across the network or through shared memory segments. In this paper, the term database machine (DBMC) is

Manuscript received May 15, 1989; revised November 15, 1989.

M. S. Lakshmi was with IBM T. J. Watson Research Center, Yorktown Heights, NY 10598 when this work was performed. She is now with IBM Application Systems Division, Dallas, TX 76299.

P. S. Yu is with the IBM Research Division, T. J. Watson Research Center, Yorktown Heights, NY 10598.

IEEE Log Number 9040092.

used to refer to the message passing architecture. A schematic of a DBMC is given in Fig. 1 and the features relevant to the performance study are discussed below.

The DBMC consists of two sets of processors—database processors and control processors. These are linked through an interconnection network. There are one or more disks attached to each database processor. Each relation in the database is horizontally partitioned, based on a key attribute, and distributed across all the disks. Each database processor is responsible for the data residing in the disks associated with it. All processors have their own memory, operating system, etc., and function autonomously in accessing the data from their local disks. However, they cooperate and communicate with each other by exchanging messages through the interconnection network. The network could be a point to point network, a bus such as Ethernet, or a token ring network such as the one used in GAMMA [9]. The function of the control processors is twofold; they interface to the users as well as control and coordinate the database activities. They do not perform any direct data manipulation. However, they have access to the information on catalog, directory, index table information, etc., and hence can determine which database processors have to be activated to access a particular tuple. In accessing tuples with a given key value, the control processors would activate only the relevant database processors. For a join or a selection based on a table scan, all the database processors would be activated.

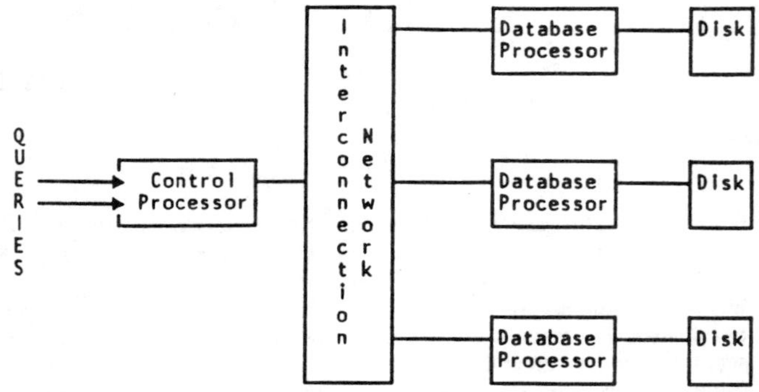

Fig. 1. Database machine.

III. Join Algorithm

Nested loop, sort/merge, and hash-based algorithms are the most commonly used join algorithms. Performance of these algorithms has been reported in [4], [7], [8], [26], [33], and [34]. The nested loop algorithm has been found to be useful only when the relations to be joined are relatively small. When the relations are large, hash-based algorithms are superior to sort/merge provided 1) the relations are not already in sorted order or 2) the final result need not be sorted before presenting it to the user. In this paper, the performance of a parallel hash-based join algorithm is being evaluated. Use of semijoin and its impact on the performance are also being examined.

A. Hash Join

First, an outline of the hash join algorithm in a single processor environment is given. Subsequently, its generalization to the multiprocessor environment is described. Let R and S be the two relations to be joined, with R being the smaller relation. When R is smaller than the available memory, the hash join algorithm works as follows: for each tuple in R, the join attribute is first hashed and the hash result is used to decide where to insert the tuple into the hash table in memory. Then relation S is scanned sequentially. For each tuple in S, the join attribute is hashed and used to probe R's hash table in memory. When a match is found the corresponding tuples from the two relations are concatenated and added to the result relation.

Three extensions to the above algorithm for situations where R exceeds the size of available memory are presented in [7] and [33]. Among the three, the hybrid hash join algorithm was shown to be the most efficient algorithm. A parallel version of the hybrid hash join algorithm, for the multiprocessor system, is described below in detail.

B. Parallel Hash Join

As mentioned in Section II, the relations are horizontally partitioned based on a key attribute and equally distributed across all the processors. Let R_i and S_i be the portion of R and S residing at processor i. The parallel hybrid hash join algorithm has two phases. (In an efficient implementation the two phases may overlap.) In the first phase, called the distribution phase, the two relations are hashed on their join attribute and redistributed among the processors such that corresponding hash partitions of the two relations reside on the same processor. In the event that the join attribute of R or S is also the key attribute on which it is originally partitioned, then the relation is not hashed and redistributed. In the second phase, called the join phase, the hash partitions are joined independently by each processor in parallel.

A schematic of an example parallel hash join is shown in Fig. 2. During phase one, all the processors use a predefined hash function h_1 and number of hash partitions P. In the example, mod *3* is used as h_1. There are as many hash partitions as there are processors. The domain of the join attribute is mapped onto the P disjoint partitions by associating a set of possible hash values with each partition. Each processor allocates one or more output buffers to each of the P hash buckets. Then, it reads its portion (R_i) of relation R from the disk and hashes the join attribute of each tuple. The tuples are moved to one of the P buckets based on their hash values. As the buffers fill up, they are sent across the network to the appropriate processors. Tuples that are moved to bucket j in any processor will eventually arrive at processor j. Thus, processor i will receive a bucket (empty or full) from each of the other $(P - 1)$ processors. After the relation R has been hashed and redistributed, each processor reads and redistributes its portion (S_i) of relation S to all the processors, using the same hash function h_1. At the end of phase one, corresponding hash partitions (R_i' and S_i') of both relations R and S reside on the same processor. Tuples in R_i' will match only with the tuples in S_i'; they need not be compared against tuples in any other hash partition S_j'.

During the second phase, each processor i independently joins the hash partitions R_i' and S_i' as follows. Here again, hashing is used to divide the problem into smaller subsets. A hash function h_2 and the number of hash buckets $(B + 1)$ are predefined. In the figure, h_2 = mod 2 and $B = 1$. A set of possible hash values is associated with each bucket. The number of hash buckets in this phase is a function of the available memory alone and is not related to the number of processors in the system. It is chosen such that the hash table for each bucket will individually fit in the memory. In order for each bucket to fit in the memory, the available memory should be greater than the square root of the size of R_i' in each processor [33]. A block of memory is allocated

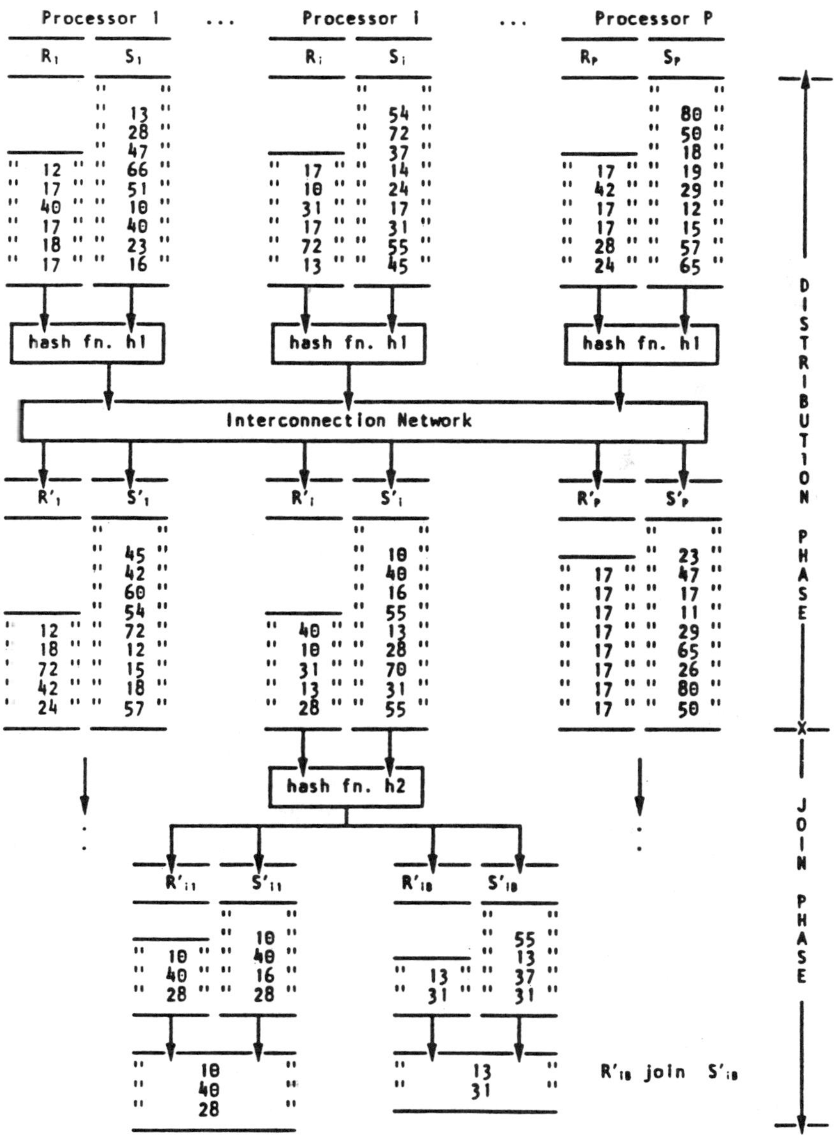

Fig. 2. Parallel hash join.

as an output buffer for each of the B buckets, $R'_{i1}, \cdots, R'_{iB}$. The rest of the memory is allocated for creating a hash table for R'_{i0}. The join operation is done in three stages. In stage one, relation R'_i is read from the disks and the join attribute of each tuple is hashed using the hash function h_2. If the hashed value belongs to bucket R'_{i0} it is placed in the hash table. If it belongs to any other bucket $R'_{i1}, \cdots, R'_{iB}$, it is moved to the output buffer corresponding to that bucket. As the buffers fill up they are saved on the disks. At the end of stage one, R'_i is hashed and the hash table for bucket R'_{i0} resides in the memory while the other buckets $R'_{i1}, \cdots, R'_{iB}$ reside on disks.

In stage two, S'_i is read from the disk, and the join attribute of each tuple is hashed using the same hash function h_2. If the tuple belongs to bucket S'_{i0} (whose values are identical to those in bucket R'_{i0}), the hash table for R'_{i0} is probed for a match. When a match is found the R and S-tuples are concatenated and output as a result tuple. If there is no match the tuple is discarded. If the tuple belongs to any other bucket $S'_{i1}, \cdots, S'_{iB}$, it is moved to the corresponding output buffer. At the end of stage two, tuples belonging to buckets R'_{i0} and S'_{i0} have been joined; and buckets $R'_{i1}, \cdots, R'_{iB}$ and $S'_{i1}, \cdots, S'_{iB}$ reside on disk. The B buckets will be nonempty only if the memory were smaller than R.

A third stage is necessary for joining the remaining buckets. The following steps are repeated for each of the B buckets. An R'_i bucket is read from the disks and its hash table is created in memory. The corresponding S'_i bucket is read from the disks, and each tuple in this bucket is hashed and used to probe the hash table for the R'_i bucket. If a match is found the corresponding R and S-tuples are concatenated and output, otherwise the tuple is discarded.

C. Semijoin

Use of semijoin in conjunction with the hybrid hash join algorithm is described here. Semijoin operation [1], when used as the preliminary step in join algorithms for parallel/distributed systems, could potentially reduce the amount of data distributed over the interconnection network as well as the size of the relations which have to be joined. In this paper, we consider the use of semijoin of S by R as the preprocessing step. When relation S is semijoined by relation R, S is restricted to those tuples which have a matching join attribute in R. Note that the following relationships are true.

$$(S \text{ semijoin by } R) = Z$$
$$(R \text{ join } S) = (R \text{ join } (S \text{ semijoin by } R)) = (R \text{ join } Z).$$

If Z is the resulting relation from semijoin, it is likely that Z is smaller than the original relation S.

The join algorithm now has three phases. In phase 0, the semijoin operation is performed. The hash join of R with the semijoin result is done in phase 1 and phase 2 as described in Section III-B. The actual steps performed by each processor i during the semijoin phase are as follows.

Semijoin S by R:

Step 1: Read the partition R_i from local disk.

Step 2: Project the join attribute from R_i. It is assumed that the projected result is in a sorted sequence—since projection may involve sorting all the join attributes in order to eliminate the duplicates.

Step 3: Send the sorted sequence of the join attributes to all the other processors in the system.

Step 4: Wait to receive the sorted sequence of R_j's join attributes from all the other processors in the system.

Step 5: Merge all the sorted sequences and eliminate any duplicate values. At the end of this step each processor has the list $R.A$ of all the distinct join attribute values in relation R.

Step 6: Read the partition (S_i) from local disk.

Step 7: Restrict S_i by $R.A$. That is, scan all the tuples in S_i and retain a tuple if its join attribute matches any in $R.A$; else discard the tuple.

At the end of Step 7, each processor has a portion Z_i of the semijoin result. The hybrid hash join, which follows the semijoin phase, joins R and Z instead of R and S.

IV. Skew

This section introduces the notion of data skew. The distribution of values taken by the join attribute can have a significant impact on the execution time of the join operation. In many real databases, certain values for an attribute occur more frequently than other values, resulting in a skewed distribution [5], [24], [27]. This phenomenon is referred to as data skew. The terms single skew and double skew are used to represent the respective cases where the join attribute of one or both the relations have a skewed distribution. For the purpose of this paper, double skew further implies that the two relations being joined are skewed at the same attribute values. The occurrence of single skew and double skew is illustrated by the following examples.

Consider the three relations, CUSTOMERS, ORDERS, and SUPPLIERS shown in Fig. 3. The 'Customerid' attribute on the CUSTOMERS relation takes unique values. However, the same attribute on the ORDERS relation can take nonunique values, since a given customer may order more than one item. It is possible for one customer (e.g., Robin) to have more outstanding orders than others, inducing the possibility of data skew. On the same note, a given item can be ordered by more than one customer and several suppliers can supply a given item. Some items (e.g., coffee) are more popular than other items. Thus, the 'Customerid' and 'Item' attributes in the ORDERS relation, and the 'Supplierid' and 'Item' attributes in the SUPPLIERS relation can have a skewed distribution. A query which needs to list all the customers with outstanding orders, would join the ORDERS and CUSTOMERS relations on the 'Customerid' column resulting in a join involving single skew. Similarly, a query which needs to list all the suppliers who can fill the outstanding orders would join the ORDERS and SUPPLIERS relations on the 'Item' column, resulting in a join involving double skew. Note that the 'Item' attribute on both ORDERS and SUPPLIERS is skewed on the value 'coffee'.

As tuples taking the same join attribute value will always be hashed into the same hash bucket, skew results in some hash buckets (and hence processors) receiving more tuples than others. For example, in the ORDERS relation, let 1000 tuples have the value 'coffee' for the 'Item' attribute. At the end of phase 1 in hash join, a single processor will receive these 1000 tuples irrespective of how many tuples go to the other processors. This load imbalance, which will occur even with the ideal hash function, limits the advantage of parallel processing architecture. A judicial selection of hash function may avoid two tuples with different join attribute values hashing into the same bucket. However, the choice of hash function has little impact on the size of the hash bucket which receives all the tuples with the skewed attribute value. Hence, the hash function is not a solution to the data skew problem. This effect is quantified in Section VIII.

Although in real applications databases do exhibit skew, an accepted value for the amount of skew or the prevalence of single skew and double skew is not reported in the open literature. Designers should, however, be aware of the skew phenomenon and evaluate the existing algorithms in the light of data skew, before scaling them to large parallel/distributed systems. To demonstrate the parallel architecture's vulnerability to skew our analysis mainly considers single skew joins with varying degrees of skew. Performance of double skew joins will be much worse, since the processing requirements under double skew increase tremendously with the join selectivity (which determines the size of the result relation).

In addition to the inherent data skew, other aspects of the system can manifest as data skew. For example, 1) simple hash functions used in distributing the relations in parallel architectures can result in high hash collision rates, leading to unequal numbers of tuples in the hash buckets; 2) when a predicate is applied to a relation before it is joined, it can further skew the distribution. The later can also result in unequal workload during phase 1.

V. Stochastic Processing Times

In parallel processing systems, a query is divided into multiple tasks which can be executed in parallel. The execution/processing time of a task can be a deterministic constant or an independent random variable. In Section IV, we illustrated how the task processing time on different processors will be different if there is skew. Even in the absence of skew, when the number of tuples to be processed by each processor is evenly distributed, the task processing time on different processors will exhibit stochastic variation (nondeterminism). Some of the factors that can contribute to the nondeterminism are: data may be placed in different locations on the disks in different processors, causing random variations in data access time in each processor; the interconnection network will introduce arbitrary delays for inter-processor communication; the join selectivity of the hash buckets, the selectivities of the predicates, and the number of predicates to be applied to filter out the unqualified tuples, etc., which are likely to be different in each processor, will lead to different processing

CUSTOMERS

Customer id	Address	"
Brooks, B	"	"
Browne, J	"	"
Fields, K	"	"
Robin, F	"	"
Smith, W	"	"

ORDERS

Customer id	Item	Qty
Robin, F	Coffee	"
Robin, F	Banana	"
Brooks, B	Coffee	"
Fields, K	Coffee	"
Robin, F	Yogurt	"

SUPPLIERS

Supplier	Item	Rate
Mountview	Coffee	"
Hillside	Coffee	"
Sunset	Coffee	"
Sunset	Raisin	"
Farmers	Yogurt	"
Sunset	Banana	"
Tropical	Banana	"

Fig. 3. Examples of data skew.

requirements for tasks in different processors. As pointed out in [32], in System R, the number of instructions required to join a matching pair of tuples far exceeds that to determine if two tuples are matching. The CPU time is dominated by the size of the join result, and not the size of the joining relations. Thus, even if the tuples are equally distributed across all the processors, and the subtasks require the same number of instructions on the average, the actual processing time on each processor may vary.

When the task times are stochastic, the different tasks will finish at different times. If all the tasks have to be completed before returning the result of this query or proceeding to the next query, there can be long synchronization delays for some tasks. We define task synchronization delay as the interval between the time when a task completes execution and the time when the last sibling task finishes execution. The synchronization delay is determined by the characteristics of the task processing times. When the task times are deterministic and equal (no skew), the synchronization delay is zero; when they are deterministic but not equal (say due to skew), the task with the longest processing time determines the overall execution time. When the task times are stochastic, however, even if they have the same mean processing time requirements, the synchronization delay is nonzero and is a function of the task time distribution.

While the task processing times are likely to be nondeterministic, the actual task time distribution characteristics are not known for database applications. In Section VII, analytical expressions for the join execution time for different task time distribution characteristics are derived. Three specific distribution functions, namely, exponential, normal, and uniform are being considered. Here, we attempt to provide the rationale behind the choice of these distributions. In join operations whether an S-tuple joins with an R-tuple is a random variable. Also, the time to join each pair of tuples is a random variable with arbitrary probability distribution. The sum of N independent random variables drawn from an identical or very similar distributions approaches a normal distribution by central limit theorem [12]. Also, by proper transformation, any continuous distribution can be converted to a normal distribution. Hence, normal is perhaps the appropriate distribution to model database joins. However, it requires two parameters to characterize normal distributions—not only the mean but also the coefficient of variation which is generally not available. Further, exact analysis of models involving normal distributions is not always straightforward. On the other hand, exponential and uniform distributions have a lot of theoretical value, and can be often solved easily for exact results. These distributions can be characterized by the single parameter, mean. These two distributions are considered in this paper as reference points for normal distribution. The exponential has a coefficient of variation of 1, the uniform has a coefficient of variation of $1/\sqrt{3}$, and the normal can have any value for the coefficient of variation.

VI. Assumptions and Parameters

To capture the effect of data skew, ideally, we need the actual distribution of the join attribute values. However, when the processing times are deterministic, the processor that receives the largest bucket determines the execution time. And the actual distribution of attribute values of the other tuples is less relevant. To simplify our analysis, we use a parameter Q $(0 \leq Q \leq 1)$ to model the skew. Q is the fraction of the relation which takes the highly skewed attribute value and hence hashes to one particular bucket during phase one. The rest of the relation is assumed to spread more or less evenly over the other values in the attribute domain. When there are P processors and $Q \leq 1/P$, at the end of phase one, all the processors are assumed to have approximately equal numbers of tuples in the hash buckets and the effect of skew is imperceptible. This is referred to as the no skew case. When $Q > 1/P$, one (skewed) processor receives the fraction Q of the relation while the rest of the relation is divided equally among the other processors. This is referred to as the skewed case with skew Q.

We assume that each tuple is 100 bytes long and there are 25K bytes per block which is approximately equal to the size of a track in a disk. Choice of these parameter values is consistent with other measurement and modeling studies [25], [3]. Relation S is always twice as large as relation R and relation R is the skewed relation in single skew joins. The hash functions are perfect, i.e., the effect of hash value collisions is not observable.

In the analysis, we use the parameter effective network bandwidth which is a function of the raw bandwidth, communication protocol used, the type of network (point to point or common access medium), and the amount of contention for the network. The effective bandwidth is usually much less than the raw bandwidth. A detailed model of the interconnection network would be necessary for computing the effective network bandwidth and it is not addressed in this paper. Instead, we assume the effective network bandwidth to be a known parameter, and examine the performance sensitivity to this parameter. This allows us the flexibility to study different scenarios easily. E.g., a higher value for the effective network bandwidth could refer to a faster network, or more efficient protocol, or to the fact that instead of sending the whole relation, only the hash values and tuple identifiers are exchanged. In the rest of the paper, the terms network bandwidth and effective network bandwidth are interchangeably used.

Other parameters (along with a representative default value) and notations used in the analysis are introduced below. The default values are chosen to be representative of real applications. The subscript i is used to denote any arbitrary processor in the DBMC; subscript k is used to denote the processor that receives the skewed bucket; and subscript j is used to denote any processor other than k.

Configuration Related

- P Number of processors (varied from 15 to 1000).
- μ Processor speed (2 MIPS).
- M Available memory in each processor (4 megabytes).
- β Effective network bandwidth (12 megabytes/s).

DB Related

- R, S The relations to be joined (2 and 4 million tuples, respectively).
- R_i, S_i Portion of R and S in processor i at the beginning of phase one $(R/P, S/P)$.
- R_i', S_i' Hash partitions (buckets) of R and S that will be joined by processor i during phase two.
- f_i Fraction of R_i' whose hash table can fit in memory M in the presence of output buffers for other hash buckets, during phase two.
- Q Measure of skew (varied from 0 to 20%).
- η Semijoin selectivity, which is the ratio of the size of semijoin S by R to the size of S (varied from 0.01 to 0.5).

Processing Related

- t_d Disk access time (20 ms).
- I_d Required pathlength for initiating an IO access (1000 instructions).
- I_{comm} Required pathlength for exchanging a message across the network (1000 instructions).
- I_1 Required pathlength for processing a tuple to create hash buckets during phase one or phase two (1000 instructions).

The following notations are used to refer to the number of blocks, tuples, etc.

- $|X|$ Number of blocks in an item X.
- $\{X\}$ Number of tuples in an item X.
- $\uparrow X$ Ceiling of an item X.

VII. Performance Models

The execution time of join queries in single user mode and the average response time of join queries in multiuser mode are evaluated here. The execution time/response time corresponds to the completion of a query and not the time until first result tuple is available. An abstract model of query execution is given in Fig. 4. The processors are assumed to be identical (same MIPS, memory, etc.) and that there is an equal number of tuples to be processed by each processor during phase one. Queries arrive from an external source and each query is split into P parallel tasks. Each task is scheduled for one of the P processors. Tasks receive several bursts of CPU time, perform many physical I/O accesses, and communicate with other processors in performing the join operation. When a task finishes execution, it waits in a synchronization box until all the sibling tasks are completed, at which time the result of the query is available. If the interconnection network is a common access medium such as a bus or a token ring, where tasks compete with each other for accessing the network, all the tasks cannot exchange data in parallel. In other words, the network delay is serialized, in which case, the network delay in the model can be moved external to the split/merge node. On the other hand, if the interconnection network is a point to point network, all the processors can send/receive in parallel and the network delay will be on a per task basis. In our analysis, we have assumed a common access medium. Thus, the query execution time is the sum of the processing delay T_{proc} and the network delay T_{net}. T_{proc} includes the time spent by a task in the processor node for CPU and I/O services as well as the synchronization delay incurred in waiting for other sibling tasks to complete. The various components of the execution time under different conditions are presented below.

A. Average Task Time

Let T_i represent the average task time in an arbitrary processor i. T_i consists of the CPU time and the physical disk access time. The CPU time includes the tuple processing time, time required for initiating I/O accesses and sending/receiving messages from other processors. Detailed expressions for the task times T_i are derived in Appendix A. The final expressions are:

Parallel Hash Join

$$T_i(\text{hash join}) = T_{cpu} + T_{io} + T_{comm} + T_{net}$$

where

$$T_{cpu} = \left(\frac{\{R\}}{P} + \frac{\{S\}}{P} + (2 - f_i)\left(\{R_i'\} + \frac{\{S\}}{P}\right)\right)\frac{I_1}{\mu}$$

$$T_{io} = \left(\frac{|R|}{P} + \frac{|S|}{P} + 2(1 - f_i)\left(|R_i'| + \frac{|S|}{P}\right)\right)\left(t_d + \frac{I_d}{\mu}\right)$$

$$T_{comm} = \left(\uparrow\frac{R}{PM} + \uparrow\frac{S}{PM}\right)(P-1)\frac{I_{comm}}{\mu}$$

$$T_{net} = \frac{R+S}{\beta}.$$

The task processing times on the skewed processor k or any of the other processors j are obtained by substituting the appropriate values for R_i' and f_i.

$$\text{When } Q \le 1/P \quad R_i' = \frac{R}{P}$$

$$\text{When } Q > 1/P \quad R_k' = QR; \quad R_j' = \frac{1-Q}{P-1}R.$$

f_i is a function of R_i', R, and M. The exact expression is given in Appendix A. From the above expressions it is evident that the T_{comm} and T_{net} do not vary with the number of processors. For small values of P and Q where $Q \le 1/P$, T_{cpu} and T_{io} are inversely proportional to the number of processors P. Increasing P tends to decrease these components. When $Q > 1/P$, up to a certain point, increasing P will decrease these components; beyond that point the effect of Q will be more pronounced. These effects are also observed in the empirical study in Section VIII.

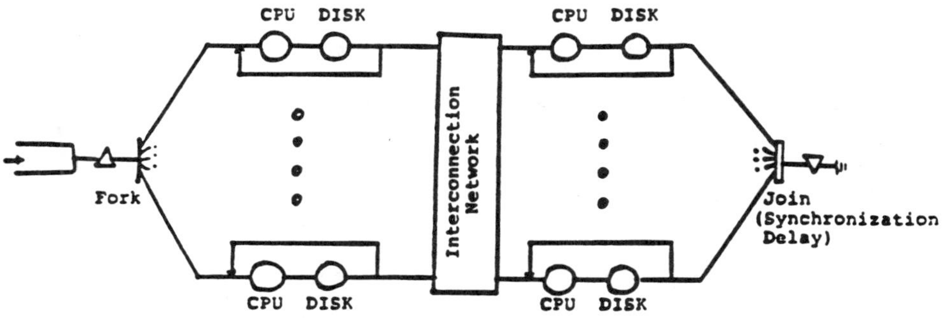

Fig. 4. Query execution on DBMC.

Hash Join with Semijoin: The use of semijoin as a preprocessing step in the hash join algorithm was described in Section III-C. The T_i under this algorithm is made of two major components, namely, the time to perform the semijoin of S by R, and the time to hash join R and a subset of S. Detailed derivation of T_i is presented in Appendix B. Due to the complexity of introducing additional parameters and notations, the equations are not reproduced here. The implications of the parameters related to the semijoin operation are also discussed in the Appendix. The semijoin selectivity, which is the ratio of the result size of S semijoin by R to the size of S, is found to be a significant parameter. Semijoin selectivity is a measure of the efficiency of the semijoin operation in the join algorithm. The impact of this parameter on the hash join performance is investigated in Section VIII.

B. Average Query Execution Time

As mentioned earlier,

$$\text{Query execution time} = T_{\text{proc}} + T_{\text{net}}$$

where T_{proc} is a function of individual task times T_i's. When the task times T_i's are deterministic constants, the processor with the maximum task time determines the execution time. Recalling that subscript k denotes the skewed processor and j denotes any of the other processors,

Deterministic Task Time:

$$\begin{aligned} T_{\text{proc}} &= \max(T_j, T_k) \\ &= T_i \quad \left(Q \le \frac{1}{P}\right) \\ &= T_k \quad \left(Q > \frac{1}{P}\right). \end{aligned}$$

When the task times are stochastic (i.e., random values drawn from a given probability distribution with mean T_i), T_{proc} is obtained by integrating a function of the probability distribution. Let $F_{T_i}(y)$ represent the probability distribution function from which the task time for processor i is drawn. In a DBMC with P processors and $(Q \le 1/P)$, P task times are drawn from the same distribution. When $(Q > 1/P)$, $P - 1$ samples are drawn from one distribution and one task time is drawn from a different distribution. T_{proc} is equal to the expected value of the maximum of these P samples. It is expressed as

$$\begin{aligned} T_{\text{proc}} &= \int_0^\infty \left(1 - (F_{T_i}(y))^P\right) dy \qquad Q \le 1/P \\ &= \int_0^\infty \left(1 - F_{T_k}(y)(F_{T_j}(y))^{P-1}\right) dy \qquad Q > 1/P. \end{aligned}$$

In the subsequent paragraphs, T_{proc} is derived under exponential, uniform, and normal distributions of task times. For brevity, the intermediate steps involved in the integrations are omitted, and only the final expressions are presented.

Exponential Distribution: The distribution function of an exponential random variable y with mean T_i is given by

$$F_{T_i}(y) = 1 - e^{-T_i y} \qquad y \ge 0.$$

Substituting the above expression (with appropriate values for T_i) in the equation for T_{proc} and integrating, we get

$$T_{\text{proc}} = H_P T_i \qquad \text{when } Q \le 1/P$$

$$T_{\text{proc}} = H_{P-1} T_j + T_k \prod_{n=1}^{P-1} \frac{n}{n + T_j/T_k} \qquad \text{when } Q > 1/P$$

where H_P is the harmonic series given by $\sum_{i=1}^{P} 1/i$. For large values of P, the harmonic series can be approximated by logarithm of P. Thus, even if T_i can be made to decrease by increasing the number of processors, T_{proc} will reduce only as $\ln(P)/P$. Note that the effect of skew (Q) is reflected in the above expressions for T_{proc} through T_j and T_k.

Uniform Distribution: When the task time is a uniform random variable with a mean of T_i, it can take any value in the interval 0 to $2T_i$. The distribution function is given by

$$\begin{aligned} F_{T_i}(y) &= \frac{y}{2T_i} \qquad 0 \le y \le 2T_i \\ &1 \qquad y > 2T_i. \end{aligned}$$

Substituting these in the general expression for T_{proc} and integrating, we get

$$T_{\text{proc}} = 2T_i \frac{P}{P+1} \qquad \text{when } Q \le 1/P$$

$$T_{\text{proc}} = T_k + \frac{T_j^2(P-1)}{T_k(P+1)} \qquad \text{when } Q > 1/P.$$

Normal Distribution: For general distribution functions such as the normal distribution, the integration is not straightforward. Consider the no skew case. In [13] and [17], it is shown that the maximum of P i.i.d. normally distributed random variables can be approximated by the characteristic maximum of the random variable, which for the task times is defined to be $\min\{x : 1 - F_{Ti}(x) < 1/P\}$. In [20], it is shown that this characteristic maximum can be approximated by $T_i(1 + C\sqrt{2 \log P})$ where C is the coefficient of variation of the normal distribution with mean T_i. Hence, under no skew condition, T_{proc} can be approximated as

$$T_{\text{proc}} = T_i(1 + C\sqrt{2 \log P}) \qquad \text{when } Q \leq 1/P.$$

Examining the different equations derived above, deterministic task times offer the best performance and hence can be considered as an upper bound.

C. Multiple Query Environment

Here we develop a model to consider the effect of data skew when there are multiple join queries to be processed. This is used in Section VIII-B to illustrate the tradeoff between DBMC's MIPS and bandwidth requirements. The model does not address any stochastic variations in task times, however, it captures the effect of variations in the execution time of different join queries. The model can be generalized to include the effects of stochastic variations in task times [23].

Although concurrent execution of multiple join queries is feasible through the multiprogramming feature, we assume that the scheduler in the DBMC will not schedule multiple nonprimary key joins (of interest in this paper) concurrently. This assumption is reasonable considering the complexity of the network protocol, and buffer manager in sending/receiving hash buckets belonging to multiple joins. Such complexity may not be justified when the DBMC is made of many small microprocessors each with relatively small main memory. Note that we do not exclude the possibility of concurrent execution of other types of queries (e.g., JOIN which does not require redistribution of relations across the network, SELECT, etc.). The performance trends observed in this paper are expected to hold even when this assumption is relaxed, since multiprogramming can only improve the throughput in multiuser mode, and not the response time. Thus, when multiple nonprimary key join queries arrive in the system, each query is run to completion before another query becomes active. Since each of these queries is likely to have different processing and network requirement, we model the multiquery scenario by an M/M/1 queue. When a query arrives in the system it joins the queue; upon reaching the head of the queue, it is executed by the system. The execution time for each query is drawn from an exponential distribution whose mean is given by

$$\begin{aligned} &T_i + T_{\text{net}} && \text{when } Q \leq 1/P \\ &T_k + T_{\text{net}} && \text{when } Q > 1/P. \end{aligned}$$

T_i and T_k are discussed in Section VII-A. The M/M/1 model is solved for the average query response time, which includes the query execution time and the queueing time [18].

VIII. Performance Results

In this section, we examine the impact of skew and stochastic variation of task processing time on parallel join performance. In order to evaluate the effectiveness of the DBMC we compare DBMC's performance to an idealized single processor architecture where the processing power and memory are concentrated in one processor. Further, in the idealized architecture, the CPU and I/O loads are assumed to be perfectly balanced. This is possible through parallel I/O feature which is achieved by disk interleaving of data and parallel access to several blocks (say 20) of data [17], [22]. Thus, I/O is not a distinct bottleneck in the idealized architecture. Since this idealized architecture avoids the issues of creating multiple tasks, balancing the load on the multiple processors, interprocessor communication overhead, and network transmission delay, etc., it serves as a good reference point to evaluate the effectiveness of parallelism. This idealized architecture is referred to as the SPPI (single processor parallel IO) architecture. Certainly, in reality, it may not be technically feasible or economical to build such a system with an arbitrarily fast processor. Analysis of the SPPI is similar to the phase two analysis of hash join algorithm presented in Appendix A. It can also be found in [21] and [23].

We use the metrics MIPS ratio and speedup, relative to the idealized SPPI architecture, to measure the effectiveness of parallel processing. Suppose the throughput and response time of the SPPI system at a given utilization are $\lambda_{\max}$ and $T_{\max}$, respectively. *MIPS ratio* is defined as the ratio of the total MIPS (i.e., the sum of the MIPS of individual processors) required in the DBMC to the single processor MIPS such that the DBMC can sustain a throughput of $\lambda_{\max}$ and provide the same or better response time than $T_{\max}$. *Speedup* is the ratio of query execution time in the SPPI to that in the DBMC.

We are interested in determining the robustness of the DBMC performance. Almost all of our results are for single skew joins as it is sufficient to demonstrate the skew phenomenon. Both regular hash join and semijoin are considered. We do present a case with double skew to illustrate how the performance can deteriorate. Although we concentrate on the performance of nonprimary key joins where both relations are transmitted over the network before they are joined, a set of curves addressing the issue of primary key join is also provided. To see the effect of stochastic variation on task processing times, we examine the speedup under constant, exponential, uniform, and normal task time distributions. We do not explicitly consider the case where some predicates are applied to the relations before they are joined. Applying a predicate can have two effects: 1) it can reduce the size of the relation and 2) it can result in higher skew. Both these effects can be captured in our model by changing the relation size and Q.

The processors in the DBMC are 2 or 4 MIPS, and the SPPI processor is chosen to be 60 MIPS. The choice of processor MIPS is in some sense arbitrary since it is intended to illustrate the speedup characteristics of many small processors relative to one large processor. The general conclusion does not change whether we choose a 30 MIPS or 120 MIPS SPPI instead. It is not intended to reflect the MIPS ratings of commercial mainframe processors or high-speed RISC processors with respect to small microprocessors. It is hard to relate the MIPS of different types of processors; a mainframe has a complex instruction set and can employ a vector facility to enhance join performance and increase its effective MIPS rating [35]. The RISC type processors have a simpler instruction set while the instruction set of microprocessors lies in between the two. However, even within the same processor architecture family like system 370 or VAX, there is a widespread performance difference (more than an order of magnitude) between the top of the line processors and the smallest processors. It may thus be interesting to examine the effectiveness of coupling many small processors relative to a single large processor even within the same architecture family.

The discussions which follow, unless stated otherwise, pertain to hash join; performance of semijoin is explicitly discussed in the Section VIII-D.

A. Maximum Throughput

In Figs. 5 and 6, the maximum join throughput in the DBMC is plotted against the number of processors for no skew and 5% skew. Since we have assumed that multiple joins are not scheduled concurrently, the maximum throughput is merely the reciprocal of the query execution time under deterministic task times. The DBMC processors are 2 MIPS and the effective network bandwidth is 12 megabytes/s. These figures also illustrate the sensitivity to relation size. The two relations have 20K and 40K tuples in Fig. 5 and they are 100 times bigger in Fig. 6. From these figures we can observe that initially throughput increases with the number of processors and after a certain number of processors, there is a diminishing marginal return. This is due to the tradeoff between the increased communication cost and reduction in tuple processing load on each processor as the number of processors is increased. Even a 5% skew on the smaller relation results in substantial reduction in throughput compared to when there is no skew. With larger relations, a larger number of processors can be more effectively utilized, as evident from Fig. 6. However, when the relations are larger, the difference in throughput between the no skew and 5% skew cases is much more significant—the 5% skew case is about 30% of the no skew case.

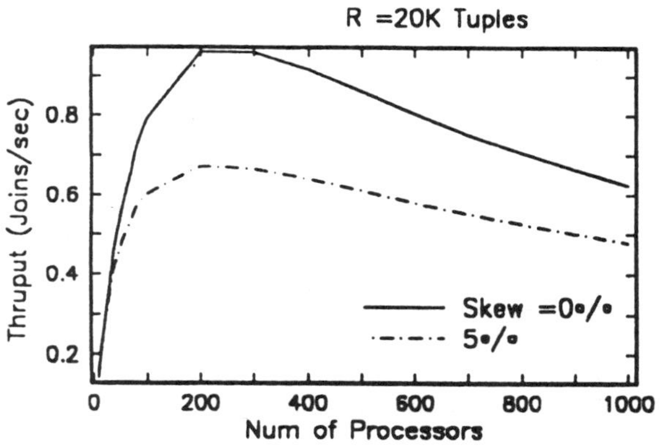

Fig. 5. $\{R\}$ = 20K tuples.

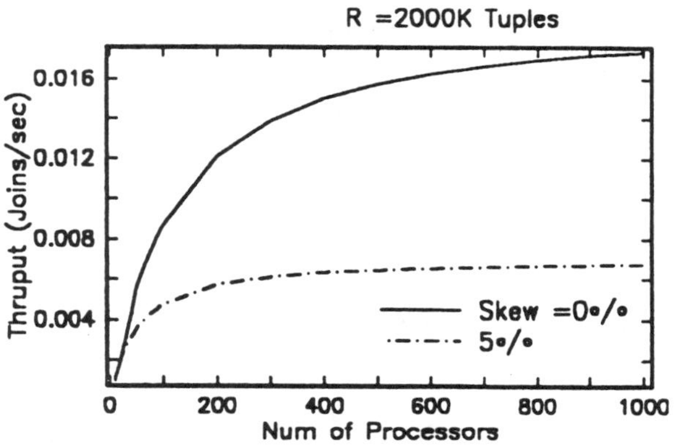

Fig. 6. $\{R\}$ = 2000K tuples.

B. MIPS Ratio Versus Bandwidth

This section examines the amount of MIPS and network bandwidth required by DBMC to match the performance of SPPI in a multiuser environment. The MIPS ratio has been identified as a useful metric for this purpose. It is defined as the ratio of total MIPS required by the DBMC to that of the SPPI to deliver the same response time at a given transaction rate, if possible. A 60 MIPS SPPI machine (with 256 megabytes of memory, IO parallelism of 20, and multiprogramming level of 5) at 70% utilization is used as a base to study the effectiveness of the DBMC. The two relations being joined consist of 2 and 4 million tuples, respectively. The response time of SPPI was computed to be 664 s at a throughput of 0.004 join/s. The DBMC response time at this throughput was computed using the multiple query models developed in Section VII-C. As both the network delay and the CPU time are significant components of the DBMC response time, a reduction in either would result in improved performance. Fig. 7 shows the MIPS ratio versus the effective bandwidth for different degrees of skew when the DBMC is made of 2 MIPS microprocessors. It reflects the tradeoff between bandwidth and total MIPS requirements. If microprocessor MIPS are cheaper than bandwidth, we can employ more microprocessors and accept a higher MIPS ratio to reduce the effective bandwidth needed to meet the throughput and response time requirements. On the other hand, if bandwidth is cheaper, more bandwidth can be employed to achieve a lower MIPS ratio. From Fig. 7, we note that if the effective bandwidth is less than 4 megabytes/s, a MIPS ratio of 5 or less cannot be achieved even in the absence of any skew. If a bandwidth of 100 megabytes/s is available, we can achieve a MIPS ratio of less than 1.5. For a given bandwidth, as the skew increases, the MIPS ratio also increases. If the relative speed of the microprocessor to the SPPI processor improves, the skew effect is reduced. For example, if the microprocessor speed increases from 2 to 4 MIPS while the SPPI processor speed remains at 60 MIPS, the 5% skew case improves (noticeably at low bandwidth), as seen in Fig. 8. With faster microprocessors only a few of them are needed in the DBMC, and hence, its performance is less

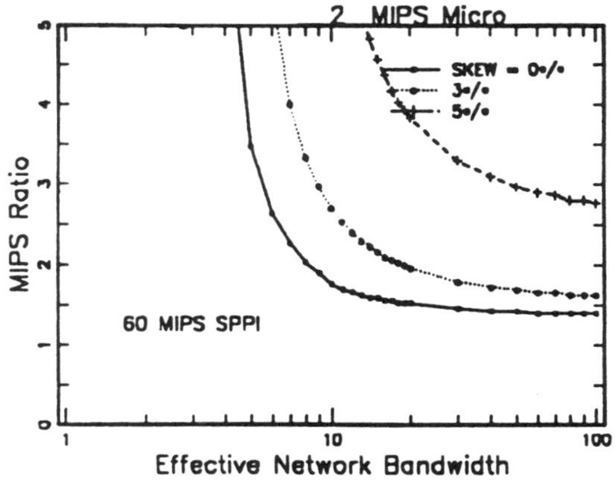

Fig. 7. 2 MIPS micro, 60 MIPS SPPI.

sensitive to skew. Taking a closer look reveals that the MIPS ratio for the no skew case increases when the processor speed increases from 2 to 4 MIPS. This is due to the reduction in IO parallelism when fewer but faster microprocessors are employed. Thus, in choosing the microprocessor size to maintain a given aggregate MIPS, there is a tradeoff between the negative impact of skew and the benefit of IO parallelism. In Fig. 9, a DBMC made of 4 MIPS microprocessors is compared to a 120 MIPS SPPI system. The sensitivity to skew is similar to Fig. 7 since the ratio of microprocessor speed to SPPI processor speed is the same in both cases.

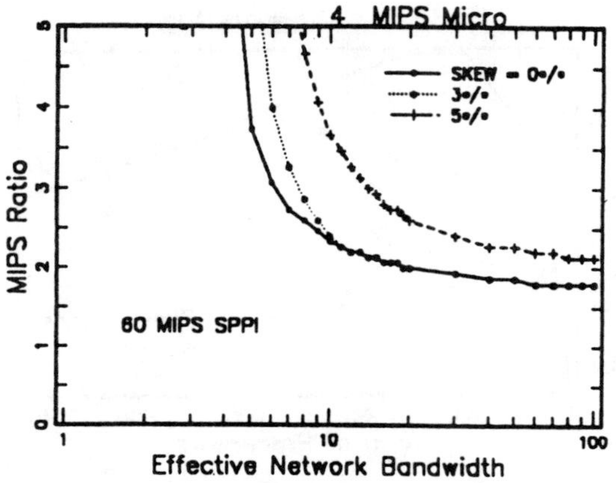

Fig. 8. 4 MIPS micro, 60 MIPS SPPI.

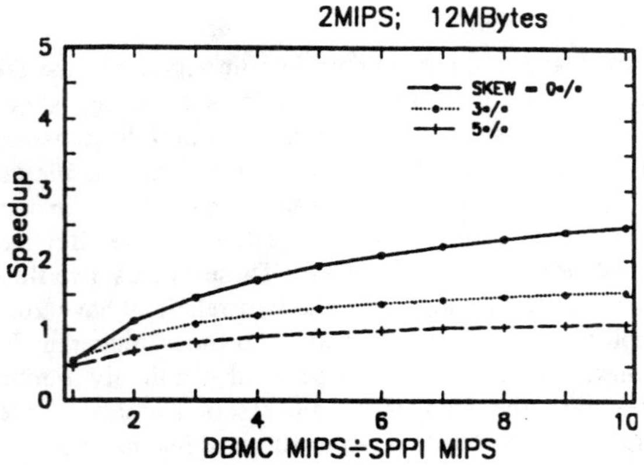

Fig. 10. 2 MIPS micro, 12 megabyte bandwidth.

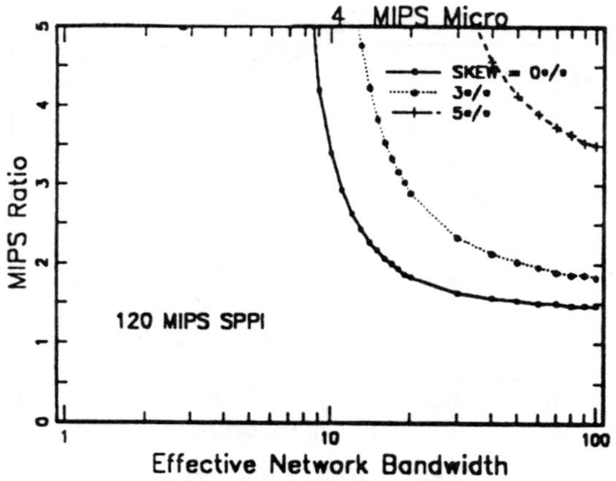

Fig. 9. 4 MIPS micro, 120 MIPS SPPI.

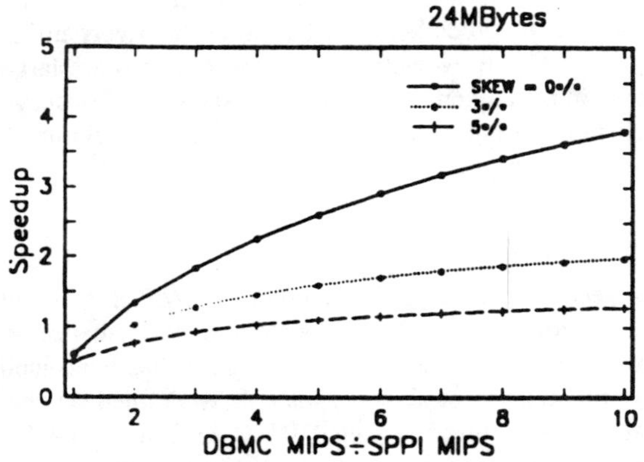

Fig. 11. 2 MIPS micro, 24 megabyte bandwidth.

C. Ultimate Speedup

The issue of the ultimate speedup (measured in single user mode) is considered here. It is a measure of the execution time improvement for a single join operation that can be achieved by the DBMC when it employs 1–10 times as many MIPS as the SPPI. The execution time of a single join in the DBMC is computed for each case and compared to the execution time on a SPPI with 128 megabytes of memory. (We did not consider SPPI with 256 megabytes of memory to evaluate single query speedup since that would lead to a special case where one of the relations would reside in memory all the time.) We consider cases with constant task processing time. In Fig. 10, the speedup is plotted against the ratio of total DBMC MIPS to SPPI MIPS. The microprocessors are 2 MIPS and the effective network bandwidth is 12 megabytes/s. Note that with 2 MIPS microprocessor, MIPS ratios of 1–10 correspond to 30–300 microprocessors in the DBMC configuration. Ideally, we would expect to see linear speedup characteristics. However, we observe that a DBMC employing 10 times the SPPI MIPS achieves a speedup of only 2.5 under no skew, 1.5 under 3% skew; under 5% skew it can achieve little speedup. Such limited speedup for the no skew case is due to bandwidth limitation and for the skew cases is due to both bandwidth and processor limitations. This is evident from Fig. 11 where the effective bandwidth is increased to 24 megabytes/s. With the increased bandwidth, the ultimate speedup for no skew case has increased to 3.7. However, the skew cases, especially the 5% skew case, show only slight improvement with a faster network. Fig. 12, where the microprocessor speed is increased to 4 MIPS, shows the impact of faster processors. The bandwidth is kept at 24 megabytes/s. Using a faster microprocessor does improve the speedup for 3% and 5% skew, but it does not help when there is no skew. This implies that when there is no skew, the DBMC speedup is basically bandwidth sensitive. With skew, it becomes sensitive to the relative speed of the microprocessors to the SPPI processor.

D. Effect of Semijoin

The benefit of using semijoin as a preprocessing step in the hash join algorithm is evaluated here. Fig. 13 illustrates the speedup of pure hash join and hash join using semijoin as a function of different semijoin selectivities and bandwidths. There is no skew in these cases, the microprocessors are 2 MIPS, and the total DBMC MIPS equals 10 times the SPPI MIPS. The selectivities considered are 0.5, 0.1, and 0.01. Selectivities less than 0.01 did not offer any significant improvement in speedup. We observe from this figure, join by semijoin does not benefit from network bandwidth greater than 12 megabytes/s, while hash join's speedup continues to improve even beyond 50 megabytes/s. The point of diminishing return of using semijoin occurs when the increase in processing delay due to semijoin phase outweighs the reduction in communication delay. Thus, semijoin can be used to improve performance when the DBMC is bandwidth limited. Fig. 14 shows the case with 5% skew. In the presence of skew, however, use of semijoin has only a

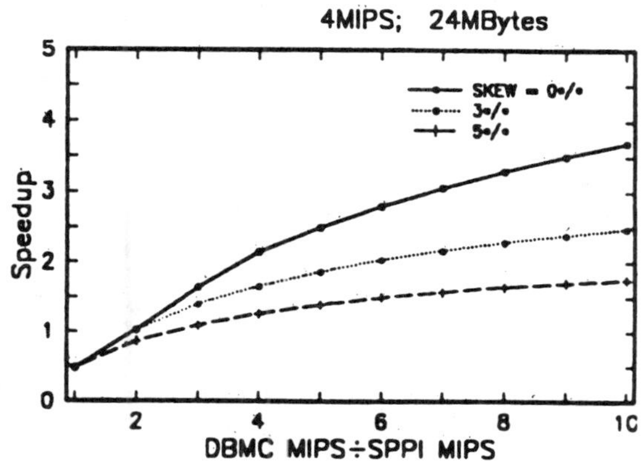

Fig. 12. 4 MIPS micro, 24 megabyte bandwidth.

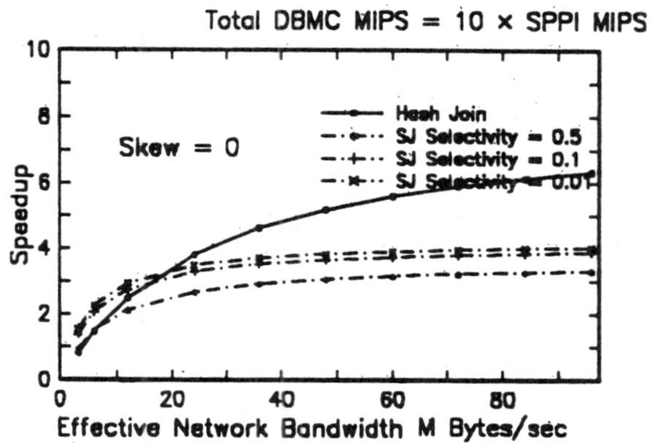

Fig. 13. Total DBMC MIPS = 10 × SPPI MIPS (skew = 0%).

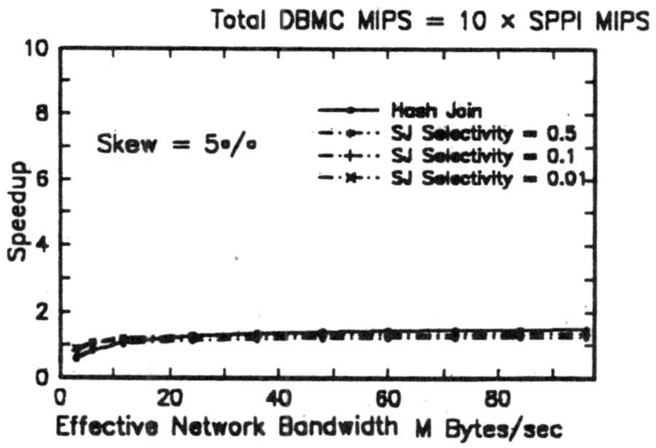

Fig. 14. Total DBMC MIPS = 10 × SPPI MIPS (skew = 5%).

marginal effect. Since skew shifts the bottleneck to the processor (CPU/disk), all curves start to saturate even at 6 megabytes/s.

Effect of skew is further illustrated in Figs. 15 and 16, where the speedups of hash join and semijoin are plotted against varying degrees of skew. The total DBMC MIPS in Fig. 15 equals the SPPI MIPS and equals 10 times the SPPI MIPS in Fig. 16. The bandwidth is assumed to be 12 megabytes/s. When the MIPS in DBMC and SPPI are equal, there are only 30 processors in the DBMC. The improvement due to semijoin is noticeable when there is no skew, but gradually diminishes as the skew increases. The relative merit of semijoin also diminishes, when the number of processors increases, as evident from Fig. 16 where the number of processors equals 300. This is due to the

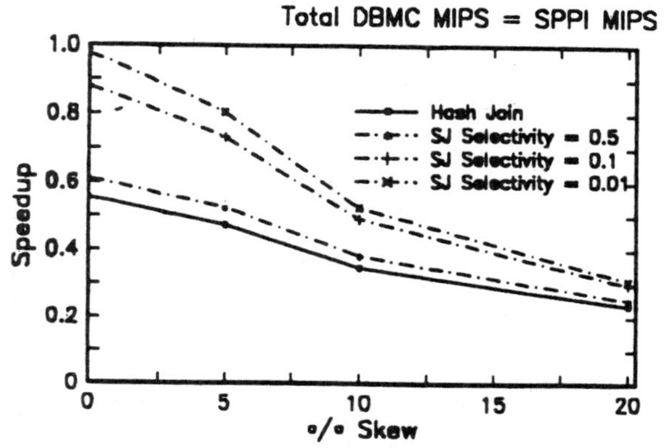

Fig. 15. Total DBMC MIPS = SPPI MIPS.

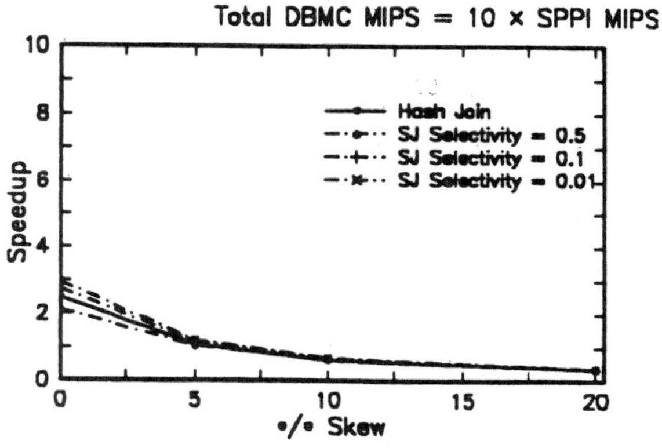

Fig. 16. Total DBMC MIPS = 10 × SPPI MIPS.

fact that, in semijoin, each processor needs to build the list of join attribute values of the whole relation R in step 5 of the semijoin algorithm in Section III-C (see analysis in Appendix B for more details). This step appears to be the bottleneck, since this time does not decrease as the number of processors increases.

E. Effect of Stochastic Task Time Variations

We now consider cases with different task time distributions. Fig. 17 presents the speedup for the no skew case under deterministic, exponential, uniform, and normal task time distributions. Normal distributions with two different values for the coefficient of variation (CV) are being used. The DBMC processors are 2 MIPS and the effective network bandwidth is 12 megabytes/s. Deterministic task time seems to offer the maximum speedup; speedup under an exponential task time distribution is always lower than that under a uniform distribution. Speedup under normal distributions varies widely depending on the coefficient of variation; the speedup decreases as the coefficient of variation increases. With a small coefficient of variation, the speedup can get close to uniform or even deterministic task time, while with a large coefficient of variation, the speedup may be worse than that of exponential task time. The 5% skew case is examined in Fig. 18 for deterministic, exponential, and uniform task time distributions. When there is 5% or more skew, the skew effect becomes dominant; there is only a marginal difference among the different distributions.

F. Effect of Primary Key Join

The situation where the join attribute of relation S is also the primary key on which the relation is originally partitioned

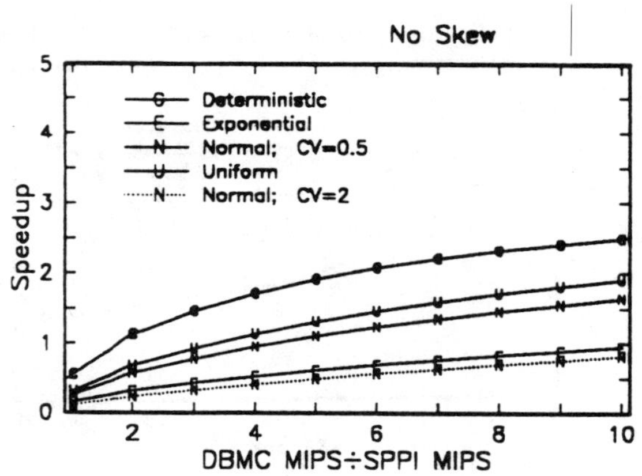

Fig. 17. No skew.

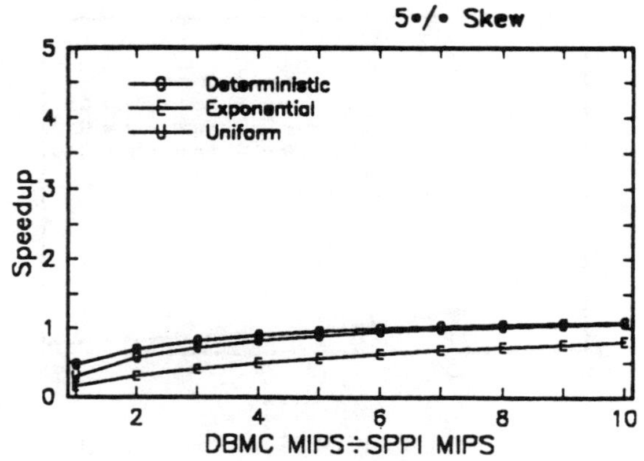

Fig. 18. 5% skew.

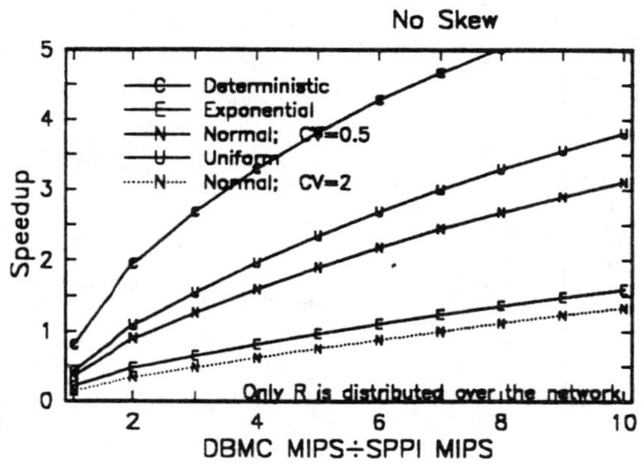

Fig. 19. No skew.

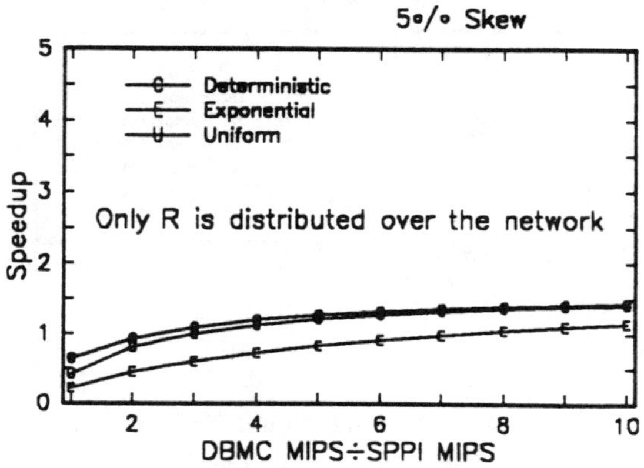

Fig. 20. 5% skew.

is considered in Figs. 19 and 20. In this case, only *R* has to be hashed and redistributed during phase one, thus reducing the network delay component of the execution time. As seen in Fig. 19, where the speedup is plotted for the no skew case, the constant task time exhibits a speedup characteristic closer to linear. Task time distributions with larger variance, such as exponential distribution and normal distribution with coefficient of variation equal to two, show little improvement as compared to the nonprimary key join case in Fig. 17 where both the relations have to be redistributed. This is due to the fact that when one of the joining attributes is a primary key the network delay decreases substantially, while the decrease in the tuple processing delay is not appreciable. Hence, the synchronization delay due to task time distributions is significant. The 5% skew case is shown in Fig. 20. It is similar to the corresponding nonprimary key join case shown in Fig. 18. Thus, in the presence of skew, the skew effect is more dominant than the effects of different task time distributions. Still perfect linear speedup may be achieved for joins involving relations that are already partitioned based on their join attribute, since no redistribution of tuples is necessary. This has been observed in [30].

G. Double Skew

Finally, joins involving double skew are investigated. We assume that both relations are skewed in the same direction. With double skew, the execution time is dominated by the actual time taken to join the two skewed buckets and it has a quadratic complexity (see explanation in the Appendix). Compared to single skew, the processing requirement for double skew increases tremendously both in the SPPI and the DBMC. Approximately the same amount of work will be done by both the SPPI processor and the microprocessor that receives the skewed buckets. However, since the microprocessor is slower than the SPPI processor, the DBMC execution time will be much larger. Table I lists the execution time in the SPPI as well as the ratio of SPPI execution time to DBMC execution time for different values of skew. As seen from this table, double skew leads to severe performance degradation in the SPPI. Its impact on the DBMC is even worse; instead of any speedup, the DBMC offers a slow down which is proportional to the ratio of the SPPI processor speed to the DBMC microprocessor speed. The increase in SPPI execution time is due to the increased processing time required to match and join all the tuples in the skewed buckets. When the two relations are not skewed in the same direction, the performance degradation may not be as severe.

H. Summary

Based on our performance study, the following observations can be made.

- Horizontal growth is an attractive feature offered by DBMC. However, perfect linear speedup can only be achieved if the load can be evenly spread across all the processors with little additional overhead.
- With the conventional join or semijoin algorithm, DBMC performance is sensitive to skew. Even with a moderate level of skew (5%), the maximum achievable speedup can

TABLE I
SPPI TO DBMC EXECUTION TIME RATIOS FOR DOUBLE SKEW

Skew	0%	1%	3%
DBMC with 30 2 MIPS micros	0.6	0.04	0.03
DBMC with 300 2 MIPS micros	2.5	0.04	0.03
DBMC with 15 4 MIPS micros	0.45	0.075	0.068
DBMC with 150 4 MIPS micros	3.6	0.075	0.068
60 MIPS SPPI execution time	179 s	1512 s	12178 s

become marginal. With large skew, the speedup relative to SPPI can be less than one. These indicate the need for new algorithms to redistribute the processing load.

- For the no skew case, the stochastic variation of task time can have a substantial impact on the speedup. As skew increases, the skew effect rather than stochastic variation dominates the performance.
- In general, there is a tradeoff between MIPS and bandwidth to meet a given performance criterion. However, faster network has more impact on the no skew case while faster processor is more important for the skewed case or the case with large task time variation when the CPU time is significant compared to the I/O time.
- Semijoin is not very helpful to address the skew problem. It may help the no skew case if the bandwidth is limited. But the improvement decreases as the number of processors or the degree of skew increases.
- The above results hold whether one or both of the relations are skewed, or one of them has the join attribute as the primary key.

IX. CONCLUSIONS

In this paper, we studied the factors that can limit the performance of parallel processing of relational queries. Parameters such as skew, task processing time distribution, relative processor speed, and network bandwidth are identified as major parameters that can affect the performance. The DBMC architecture is, in general, expected to offer horizontal growth capability. However, our study shows that the speedup achievable through horizontal growth is quite sensitive to the skew and stochastic variations in task time.

To take full advantage of parallel processing, we need to be able to divide the work evenly across all the processors. Straightforward generalization of conventional algorithms may not be adequate to handle the skew problem in environments with a large number of processors. There is clearly a need for more clever algorithms. However, algorithms which ensure better load balancing, in general, require more synchronization and communication overhead. Future efforts will be directed towards developing schemes that evenly distribute the load across a large number of processors with minimum overhead.

APPENDIX A

Hash Join under Single Skew

General expressions for the average task execution time T_i on an arbitrary processor i and the average network delay T_{net} in the DBMC are derived here. T_i consists of the CPU time due to tuple processing, CPU time required for initiating an I/O access and to send/receive hash buckets from other processors, and the physical I/O access time. The task execution time on a specific processor is obtained by substituting the appropriate values for the parameters f_i, R_i', and S_i'.

We know that R_i and S_i are processed in phase 1 and R_i' and S_i' are processed during phase 2. Further, depending on the available memory, phase 2 processing is performed in a number of stages. We first determine the fraction f_i of R_i' that will be processed in stage one of phase 2. The number of hash buckets $(B + 1)$ used in phase 2 processing is chosen such that

$$B = \frac{|R_i'| - |M|}{M - 1}.$$

f_i is the fraction of R_i' that can fit in the memory after allocating B blocks as buffers. Thus,

$$f_i = \frac{|M| - B}{|R|}.$$

B and f_i are, of course, positive values.

Phase 1 Cost: The equations are derived under the assumption that phase 1 and phase 2 computations proceed concurrently. I.e., as the hash partitions of relation R are received, phase 2 processing of these partitions starts; $(1 - f_i)$ fraction of these partitions are saved on the disk and the remaining stay in memory, thus reducing the number of I/O's.

Number of I/O's, $N_{\text{IO}}^1 = |R_i| + |S_i| + (1 - f_i)(|R_i'| + |S_i'|)$

I/O access time $= N_{\text{IO}}^1 \times t_d$

$$\text{CPU time to process tuples} = (\{R_i\} + \{S_i\})\frac{I_1}{\mu}$$

$$\text{CPU time to initiate I/O's} = N_{\text{IO}}^1 \times \frac{I_d}{\mu}.$$

In addition to tuple processing and I/O time, there is a component of CPU time which is due to the communication protocol involved in exchanging hash buckets among the processors. This depends on the number of processors, the size of the relations, and memory in each processor. Since only as much of R_i and S_i as the available memory can be read from the disk and processed at any time, the distribution phase is performed in a number of stages. In each stage, processor i sends a message to all the other processors. Since all the processors are assumed to be identical, processor i receives a message from each of the $(P - 1)$ processors. Thus,

CPU time to send/receive hash buckets to other processors

$$= \left(\uparrow \frac{R}{PM} + \uparrow \frac{S}{PM}\right)(P - 1)\frac{I_{\text{comm}}}{\mu}.$$

Phase 2 Cost: During phase 2, only $(1 - f_i)$ of the relations are read from the disk.

Total number of I/O's, $N_{\text{IO}}^2 = (1 - f_i)(|R_i'| + |S_i'|)$.

$$\text{CPU time} = (2 - f_i)(\{R_i'\} + \{S_i'\})\frac{I_1}{\mu}$$

Hence, the final expressions for the CPU time and I/O time of a task are

$$N_{\mathrm{IO}} = |R_i| + |S_i| + 2(1 - f_i)(|R'_i| + |S'_i|)$$

$$\text{I/O time} = N_{\mathrm{IO}} t_d$$

$$\text{CPU time} = \frac{I_1}{\mu}(\{R_i\} + \{S_i\} + (2 - f_i)(\{R'_i\} + \{S'_i\})) + \frac{I_d}{\mu} N_{\mathrm{IO}} + \frac{I_{\mathrm{comm}}}{\mu}\left(\frac{R}{PM} + \frac{S}{PM}\right)(P - 1)$$

and $T_i =$ I/O time + CPU time.

The actual transmission of relations over the communication medium causes a network delay which can be a substantial portion of the overall execution time. During the distribution phase, each processor sends its portion of R and S (except for a small fraction which belongs to its own hash bucket) across the network. If we ignore the small fraction, the network delay is due to the transmission time of both the relations. It is given by

$$T_{\mathrm{net}} = \frac{R + S}{\beta}.$$

Hash Join under Double Skew

When both the relations are skewed, the CPU time in phase 2 of hash join increases tremendously. Since we have assumed that double skew implies both the relations are skewed on the same join attribute value, each of the R-tuples with the specific skewed attribute value will match with every S-tuple with that skewed attribute value. If I_1 is the number of instructions required to join the first matching tuple and ζ is the fraction of I_1 required to join an additional tuple with the same attribute value, the CPU processing time (in the skewed processor) for phase 2 is given by

$$\frac{I_1}{\mu}(2 - f_i)(\{R'_i\} + \{S'_i\}) + \frac{I_1\zeta}{\mu}\{S'_i\}\{R'_i\}$$

$$= \frac{I_1}{\mu}(2 - f_i)Q(\{R\} + \{S\}) + \frac{I_1\zeta}{\mu}Q^2\{R\}\{S\}.$$

Note that the skewed processor performs a cross product join whose complexity is quadratic on the number of tuples in the skewed buckets.

Appendix B

Analysis of Semijoin

For the analysis of semijoin, the following parameters are introduced.

- I_s Required pathlength to process a tuple during either Step 2 or 7 of Section III-C ($0.25 I_1$ instructions)
- I_m Required pathlength to process a tuple during Step 5 ($30 \times \log P$ instructions)
- α Ratio of join attribute size to tuple size (0.1).

The execution time of semijoin is determined by summing the time required to perform the seven steps identified in Section III-C.

$$\text{IO time} = (|R_i| + |S_i|)\left(t_d + \frac{I_d}{\mu}\right)$$

$$\text{CPU time} = (\{R_i\} + \{S_i\})\frac{I_s}{\mu} + \{R_i\}\frac{I_m}{\mu}$$

$$\text{Network delay} = \frac{2R\alpha}{\beta}.$$

During our empirical study it was found that the choice of value for I_m has a significant impact on the execution time while I_s has only secondary effect. I_s is assumed to be a fraction, say 0.25, of I_1 (defined for hash join algorithm). Choice of value for I_m is elaborated here. Step 5 involves merging P sorted sequence of approximately R/P join attribute values. The complexity of the most efficient algorithm for performing this is $O(P \log P)$ [19]. Thus, the CPU time for Step 5 is proportional to $(R/P)P \log P = R \log P$. Unlike other steps, it cannot be decreased by increasing the number of processors. In our analysis, I_m was assumed to be $30 \log P$ instructions. Thus, the final expression for semijoin execution time is

$$\left(\frac{|R|}{P} + \frac{|S|}{P}\right)\left(t_d + \frac{I_d}{\mu}\right) + \left(\frac{\{R\}}{P} + \frac{\{S\}}{P}\right)\frac{0.25 I_1}{\mu} + \{R\}\frac{30}{\mu} + \frac{2R\alpha}{\beta}.$$

Hash Join with Semijoin

When semijoin is used as a preprocessing step, the hash join phases process relations R and Z which is a subset of relation S. Let η be the semijoin selectivity. Further, let all the processors have an equal size partition of Z in their local disks, i.e.,

$$Z = \eta S$$

$$Z_i = \eta S_i = \frac{\eta S}{P}$$

$$Z'_i = \eta S'_i.$$

The cost of the hash join phases is evaluated as before after substituting Z for S. The overall cost of using semijoin with hash join is obtained by adding the semijoin cost to the hash join cost. It is given by

N_{IO} (hash join with semijoin) $= 2|R_i| + (1 + \eta)|S_i| + 2(1 - f_i)(|R'_i| + |\eta S'_i|)$.

I/O time (hash join with semijoin) $= N_{\mathrm{IO}} t_d$.

CPU time (hash join with semijoin)

$$= \frac{0.25 I_1}{\mu}\left(\frac{\{R\}}{P} + \frac{\{S\}}{P}\right) + \{R\}\frac{30}{\mu} + \frac{I_1}{\mu}(\{R_i\} + \{\eta S_i\} + (2 - f_i)\{R'_i\} + \{\eta S'_i\}) + \frac{I_d}{\mu} N_{\mathrm{IO}} + \frac{I_{\mathrm{comm}}}{\mu}\left(\frac{R}{PM} + \frac{\eta S}{PM}\right)(P - 1)$$

Network delay (hash join with semijoin)

$$= \frac{2R\alpha + R + \eta S}{\beta}.$$

Execution time (hash join with semijoin) = IO time + CPU time + Network delay.

REFERENCES

[1] A. P. Bernstein and D. W. Chiu, "Using semijoins to solve relational queries," *J. ACM,* vol. 28, no. 1, pp. 25–40, 1981.

[2] L. Bic and R. L. Hartman, "Hither hundreds of processors in a database machine," in *Proc. 1985 Int. Workshop Database Machines,* Springer-Verlag, pp. 153–168.

[3] D. Bitton, D. J. DeWitt, and C. Turbyfill, "Benchmarking database systems—A systematic approach," in *Proc. 9th Int. Conf. Very Large Databases,* 1983.

[4] K. Bratsbergsengen, "Hashing methods and relational algebra operations," in *Proc. 10th Int. Conf. Very Large Databases,* 1984, pp. 323–333.

[5] S. Christodoulakis, "Estimating record selectivities," *Inform. Syst.,* vol. 8, no. 2, pp. 105–115, 1983.

[6] S. A. Demurjian, D. K. Hsiao, D. S. Kerr, J. Menon, P. R. Strawser, R. C. Tekampe, J. Trimble, and R. J. Watson, "Performance evaluation of a database system in multiple backend configurations," in *Proc. 1985 Int. Workshop Database Machines,* Springer-Verlag, pp. 91–111.

[7] D. J. DeWitt, R. H. Katz, F. Olken, L. D. Shapiro, M. R. Stonebraker, and D. Wood, "Implementation techniques for main memory database systems," in *Proc. SIGMOD'84,* Sigmod Record, vol. 14, no. 2, 1984, pp. 1–8.

[8] D. J. DeWitt and R. H. Gerber, "Multiprocessor hash-based join algorithms," in *Proc. 11th Int. Conf. Very Large Data Bases,* 1985, pp. 151–164.

[9] D. J. DeWitt, R. H. Gerber, G. Graefe, M. L. Heytens, K. B. Kumar, and M. Muralikrishna, "GAMMA—A high performance dataflow database machine," in *Proc. 12th Int. Conf. Very Large Data Bases,* 1986, pp. 228–237.

[10] D. J. DeWitt, M. Smith, and H. Boral, "A single-user performance evaluation of the teradata database machine," MCC Tech. Rep. DB-081-87, 1987.

[11] D. M. Dias, B. R. Iyer, and P. S. Yu, "Tradeoffs between coupling small and large processors for transaction," *IEEE Trans. Comput.,* vol. 37, no. 3, pp. 310–320, 1988.

[12] W. Feller, *An Introduction to Probability Theory and Its Applications, Vol. 1,* 3rd ed. New York: Wiley, 1967.

[13] A. Gravey, "A simple construction of upper bound for the mean of the maximum of N identically distributed random variables," *J. Appl. Probability,* vol. 22, pp. 844–851, 1985.

[14] P. Heidelberger and M. S. Lakshmi, "A performance comparison of multimicroprocessor and mainframe database architectures," *IEEE Trans. Software Eng.,* vol. 14, no. 4, pp. 522–531, 1988.

[15] D. K. Hsiao, *Advanced Database Machine Architecture.* Englewood Cliffs, NJ: Prentice-Hall, 1983.

[16] M. Y. Kim, "Parallel operation of magnetic disk storage devices: Synchronized disk interleaving," in *Proc. 1985 Int. Workshop Database Machines,* Springer-Verlag, pp. 299–329.

[17] M. Y. Kim and A. N. Tantawi, "Asynchronous disk interleaving: Approximating access delays," IBM Res. Rep. RC12497, IBM T. J. Watson Research Center, Yorktown Heights, NY 10598, 1988.

[18] L. Kleinrock, *Queueing Systems, Vol. 1: Theory.* New York: Wiley, 1975.

[19] D. E. Knuth, *The Art of Computer Programming, Vol. 3: Sorting and Searching,* Reading, MA: Addison-Wesley, 1973.

[20] C. Kruskal and A. Weiss, "Allocating independent subtasks on parallel processors," *IEEE Trans. Software Eng.,* vol. SE-11, no. 10, pp. 1001–1016, 1985.

[21] S. Lakshmi and P. S. Yu, "Performance of relational join operations on parallel architectures," IBM Res. Rep. RC13370, IBM T. J. Watson Research Center, Yorktown Heights, NY 10598, 1987.

[22] ——, "Effect of skew on join performance in parallel architectures," in *Proc. Int. Symp. Databases in Parallel Distributed Syst.,* 1988, pp. 107–120.

[23] ——, "Effectiveness of parallel processing in database systems," *Comput. Sci. Eng.,* vol. 5, no. 2, pp. 73–81, 1990.

[24] C. A. Lynch, "Selectivity estimation and query optimization in large databases with highly skewed distributions of column values," in *Proc. 14th Int. Conf. Very Large Databases,* 1988, pp. 240–251.

[25] L. F. Mackert and G. M. Lohman, "Index scans using a finite LRU buffer: A validated I/O model," IBM Res. Rep. RJ 4836, IBM T. J. Watson Research Center, Yorktown Heights, NY 10598, 1985.

[26] J. Menon, "Sorting and join algorithms for multiprocessor database," IBM Res. Rep. RJ 5049, IBM T. J. Watson Research Center, Yorktown Heights, NY 10598, 1986.

[27] A. Y. Montgomery, D. J. D'Souza, and S. B. Lee, "The cost of relational algebraic operations on skewed data: Estimates and experiments," *Inform. Processing 83,* IFIP, 1983, pp. 235–241.

[28] P. M. Neches and J. E. Shemer, "The genesis of a database computer," *IEEE Comput. Mag.,* vol. 17, no. 11, pp. 42–56, 1984.

[29] G. Z. Qadah, "The equi-join operation on a multiprocessor database machine: Algorithms and the evaluation of their performance," in *Proc. 1985 Int. Workshop Database Machines,* Springer-Verlag, 1985, pp. 35–67.

[30] Measurement Concepts Corp., "C3 teradata study," Tech. Rep. RADC-TR-85-273, Rome Air Development Center, NY, Mar. 1986.

[31] S. Salza, M. Terranova, and P. Velardi, "Performance modeling of the DBMAC architecture," in *Proc. 1983 Int. Workshop Database Machines,* Springer-Verlag, pp. 74–90.

[32] P. G. Selinger, M. M. Astrahan, D. D. Chamberlin, R. A. Lorie, and T. G. Price, "Access path selection in a relational database management system," in *Proc. SIGMOD'79,* pp. 23–34.

[33] L. D. Shapiro, "Join processing in database systems with large memories," *ACM Trans. Database Syst.,* vol. 11, no. 3, pp. 239–264, 1986.

[34] P. Valduriez and G. Gardarin, "Join and semi-join algorithms for a multiprocessor database machine," *ACM Trans. Database Syst.,* vol. 9, no. 1, pp. 133–161.

[35] S. Yoshizumi, S. Torii, K. Kojima, A. Sakata, and T. Imon, "Vector-type high-speed database processor—Fundamental concepts," in *Proc. 32nd Nat. Convention Inform. Processing Soc.,* Japan.

[36] G. K. Zipf, *Human Behavior and the Principle of Least Effort.* Reading, MA: Addison-Wesley, 1949.

M. Seetha Lakshmi received the B.E. degree in electrical engineering from Madras University, India, in 1972, and the M.S. and Ph.D. degrees in computer sciences from The University of Texas at Austin, in 1979 and 1983, respectively.

She joined IBM Thomas J. Watson Research Center, Yorktown Heights, NY, in 1983. She is currently involved in the IBM Office Vision product at the IBM Applications Systems Division Lab, Dallas, TX. Her research interests include performance modeling, database systems, distributed/parallel systems, and computer architecture.

Dr. Lakshmi is a member of the IEEE Computer Society.

Philip S. Yu (S'76–M'78–SM'87) received the B.S. degree in electrical engineering from National Taiwan University, Taipei, Taiwan, Republic of China, in 1972, the M.S. and Ph.D. degrees in electrical engineering from Stanford University, in 1976 and 1978, respectively, and the M.B.A. degree from New York University in 1982.

Since 1978 he has been with the IBM Thomas J. Watson Research Center, Yorktown Heights, NY. Currently he is a manager of the Architecture Analysis and Design group. His current research interests include database systems, parallel and distributed processing, computer architecture, performance modeling, workload analysis, and computer networking. He has published about 70 papers in referred journals and conferences and has published over 60 research reports and 50 technical disclosures.

Dr. Yu is a member of the Association for Computing Machinery.

Performance Analysis of a Load Balancing Hash-Join Algorithm for a Shared Memory Multiprocessor

Edward Omiecinski

College of Computing
Georgia Institute of Technology
Atlanta, Georgia 30332
U. S. A.

Abstract

Within the last several years, there has been a growing interest in applying general multiprocessor systems to relational database query processing. Efficient parallel algorithms have been designed for the join operation but usually have a failing in that their performance deteriorates greatly when the data is nonuniform. In this paper, we propose a new version of the hash-based join algorithm that balances the load between the processors, for any given bucket, in a shared everything environment. We develop an analytical model of the cost of the algorithm and implement the algorithm on a shared memory multiprocessor machine. We also perform a number of experiments comparing our model with our empirical results.

1. Introduction

Applying multiprocessor machines to database query processing has been an active area of research. The motivation for using a multiprocessor machine stems from the fact that databases are getting larger and that an adequate level of performance, e.g. response time, is required. Most of the proposed multiprocessor database systems are based on a shared nothing [BF87,DGGHKM86,KO90] architecture. That is, where each processor has its own local memory and processors communicate via message passing. In addition, a disk or set of disks is connected to each processor, allowing processors to read/write to a disk in parallel. There have also been proposed systems that follow a shared everything [DKT90,MR89,OS90,QI88,SKPO88] paradigm. In these schemes memory and disks are shared by all processors. Once again, a disk (or set of disks) would have its own I/O controller so that a read/write to different disks can be done in parallel.

For relational database systems, there have been a number of algorithms developed for implementing the join operation in parallel [BF87,DG85,QI88]. They include the nested-loop method [BF87,SD89], the sort-merge method [QI88,SD89] and the hash-join method [QI88,SD89]. The performance of the algorithms is usually predicted by analytical modelling or simulation. In the performance analysis it is assumed that the data (relations) are uniformly distributed. However, as pointed out in [LY88,SD89], a non-uniform data distribution (also referred to as data skew) can have a severe affect on the performance of the join algorithm.

In this paper we develop a hash-join algorithm that is robust in the face of data skew. It is specifically designed for a shared everything architecture. We present some of the previous work that has been done to devise a join algorithm that will be immune to data skew in the next section. In section 3, we present our hash-join algorithm that balances the load when the data is skewed. In section 4, we present an analytical cost model for our algorithm and in section 5, we show the results of implementing our algorithm on a shared memory multiprocessor machine.

2. Previous Work

In [WDY90], the shared nothing model of parallelism is assumed and a parallel join algorithm based on the sort-merge method is presented to handle data skew. The algorithm is based on the divide-and-conquer approach. It adds an extra scheduling phase to the usual sort, transfer and join phases. During the scheduling phase, an optimization algorithm is used, which takes the output of the sort phase and determines how the join is to be divided into multiple tasks and how those tasks are to be assigned to proces-

"Performance Analysis of a Load Balancing Hash-Join Algorithm for a Shared-Memory Multiprocessor" by E. Omiecinski from *Proc. 17th Int'l Conf. Very Large Data Bases,* 1991, pp. 375-385.

sors so as to balance the load. They present an analytical model of their algorithm's performance and show that it achieves a good load balancing for the join processing phase in a CPU-bound environment.

In [KO90], a robust hash-join based algorithm is devised for a specific parallel database computer architecture. This architecture is also based on a shared nothing model. Instead of their previous approach [KNHT90] of allocating buckets to processors, they dynamically allocate buckets to processors so as to balance the load. They propose a bucket spreading strategy which partitions buckets into fragments and in a subsequent phase these fragments are assigned to processors. The bucket spreading strategy is similar to the idea of disk striping. They also use a specific network structure, i.e., an omega network, to assist in the bucket spreading strategy. They present a simulation model of their system and show that the performance of their algorithm is not affected very much by the presence of data skew. The cost of writing the result of the join to a file and to disk is not considered.

In [SD89], the effect of limited data skew on four different join algorithms is examined. They conclude that the performance of the hash-based join algorithms degrade when the join values of the inner relation are highly skewed and that a non-hash-based algorithm should be used in those cases, e.g. sort-merge. However, the double skew case was not considered.

Some work has appeared in the recent literature dealing with hash-join algorithms for a shared everything architecture [LTS90,QI88]. In [QI88], they present a large set of parallel algorithms, including hash-join, for implementing a join operation on a shared memory database machine. An analytical model of the various algorithm's performance is presented. However, the problem of data skew was not considered.

In [LTS90], they examine only hash-based join algorithms for a general purpose shared memory multiprocessor. The amount of available memory is assumed to be proportional to the number of processors. In this approach a global hash table is built for each bucket. They use a locking mechanism to provide exclusive access for a write to this hash table but they allow multiple reads to occur simultaneously. They provide an analytical model of the total processing time for their join algorithms. As in the previously mentioned work in this section, data skew is not considered.

3. Hash Join Algorithms for a Shared Everything Architecture

The basic architecture that we assume is that of a shared everything machine. Each processor shares common memory with other processors and each processor may have some local (nonshared) memory as well. Processors also share secondary storage devices. We assume that for secondary storage, we have the same number of disk drives as we do processors. We do not have to limit our approach to this but we had to make a decision regarding this feature and this seemed reasonable. The processors, disks and memory are linked by an interconnection network. We assume that disk reads/writes of different pages can be done concurrently as can memory accesses to distinct variables. Although main memory sizes are increasing rapidly, we assume that neither of the two relations to be joined will fit entirely in main memory.

The hash-join algorithm that we consider for a shared memory multiprocessor is the GRACE hash-join method [KTM83]. This algorithm will also form the basis for our load balancing hash-join algorithm. Since the number of processors will be relatively small in a shared memory multiprocessor, the number of buckets produced will be greater than the number of processors.. Hence, a single processor will handle multiple buckets. The GRACE hash-join algorithm can be summarized by the following phases for performing R ⋈ S.

I. Read relation R, partition the tuples into buckets based on a given hash function applied to the joining attribute value and write those buckets to secondary storage;

II. Read relation S, partition the tuples into buckets based on the same hash function as used in prior phase and write those buckets to secondary storage;

III. For each bucket created in phase I, read the R bucket from secondary storage, build an in memory hash table using some hash function applied to the joining attribute value, read the corresponding S bucket from secondary storage and for each tuple probe the hash table for an R tuple with the matching value for the joining attribute. The join result is formed by the matching tuples.

One can see that if the data for each relation is partitioned across all the disks, then each phase can be done in parallel. As seen in [LTS90], one has to be careful in phases I and II that multiple processors do not try to write to the same bucket at the same time. In [LTS90], they used locks to avoid the problem. However, when the data is highly skewed the lock conflict rate can be quite high for both phases. For our adaptation of this algorithm, we avoid the use of locks. In phase I (or phase II) each processor determines the bucket that a tuple belongs in but does not write it to the bucket at that time. Instead that information is stored in a small array. The array is small since we are processing a page of a relation at a time on each processor. Hence, the number of entries in the array is equal to the number of tuples in a page. Each processor sorts its array in increasing order of bucket number and builds a small index on that information, i.e., linking a bucket number with the tuples that belong to that bucket. After that, the processors are assigned buckets. The tuples for each given bucket will be placed in a buffer page by only one processor. To accomplish this, a given processor will access a distinct entry in the index of each of the processors. For example, if a processor is responsible for bucket 0, then that processor will access entry 0 in the index created by each of the processors. With this scheme only one buffer page per bucket is needed and there is no contention between processors.

In contrast to the approach in [LTS90], one hash table is not built at a time and all processors do not probe that hash table in parallel during phase III. As previously mentioned, if the data is highly skewed, then building and probing a single hash table in parallel can result in a high conflict rate that degrades performance. Instead, if there are n processors then hash tables for n buckets will be created in parallel and probed in parallel.

Our load balancing hash-join approach is similar to the approach in [KO90] but with the following notable differences: our method is designed for a shared everything system as opposed to a shared nothing system, we make use of no special hardware and we assign a bucket to one or more processors based on a first-fit decreasing heuristic, similar to that used for the bin-packing problem [HS78]. In addition, we develop an analytical model of our algorithm's cost and implement the algorithm so that we can validate our model.

For our load balancing hash-join approach, we need to modify the three phases and to add a scheduling phase prior to phase III. In phase I, we keep a count of the number of tuples that hash into each bucket for relation R. In addition, since one bucket may need to be processed by several processors in phase III, we must stripe the pages of a bucket across the disks. This will allow us to read in a portion of one bucket in parallel and to process each portion in parallel. We need to do the same for phase II but for relation S. Having the size (in number of tuples) for each bucket we can decide on the number of processors to handle each bucket and the schedule of buckets to processors. For a given bucket, we use the maximum of the sizes of the corresponding R and S buckets for the following calculation. To determine the number of processors that are needed to handle a bucket, we calculate the size of a uniform bucket, *usize*, i.e., as if the tuples were uniformly distributed to buckets. We then divide each actual bucket size by *usize* and take the ceiling of that result, which yields the number of needed processors per bucket, *processors_per_bucket*. The scheduling phase, which precedes phase III, sorts the *processors_per_bucket* information in increasing order. Next a schedule is produced by using a first-fit decreasing heuristic to allocate buckets to individual steps in the schedule so that the number of steps is minimized. In the first-fit decreasing heuristic, buckets are allocated to a step in non-increasing order of the number of processors needed. If the required number of processors for the bucket to be scheduled is not available in the current set of steps in the schedule, then a new step is added to the schedule and the bucket is allocated to the processors in that new step.

Once the scheduling phase is complete, which is done by a single processor, phase III may begin using the schedule as a driver. The schedule is a global array and as such is accessible by all processors. Using the schedule information, each processor involved with a given bucket can read a disjoint subset of the pages of that bucket since the pages are striped across the disks and can build an in-memory hash table of the tuples on those pages. Now, since there does not exist just a single hash table for a given bucket but, let say n hash tables where n is the number of processors needed to process the bucket, the tuples in the corresponding S bucket must be processed against each of those n hash tables. Once again, since the pages of the S bucket have been striped across the disks, a disjoint subset of those pages can be processed by each of the n processors. At this point the process resembles the nested-loop join method since a page read (by processor i) and processed against hash table i has to be processed against the remaining $n-1$ hash tables. This is accomplished in a circular fashion, i.e., processor i processes a data page with hash tables $i, i+1, \ldots, n, 0, \ldots, i-1$ in that order. The circular approach is also used for reading pages from the disks so that contention is minimized due to multuple processors trying to read distinct pages from the same disk at the same time.

Table I. Model Parameters

Parameter	Description/ Value
$\|R\|$	size of relation R = 1000 (in pages)
$\|S\|$	size of relation S = 1000 (in pages)
$\{R\}$	number of R tuples = 10000
$\{S\}$	number of S tuples = 10000
JV_R	number of unique join values in relation R = 1000
t_R	number of tuples per page of relation R = 10
t_S	number of tuples per page of relation S = 10
P	number of processors = 2 thru 9
B	number of buckets = 25
D	number of disks = 2 thru 9
IO	time to perform an I/O operation = 24 ms
Comp	time to compare two attributes = 0.007 ms
Assign	time to assign a value to a variable = 0.007 ms
C	sorting constant = 2
F	scheduling constant = 2
Hash	time to compute hash value of an attribute = 0.015 ms
Move	time to move a tuple in memory = 0.040 ms
Rskew	fraction of R tuples with skew data value = 0.1 to 0.4
Sskew	fraction of S tuples with skew data value = 0.1 to 0.4

4. Analytical Models for Hash Join Algorithms

In this section we present the analytical models for both hashing schemes. To make the modelling more tractable we make a few assumptions. We should note that these assumptions are not restrictions on the algorithms. The main assumption regards the data skew. We assume that only one bucket contains a disproportionate number of tuples, which is a percentage of the total number of tuples in the relation. The other tuples are uniformly distributed across the remaining buckets. To accomplish this we have a single data skew value for the joining attribute and we generate a specified fraction of the tuples with that value. The remaining tuples will actually be distributed across all of the buckets, including the skew bucket. In addition, when we consider the double skew case, the corresponding buckets in the other relation have the same structure. This is in agreement with the assumptions made in other work [LY88]. We also assume that there is enough main memory to process any given bucket, since we are primarily interested in how data skew affects load balancing and not how data skew may cause overflow in a hash bucket. Table I describes the different parameters and their values used with the analytical models. They are similar to the values found in [LTS90,QI88,Sha86].

We will first present the model for the basic hash-join approach and then for the load balancing approach. Since the processors are working in parallel, the one processor that takes the longest time to finish in each step will dictate the overall cost of the algorithm. That processor is the one that is assigned the skew bucket. As already mentioned, that processor will also handle an equal share of the other buckets. Hence, the cost formulas will be derived for just that processor. In phase I, we have the following steps:

(a) Read pages of R relation:

$$\left\lceil \frac{|R|}{P} \right\rceil \cdot IO$$

(b) Find bucket address of tuple:

$$\left\lceil \frac{|R|}{P} \right\rceil \cdot t_R \cdot Hash$$

(c) Store address of tuple and bucket address in an array:

$$2 \cdot \left\lceil \frac{|R|}{P} \right\rceil \cdot t_R \cdot Assign$$

(d) Sort array by bucket number:

$$C \cdot \left\lceil \frac{|R|}{P} \right\rceil \cdot t_R \log_2 t_R \cdot (Compare + Assign)$$

(e) Build index on bucket number:

$$\left\lceil \frac{|R|}{P} \right\rceil \cdot (t_R \cdot Compare + 2 \cdot B \cdot Assign)$$

(f) Move tuples to their associated buckets: Note, based on our assumptions, one processor will handle the skew bucket as well as $\left\lceil \frac{B}{P} \right\rceil - 1$ other buckets since the bucket to processor assignment is static and since all processors will handle approximately the same number of buckets. So the skew value contributes $\lceil Rskew \cdot \{R\} \rceil$ tuples to the skew bucket. Since the other tuples are uniformly distributed across all B buckets, each bucket will have $\left\lceil (1 - Rskew) \cdot \frac{\{R\}}{B} \right\rceil$ tuples. So the total number of tuples in any nonskew bucket can be defined as

$$t_{nonskewbucket} = \left\lceil (1 - Rskew) \cdot \frac{\{R\}}{B} \right\rceil$$

and the total number of tuples in the skew bucket can be defined as

$$t_{skewbucket} = \lceil Rskew \cdot \{R\} \rceil + t_{nonskewbucket}$$

So we have the following cost for this step:

$$2 \cdot \left\lceil \frac{B}{P} \right\rceil \cdot P + t_{skewbucket} \cdot Move + \left(\left\lceil \frac{B}{P} \right\rceil - 1 \right) \cdot t_{nonskewbucket} \cdot Move$$

(g) Write pages of buckets to disk:

$$\left[\left\lceil \frac{t_{skewbucket}}{t_R} \right\rceil + \left(\left\lceil \frac{B}{P} \right\rceil - 1 \right) \cdot \left\lceil \frac{t_{nonskewbucket}}{t_R} \right\rceil \right] \cdot IO$$

Phase II has the same cost formulas as phase I except that the R relation is replaced by the S relation, Rskew replaced by Sskew and t_R replaced by t_S.

Phase III consists of the following steps:

(a) Read R pages for skew bucket and $\left\lceil \frac{B}{P} \right\rceil - 1$ other buckets:

This is the same cost as in Phase I, step (g).

(b) Build an in-memory hash table for each bucket:

$$t_{skewbucket} \cdot (Hash + Move) + \left(\left\lceil \frac{B}{P} \right\rceil - 1 \right) \cdot t_{nonskewbucket} \cdot (Hash + Move)$$

(c) Read S pages for skew bucket and $\left\lceil \frac{B}{P} \right\rceil - 1$ other buckets:

This is the same cost as in Phase II, step (g).

(d) Probe the hash table and form the join:

The cost for the non skew buckets is

$$\left(\left\lceil \frac{B}{P} \right\rceil - 1 \right) \cdot \left(\frac{(1 - Sskew) \cdot \{S\}}{B} \right) \cdot (Hash + (Comp + Move) \cdot \frac{(1 - Rskew) \cdot \{R\}}{JV_R - 1})$$

The cost for the skew bucket is

$$(1 - Fskew) \cdot (Sskew \cdot \{S\} + \frac{(1 - Skew) \cdot \{S\}}{B}) \cdot (Hash + (Comp + Move) \cdot \frac{(1 - Rskew) \cdot \{R\}}{JV_R - 1})$$

$$+ \ Fskew \cdot (Sskew \cdot \{S\} + \frac{(1 - Skew) \cdot \{S\}}{B})$$

$$\cdot (Hash + (Comp + Move) \cdot Rskew \cdot \{R\})$$

where *Fskew* is the fraction of tuples in relation S that match the skew value in relation R, i.e.,

$$\frac{Sskew \cdot \{S\}}{Sskew \cdot \{S\} + (1 - Sskew) \cdot \frac{\{S\}}{B}}$$

We now present the analytical cost model for our load balancing hash-join algorithm.

Phase I has the same cost formulas as phase I for the hash-join model.

Phase II has the same cost formulas as phase II for the hash-join model.

Scheduling phase:

$$F \cdot B^2 \cdot Assign$$

where F is a scheduling constant.

Phase III consists of the following steps:

(a) Read R pages for skew bucket and other buckets:

$$IO \cdot [\left\lceil \frac{B - (P - N + 1)}{P} \right\rceil \cdot \left\lceil \frac{(1 - Rskew) \cdot |R|}{B} \right\rceil + \frac{Rskew \cdot |R| + \left\lceil \frac{(1 - Rskew) \cdot |R|}{B} \right\rceil}{N}]$$

where N is the number of processors needed to handle the skew bucket. N is defined as

$$Max(\frac{Rskew \cdot \{R\} + (1 - Rskew) \cdot \{R\} / B}{\{R\} / B}, \frac{Sskew \cdot \{S\} + (1 - Sskew) \cdot \{S\} / B}{\{S\} / B})$$

The first term gives the number of other buckets that will be handled by the processor that handles the skew bucket times the number of pages for non skew buckets. The second term gives the number of pages per processor for the skew bucket, i.e., number of pages of skew data plus number of pages for non skew data in skew bucket divided by the number of processors that will process the skew data bucket.

(b) Build an in-memory hash table for each bucket:

$$\left\lceil \frac{B - (P - N + 1)}{P} \right\rceil \cdot \left\lceil \frac{(1 - Rskew) \cdot |R|}{B} \right\rceil$$

$$\cdot t_R \cdot (Hash + Move)$$

$$+ \frac{Rskew \cdot |R| + \left\lceil \frac{(1 - Rskew) \cdot |R|}{B} \right\rceil}{N}$$

$$\cdot t_R \cdot (Hash + Move)$$

(c) Read S pages for skew bucket and other buckets:

$$IO \cdot [\left\lceil \frac{B - (P - N + 1)}{P} \right\rceil \cdot \left\lceil \frac{(1 - Sskew) \cdot |S|}{B} \right\rceil + \frac{Sskew \cdot |S| + \left\lceil \frac{(1 - Sskew) \cdot |S|}{B} \right\rceil}{N}]$$

(d) Probe the hash table and form the join:

$$\left\lceil \frac{B - (P - N + 1)}{P} \right\rceil \cdot \left\lceil \frac{(1 - Sskew) \cdot |S|}{B} \right\rceil \cdot t_S$$

$$\cdot (Hash + (Comp + Move) \cdot \frac{(1 - Rskew) \cdot \{R\}}{JV_R - 1},$$

$$+ \ N \cdot [\ (1 - Fskew) \cdot (Sskew \cdot \{S\} + \frac{(1 - Skew) \cdot \{S\}}{B})$$

$$\cdot (Hash + (Comp + Move) \cdot \frac{(1 - Rskew) \cdot \{R\}}{JV_R - 1})$$

$$+ \ Fskew \cdot (Sskew \cdot \{S\} + \frac{(1 - Skew) \cdot \{S\}}{B})$$

$$\cdot (Hash + (Comp + Move) \cdot \frac{Rskew \cdot \{R\}}{N})\ ]$$

5. Comparison of Analytical and Experimental Results

In this section we present the results of some of our experiments as well as the results of our analytical models. The hash-join algorithms were executed on a 10 node Sequent Symmetry multiprocessor, in a single user environment. Since the multiprocessor we used does not have a parallel I/O capability, that part of the algorithm had to be simulated. When a page I/O was required, a procedure was called that did a busy wait for the required amount of time, e.g., 24 ms. We ran experiments with a uniform data distribution, single skew in the inner relation, single skew in the outer relation and skew in both relation, i.e., double skew. For the single skew cases, the join selectivity was the same, i.e., 0.0001. For the double skew case, the join selectivity was 0.0406, the result was considerably larger than in the single skew cases. Also, in the double skew case, the CPU processing became the dominating factor in the response time of the algorithms. We also ran experiments that included the cost of writing the resultant relation to secondary storage. We should note that our analytic models were adjusted to accomodate the extra I/O cost, although for brevity we did not show the changes of the cost formulas in the paper. We should note that the data used for the graphs are an average of several runs of the algorithms on the multiprocessor. We should also point out that in our experiments we assumed that enough memory exists to permit an in memory hash table to be built for the maximum bucket size. So for the basic hash-join method, we would not incur bucket overflow. Hence, our experiments deal solely with the load balancing aspect of the hash-join approach in a shared memory multiprocessor.

In figure 1, we show the effect of data skew on the basic hash-join algorithm. An interesting observation concerning the 6 processor case, is that the decrease in response time over the 5 processor case is small. The reason for this, is that for both the 5 and 6 processor cases, a maximum of 5 buckets will be processed during phase III by at least one processor, i.e., the processor that dictates the overall performance. A similar situation occurs for the 8 processor case.

As one would imagine, the response time increases as the data skew increases, as shown in figure 1. For the 2 processor run, the difference between the time taken by the algorithm for a uniform data distribution versus a data skew of 0.4 was only 13.76%. When we used 4 processors the difference increased to about 55.79% and when we used 9 processors the difference reached 97.62%.

In figure 2, we show the effect of data skew on the load balancing hash-join algorithm. Again, as the data skew increases, so does the response time, but not as much as for the basic method. For the 2 processor case, there is a difference of 8.37%, for the 5 processor case there is a difference of 31.85% and for the 9 processor case there is a difference of 52.17%. If we examine the case with skew equal to 0.4, we see that the difference in response time for the basic method and the load balancing method for 2, 5 and 9 processors is 3.93%, 16.96% and 28.75%, respectively. So, we see a reasonable decrease in response time with the load balancing hash-join method.

In figure 3, we compare the basic hash-join method with the load balancing hash-join method for a uniform data distribution. We see that there is little difference between the two. The maximum difference is approximately 1.09%. Hence, the scheduling overhead for the load balancing algorithm is insignificant compared to the entire cost. In addition, we show the results of the models for each of the two algorithms. The maximum difference between the basic method and its model is about 6.97%. The maximum difference between the load balancing method and its model is about 5.43%.

In figure 4, we again compare the basic hash-join algorithm with the load balancing hash-join algorithm but for the case where there is single skew in the inner relation. The skew value of 0.2 indicates that 20% of the tuples in the R relation have the same value. The total percentage of tuples hashing into the skew bucket is 23.2%. For the 8 processor case, the load balancing hash-join algorithm reduces the response time by about 13.83%. The average improvement for 6 to 9 processors is about 10.4%. The results of the models are also shown in figure 4. For the basic algorithm, the maximum difference between the actual run and the model is 3.15%. In the case of the load balancing algorithm and model, the maximum difference is only 8.46%.

For the next set of experiments, we wanted to see the effect of having to write the join result to disk. Writing the resulting relation back to disk dominated the overall cost of the join as can be seen by comparing figure 5 with figure 4. We can

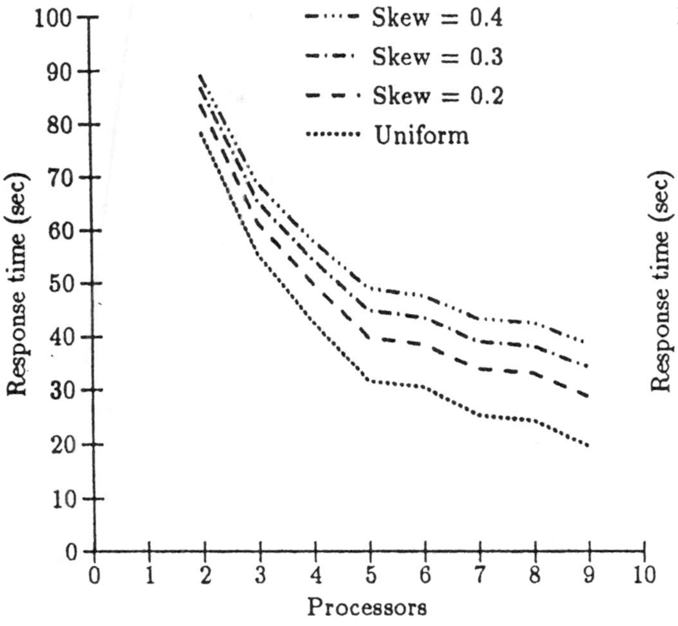

Figure 1: Basic Hash-Join Method

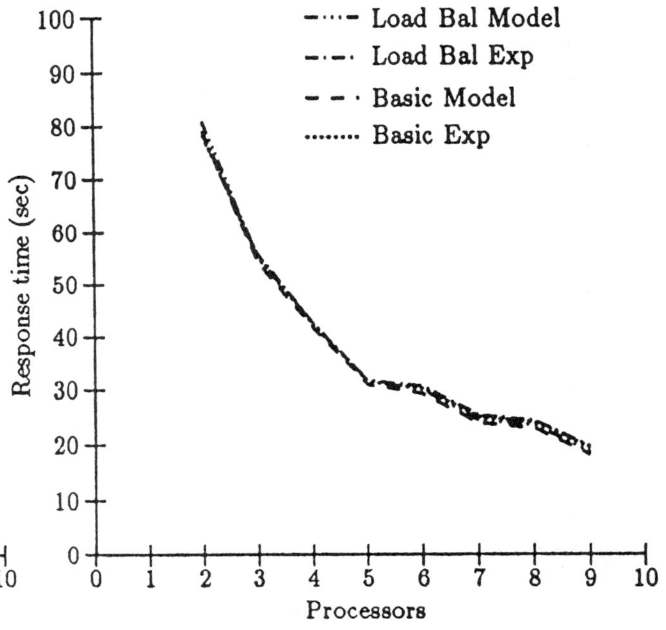

Figure 3: Basic and Load Balancing Hash-Join (uniform data)

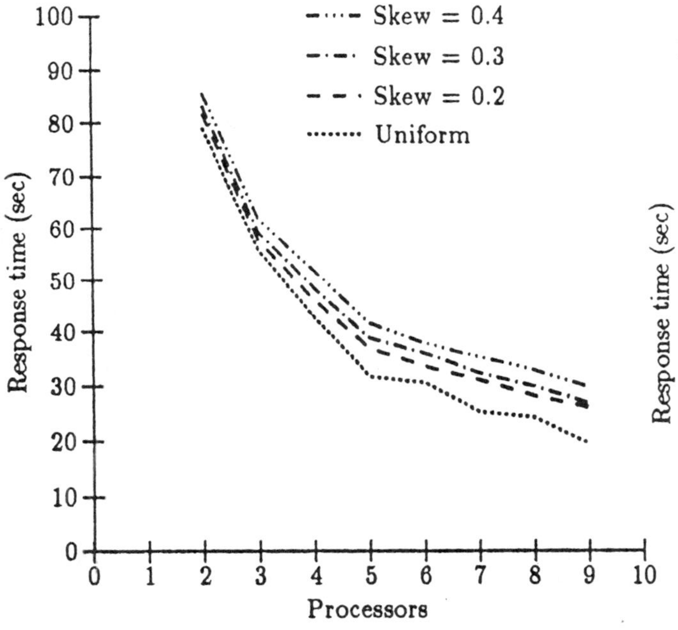

Figure 2: Load Balancing Hash-Join Method

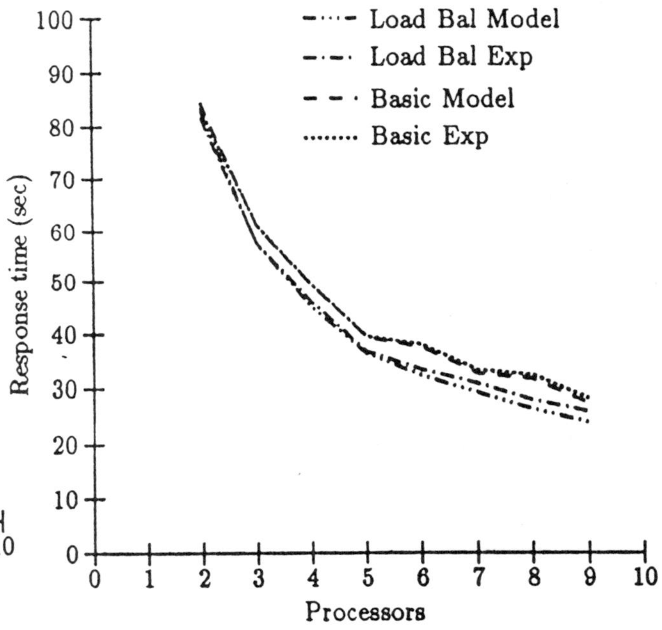

Figure 4: Basic and Load Balancing Hash-Join (R skew = 0.2)

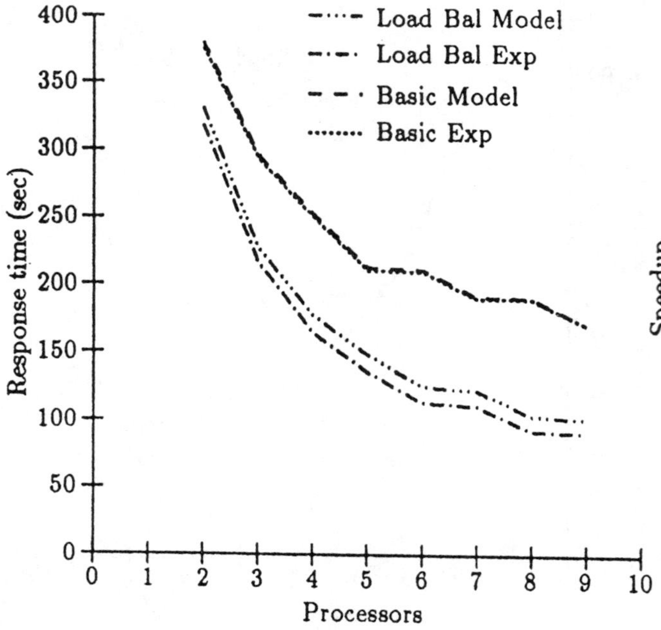

Figure 5: Basic and Load Balancing Hash-Join (R skew = 0.2) with result written to disk

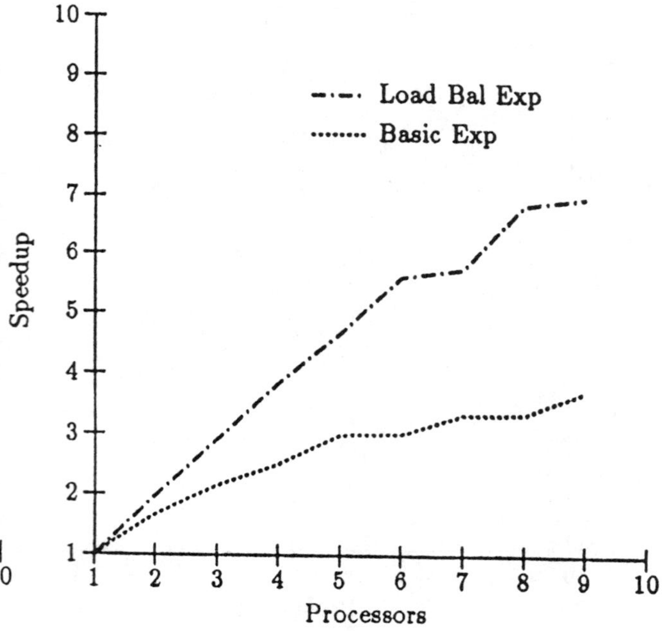

Figure 7: Speedup for Basic and Load Balancing Hash-Join (R skew = 0.2) with result written to disk

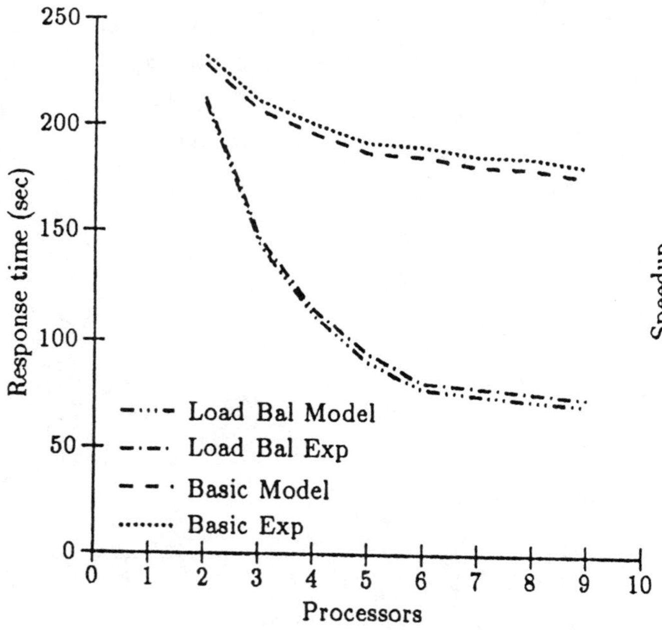

Figure 6: Basic and Load Balancing Hash-Join (R skew = S skew = 0.2)

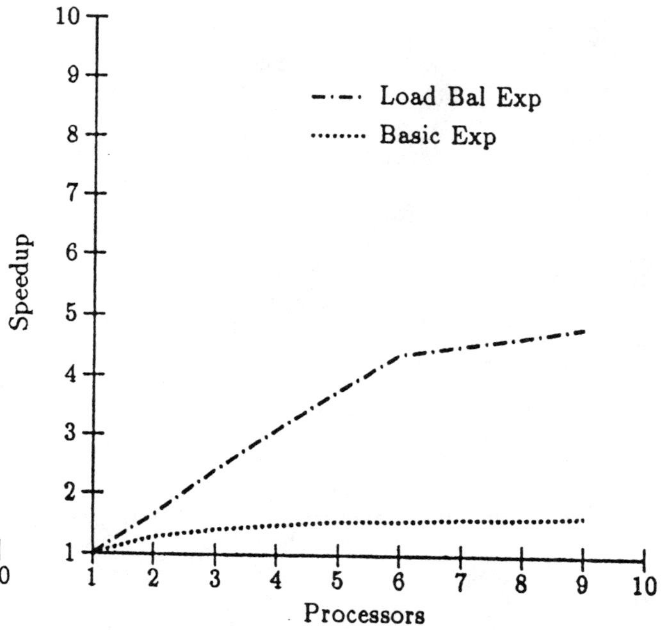

Figure 8: Speedup for Basic and Load Balancing Hash-Join (R skew = S skew = 0.2)

also see in figure 5 that the difference between the two algorithms is even more pronounced. This is due to the fact that in the basic method, one processor writes out the join result from the skewed bucket whereas in the load balancing method multiple processors write out the join result in parallel. In the 2 processor case, the load balancing method shows a decrease of about 15.4% as compared with the basic method. In the 8 processor case, the difference between the two algorithms increases to 51.19%. The average difference for the 2 to 9 processor cases is 33.1%. In addition, the model for both algorithms is quite good. The maximum difference between the observed time and the calculated time for the load balancing case is only 11.83%, while for the basic hash-join case it is less than 1%.

In addition to the response time graph in figure 5, we also include the companion graph, figure 7, of the speedup for the basic hash-join method and the load balancing method. As can be seen in figure 7, the speedup for the basic method is dismal. This can be attributed to the fact that a single processor is responsible for handling the skewed bucket. The small increase in speedup as proccessors are added is probably due to the distribution of some of the I/O costs across the additional disks. As a reminder, the number of disks is set equal to the number of processors. For the load balancing method, the speedup is close to linear, especially up to the 6 processor case. As calculated by the load balancing algorithm, the number of processors needed to handle the skewed bucket, so as to distribute the load evenly, is 6. Hence, the improvement as shown in figure 7. For the 7 processor case, the number of steps needed by the algorithm is the same as for the 6 processor case. A similar situation occurs for the 9 processor and 8 processor cases.

For the final set of experiments to be reported in this paper, we examined the situation of double skew. The results are shown in figure 6. Both the inner and outer relations had a skew value of 0.2. That is, as mentioned previously, 23.2% of the tuples of each relation hashed into one bucket, which was the same bucket, i.e., bucket 0, for each relation. This produced a join selectivity of 0.0406. For the case of double skew as with the case of writing the result to disk, the difference between the performance of the two methods is considerable. The maximum difference occurs for the 9 processor case, i.e., the load balancing algorithm shows a reduction in response time of approximately 59.28%. The average reduction in response time, considering the 2 to 9 processor cases, is 40.7%, with the 2 processor case having the least reduction, i.e., 8.5%. It can also be seen from figure 6 that the cost model is again a good reflection of the algorithm's cost.

In addition to the response time graph in figure 6, we also include the companion graph, figure 8, of the speedup for the basic hash-join method and the load balancing method. As can be seen in figure 8, the speedup for the basic method is virtually nonexistent. This is due to the fact that a single processor is responsible for handling the skewed R and S buckets. The amount of work done by this processor overshadows the total work done by all the other processors. For the load balancing method, we see a reasonable speedup, although not as good as in figure 7. This can be attributed to the fact that the load balancing algorithm calculates the number of needed processors based on the maximum size of the R bucket and S bucket. For the double skew case, the decision should be made based on the combined sizes. Hence, more than 6 processors should be allocated to the skewed bucket.

6. Conclusion

In this paper, we have adapted the Grace hash-join method for a shared everything environment and have designed and implemented a modified version that trys to balance the load on the processors when the data is skewed. We also developed cost models for our algorithms and showed that they accurately reflect the performance of the algorithms, under our assumptions. The algorithms were run on a 10 node Sequent multiprocessor machine with the parallel I/O capability simulated. From our experiments, we saw that even single skew affects the performance of the basic hash-join approach for a shared-everything system. The performance degrades greatly when the result of the join is written to disk or when there is double skew. Our load balancing algorithm has also been shown to have a much better performance when compared with the basic method in all of those cases.

7. Acknowledgments

The author would like to thank the anonymous referees for their insightful and constructive comments.

8. References

[BF87] C. Baru and O. Frieder, "Implementing Realtional Database Operations in a Cube-Connected Multicomputer," Proc. of IEEE Data Engineering Conference, 1987, 36-43.

[DKT90] S. Deen, D. Kannangara and M. Taylor, "Multi-Join on Parallel Processors," IEEE Symposium on Databases in Parallel and Distributed Systems, 1990, 92-102.

[DG85] D. DeWitt and R. Gerber, "Multiprocessor Hash-Based Join Algorithms," Proc. of 11th VLDB Conference, 1985, 151-164.

[DGGHKM86] D. DeWitt, R. Gerber, G. Graefe, M. Heytens, K. Kumar and M. Muralikrishna, "GAMMA - A High Performance Dataflow Database Machine," Proc. of VLDB Conference, 1986, 228-237.

[HS78] E. Horowitz and S. Sahni, Fundamentals of Computer Algorithms, Computer Science Press, Potomac, MD, 1978.

[KNHT90] M. Kitsuregawa, M. Nakano, L. Harada and M. Takagi, "Performance Evaluation of Functional Disk System with Nonuniform Data Distribution," Proc. of IEEE Symposium on Databases in Parallel and Distributed Systems, 1990, 80-89.

[KO90] M. Kitsuregawa and Y. Ogawa, "Bucket Spreading Parallel Hash: A New Robust, Parallel Hash Join Method for Data Skew in the Super Database Computer (SDC)," Proc. of 16th VLDB Conference, 1990, 210-221.

[KTM83] M. Kitsuregawa, H. Tanaka and T. Moto-Oka, "Application of Hash to Database Machine and its Architecture," New Generation Computing, 1, 1983, 63-74.

[LY88] S. Lakshima and P. Yu, "Effect of Skew on Join Performance in Parallel Architectures," IEEE Symposium on Databases in Parallel and Distributed Systems, 1988, 107-120.

[LTS90] H. Lu, K. Tan and M. Shan, Hash-Based Join Algorithms for Multiprocessor Computers with Shared Memory," Proc. of 16th VLDB Conference, 1990, 198-209.

[MR89] M. Murphy and D. Rotem, "Effective Resource Utilization for Multiprocessor Join Execution," Proc. of 15th VLDB Conference, 1989, 69-75.

[OL89] E. Omiecinski and E. Lin, "Hash-Based and Index-Based Join Algorithms for Cube and Ring Connected Multicomputers," IEEE Trans. on Knowledge & Data Eng., 1, 3, September 1989, 329-342.

[OS90] E. Omiecinski and R. Shonkwiler, "Parallel Join Processing using Nonclustered Indexes for a Shared Memory Multiprocessor," 2nd IEEE Symposium on Parallel & Distributed Processing, December 1990, pp. 144-151.

[QI88] G. Qadah and K. Irani, "The Join Algorithms on a Shared-Memory Multiprocessor Database Machine," IEEE Trans. on Software Eng., 14, 11, November 1988, 1668-1683.

[SD89] D. Schneider and D. DeWitt, "A Performance Evaluation of Four Parallel Join Algorithms in a Shared-Nothing Multiprocessor Environment," ACM SIGMOD Proceedings, 1989, 110-122.

[Sha86] L. Shapiro, "Join Processing in Database Systems with Large Main Memories," ACM Trans. on Database Sys., 11, 3, 1986, 239-264.

[SKPO88] M. Stonebraker, R. Katz, D. Patterson and J. Ousterhout, "The Design of XPRS," Proc. of 14th VLDB Conference, 1988, 318-330.

[WDY90] J. Wolf, D. Dias and P. Yu, "An Effective Algorithm for Parallelizing Sort Merge Joins in the Presence of Data Skew," IEEE Symposium on Databases in Parallel and Distributed Systems, 1990, 103-115.

Handling Data Skew in Multiprocessor Database Computers Using Partition Tuning

Kien A. Hua

Department of Computer Science
University of Central Florida
Orlando, FL 32816-0362
U. S. A.

Chiang Lee

Institute of Information Engineering
National Cheng Kung University
Tainan, Taiwan, 70101
Republic of China

Abstract

Shared nothing multiprocessor architecture is known to be more scalable to support very large databases. Compared to other join strategies, a hash-based join algorithm is particularly efficient and easily parallelized for this computation model. However, this hardware structure is very sensitive to the data skew problem. Unless the parallel hash join algorithm includes some load balancing mechanism, skew effect can deteriorate the system performance severely.

In this paper, we propose two *skew avoidance techniques* and one *skew resolution method*. In particular, three new parallel hash join algorithms are presented. We developed an analytical model to study the effectiveness of these algorithms. The performance study indicates that the proposed techniques offer substantial improvement over the conventional strategies in the presence of data skew. It is also interesting to observe that the skew avoidance techniques provide join strategies that are robust against data skew; where as the skew resolution method offers an adaptive join strategy that outperforms the conventional algorithms for any skew condition.

1 Introduction

There are several architectures for designing multiprocessor database computers. However, The multicomputer model [1], is most popularly used for its scalability to support very large databases [2, 3, 4, 5, 6]. The hardware structure of this computation model consists of a number of *processing nodes* (PN) interconnected through a communication network. Each PN has its own private memory and dedicated disk drives. This architecture is also known as message passing or shared nothing [7] multiprocessor structure. In this environment, the relations are typically declustered into fragments and spreaded across the PNs. Since in this model each PN processes the portion of the database on its disks, the degree of parallelism is determined by the distribution of data in the system. When serious data skew occurs, balancing the load on all the PNs is needed to ensure high system performance.

The join operation has been the most intensively studied among the relational operations for this structure. Since join operations are generally very expensive, a query optimizer typically defers the join operations until the data reduction process is performed by less costly operations, such as selections and projections. For this reason, the distribution of the input relations to a join operation is typically hard to predict. Most likely the data fragments result from the earlier data reduction operations will vary in size, and a load balancing mechanism will be necessary to ensure the efficient performance of the succeeding join operation [8].

Several parallel join algorithms have been proposed. Among them, hash-based algorithms [9, 10] are particularly suitable for the multicomputer model. In these strategies the relations are hashed (partitioned) into buckets, and each bucket is allocated to a distinct PN. Since tuples of a relation in one bucket are never joined with tuples of the other relation in other buckets, matching buckets can be joined independently in parallel by all PNs. The effectiveness of these schemes depends on the uniformity of the tuple distribution. Although they have been demonstrated to be very effective, these techniques do not guarantee the balanced workload among the local join operations. When severe fluctuation occurs among the bucket sizes, the skew effect deteriorates the performance of the join operations. A *Bucket Spreading Parallel Hash Join* (BSJ) was introduced in [11] to correct this problem.

Unlike the conventional hash-based join algorithms that statically assigned the buckets to the PN prior to the data partitioning process, BSJ algorithm defers the bucket allocation until the data partitioning process is completed. Since the distribution of the data among the buckets then becomes known, the buckets can be assigned to the PNs dynamically based on the bucket sizes to ensure a balanced data load at each PN. However, when buckets are to be allocated dynami-

"Handling Data Skew in Multiprocessor Database Computers Using Partition Tuning" by K.A. Hua and C. Lee from *Proc. 17th Int'l Conf. Very Large Data Bases,* 1991, pp. 525-535.

cally, the destination of a tuple cannot be determined during partitioning because "which PN to handle the tuple" is not assigned yet. BSJ solves this problem by spreading the original buckets across all PNs, and collecting them later to the appropriate destinations just prior to the join operations. To avoid a bottleneck during the bucket collection phase, BSJ uses a special Omega network [12] to ensure that the buckets evenly spread across all PNs. The implementation of this switch includes at each switch element, as many number of counters as there are number of buckets involved. Such a switch design may face two problems. First, it does not scale well with the rest of the system. As the number of PNs increases to support larger databases, the number of buckets increases causing the increase in the complexity of the switch elements (i.e., need more counters). Even when the system does not yet have a large number of PNs, the switch element must have enough number of counters to anticipate system growth. In other words, the complexity in the switch design could penalize the smaller system configurations. Secondly unless other operations can be designed to take advantage of the data spreading feature of the functional switch, the complexity in the switch design may affect the communication performance of the switch, and consequently the performance of the whole system. Depending on the transaction mix, it may not be worthwhile to improve the performance of joins on the expense of other operations. Finally the complexity explodes when we consider a multiuser environment. Managing different sets of counters for different users becomes quite expensive.

In [13], we proposed an adaptive load balancing strategy using *Partition Tuning*. In this approach, a relation is organized as a set of data cells (data fragments), and balanced work load is achieved by reassigning data cells from overflow PNs to underflow PNs using a *Best Fit Decreasing* strategy. In this paper, we discuss the load balancing technique in the context of join operation. We will introduce three parallel join algorithms with dynamic load balancing capability using the partition tuning concept:

1. **Tuple Interleaving Parallel Hash Join (TIJ)**: This scheme is similar to BSJ algorithm. However, instead of relying on a specially designed switch to maintain uniform bucket spreading across PNs, it uses software control to interleave the tuples among PNs as they are being spread to their destinations.

2. **Adaptive Load Balancing Parallel Hash Join (ABJ)**: This technique introduces an additional step to the conventional parallel hash join algorithms [9, 10]. This added process relocates the excess buckets from the larger PNs to the smaller PNs attempting to balance the data load prior to the join operations.

3. **Extended Adaptive Load Balancing Parallel Hash Join (ABJ^+)**: In this strategy, each PN hashes its local portion of the relations into local subbuckets. These local subbuckets are stored back in the local disks. After this partitioning process is complete, the distribution of the data in each bucket can be computed. The matching local subbuckets are then collected to their final destination to form the corresponding buckets. The gathering of the subbuckets are based on the bucket sizes to ensure balanced work load for each of the PNs during the join phase.

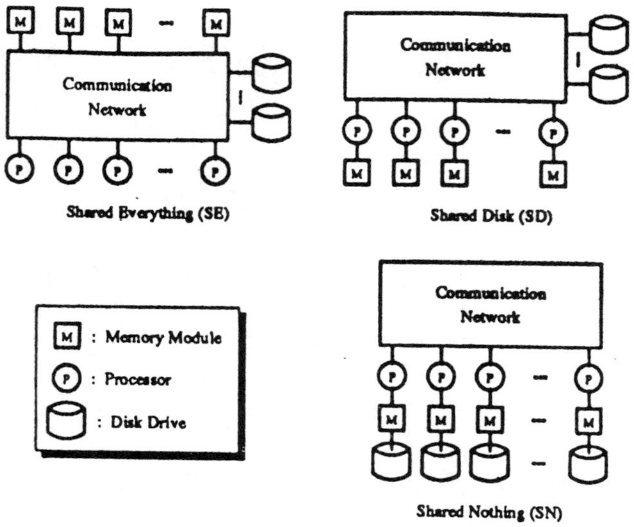

Figure 1: Architectures for multiprocessor database computers.

In the following sections we will describe these algorithms in more details. A performance model will be introduced and it will be used to compare the performance of these strategies.

The rest of this paper is organized as follows. The design environment and assumptions are described in Section 2. Some problems in hash-based join strategy is discussed, and the proposed join algorithms are presented in Section 3. In Section 4, we introduce an analytical model and discuss the performance comparison of the proposed schemes. Finally, we offer our conclusions in Section 5.

2 System Environment

Basically, there are three different architectures for multiprocessor database computers: *Shared Everything* (SE), *Shared Disk* (SD), and *Shared Nothing* (SN) (Figure 1). There has been a lot of debate in the database management community about which architecture is most suitable for a database management system. The coherency control problem limits the number of processors that can efficiently cooperate in a SE or a SD system. In a SE system, processors share a single global memory address space. The shared memory is typically a physically distributed memory to accommodate the aggregate demand on the shared memory from a large number of processors. An interconnection network is usually used to allow any processor to access any memory module. This communication network, however, increases the memory-access latency. The performance of conventional processors is quite sensitive to memory-access latency. If the memory-access latency exceeds one instruction time, the processor must idle until the storage cycle completes. A popular solution to this problem is to have cache memory with each processor. However, the use of caches requires a mechanism to ensure cache coherency. As we increase the number of processors, the number of messages due to cache coherency control (i.e., cross-interrogation) increases. Unless this problem can be solved, scaling a SE system into the range of hundreds of processors will be impractical. Similarly in a SD system, it is obvious that inter-processor coherency control is necessitated due to the caching of the shared database pages in main memory database buffers. The buffer invalidation problem tends to be the limiting factor for the size of a SD system.

In contrast, data coherency control is not a problem in a SN system. Besides, the processor and memory are physically localized in a node, and memory-access latency is not a problem. Nevertheless, SN systems are very sensitive to the data skew problem [8]. When the data are seriously skewed, rebalancing the data load among the PNs is necessary to resume good system performance.

From the above discussion, it seems that there is no absolute winner. When the individual processors are very powerful as in the case of mainframe computers, since we don't need a lot of processors in order to achieve the required performance level a small number of very high performance processors can be interconnected in a shared memory structure to avoid the communication overhead and the data skew problems (e.g., IBM 3090 Model 600). On the other hand if the applications demand a performance level far exceeding the capability of typical mainframe systems, then a microprocessor-based SN structure offers a solution for handling very large databases (e.g., iPSC/2 version of GAMMA [3], NonStop SQL [4], [5], Super Database Computer (SDC) [11], DBC/1024 [6]). In this paper we assume the latter environment and discuss dynamic load balancing strategies for parallel join operations in these systems. We would like to note that a combination of the three generic parallel architectures can also be employed to benefit from the advantages of each scheme. One such hybrid structure was discussed independently in [14] and [11].

3 New Parallel Hash Join Algorithms

There are two major problems associated with hash-based parallel join algorithms:

1. **Bucket overflow**: In hash-based join algorithms, the size of each bucket should be smaller than the memory capacity. However, nonuniform distribution of the join attribute values occasionally generates *bucket overflow*, in which the sizes of the buckets exceed the memory capacity. The performance diminishes because it requires extra I/O to repartition the buckets into smaller fragments so that each will fit in the memory.
2. **Data skew**: The performance of the conventional parallel hash join algorithms relies on the randomizing hash function to redistribute the tuples of the join relations evenly across all PNs in the system. Their performance degrades when the join attribute values of the relations are non-uniformly distributed [9, 8, 15]. This phenomenon is known as the *data skew* problem, in which some PNs have significantly more tuples than the remaining PNs.

To overcome the bucket overflow problem, Hybrid Hash Join [10] uses a second hash function, h_2, to stream the overflow tuples to a temporary file on disk. In other words, h_2 redistributes the overflow bucket between an in-memory hash table and overflow buckets on disk. GRACE Hash Join [9] tries to avoid the bucket overflow problem by splitting the relations into a large number of smaller buckets, and then these small buckets are combined into buckets to fit the memory capacity. This process is referred to as *bucket tuning* in [9]. Although these conventional parallel hash join algorithms effectively resolves the bucket overflow problem, no mechanism is provided to avoid the data skew effect. This problem is addressed in the *Bucket Spreading Parallel Hash Join* (BSJ) algorithm [11] by deferring the bucket allocation process until after the data partitioning procedure is completed. The delay allows the buckets to be allocated to PNs based on the bucket sizes to ensure a balanced data load in the system.

BSJ algorithm provides an effective parallel algorithm for performing join under skew conditions. This scheme, however, requires an expensive specially designed network to support the bucket spreading mechanism. As discussed in Section 1, the additional complexity in the communication network may also cause the following problems:

1. It does not scale well with the rest of the system.
2. It could degrade the communication performance of the network.

In this section we present three new efficient algorithms that require only conventional hardware. Therefore, they are immediately applicable to many existing parallel database computers.

3.1 Tuple Interleaving Parallel Hash Join

The purpose of the special hardware used in [11] is to ensure the uniform distribution of each bucket across all PNs. Alternatively, the bucket spreading effect can be achieved by software control. One way to achieve the uniform bucket distribution effect is to send each tuple to the PN currently containing the smallest subbucket among all the subbuckets of its bucket. Thus to determine the destination of a tuple, each PN has to keeps track of data distribution on every PN. As criticized in [11], this approach would require a high volume of data transfer between PNs, resulting in considerable performance degradation. For this reason, a highly functional Omega network is used in [11] to resolve the problem. Alternatively, this problem can be avoided by having each PN interleaving the tuples among the PNs as they were spread out from a bucket. This tuple interleaving strategy is described in more details in the *Tuple Interleaving Parallel Hash Join* (TIJ) algorithm given below.

1. **Split Phase**: R and then S are partitioned in parallel. Each PN independently divides its partition of each of the relations R and S stored therein into p buckets where p is considerably larger than the number of PNs in the system. During this partitioning process, tuples belonging to each of these buckets are spread across the PNs. The spreading is done by interleaving the consecutive tuples from each bucket among the PNs in the system. For each PN, the ith tuple of a bucket is sent to the $(((i-1) \bmod N)+1)$th PN, where N is the number of PNs in the system. Since this spreading strategy guarantees that each bucket is spread evenly among PNs, the N subbuckets of each bucket such derived, therefore, should be uniform in size.
2. **Bucket Tuning Phase**: Since buckets are distributed evenly among the PNs, the distribution of subbuckets in each PN is representative of the distribution of buckets among all PNs. Therefore a predetermined coordinating PN can decide how to tune the size of buckets to fit the memory capacity based only on its local distribution of subbuckets. The remaining PNs can then tune their subbuckets accordingly as directed by the coordinator.
3. **Partition Tuning Phase**: The coordinating PN groups the buckets into N equal partitions, and allocates each partition to a distinct PN. The bucket-to-PN mapping information is then broadcast to all the remaining PNs. Each PN then forms its partition by sending and receiving tuples as directed in the mapping information. Even after bucket size tuning, the buckets vary slightly in size. To reduce the effect of this nonuniformity, we can sort the buckets according to size. Then the sorted buckets are allocated to the PNs in a round-robin fashion [11]. In the case that the buckets vary greatly in size, a partition tuning strategy as described in [13] can be employed, in which the tuning algorithm is performed by first sorting in descending order the bucket according to size. The buckets are then allocated to the PNs in the sorted order. The assignment is done by allocating the currently largest buckets in the sorted list to the currently smallest PN. The bucket is then removed from the list. This process is repeated until the sorted list is exhausted. Hereafter, we will refer to this process as the *Best Fit Decreasing* strategy.
4. **Join Phase**: Each PN performs the local joins of respectively matching buckets.

We note that TIJ algorithm is a variation of the BSJ algorithm originally proposed in [11]. Except for the Split Phase, the remaining three phases of TIJ are similar to the corresponding steps in the BSJ algorithm. Our bucket spreading strategy employs software control at each PN instead of using special hardware as proposed in the original BSJ algorithm. The overhead associated with the software control is essentially negligible. For instance, a simple round-robin strategy is sufficient to keep track of the next destination for each bucket in a PN. This mechanism can also be implemented in hardware by providing a simple *spreading processor* at each of the input to the communication network. This spreading processor maintains a set of round-robin counters, one for each bucket involved. When a tuple is received by the spreading processor, the content of the round-robin counter is used as the destination for the tuple transfer. The counter is then incremented by one (modulo N, where N is the number of PNs). Comparing this scheme to the hardware design proposed in [11], we see two advantages. First, the number of counters used in the proposed scheme is proportional to N; whereas the complexity of the scheme proposed in [11] is $O(N \log N)$. Second, decoupling the complexity of the bucket spreading hardware from the communication media is a good idea to maintain the high communication throughput for all operations. An alternative to this design is to emulate the round-robin mechanism in the communication processor at each PN. Most today's communication processor should be capable of performing this additional simple task without becoming a bottleneck in the system.

We note also that the data transfer as described in the TIJ algorithm does not have to be performed at the tuple level. In practice, each PN maintains N outgoing buffers. Tuples belonging to the same destination are piggybacked to the same buffer, and the buffer is sent to its destination when it is full. In addition, if an appropriate network (e.g., Omega) is used the transfer of buffers can be synchronized to follow the cyclic shift pattern [16] in order to avoid access conflict. The four possible cyclic shift patterns for a 4-PN system is depicted in Figure 2.

Furthermore, if the system is designed for a multiuser environment it is advantageous to employ a partitionable communication network [17] (e.g., multistage shuffle-exchange networks) so that the system can be reconfigured dynamically into smaller "independent" parallel engines to serve different queries if necessary. In such an environment, not all base relations are large; smaller relations need to store on fewer

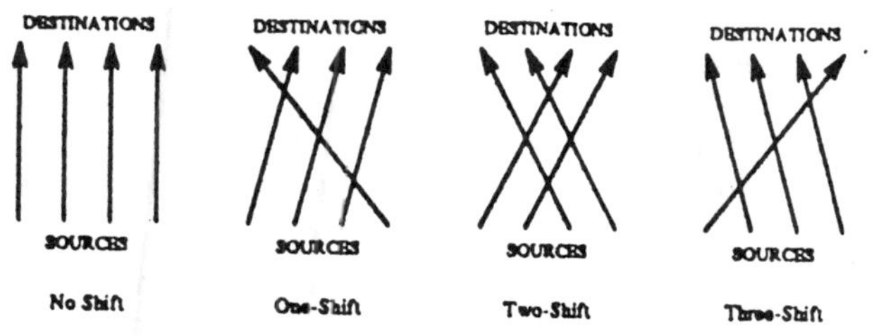

Figure 2: Cyclic shift patterns.

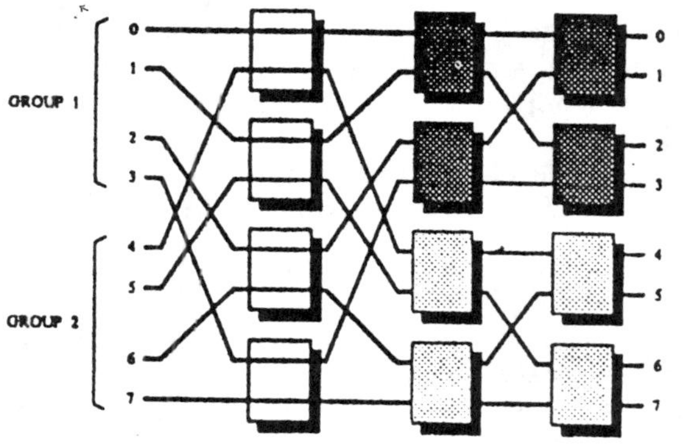

Figure 3: Cube network of size eight partitioned into two subnetworks of sizes four.

PNs only to reduce the skew effect and communication overhead. They are assigned to the PNs in such a way to take advantages of the partitioning properties of the communication network. Similarly for non-base relations, the intermediate operations can be centralized to as little or to as great an extent as is appropriate to maximize the system throughput. These individual operators can be scheduled to run on different partitions of the hardware in order to eliminate network contention among concurrent queries. In addition, the data transmission due to an individual query is synchronized within a hardware partition to follow a cyclic shift pattern [16] in order to avoid regional access conflict. For example, Figure 3 shows a cube network of size eight partitioned into two independent subnetworks. The first group consists of PNs connected to ports 0 to 3. The second group consists of PNs connected to ports 4 to 7. Since the original network supports the cyclic shift permutations without conflicts, the partitioning properties of the cube network guarantee that each of the two subnetworks will have all the connection properties of a cube network including the cyclic shift communication patterns. In a multiuser environment, we are concerned about system throughput in addition to response times. The use of a partitionable network reduces network contention among concurrent queries, and consequently improves the throughput of the multiprocessor system.

3.2 Adaptive Load Balancing Parallel Hash Join

A major advantage of the TIJ algorithm is that the work load is very balanced at each PN for all phases of the algorithm. A drawback of this strategy, however, lies in the fact that it shuffles the whole tuple space entirely during their load balancing process regardless of the degree of data skew. When the skew condition is mild, this strategy tends to result in unnecessary communication and computation overhead. The *Adaptive Load Balancing Parallel Hash Join* (ABJ) algorithm given in the following addresses this problem.

1. **Split Phase**: R and then S are partitioned into a large number of buckets in parallel. Each bucket is statically allocated to a PN as in GRACE Hash Join algorithm. Each tuple in a bucket is collected to the corresponding PN through the interconnection network.
2. **Partition Tuning Phase**: This phase consists of two stages.
   (a) **Bucket Retaining Stage**: For each relation, each PN_i retains n buckets using some best-fit strategy so that their aggregated size satisfies the following condition:

   $$\sum_{j=1}^{n} |B_{ij}| \leq \frac{|A|}{N} \quad and \quad \sum_{j=1}^{n+1} |B_{ij}| > \frac{|A|}{N}$$

   where $|A|$ is the size of the corresponding relation, and $|B_{ij}|$ is the size of the jth bucket of PN_i. The remaining buckets not retained in this stage are termed the *excess buckets*.
   (b) **Bucket Relocating Stage**: Each PN reports its size and the size of the excess buckets to a designated coordinating PN. The coordinator then use these information to reallocate the excess buckets to the underflow PNs using the Best Fit Decreasing strategy described in the last subsection. Once the destination of the excess buckets has been determined, this information is broadcast to the PNs, and the excess buckets are physically collected by the PNs accordingly.
3. **Bucket Tuning Phase**: Each PN combines the small buckets to form more optimal size join buckets.
4. **Join Phase**: Each PN performs the local joins of respectively matching buckets.

We note in the Bucket Retaining Stage that each PN should try to retain the larger buckets since the Best Fit Decreasing Strategy employed by the following Bucket Relocation Stage works better with smaller buckets. Comparing the Bucket Relocating Stage of this algorithm with the Partition Tuning Phase of the TIJ algorithm, we see that the former attempts to keep the data transfer to minimal, whereas the latter strategy shuffles on average $\frac{N-1}{N}$ of the tuples of each relation. When the skew condition is mild, the number of tuples at each PN varies very slightly and only little data movement will be needed during the Bucket Relocating Phase of the ABJ algorithm. In this sense, ABJ is capable of adapting dynamically to the degree of skew. For this reason, we call this strategy Adaptive Load Balancing Parallel Join algorithm. Since the skew conditions are typically mild (that is why the conventional hash join algorithms are so effective e.g., GRACE Hash Join, Hybrid Hash Join), we expect the proposed ABJ algorithm to have good performance for many applications.

3.3 Extended Adaptive Load Balancing Parallel Hash Join

When the skew condition is serious, disk overflow may occur during the Split Phase of the ABJ strategy. In addition, the severe skew condition causes the transfer of tuples concentrate on the skewed PN resulting in communication hot spot. Moreover, it further degrades the performance since these excess tuples must be reallocated to the underflow PNs during the Partition Tuning Phase. The *Extended Adaptive Load Balancing Parallel Hash Join* (ABJ^+) algorithm presented in this subsection corrects this problem by deferring the tuple transfer until the Partition Tuning Phase. The details of the algorithm is outlined bellow.

1. **Split Phase**: Each PN partitions its portion of each relation into considerably small subbuckets. Each subbucket is stored back in the local disks (no disk overflow).
2. **Partition tuning**: Each PN reports the sizes of its subbuckets to a designated coordinating PN. The coordinator adds up the sizes of the matching subbuckets distributed across the PNs to derive the sizes of the corresponding buckets. The coordinator then allocates the buckets to the PNs using the following strategy:
   (a) The buckets are sorted into descending order according to their sizes.
   (b) The buckets are then allocated to the PNs in the sorted order. For each bucket, it is assigned to the PN with the largest matching subbucket among the qualified PNs[1] in order to minimize communication overhead. The size of that PN is then updated to reflect the addition of the new bucket. When the size of a PN satisfies the following condition:

   $$\sum_{j=1}^{n} |B_{ij}| \leq \frac{|A|}{N} \quad and \quad \sum_{j=1}^{n+1} |B_{ij}| > \frac{|A|}{N}$$

   where $|A|$ is the size of the corresponding relation, and $|B_{ij}|$ is the size of the jth bucket of PN_i, it is disqualified from consideration for any further bucket allocation.

   This iterative process continues until all buckets are allocated. Once this process is complete, the allocation information is broadcast to all PNs, and the subbuckets are physically collected accordingly to their respective destination to form the corresponding local buckets.
3. **Bucket Tuning Phase**: Each PN combines the small buckets to form more optimal size (i.e., fit the memory capacity) join buckets.
4. **Join Phase**: Each PN performs the local joins of respectively matching buckets.

We note in this strategy that no tuple travels across a PN boundary more than once during the entire algorithm. Furthermore, it takes advantage of the already balanced portion of the tuple space to minimize the disk I/O and communication overheads. In this sense, it is capable of adapting dynamically to the current condition of the tuple distribution in the system.

4 Performance Analysis

In this section, we develop an analytical model for the four parallel join algorithms: TIJ, ABJ, ABJ^+ and GRACE. First we describe the performance model, and present the cost function for each of the join algorithms. These cost functions are then used to perform sensitivity analysis with respect to three parameters: degree of data skew, I/O bandwidth, and communication bandwidth. In this paper, GRACE algorithm which does not handle skew problems is used as the reference for the comparison of the three proposed techniques.

4.1 Performance Model

The following parameters are designed for cost evaluation. They are similar to those used in [8].

- **Workload Parameters:**
  $|R|$: Relation size in tuples for each of the joining relations.
  $|P_s|$: Size in tuples of the skewed partition.
  $|P_u|$: Size in tuples of each of the remaining unskewed partitions.
  σ: The degree of data skew which is defined as $\sigma = \frac{|P_s| - |P_u|}{|P_s|}$.
  t: Size in bytes of each tuple.
- **System Parameters**:
  N: Number of PNs in the system.
  M: Memory capacity in bytes for each PN.
  μ: CPU processing rate in million-instructions-per-second (MIPS).
  ω_{io}: I/O bandwidth between a processor and its secondary storage.
  ω_{comm}: Effective communication channel bandwidth per PN.

[1] PNs which have a matching subbucket

I_{cpu}: CPU pathlength for processing a tuple in any step of the join operation.

- **Measurement Parameters**

T_{split}: Time cost in seconds due to a Split Phase.

T_{parti}: Time cost in seconds due to a Partition Tuning Phase.

T_{bucket}: Time cost in seconds due to a Bucket Tuning Phase.

T_{join}: Time cost in seconds due to a Join Phase.

T_{split_io}: Time cost in seconds for disk accesses during a Split Phase.

T_{split_cpu}: Time cost in seconds for processing tuples during a Split Phase.

T_{split_comm}: Time cost in seconds for transferring data among PNs during a Split Phase.

T_{parti_io}: Time cost in seconds for disk accesses during a Partition Tuning Phase.

T_{parti_comm}: Time cost in seconds for transferring data among PNs during a Partition Tuning Phase.

T_{join_hash}: Time cost is seconds for building a hash table for a bucket in memory.

T_{join_probe}: Time cost in seconds for probing the in-memory hash table using tuples from the matching bucket.

T_{TIJ}: Time cost in seconds for joining two relations using the TIJ algorithm.

T_{ABJ}: Time cost in seconds for joining two relations using the ABJ algorithm.

T_{ABJ^+}: Time cost in seconds for joining two relations using the ABJ$^+$algorithm.

T_{GRACE}: Time cost in seconds for joining two relations using the GRACE Hash Join algorithm.

In this study, the system environment as described in Section 2 is assumed. we assume that initially both relations are horizontally partitioned and evenly distributed among the PNs (i.e., the sizes of all partitions of a relation are equal). In the join operation, we further assume that under the skew condition the relations are evenly distributed among all PNs, except one (i.e., The skewed PN) which has excess data. In other words, for each of the joining relations the skewed PN has $\sigma \times 100\%$ more tuples than each of the remaining PNs. σ is called the degree of skew, and it has value ranging between 0 and 1. This assumption is based on the fact that the most seriously skewed PN constitutes the bottleneck in our shared nothing environment. It dictates the performance of the parallel execution regardless of those less severely skewed PNs. Therefore, it is sufficient to assume a single skewed PN for our purpose. Based on this assumption, we thus have:

$$|P_s| + (N-1)|P_u| = |R| \Longrightarrow \begin{cases} |P_s| = \frac{|R|}{1+(N-1)(1-\sigma)} \\ |P_u| = \frac{(1-\sigma)|R|}{1+(N-1)(1-\sigma)} \end{cases}$$

$|P_s|$and $|P_u|$derived here will be used in the following subsections to compute the time costs for the parallel join algorithms.

4.2 Cost Functions

In this subsection, we present the cost functions for the join algorithms based on the described architecture and workload. Since partial overlap can exist between the phases of the join algorithms, the total join cost, T_{total} is bounded by:

$$\max(T_{phase\_1}, T_{phase\_2}, \cdots T_{phase\_n}) \le T_{total}$$
$$\le T_{phase\_1} + T_{phase\_2} + \cdots + T_{phase\_n}$$

Where max represents the maximum function. Similarly, each phase consists of several steps (disk accesses, tuple processing, communication). Overlapping of those steps is also achievable. A performance upper bound and lower bounds for the phases can be derived accordingly. In our study, we made the following assumptions:

- The overlap within each phase is perfect. The system is assumed to include a separate I/O processor and a separate communication processor which allow the overlap among disk I/O, CPU computation, and data communication [5].
- The overlap between two phases is not allowed. That is, a simple barrier type synchronization [18] is used between the phases to guarantee the correct parallel execution.

Therefore, the join time can be computed as:

$$T_{total} = T_{phase\_1} + T_{phase\_2} + \cdots + T_{phase\_n}$$

4.2.1 Time Cost for GRACE Hash Join

GRACE Parallel Hash Join consists of two distinct phases. Its cost is computed below:

$$T_{GRACE} = T_{split} + T_{join}$$

$$T_{split} = \max(T_{split\_io}, T_{split\_cpu}, T_{split\_comm})$$

$$T_{split\_io} = \frac{2|R|}{N} \cdot \frac{t}{\omega_{io}} + \frac{2|P_s|t}{\omega_{io}}$$

$$T_{split\_cpu} = \frac{2|R|}{N} \cdot \frac{I_{cpu}}{\mu}$$

$$T_{split\_comm} = \left(2|P_s| + \frac{N-2}{N} \cdot \frac{2|R|}{N}\right) \cdot \frac{t}{\omega_{comm}}$$

$$T_{join} = \left\lceil \frac{|P_s| \cdot t}{M} \right\rceil \cdot (T_{join\_hash} + T_{join\_probe})$$

$$T_{join\_hash} = \max\left(\frac{M}{\omega_{io}}, \frac{M}{t} \cdot \frac{I_{cpu}}{\mu}\right)$$

$$T_{join\_probe} = \max\left(\frac{M}{\omega_{io}}, \frac{M}{t} \cdot \frac{I_{cpu}}{\mu}\right)$$

$$\Longrightarrow \quad T_{join} = 2 \cdot \left\lceil \frac{|P_s|t}{M} \right\rceil \cdot \left[\max\left(\frac{M}{\omega_{io}}, \frac{M}{t} \cdot \frac{I_{cpu}}{\mu}\right)\right]$$

4.2.2 Time Cost for Tuple Interleaving Parallel Hash Join Algorithms

TIJ algorithm consists of four phases. Its time cost is computed below:

$$T_{TIJ} = T_{split} + T_{parti} + T_{bucket} + T_{join}$$

$$T_{split} = \max(T_{split\_io}, T_{split\_cpu}, T_{split\_comm})$$

$$T_{split\_io} = 2 \cdot \left(\frac{2|R|t}{N\omega_{io}}\right) \qquad T_{split\_cpu} = \frac{2|R|}{N} \cdot \frac{I_{cpu}}{\mu}$$

$$T_{split\_comm} = 2 \cdot \frac{N-1}{N} \cdot \frac{2|R|t}{N\omega_{comm}} = \frac{4(N-1)|R|t}{N^2 \cdot \omega_{comm}}$$

$$T_{bucket} \approx 0$$

$$T_{parti} = \max(T_{parti\_io}, T_{parti\_comm})$$

$$T_{parti\_io} = 2 \cdot \frac{N-1}{N} \cdot \frac{2|R|t}{N\omega_{io}} = \frac{4(N-1)|R|t}{N^2 \cdot \omega_{io}}$$

$$T_{parti\_comm} = 2 \cdot \frac{N-1}{N} \cdot \frac{2|R|t}{N\omega_{comm}} = \frac{4(N-1)|R|t}{N^2 \cdot \omega_{comm}}$$

$$T_{join} = \left\lceil \frac{|R|t}{N \cdot M} \right\rceil \cdot (T_{join\_hash} + T_{join\_probe})$$

$$T_{join\_hash} = \max\left(\frac{M}{\omega_{io}}, \frac{M}{t} \cdot \frac{I_{cpu}}{\mu}\right)$$

$$T_{join\_probe} = \max\left(\frac{M}{\omega_{io}}, \frac{M}{t} \cdot \frac{I_{cpu}}{\mu}\right)$$

$$\Longrightarrow \quad T_{join} = 2 \cdot \left\lceil \frac{|R|t}{N \cdot M} \right\rceil \cdot \max\left(\frac{M}{\omega_{io}}, \frac{M}{t} \cdot \frac{I_{cpu}}{\mu}\right)$$

4.2.3 Time Cost for Adaptive Load Balancing Parallel Hash Join Algorithm

ABJ algorithm consists of four phases. Its time cost is computed below:

$$T_{ABJ} = T_{split} + T_{parti} + T_{bucket} + T_{join}$$

$$T_{split} = \max(T_{split\_io}, T_{split\_cpu}, T_{split\_comm})$$

$$T_{split\_io} = \frac{2|R|t}{N\omega_{io}} + \frac{2|P_s|t}{\omega_{io}} \qquad T_{split\_cpu} = \frac{2|R|}{N} \cdot \frac{I_{cpu}}{\mu}$$

$$T_{split\_comm} =$$

$$\left\{\frac{N-1}{N} \cdot \frac{2|R|}{N} + \left[2|P_s| - \frac{1}{N} \cdot \frac{2|R|}{N}\right]\right\} \cdot \frac{t}{\omega_{comm}}$$

$$T_{parti} = \max(T_{parti\_io}, T_{parti\_comm})$$

$$T_{parti\_io} = \frac{N-1}{N} \cdot (|P_s| - |P_u|) \cdot \frac{t}{\omega_{io}}$$

$$T_{parti\_comm} = \frac{N-1}{N} \cdot (|P_s| - |P_u|) \cdot \frac{t}{\omega_{comm}}$$

As in TIJ algorithm, we let $T_{bucket} \approx 0$. Also, the time cost for the Join Phase, T_{join}, is the same as that of TIJ algorithm (Section 5.2.2).

4.2.4 Time Cost for Extended Adaptive Load Balancing Parallel Hash Join Algorithm

ABJ$^+$ algorithm consists of four phases. Its time cost is computed below:

$$T_{ABJ+} = T_{split} + T_{parti} + T_{bucket} + T_{join}$$

$$T_{split} = \max(T_{split\_io}, T_{split\_cpu}, T_{split\_comm})$$

$$T_{split\_io} = 2 \cdot \left(\frac{2|R|t}{N\omega_{io}}\right) \qquad T_{split\_cpu} = \frac{2|R|}{N} \cdot \frac{I_{cpu}}{\mu}$$

$$T_{split\_comm} = 0$$

$$T_{parti} = \max(T_{parti\_io}, T_{parti\_comm})$$

$$T_{parti\_io} = 2 \cdot \frac{N-1}{N} \cdot \frac{2|R|t}{N\omega_{io}} = \frac{4(N-1)|R|t}{N^2 \cdot \omega_{io}}$$

$$T_{parti\_comm} = 2 \cdot \frac{N-1}{N} \cdot \frac{2|R|t}{N\omega_{comm}} = \frac{4(N-1)|R|t}{N^2 \cdot \omega_{comm}}$$

Finally $T_{bucket} \approx 0$ and the time cost for the Join Phase can be computed as in TIJ algorithm (Section 5.2.2).

4.3 Sensitivity Analysis

With the model we developed, we are able to do the performance sensitivity study for the proposed parallel join algorithms under different parameters. The values of the parameters we used in our study are listed in the following:

1. **Workload Parameters**:
   - Relation size ($|R|$): 1 million tuples each
   - Tuple size (t): 200 Bytes per tuple
   - Degree of skew (σ): varies from 0.1 to 1.0
2. **System Parameters**:
   - Number of PNs (N): 64
   - Memory Capacity (M): 2 MBytes per PN
   - CPU processing rate (μ): 20 MIPS
   - I/O bandwidth (ω_{io}): varies from .25 to 4 MBytes/Second per PN
   - Effective communication channel Bandwidth (ω_{comm}): varies from .25 to 4 MBytes/Second per PN
   - Instruction pathlength (I_{cpu}): 1,000 instructions

Among these parameters, we select the degree of data skew, disk I/O bandwidth, and communication bandwidth for the sensitivity analysis.

We note that the I/O bandwidth is set to 4 MBytes/sec which is typical for the industry standard SCSI bus. The communication bandwidth for each port of the communication network is also set to 4 MBytes/sec to match the data transfer rate of the disk controller. We could have set the bandwidth of the communication network to a fixed number independent of the number of PNs in the system. In practice,

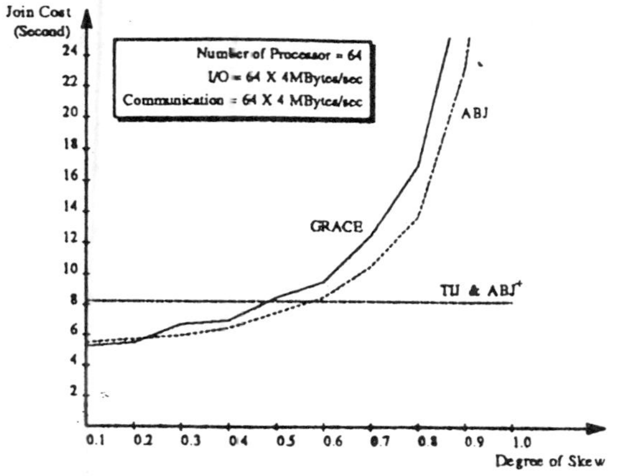

Figure 4: Skew effect on the parallel join algorithms.

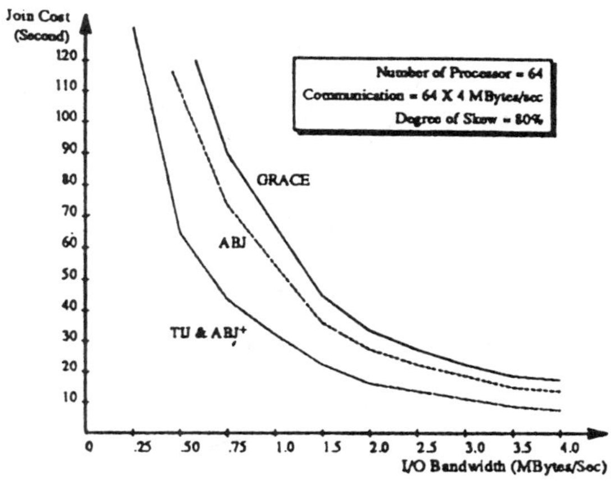

Figure 5: Effect of I/O bandwidth on the parallel join algorithms.

this is the case for systems using a common bus for interprocessor communication. For instance, Tandem NonStop Computer consists of 2 to 16 PNs connected by two high-speed 20Mb/sec buses [19]. Our model represents communication network topologies whose bandwidth increases with the increase in the number of communication ports. Crossbar switches, multi-stage networks are examples of this category. For simplicity, we assume the effective bandwidth of the communication network increases linearly with the number of PNs.

To prevent the processor from becoming a bottleneck, the processing rate of each PN is set to 20 MIPS which is derived as follows:

$$\mu = I_{cpu} \cdot \frac{\omega_{io}}{t} = 20MIPS$$

We present the results of the sensitivity analysis in the following subsections.

4.3.1 Skew Effect

The three parallel hash join algorithms proposed in this papers can be loosely grouped into two categories: TIJ and ABJ$^+$are *skew avoidance techniques*, whereas ABJ is a *skew resolution method*. This classification is based on the fact that TIJ and ABJ$^+$maintain balanced data load for each PN at all time to prevent the skew problems. On the other hand, ABJ attempts to resolve the skew problems as they arise.

The effect of the data skew on the parallel join algorithms is plotted in Figure 4. The corresponding data are also given wherein. It is interesting to observe that the algorithms TIJ and ABJ$^+$are robust against the skew effect. Their time costs are constant regradless of the degree of skew. Furthermore the two algorithms share the same performance curve in this study. This is due to the fact that I/O operation can be overlapped with the data communication process in our model. Although ABJ$^+$reduces one round of data transfer in the Split Phase as compared to TIJ, this communication reduction does not have an effect on the savings unless the communication network becomes the bottle neck in the system ($\omega_{comm} < \omega_{io}$). In order to perform the sensitivity analysis with respect to the skew effect, we designed the perfect parameters (i.e., $\omega_{comm} = \omega_{io}$) to avoid this bottleneck.

The drawbacks of TIJ and ABJ$^+$are the I/O and communication overheads associated with the deferred bucket allocation strategies. In TIJ, subbuckets of a bucket are temporarily saved at all PNs, and must be collected to their appropriate PN later. In ABJ$^+$, the subbuckets of a bucket are stored back to the local disks during the Split Phase, and must be reloaded in order to send them to their final destination. Due to these disk I/O and communication overheads, TIJ and ABJ$^+$cannot provide savings over GRACE algorithm until $\sigma > 45\%$ (i.e., one of the 64 PNs has 2.8% of the total tuples) as depicted in Figure 4. Similarly, ABJ performs better than TIJ and ABJ$^+$for $\sigma < 60\%$. Since the skew conditions are typically mild for many applications, it makes ABJ attractive for some environments. Nevertheless, both GRACE and ABJ are sensitive to data skew, the robustness of the TIJ and ABJ$^+$against skew conditions makes them uniquely appealing to highly parallel database systems.

In comparing ABJ to GRACE, we see that ABJ performs better for $\sigma > 20\%$ (i.e., one of the 64 PNs has 1.94% of the total tuples). In practice, at the beginning of the Partition Tuning Phase of ABJ, we can decide whether to proceed with the tuning process based on the skew condition. With this extension, it is possible to implement ABJ to perform at least as well as, or better than GRACE for any skew condition.

4.3.2 Effect of I/O Bandwidth

In the sensitivity study with respect to the degree of data skew, we assume that the hardware design is "perfect" - the processors, the I/O subsystems, and the communication processors are tuned for the join operation. In this and the following subsection, we are

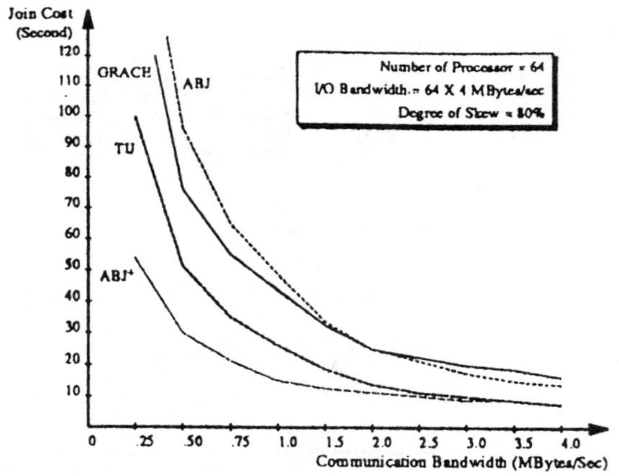

Figure 6: Effect of communication bandwidth on the parallel join algorithms.

interested in an environment that is less than ideal. In this subsection, we study how the performance of the I/O subsystems can affect the algorithms. In particular, how the overhead due to load balancing is related to the I/O bandwidth. In order to compare the three load balancing strategies over a wide range of I/O bandwidths, we purposely set the skew condition to a large number, namely $\sigma = 80\%$. This means that one of the 64 PNs has 7.3% of the total tuples according to our model. The results of this study is ploted in Figure 5. The corresponding data are also given wherein.

This study shows that TIJ and ABJ$^+$are the better choices when the I/O bandwidth is low. Furthermore, the savings due to the load balancing strategies with respect to GRACE algorithm increases as the I/O bandwidth decreases. This suggests that load balancing will become even more critical when the performance gap between the processor technology and I/O technology widen - a phenomenon we are observing today.

Finally, we also observe here that TIJ and ABJ$^+$share the same performance curve. This is due to the fact that $\omega_{io} < \omega_{comm}$ in this sensitivity study.

4.3.3 Effect of Communication Bandwidth

We are also interested in the effect of the communication bandwidth on the proposed join algorithms. Again, we set $\sigma = 80\%$ for this sensitivity analysis. The results of this study is ploted and the corresponding data are given in Figure 6.

We observe that ABJ$^+$is the best scheme in this study. We also note that although TIJ and ABJ$^+$perform equally well in Figure 4 and Figure 5, ABJ$^+$outperforms TIJ in systems with limited communication capability as shown in Figure 6. From this study, it suggests that ABJ$^+$is the better approach of the two proposed skew avoidance techniques.

Finally, comparing Figure 5 to Figure 6 we see that load balancing is even more critical in a system with limited communication capability than in a system with inadequate I/O performance. In Figure 4, we made the assumption that the effective bandwidth of the communication network increases linearly with the number of PNs. This is over optimistic. In practice, the rate of increase in communication bandwidth decreases as the number of PNs increases, and we expect to see the benefits of the proposed schemes at even lower skew conditions than those suggested in Figure 4.

5 Conclusion

In this paper, we discussed dynamic load balancing strategies for parallel hash join algorithms. In particular, we proposed three new parallel hash join strategies. They are categorized as follows:

1. **Skew Resolution Technique:**
   - *Adaptive Load Balancing Parallel Hash Join Algorithm* (ABJ)
2. **Skew Avoidance Techniques:**
   - *Tuple Interleaving Parallel Hash Join Algorithm* (TIJ)
   - *Extended Adaptive Load Balancing Parallel Hash Join Algorithm* (ABJ$^+$)

We developed a performance model, and did sensitivity analysis to study the effect of data skew, I/O bandwidth, and communication bandwidth on the proposed schemes. The results of our study indicate that:

- ABJ algorithm should be used if the degree of skew is mild.
- ABJ$^+$algorithm should be used if the degree of skew is significant.
- TIJ algorithm should be used in lieu of ABJ$^+$algorithm if
  1. the relations are very seriously skewed initially, and
  2. the communication bandwidth is sufficiently large.

Overall, the proposed schemes are able to provide savings over conventional parallel hash-based join algorithms even at low skew conditions.

In addition to the comparison results, we also observed that load balancing is more critical to systems with limited I/O and communication capabilities. With the cost of communication hardware remains expensive, and the performance gap between microprocessor technology and I/O technology widen rapidly, the benefits of the proposed join strategies are evident for today's multicomputer database management systems.

Finally, although we assumed a barrier synchronyzation between join phases in our performance model for simplicity, in practice techniques used in the popular Hybrid Hash Join algorithm [20] can be employed to overlap the join phases whenever possible. This strategy is particularly beneficial when the memory capacity is large. In addition, the concept of *cell* as described in [13] can also be used, in which tuples are organized into cells to facilitate the environment for efficient execution of the Best Fit Decreasing algorithm during partition tuning.

References

[1] Danial A. Reed and Richard M. Fujimoto. *Multicomputer Networks: Message-Based Parallel Processing*. Scientific Computation. MIT Press, 1987.

[2] H. Boral, W. Alexander, L. Clay, G. Copeland, S. Danforth, M. Franklin, B. Hart, M. Smith, and P. Valduriez. Prototyping bubba, a highly parallel database system. *IEEE Transactions on Knowledge and Data Engineering*, 2(1):4–24, 1990.

[3] D. J. DeWitt, S. Ghandeharizadeh, D. A. Schneider, A. Bricker, H.-I Hsiao, and R. Rasmussen. The gamma database machine project. *IEEE Transactions on Knowledge and Data Engineering*, 2(1):44–62, 1990.

[4] Susanne Englert, Jim Gray, Terry Kocher, and Praful Shah. A benchmark of nonstop sql release 2 demonstrating near-linear speedup and scaleup on large databases. Technical Report 89.4, Tandem Computer Inc., 1989.

[5] Kien A. Hua and Honesty C.Young. Designing a highly parallel database server using off-the-shelf components. In *Proceedings of The International Computer Symposium*, Hsinchu, Taiwan, December 1990.

[6] Teradata Corporation, Los Angesles, Calafornia. *Teradata DBC/1012 Data Base Computer Concepts and Facilities*, release 3.1 edition, 1988. Teradata Document C02-0001-05.

[7] M. Stonebraker. The case for shared nothing. *IEEE Database Engineering*, 9(1), 1986.

[8] S. Lakshmi and P. S. Yu. Effect of skew on join performance in parallel architectures. In *Proceedings of International Symposium on Databases in Parallel and Distributed Systems*, pages 107–117, Austin, Texas, December 1988.

[9] M. Kitsuregawa, H. Tanaka, and T. Moto-oka. Application of hash to database machine and its architecture. *New Generation Computing*, 1(1):66–74, 1983.

[10] D. A. Schneider and D. J. DeWitt. A performance evaluation of four parallel join algorithms in a shared-nothing multiprocessor environment. In *Proceedings of the SIGMOD Conference*, pages 110–121, 1989.

[11] M. Kitsuregawa and Yasushi Ogawa. Bucket spreading parallel hash: A new, robust, parallel hash join method for data skew in the super database computer (sdc). In *Proceedings of 16th International Conference on Very Large Data Bases*, pages 210–221, Brisbane, Australia, August 1990.

[12] D. H. Lawrie. Access and alignment of data in an array processor. *IEEE Transaction on Computers*, c-24(12):1145–1155, December 1975.

[13] Kien A. Hua and Chiang Lee. An adaptive data place scheme for parallel database computer systems. In *Proceedings of 16th International Conference on Very Large Data Bases*, pages 493–506, Brisbane, Australia, August 1990.

[14] Kien A. Hua, Chiang Lee, and Jih-Kwon Peir. A high-performance hybrid architecture for concurrent query execution. In *Proceedings of Symposium on Parallel and Distributed Processing*, Dallas, Texas, December 1990.

[15] S. Lakshmi and P. S. Yu. Limiting factors of join performance on parallel processors. In *Proceedings of 5th International Conference on Data Engineering*, pages 488–496, 1989.

[16] Jacques Lenfant. Parallel permutations of data: A benes network control algorithm for frequently used permutations. *IEEE Transaction on Computers*, c-27(7):637–647, July 1978.

[17] Howard Jay Siegel. The theory underlying the partitioning of permutation networks. *IEEE Transaction on Computers*, c-29(9):791–800, September 1980.

[18] Harry F. Jordan. A special purpose architecture for finite element analysis. In *Proceedings of 1978 International Conference on Parallel Processing*, pages 263–266, 1978.

[19] Robert Holbrook. Nonstop sql - a distributed relational dbms for oltp. In *Proceedings of Compson '88*, San Francisco, California, Februaray 1988.

[20] D. J. DeWitt, R. Katz, F. Olken, L. Shapiro, M. Stonebraker, and D. Wood. Implementation techniques for main memory database systems. In *Proceedings of the 1984 SIGMOD Conference*, pages 1–8, Boston, MA, June 1984.

Dynamic and Load-balanced Task-Oriented Database Query Processing in Parallel Systems

Hongjun Lu *Kian-Lee Tan*

Department of Information Systems and Computer Science
National University of Singapore

ABSTRACT

Most parallel database query processing methods proposed so far adopt the task-oriented approach: decomposing a query into tasks, allocating tasks to processors, and executing the tasks in parallel. However, this strategy may not be effective when some processors are overloaded with time-consuming tasks caused by some unpredictable factors such as data skew. In this paper, we propose a dynamic and load-balanced task-oriented database query processing approach that minimizes the completion time of user queries. It consists of three phases: task generation, task acquisition and execution and task stealing. Using this approach, a database query is decomposed into a set of tasks. At run-time, these tasks are allocated dynamically to available processors. When a processor completes its assigned tasks and no more new tasks are available, it steals subtasks from other overloaded processors to share their load. A performance study was conducted to demonstrate the feasibility and effectiveness of this approach using join query as an example. The techniques that can be used to select task donors from overloaded processors and to determine the amount of work to be transferred are discussed. The factors that may affect the effectiveness, such as the number of tasks to be decomposed to, is also investigated.

1. Introduction

Today's DBMS will have to deal with complex queries that take a long time to complete. The conventional von-Neumann architecture will soon reach its speed limit, and parallelism represents the most feasible alternative to achieve any significant breakthrough in performance. With the advances in hardware technology and computer architecture, a large number of parallel computers are already being employed to solve database applications [DeWi90, Engl89, Ozka86, Su88, Tera88].

To explore parallelism and to fully utilize the system resources, most proposed parallel database query processing methods use a *task-oriented* approach. In general, the approach consists of three phases: *task generation, task allocation* and *task execution*. In the task generation phase, a query is decomposed into a set of tasks that are allocated to all available processors in the second phase, the task allocation phase. Tasks are assigned to processors according to some criteria such as the tuple sizes of data associated to tasks [Hua91, Kits90] or

"Dynamic and Load-Balanced Task-Oriented Database Query Processing in Parallel Systems" by H. Lu and K.-L. Tan from *Proc. Third Int'l Conf. Extending Data Base Technology,* 1992, pp. 357-372.

the estimated execution time of tasks [Wolf90, Wolf91]. Finally, in the third phase, *task execution phase*, all the processors concurrently execute the tasks allocated to them according to some predetermined order. This task-oriented approach is most effective when the load of tasks to be executed concurrently at each processor is approximately the same. In this case, the completion time of the query is near-optimal if not optimal. However, in real situation, the processing load across the processors will not be the same for the following reasons:

1. Some tasks are more time-consuming or expensive, for example join in relational database systems is often recognized as the most costly operation.
2. The criteria on which the tasks are assigned to processors fail to allocate the tasks evenly across the system.
3. Even when all tasks seem evenly distributed across the processors, some unpredictable factors such as the skew in the data may cause a load-imbalance across the processors during execution [Laks90, Walt91].

In such cases, the minimum completion time for the query depends on the task(s) that finishes last. Moreover, under-loaded processors will soon become idle. All these indicate the need to develop new algorithms to evenly distribute the processing load across the processors.

The problem has been addressed by researchers from different directions — intra-operation [Hua91, Kits90, Omic91, Wolf90, Wolf91] and inter-operation [Deen90, Lu91, Murp91]. Wolf, Dias and Yu propose a parallel sort-merge join algorithm [Wolf90] and a parallel hash-based join algorithm [Wolf91] to handle data skew. Both algorithms introduce a *scheduling phase* that employs two optimization algorithms iteratively to minimize the overall completion time of the join based on the estimated execution time of the tasks. Instead, in [Hua91, Kits90] the skew problem is alleviated by allocating the tasks to the processors such that the bucket sizes are balanced. Omiecinski's approach to handle skew, in a shared-everything environment, is to allocate more processors for large buckets [Omic91]. In [Deen90], the processors are distributed evenly across the number of joins. Lu, Shan and Tan allocate more processors to more expensive joins such that the completion time for the joins is minimized [Lu91]. In [Murp91], the *execution plan balancing* strategy prioritizes the operations and allocates resources (memory and processors) to the most critical operation first.

In this paper, we propose a dynamic task-oriented query processing method with load-balancing capabilities. The proposed approach is robust to data skew and is able to achieve a minimum completion time for a query. It is different from the conventional method in the following ways. First, our approach is a *dynamic* approach and task allocation is *demand-driven*. For most of the previous work, the allocation of tasks to processors is *static*, that is, all the tasks are allocated to the processors before the execution of any tasks. Thus each processor knows exactly which (and how many) tasks are allocated to it. In our approach, a processor *acquires* a task to be processed at run-time. Each processor has, at any time, at most one task to process and it does not know which is the next task to process until the current task finishes. Once the current task is completed, the processor will acquire another task until there is no more tasks. Second, a *task transfer* strategy is employed to handle load-imbalances across the processors when there is no more tasks in the system. Most of the existing work does not transfer any task or sub-tasks once it is allocated to a processor. Once a task is allocated to a processor, it will only be executed by the processor. In our approach, an idle processor can *steal* some load — pages of data that have not been processed — from an overloaded processor.

In the next section, we discuss the general dynamic and load-balanced task-oriented query processing approach. Section 3 describes the detailed implementation of the approach when apply to single join queries. A performance study and its results are also presented. We summarize this research and briefly discuss some future work in section 4.

2. The General Approach

In this paper, we assume the system to be a multiprocessor system with *shared disks (SD)*. In SD systems, each processor has its own private memory but each processor can directly access any disk. The processors cooperate by message passing through an interconnection network connecting processors. Each relation is horizontally partitioned across the disks in the system. However, we assume that the system has a certain amount of global memory and the global memory is used to keep up-to-date information of the tasks. We also assume a locking mechanism is used to regulate access to the global memory.

The proposed approach, a *dynamic and load-balanced task-oriented query processing method* provides a solution to the problem of minimizing the completion time of a query by using the system resources to the fullest. The approach comprises three phases — *task generation, dynamic task acquisition and execution* and *task stealing (load-balancing)*.

2.1. Task generation

The first phase of our approach is the task generation phase where a query is decomposed into a set of tasks as in conventional methods. In the database query processing environment, task decomposition can be *operation oriented*, that is, a *task* represents a single operation on the associated data. However, task decomposition can also be *data oriented*. That is, data to be operated on by certain operations can be partitioned into subsets and a task becomes the application of the same operation(s) on a subset of the data. By applying these two decomposition techniques alternatively and recursively, a database query can be decomposed into a set of tasks that can be ordered and allocated to processors in the task allocation phase.

First issue in task generation is that the decomposition should guarantee the correctness of the operation. That is, the results from subtasks should be easily assembled into the same final result as that from the operation without decomposition. This is especially important to data oriented decomposition. With different operations, the way in which the data is partitioned to form tasks will be different to guarantee the correctness. For example, for the hash-based joins, both participating relations, say R and S, can be partitioned into corresponding buckets. A task will then be the join operation on a set of two buckets from two relations. However, if a nested-loops join method is used, a task could be a join on whole relation R and any subset of S.

Second issue in task generation is the optimal number of tasks to be generated. The number of tasks to be generated is limited by the decomposibility of the tasks. It is also limited by the amount of memory at each processor. The optimal number of tasks to be generated is closely associated with the size of the data that an operation works on. A large number of tasks may be generated such that an operation is applied on only few tuples of data. This may result in poor performance because of the overhead incurred in splitting the data and duplicating the operation. Fragmentation may also cause additional I/Os. On the other hand, a small number of tasks will limit the flexibility of allocating tasks to the processors and result in uneven load among the processors.

Our task generation, or query decomposition follows the same strategy as that in conventional methods. However, the portions of data across the disks that correspond to a task are *not transferred* until the task is to be executed during the execution phase. Instead, these data form a logical system pool of tasks with the following information for each task stored in the global memory: 1) what is the operation, 2) the number of tasks associated with the operation, and 3) the addresses of the data that is associated with this task. The global memory also stores the information of the processing at each processor. Such information includes 1) the size of data left (in pages) and 2) the size of the resultant relations generated so far.

2.2. Dynamic task acquisition and execution

In the second phase, processors acquire tasks from the system task pool and execute them if the acquisition is successful. Initially, the size of the task left is the number of pages of data associated with the task and the size of the result generated is zero. Whenever a page of data is processed, the global information is updated accordingly. Whenever a processor finishes the processing of the acquired task, it checks whether there are more tasks in the system. If there are tasks available in the system, the processor will be assigned the next task for execution. This process of *dynamic acquisition and execution* of tasks is repeated until all the tasks have been allocated.

2.3. Task stealing

In the third phase, a load-balançing strategy is employed when there is no more tasks to be assigned. When all the tasks have been assigned, idle processors may help to bear the burden of overloaded processors to minimize the completion time. This may require the *stealing* of some load from overloaded processors. Based on the global information, the idle processor determines the *donor* (the overloaded processor) and the amount of load to be transferred. This process of stealing is repeated until some criterion, which indicates that the minimum completion time has been achieved, is satisfied. In this case, no further transfer is necessary and each processor may finish up its processing for the entire query to complete. In this way, the load is balanced across all the processors and the completion time is minimized.

3. DLPJ: A Dynamic and Load-balanced Parallel Join Processing Algorithm

In this section, we present a detailed implementation of the above dynamic and load-balanced query processing method for join queries. The join algorithm obtained is *dynamic* as there is no prior allocation of tasks to any processor before execution begins. Tasks are assigned at run-time. As such, some processors in the system may perform more "light" tasks while others may perform few tasks with "heavy" load. The task generation is *hash-based* as in conventional hash-based join methods. We will describe the three phases of the join algorithm that corresponds to the three phases of the proposed approach followed by a discussion of the experiments conducted and their results.

3.1. Phase 1: Task Generation — Partitioning Phase

The task generation phase of the join algorithm is essentially a partitioning phase since the number of buckets determines (equals) the number of tasks. As in all previous parallel hash-based algorithms, this phase scans the relations R and S and creates partitions for the joining phase. Each processor i $(1 \leq i \leq p)$ allocates one output buffer for each of the B partitions where B is the number of partitions desired (the number of partitions is limited by the amount of memory that is available). Each processor reads a subset R_i of relation R and hashes the tuples to the corresponding output buffers based on the hash results. When the buffer is full, it is written out to the disk. The same hash function is used to create partitions for relation S. We call the portions of R_i (S_i) that hash into the jth output buffer the sub-buckets of R_i (S_i) and denote them as R_{ij} (S_{ij}), where $1 \leq j \leq B$.

During the partitioning of data, each sub-bucket on each disk has associated with it a *directory*. The directory for a sub-bucket stores the *disk identifier* and *page identifier* for pages belonging to a partition. With this directory, a processor assigned a partition will have direct access to the pages. Moreover, such a structure facilitates the balancing of load in the joining phase, which we will describe in Section 3.3. It should be noted that the sizes of the directories are not large. Assuming the disk identifier requires 1 byte and the page identifier requires 2 bytes, a 4 Kbytes page can house the addresses for more than 1300 pages of data.

For hash-based join algorithms, the number of partitions may have an impact on the performance of the algorithm [Naka88, Kits89]. When the number of buckets is small, more tuples will be hashed to a bucket and the probability of the size of a bucket exceeding the main memory size increases. Such overflow buckets will degrade the performance of the algorithm. On the other hand, too many buckets may also lead to poor performance as the number of fragmented pages increases resulting in more I/Os. A compromise is to generate a large number of buckets first. The small buckets are then merged into larger ones that can still be staged in memory [Kits83]. The maximum number of partitions is constrained by the memory size since each page corresponds to a partition. We do not consider the case when a partition is recursively split to generate more partitions since this will incur additional I/Os. Once the partitioning is performed, each processor will store the information of the sub-buckets in the global memory. Such information includes 1) the task number, 2) the size of the sub-buckets of the source and target relations and 3) the addresses to the directories of the sub-buckets. A processor (with smallest index) will then build a single *task table* containing the task number with its associated information for a partition of R and S. This task table is used in subsequent phases. Figure 3.1 illustrates this process. The size of each partition is the sum of the corresponding sub-buckets. The addresses of the directories are stored as it is.

Information on disk 1				
j	$\lvert R_{1j}\rvert$	$\lvert S_{1j}\rvert$	$AddrR_{1j}$	$AddrS_{1j}$
1	100	100	(1, 2)	(1, 7)
...	...	...	...	...
.	.	.	.	.
.	.	.	.	.
B	...	...	...	...

Information on disk n				
j	$\lvert R_{nj}\rvert$	$\lvert R_{nj}\rvert$	$AddrR_{nj}$	$AddrS_{nj}$
1	100	100	(n, 5)	(n, 9)
...	...	...	...	...
.	.	.	.	.
.	.	.	.	.
B	...	...	...	...

(a) Initial set of tables.

Task# j	$\lvert R_j\rvert$	$\lvert S_j\rvert$	$AddrR_{1j}$	.....	$AddrR_{nj}$	$AddrS_{1j}$	.....	$AddrS_{nj}$
1	1000	1000	(1, 2)	.....	(n,5)	(1, 7)	.....	(n,9)
...	...	...	...	...	...	...	...	...
.	.	.	.	..	.	.	.	
.	.	.	.	..	.	.	.	
B	...	...	...	...	...	...	...	...

(b) Task table.

Figure 3.1. Build information in global memory

3.2. Phase 2: Task Acquisition and Execution — Joining Phase

This phase is the joining phase of the algorithm. During the joining phase, a free processor reads the global information and acquires a task to process. Once a task is available, the directories associated with the sub-buckets of R and S that correspond to this task are collected at the processor. The directories from all disk are then linked as shown in Figure 3.2(a). In this way, each processor has the addresses to all pages that correspond to the task. The task is then executed, that is the join is performed, as in a uniprocessor environment. Any uniprocessor join algorithm may be employed. In our study, we use the *hash-based nested-loops join* (HNL) algorithm for simplicity. The result can be easily generalized. This algorithm is shown to be superior over the other algorithms when we handle medium-sized source relations, that is the size of the source relation is no more than 5 times the size of the memory [Naka88]. The algorithm comprises two phases: 1) Several pages of the source relation, which is determined by the available memory, is read and the hash table is built; 2) The whole of target relation is read a page at a time and each tuple is probed for joinability with the partially staged hash table. These two phases are repeated until all the pages of the source relation are read. We denote the time for the entire join to be $T_{HNL}(|R|, |S|, |Res|)$ where $|R|$, $|S|$ and $|Res|$ represent the size (in pages) of the source, target and result relations respectively. We also denote the time to perform phase 2 when r pages are of R are staged in memory and s pages of S are used to probe for a match to generate result res as $T_{join}(r, s, |res|)$.

As each page is read, the processor will update the global information — number of pages of each relation left and the number of pages of the result relation generated thus far. Whenever a processor finishes the processing of the allocated task, it acquires a new task. This process of *acquisition and execution* of tasks is repeated until all the B tasks have been allocated. When there is no more tasks, the processor will enter into the *task stealing (load-balancing) phase.*

3.3. Phase 3: Task Stealing — Load-balancing Phase

Once all the tasks have been acquired, that is there is no more tasks from the system task pool for the idle processor to process, the processor will try to *steal* some load from a processor that has not completed the execution of its acquired task. The load at a processor is the amount of unfinished work to be performed and is measured as the estimated time needed to finish up the task. We will discuss how to determine the appropriate candidate processor(s) that is overloaded and the amount of load to steal in the subsequent sub-sections. The stealing process is realized by transferring bucket directories among two processors. Let p_a be the candidate over loaded processor and p_a is the idle one. After the amount of work to steal has been determined, the work load of p_a, represented by a chain of directories are divided into two portions. That is, each directory in the chain is split into two. The upper portion remains in p_a, that is to be processed by p_a. The lower portion is chained up and sent to p_b. Thus the load is shared between p_a and p_b without physical movement of data — only the directories are shipped. Figure 3.2 illustrates the process. This process of *stealing* is repeated until the criterion, which indicates that the minimum completion time has been achieved, is satisfied. In this case, one just need to wait for all the processors to finish up its processing for the entire join operation to complete.

3.3.1. Determination of donor

Any processor that is executing its acquired task when an idle processor tries to steal some load from other processors can be a donor. Naturally, we hope that the donor is the most heavily loaded processor since it will be the last processor to finish up the entire processing. However, it is impossible to provide an exact measure of the load of a processor. We propose to use the *estimated finish time (EFT)* as the measure of the load of a processor. When task stealing happens, the EFTs of those processors with tasks are computed and the processor with the maximum EFT will be chosen as the donor, that is, processor i is the donor (ties are arbitrary broken) when

$$EFT_i = \max_{j=1}^{p}(EFT_j)$$

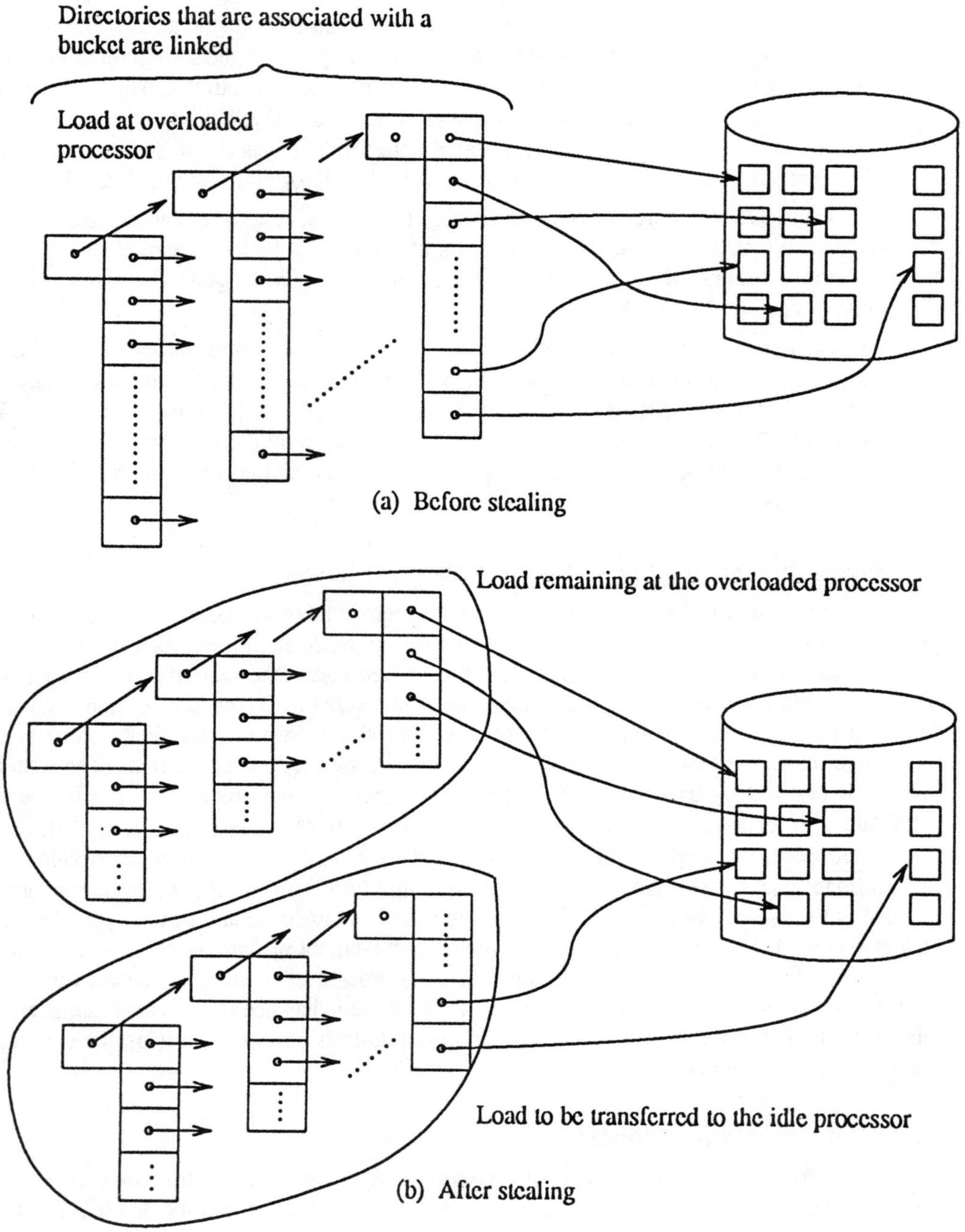

Figure 3.2. Stealing of load.

Note that the estimated finish time is both data and operation dependent since a task is defined as an operation on certain amount of data. In our example, where each task is a hash-based nested loops join on two buckets T_1 and T_2, the finish time will depend on the relative size of the outer bucket, say T_1, on which a hash table is built.

1. If $|T_1| \times F \leq |M|$ (we assume a hash table for R occupies $|R| \times F$ pages), the hash table for T_1 is staged in memory, and the joining process is to scan T_2 once and probe for a match for each tuple of T_2 scanned. The load of the processor at any time after building the hash table is determined by the unprocessed pages of T_2.
2. If T_1 is too large for the available memory, that is $|T_1| \times F > |M|$, T_2 needs to be scanned several times, each with a portion of T_1 that can be staged in memory. The load therefore is dependent on both the unprocessed pages of T_1 and T_2.

With this in mind, we can proceed to estimate the EFT for a processor.

Case 1: $|T_1| \times F \leq |M|$.

The time to perform the join of T_1 and T_2 with result *Result* is estimated by

$$T_{HNL}(|T_1|, |T_2|, |Result|) = T_{HNL}(|T_1|, n_2, |Res|) + EFT$$

where n_2 denotes the number of pages of T_2 that have been processed, inclusive of the page that is processed at the time of the task request and $|Res|$ is the size of the resultant relation generated so far, using n_2 pages of T_2, inclusive of the page that is being generated. The size of *Result* may be estimated by [1]

$$\frac{|Result|}{|Res|} = \frac{|T_2|}{n_2}$$

Therefore,

$$EFT = T_{HNL}(|T_1|, |T_2|, |Result|) - T_{HNL}(|T_1|, n_2, |Res|) \qquad (1)$$

Case 2: $|T_1| \times F > |M|$.

The number of loops required to scan T_2 is Loop = $|T_1| \times F/|M|$. Let n_1 denotes the number of pages of T_1 processed. If $n_1 = |T_1|$, then all the pages of T_1 have already been read and the current loop is the last loop. In this case, *EFT* is derived in the same way as the case when $|T_1| \times F \leq |M|$ using Equation (1) (It should be noted the value of $|T_1|$ in Equation (1) should be replaced by $|T_1| - (Loop - 1) \times |M|/F$). Otherwise, the following computation is done. Let n_2 denotes the number of pages of T_2 processed in the current loop. Then the number of loops processed, inclusive of the loop that is currently being processed, is LoopProcessed = $n_1/T_1 \times$ Loop. The estimated time to perform the join is

$$T_{HNL}(|T_1|, |T_2|, |Result|) = T_{HNL}((LoopProcessed - 1) \times \frac{|M|}{F}, |T_2|, |Res1|) + T_{HNL}(\frac{|M|}{F}, n_2, |Res2|) + EFT$$

where |Res1| and |Res2| are estimated using the following two expressions:

$$\frac{|Res1|/(LoopProcessed - 1)}{|Res2|} = \frac{|T_2|}{n_2} \quad \text{and} \quad |Res1| + |Res2| = |Res|$$

---

[1] In the case when $|Res| = 0$, that is when no tuple has been generated yet, *Result* can be estimated using the number of distinct join attribute values in T_1 and T_2 respectively.

[2] We have ignored the transmission of directories since their sizes are expected to be small (in number of pages).

where |Res| is the size of results generated thus far. Therefore,

$$EFT = T_{HNL}(|T_1|, |T_2|, |Result|) -$$

$$T_{HNL}((LoopProcessed - 1) \times \frac{|M|}{F}, |T_2|, |Res1|) -$$

$$T_{HNL}(\frac{|M|}{F}, n_2, |Res2|)$$

3.3.2. Determination of the amount of data to be transferred

The amount of data to be transferred is determined in such a way that two processors sharing the load are expected to complete their tasks at the same time.

Case 1: $|T_1| \times F \le |M|$.

If $|T_1| \times F \le |M|$, then the idle processor needs the entire relation T_1 and portion of the unprocessed T_2. Let k be the number of pages of T_2 to be stolen. k should satisfy the following expression:

$$EFT - T_{join}(|T_1|, k, Res_k) \ge \begin{cases} T_{HNL}(|T_1|, k, Res_k) & \text{if } k \ge |T_1| \\ T_{HNL}(k, |T_1|, Res_k) & otherwise \end{cases}$$

where Res_k, the result size of the k pages, is estimated as follows:

$$\frac{|Res_k|}{|Res|} = \frac{k}{n_2}$$

We can determine the optimal number of pages to be transferred by solving the following equation:

$$EFT - T_{join}(|T_1|, k, Res_k) = \begin{cases} T_{HNL}(|T_1|, k, Res_k) & \text{if } k \ge |T_1| \\ T_{HNL}(k, |T_1|, Res_k) & otherwise \end{cases}$$

Case 2: $|T_1| \times F > |M|$.

On the other hand, if $|T_1| \times F > |M|$, then we should transfer portion of the unprocessed T_1 and the entire T_2. We would like to transfer enough pages of T_1 such that a hash table can be built in memory for these pages. If all pages of T_1 have already been read, the number of pages to be transferred is determined in the same way as case (1) using the number of pages processed in the last loop instead of T_1. Otherwise, the k pages of T_1 to be transferred should satisfy the following expression:

$$T_{HNL}(k, |T_2|, Res_k) \le EFT - T_{HNL}(k, |T_2|, Res_k)$$

where $|Res_k|$ may be estimated using

$$\frac{|Res_k|}{|Res1|/(LoopProcessed - 1)} = \frac{k}{|M|/F}$$

where |Res| is the size of results generated thus far. We can determine the number of pages to be transmitted that will optimize the load-balancing, that is

$$T_{HNL}(k, |T_2|, Res_k) = \frac{EFT}{2}$$

However, if k pages turn out to be too large to be staged in memory, we will only transmit sufficient amount that can be staged in memory. This, we believe, will minimize thrashing, that is too much load may be transferred to an idle processor which forces it to become overloaded leading to its load being stolen.

3.4. Performance Study of DLPJ

We conducted a simulation study for join algorithm DLPJ described above. We vary the skewness of the join attribute (which follows the Zipf-distribution) and the number of processors involved. We also study different memory sizes, different relation sizes and obtained similar results reported here.

To evaluate the performance of the proposed algorithm, we assume that the values of the join column follow a *Zipf-like distribution* [Knut73]. For a relation R with a domain of D distinct values, the ith distinct join column value, for $1 \le i \le D$, has such number of tuples as given by the following expression:

$$\|D_i\| = \frac{\|R\|}{i^{\theta} \cdot \sum_{j=1}^{D} \frac{1}{j^{\theta}}} \tag{2}$$

where θ is the skew factor. When $\theta = 0$, the distribution becomes *uniform*. With $\theta = 1$, it corresponds to the highly skewed *pure* Zipf distribution [Zipf49]. Though the join column is skewed, we assume that the relations to be joined are, initially, evenly distributed among the processors to facilitate full concurrent access to the relation.

We also study the effect of different correlations between the skew values in the two relations. Two types of correlation are modeled: *Ordered correlation* and *random correlation*. For ordered correlation, the values in both the attributes have the same ranking sequences. For example, the highest ranked value in attribute R_A of relation R is also the highest ranked value in the corresponding attribute S_A in relation S. On the other hand, random correlation randomly correlates the attribute in R and S.

We compare the performance of DLPJ with 3 other algorithms. The first, *join algorithm 1* (JA1) is similar to DeWitt's approach where the number of partitions generated is the same as the number of processors available [DeWi85]. Using this approach, given p processors, the relations are partitioned into p partitions generating p tasks. Each task is allocated to a processor and the p tasks are simultaneously executed. The second algorithm, *join algorithm* 2 (JA2) is similar to Kitsuregawa's method where a large number of tasks will be generated first. These partitions are then merged into p partitions so that each partition of the source relation will have approximately equal size [Kits83]. The last algorithm, *no load balancing* (NLB) is essentially equal to the DLPJ but no load-balancing is performed.

As in [Wolf90, Wolf91], we substitute the *actual* distribution of data into the cost formulas for the join algorithm HNL to compute the elapsed time. That is, the actual number of pages (and tuples) of the source, target and result relations of each partition are used in the computation. The distribution of data for the source and target relations is generated using Equation (2). A hashing function is then used to partition the relations into B partitions. Two hashing functions are used — *range-based* where partition i contains tuple in the range $\left[1 + (i-1) \times \frac{D}{B}, \ i \times \frac{D}{B}\right]$, for $1 \le i \le B$, and *modulo-based* where tuple with value *tu* belongs to partition [*tu* MOD B + 1]. Both hashing functions show similar results. To compute the result size, we introduce a selectivity factor of the join operation, *Sel*. *Sel* gives the number of distinct tuples in the source relation that has a matching value in the target relation. For example, *Sel* = 0.5 means that for each tuple in the source relation, there is a probability of 0.5 that it will find a match in the target relation. *Sel* is modeled using a uniform distribution UD(0,1). When the ordered correlation is used, for each distinct value of the source relation examined, if the value of UD(0,1) is in the range 0 — *Sel*, the corresponding distinct value in the target relation is a match and the join result size equal to the product of the number of tuples with this value in the source and target relations. Otherwise, the result size is 0. For random correlation, for each distinct value of the source relation examined, a random tuple is picked from the target relation and the result size is computed in the same manner as that of ordered correlation.

For purpose of illustrating the performance study here, the following test values are used: The system has 16 disks. The number of processors is varied from 2 — 32 and each processor has 512K of memory. The CPU processing rate is 10 MIPS and the I/O bandwidth 10 Mbytes/s. It takes 50 instructions to compare two keys/attributes. The computation of hash function of a key costs 100 instructions. The time to move a tuple in memory is 500 instructions. We also vary the number of tuples in relation R (S) from 100K — 1M. Each page of relation R(S) and the resultant relation contains 50 tuples. The number of distinct tuples in relations R and S is 10K. Three skew factors, 0.1, 0.5 and 1.0, are used to represent low, medium and high skew respectively. The selectivity factor (*Sel*) is 0.5.

3.4.1. Experiment 1: Vary the number of processors

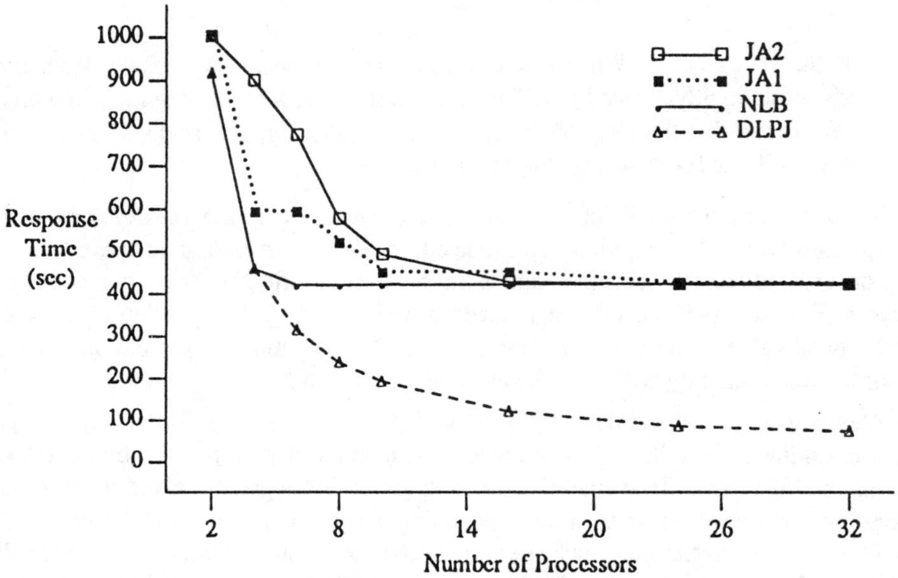

Graph 3.1. Response time as the number of processors varies.

In this experiment, we study the performance of the algorithms as the number of processors varies. We present here only the results when both relations are highly skewed. With the other parameter settings, similar behaviors are obtained. Graph 3.1 shows the result of the experiment. While the response time for all the algorithms decreases as the number of processors increases, the 3 algorithms, *JA* 1, *JA* 2 and *NLB*, perform poorly as compared to the DLPJ algorithm. This is so because of data skew which results in some tasks dominating in the join outputs. As the number of processors increases, the response time becomes dominated by a few partitions. Since there is no load-balancing in all these 3 algorithms, the most time-consuming task will determine the completion time of the algorithms. The NLB algorithm performs slightly better than the other 2 approaches since it generates a larger number of tasks (partitions). This implies that lesser number of tuples per partition and this may avoid some overflow partitions that the other 2 approaches may generate.

It is obvious that DLPJ outperforms other algorithms as it is able to balance the load across the processors. Idle processors for the JA1, JA2 and NLB algorithms remain idle once every task is allocated and the processor finishes the tasks that are allocated to it. On the other hand, for DLPJ, idle processors steal some load from some overloaded processors. However, DLPJ may not be able to achieve 100% speedup. In particular, the gain in performance is significant with each additional processor when the number of processors is small (between 2 to 10). Once the number of processors reaches a certain value, the gain is not significant (from 16 processors onwards). This is so for the following reasons. First, less than half the load from the candidate processor is transferred each time. Second, especially for high data skew, when a single processor is active (no transfer is possible because the page is currently being executed or because the estimation criterion is inaccurate), the currently executing page and any remaining pages may be the most time-consuming pages that generate a huge number of output. Since *JA* 1 and *JA* 2 perform poorly, we will not present their results subsequently but will compare only *NLB* with *DLPJ*.

3.4.2. Experiment 2: Vary the skewness of the data

Next, we study how the skew factor will affect the performance of the algorithms. We will present only the case when the correlation is ordered as random correlation of data shows similar results.

Skew/Skew	Partition	NLB		DLPJ		Gain (%) w.r.t.	
		Join	Total	Join	Total	Join	Total
Low/Low	0.702	5.985	7.389	5.600	7.004	6.428	5.207
Low/Medium	0.702	5.940	7.355	5.632	7.047	5.183	4.185
Low/High	0.702	23.426	24.833	8.352	9.759	64.349	60.701
Medium/Medium	0.713	26.498	27.925	14.572	15.998	45.008	42.709
Medium/High	0.713	515.232	516.651	74.448	75.867	85.550	85.316
High/High	0.706	2613.277	2614.688	254.249	255.661	90.271	90.222

Table 3.1. Comparison of DLPJ and NBL.

Table 3.1 summarizes some tests conducted with 16 processors. The column labeled "Skew/Skew" represents the skews for the source and target relations respectively and the values for Low, Medium and High correspond to the skew factor of 0.1, 0.5 and 1 respectively. From the table, we see that DLPJ is superior over the other approaches. The performance gain ranges from 5% to 90%. When the skew is low, the performance gain is not significant. The reason is that, with low skew, most of the tasks have approximately the same processing times. As such, there is little or even no load being transferred between processors. However, as the skew increases, some tasks are more time-consuming than others. Without balancing the load, some processors will remain lightly loaded while the heavily loaded ones will determine the completion time of the join. By balancing the load, the completion time may be, as discussed above, drastically reduced.

3.4.3. Experiment 3: Vary the number of partitions

For hash-based join algorithms, the number of partitions may have an impact on the performance of the algorithm [Naka88, Kits89]. When the number of partition is small, more tuples will be hashed to a partition and the probability of the size of a partition exceeding the main memory size increases. Such overflow partitions will degrade the performance of the algorithm. On the other hand, too many partitions may also lead to poor performance as the number of fragmented pages increases resulting in more I/Os.

In this experiment, we perform two tests on DLPJ. The first varies the number of partitions statically, that is the number of tasks to be generated. The second is more complicated. After the relations are partitioned, the number of partitions is further fined-tuned as in [Kits83] by merging partitions of smaller size to form larger-sized partitions that can still be staged in memory. The joining phase will then work with the new number of tasks.

The results of the experiment are shown in Graph 3.2. [3] First, it is observed that, for test

[3] The curve for test 2 is drawn according to the initial number of partitions and not the final number of

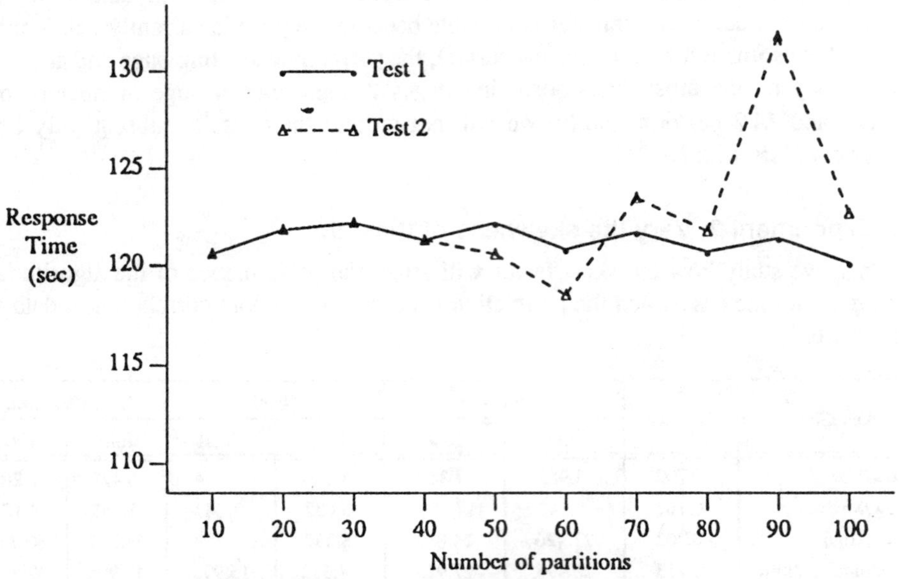

Graph 3.2. Response time as the number of partitions varies.

1, the number of partitions does not seem to affect the performance significantly. This is because the tasks are CPU-bound and so the algorithm is able to balance the load across all the processors. [4] The performance difference between the best and worst case is less than 5% of the response time. Second, both tests 1 and 2 have the same performance when the number of partitions is small. For test 2, when the initial number of partitions is small, the partition size is large and the opportunity for merging decreases. However, when the initial number of partitions is larger, the opportunity for merging increases. While this has the benefit of reducing I/Os for fragmented pages, it also has the overhead cost during the balancing stage of the joining phase. During the balancing phase, if the partition whose load is to be transferred is a merged partition (that is it has been merged from several smaller partitions), additional cost would be incurred for building a larger hash table by the idle processor than it would if no merging has been performed. In Graph 3.2, when the number of partitions is large (> 70), each partition contains lesser tuples. Therefore, there are more opportunity for merging smaller partitions to form a larger one. Thus during the balancing stage, the overhead incurred exceeds the benefit gained. As the result, the performance is poorer than the case when no fine-tuning is performed. On the other hand, as shown in Graph 3.2, when the number of partitions is moderate, fewer partitions need to be integrated and therefore the gain is greater than the overhead. Thus, we propose that the number of partitions be chosen to be as large as possible to avoid overflow partitions. Moreover, partition-size tuning is not necessary for CPU-bound tasks.

4. Conclusion

The traditional query processing method that distributes the processors across the number of operations suffers from two problems: 1) some operations are more expensive than others, and 2) load imbalance between tasks of the same operation. In this paper, we proposed a dynamic and load-balancing task-oriented approach to query processing that not only minimizes the completion time of a query but is also robust to data skew. A query is first

---

partitions after partition-size tuning.

[4] We assume a quite high I/O bandwidth. With a low I/O bandwidth, the I/O will always be the bottleneck and the performance will not be improved much by increasing the number of processors. With new technology, such as optical erasable disks and parallel I/Os, the high bandwidth is also realizable.

decomposed to a set of tasks. These tasks are then dynamically allocated to the available processors one at a time. Once a processor finishes the execution of the assigned task, it requests for another one. When there is no more tasks, some load of a busy processor may be transferred to the idle processor.

We study the performance of this approach for single join queries in shared-disk environment. The data skew is modeled by Zipf-like distribution. Moreover, we use the actual data distribution of each task to measure the elapsed time in our simulation. A task is to join a partition of the source relation with the corresponding partition of the target relation. A directory of the addresses of the pages belonging to a partition is created during partitioning. This structure facilitates the balancing of the load easily. Our results show that the new approach is superior compared to traditional hash-based join methods. The performance gain is in the range of 5% to 90% depending on the data skew. Our study also shows that the performance of the approach is not sensitive to the number of partitions. This is an important feature since it can simplify the algorithm design and implementation.

We plan to extend this work in the following area. First, we are planing to extend our study to more general queries. We have applied the same approach to multi-join queries. The preliminary results are very promising. With more general query plans, some other issues, such as task ordering, pipelined processing versus task stealing, etc. make the problem more complicated. Second, we can enhance the load-balancing strategy for the join algorithm when the source relations can be staged in memory. Instead of reading the source relations and built the hash table by the idle processor, we may transfer the content from memory to memory, that is from the candidate processor to the idle processor. Since the cost of communication is expected to be cheaper than that of disk I/Os, this enhancement may provide a slightly better performance. Finally, we have considered only hash-based nested loop join algorithm in which the load to be transferred can be determined easily. It would be interesting to explore how the load for other algorithms, such as sort-merge join, may be determined and transferred.

References

[Deen90] Deen, S. M., Kannangara, D. N. P. and Taylor, M. C., "Multi-join on Parallel Processors," *Proc. 2nd Intl. Symp. Databases in Parallel and Distributed Systems*, Dublin, Ireland, Jul. 1990, pp. 92-102.

[DeWi85] DeWitt, D. J., and Gerber, R., "Multiprocessor Hashed-Based Join Algorithms," *Proc. VLDB 85*, Stockholm, Aug. 1985, pp. 151-164.

[DeWi90] DeWitt, D. J., *et al.*, "The GAMMA Database Machine Project," *IEEE Trans. Knowledge and Data Engineering*, Vol. 2, No. 1, Mar. 1990, pp.44-62.

[Engl89] Englert, S., *et al.*, "A Benchmark of Nonstop SQL Release 2 Demonstrating Near-linear Speedup and Scaleup on Large Databases," Tandem Tech. Rep. 89.4, May 1989.

[Hua91] Hua, K. A. and Lee, C., "Handling Data Skew in Multicomputer Database Systems Using Partition Tuning," to appear in *Proc. VLDB 91*, Barcelona, Spain, Sept. 1991.

[Kits83] Kitsuregawa, M., Tanaka, H. and Motoka, T., "Application of Hash to Database Machines and its Architecture," *New Generation Computing*, Vol. 1, No. 1, 1983, pp. 63-74.

[Kits89] Kitsuregawa, M., Nakayama, M. and Takagi, M., "The Effect of Bucket Size Tuning in the Dynamic Hybrid GRACE Hash Join Method," *Proc. VLDB 89*, Amsterdam, Netherlands, Aug. 1989, pp. 257-266.

[Kits90] Kitsuregawa, M. and Ogawa, Y., "Bucket Spreading Parallel Hash: A New, Robust, Parallel Hash Join Method for Data Skew in the Super Database Computer (SDC)," *Proc. VLDB 90*, Brisbane, Australia, Aug. 1990, pp. 210-221.

[Knut73] Knuth, D. E., The Art of Programming, Vol. 3: Sorting and Searching, Addison-Wesley, 1973.

[Laks90] Lakshmi, M. S., and Yu, P. S., "Effectiveness of Parallel Joins," *IEEE Trans. Knowledge and Data Engineering*, Vol. 2, No. 4, Sept. 1990, pp.410-424.

[Lu91] Lu, H., Shan, M. C., and Tan, K. L., "Optimization of Multi-Way Join Queries for Parallel Execution," to appear in *Proc. VLDB 91*, Barcelona, Spain, Sept. 1991.

[Murp91] Murphy, M. C., and Shan, M. C., "Execution Plan Balancing: A Practical Technique for Multiprocessor Query Optimization," *Proc. 7th Intl. Conf. on Data Engineering*, Kobe, Japan, Apr. 1991, pp. 698-706.

[Naka88] Nakayama, M. and Kitsuregawa, M., "Hash-partitioned Join Method Using Dynamic Destaging Strategy," *Proc. VLDB 88*, Los Angeles, CA., Aug. 1988, pp. 468-478.

[Omic91] Omiecinski, E., "Performance Analysis of a Load Balancing Relational Hash-Join Algorithm for a Shared Memory Multiprocessor," to appear in *Proc. VLDB 91*, Barcelona, Spain, Sept. 1991.

[Ozka86] Ozkarahan, E., Database Machines and Database Management, Prentice Hall, 1986.

[Su88] Su, S. Y. W., Database Computers, McGraw-Hill, 1988.

[Tera88] Teradata Corporation, DBC/1012 Data Base Computer Concepts and Facilities, Teradata Document C02-0001-05, Los Angeles, CA, 1988.

[Walt91] Walton, C. B., Dale, A. G., and Jenevein, R. M., "A Taxonomy and Performance Model of Data Skew Effects in Parallel Joins," to appear in *Proc. VLDB 91*, Barcelona, Spain, Sept. 1991.

[Wolf90] Wolf, J. L., Dias, D. M. and Yu, P. S., "An Effective Algorithm for Parallelizing Sort Merge Joins in the Presence of Data Skew," *Proc. 2nd Intl. Symp. Databases in Parallel and Distributed Systems*, Dublin, Ireland, Jul. 1990, pp. 103-115.

[Wolf91] Wolf, J. L., Dias, D. M. and Yu, P. S., "An Effective Algorithm for Parallelizing Hash Joins in the Presence of Data Skew," *Proc. 7th Intl. Conf. on Data Engineering*, Kobe, Japan, Apr. 1991, pp. 200-209.

[Zipf49] Zipf, G. K., Human Behavior and the Principle of Least Effort, Addison Wesley, 1949.

Chapter 6: Parallel Query Optimization

As applications and queries become more complex, it is not uncommon for queries to involve several relations. In fact, queries with a large number of joins are expected of novel applications, such as knowledge-based systems, which could be built on top of relational systems. Query optimization refers to the important process in relational database management systems that selects an optimal execution plan for a query from a set of feasible plans, based on some predefined optimization objectives such as minimizing the response time and maximizing throughput. This execution plan specifies the operations, the operands (relations), and their execution order. The different methods used to implement the operations, such as the join methods and access methods previously discussed are also specified. Since the search space for the optimal plan is usually very large and will often incur unreasonable overhead if the best plan must always be chosen, most query optimizers aim at finding a near-optimal plan within reasonable time. Nevertheless, the process is traditionally referred to as "query optimization."

Because of the importance and complexity of query optimization, a large amount of effort has been spent on developing efficient optimization algorithms for various systems, including centralized, distributed, and parallel database systems.[1-10] Most of these works concentrate on the optimization of multi-way join queries as the optimization of selection or projection is relatively easier. Furthermore, most of the work focus on determining the order in which the joins should be executed and the join method used by each join, as these are the most important factors in determining the optimality of a plan. In this chapter, we first give some background information, including the search space for multi-way join query optimization and the basic optimization strategies used in uniprocessor systems. A brief discussion on optimization for parallel database systems is also given.

Plan representation

In relational database systems, each query execution plan can be represented by a processing tree where the leaf nodes are the base relations and the internal nodes represent operations. Figure 6-1 shows the four typical tree shapes that have been used in the literature. If all the internal nodes of an execution tree have at least one leaf as a child, then the tree is called deep. Otherwise, it is called bushy. A left-deep tree is a deep tree where all the right children must be leaf nodes. Conversely, a right-deep tree is a deep tree where all the left children are leaf nodes. The left-deep and right-deep plans are not the same because different join algorithms use their two inputs differently. As defined, the search space of bushy trees includes deep trees, which in turn include left-deep and right-deep trees.

Figure 6-1. Examples of different query trees.

Strategy space

Consider the problem of evaluating the multi-way join query $R_1 \bowtie R_2 \bowtie R_3 \dots \bowtie R_n$ where there are n relations $R_1, R_2, \dots, R_n$ and $n-1$ joins. Since join operations are commutative, there are many different processing trees that can represent this query. An upper bound on the number of processing trees that corresponds to the query is given in Reference 9 as

$$\binom{2n}{n} \cdot n!$$

However, this number merely considers the join orders without the join methods. Here, we will first derive the number of feasible processing trees that correspond to a join expression.

Each processing tree, *PT*, that identifies the order of evaluating the joins in a multi-way join query can be represented as a triple (T_k, r, T_{n-k}) where r is a distinguished node called the join result of T_n, T_k is a PT of k relations for some $k = 1, \ldots, n-1$, called the left subtree of T_n, and T_{n-k} is a PT of $n - k$ relations, called the right subtree of T_n. From this definition, we can deduce that x_n, the number of possible PTs for n relations, is given by the recurrence relation:

$$x_n = \sum_{k=1}^{n-1} \binom{n}{k} \cdot x_k \cdot x_{n-k} \text{ where } x_1 = 1$$

Since for every triple (T_k, r, T_{n-k}), there is a corresponding triple (T_{n-k}, r, T_k) and the two are indistinguishable, we have y_n, the number of distinct processing trees, as

$$y_n = \frac{1}{2} \cdot \sum_{k=1}^{n-1} \binom{n}{k} \cdot y_k \cdot y_{n-k} \text{ where } y_1 = 1 \qquad (6.1)$$

$$= \binom{2(n-1)}{n-1} \cdot \frac{(n-1)!}{2^{n-1}}$$

With Equation (6.1), the number of distinct PTs for 2, 3, 4, 5, 6, and 7 relations are, respectively, 1, 3, 15, 105, 945, and 10,385.

In a uniprocessor environment, besides choosing the join order, a query execution plan needs to specify the join method for each of the joins as well. Given m join methods supported by the DBMS, the total number of query evaluation plans becomes

$$z_n = m^{n-1} \cdot y_n$$

In a multiuser environment, the allocation of resources such as memory will also increase the search space drastically. One could further expand the search space derived above by considering buffer space allocation and access methods.

With such a huge search space, it is computationally expensive to perform an exhaustive search to obtain the optimal execution plan. The challenge to the database community is to develop efficient heuristics that are not only able to prune the search space effectively but also to ensure that the plan obtained from the restricted space is near-optimal, if not optimal.

Uniprocessor optimization techniques

Most relational database systems support join as a primitive relation and their optimizers visualize an M-way join as a sequence of 2-way joins. For example, a 4-way join query of the form

$$R_1 \bowtie R_2 \bowtie R_3 \bowtie R_4$$

may be processed as

$$(((R_1 \bowtie R_2) \bowtie R_3) \bowtie R_4)$$

Therefore, the two essential tasks of a query optimizer for uniprocessor systems are to select

- an appropriate join method for each join operation and
- the order in which the joins are performed

to achieve some predefined optimization objectives. A large number of optimization algorithms for uniprocessor systems have been developed. The basic techniques used include exhaustive search, dynamic programming with branch and bound,[8] combinatorial algorithms,[3,9,10] and polynomial heuristics.[4]

Exhaustive. By exhaustive, we mean that every plan is generated and the plan with the least cost is taken as the optimal solution. Although this approach generates the optimal solution, it is clearly not feasible for a large number of relations since the total number of plans grows exponentially with the number of relations. Because of its costliness, this approach has not been implemented in real systems; it is mainly used as a reference in performance comparisons.

Dynamic programming with branch and bound. The most commonly used branch and bound technique is dynamic programming. The basic dynamic programming strategy works iteratively in the following manner: it builds a plan of i relations from two plans of $(i-j)$ and j relations $(j<i)$. For dynamic programming to produce an optimal solution, the cost metric used must abide by two fundamental assumptions: (1) whenever two plans share a common subplan, the cheaper plan is the better plan, and (2) the cost of the plans can be totally ordered.

The System R optimizer employs this approach.[8] The algorithm for dynamic programming for left-deep trees is shown below:

Algorithm *Dynamic Programming*
Input: a multi-way join query with n relations
Output: an optimal plan P_{opt} with optimal work

for i := 1 to n do
    $optPlan(\{R_i\}) \leftarrow accessPlan(R_i)$
endfor
for i := 1 to n do
    forall $S \subseteq \{R_1, \ldots, R_n\}$ such that $cardinality(S) = i$ do
        $bestPlan \leftarrow$ dummy plan with infinite cost
        forall R_j, S_j such that $S = \{R_j\} \cup S_j$ do
            $p \leftarrow joinPlan(optPlan(S_j), R_j)$
            if $cost(p) \leq cost(bestPlan)$ do
                $bestPlan \leftarrow p$
            endif
            $optPlan(S) \leftarrow bestPlan$
        endfor
    endfor
endfor
$P_{opt} \leftarrow optPlan(\{R_1, \ldots, R_n\})$

In the algorithm, several functions are used. Function $accessPlan(R)$ generates the optimal access plan for relation R. The function $joinPlan(p, R)$ produces a new plan p' from plan p and relation R, which is obtained by joining p with R in the best way. The function $cost(p)$ returns the cost of plan p. The cost metric used in system R is the resource consumption (that is, the total CPU and I/O cost) of the plan.

In System R, only linear processing trees are explored. To further restrict the search space to linear processing trees, heuristics are used to prune the restricted search space. Join orders which have join predicates relating the inner relation to the other relations participating in the join are considered first; cartesian products are postponed until as late as possible. The intuition is that cartesian products are expensive and result in large intermediate results. However, these heuristics do not change the combinatorial nature of the problem. With large numbers of joins, as in the exhaustive case, these algorithms become impractical.

In Reference 11, the optimization of a multi-way join query is studied using the nested-block join algorithm. Using the nested-block join algorithm, a three-way join would be executed as follows. Each relation is assigned a block of memory (which need not be the same size). For each block of the outer relation, we loop over the middle relation once; for every pair of blocks — one from the outer and one from the middle — we loop over the inner relation once. Since different block sizes result in different cost, the optimization problem may be reduced to finding an optimal allocation of memory to the relations.[11] The DYNAMIC algorithm that employs both dynamic programming and branch-and-bound is proposed to give an optimal allocation.

Polynomial heuristics. Since the optimization cost could be substantial, this prompted the need to develop new query optimization algorithms. In particular, the class of polynomial algorithms is of interest since the optimization cost of such algorithms is low. The most straightforward polynomial algorithms come under the greedy paradigm. Greedy algorithms are usually iterative in nature. For each iteration, the algorithms greedily obtain the partial plan that has the lowest cost during the current iteration. A generic greedy algorithm works as follows:

Algorithm *Greedy*
Input: a multi-way join query with n relations
Output: an optimal plan P_{opt}

$setR \leftarrow \{R_1, \ldots, R_n\}$
for $i = 1$ to $n - 1$ do
    select R and S from $setR$ such that joinCost($R \bowtie S$) is cheapest
    $setR \leftarrow setR - \{R\} - \{S\} \cup \{R \bowtie S\}$
    $P_{opt} \leftarrow joinPlan(R, S)$
endfor
return(P_{opt})

Here, the function *joinCost*($R \bowtie S$) computes the cost to join two relations R and S. The function *joinPlan*(R, S) builds the plan for relations R and S.

In Reference 4, an $O(n^2)$ algorithm known as a KBZ heuristic for multi-way join optimization is presented. (The name of the algorithm, KBZ, is derived from the initials of the three authors.) The algorithm is based on the notion of differential cost of a join method where the join cost may be estimated independently of the join order. Thus the ordering of two sub-sequences of joins can be decided independently of the rest of the sequence. The decision is based on a rank function defined only for the sub-sequences. The rank of a sub-sequence measures the increase in the intermediate result, normalized by the cost of doing the joins in the sub-sequence. A minimized rank implies optimality.

Combinatorial algorithms. Another viable alternative to the exhaustive search approach is the use of randomized algorithms, such as simulated annealing and iterative improvement, which have been successfully applied to various combinatorial optimization problems. In a combinatorial optimization problem, a solution can be thought of as a state in a state space; that is, a node in a graph that includes all possible solutions. Each state has a cost associated with it, which is given by some problem-specific cost function. The goal of the optimization algorithm is to find a state with the globally minimum cost. Randomized algorithms usually perform random walks in the state space via a series of moves. The states that can be reached in one move from a state S are called the neighbors of S. A move that takes a state to another one with a lower cost is called a downward move; otherwise it is called an upward move. A state is a local minimum if its cost is lower than that of all neighboring states. A state is a global minimum if it has the lowest cost among all local minima and hence all moves are upward moves. A state is on a plateau if it has no lower cost neighbor and yet it can reach lower states without uphill moves.

We briefly discuss two of the most commonly used combinatorial algorithms — iterative improvement (II) and simulated annealing (SA). The iterative improvement algorithm is essentially a greedy algorithm. Starting from an initial state (S), the inner loop improves the solution by repeatedly accepting random downward moves until a local minimum is reached. By using different initial states, different local minima would be obtained. The best of these local minima could then be chosen. It is shown that as time approaches ∞, the probability of obtaining the global minimum using this algorithm approaches 1 (see Reference 12). Algorithmically, II works as follows:

```
Algorithm Iterative Improvement
minS ← S∞
while not (stopping condition) do
        S ← random state
        while not (local_minimum(S)) do
                newS ← random state in neighbor(S)
                if (cost(newS) < cost(S)) do
                        S = newS
                endif
        endwhile
        if cost(S) < cost(minS) then minS = S
endwhile
return(minS)
```

Whereas the iterative improvement approach accepts moves that decrease only the cost, SA accepts upward moves with some probability, to prevent it from being trapped in a high-cost local minimum. The inner loop of SA is called a stage. During each stage, upward moves are accepted with a probability of $e^{-\Delta C/T}$, where ΔC is the cost difference between the new and original state and T is the temperature. (The term "temperature" was borrowed from the original application of the algorithm.)[13] It is obvious that the probability of accepting an upward move increases as the value of T increases, and as the value of the cost difference decreases. Each stage terminates when the algorithm reaches equilibrium. The temperature is then reduced and a new stage begins. The algorithm halts when it is frozen, that is, when the temperature is reduced to zero. The algorithm is given here:

```
Algorithm Simulated Annealing
S ← S0
T ← Tc
minS ← S
while not(frozen) do
        while not (equilibrium) do
                newS ← random state in neighbor(S)
                ΔC ←cost(newS) - cost(S)
                if (ΔC <= 0) do
                        S = newS
                endif
                if (ΔC > 0) do
                        S - newS with probability e^(-ΔC/T)
                endif
        endwhile
        T ← reduce(T)
endwhile
return(minS)
```

In the context of a database, each state in a query optimization corresponds to an access plan of the query to be optimized. For join queries, this corresponds to the join processing tree. The neighbors of a state, which are join processing trees, are determined by a set of transformation rules, such as join commutativity and join associativity. The cost of each access plan is determined by the supported cost function.

In References 9 and 10, the multi-way join optimization problem is shown to be a hard combinatorial optimization problem. As such, Swami and Gupta adapted some general combinatorial optimization techniques to the problem. They studied techniques such as iterative improvement, simulated annealing, perturbation walk, and quasi-random sampling. Heuristics such as augmentation heuristics, KBZ heuristics, and local improvement are also used to aid the combinatorial techniques. Their studies show that iterative improvement that uses the augmentation heuristics performs best, whereas the use of KBZ heuristics and simulated annealing approaches is not encouraging.

In Reference 3, the use of combinatorial algorithms for optimization of large join queries was re-examined. Several aspects of this work are different from that of References 9 and 10. First, the strategy space for this work is larger. The processing trees examined included both linear and bushy ones. Furthermore, two join methods, both nested-loops and merge-join, are considered instead of one. Second, the environment of study is different. Swami assumes a main memory database, whereas no such assumption is made in Reference 3. Third, a different approximation for the local minimum is considered. Finally, the set of transformation rules is not only larger but is also based on algebraic properties of joins. The results indicated that II outperforms SA initially, but when enough time is given to SA, it performs better than II. The work also proposes the two-phase optimization algorithm, which is a hybrid of II and SA. This algorithm is shown to outperform II and SA all the time.

The disadvantage of using combinatorial approaches is that the query optimization time may be substantial before a good solution can be obtained.

Parallel optimization techniques

In a parallel system, the optimization problem is more complicated, with new dimensions introduced by parallelism. First, the number of feasible plans increases dramatically[14] because of the availability of more resources such as processors and memory. Bushy plans, which have been ignored in most uniprocessor systems, tend to give better overall system performance. In fact, any form of restriction of the search space (for example, using only linear execution plans), incurs the risk that the optimal and even the suboptimal solutions might be excluded from the restricted search space. Second, proper scheduling and allocation of resources such as processors and memory are critical to parallel database systems. A poor schedule or allocation will result in poor system performance. Thus, besides determining a good join order and the join strategies used, the optimizer for parallel systems must also determine

- the number of operations to perform in parallel and the relations involved in each of these operations, and
- the scheduling and allocation of resources to the concurrent operations.

The plan will include information such as the ordering of the joins and the resource allocation (number of processors and amount of memory assigned) for each operation. Hence, optimization of a query is more expensive and complicated in parallel database systems.

The optimization techniques developed so far can be classified into two types: one-phase and two-phase. For the two-phase approach, the first phase, called plan generation, generates a query processing plan without considering the run time resources. In this phase, the best strategy is also selected for each operation from among all available methods. The second phase, known as resource scheduling, ensures that the scheduling of resources is optimal for the plan generated in the first phase. Such an approach not only simplifies the optimization process, it also allows the first phase to be moved to compilation time so as to reduce the run time overhead. On the contrary, the one-phase approach packs all operations into one integrated component. The rationale is that a generated plan may not be optimal without considering resource allocation during the generation phase. In this section, we describe these two types of optimization techniques.

Two-phase optimization

All optimization strategies employed in uniprocessor systems can easily be extended for parallel systems using the two-phase approach. This is so because any of the algorithms can be used to generate a plan (without resource allocation) in the first phase. A resource scheduling algorithm may then be employed to schedule the resources for the plan generated.

Besides extending the uniprocessor algorithms, several works directly address the problem for parallel database systems.[1,15,16]

In Reference 16, the optimizer of XPRS used the two-phase approach to achieve intraquery parallelism. First, a collection of good sequential plans for various memory sizes is obtained. Second, ways to parallelize this collection of plans are then explored. At the time of execution, the best plan that fits the amount of memory available would be selected.

In Reference 1, the first phase was not discussed. Instead, it assumed that the query execution plan is available. To handle multiple joins on parallel processors, several strategies are considered. The basic idea is to form clusters of (approximately) equal numbers of processors and distribute the join operations across these clusters. The one-join in parallel approach allocates all processors to parallelize a single join operation. To process five joins, the algorithm will process the five joins one at a time, and all the processors are used in each join. In the *k*-separate joins in parallel strategy, *k* joins are performed in parallel at the same time. The processors are distributed evenly over the number of joins. If there are ten processors and two joins, then five processors will be assigned to work on each join. An experimental study is done for two and three joins using a small-scale multiprocessor (11 processors), and it is assumed that all the relations fit in the memory of the system. The result of the study shows that employing *k* one-join in parallel outperformed *k*-separate joins in parallel. In other words, it is better to use all processors to perform the joins one after another than to perform the *k* joins in parallel with fewer processors per join. This is because the one-join in parallel algorithm requires fewer scheduling and control overheads.

In Reference 17, a different result from that of Reference 1 is observed when the number of processors is large. It is shown that splitting the number of processors into several clusters and processing several join operations on different clusters may be advantageous in the case of a large number of processors. This is because for join operations, the gain in response time is more significant when the number of processors is small. When the number of processors exceeds a certain value (say, p_0), the gain in response time is not great. Thus, for a large number of processors, it becomes beneficial to execute several joins in parallel rather than process them one at a time.

Another two-phase optimization technique was proposed in Reference 18. Several heuristics are studied to generate a good sequential plan that facilitates parallelism. In particular, the Huffman algorithm[19] is used to derive three algorithms that would generate bushy plans: minimal cost, minimal resulting relation, and minimal expansion. For the second phase, several processor scheduling algorithms are also proposed and studied. In the bottom-up approach, the number of processors allocated to a join could be the smallest number that minimizes the execution time of the join or the smallest number that optimizes the processor utilization. Using the top-down approach, the processors are allocated such that the execution time of the left and right subtrees are approximately the same.

In the two-phase optimization approach, scheduling of resources is a key issue that will affect the system performance. Most of the previous work has simplified the allocation of resources to a mere allocation of processors. In Reference 1, it was assumed that the system has infinite memory. In Reference 5, the amount of memory allocated for an operation is proportional to the number of processors allocated for the operation. Murphy and Shan attempt to allocate both memory and processor resources for a two-phase optimization approach.[6] For each level of a query plan, their execution plan balancing strategy allocates resources to operations based on how critical they are. An operation is regarded as critical if it takes a long time to execute. Resources are first allocated to the most critical operation so that it can be completed in minimum time. The remaining resources are then assigned to the remaining operations so that all operations at the same level finish at approximately the same time. When the total amount of resources demanded exceeds that which is available, the completion time is adjusted (increased) and the resource allocation rebalanced. This process is repeated until the amount of resources demanded is no more than what is available.

One-phase optimization

Although the two-phase optimization approach seems to be more popular, it is not clear how an optimal ordering may be achieved without taking resources (memory and processors) into consideration in the plan generation phase. The one-phase approach has been studied in References 5, 15, and 20 through 24.

Exploiting deep plans. Schneider and DeWitt are among the first to study how pipelining may be exploited for multiway join optimization.[22] However, their work concentrates on the effect of query tree representations in processing multi-way join queries (using hash-based join algorithms) in shared-nothing architecture. In particular, left-deep, right-deep, and bushy query trees are studied. The right-deep representation strategy is shown to perform well in most instances because of its potential for pipelining to achieve the highest degree of parallelism. Pipelining is a desirable feature since it may reduce both the elapsed time and initial response time of a query. Furthermore, it reduces the importance of correctly estimating join selectivities. Three pipelined algorithms that generate parallel plans that are right-deep have been developed. The static right-deep scheduling strategy splits a right-deep tree into disjoint segments such that the total amount of memory consumption for each segment will not be more than the memory available. The dynamic bottom-up scheduling strategy builds a hash table in memory one at a time in a bottom-up manner and determines the segment boundary dynamically based on memory availability. The right-deep hybrid scheduling reduces the memory requirement for the query by partitioning the relations into buckets and processing the buckets in a pipeline manner.

Ziane et al.[24] introduces the notion of a zigzag tree, which is essentially a deep tree built out of a right-deep tree. In a zigzag tree, the intermediate result of a right-deep segment is not written to disk, if possible. Instead, the intermediate result is materialized in memory and used as the building relation in the next segment to be executed (provided enough memory is available). Implementation results are presented to demonstrate the advantages of zigzag trees over purely right-deep trees in a shared-memory environment.

Exploiting bushy plans. As mentioned earlier, restricting plans to left-deep or right-deep trees may lead to poor-quality plans. On the other hand, bushy plans allow several operations that are unrelated or independent of one another to be executed concurrently. Early works that attempted to exploit bushy plans did so at the expense of ignoring pipelining during optimization.[5,20]

In Reference 5, both the plan generation phase and the resource allocation phase are integrated into one so that resource allocation can be taken into consideration as the plan is generated. The proposed greedy algorithm, Greedy Parallel (GP), is shown below:

> **Algorithm** *Greedy Parallel*
> Input: $G \leftarrow (T, E)$
> Output: S, the join sequence consisting of relation pairs
> S ← ∅
> while Size(T) > 3 do
>   R ← *Select_rel_pairs* (G);
>   S ← S ∪ R;
>   T ← T - R ∪ *Join_result* (R);
>   for each pair (R_1, R_2) in R do
>   E ← E – { edges adjacent to R_1 and R_2 }
>   ∪ { edges from $R_1$and R_2 to *Join_Result* ((R_1, R_2)) } ;
> endwhile
> R ← *Two_way_seq*(G);
> S ← S ∪ R;

Algorithm GP generates plans that are bushy and flat. The plan will include information such as the ordering of the joins and the resource allocation (number of processors assigned) for each join. Algorithm GP selects, at each step, as many pairs of relations as possible to be joined concurrently. This is guided by a cost evaluation function. For the selection of pairs of relations to be joined, four criteria to be used as heuristics to guide the selection process were studied. The results show that the performance of the criteria turns out to be relatively close in the multiprocessor environment. Two cost evaluation functions — total cost evaluation and partial cost evaluation — were studied and used as heuristics to determine the number of pairs of relations to be executed at each step. The total cost evaluation function uses the total cost to compute the multi-way join at each step to determine the number of join operations for each step. On the other hand, the partial cost evaluation function only considers the cost to execute joins of the current step. The results of the study show that algorithm GP (with either cost heuristic) performs well for a small number of joins, with costs of no more than 120% of the optimal plans. Moreover, the study shows that the total cost evaluation function is a better heuristic, though at the expense of taking a longer time to generate the plan.

A more recent work investigates load-balancing issues in the optimization of multi-way join queries.[20] As in Reference 25, each tree is composed of several synchronized steps. The linear tree with load-balancing algorithm generates a linear tree first and employs the partition tuning algorithm of Reference 26 on each join operation. The no load-balancing optimization algorithm first generates a bushy plan using the algorithm proposed in Reference 5 and then performs load-balancing within each join operation. The load-balancing optimization algorithm integrates load-balancing into the optimization process. When several joins are selected to be processed concurrently, these joins are viewed collectively as a single large join and load-balancing is then performed on these joins as if they were a single large join. As such, the joins may be processed in an interleaved fashion, as in Reference 17.

More recently, several works have been published that emphasized generating bushy plans that exploit pipelining.[15,21,23,27] To further improve the execution of pipelined multi-way joins, two heuristics that generate segmented right-deep trees were proposed.[15] The main feature of these heuristics is that the generated tree is a bushy structure of right-deep segments and is called a segmented right-deep tree. Unlike right-deep trees, segmented right-deep trees allow the result of a right-deep segment to be either the inner or the outer relations of any of the subsequent segments. In the first heuristic — minimal work — relations are selected to minimize the total work done for the current segment. As a result, small relations are more likely to be included in earlier segments and large relations are delayed to the later segments. To avoid this scenario, the second heuristic — balanced consideration — introduces the notion of penalty, which is the work done in the current segment, and benefit, which is the size reduction. By minimizing the weighted difference of the penalty and the benefit, large relations (which will contribute to more work, that is, higher penalty) that give a small result for the segment (which will contribute to large size reduction, that is, more benefit) could potentially be selected in the earlier segments.

In Reference 27, the query evaluation plan is constructed in a bottom-up manner. At each step, several joins are performed as in Reference 5. However, the left operand of each join must fit in the memory. Thus, a right-deep pipelining may be achieved. The selection of the number of joins is guided by the lower and upper bounds on the estimated time to process these joins.

Lanzelotte et al.[21] studied the trade-offs between optimization cost and processing cost. The results show that instead of restricting the search space to left-deep or right-deep trees, the optimization cost could be reduced by controlling the search strategy. A parallel version of simulated annealing that generates bushy plans, Toured Simulated Annealing, is proposed. It is shown to yield the best optimization/processing cost ratio.

Incorporation memory resource. Query optimizers have traditionally ignored memory resources. This is not unreasonable since computer memories were small in the past and there was little opportunity for caching data in memory. However, this is no longer true, and the need for the optimizer to be aware of memory resources in order to generate good-quality plans cannot be overemphasized.[15,22,24] As such, a cost model of memory resources is needed to fully exploit available memory resources. Otherwise, suboptimal execution plans may be generated.

In Reference 23, optimization algorithms using dynamic programming and greedy heuristics are described. Unlike traditional methods, these new heuristics include both memory resources and pipelining in their cost model. Extensive experiments highlight the advantages of using bushy and deep execution trees. Execution plans for bushy and deep trees were found to be able to do a better job of exploiting memory resources. Consequently, they were able to generate less I/O for intermediate results, and this led to a reduction in execution times.

Papers in this chapter

We have included five papers in this chapter to give some idea of the difficulty of the optimization problem. The first paper, "Scheduling and Processor Allocation for the Execution of Multi-join Queries in a Multiprocessor System," is by Chen, Yu, and Wu. The two-phase optimization approach is adopted in this paper. A large number of interesting algorithms proposed both for the plan generation phase and the resource allocation phase deserve the attention of the reader.

The second paper is by Shasha and Wang and is entitled "Optimizing Equijoin Queries in Distributed Databases where Relations Are Hash Partitioned." This paper is among the first to address the optimization problem in a shared-nothing environment. The importance and benefits of computing the closure of the join graph are pointed out. An algorithm that optimizes a special class of join queries, closed-chain queries, is proposed. Heuristics based on algorithms that compute the minimum cost spanning trees are also proposed for general queries.

The structure of a query tree, whether it be linear or bushy, can affect performance in parallel database systems. This is studied and explored in the next paper by Schneider and DeWitt, "Tradeoffs in Processing Complex Join Queries via Hashing in Multiprocessor Database Machines." Arguments in favor of right-deep trees are given. Experimental studies show that right-deep trees have the greatest potential for parallelism and are best suited for pipelined parallelism. Several scheduling algorithms are then proposed to pipeline the execution of multi-way join queries.

The last two papers address the optimization problem in the context of Select-Project-Join queries. The paper by Hong, "Exploiting Interoperation Parallelism in XPRS," describes how interoperation parallelism is achieved in the shared-memory XPRS system. In particular, a scheduling algorithm is proposed to allocate the I/O-bound and CPU-bound tasks such that maximum resource utilizations may be achieved. The other paper is "Query Optimization for Parallel Execution" by Ganguly, Hasan, and Krishnamurthy. The paper points out that the basic dynamic programming approach does not provide the correct optimal solution when response time is taken as the cost metric. Moreover, the paper extends dynamic programming to accurately predict the response time subjected to some classes of optimization metrics.

References

1. S.M. Deen, D.N.P. Kannangara, and M.C. Taylor, "Multi-Join on Parallel Processors," *Proc. Second Int'l Symp. Databases in Parallel and Distributed Systems,* IEEE CS Press, Los Alamitos, Calif., 1990, pp. 92-102.
2. J.C. Freytag, "A Rule-Based View of Query Optimization," *Proc. ACM Int'l Conf. Management of Data,* Assoc. for Computing Machinery, New York, N.Y., 1987.
3. Y.E. Ioannidis and Y. Kang, "Randomized Algorithms for Optimizing Large Join Queries," *Proc. ACM Int'l Conf. Management of Data,* Assoc. for Computing Machinery, New York, N.Y., 1990, pp. 312-321.
4. R. Krishnamurthy, H. Boral, and C. Zaniolo, "Optimization of Non-Recursive Queries," *Proc. 12th Int'l Conf. Very Large Data Bases,* Morgan Kaufman, San Mateo, Calif., 1986, pp. 128-137.
5. H. Lu, M.C. Shan, and K.L. Tan, "Optimization of Multi-Way Join Queries for Parallel Execution," *Proc. 17th Int'l Conf. Very Large Data Bases,* Morgan Kaufman, San Mateo, Calif., 1991.
6. M.C. Murphy and M.C. Shan, "Execution Plan Balancing: A Practical Technique for Multiprocessor Query Optimization," *Proc. Seventh Int'l Conf. Data Eng.,* IEEE CS Press, Los Alamitos, Calif., 1991, pp. 698-706.
7. K. Ono and G. Lohman, "Measuring the Complexity of Join Enumeration in Relational Query Optimization," *Proc. 16th Int'l Conf. Very Large Data Bases,* Morgan Kaufman, San Mateo, Calif., 1990, pp. 314-324.
8. P.G. Selinger et al., "Access Path Selection in a Relational Database Management System," *Proc. ACM Int'l Conf. Management of Data,* Assoc. for Computing Machinery, New York, N.Y., 1979, pp. 23-34.
9. A. Swami and A. Gupta, "Optimization of Large Join Queries," *Proc. ACM Int'l Conf. Management of Data,* Assoc. for Computing Machinery, New York, N.Y., 1988, pp. 8-17.
10. A. Swami, "Optimization of Large Join Queries: Combining Heuristics and Combinatorial Techniques," *Proc. ACM Int'l Conf. Management of Data,* Assoc. for Computing Machinery, New York, N.Y., 1989, pp. 367-376.
11. J.L. Wolf et al., "Optimal Buffer Partitioning for the Nested Block Join Algorithm," *Proc. Seventh Int'l Conf. Data Eng.,* IEEE CS Press, Los Alamitos, Calif., 1991, pp. 510-519.
12. S. Nahar, S. Sahni, and E. Shragowitz, "Simulated Annealing and Combinatorial Optimization," *Proc. 23rd Design Automation Conf.,* IEEE CS Press, Los Alamitos, Calif., 1986, pp. 293-299.
13. S. Kirkpatrick, C.D. Gelatt, and M.P. Vecchi, "Optimization by Simulated Annealing," *Science,* Vol. 220, No. 4598, May 1983, pp. 671-680.
14. K.L. Tan and H. Lu, "On the Strategy Space of Multi-Way Join Query Optimization," *SIGMOD RECORD,* Vol. 20, No. 4, Assoc. for Computing Machinery, New York, N.Y., 1991, pp. 81-82.

14. K.L. Tan and H. Lu, "On the Strategy Space of Multi-Way Join Query Optimization," *SIGMOD RECORD,* Vol. 20, No. 4, Assoc. for Computing Machinery, New York, N.Y., 1991, pp. 81-82.
15. M.S. Chen et al., "Using Segmented Right-Deep Trees for the Execution of Pipelined Hash Joins," *Proc. 18th Int'l Conf. Very Large Data Bases,* Morgan Kaufman, San Mateo, Calif., 1992, pp. 15-26.
16. M. Stonebraker et al., "The Design of XPRS," *Proc. 14th Int'l Conf. Very Large Data Bases*, Morgan Kaufman, San Mateo, Calif., 1988, pp. 318-330.
17. K.L. Tan and H. Lu, "Processing Multi-Join Query in Parallel Systems," *Symp. Applied Computing,* IEEE CS Press, Los Alamitos, Calif., 1992.
18. M.S. Chen, P.S. Yu, and K.L. Wu, "Scheduling and Processor Allocation for Parallel Execution of Multi-Join Queries," *Proc. Eighth Int'l Conf. Data Eng.,* IEEE CS Press, Los Alamitos, Calif., 1992, pp. 58-67.
19. D.E. Knuth. *The Art of Programming, Vol. 3: Sorting and Searching,* Addison-Wesley, Reading, Mass., 1973.
20. K.A. Hua, Y.L. Lo, and H.C. Young, "Including the Load Balancing Issue in the Optimization of Multi-Way Join Queries for Shared-Nothing Database Computers," *Proc. Second Int'l Conf. Parallel and Distributed Information Systems,* IEEE CS Press, Los Alamitos, Calif., 1993, pp. 74-83.
21. R.S.G. Lanzelotte, P. Valduriez, and M. Zait, "On the Effectiveness of Optimization Search Strategies for Parallel Execution Spaces," *Proc. 19th Int'l Conf. Very Large Data Bases,* Morgan Kaufman, San Mateo, Calif., 1993.
22. D.A. Schneider and D.J. DeWitt, "Tradeoffs in Processing Complex Join Queries via Hashing in Multiprocessor Database Machines," *Proc. 16th Int'l Conf. Very Large Data Bases,* Morgan Kaufman, San Mateo, Calif., 1990.
23. E.J. Shekita, H.C. Young, and K.L. Tan, "Multi-Join Query Optimization for Symmetric Multi-Processors," *Proc. 19th Int'l Conf. Very Large Data Bases,* Morgan Kaufman, San Mateo, Calif., 1993.
24. M. Ziane, M. Zait, and P. Borla-Salamet, "Parallel Query Processing in dbs3," *Proc. Second Int'l Conf. Parallel and Distributed Information Systems,* IEEE CS Press, Los Alamitos, Calif., 1993, pp. 93-102.
25. H. Lu and K.L. Tan, "Dynamic and Load-Balanced Task-Oriented Database Query Processing in Parallel Systems," *Proc. Third Int'l Conf. Extending Data Base Technology,* 1992, pp. 357-372.
26. K.A. Hua and C. Lee, "Handling Data Skew in Multiprocessor Database Computers Using Partition Tuning," *Proc. 17th Int'l Conf. Very Large Data Bases,* Morgan Kaufman, San Mateo, Calif., 1991, pp. 525-535.
27. J. Srivastava and G. Elsesser, "Optimizing Multi-Join Queries in Parallel Relational Databases," *Proc. Second Int'l Conf. Parallel and Distributed Information Systems,* IEEE CS Press, Los Alamitos, Calif., 1993, pp. 84-92.

SCHEDULING AND PROCESSOR ALLOCATION FOR PARALLEL EXECUTION OF MULTI-JOIN QUERIES

Ming-Syan Chen, Philip S. Yu and Kun-Lung Wu

IBM Thomas J. Watson Research Center
P.O. Box 704, Yorktown Heights, New York 10598

ABSTRACT

We explore in this paper inter-operator parallelism within a multi-join query to minimize the execution time of the query in a multiprocessor system. Specifically, we focus on two major issues: (i) scheduling the execution sequence of multiple joins within a query, and (ii) determining the number of processors to be allocated for the execution of each join operation obtained in (i). For the first issue, we propose and evaluate by simulation several methods to determine the general join sequences, or the bushy execution trees. Despite their simplicity, the heuristics proposed can lead to the general join sequences which significantly outperform the optimal sequential join sequence. In addition, several heuristics to determine the processor allocation, categorized by bottom up and top down approaches, are derived and evaluated by simulation. As confirmed by our simulation, by first using the join sequence heuristics to build a bushy tree and then applying the concept of the synchronous execution time to the bushy tree for processor allocation, we have an efficient two-step approach to schedule and execute multi-join queries in a multiprocessor system.

1. Introduction

In recent years, multiprocessor-based parallel database machines have drawn considerable attention from both the academic and industrial communities due to the high potential for parallel execution of complex database operations [6] [14] [20][22]. In relational database systems, joins are the most expensive operations to execute, especially with the increasing database sizes [25]. Furthermore, several applications which involve decision support and complex objects usually have to specify their desired results in terms of multi-join queries. As a result, some complex queries in such systems may take hours or even days to complete and the system performance is thus degraded. Consequently, the development of effective schemes to exploit parallelism in the execution of multi-join queries has become increasingly attractive and important.

As pointed out in [18], the methods to exploit parallelism in the execution of database operations in a multiprocessor system can be divided into three categories. First, parallelism can occur in each operator within a query in such a way that several processors can work, in parallel, on a single database operation. This form of parallelism is termed *intra-operator* parallelism. Various solutions for exploiting intra-operator parallelism in multiprocessor database systems have been reported in the literature. Several algorithms were proposed for parallel execution of two-way joins in multiprocessor systems [1] [5] [12][16] [17]. The effect of data skew on the performance of parallel joins has been analyzed in [10] [24]. The second form of parallelism is termed *inter-operator* parallelism, meaning that several operators within a query can be executed in parallel. Third, parallelism can be achieved by executing several queries simultaneously within a multiprocessor system, which is termed *inter-query* parallelism. It can be seen that to exploit the third form of parallelism, one has to resort to the results derived for inter-operator parallelism within a query. However, despite its importance, inter-operator parallelism has not yet been fully studied, although during the past few years some light has been shed on this issue [4] [8][15] [18]. In view of this, the objective of this paper is to study and improve the execution of multi-join queries with the focus on deriving efficient schemes to exploit inter-operator parallelism in a multiprocessor system.

Note that different execution sequences of joins in a query will result in different execution costs [19]. Also, in a multiprocessor system the execution time of each join strongly depends on the number of processors allocated for the execution of the join [10]. Thus, the subject of exploiting inter-operator parallelism for the execution of a multi-join query mainly consists of the following two major issues: (i) join sequence scheduling, i.e., scheduling the execution sequence of joins in the query, and (ii) processor allocation, i.e., determining the number of processors for each join obtained in (i) so that the execution time required for the query can be minimized. To facilitate our discussion, the efficiency of the join sequence, measured by its execution on a single processor system, is termed *join sequence efficiency*, and the effectiveness of processor allocation, determined by the speedup achieved over the single processor case, is termed *processor allocation efficiency*. The overall efficiency for dealing with the above two issues then depends closely on the two factors.

For the issue of join sequence scheduling, we develop and evaluate by simulation several heuristics to determine the sequence of joins for a multi-join query with the focus on optimizing the join sequence efficiency, i.e., minimizing the total amount of work required in the join sequence. Specifically, we investigate two sorts of join sequences, namely *sequential join sequences* and *general join sequences*. A join sequence in which the resulting relation of an intermediate join can only be used in the next join is termed a sequential join sequence. An example of a sequential join sequence can be found in Fig. 1a where every non-leaf node (internal node) represents the resulting relation from joining its child nodes and the join sequence is performed in the manner of bottom up. For notational simplicity, such an execution tree in Fig. 1a will be denoted by the expression $((((R_1,R_2),R_3),R_4),R_5)$. A join sequence

0-8186-5452-X/94 $3.00

Reprinted from *Proc. 8th Int'l Conf. Data Engineering*, 1992, pp. 58-67.

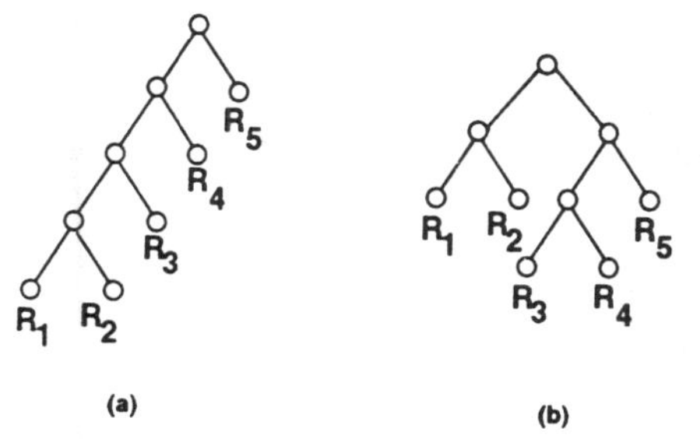

Figure 1. Illustration of different join sequences.

in which the resulting relation of a join is not required to be only used in the next join is termed a general join sequence. For example, the sequence of joins specified by the join sequence tree in Fig. 1b is a general join sequence. Such an execution tree of a general join sequence is called a *bushy tree* [8], or a *composite inner* [13]. The general join sequence in Fig. 1b can be denoted as $((R_1,R_2),((R_3,R_4),R_5))$. Note that the cost of a join is usually proportional to the sizes of its operands. In view of this and the fact that the size of the resulting relation of a join is often larger than those of its operands, it is important to explore the general join sequence in order to reduce the total cost incurred, particularly for complex queries, i.e., queries consisting of joins involving many relations. However, prior approaches on executing multi-join queries mostly focused on the use of sequential join sequences [19]. This mainly results from the fact that the problem of finding the optimal general join sequence is inherently difficult, if not infeasible, for complex queries due to its exponential complexity [13] [21], and also that the improvement achievable on the join sequence efficiency by employing general join sequences has not yet been clearly shown. Consequently, we propose and evaluate by simulation several join sequence heuristics in this paper to efficiently determine general join sequences of good efficiency. As can be seen from our results, the heuristics proposed, despite their simplicity, result in general join sequences whose join sequence efficiencies are significantly better than that of the optimal sequential join sequence. This is especially true for complex queries. More importantly, it is shown that the join sequence efficiencies obtained by our general join sequence heuristics are rather close to that of the optimal general join sequence, meaning that by employing appropriate heuristics we can avoid excessive search costs and obtain join sequences with very high quality.

Next, we explore the issue of processor allocation to join operations. Note that in the study of intra-operator parallelism, the objective is usually to determine the processor allocation which achieves the minimum execution time of a single join. Such a selection is referred to as *operational point selection* in this paper. However, in exploiting inter-operator parallelism, we, in contrast, are dealing with the execution of a complex query with multiple joins where different joins are allowed to be executed in parallel in different clusters of processors. As will be seen later, minimizing the execution time of a multi-join query, in addition to the operational point selection as in the study of intra-operator parallelism, requires more factors, such as *execution dependency* and *system fragmentation*, to be considered. Execution dependency means that some joins cannot be performed until their operands generated by prior joins are available. Also, after a sequence of processor allocation and release, there might be a few processors left idle since they do not form a cluster large enough to execute any remaining join efficiently. This phenomenon is termed system fragmentation. Clearly, execution dependency and system fragmentation, as well as the operational point selection, have to be taken into account for a better processor allocation efficiency, thus complicating the minimization procedure for the query execution time. To deal with this problem, we propose and evaluate several heuristics to determine the number of processors for each join. The processor allocation heuristics proposed can be divided into two categories: (1) the bottom up approach, which determines the join sequence and processor allocation at the same time, i.e., the number of processors allocated to each internal node (join) in a bushy tree is determined as the bushy tree is being built bottom up, and (2) the top down approach which is based on the concept of *synchronous execution time* to determine the processor allocation based on a given bushy tree. The concept of synchronous execution time is to partition the processors allocated to an internal node in the bushy tree into two clusters of processors for the execution of the two joins associated with its two child nodes in such a way that the resulting relations from the two child nodes can be made available approximately the same time. It is shown that the concept of synchronous execution time will significantly alleviate execution dependency and system fragmentation, and hence improve the query execution time.

Note that the schemes on join sequence scheduling and processor allocation can be combined to form a final scheduler for the execution of a multi-join query in a multiprocessor system. As shown by our simulation results, the join sequence efficiency is in general the dominating factor for the query execution time whereas the processor allocation efficiency becomes significant as the number of processors increases. Thus, as confirmed by our simulation, among all the schemes investigated, the two-step approach of first applying the join sequence heuristics to build a bushy tree as if under a single processor system, and then determining the processor allocation in light of the concept of synchronous execution time for the bushy tree built is shown to be the best solution to minimize the query execution time.

This paper is organized as follows. The notation and assumptions used are given in Section 2. In Section 3, we study several join sequence heuristics. Processor allocation is dealt with in Section 4. This paper concludes with Section 5.

2. Preliminaries

We assume that a query is of the form of conjunctions of equi-join predicates. A join query graph can be denoted by a graph $G = (V, E)$, where V is the set of nodes and E is the set of edges. Each node in a join query graph represents a relation. Two nodes are connected by an edge if there exists a join predicate on some attribute of the two corresponding relations. Notice that when a join operation between the two relations R_i and R_j in a given query graph is carried out, we can obtain the resulting query graph by shrinking the edges between R_i and R_j and merging the two relations together to represent the resulting relation from the join operation.

We use $|R_i|$ to denote the cardinality of a relation R_i and $|A|$ to denote the cardinality of the domain of an attribute A. The notation (R_i,R_j) is used to mean the join between R_i and R_j, and R_i*R_j denotes the resulting relation of (R_i,R_j). As in most prior work, we assume that the execution time incurred is the primary cost measure for the processing of database operations. Also, we focus on the execution of complex queries [21]. Note that there are various join algorithms applicable to execute a join operation in a multiprocessor system, such as the sort-merge join, the hash join and the nested loop join. Different join methods and different multiprocessor systems will result in different execution costs for a join, for which various formulas have been derived in [23]. Since our objective in this paper is to study the execution sequence of multiple joins in a query and the processor allocation for each join so as to minimize the execution time (i.e., the response time) required, we shall focus on the sort-merge join in what follows to have a specific cost model, and the cost function of joining R_i and R_j will be expressed by $|R_i|+|R_j|+|R_i*R_j|$ as in [24]. This formula is believed to be general and reasonable for joining large relations by sort-merge joins in a multiprocessor system (either with shared disks or with shared everything [2]) as assumed in our discussion. The amount of memory available to execute a join is assumed to be in proportion to the number of processors involved. Clearly, for other join methods the cost model has to be changed accordingly, and additional provisions might be needed to handle some more issues, such as pipelining that is possible under the hash join, which is beyond the scope of this paper. Readers interested in the study of pipelined hash joins are referred to a companion paper [11]. In addition, we assume that the values of attributes are uniformly distributed over all tuples in a relation and that the values of one attribute are independent of those in another. The cardinalities of the resulting relations from join operations can thus be estimated according to the formula used in [3], which is given in the Appendix for reference. This assumption is not essential but will simplify our presentation. In the presence of data skew, we only have to modify the formula for estimating the cardinalities of resulting relations from joins accordingly [7].

3. Determining the Join Sequence

For the objective of showing the effect of a join sequence on the total work incurred, we in this section assume that the execution of joins is under a single processor system. The join sequence efficiencies of various join sequences can thus be compared with one another.

3.1 Sequential join sequences

First, we investigate the sequential join sequences resulted by the following two methods: (1) the greedy method, denoted by S_{GD}, and (2) the optimal permutation, denoted by S_{OPT}, where S means "sequential join sequence" and the subscripts mean the methods used. The greedy scheme S_{GD} can be outlined as follows. First, the scheme starts with the join which requires the minimal execution cost. Then, the scheme tries to join the composite with the relation which has the minimal-cost join with the existing composite. The above step is repeated until all joins are finished. An algorithmic form of this scheme is shown below.

Scheme S_{GD}:

1. Choose the join (R_i,R_m) from $G=(V,E)$ such that $cost(R_i,R_m) = \min_{\forall R_p R_q \in V} \{cost(R_p, R_q)\}$.
2. Perform (R_i,R_m).
3. Merge R_i and R_m in G and denote the resulting relation as R_i. Update the profile accordingly.
4. **repeat until** $|V|=1$
5. **begin**
6.   Choose a relation R_j from G such that $cost(R_i,R_j) = \min_{\forall R_p \in V} \{cost(R_i, R_p)\}$.
7.   Perform (R_i,R_j).
8.   Merge R_i and R_j into R_i in G. Update the profile accordingly.
9. **end**

It can be seen that the complexity of the operation in line 6 of S_{GD} is $O(|V|)$, and that of the whole scheme is thus $O(|V|^2)$. Moreover, we also investigate the optimal sequential join sequence which can be obtained by the optimal permutation of relations to be joined. It can be seen that the number of different sequential join sequences for a query of n relations is $\frac{n!}{2}$, which is half of the total number of permutations of n objects since the first two relations can be interchanged. To evaluate the optimal sequential join sequence in Section 3.3 where different join sequences are compared by simulation, we implemented scheme S_{OPT} in which the technique of branch and bound is used to avoid exhaustive enumeration and reduce the cost of search. For better readability, the detail of S_{OPT}, which is irrelevant to the quality of the join sequence resulted, is not included in this paper.

To show the resulting join sequences by S_{GD} and S_{OPT}, consider the query in Fig. 2a whose profile is given in Table 1. From the operations of S_{GD} and the formula in the Appendix, it can be seen that the join between R_2 and R_4 is the one with the minimal cost among all joins. After the join (R_2,R_4), the resulting query graph is given in Fig. 2b where R_2 now represents the resulting composite. Then, it can be verified that R_5 is the relation which will have the minimal-cost join with R_2, and the execution of (R_2,R_5) in Fig. 2b is executed. Following the above procedure, we have the resulting join sequence by S_{GD}, $(((((R_2,R_4),R_5),R_6),R_3),R_1)$ whose total cost is 45,246.43. On the other hand, it can be obtained that for the query in Fig. 2a, the optimal sequential join sequence by S_{OPT} is $(((((R_1,R_3),R_6),R_5),R_2),R_4)$ whose total cost is 36,135.92, which is less than that required by S_{GD}.

3.2. General join sequences (bushy trees)

To determine a join sequence of the minimal cost, consider the problem of adding up n numbers using the Huffman algorithm [9], which performs the additions of two numbers in the set that results in the minimal intermediate sum, replaces the two numbers with the intermediate sum and repeats the above procedure until the final sum is obtained. Suppose that the cost of adding two numbers is equal to the value of their sum. The Huffman algorithm is proved to produce the addition sequence that requires the minimal total cost of additions. Note that there is a similarity between this problem and the one to find the join sequence of minimal cost, since in both problems, we would like to minimize the total cost of a sequence of operations (additions and joins, respectively). This similarity suggests us to perform the minimal-cost join first, and then, from the resulting query, choose the minimal-cost join to perform. This procedure repeats until all joins are finished. Based on this heuristic, scheme G_{MC}, where G means that the resulting sequence is a general join sequence and the subscript MC is from

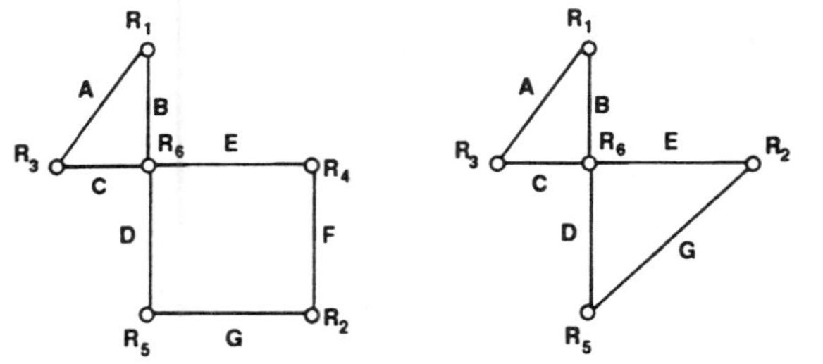

(a) an example query graph **(b) after joining R2 and R4.**

Figure 2. A query graph to show join sequences.

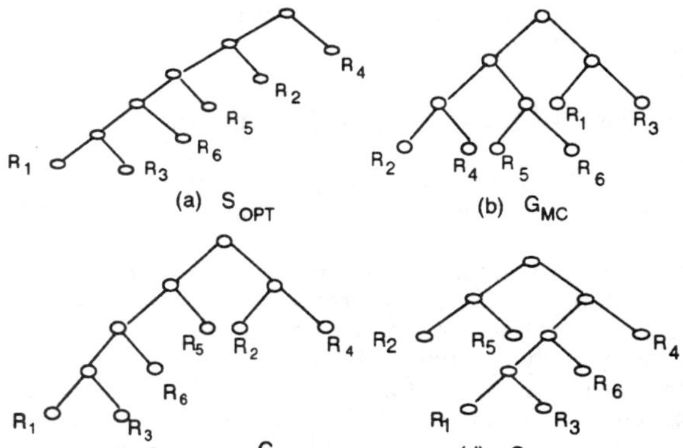

(a) S_{OPT} (b) G_{MC} (c) G_{MR} and G_{ME} (d) G_{OPT}

Figure 3. Different join execution trees resulted by different approaches.

Rel.	R_1	R_2	R_3	R_4	R_5	R_6
Card.	118	102	106	100	131	120

(a). Profile for relations

Att.	A	B	C	D	E	F	G
Card.	19	15	17	19	16	15	18

(b). The domain size of each attribute

Table 1. Profile for the query in Figure 2a.

"minimal cost", is outlined below. It can be seen that unlike S_{GD}, the resulting composite of a join by G_{MC} need not participate in the next join.

Scheme G_{MC}: /* A scheme to execute the join with the minimal cost. */
1. **repeat until** $|V| = 1$
2. **begin**
3. Choose the join (R_i,R_j) from $G=(V,E)$ such that $cost(R_i,R_j) = \min_{\forall R_p R_q \in V} \{cost(R_p, R_q)\}$.
4. Perform (R_i,R_j).
5. Merge R_i and R_j into $R_{min(i,j)}$ in G. Update the profile accordingly.
6. **end**

For the example query in Fig. 2a, it can be verified that after the first minimal-cost join (R_2,R_4) is performed, the next minimal-cost join to be executed by G_{MC} is (R_5,R_6), rather than (R_2,R_5) as in S_{GD}. The resulting sequence is $(((R_2,R_4),(R_5,R_6)),(R_1,R_3))$ whose total cost is 13,958.62, significantly less than those required by S_{GD} and S_{OPT}. The execution trees resulted by S_{OPT} and G_{MC} are shown in Figs. 3a and 3b, respectively. It can be seen that the complexity in the operation in line 3 of scheme G_{MC} is $O(|E|)$, and that of the scheme is $O(|V||E|) \leq O(|V|^3)$, rather close to $O(|V|^2)$ required by S_{GD}.

Note that in a sequence of joins, the cardinalities of intermediate relations resulting from the early joins affect the costs of joins to be performed later. Since the objective taken is to minimize the total cost required to perform a sequence of joins, one may want to execute the joins which produce smaller resulting relations first. In view of this fact, we develop and evaluate the following two heuristic schemes which are variations of G_{MC}, namely the minimal resulting relation (G_{MR}) and the minimal expansion (G_{ME}). Instead of finding the minimal-cost join as in G_{MC}, these two schemes look for joins which result in, respectively, the minimal resulting relation and the minimal expansion, where the expansion of a join (R_i,R_j) is defined as the size increase, i.e., $|R_i{*}R_j| - |R_i| - |R_j|$. Clearly, the heuristic schemes G_{MR} and G_{ME} are of the same complexity, $O(|V||E|)$, as scheme G_{MC}. Algorithmic forms of G_{MR} and G_{ME} are similar to the one of G_{MC}, except that the statement 3 in G_{MC} is changed to 3A and 3B below for G_{MR} and G_{ME}, respectively.

3A. (for G_{MR}): Choose the join (R_i,R_j) from $G=(V,E)$ such that $|R_i{*}R_j| = \min_{\forall R_p R_q \in V} \{|R_p{*}R_q|\}$.

3B. (for G_{ME}): Choose the join (R_i,R_j) from G such that $(|R_i{*}R_j| - |R_i| - |R_j|) = \min_{\forall R_p R_q \in V} \{|R_p{*}R_q| - |R_p| - |R_q|\}$.

Following G_{MR}, the resulting join sequence for the query in Fig. 2a is $((((R_1,R_3),R_6),R_5),(R_2,R_4))$, whose bushy tree is shown in Fig. 3c. The associated cost is 13,288.38, showing a better join sequence efficiency than the one obtained by G_{MC}. This fact can be further justified by the simulation results in Section 3.3. It can be seen that the resulting join sequence by G_{ME}, where the expansion of a join operation is of concern, is also $((((R_1,R_3),R_6),R_5),(R_2,R_4))$ for the query in Fig. 2a. Moreover, to assess the performance of the heuristics, we implemented scheme G_{OPT} to determine the optimal general join sequence for a multi-join query. Same as in S_{OPT}, we enumerate possible candidate sequences in our implementation of G_{OPT} and employ the technique of branch and bound to prune the search. Using G_{OPT}, we obtain that the optimal general join sequence for the query in Fig. 2a is $((R_2,R_5),(((R_1,R_3),R_6),R_4))$ with its bushy tree shown in Fig. 3d, requiring only a cost of 13,013.57, which is in fact rather close to those obtained by G_{MC}, G_{MR} and G_{ME}. Clearly, such an optimal scheme, though leading to the optimal solution sequence, will incur excessive computational overhead which is very undesirable in some applications and might outweigh the improvement it could have over the heuristic schemes. As can be seen in the following, the heuristic schemes G_{MC}, G_{MR} and G_{ME}, despite their simplicity, perform significantly better than S_{GD} and S_{OPT}, and result in join sequences whose execution costs are reasonably close to that of the optimal one.

3.3. Simulation results and remarks

To perform the simulation, the number of relations in a query, denoted by n, is chosen to be 4, 6, 8 and 10, respectively. For each value of n, 300 queries were randomly generated. The occurrence of an edge between two relations in the query graph is determined according to a given probability, denoted by *prob*. Without loss of generality, only queries with connected query graphs are deemed valid and used for our study. The cardinalities of relations and attributes are also randomly generated within a reasonable range. The simulation program is coded in C. In that program, for each query the six scheduling schemes, i.e., S_{GD}, S_{OPT}, G_{MC}, G_{MR}, G_{ME} and G_{OPT}, are performed to determine join sequences to execute the query. When two relations not having join predicates are to be joined together, a Cartesian product is performed. The average execution cost for join sequences obtained from each scheme when $prob = 0.32$ is shown in Table 2. Also, we divide the average execution costs of the first five schemes by that of G_{OPT} for a comparison purpose, and show the results associated with Table 2 in Fig. 4.

rel. no.	S_{GD}	S_{OPT}	G_{MC}	G_{MR}	G_{ME}	G_{OPT}
n=4	6905	6001	5112	5087	5098	4762
n=6	23917	18135	14192	13927	13940	13141
n=8	136505	74151	52085	46760	47187	42131
n=10	606518	237223	112723	104311	107675	84121

Table 2. Average execution cost for various join sequences.

From Table 2 and Fig. 4, it can be seen that except for G_{OPT}, the join sequence efficiency of join sequences obtained by G_{MR} is the best among those obtained by the five remaining schemes, and then, in order, those by G_{ME}, G_{MC}, S_{OPT} and S_{GD}. The join sequence efficiencies of the sequences resulted by G_{MC}, G_{MR} and G_{ME} are quite close to the optimal one and significantly better than those by S_{GD} and S_{OPT}, especially when the number of relations increases. For the sizes of queries simulated here, the run times of S_{GD}, G_{MC}, G_{MR} and G_{ME} under the DOS/PS2-80 environment are very close to one another whereas those of S_{OPT} and G_{OPT} are larger than them by more than three orders of magnitude due to their exponential complexity.

4. Processor Allocation for Each Join

The execution time required for a join operation within a multiprocessor system depends on the number of processors allocated to perform the join [10]. Basically, increasing the number of processors will reduce the execution time of a join until a saturation point is reached, above which point adding more processors to execute the join will, on the contrary, increase its execution time. This is mainly due to the combining effects of limited parallelism exploitable and excessive communication and coordination overhead over too many processors. An example of an operational curve for this phenomenon is shown by the solid curve in Fig. 5, where a dotted curve $xy = 30$ is given for reference. In such a curve, the operational point chosen from the curve, depending on the design objective, is generally between the point which minimizes the execution time of the join, referred to as *the minimum time*

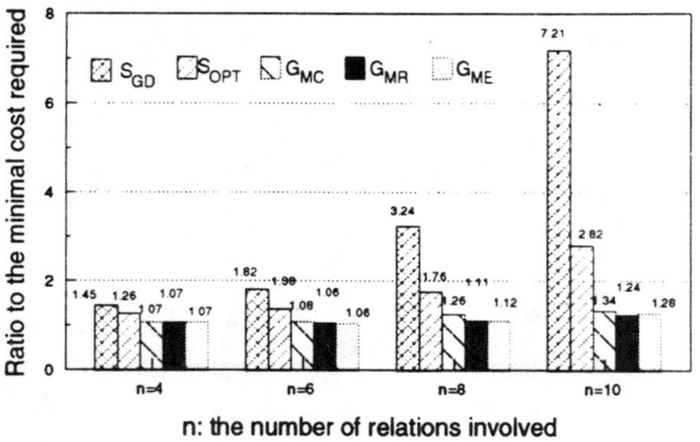

Figure 4. The results of different heuristics for join sequences.

point, denoted by p_M, and the one which optimizes processor utilization, i.e., minimizes the product of the number of processors and the execution time, referred to as *the best efficiency point*, denoted by p_B. For example, $p_B = 5$ and $p_M = 16$ for the operational curve in Fig. 5. To improve the processor allocation efficiency, we not only have to utilize the information provided in the operational curve for the operational point selection, but are also required to comply with execution dependency and avoid system fragmentation as much as possible so as to minimize the execution time of the query.

Consequently, we propose and evaluate in the following several heuristics for processor allocation. The heuristics proposed can be divided into two categories: (1) the bottom up approach in Section 4.1, and (2) the top down approach in Section 4.2.

4.1. Bottom up approach

(a). Sequential execution (SE):
This heuristic is to use all the processors in the system to execute each join in the query sequentially. It can be seen that inter-operator parallelism is absent when this heuristic is used, and the join sequence is the key factor to the performance in such a case.

(b). Fixed cluster size (FS):
This heuristic is to allocate a fixed number of processors for the execution of each join to avoid system fragmentation. Clearly, by taking the total number of processors as the cluster size, we have a special case equivalent to heuristic SE.

Note that by using the above heuristics, system fragmentation is avoided. Moreover, under heuristic SE, execution dependency is inherently observed, since join operations are executed sequentially. However, the two heuristics may suffer from poor operational point selection because the information provided by the operational curve is not utilized to determine the operational point of a join.

(c). Minimum time point (MT):
This heuristic is based on the minimum time point in the operational curve, i.e., p_M. Note that even though this operational point obtains the minimum execution time for each join, it may not minimize the execution time of a multi-join query as a whole due to the effect of execution dependency and system fragmentation.

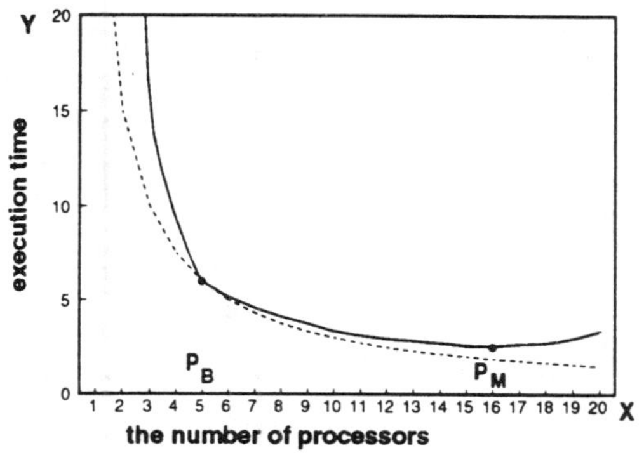

Figure 5. An example operational curve of a join in a multiprocessor.

(d). Time-efficiency point (TE):
Recall that the best efficiency point is the operational point where processors are most efficiently used to execute the join. However, a scheme based on the the best efficiency point might suffer from execution dependency, since some join operating at its best efficiency point might take a long execution time to complete due to a small number of processors used, thus causing long waiting time for subsequent joins. On the other hand, a scheme based on MT may not use processors efficiently since it may require too many processors to reach the minimum time point. Clearly, the number of processors associated with an operational point which can strike a compromise between the execution time and the processor efficiency should be within the region $[p_B, p_M]$. In view of this, we shall use a combination of the minimum time point and the best efficiency point, termed as *the time-efficiency point*, as a heuristic for our study, i.e., the number of processors, $k^* p_M + (1-k)^* p_B$, is used to execute each join, where $0 \le k \le 1$.

Note that the above heuristics for processor allocation can be combined with the schemes for scheduling join sequences developed in Section 3 to form a final scheduler which handles the scheduling and processor allocation of a multi-join query in a multiprocessor system. That is, we use a join sequence heuristic, say G_{MR}, to determine the next join to be considered and employ the appropriate processor allocation heuristic to determine the number of processors to be allocated for the execution of that join. The operations for processor allocation and deallocation can be outlined as follows where the processor allocation heuristic, denoted by h_P, can be any of SE, FS, MT and TE described above and $h_P(J)$ is the number of processors allocated to execute a join J under the heuristic h_P.

Processor Allocation:
/* P is the number of processors available and initialized as the total numbers of processors. */
Step 1: Use the join sequence heuristic to determine the next join operation J such that $h_P(J) \le P$ and execution dependency is observed, i.e., the two input relations of J are available then. If no such a join exists, go to processor deallocation.
Step 2: Allocate $h_P(J)$ processors to execute the join J. $P := P - h_P(J)$.
Step 3: Update the profile by marking J as an ongoing join.
Step 4: Determine the completion time of J and record it in the completion time list of ongoing joins.
Step 5: Go to Step 1.

Processor Deallocation:

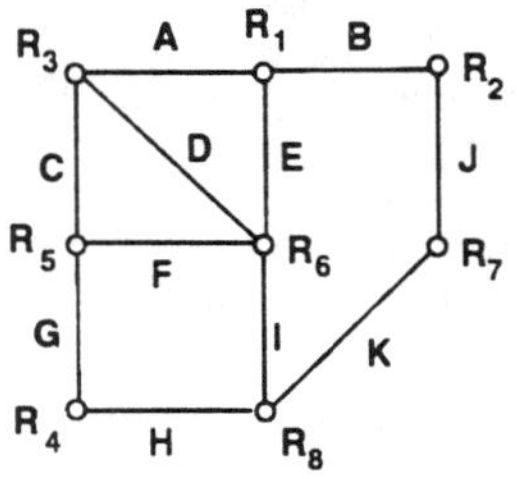

Figure 6. A query to show processor allocation.

Rel.	R_1	R_2	R_3	R_4	R_5	R_6	R_7	R_8
Card.	100	85	93	106	102	90	101	94

(a). Profile for relations

Att.	A	B	C	D	E	F	G	H	I	J	K
Card.	9	8	7	9	9	10	9	7	7	10	8

(b). The domain size of each attribute

Table 3. Profile for the query in Figure 6.

Step 1: From the completion time list, determine the next completion of an ongoing join, say J.
Step 2: Update the profile to reflect that J is completed. $P := P + h_P(J)$.
Step 3: If there is any executable join in the updated query profile, go to processor allocation.
Step 4: Go to Step 1.

Using the above procedures, the execution tree can be built bottom up. To demonstrate the processor allocation and deallocation, we shall show the operations using heuristics SE and TE. The operations by FS and ME follow similarly. Consider the query in Fig. 6 with the profile in Table 3. For illustration, the operational curve of a join is approximated by the function,

$$T_{exe} = \frac{a|R_i| + b|R_j| + c|R_i{}^*R_j|}{N_p} + dN_p$$

where N_p is the number of processors employed, parameters a, b and c are determined by the path length of the system in processing and joining tuples [24], and parameter d is determined by the inter-processor communication protocol. Also, to each join we determine the minimal number of processors required for its execution according to the sizes of its operands. p_B is thus obtained. Note that the operational area where the number of processors is less than p_B can be ignored, since only the operational region $[p_B, p_M]$ is of interest in this study. Without loss of generality, G_{MR} is used to determine the next join operation to be executed. Then, for heuristics SE in a multiprocessor system of 32 nodes with $a = b = c = 1$ and $d = 20$, we have the execution sequence as shown in Table 4a, where the meaning of the column $W(R_i)$ will be explained in Section 4.2. The bushy tree and its corresponding processor allocation by SE is shown in Fig. 7a. The execution scenarios using TE are shown in Table

4b, where the time-efficiency point used is determined by $0.3p_B+0.7p_M$[1]. The bushy tree and its corresponding processor allocation by TE is shown in Fig. 7b. Note that though the same scheme G_{MR} is used to determine the next join to be performed in both cases, the resulting join sequences are different from each other due to different processor allocation scenarios. It can be seen that the bushy tree in Fig. 7b is different from the one in Fig. 7a.

4.2. Top down approach

Note that when an execution tree is built bottom up, the following two constraints have to be followed: (1) execution dependency is observed, and (2) the processor requirement is satisfied according to the processor allocation heuristic employed. As can be seen in Tables 4a and 4b, the above two constraints lengthen the execution time of a query. Naturally, one wants to achieve some degree of execution synchronization, meaning that processors are allocated to joins in such a way that the two input relations of each join can be made available approximately the same time. Also, idleness of processors should be avoided. As a result, we propose the top down approach for processor allocation which uses the concept of synchronous execution time to alleviate the two constraints and improve the query execution time.

To describe the processor allocation using the synchronous execution time, consider the bushy tree in Fig. 7a for example. Recall that every internal node in the bushy tree corresponds to a join operation, and we determine the number of processors allocated to each join in the manner of top down. Clearly, all processors are allocated to the join associated with the root in the bushy tree since it is the last join to be performed. Then, the processors allocated to the join on the root are partitioned into two clusters which are assigned to execute the joins associated with the two child nodes of the root in the bushy tree in such a way that the two joins can be completed approximately the same time. The above step for partitioning the processors for the root is then applied to all internal nodes in the tree in a top down manner until each internal node (join) is assigned with a number of processors. More formally, define the *cumulative execution costs* of an internal node as the sum of the execution costs of all joins in the subtree under that internal node. Also, define the cumulative execution cost of a leaf node (an original relation) as zero. Let R_i be a relation associated with an internal node in the bushy tree and R_x and R_y be the relations corresponding to its two child nodes. Then, the cumulative execution cost of the node with R_i, denoted by $W(R_i)$, is determined by,

$$W(R_i) = W(R_x) + W(R_y) + cost(R_x, R_y).$$

Note that the cumulative execution cost of each node can be determined when the bushy tree is built bottom up. The cumulative execution costs of internal nodes for the bushy trees in Figs. 7a and 7b can be found in Tables 4a and 4b, respectively. Then, it is important to see that to achieve the synchronous execution time, when partitioning the processors of a node into two clusters for its child nodes, one has to take into account the cumulative execution costs of the two child nodes, rather than the execution costs of the two joins associated with the two child nodes. Let R_i be a relation associated with an internal node in the bushy tree and R_x and R_y be the relations corresponding to its two child nodes such that $W(R_x) \geq W(R_y)$. Denote the number of processors allocated to perform the join generating R_i as $P(R_i)$. Then, $P(R_x)$ and $P(R_y)$ are determined, respectively, by,

$$P(R_x) = \left\lceil P(R_i)\frac{W(R_x)}{W(R_x)+W(R_y)} \right\rceil \text{ and}$$

$$P(R_y) = P(R_i) - P(R_x).$$

Since $W(R_y)=0$ if R_y is an original relation, we know that when only one child node corresponds to a join and the other is a leaf node, the former inherits all processors. Note that if the number of processors allocated to an internal node (join) of a bushy tree, say r processors, exceeds p_M, we shall employ p_M processors to perform that join whereas using r processors for the subsequent

join seq.	start time	end time	$W(R_i)$
(R_2,R_7)	0.0	289.2	1044.5
(R_4,R_5)	289.2	625.3	1409.9
(R_1,R_3)	625.3	940.5	1226.3
(R_1,R_6)	940.5	1367.7	3497.8
(R_2,R_8)	1367.7	2307.7	12084.3
(R_1,R_4)	2307.7	4636.8	26961.0
(R_1,R_2)	4636.8	22553.3	565892.7

Table 4a. Execution sequence for heuristic SE.

join seq.	start time	end time	$W(R_i)$
(R_2,R_7)	0.0	308.9	1044.5
(R_1,R_3)	0.0	345.2	1226.3
(R_6,R_8)	0.0	378.5	1392.5
(R_4,R_5)	0.0	381.8	1409.9
(R_1,R_6)	378.5	1661.5	20278.7
(R_1,R_4)	1661.5	4002.1	76107.7
(R_1,R_2)	4002.1	21695.6	622866.5

Table 4b. Execution sequence for heuristic TE.

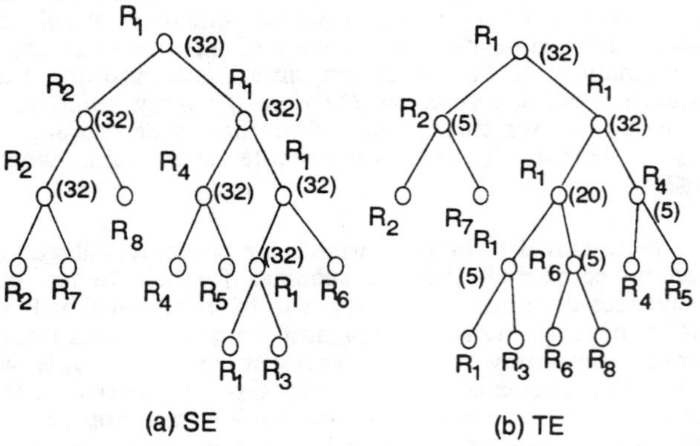

Figure 7. Bottom up processor allocation.

---
[1] Different values for k have been evaluated. The choice for k = 0.3 is made for its reasonably good performance.

partitioning for the subtree under that internal node. Also, when the number of processors passed to an internal node in a lower level of the tree is too few to be further partitioned for efficient execution of joins, sequential execution for the joins in its child nodes is employed for a better performance. Clearly, there are many different bushy execution trees for a query. The problem of determining the optimal bushy tree to minimize the execution time by the concept of synchronous execution time is of exponential complexity. For an efficient solution, we apply the concept of synchronous execution time to the bushy trees obtained by the heuristics introduced in Section 4.1.

Different bottom up processor allocation heuristics used may result in different bushy trees even when the same join sequence heuristic is applied. It is important to see that although execution time for the sequence in Table 4a (by SE) is larger than that in Table 4b (by TE), the join sequence efficiency of the bushy tree in Fig. 7a is in fact better than that of the tree in Fig. 7b, as shown by their cumulative execution costs in Tables 4a and 4b. Note that the constraints on execution dependency can get introduced when a bushy tree is being built by heuristic TE, as well as by FS and MT. Such constraints are absent when heuristic SE is employed to form the bushy tree. (This explains why the tree in Fig. 7a is different from that in Fig. 7b.) Thus, the bushy tree by SE is in fact superior to those by other heuristics in that the former has a better join sequence efficiency owing to full exploitation of the join sequence heuristics. Therefore, we shall apply the concept the synchronous execution time to the bushy tree built by SE, denoted by ST_{SE}. For a comparison purpose, we also investigate the use of the synchronous execution time on the bushy tree built by TE, denoted by ST_{TE}.

The execution scenario using the heuristic ST_{SE} is shown in Table 4c, and the corresponding bushy tree and processor allocation is shown in Fig. 8a. In spite of the fact that the bushy tree in Fig. 8a is the same as that in Fig. 7a, the resulting execution times differ due to the difference in processor allocation. It can be seen that under ST_{SE}, processors are allocated to the execution of each join in such a way that two joins generating the two operands for a later join can be completed approximately the same time, thus alleviating execution dependency. Moreover, since the processors allocated to a node in a bushy tree are partitioned for the allocation to its child nodes, system fragmentation is eased. This explains why ST_{SE} outperforms SE despite both of them have the identical bushy trees and the same join sequence efficiency. It can be obtained that the execution time for ST_{TE} is 20557.2. The bushy tree and its processor allocation by ST_{TE} is shown in Fig. 8b which has the same bushy tree as the one in Fig. 7b, but differs from the latter in processor allocation. It is important to see that despite TE outperforms SE, ST_{SE} performs better than ST_{TE}, and in fact is the best one among the processor allocation heuristics evaluated in Section 4.3.

4.3. Simulation results and remarks

As in Section 3.3, 300 queries with a given number of relations involved were randomly generated. For each query, the six scheduling schemes, according to the heuristics of SE, FS, MT, TE, ST_{SE} and ST_{TE}, respectively, are performed to determine the number of processors for each join to execute the query, where the cluster size of FS is chosen to be half of the total processors. For a multiprocessor of 48 nodes, the average execution times

join seq.	start time	end time	$W(R_i)$
(R_2,R_7)	0.0	289.2	1044.5
(R_4,R_5)	0.0	354.8	1409.9
(R_1,R_3)	0.0	315.1	1226.3
(R_1,R_6)	315.1	742.3	3497.8
(R_2,R_8)	289.2	1593.2	12084.3
(R_1,R_4)	742.3	1684.7	26961.0
(R_1,R_2)	1684.7	19101.2	565892.7

Table 4c. Execution sequence for heuristic ST_{SE}.

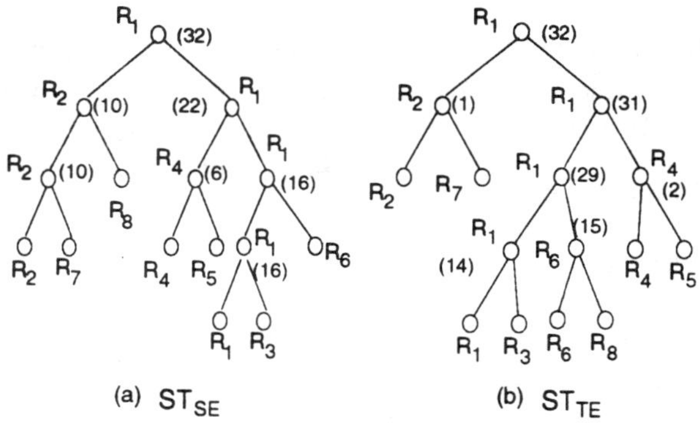

Figure 8. Top down processor allocation (synchronous execution time).

obtained by each heuristic for queries of 10, 15, 20 and 25 relations are shown in Fig. 9. It can be seen that SE, i.e., the one using intra-operator parallelism only, performs well when the number of relations is 10, but performs worse when the number of relations increases. Also, FS is in general outperformed by others due mainly to execution dependency and poor operational points selection. Among the heuristics on bottom up approaches, the shortest execution time is usually achieved by TE, especially when the number n is large. This can be explained by the reason that execution dependency is eased when the number of relations is large, and the execution time of each join thus becomes the primary factor in determining the execution time of a multi-join query.

Also, from 300 randomly generated queries, the average execution times obtained by the six heuristics for a query of 15 relations are shown in Fig. 10 where the number of processors in the system is varied from 16 to 64. It can be seen that when the number of processors increases, SE suffers from the inefficient use of processors, and is thus outperformed by MT, TE, ST_{SE} and ST_{TE} by a wide margin. It can also be observed that heuristic TE which uses processors efficiently to achieve a nearly minimum execution time performs well when the number of processors is large. However, MT performs better than TE when pn = 64, which can be explained by the fact that when the supply of processors is sufficient, achieving minimum time point (by MT) becomes a better heuristic than using processors efficiently (by TE). In all, when the number of processors is small, utilizing intra-operator parallelism (i.e., SE) will suffice to provide a reasonably good performance. On the other hand, for a large multiprocessor system, one has to resort to inter-operator parallelism to fully exploit the resources in the system. Note, however, that without using synchronous execution

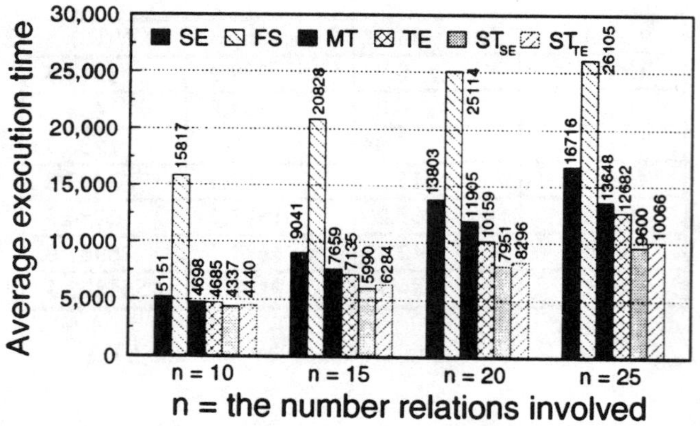

Figure 9. The average execution time for each heuristic when the number of processors is 48.

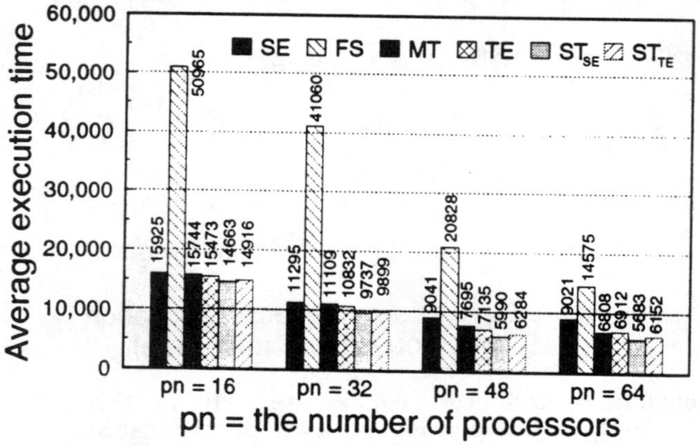

Figure 10. The average execution time for each heuristic when the number of relations is 15.

time, ME and TE, though having a good operational point selection for each join, cannot improve the query response time in a global sense due to the nature of a bottom up approach, and are thus outperformed by ST_{SE} and ST_{TE}. This fact strongly justifies the necessity of taking execution dependency and system fragmentation into consideration when inter-operator parallelism is exploited.

Although SE is outperformed by TE due to its poor operational point selection, ST_{SE} remedies this defect by properly reallocating processors using the concept of synchronous execution time. ST_{SE} can thus outperform ST_{TE}. Note that the sequential join sequences, such as the one shown in Fig. 3a, will not benefit from the concept of synchronous execution time, since in this case, joins have to be executed sequentially and there is no inter-operator parallelism exploitable. This fact, together with the fact that the sequential join sequences usually suffer from poor join sequence efficiency, accounts for the importance of exploring the general join sequences.

Similar to the heuristics in Section 3, the heuristics we investigated here are very straightforward and require little implementation overhead. Our results showed that the join sequence efficiency is in general the dominating factor for the query execution time whereas the processor allocation efficiency becomes significant as the number of processors increases. This suggests that for an efficient solution, one can attempt to optimize the join sequence efficiency by building a good bushy tree first and then improve the processor allocation efficiency by appropriately allocating processors for the execution of each join. This is in fact how the heuristic ST_{SE} is constructed. Note that after the initial processor allocation by ST_{SE}, it is possible to further improve the query execution time by iteratively refining the number of processors allocated to each join. Nevertheless, such a revision should be system dependent.

5. Conclusion

In this paper we dealt with two major issues to exploit inter-operator parallelism within a multi-join query: (i) join sequence scheduling and (ii) processor allocation. We explored the general join sequence so as to exploit the parallelism achievable in a multiprocessor system. The heuristics proposed, despite their simplicity, were shown to lead to general join sequences whose join sequence efficiencies are close to that of the optimal one (G_{OPT}), and significantly better than what is achievable by the optimal sequential join sequence (S_{OPT}), particularly when the number of relations in the query is large. Also, we explored the issue of processor allocation. Several processor allocation heuristics, categorized by bottom up and top down approaches, were proposed and evaluated by simulation. Among all the schemes evaluated, the two-step approach by ST_{SE}, which first applies the join sequence heuristic to build a bushy tree as if under a single processor system, and then, in light of the concept of synchronous execution time, allocates processors to the internal nodes of the bushy tree in a top down manner, is shown to be the best solution to minimize the query execution time.

Acknowledgement

The authors would like to thank S. Lavenberg, H. Young, M. Lo and J. Chen at IBM for their helpful comments and technical assistance on improving this paper.

REFERENCES

[1] C. K. Baru and O. Frieder, "Database Operations in a Cube-Connected Multiprocessor System," *IEEE Trans. on Computers*, vol. 38, no. 6, pp. 920-927, June 1989.

[2] A. Bhide and M. Stonebraker, "A Performance Comparison of Two Architectures for Fast Transaction Processing," *Proceedings of the 4th Intern'l Conf. on Data Engineering*, pp. 536-545, Feb. 1988.

[3] M.-S. Chen and P. S. Yu, "Interleaving a Join Sequence with Semijoins in Distributed Query Processing," *IEEE Trans. on Parallel and Distributed Systems*, vol. 3, 1992.

[4] S. M. Deen, D. N. P. Kannangara, and M. C. Taylor, "Multi-Join Parallel Processors," *Proceedings of the 2nd Intern'l Symp. on Databases in Parallel and Distributed Systems*, pp. 92-102, July 1990.

[5] D. J. DeWitt and R. Gerber, "Multiprocessor Hash-Based Join Algorithms," *Proceedings of the 10th Int'l Conf. on Very Large Data Bases*, pp. 151-162, Aug. 1985.

[6] D. J. DeWitt, S. Ghandeharizadeh, D. A. Schneider, A. Bricker, H.I. Hsiao, and R. Rasmussen, "The Gamma Database Machine Project," *IEEE Trans. on Knowledge and Data Eng.*, vol. 2, no. 1, pp. 44-62, March 1990.

[7] D. Gardy and C. Puech, "On the Effect of Join Operations on Relation Sizes," *ACM Trans. on Database Syst.*, vol. 14, no. 4, pp. 574-603, Dec. 1989.

[8] G. Graefe, Rule-Based Query Optimization in Extensible Database Systems, Madison, WI: Computer Science Department, Univ. Wisconsin-Madison, 724, Nov. 1987.

[9] D. E. Knuth, *The Art of Computer Programming: Sorting and Searching, Vol 3*, MA.: Addison-Wesley, 1972.

[10] M. S. Lakshmi and P. S. Yu, "Effectiveness of Parallel Joins," *IEEE Trans. on Knowledge and Data Eng.*, vol. 2, no. 4, pp. 410-424, Dec. 1990.

[11] M.-L. Lo, M.-S. Chen, and P. S. Yu, "Using Segmented Right-Deep Trees for the Execution of Pipelined Hash Joins," *IBM Research Report*, Dec. 1991.

[12] E. R. Omiecinski and E. T. Lin, "Hash-Based and Index-Based Join Algorithms for Cube and Ring Connected Multicomputers," *IEEE Trans. on Knowledge and Data Eng.*, vol. 1, no. 3, pp. 329-343, Sep. 1989.

[13] K. Ono and G. Lohman, "Measuring the Complexity of Join Enumeration in Query Optimization," *Proceedings of the 16th Int'l Conf. on Very Large Data Bases*, pp. 314-325, Aug. 1990.

[14] F. N. Parr, D. M. Dias, and A. Goyal, "ADB/QDB: A Composite System for High-End Transaction Throughput and Parallel Query Processing," *IBM Research Report RC 15428*, Jan. 1990.

[15] H. Pirahesh, C. Mohan, J. Cheng, T. S. Liu, and P. Selinger, "Parallelism in Relational Data Base Systems: Architectural Issues and Design Approaches," *Proceedings of the 2nd Intern'l Symp. on Databases in Parallel and Distributed Systems*, pp. 4-29, July 1990.

[16] G. Z. Qadah and K. B. Irani, "The Join Algorithms on a Shared-Memory Multiprocessor Database Machine," *IEEE Tran. on Software Engineering*, vol. 14, no. 11, pp. 1668-1683, Nov. 1988.

[17] J. Richardson, H. Lu, and K. Mikkilineni, "Design and Evaluation of Parallel Pipelined Join Algorithms," *Proceedings of ACM SIGMOD*, pp. 399-409, May 1987.

[18] D. Schneider and D. J. DeWitt, "Tradeoffs in Processing Complex Join Queries via Hashing in Multiprocessor Database Machines," *Proceedings of the 16th Int'l Conf. on Very Large Data Bases*, pp. 469-480, Aug. 1990.

[19] P. G. Selinger, M. M. Astrahan, D. D. Chamberlin, R. A. Lorie, and T. G. Price, "Access Path Selection in a Relational Database Management System," *Proceedings of ACM SIGMOD 20*, pp. 23-34, 1979.

[20] M. Stonebraker, R. Katz, D. Patterson, and J. Ousterhout, "The Design of XPRS," *Proceedings of the 14th Int'l Conf. on Very Large Data Bases*, pp. 318-330, 1988.

[21] A. Swami, "Optimization of Large Join Queries: Combining Heuristics with Combinatorial Techniques," *Proceedings of ACM SIGMOD*, pp. 367-376, 1989.

[22] Teradata, "DBC/1012 Database Computer System Manual Release 2.0," *Document C10-0001-02*, Nov. 1985. Teradata Corp.

[23] P. Valduriez and G. Gardarin, "Join and Semijoin Algorithms for a Multiprocessor Database Machine," *ACM Trans. on Database Syst.*, vol. 9, no. 1, pp. 133-161, March 1984.

[24] J. L. Wolf, D. M. Dias, and P. S. Yu, "An Effective Algorithm for Parallelizing Sort Merge Joins in the Presence of Data Skew," *Proceedings of the 2nd Intern'l Symp. on Databases in Parallel and Distributed Systems*, July 1990.

[25] P. S. Yu, M.-S. Chen, H. Heiss, and S. H. Lee, "On Workload Characterization of Relational Database Environments," *IEEE Trans. on Software Eng.*, vol. 18, no. 1, Jan. 1992.

Appendix

Proposition: Let $G=(V,E)$ be a join query graph. $G_B=(V_B, E_B)$ is a connected subgraph of G. Let $R_1, R_2, \ldots, R_p$ be the relations corresponding to nodes in V_B, $A_1, A_2, \ldots, A_q$ be the distinct attributes associated with edges in E_B and m_i be the number of different nodes (relations) that edges with attribute A_i are incident to. Suppose R_M is the relation resulting from all the join operations between relations in G_B and $N_T(G_B)$ is the expected number of tuples in R_M. Then,

$$N_T(G_B) = \frac{\prod_{i=1}^{p} |R_i|}{\prod_{i=1}^{q} |A_i|^{m_i - 1}} .$$

Optimizing Equijoin Queries In Distributed Databases Where Relations Are Hash Partitioned

DENNIS SHASHA and TSONG-LI WANG
New York University

Consider the class of distributed database systems consisting of a set of nodes connected by a high bandwidth network. Each node consists of a processor, a random access memory, and a slower but much larger memory such as a disk. There is no shared memory among the nodes. The data are horizontally partitioned often using a hash function. Such a description characterizes many parallel or distributed database systems that have recently been proposed, both commercial and academic. We study the optimization problem that arises when the query processor must repartition the relations and intermediate results participating in a multijoin query. Using estimates of the sizes of intermediate relations, we show (1) optimum solutions for closed chain queries; (2) the NP-completeness of the optimization problem for star, tree, and general graph queries; and (3) effective heuristics for these hard cases.

Our general approach and many of our results extend to other attribute partitioning schemes, for example, sort-partitioning on attributes, and to partitioned object databases.

Categories and Subject Descriptors: F.2 [**Theory of Computation**]: Analysis of Algorithms and Problem Complexity; H.2.4 [**Database Management**]: Systems—*distributed systems; query processing*; H.2.6 [**Database Management**]: Database Machines

General Terms: Algorithms, Performance, Theory

Additional Key Words and Phrases: Equijoin, hashing, NP-complete problems, relational data models, spanning trees, systems

1. INTRODUCTION

We consider the class of distributed database systems consisting of a collection of nodes (sites), each having a processor, local memory, and local disk. The nodes communicate with one another across a high bandwidth (and high latency) network. Each relation is horizontally partitioned to different nodes

This work was partially supported by the National Science Foundation under grants DCR8501611 and IRI-8901699, and by the Office of Naval Research under grant N00014-85-K-0046.
Authors' addresses: D. Shasha, Courant Institute of Mathematical Sciences, New York University, New York, NY 10012; J. T. L. Wang, Department of Computer and Information Science, New Jersey Institute of Technology, University Heights, Newark, New Jersey, 07102.

Node 1:

R_1	Emp #	Salary
	2	55,000
	4	24,000

S_1	Emp #	Name	Age
	2	John	35
	4	Mary	25

Node 2:

R_2	Emp #	Salary
	1	38,000
	3	42,000

S_2	Emp #	Name	Age
	1	Andy	50
	3	Ann	40

Fig. 1. Example of two partitioned relations.

by hashing: use a hash function h whose domain is the domain of some attribute A of relation R and whose range is the number of processing nodes. For each tuple t of R, we put t in processing node $h(t.A)$.[1] When performing joins, we use the same function for any pair of relations that could possibly be joined together.

Example 1. Suppose we have a system composed of two nodes, node 1 and node 2, and a hash function $h(x) = (x \bmod 2) + 1$. Figure 1 shows two relations that are partitioned on the join attribute emp#: $R(S)$ is partitioned into R_1 and R_2 (S_1 and S_2), which are stored at node 1 and node 2, respectively.

Such a loosely coupled hash-partitioned architecture characterizes many parallel or distributed database systems that have recently been developed, including commercially available ones such as the Teradata machine [33], as well as research prototypes such as Bubba [9], Gamma [11], Grace [18], and Sabre [34].

In this paper we are concerned with optimizing equijoin queries in such systems. We restrict ourselves to queries that retrieve all fields of joined relations.[2] For our purposes, we assume that relations are not replicated, that is, each node holds a unique fragment for each relation. We also assume that there is no answer site in the systems. Thus we mainly concentrate on join processing, ignoring unioning results at the answer site.

For example, consider doing the join between R and S in Figure 1, based on the condition R.emp# = S.emp#. Since both relations are partitioned on emp#, no communication is required. On the other hand, if R is partitioned on emp#, whereas S on age, each S tuple t needs to be sent to processing

[1]Though one may partition on a set of attributes, for the purpose of this paper, we assume partitioning on a single attribute only. Some partitioning schemes (see, e.g., [18]) also allow the range to be k times the number of processing nodes, with each node having k buffers that can receive data. In that case, $h(t.A)$ designates a buffer as well as a node. The results in this paper hold for that generalization.

[2]This restriction is made mainly for simplifying cost computation. It is not difficult, however, to extend our techniques to handle queries whose outputs contain only certain fields of joined relations.

Table I. Effect of Repartitioning on Join Performance

Join Size	With Repartitioning (seconds)	Without (seconds)
10,000 with 1,000	35.4	18.0
100,000 with 10,000	286.4	122.0
1,000,000 with 100,000	3,144.0	1,143.0

Source: DeWitt et al. [12].

node $h(t.\mathrm{emp}\#)$. Such data transmission is called *repartitioning*. The overhead caused by repartitioning is not negligible. If communication among nodes is slow, then most time will be spent in routing data in a network when repartitionings occur. Even if communication is fast, repartitioning may reduce throughput because it entails more disk accesses.

To understand the importance of such overhead, let us review an experiment by DeWitt et al. on the Teradata machine [12]. The machine consisted of 20 nodes and 40 disk storage units, which were interconnected with a 12-Mbyte/second-bandwidth network. The data consisted of 200 byte tuples. DeWitt et al. performed joins between two relations having different sizes (10,000 tuples with 1,000 tuples, 100,000 tuples with 10,000 tuples, 1,000,000 tuples with 100,000 tuples, respectively) and recorded the time for executing these joins with and without repartitionings. Table I shows the result of their experiment. By comparing the values listed in the second and third columns of the table, we see that there exist ratios of between 2 or 3 to 1 for the same size joins. This indicates that when processing queries in a loosely coupled multiprocessor system, the repartitioning cost can dominate the local processing cost. The authors also measured the influence of the bandwidth of the network. They observed that repartitioning a relation of 200 Mbyte took 2,000 seconds and used less than 1 percent of network capacity on the average. This result reveals that repartitioning large relations is expensive even when a network is fast.

But can we control the repartitionings necessary to process a query, thereby minimizing response time in such an environment?

Example 2. Suppose we have a suppliers-and-parts database containing relations SUP(s#, sname, city), PART(p#, pname, city), and SUP-PART(s#, p#, qty). Suppose that SUP is partitioned on s#, PART on p#, and SUP-PART on s#. Consider the following SQL query:

```
SELECT  SUP.*, PART.*, SUP-PART.*
FROM    SUP, PART, SUP-PART
WHERE   SUP.s# = SUP-PART.s#
AND     SUP-PART.p# = PART.p#
```

One way to process this query is to join SUP-PART with PART first, obtaining a result T_1, and then join T_1 with SUP. Assume that joining two relations takes 100 seconds and repartitioning a relation takes 100 seconds, as indicated in Table I. The cost of this strategy would be (the cost of repartitioning SUP-PART) + (the cost of joining SUP-PART with PART) + (the cost of repartitioning T_1) + (the cost of joining T_1 with SUP) = 100 + 100 + 100 + 100 = 400 seconds. On the other hand, joining SUP with SUP-PART first requires no repartitioning. Then joining the intermediate result T_2 with PART requires repartitioning T_2. The cost of this strategy is thus 100 + 100 + 100 = 300 seconds.

Clearly, the second strategy is better for processing the given query. This example demonstrates that by properly arranging the order of joins among relations, better performance can be achieved. Exactly how to do this to minimize the cost for various important queries is the main concern of this paper. In Section 2, we present an overview of previous work in the area. Section 3 discusses basic assumptions and formally defines the optimization problem. Section 4 then gives a dynamic programming algorithm to solve the problem in the context of closed chain queries. Section 5 establishes the NP-completeness of the problem for star, tree, and general graph queries. Section 6 presents and analyzes heuristic procedures. In Section 7, we report the results of computational experiments. Finally we conclude the paper with some directions for future research in Section 8.

2. RELATED WORK

A considerable amount of work has been performed in the area of query processing using partitioning schemes. Bernstein et al. [3], Stonebraker and Neuhold [31], and Williams et al. [35] discussed horizontal partitioning (fragmentation) in the context of distributed database management systems (DDBMSs). In these systems, fragmentation is used as part of processing strategy to increase parallelism, thus increasing throughput and saving response time.

A common objective adopted by researchers in the area of DDBMS is to minimize the communication cost incurred in processing a query. Segev [25], for example, introduced the notion of remote semijoin, which can significantly reduce the communication cost while incurring higher processing cost. Fragments may also be replicated at different sites. Yu et al. [38] distinguished queries as locally processable and nonlocally processable. If a query is locally processable, then the query can be processed without data transfer. They proposed a linear time "fragment and replicate" algorithm for nonlocally processable queries. Relevant work has also been discussed by Apers et al. [1], Wong [36], Pramanik and Vineyard [22], Stamos and Young [30], and others. What distinguishes us from these workers is that we seek the optimal join order when processing queries, starting with partitioned data and ending with partitioned data. Moreover, our main concern is on the environment without data replication. We defer to Section 8 the possibility of replicating data.

The idea of using hash partitioning for joins in multiprocessor systems comes from [2]. This scheme is then adopted by Kitsuregawa et al. on the Grace database machine project [18], though their emphasis is on the speed of the sort engine rather than on the performance of the join algorithm. Valduriez and Gardarin [34] described also various join and semijoin strategies, but hashing is applied only during the partition phase. DeWitt and Gerber [10] proposed two algorithms that exploit hashing thoroughly in both partition and join phases. They applied the algorithms to a number of simple join operations and concluded that both algorithms have satisfactory performance.

In contrast to the previous work on hash partitioning, this paper examines *multijoin* queries arising in systems that use hash methods to execute joins and partition data. Thus, we are not concerned with the particular hash-join strategy used, but rather with reducing the cost of a query involving many joins by minimizing communication, I/O, and processing time. In [28], we developed a model for processing such queries without considering the size of relations and intermediate results participating in a join. Here, we address more general cases and explore strategies for taking size into account. We present a polynomial time algorithm for optimizing queries whose closure is a chain. We then show that finding optimal solutions to a simpler problem is NP-complete for star and tree queries. In view of the NP-hardness for the simpler problem, we consider various heuristics for the general problem. We find that combining our chain algorithm with a heuristic related to Kruskal's spanning tree algorithm [20] achieves the best performance over a wide range of query topologies and cost assumptions.

3. FORMULATION OF THE PROBLEM

3.1 Basic Assumptions

Our objective is to minimize response time when processing a query. We approximate this goal by considering both processing and repartitioning costs. Processing cost refers to the time spent for performing joins at each node. Repartitioning cost refers to the time spent for repartitionings, which is determined by (1) the total amount of data transmitted in the network, and (2) system parameters of a given architecture. System parameters include the bandwidth of the network, as well as the speed of the I/O and processors.

To simplify the model developed in this paper, we make the following assumptions.

Assumption 1. The processing speeds and I/O speeds at different nodes are the same. The bandwidth of the network is a constant.

Assumption 2. Each processing node uses the same hashing technique to execute joins (e.g., DeWitt and Gerber's).

Assumption 3. For each repartition (or partition) of a relation, the hash function applied to its attribute evenly distributes tuples to each node.

Assumptions 1 and 2 deal with parameters related to a given system. The two assumptions, together with Assumption 3, ensure that the processors complete joins and transfer data at the same time. (The data could be transferred either in pipelined fashion or one batch at a time.) Assumption 3 is reasonable when the attribute is a key and the hash function is "good," that is, it acts as a random function from the set of tuples to the set of n

nodes such that each tuple has probability $1/n$ of being sent to any node. This has been established analytically in [29] where we show that the probability that any of the n nodes has more than twice the average number of tuples is very small, provided that the number of tuples $> 4n \log n$. If the attribute is not a key or the hash function is biased, our results should be taken as heuristics.

3.2 Terminology

We assume the reader is familiar with the standard terms, attribute, tuple, join, used in relational database systems. Define a *relation schema* $\mathbf{R}$ as a finite set of attributes $\{A_1, A_2, \ldots, A_n\}$ [16]. Associated with each attribute A_i, $1 \le i \le n$, is a domain, denoted $\mathrm{dom}(A_i)$. A relation instance (or simply *relation*) R on schema $\mathbf{R}$ is a finite set of mappings $\{t_1, t_2, \ldots, t_m\}$ from $\mathbf{R}$ to the set of domains such that for each $t \in R$, $t(A_i) \in \mathrm{dom}(A_i)$, $1 \le i \le n$. Let B be an attribute in $\mathbf{R}$. We write $t.B$ for $t(B)$. We define $R.B$ to be $\{t_1.B, t_2.B, \ldots, t_m.B\}$.

An equijoin clause, or *clause* for short, is a pair of the form $\{R.B, S.C\}$ where B and C are attributes of R and S, respectively. This clause represents the join condition $R.B = S.C$. We are only interested in queries whose qualification is a conjunction of such join conditions. Therefore, we define a *query* as a set of clauses.[3] To represent a join that links different tuples of the same relation, we consider the two arguments of the join to be different relation instances for the purpose of the query. For example, to find the salary of each employee's current manager, given an EMP(name, sal, manager) schema, we assume two employee relation instances EMP1 and EMP2. These would be represented as distinct relations in the query.

In order to find an optimal join strategy, it is helpful to consider the *query graph* $QG_q = (QV_q, QE_q)$ for a query q, where

$$QV_q = \{\text{relations referenced by the clauses in } q\}$$

$$QE_q = \{\{R, S\} \mid \text{some member of } q \text{ references both } R \text{ and } S\}.$$

An example of a query graph is given in Figure 2a. Notice that a query graph is never a multigraph, though there may be many clauses associated with each edge. We write clauses($\{R, S\}$, q) to denote the set of equijoin clauses referencing both R and S in q. We assume that the query graph of a query is connected. Otherwise we consider the queries to correspond to the connected components of the query graph; the resulting query would then be a Cartesian product of these individual queries.

Observe that in processing a query graph, one can always execute a spanning tree of it, treating all other clauses as selections. Furthermore, in executing a spanning tree, we can take only one clause, for each edge, as the

---

[3] Because all attributes of joined relations appear in the output of a query, as marked in Section 1, we exclude the target list in defining a query.

SELECT	$S.*$, $T.*$, $R.*$
FROM	S, T, R
WHERE	$S.C = T.B$
AND	$S.G = T.H$
AND	$S.F = R.E$
AND	$T.B = R.D$

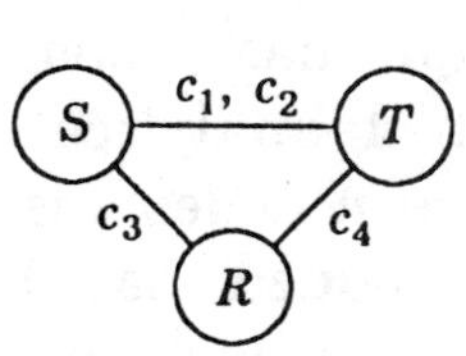

$c_1 = \{S.C, T.B\}$

$c_2 = \{S.G, T.H\}$

$c_3 = \{S.F, R.E\}$

$c_4 = \{T.B, R.D\}$

(a)

(1) Consider the query graph in Figure 2a just above. We can execute the graph by joining S with T first, and then ST with R. (The juxtaposition of two relation names represents the join result of the relations.)

(2) While joining S and T based on, say $\{S.C, T.B\}$, the selection condition $S.G = T.H$ is also processed.

(3) Then when joining ST with R based on, say $\{S.F, R.E\}$, the clause $\{T.B, R.D\}$ enforces another selection condition on tuples of ST and R (see Figure 2c).

(b)

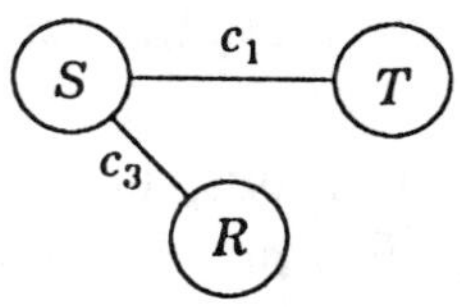

(c)

(4) Consider the query graph in Figure 2a. When joining S and T on the clause $\{S.C, T.B\}$, S needs to be partitioned on C and T on B. Then in joining ST and R,

(i) if $\{S.F, R.E\}$ is used as the join clause, ST needs to be repartitioned on F; such a repartitioning causes part(T) to be empty;

(ii) if $\{T.B, R.D.\}$ is used as the join clause, since no repartitioning of ST is needed, part(T) = $\{B\}$.

Fig. 2. Example of query graph and its single-clause spanning tree.

join clause, applying the other clauses as selections (see Figure 2b). This motivates us to introduce the following.

Definition 1. A *spanning tree* of a query graph $QG_q = (QV_q, QE_q)$ is a graph $QG_{Treeq} = (QV_{Treeq}, QE_{Treeq})$ with the following properties:

(i) $QV_{Treeq} = QV_q$.

(ii) $QE_{Treeq} \subseteq QE_q$ and (QV_{Treeq}, QE_{Treeq}) is a tree.

(iii) For each $e \in QE_{Treeq}$, clauses(e, *Treeq*) $\subseteq$ clauses(e, q) and clauses(e, *Treeq*) $\neq \emptyset$.

If clauses(e, *Treeq*) is a singleton set for each $e \in QE_{Treeq}$, QG_{Treeq} is called a single-clause spanning tree (ss tree) of QG_q.

Figure 2c shows an ss tree for the query graph in Figure 2a, which corresponds to the execution sequence in Figure 2b.

3.3 Cost Model

We denote as part(R) the set of attributes on which a relation R is partitioned sometime in the query execution. By the assumption stated in Section

1, the initial value of part(R) is always a singleton set. However, when repartitionings occur, part(R) may become empty. Figure 2d illustrates such a case.

In order to evaluate a join strategy effectively, we need to have a measure that reflects the cost. We begin with the definition of the cost for a clause.

Definition 2. Let $|R|$ denote the number of tuples in relation R and $|t_R|$ the width (in bytes) of a tuple in R. The cost of a clause $\{R.A, S.B\}$ equals PC + RC; PC $= \alpha \times (|R| \times |t_R| + |S| \times |t_S|)$ is the processing cost, and RC $= \beta \times Move$ is the repartitioning cost, where α, β are nonzero constants (e.g., in the Teradata case $\beta = 2\alpha$), and

$$Move = \begin{cases} 0 & \text{if } (A \in \text{part}(R)) \wedge (B \in \text{part}(S)) \\ |S| \times |t_S| & \text{if } (A \in \text{part}(R)) \wedge (B \notin \text{part}(S)) \\ |R| \times |t_R| & \text{if } (A \notin \text{part}(R)) \wedge (B \in \text{part}(S)) \\ |R| \times |t_R| + |S| \times |t_S| & \text{otherwise.} \end{cases}$$

Thus we are assuming that both PC and RC are linearly proportional to the sizes of the relations. This assumption is consistent with the Teradata benchmarks shown in Section 1 and the Grace measurements [18, 19]; it is also consistent with the cost equations derived elsewhere [27]. *Move* represents the amount of data transmitted in the network, where case 1 refers to the situation in which neither R nor S will be repartitioned; cases 2 and 3 represent the situation where one of the relations will be repartitioned, and case 4 represents the situation where both relations need to be repartitioned.

Also, we consider the measure of processing cost to be the number of bytes moved from disks, as opposed to the number of page fetches from disks often assumed in the literature [4, 17, 24], though the two measures differ by only a constant additive factor. By including factors such as page size, I/O speed, and bandwidth, one can convert the byte units to corresponding time unit.

Next, as noted in Section 1, in executing the same ss tree of a graph, joining nodes in different order can yield different costs.[4] We thus introduce the following.

Definition 3. A clause string, or *string* for short, associated with an ss tree $QG_{Treeq} = (QV_{Treeq}, QE_{Treeq})$ is an *ordered* clause sequence

$$c_{i1}\, c_{i2} \ldots c_{in}$$

where $QE_{Treeq} = \{e_i \mid 1 \le i \le n\}$, $i1, i2, \ldots, in$ is a permutation of $1, 2, \ldots, n$, and $c_{ij} \in \text{clauses}(e_{ij}, Treeq)$.

The order of clauses in a string indicates the order in which nodes of the associated tree are joined. There are $n!$ strings associated with QG_{Treeq} if there are n edges in it.

[4]Since the results obtained in this paper depend on the properties of graphs, we use the terms node and relation interchangeably.

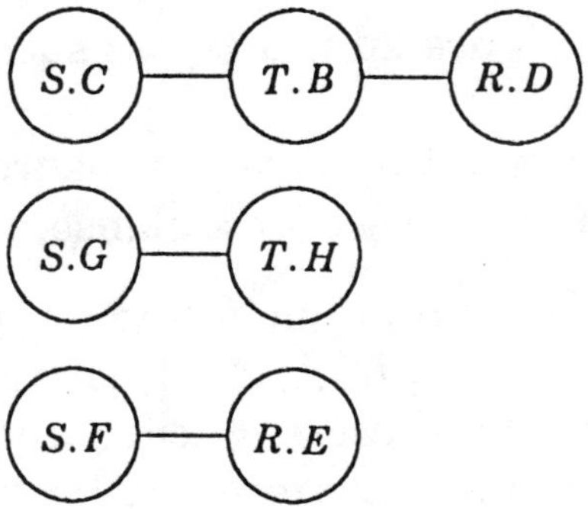

Fig. 3. Join graph of query shown in Figure 2a.

We define the cost of a string as the sum of the costs of its component clauses. However, since the cost of a clause is dependent on the sizes and partition attributes of its two corresponding relations, which in turn are influenced by the order in which relations of the query tree are joined, it is required that, when calculating the cost of a string, one follow the exact order specified in the string.

Finally, we define the cost of an ss tree QG_{Treeq} as

$$\text{Cost}(QG_{Treeq}) = \min_{cs \in CS} \{\text{Cost}(cs)\}$$

where CS is the set of all strings associated with QG_{Treeq}. A *minimum cost spanning tree* of a query graph QG_q is an ss tree of QG_q such that no other ss tree of QG_q has a smaller cost. For a given query graph, executing its minimum cost spanning tree yields minimum response time.

3.4 Exploiting Redundant Clauses to Optimize Queries

Our goal is to minimize response time when processing a query. Thus far we have concentrated on query graphs, rather than on queries. However, different query graphs may refer to the same query. To have a clear view of this, we need another graph model.

Define the *join graph* for a query q, denoted JG_q, as a pair (JV_q, JE_q), where

$$JV_q = \{R.A \mid R.A \text{ is an attribute of } R \text{ that occurs in some clause of } q\}$$

$$JE_q = \{\{R.A, S.B\} \mid \{R.A, S.B\} \text{ is some clause in } q\}.$$

Intuitively a join graph represents an equivalence relation on attributes from different relations. (This is because we consider only queries with equijoin clauses.) Each equivalence class of attributes is a connected component of the graph. Figure 3 shows the join graph of the query in Figure 2a.

We say two queries are *equivalent* if their join graphs have the same connectivity. For any state of a database, equivalent queries give the same result. A clause c of a query q is *redundant* if c is an edge in a cycle of JG_q. The *closure* of a query q is an equivalent query, denoted q^+, to which one cannot add more redundant clauses. Figure 4 illustrates the above concepts. A query is a *chain query* (*star query*, *tree query*, respectively) if it is equivalent to some query whose query graph is a chain (star, tree,

(1) Consider the query $q = \{\{R.A, T.B\}, \{T.B, S.C\}, \{R.A, S.C\}, \{T.B, U.D\}\}$.
(2) q's join graph

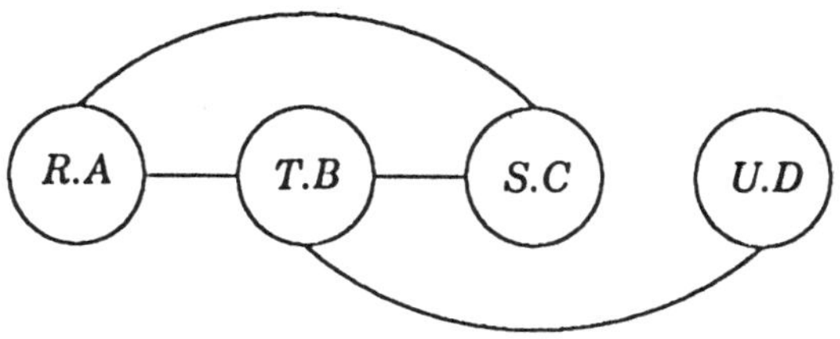

(3) $q' = \{\{R.A, T.B\}, \{T.B, S.C\}, \{T.B, U.D\}\}$ is equivalent to q.
(4) $\{R.A, S.C\}$ is redundant.
(5) $q^+ = \{\{R.A, T.B\}, \{T.B, S.C\}, \{R.A, S.C\}, \{T.B, U.D\}, \{R.A, U.D\}, \{S.C, U.D\}\}$.

Fig. 4. Join graph representation of a query and its closure.

(1) Consider the query q and its closure (expressed in terms of their query graphs):

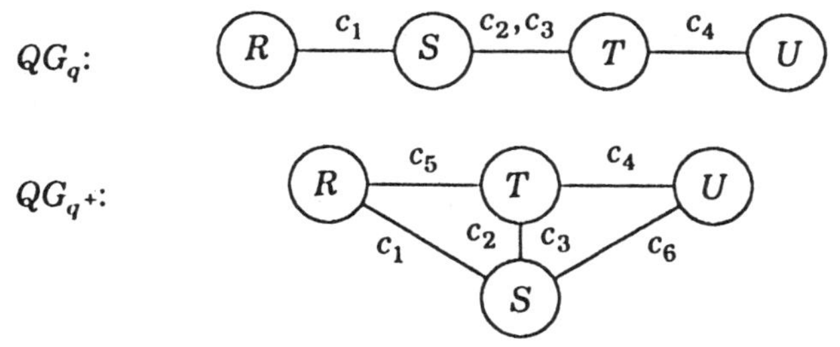

$c_1 = \{R.A, S.B\}$
$c_2 = \{S.B, T.D\}$
$c_3 = \{S.C, T.E\}$
$c_4 = \{T.E, U.F\}$
$c_5 = \{R.A, T.D\}$
$c_6 = \{S.C, U.F\}$

(2) Assume that all relations and intermediate results have the same size, K. Moreover, part(R) = A, part(S) = C, part(T) = D, and part(U) = F.
(3) If we only consider QG_q, we get the best strings (e.g., $\{R.A, S.B\}\{S.B, T.D\}\{T.E, U.F\}$) with cost 10K.
(4) If we consider the redundant clauses in QG_{q^+}, we can get the string $\{R.A, T.D\}\{T.E, S.C\}\{T.E, U.F\}$ with cost 8K.

Fig. 5. Example showing the need to compute the query closure.

respectively). The importance of these queries and their processing in distributed database systems have been discussed extensively in the literature [5–7, 16, 37].

In order to minimize costs when processing a query, one might conjecture that it is enough to look at the spanning trees of its query graph. But this is wrong. Figure 5 illustrates such a case.[5] This example highlights an important idea: redundant clauses may lead to cheaper strings (and ss trees). It also suggests that when processing a query, we should begin with the closure of the query.

[5]For concreteness, in this and subsequent examples, we set the constants α and β in the cost model (cf. Definition 2) to 1 and 2, respectively (two values that are consistent with the Teradata benchmark result).

Computing closures may sometimes introduce *self-loops* (i.e., edges from nodes to themselves) in the query graph. For example, suppose a given query q has clauses $\{R.A, S.B\}$, $\{S.B, T.C\}$, and $\{T.C, R.D\}$. Then QG_{q+} will contain $\{R.A, R.D\}$, an edge from R to R. In general, one can eliminate a loop $\{R.X, R.Y\}$ by replacing either $R.X$ by $R.Y$ or $R.Y$ by $R.X$ in all clauses of the query. The choice is arbitrary unless one of them, say $R.Y$, is the initial partition attribute of R, in which case we replace $R.X$ by $R.Y$. $\{R.X, R.Y\}$ will then be removed from the query graph and used as a selection condition. Eliminating self-loops is useful, since by renaming identical attributes we may reduce costs. Henceforth, we restrict our attention to loop-free query graphs.

Based on the above formulation, the problem of minimizing response time (MRP) becomes

> **Given** a query q,
> **Find** (1) QG_{q+}; (2) a minimum cost spanning tree $\mathcal{T}$ of QG_{q+} and the clause string *cs* that yields $\mathcal{T}$'s cost.

In the following sections, the problem is addressed for chain, star, tree, and general graph queries. It is important to note that when processing these queries, once the spanning tree $\mathcal{T}$ and associated string *cs* are found, we can process them by executing $\mathcal{T}$ based on the clauses and join order specified in *cs*.

4. CLOSED CHAIN QUERIES

As shown in Figure 5, the closure of a chain in the query graph does not necessarily remain a chain. If it is not a chain, it will contain a cycle.[6] In this section, we focus on queries q whose QG_{q+} is a chain. (Such a class of queries are called *closed chain queries*.) More general queries are treated in the next section.

A dynamic programming technique is used to solve the MRP problem for closed chain queries. The dynamic programming algorithm computes the best order of joins. The algorithm, in its style, is similar to that proposed independently by Sun et al. [32] for optimizing chain queries in object-oriented database systems.

The following notation is needed to describe our algorithm. For $1 \le i \le j \le n$,

(1) $cs(i, j)$: a minimum cost string associated with the chain segment $R_i, R_{i+1}, \ldots, R_j$;
(2) $\text{Cost}(i, j)$: the cost of $cs(i, j)$;
(3) R_{ij}: the intermediate relation obtained by joining the relations $R_i, R_{i+1}, \ldots, R_j$ based on the clauses and join order specified in $cs(i, j)$.

In general, when joining any two (possibly intermediate) relations, say R_{ip} and R_{p+1j} for some p, $i \le p < j$, among the clauses between the two

[6] To see this, notice that connecting two nonadjacent nodes on a single path results in a node becoming a descendant of the two nodes.

relations, we want to choose a pair with the lowest cost as the join clause. Observe that the processing cost depends solely on the sum of the sizes of the two relations, and hence is the same for all these clauses. We thus choose an attribute, if any, on which no repartitioning is needed, thereby minimizing the communication cost.

After joining the two relations on a clause $\{R_p.X, R_{p+1}.Y\}$, the cardinality of the new intermediate relation R_{ij} is $|R_{ip}| \times |R_{p+1j}| \times \alpha$, where α is the selectivity factor between R_{ip} and R_{p+1j},[7] and the width of tuples in R_{ij} is $|t_{Rip}| + |t_{Rp+1j}|$.[8] Algorithm CHAIN summarizes the procedure.

Algorithm CHAIN

1. (*Initialization*) For $1 \le i \le n$, $cs(i, i)$ = null, $\text{Cost}(i, i) = 0$, $R_{ii} = R_i$, part(R) is the attribute that R is initially partitioned on;
2. **for** $k = 1$ **to** $n - 1$ **do**
3.   **for** $i = 1$ to $n - k$ **do**
4. $j = i + k$;
5.   **for** $p = i$ **to** $j - 1$ **do**
6.   choose clause $\{R_p.X, R_{p+1}.Y\}$ such that
               $\text{Cost}(\{R_p.X, R_{p+1}.Y\}) = \min_{c \in \text{clauses}(\{R_p, R_{p+1}\}, q)}\{\text{Cost}(c)\}$;
7.   concatenate $cs(i, p)$, $cs(p + 1, j)$, $\{R_p.X, R_{p+1}.Y\}$ to form a string cs;
            set $\text{Cost}(cs) = \text{Cost}(i, p) + \text{Cost}(p + 1, j) + \text{Cost}(\{R_p.X, R_{p+1}.Y\})$;
            put cs in set(i, j);
         end for
8.   construct $cs(i, j)$ where $\text{Cost}(i, j) = \min_{cs \in set(i,j)}\{\text{Cost}(cs)\}$;
         compute the size of R_{ij} as described above;
      end for
   end for

It should be noted that $cs(1, n)$ is not unique if all the clauses (strings) with the same minimum cost are selected at steps 6 and 8.

To show that the algorithm solves the MRP problem for closed chain queries, it suffices to prove the following.

THEOREM 1. *Given a chain segment with relations $R_i, R_{i+1}, \ldots, R_j$, algorithm CHAIN finds a minimum cost string of the segment.*

PROOF. The proof is by induction on $j - i$, the length of the segment. The base case $(j - i = 1)$ is straightforward. Assume the theorem holds for any chain with length less than or equal to $k - 1$. Let $\tilde{cs}(i, j)$ be a string of the segment with the actual minimum cost, where $j - i = k$. It will be proved that $\text{Cost}(\tilde{cs}(i, j)) = \text{Cost}(i, j)$. Note that $\tilde{cs}(i, j)$ is not necessarily equal to

[7] It may happen that, when joining two (intermediate) relations, there exist clauses whose selectivities differ from that of the chosen join clause. As an example, consider the optimal string $\{R.A, T.D\}\{T.E, S.C\}\{T.E, U.F\}$ in Figure 5. When joining RT with S, the selectivity of the clause $\{R.A, S.B\}$ may differ from that of $\{T.E, S.C\}$. For simplicity, we define the selectivity factor between two (intermediate) relations R and S as the fraction of tuple pairs from R and S satisfying *all* clauses between them. Note that, under this definition, the cardinality of a join result is independent of which clause is used as the join clause.

[8] Strictly speaking, the width should be $|t_{Rip}| + |t_{Rp+1j}| - |X|$—it is sufficient to retain one join attribute in the resulting relation because equijoins are involved. For exposition purpose, we omit the last term and include it only in the simulation study (Section 7).

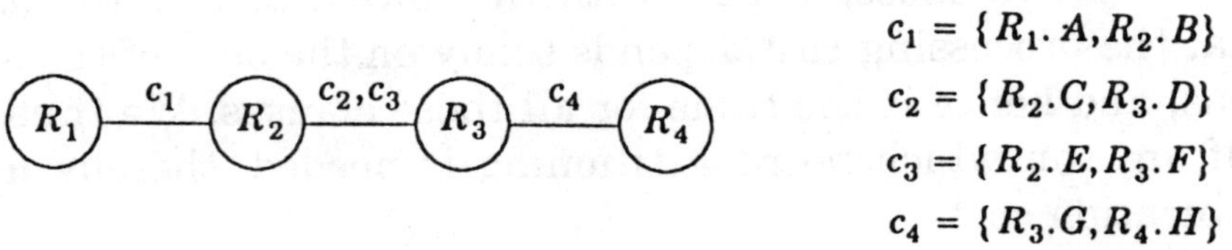

Fig. 6. Query graph for closed chain query example.

$cs(i, j)$, the minimum cost string obtained by algorithm CHAIN for this segment.

Assume that the last clause joined in $\tilde{cs}(i, j)$ is $\{R_p.U, R_{p+1}.V\}$. Let $\tilde{cs}(i, p)$ be the string obtained by concatenating the clauses from $\tilde{cs}(i, j)$ that are on the edges between R_i and R_p, and $\tilde{cs}(p + 1, j)$ be the string formed by concatenating the remaining clauses except $\{R_p.U, R_{p+1}.V\}$, with the constraint that the order of clauses in the two strings obeys that in $\tilde{cs}(i, j)$. By induction hypothesis, $\text{Cost}(\tilde{cs}(i, p)) \geq \text{Cost}(i, p)$ and $\text{Cost}(\tilde{cs}(p + 1, j)) \geq \text{Cost}(p + 1, j)$.

Now, $\text{Cost}(\tilde{cs}(i, j)) = \text{Cost}(\tilde{cs}(i, p)) + \text{Cost}(\tilde{cs}(p + 1, j)) + \text{Cost}(\{R_p.U, R_{p+1}.V\}) \geq \text{Cost}(i, p) + \text{Cost}(p + 1, j) + \text{Cost}(\{R_p.U, R_{p+1}.V\}) \geq \text{Cost}(i, j)$ (steps 6 and 8). Since $\text{Cost}(\tilde{cs}(i, j))$ is the known minimum, we have $\text{Cost}(\tilde{cs}(i, j)) = \text{Cost}(i, j)$. □

The following shows the time complexity of the algorithm.

THEOREM 2. *Algorithm CHAIN runs in $O(n^3 + n^2 l)$ time, or $O(n^3)$ when n is greater than l, where n is the number of nodes in a closed chain and l is the maximum number of clauses on an edge.*

PROOF. Consider the following two cases. When $k = 1$, we are joining two relations rather than intermediate results. Thus in order to find the lowest cost clause, we need to examine all clauses between the two relations, checking whether their component attributes are the same as the initial partition attributes of the two relations. This requires $O(nl)$ time.

When $k > 1$, in joining R_{ip} and R_{p+1j} for some p, $i \leq p < j$, we need to examine all clauses between them only when $i = p$ but $p + 1 < j$ (or $i < p$ but $p + 1 = j$), because in such situations we are joining a relation with an intermediate result, and we need to check whether any attribute matches the initial partition attribute of the relation. In the other situations, in which we are joining two intermediate relations, we can arbitrarily choose a clause, since a closed chain does not allow the same attribute to occur on distinct edges (because then the closure would not be a chain). Therefore, both intermediate relations need to be repartitioned anyway. Thus, this requires $O(n^2 + nl)$ time.

The value of k ranges from 1 to n. Hence, there are $O(n^3 + n^2 l)$ operations to be performed in total. □

Example 3. Consider the query graph in Figure 6. Both the initial data and results obtained by applying algorithm CHAIN to this graph are shown

Table II. Data for the Closed Chain Query Example

i	1	2	3	4
		Cardinality of Relation		
$\|R_i\|$	30	10	10	20
		Initial Partition Attribute		
part(R_i)	U	C	D	V
		Tuple Size		
$\|t_{Ri}\|$	3	2	1	4

Selectivity Factor

α_{12} [a]	α_{23}	α_{34}
0.2	0.1	0.2

Results

i	j	Cost(i, j)	$cs(i, j)$	$\|R_{ij}\|$	$\|t_{Rij}\|$
1	2	330	c_1	60	5
2	3	30	c_2	10	3
3	4	270	c_4	40	5
1	3	390	$c_2 c_1$	60	6
2	4	360	$c_2 c_4$	40	7
1	4	1470	$c_2 c_4 c_1$	240	10

[a] α_{ij} is the selectivity factor between R_i and R_j.

in Table II. Thus the minimum cost required to process the query is 1470 and the corresponding string is $\{R_2.C, R_3.D\}\{R_3.G, R_4.H\}\{R_2.B, R_1.A\}$.

5. MORE GENERAL QUERIES

Solving the MRP problem for a complex query whose graph has multiple edges, with each edge being associated with multiple clauses, is NP-complete. The difficulty stems from simultaneous choices among multiple clauses for multiple edges. In this section, we address the time complexity of the MRP problem for such complex queries. In particular, we focus on star queries, a particularly simple form of tree queries.

THEOREM 3. *Given a star query q without redundant clauses, finding a minimum cost spanning tree from QG_q is NP-complete.*

PROOF. The proof that this problem can be solved by a nondeterministic algorithm in polynomial time is straightforward: given a target cost, just guess a single-clause spanning tree and see whether its cost is less than the target cost. To show that the problem is NP-hard, we consider the following easier case. The size of each relation in QG_q is the same, and the result of each join is as large as the relations participating in the join. Under these restrictions, minimizing response time is equivalent to minimizing the *number* of repartitionings.

We therefore modify the cost of an ss tree $QG_{Treeq} = (QV_{Treeq}, QE_{Treeq})$ to be

$$\text{Cost}(QG_{Treeq}) = \sum_{R \in QV_{Treeq}} \text{nodecost}(R)$$

where the nodecost of a relation is the number of nonpartitioning attributes in clauses touching that relation.

Intuitively this cost reflects the smallest number of repartitionings that the execution of an ss tree requires. To show this, consider some node R in QG_{Treeq}. Since QG_{Treeq} is a single-clause spanning tree, if $R.A$ appears in a clause, then R or an intermediate result containing R will have to be partitioned on A at some point in the query execution. If A is the partition attribute of R, then R may not have to be repartitioned to allow the joins associated with $R.A$ to occur. Thus, the nodecost of R is in fact the minimum number of times R will have to be repartitioned during the execution of the query. The same holds for any other relation in the tree.[9] So the number of repartitionings must be at least the sum of these nodecosts.

We show that the special case is NP-hard by transforming the following hitting set problem [14] to it.

Hitting Set. Given a collection $\mathscr{C}$ of subsets of a finite set S and a positive integer K, decide whether there is a subset S' of S with $\|S'\| \leq K$ such that S' contains at least one element from each subset in $\mathscr{C}$.

We construct a query graph QG by the following steps:

(1) For each subset $C_i \in \mathscr{C}$, create a node R_i. Create an additional distinguished node R.
(2) If C_i contains members $B_{i1}, B_{i2}, \ldots, B_{ik_i}$, associate the edge $\{R, R_i\}$ with the clauses $\{R.B_{i1}, R_i.B_{i1}\}, \{R.B_{i2}, R_i.B_{i2}\}, \ldots, \{R.B_{ik_i}, R_i.B_{ik_i}\}$.

See Figure 7 for an example of the above construction, where $\|\mathscr{C}\| = m$. Assume that none of the B_{ij} are partition attributes. It is easy to verify that the resulting graph has the following properties.

(a) All clauses between R and each R_i are of the form $\{R.X, R_i.X\}$ for some attribute X.
(b) None of the clauses are redundant.
(c) Each R_i has a nodecost of one in any ss tree of QG.

Consider QG as the query graph of a certain star query q. Let us suppose that there is a single-clause spanning tree of QG_q with cost $\|\mathscr{C}\| + K$. It is then easily seen that there is a hitting set of $\mathscr{C}$ with K elements (by property (c) above and the fact that R has a nodecost of K). Conversely if $\mathscr{C}$ has a

---

[9] One might think that repartitioning intermediate relations might achieve two repartitionings at the cost of one. For example, if the A and B attributes are equal in some intermediate relation created by the join $R.A = S.B$, any repartitioning on A would also cause a repartitioning of B. This is true but irrelevant, since immediately after the join corresponding to $R.A = S.B$, the intermediate relation was already partitioned on those attributes.

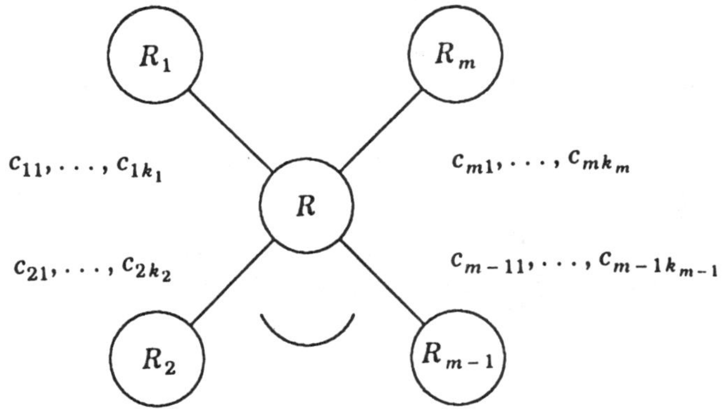

Fig. 7. Transforming $\mathscr{C} = \{C_1, C_2, \ldots, C_m\}$, where $C_i = \{B_{i1}, B_{i2}, \ldots, B_{ik_i}\}$, $1 \le i \le m$, into QG. R is a distinguished relation; each R_i corresponds to C_i; each clause c_{ij} corresponds to the join condition $R_i.B_{ij} = R.B_{ij}$, $1 \le j \le k_i$, that is, $c_{ij} = \{R_i.B_{ij}, R.B_{ij}\}$, $1 \le j \le k_i$, $1 \le i \le m$.

hitting set H with K elements, we can construct a single-clause spanning tree of QG_q by associating one clause $\{R.X, R_i.X\}$ with each edge where $X \in H \cap C_i$. (Note that if H includes more than one element from a subset C_i, we arbitrarily choose one element as the attribute in the corresponding clause.) The cost of this tree is at most $\|\mathscr{C}\| + \text{K}$. Thus, the special case is NP-hard. It follows that our problem is also NP-hard. □

The above theorem says that it is already hard when only considering the query, rather than its closure. The next theorem shows that the same result holds for the query's closure.

THEOREM 4. *Problem (MRP) is NP-complete for star queries.*

PROOF. We adopt the cost formula in Theorem 3 and again transform the hitting set problem to the current problem; that is, we must show that there is an ss tree of QG_{q+} with cost $\|\mathscr{C}\| + \text{K}$ iff there is a hitting set with K elements.

(1) If. This follows from the proof in Theorem 3 since there would then be an ss tree of QG_q with cost $\|\mathscr{C}\| + \text{K}$. That tree would also be an ss tree of QG_{q+}.
(2) Only if. Let $\mathscr{T}$ be an ss tree of QG_{q+} with cost $\|\mathscr{C}\| + \text{K}$. We construct an ss tree of QG_q with the same or less cost. The proof in Theorem 3 then implies the existence of a hitting set of $\mathscr{C}$ with at most K elements.

Observe that the cost of any ss tree in QG_{q+} or QG_q is the sum of the number of distinct attributes touching each node. Let us make the distinguished relation R be the root of the given ss tree $\mathscr{T}$. Let the nodes of depth 1 in $\mathscr{T}$ be the neighbors of R. In general, the nodes of depth i, $i \ge 1$, in $\mathscr{T}$ will be those whose shortest simple path to R contains i edges. Now, for each attribute X, we reconnect edges by the following steps. As a result, certain nodes that were not neighbors of R will become R's neighbors.

For each clause $\{R_{k1}.X, R_{k2}.X\}$ that connects the depth $i + 1$ node R_{k1} to the depth i ($i \geq 1$) node R_{k2} (we know that the two nodes share a common attribute, here X, by the construction of q and the definition of redundancy),

—eliminate that clause and its corresponding edge;
—create the edge $\{R_{k1}, R\}$, associating the edge with $\{R_{k1}.X, R.X\}$. (We know that q has $\{R_{k1}.X, R.X\}$ and $\{R_{k2}.X, R.X\}$, because q and qt are equivalent and $\{R_{k_1}.X, R_{k_2}.X\}$ could not be inferred from q otherwise.)

Two cases may arise.

Case 1. There is already a clause connecting to R using attribute X. So, the nodecost of R does not change, and the nodecost of R_{k_1} may or may not decrease, but certainly will not increase.

Case 2. There is no clause connecting to R using attribute X. Therefore, some edge in the path from R_{k_2} to R does not have X on it; say the edge from R_{k_3} to R_{k_4} is the first one. In that case, removing the edges leading to R_{k_3} that contain a clause with attribute X will reduce the nodecost of R_{k_3} by one. At most, the nodecost of R can increase by one, so the cost of the resulting tree cannot increase.

We perform such reconnections for each attribute in turn, so that each node other than R in the resulting tree is connected only to R by a single clause in q. Thus, the resulting tree is an ss tree of QG_q. Furthermore, since the reconnections for each attribute do not increase any cost, the cost of the ss tree will be at most $\| \mathscr{C} \| + K$. □

Because stars are subcases of trees and general graphs, we obtain the following immediately.

COROLLARY 1. *Problem (MRP) is NP-complete for tree queries.*

COROLLARY 2. *Problem (MRP) is NP-complete for general graph queries.*

The results obtained so far give us a picture for various queries shown in Figure 8.[10] These results are discouraging as they indicate that even for simple queries, an enumerative algorithm must be used to find the optimal join strategy. In the next section, we develop heuristics that approximate the optimal solution while having a polynomial time complexity.

6. HEURISTIC ALGORITHMS

Our general approach to processing a complex query is as follows. Given a query q, we first construct the query graph of its closure, QG_{q+}. We then

[10] *Closed tree queries* in the figure are defined in a similar way as closed chain queries; namely, they refer to tree queries whose closures are trees. As the reader may have noticed, the construction of QG_q in Theorem 3 implies that QG_{q+} may contain a cycle. This then raises an interesting question as to whether there exists a polynomial time algorithm for closed tree queries. The problem remains open and deserves further investigation.

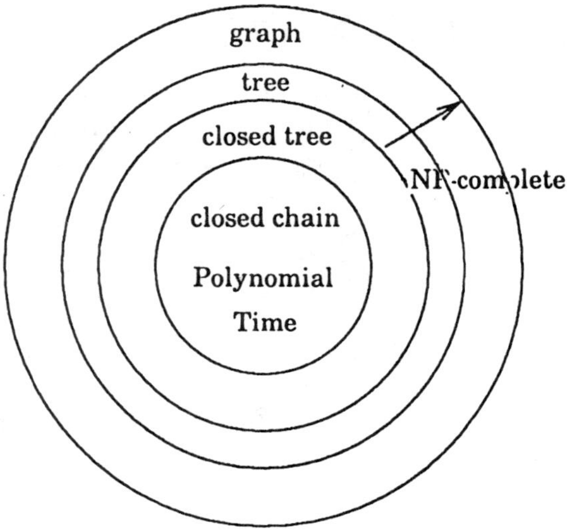

Fig. 8. Complexity of problem MRP for various queries. Note that the problem of finding the best join strategy for queries whose closure is a tree (closed trees) remains open.

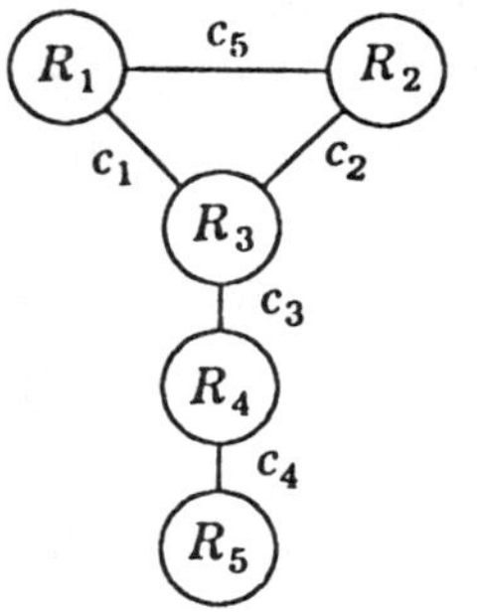

$c_1 = \{R_1.A,\ R_3.C\}$
$c_2 = \{R_2.B,\ R_3.C\}$
$c_3 = \{R_3.D,\ R_4.E\}$
$c_4 = \{R_4.F,\ R_5.G\}$
$c_5 = \{R_1.A,\ R_2.B\}$

Fig. 9. Initial query graph for heuristics examples.

Table III. Data for the Heuristic Examples

i	1	2	3	4	5
		Cardinality of Relation			
$\lvert R_i \rvert$	10	60	95	30	50
		Tuple Size			
$\lvert t_{R_i} \rvert$	4	4	3	1	5

Note. Initially, part$(R_i) = X$, $1 \le i \le 5$. Selectivity factor between any two relations is 0.02.

apply the algorithms developed in this section to construct a clause string from the graph. The behavior of the heuristics is analyzed in Section 7. One of our heuristics is a consistent generalization of algorithm CHAIN in the sense that an optimal solution will be found if q is a closed chain.

For each algorithm, a numerical example and graphical description are given based on the query graph in Figure 9 and data presented in Table III.

6.1 Kruskal Heuristic

The Kruskal heuristic (KH) is a greedy strategy similar to Kruskal's algorithm [20] for finding a minimum cost spanning tree from a weighted graph. Each time a lowest cost clause, say $\{R.A, S.B\}$, is selected; the two nodes R

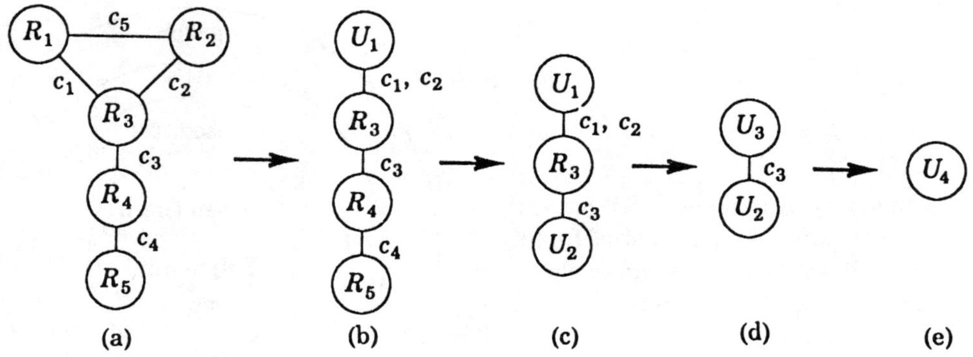

Fig. 10. Query graph reduction by algorithm KH.

and S are then collapsed to a single node U. Since U represents the join result of R and S, its cardinality with be $|R| \times |S| \times \alpha$, where α is the selectivity factor between R and S, and the width of its tuples is $|t_R| + |t_S|$. The partition attributes of U are calculated as follows:

(1) If R needs to be repartitioned (such a repartitioning destroys the original partition attributes of R), set newpart(R) to $\{A\}$; otherwise newpart(R) = part(R).
(2) Similarly, if S needs to be repartitioned, set newpart(S) to $\{B\}$; otherwise newpart(S) = part(S).
(3) part(U) = newpart(R) $\cup$ newpart(S).

The algorithm repeats the above steps until the query graph becomes a single node.

Since clauses on an edge share common relations, it is likely that many clauses have the same minimum cost. The essence of the algorithm is to assign a *number value* to each clause $\{R.A, S.B\}$, where number($\{R.A, S.B\}$) is defined as the total number of clauses on distinct edges (after collapsing R and S) that have $R.A$ or $S.B$ as a component attribute. Among the clauses with the same minimum cost, the algorithm selects among those with the largest number value. Performing a join on such a clause is good, because its two component attributes become the partition attributes of the new node and other clauses may be able to exploit them.

Example 4. Figure 10 shows the application of algorithm KH to the query graph in Figure 9. First, since both $\{R_1.A, R_2.B\}$ and $\{R_4.F, R_5.G\}$ have the lowest cost, 840, and number($\{R_1.A, R_2.B\}$) = 1 > number($\{R_4.F, R_5.G\}$) = 0, $\{R_1.A, R_2.B\}$ is selected. R_1 and R_2 are collapsed to U_1 (Figure 10b). We get $|U_1| = 12$; $|t_{U_1}| = 8$; part(U_1) = $\{A, B\}$. Next, $\{R_4.F, R_5.G\}$ is selected. R_4 and R_5 are collapsed to U_2 (Figure 10c). We get $|U_2| = 30$; $|t_{U_2}| = 6$; part(U_2) = $\{F, G\}$. Then, since both $\{R_1.A, R_3.C\}$ and $\{R_2.B, R_3.C\}$ have cost 951 and number value 0, we arbitrarily choose one,

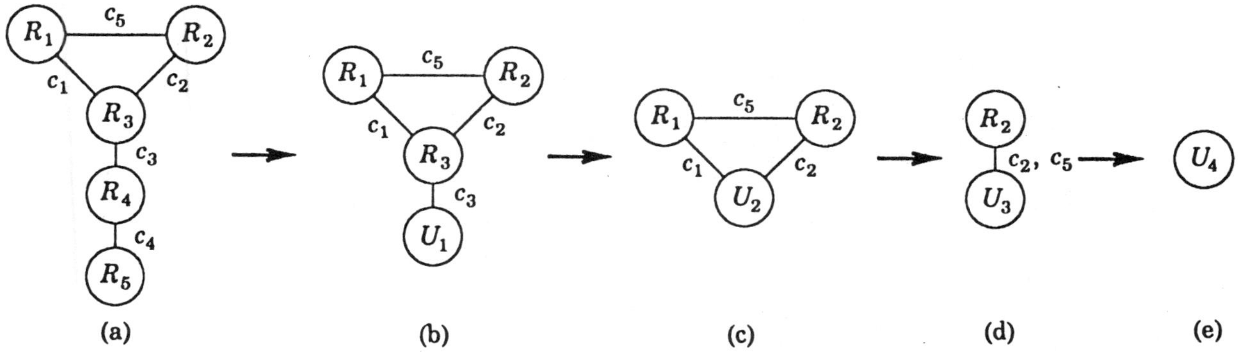

Fig. 11. Query graph reduction by algorithm PH.

say $\{R_1.A,\ R_3.C\}$. U_1 and R_3 are collapsed to U_3 (Figure 10d). We get $|U_3| \approx 22$; $|t_{U_3}| = 11$; part(U_3) = $\{A, B, C\}$. Finally, the clause $\{R_3.D,\ R_4.E\}$ with cost 1266 is selected. The string produced by the algorithm is $\{R_1.A,\ R_2.B\}\{R_4.F,\ R_5.G\}\{R_1.A,\ R_3.C\}\{R_3.D,\ R_4.E\}$ and the cost is 840 + 840 + 951 + 1266 = 3897.

6.2 Prim Heuristic

The Prim heuristic (PH) is similar to Prim's algorithm [23] for finding a minimum cost spanning tree from a weighted graph. At each step, a node in the graph is designated as a "pivot." (Heuristically, the initial pivot is a relation of smallest size.) The algorithm considers only the clauses that are on the edges connected to the pivot and selects a clause, say $\{R.A,\ S.B\}$, with the lowest cost and largest number value. R and S are then collapsed to a single node U. U becomes the new pivot, and its size and partition attributes are calculated as described previously. The algorithm repeats the above steps until the graph is reduced to a single node.

Example 5. Figure 11 shows the application of algorithm PH to the query graph in Figure 9. Initially, pivot = R_4. The clause $\{R_4.F,\ R_5.G\}$ with cost 840 is selected. R_4 and R_5 are collapsed to U_1 (Figure 11b). We get $|U_1| = 30$; $|t_{U_1}| = 6$; part(U_1) = $\{F, G\}$. The pivot becomes U_1. Next, $\{R_3.D,\ R_4.E\}$ with cost 1395 is selected. U_1 and R_3 are collapsed to U_2 (Figure 11c). We get $|U_2| = 57$; $|t_{U_2}| = 9$; part(U_2) = $\{D, E\}$; pivot = U_2. Then $\{R_1.A,\ R_3.C\}$ with cost 1659 is selected. U_2 and R_1 are collapsed to U_3 (Figure 11d). We get $|U_3| \approx 11$; $|t_{U_3}| = 13$; part(U_3) = $\{A, C\}$; pivot = U_3. Finally, since both $\{R_1.A,\ R_2.B\}$ and $\{R_2.B,\ R_3.C\}$ have cost 863 and number value 0, we arbitrarily choose one, say $\{R_1.A,\ R_2.B\}$. The string produced by the algorithm is $\{R_4.R,\ R_5.G\}\{R_3.D,\ R_4.E\}\{R_1.A,\ R_3.C\}\{R_1.A,\ R_2.B\}$ and the cost is 840 + 1395 + 1659 + 863 = 4757.

6.3 Hybrid Heuristics

A given graph may have several chains, that is, paths on which all nodes except the (distinct) endpoints (referred to as boundaries) are connected with

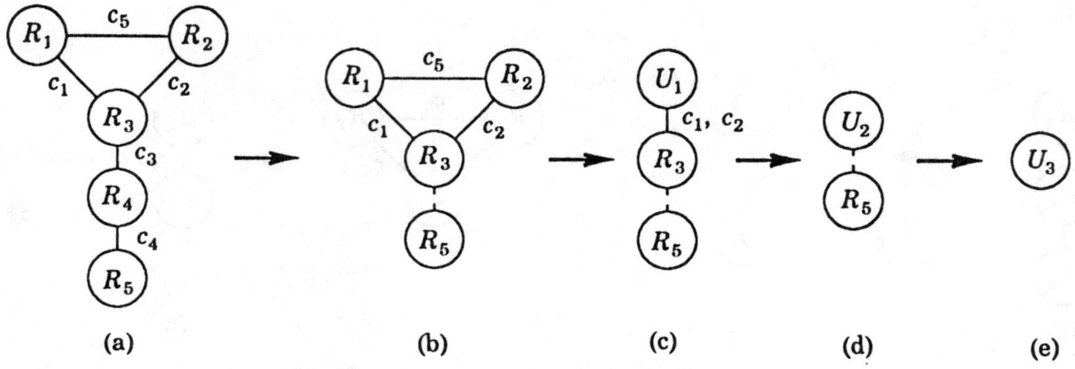

Fig. 12. Query graph reduction by algorithm HKH; dashed line represents generalized clause.

exactly two other nodes. It may be beneficial to process these chains based on algorithm CHAIN while applying the previous heuristics to the remaining part of the graph. This is also intuitively reasonable because by so doing, the optimal solution can be achieved when the given graph is a closed chain.

The algorithm first replaces each chain with a generalized clause. The component attributes of the generalized clause are the partition attributes of the boundaries after executing the chain's minimum cost string, and the cost of it is given by that of the string, which is calculated (by algorithm CHAIN) as a function of the sizes and partition attributes of the boundaries. Notice that, because it depends on the current sizes and partition attributes of a chain's boundaries, the generalized clause may vary during the execution of the algorithm (see the example below).

The algorithm then simulates algorithm KH or PH on the resulting graph. (The former is referred to as algorithm HKH, and the latter as HPH). During the course of execution, if a generalized clause is selected, its corresponding chain is collapsed to a single node. Since several chains may share the same two boundaries, collapsing one of them may cause the generalized clauses of the other chains to become self-loops in the query graph. When the algorithm detects this situation, it removes the loops, putting back nodes on their corresponding chains into the graph.

Example 6. Figure 12 shows the application of algorithm HKH to the query graph in Figure 9. First, the chain $\{\{R_3, R_4\}, \{R_4, R_5\}\}$ is replaced by the generalized clause $\{R_3.D, R_5.\perp\}$ with cost 2235, where $\perp$ indicates that after executing the minimum cost string $\{R_4.F, R_5.G\}\{R_4.E, R_3.D\}$, part($R_5$) is empty (Figure 12b). Next, the clause $\{R_1.A, R_2.B\}$ with cost 840 is selected. R_1 and R_2 are collapsed to U_1 (Figure 12c). We get $|U_1| = 12$; $|t_{U_1}| = 8$; part(U_1) = $\{A, B\}$. Then, since both $\{R_1.A, R_3.C\}$ and $\{R_2.B, R_3.C\}$ have cost 951 and number value 0, we arbitrarily pick one, say $\{R_2.B, R_3.C\}$. U_1 and R_3 are collapsed to U_2 (Figure 12d). We get $|U_2| \approx 22$; $|t_{U_2}| = 11$; part(U_2) = $\{A, B, C\}$. Since the size of one of the boundaries of the chain is changed, the generalized clause now becomes $\{R_3.\perp, R_5.G\}$ with cost 2034. Finally, U_2 and R_5 are collapsed to U_3 (Figure 12e). The string produced by the algorithm is $\{R_1.A, R_2.B\}\{R_2.B, R_3.C\}\{R_3.D, R_4.E\}\{R_4.F, R_5.G\}$ and the cost is 840 + 951 + 2034 = 3825.

7. PERFORMANCE ANALYSIS

In this section we discuss experiments to compare the results produced by each heuristic with the optimums obtained from exhaustive search and evaluate the relative performance of these heuristics.

7.1 Experimental Parameters

Parameters used in the experiments can be classified into two categories: those related to databases and those specific to a query graph.

(1) *Database-Dependent Parameters*

$\|R\|$	Number of tuples in relation R
$\|t_R\|$	Width (in bytes) of a tuple in R
part(R)	Initial partition attribute of R
$\alpha_{R,S}$	Join selectivity factor between relations R and S.

(2) *Query-Dependent Parameters*

$\|QG\|$	Size (in number of nodes) of a query graph QG
$\|cn\|$	Size (in number of nodes) of a chain in the graph (including boundaries)
Num	Number of chains in the graph
$\|\text{clauses}(e, QG)\|$	Number of clauses on edge e in the graph.

To construct a query graph, we used a random-number generator to produce edges between nodes and to choose nodes in chains. Clauses on edges were also generated randomly and join attributes were drawn randomly from the range A to D. Such a range was chosen because in actual applications, relations generally contain no more than this number of join attributes, even in a fairly complex query.[11] After generating a query graph, we used its closure as a test graph for the algorithms.

In all the experiments presented here, the constants α and β for processing cost and repartitioning cost (cf. Definition 2) were fixed at 1 and 2, respectively. In fact, the constants have little effect on the relative behavior of our algorithms. In further experiments, we ran the algorithms with various constants (e.g., with $\alpha = 1$, $\beta = 10$; $\alpha = 10$, $\beta = 1$, etc.). It was found that both the relative performance of the heuristics and their performance relative to optimums are insensitive to these parameters.

7.2 Heuristic Performance Relative to Optimal Value

Suppose there are m spanning trees for a given graph, named $T_1, T_2, \ldots, T_m$, and edges in T_j, $1 \le j \le m$, are denoted by e_i^j, $1 \le i \le |QG| - 1$. The

[11] Part(R) used in the experiments was drawn randomly from the range A to G, as relations may not be partitioned on any of their join attributes initially.

Table IV. Heuristic Performance/Optimal Performance

	KH		PH		HKH		HPH	
Size of graph	Mean	Variance	Mean	Variance	Mean	Variance	Mean	Variance
6	1.04	0.00628	1.09	0.01292	1.02	0.01314	1.06	0.00823
7	1.05	0.01034	1.10	0.01125	1.04	0.00909	1.07	0.00931
8	1.07	0.01045	1.09	0.01296	1.05	0.00825	1.08	0.00911
9	1.06	0.01172	1.10	0.01325	1.04	0.00877	1.08	0.01175
10	1.09	0.01188	1.12	0.01475	1.08	0.00984	1.11	0.00928
11	1.08	0.01081	1.11	0.01407	1.07	0.00866	1.09	0.01318
12	1.10	0.01562	1.13	0.01368	1.08	0.02182	1.11	0.01236

Notes. (1) Query parameters: Number of chains = 1; chain size = $k \times$ graph size, where k was drawn from [1/2, 2/3]; number of clauses on an edge was drawn from [1, 3].

(2) Database parameters: Relation's cardinality was drawn from $[1 \times 10^a, 2 \times 10^a]$, where a can vary; tuple's width was drawn from [1, 10]; selectivity factor from $[0.1 \times 10^{-a}, 1 \times 10^{-a}]$; part($R$) from $[A, G]$.

number of clause strings that need to be examined by exhaustive search is

$$\prod_{j=1}^{m} \left\{ \left(\prod_{i=1}^{|QG|-1} |\text{clauses}(e_i^j, QG)| \right) \times (|QG| - 1)! \right\}.$$

As can be seen from the formula, the price paid for examining all possible strings becomes prohibitively high when the size of a graph is large. To keep the experiments manageable, the data were drawn from the following moderate ranges.[12] $|QG|$ was ranged from 6 to 12, Num was fixed at 1, $|cn|$ was drawn from the range [1/2, 2/3] of $|QG|$, $|R|$ was drawn from the range $[1 \times 10^a, 2 \times 10^a]$, $|t_R|$ from the range [1, 10], and $|\text{clauses}(e, QG)|$ from the range [1, 3] for any edge e in the graph. The selectivity factor between each two relations was drawn from the range $[0.1 \times 10^{-a}, 1 \times 10^{-a}]$. Special care was taken to generate the selectivity factors to ensure that joining nodes in different order yields the same size result.

The experimental results are summarized in Table IV. Each mean in the table represents the average value of the relative costs obtained by applying an algorithm to ten test graphs. A relative cost is the quotient of the solution's cost of the algorithm divided by the optimum. The means show that all the algorithms have satisfactory performance for random spanning trees and low selectivity factors, and in many situations, algorithms KH and HKH seem a bit superior to the other two algorithms. In addition, the small variances for each algorithm indicate that the algorithms exhibit consistent behavior.

7.3 Effect of Database Parameters

The purpose of this subsection is to analyze the effect of varying the database-dependent parameters on the relative performance of the heuristic

[12] In the sequel, "a parameter was drawn from the range $[a, b]$" actually means that the parameter was drawn randomly from a uniform distribution with the range $[a, b]$.

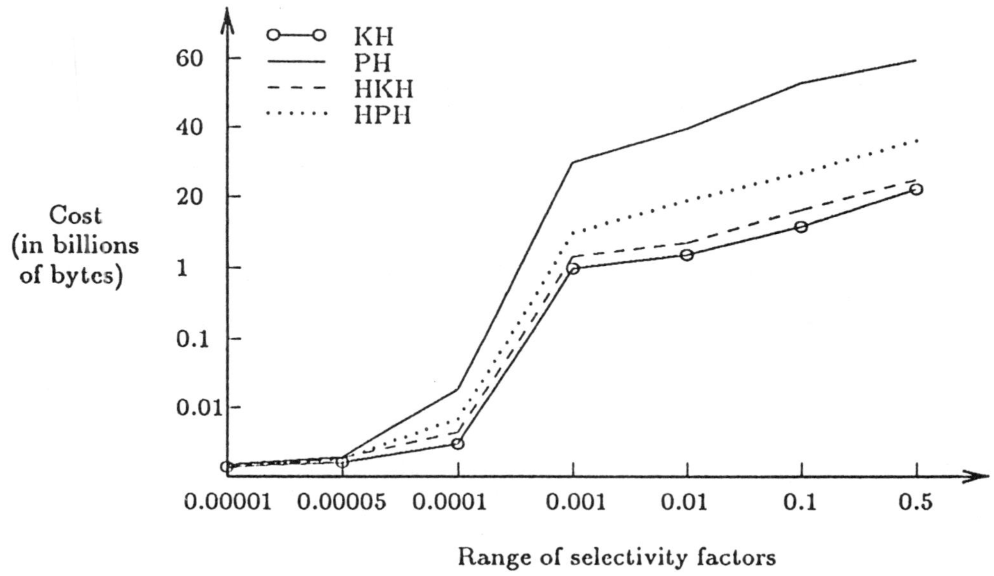

Fig. 13. Effect of selectivity factors (relation's cardinality was drawn from [10,000, 20,000], tuple's width from [1, 10], graph size = 12, chain numbers = 2, chain size = 4, number of clauses on an edge = 2).

procedures. To avoid the mutual influence of parameters, the analysis was carried out by fixing the parameters related to query graphs, which were set as follows: $|QG| = 12$, $Num = 2$, $|cn| = 4$, $|\text{clauses}(e, QG)| = 2$ for any edge e in QG. The chains have been included in order to distinguish the simple heuristics from their hybrid counterparts.

Figure 13 illustrates the behavior of the algorithms for varying join selectivity factors.[13] Examining the figure, we see that all the heuristics have close behavior for low selectivity factors ($\alpha_{R,S} \leq 0.00005$).

Notice also that algorithm PH deteriorates significantly as the selectivity factors increase. When selectivity factors are high, the more nodes are joined, the larger the pivot becomes. Consequently, joining the pivot with even more nodes will incur an intolerable cost.

Figure 14 shows the effect of varying the relation sizes on the relative performance of the algorithms. The figure shows clearly that algorithm PH becomes unattractive when the sizes of relations increase.

7.4 Effect of Query Parameters

The main distinction between the hybrid heuristics and simple ones lies in the way they handle chains. The objective of this subsection is to explore the effect of varying chains in a query graph on the behavior of the heuristics. The following parameters' values were assumed throughout the experiments: $|R|$ was drawn from the range [100, 1,000,000], $|t_R|$ was drawn from [1, 10], $\alpha_{R,S}$ was fixed at 0.1, and $|\text{clauses}(e, QG)|$ was fixed at 2.

[13] In subsequent experiments, ten query graphs were tested for each algorithm and the average value of the solutions' costs produced by each algorithm was plotted.

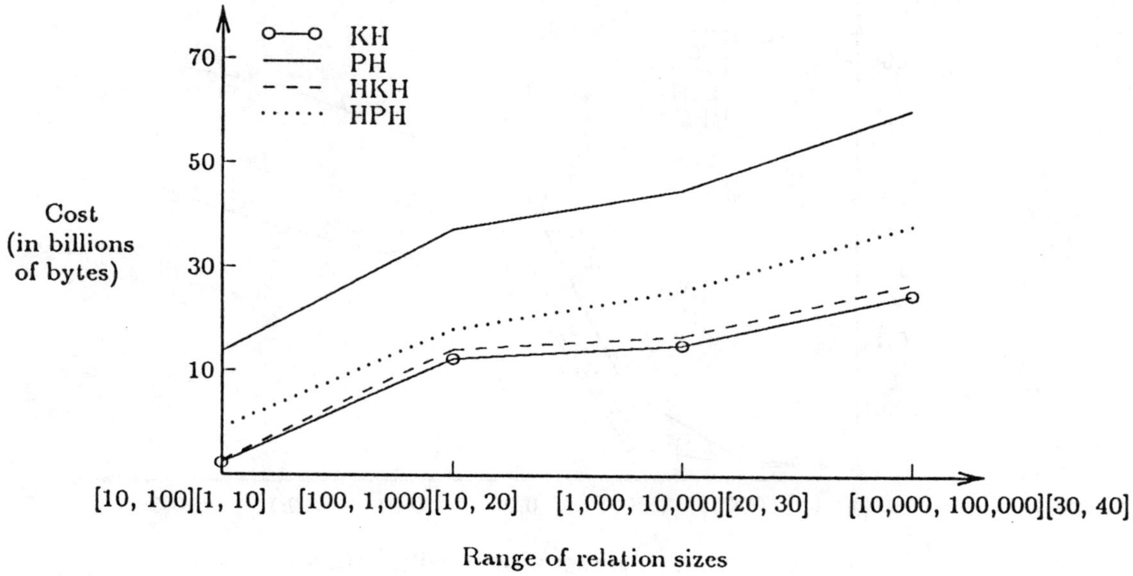

Fig. 14. Impact of relation size, where relation size = relation's cardinality × tuple's width (the first item of each label on the *x* axis gives the range of relation's cardinality and the second item gives the range of tuple's width; selectivity factor = 0.1, graph size = 12, chain numbers = 2, chain size = 4, number of clauses on an edge = 2).

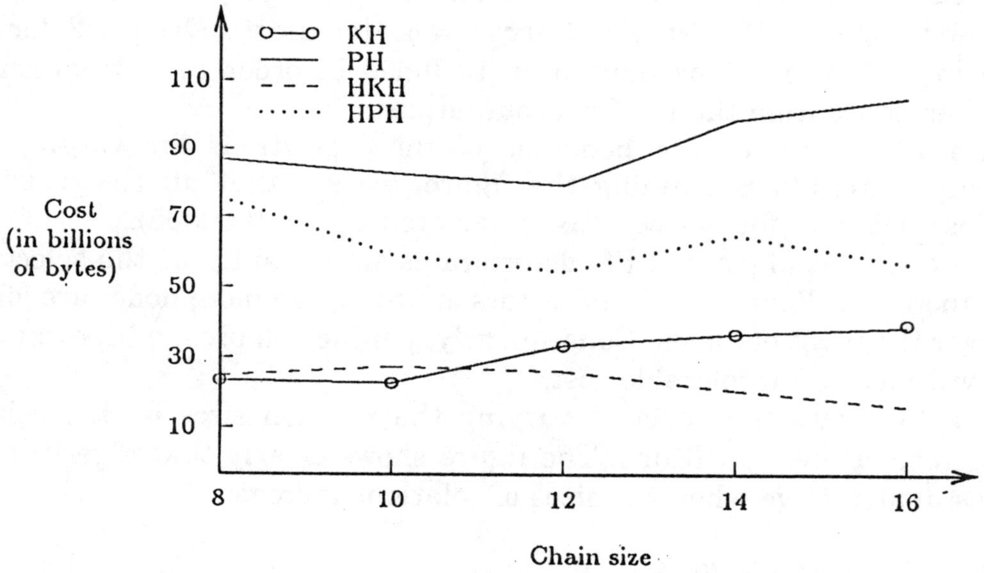

Fig. 15. Cost of heuristics as a function of chain size (graph size = 20, number of chains = 1, selectivity factor = 0.1, number of clauses on an edge = 2, relation's cardinality was drawn from [100, 1,000,000], tuple's width from [1, 10]).

Figure 15 shows the effect of changing the chain size in a graph, where the size of the graph was fixed at 20 and *Num* at 1. It is apparent that as the chain becomes a major portion of a graph, the hybrid heuristics become better than the simple ones. One expects this because the hybrid heuristics guaran-

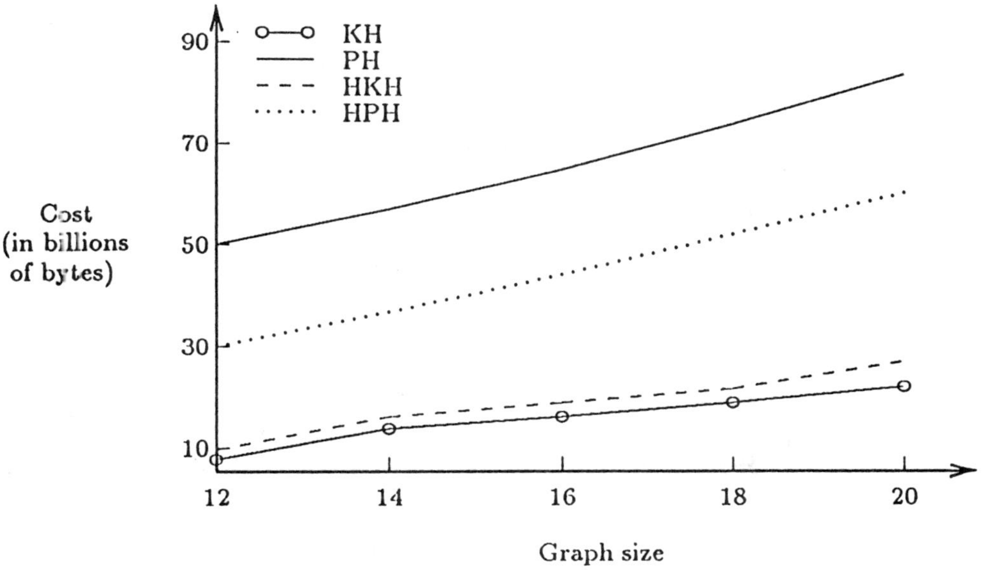

Fig. 16. Cost of heuristics as a function of graph size (chain size = 1/2 × graph size, number of chains = 1, selectivity factor = 0.1, number of clauses on an edge = 2, relation's cardinality was drawn from [100, 1,000,000], tuple's width from [1, 10]).

tee that an optimal solution can be achieved on a chain. The poor performance of algorithm PH when the chain size becomes large is due to the way it picks clauses, which is limited by its inherently local view. This situation tends to be worse if it starts searching inside a chain—very few choices can be made in determining which of the clauses should be picked at each step.

On the other hand, the size of a graph has very little impact on the performance of the heuristics. Figure 16 illustrates the effect of varying the size of a graph while fixing the portion of the chain in it (this portion was fixed at 1/2). It is clear that increasing only the graph size does not affect the relative performance of the heuristics—the gaps between these algorithms remain and gradually become larger.

Figure 17 shows the effect of varying the number of chains in a graph (where $|QG|$ was fixed at 20 and $|cn|$ at 4). Although the number of chains also influences the performance of the hybrid heuristics, it has a less significant effect than the size of a chain. The big gap between algorithms HPH and KH (HKH) may be due to the fact that the chosen size of chains is too small, as compared with that of the whole graph. Notice that there is a slight increase of the gap between algorithms HKH and KH when the number of chains is 4. This indicates that the existence of many short chains in a graph can have a negative effect on the performance of algorithm HKH. A possible explanation for this is that these chains decrease the number of nonchain edges in the graph and consequently restrict the total number of choices that can be made when globally picking a clause.

In conclusion, when selectivity factors are low, the proposed heuristics have close performance. In the presence of high selectivity factors, algorithm PH becomes less competitive while algorithm KH (and HKH) remain good. If

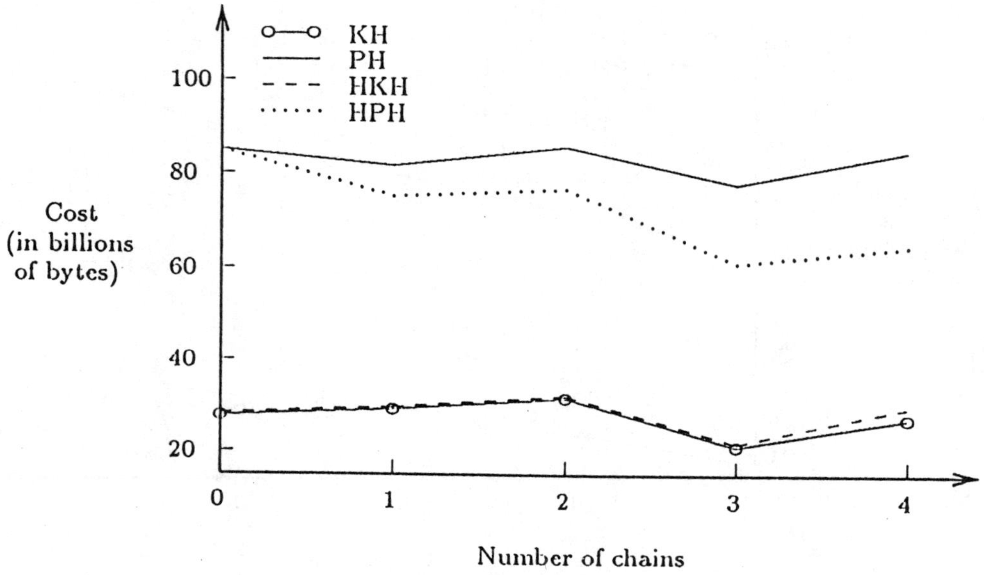

Fig. 17. Cost of heuristics as a function of number of chains (graph size = 20, chain size = 4, selectivity factor = 0.1, number of clauses on an edge = 2, relation's cardinality was drawn from [100, 1,000,000], tuple's width from [1, 10]).

a graph contains long chains (with size being over half of the number of nodes in the graph), we suggest to use the hybrid Kruskal heuristic (HKH).

8. SUMMARY

In this paper, we investigated ways of minimizing response time for various important queries in loosely coupled multiprocessor systems using a hash-partitioned data distribution scheme. First, we developed a dynamic programming algorithm for closed chain queries. Next, we proved the NP-completeness for more general queries and proposed four heuristics for them. Our simulation results show that an algorithm similar to Kruskal's spanning tree algorithm performs well when chains in a query graph are small. When chains are long, then a hybrid algorithm using the chain algorithm with Kruskal's is best.

Like other relevant work [15, 25], the heuristics presented in the paper relied on the knowledge of selectivity factors, which were used to find out the sizes of intermediate results. This information, however, is not known a priori in actual environments.[14] Fortunately, our qualitative conclusions were independent of the selectivity factors.

Our results have all assumed that relations were partitioned on a single attribute. Generalizing beyond this is not difficult. For example, consider a join between R and S based on the clauses $\{\{R.A, S.C\}, \{R.B, S.D\}\}$, where R is partitioned on A and S on C. One can process the join based on

[14]A practical approach would be to estimate the selectivity factors like those used in most real systems (see, e.g., [26]). Readers may also refer to Gardy and Puech [13] and Lipton and Naughton [21] for theoretical analyses of the sizes of intermediate relations.

$\{R.A, S.C\}$, treating $\{R.B, S.D\}$ as a selection condition. On the other hand, if the join were based on $\{R.A, S.C\}$ and R were partitioned on AB and S on CD, both relations would have to be repartitioned to A and C, respectively. Therefore, the set of repartitionings required when R is partitioned on A alone is always a subset of those required when R is partitioned on AB. To handle multiattribute partitions, we can treat the partition attributes (e.g., AB) as if they were a single attribute. Thus, to perform the join having clauses $\{R.A, S.C\}$, $\{R.B, S.D\}$, and $\{R.E, S.F\}$, given AB and CD as partition attributes, we process $\{\{R.A, S.C\}, \{R.B, S.D\}\}$ and use $\{R.E, S.F\}$ as a selection condition.

We have not discussed the possibility of using multiple copies of relations, perhaps partitioned on different attributes. Often, keeping multiple copies at each node reduces the cost of repartitionings considerably. As an example, consider again the suppliers-and-parts database and SQL query presented in Section 1. Suppose one copy of SUP is partitioned on s#, one copy of PART on p#, one copy of SUP-PART on s#, and another copy of SUP-PART on p#. When repartitioning T_2 to SUP-PART.p#, instead of sending its complete tuples, the second strategy could send the *surrogates* [8] of tuples in SUP-PART, along with the complete tuples in SUP. These surrogates would then be materialized at each node by consulting the local fragment of SUP-PART that is partitioned on p#. Suppose sending surrogates takes 10 seconds. Then the cost of this scheme would be 100 + 10 + 100 = 210 seconds, which achieves a significant improvement over the original scheme. Investigating how queries can be optimized in such a highly parallel environment with replicated data seems to be a very interesting problem for future research.

ACKNOWLEDGMENTS

The authors are deeply indebted to the anonymous referees and the editor, Won Kim, for their encouragement and thoughtful recommendations. They also wish to thank Richard Cole, Zvi Kedem, Bud Mishra, and Paul Spirakis for helpful discussions in the formative stages of this work.

REFERENCES

1. APERS, P. M. G., HEVNER, A. R., AND YAO, S. B. Optimization algorithms for distributed queries. *IEEE Trans. Softw. Eng. SE-9*, 1 (Jan. 1983), 57–68.
2. BABB, E. Implementing a relational database by means of specialized hardware. *ACM Trans. Database Syst. 4*, 1 (Mar. 1979), 1–29.
3. BERNSTEIN, P. A., GOODMAN, N., WONG, E., CHRISTOPHER, L. R. AND ROTHNIE, J. B., JR. Query processing is a system for distributed databases (SDD-1). *ACM Trans. Database Syst. 6*, 4 (Dec. 1981), 602–625.
4. BITTON, D., BORAL, H., DEWITT, D. J., AND WILKINSON, W. K. Parallel algorithms for the execution of relational database operations. *ACM Trans. Database Syst. 8*, 3 (Sept. 1983) 324–353.
5. CHEN, A. L. P., AND LI, V. O. K. An optimal algorithm for processing distributed star queries. *IEEE Trans. Softw. Eng. SE-11*, 10 (Oct. 1985), 1097–1107.
6. CHIU, D. M., BERNSTEIN, P. A., AND HO, Y. C. Optimizing chain queries in a distributed database system. *SIAM J. Comput. 13*, 1 (Feb. 1984), 116–134.
7. CHIU, D. M., AND HO, Y. C. A methodology for interpreting tree queries into optimal

semi-join expressions. In *Proceedings of the ACM-SIGMOD International Conference on the Management of Data* (May 1980). ACM, New York, 1980, pp. 169–178.

8. Codd, E. F. Extending the database relational model to capture more meaning. *ACM Trans. Database Syst. 4*, 4 (Dec. 1979), 397–434.
9. Copeland, G., Alexander, W., Boughter, E., and Keller, T. Data placement in Bubba. In *Proceedings of the ACM-SIGMOD International Conference on the Management of Data* (1988). ACM, New York, 1988, pp. 99–108.
10. DeWitt, D. J., and Gerber, R. Multiprocessor hash-based join algorithms. In *Proceedings of the 11th International Conference on Very Large Data Bases* (Stockholm, Aug. 1985), pp. 151–164.
11. DeWitt, D. J., Gerber, R. H., Graefe, G., Heytens, M. L., Kumar, K. B., and Muralikrishna, M. GAMMA—A high performance dataflow database machine. In *Proceedings of the 12th International Conference on Very Large Data Bases* (Kyoto, Japan, Aug. 1986), pp. 228–237.
12. DeWitt, D. J., Smith, M., and Boral, H. A single user performance evaluation of the Teradata Database Machine. MCC Tech. Rep. DB-081-87, 1987.
13. Gardy, D., and Puech, C. On the effect of join operations on relation sizes. *ACM Trans. Database Syst. 14*, 4 (Dec. 1989), 574–603.
14. Garey, M. R., and Johnson, D. S. *Computers and Intractability – A Guide to the Theory of NP-Completeness*. Freeman, San Francisco, Calif., 1979.
15. Gavish, B., and Segev, A. Set query optimization in distributed database systems. *ACM Trans. Database Syst. 11*, 3 (Sept. 1986), 265–293.
16. Goodman, N., and Shmueli, O. Tree queries: A simple class of relational queries. *ACM Trans. Database Syst.* 7, 4 (Dec. 1982), 653–677.
17. Kim, W. A new way to compute the product and join of relations. In *Proceedings of the ACM-SIGMOD International Conference on the Management of Data* (Santa Monica, Calif., May 1980). ACM, New York, 1980, pp. 179–187.
18. Kitsuregawa, M., Tanaka, H., and Moto-oka, T. Relational algebra machine GRACE. In *RIMS Symposium on Software Science and Engineering* (1982). *Lecture Notes in Computer Science*. Springer-Verlag, New York, 1983, pp. 191–212.
19. Kitsuregawa, M., et al. Application of hash to data base machine and its architecture. *New Generation Comput. 1* (1983), 62–74.
20. Kruskal, J. B., Jr. On the shortest spanning subtree of a graph and the traveling salesman problem. *Proc. Amer. Math. Soc.* 7, 1 (1956), 48–50.
21. Lipton, R. J., and Naughton, J. F. Query size estimation by adaptive sampling. In *Proceedings of the 9th ACM SIGACT-SIGMOD-SIGART Symposium on Principles of Database Systems* (Apr. 1990). ACM, New York, 1990, pp. 40–46.
22. Pramanik, S., and Vineyard, D. Optimizing join queries in distributed databases. *IEEE Trans. Softw. Eng. 14*, 9 (Sept. 1988), 1319–1326.
23. Prim, R. C. Shortest connection networks and some generalizations. *Bell Syst. Tech. J.* (1957), 1389–1401.
24. Sacco, G. M. Fragmentation: A technique for efficient query processing. *ACM Trans. Database Syst. 11*, 2 (Jun. 1986), 113–133.
25. Segev, A. Optimization of join operations in horizontally partitioned database systems. *ACM Trans. Database Syst. 11*, 1 (Mar. 1986), 48–80.
26. Selinger, P. G., Astrahan, M. M., Chamberlin, D. D., Lorie, R. A., and Price, T. G. Access path selection in a relational database system. In *Proceedings of the ACM-SIGMOD International Conference on the Management of Data* (Boston, Mass., May 1979). ACM, New York, 1979, pp. 23–34.
27. Shapiro, L. Join processing in database systems with large main memories. *ACM Trans. Database Syst. 11*, 3 (Sept. 1986), 239–264.
28. Shasha, D. Query processing in a symmetric parallel environment. In *Proceedings of the Advanced Database Symposium* (Tokyo, Japan, Aug. 1986), pp. 183–192.
29. Shasha, D., and Spirakis, P. Fast parallel algorithms for processing of joins. In *Proceedings of the International Conference on Supercomputing* (Athens, Greece, June 1987).

30. Stamos, J. W., and Young, H. C. A symmetric fragment and replicate algorithm for distributed joins. Res. Rep. RJ7188, IBM Corp., San Jose, Dec. 1989.
31. Stonebraker, M., and Neuhold, E. A distributed database version of INGRES. In *Proceedings of the 3rd Berkeley Workshop on Distributed Data Management and Computer Networks* (May 1977).
32. Sun, W., Meng, W., and Yu, C. Query optimization in object-oriented database systems. Unpublished manuscript, Department of Electrical Engineering and Computer Science, University of Illinois at Chicago, 1990.
33. Teradata Corporation. Database computer system concepts and facilities. Document C02-0001-01, Teradata Corporation, Los Angeles, Oct. 1984.
34. Valduriez, P., and Gardarin, G. Join and semijoin algorithms for a multiprocessor database machine. *ACM Trans. Database Syst. 9*, 1 (Mar. 1984), 133-161.
35. William, R., et al. R*: An overview of the architecture. Res. Rep. RJ3325, IBM Corp., San Jose, Dec. 1981.
36. Wong, E. Dynamic rematerialization: Processing distributed queries using redundant data. *IEEE Trans. Softw. Eng. SE-9*, 3 (May 1983), 228-232.
37. Yu, C. T., Ozsoyoglu, M. Z., and Lam, K. Distributed query optimization for tree queries. *J. Comput. Syst. Sci. 29* (1984), 409-445.
38. Yu, C. T., Guh, K. C., Zhang, W., Templeton, M., Brill, D., and Chen, A. L. P. Algorithms to process distributed queries in fast local networks. *IEEE Trans. Comput. C-36*, 10 (Oct. 1987), 1153-1164.

Received January 1988; revised May 1989 and April 1990; accepted April 1990

Tradeoffs in Processing Complex Join Queries via Hashing in Multiprocessor Database Machines

Donovan A. Schneider
David J. DeWitt

Computer Sciences Department
University of Wisconsin
Madison, WI 53706

ABSTRACT — In this paper we examine the problem of processing multi-way join queries (on the order of 10 joins) through hash-based join methods in a shared-nothing database machine. We first discuss how the choice of a format for a complex query can significantly affect performance in a multiprocessor database machine. Several query processing algorithms are then proposed and experimental results obtained from a simulation study are presented to demonstrate the tradeoffs of left-deep and right-deep scheduling strategies for complex join query evaluation. These results demonstrate that right-deep scheduling strategies can provide significant performance advantages in large multiprocessor database machines under many circumstances, even when memory is limited.

1. Introduction

Several important trends have occurred in the last ten years which have combined to change the traditional view of database technology. First, microprocessors have become much faster while simultaneously becoming much cheaper. Next, memory capacities have risen while the cost of memory has declined. Finally, high-speed communication networks have enabled the efficient interconnection of multiple processors. All these technological changes have combined to make feasible the construction of high performance multiprocessor database machines.

Of course, as with any new technology, there are many open questions regarding the best ways to exploit the capabilities of these multiprocessor database machines in order to achieve the highest possible performance. Because the join operator is critical to the operation of any relational DBMS, a number of papers have addressed parallel implementations of the join operation including [BARU87, BRAT87, DEWI85, DEWI88, KITS88, LU85, SCHN89a]. However, these papers have not addressed the processing of queries with more than one or two joins. Also, the performance impact of alternative formats for representing multi-way join queries has received little attention in the context of this new environment. The related work that has been done is discussed in Section 2.

In this paper we examine the tradeoffs imposed by left-deep, right-deep and bushy query trees in a multiprocessor environment when queries contain on the order of ten joins. We focus on hash-based join methods because their performance has been demonstrated bo be superior in systems with large memories [BRAT87, DEWI84, SCHN89a, SHAP86], although we include a brief discussion of the sort-merge join algorithm. The tradeoffs we consider include the potential for exploiting intra-query parallelism (and its corresponding effect on performance), resource consumption (primarily memory), support for dataflow processing, and the cost of optimization. The examination of these tradeoffs demonstrated the feasibility of the right-deep representation strategy and resulted in several new algorithms for processing query trees in this format. As well as providing superior opportunities for exploiting parallelism within a query tree, a right-deep representation strategy can also reduce the importance of correctly estimating join selectivities. This analysis of the tradeoffs of the alternative query tree representation strategies and a description of several new algorithms for processing right-deep query trees is presented in Section 3.

Because left-deep and right-deep representation strategies present the extreme cases among the alternative query representation strategies, we were interested in quantitatively examining the performance tradeoffs between these two strategies. To perform this analysis, we constructed a multiprocessor database machine simulator and implemented scheduling algorithms for both of these tree formats. The description of the simulation model, its validation, and the experimental results obtained are contained in Section 4. Results from this experimental analysis confirm the more qualitative results which indicate that right-deep trees can indeed provide substantial performance improvements under many different experimental conditions but that this strategy is not optimal under all circumstances. Our conclusions and plans for future work are presented in Section 5.

This research was partially supported by the Defense Advanced Research Projects Agency under contract N00039-86-C-0578, by the National Science Foundation under grant DCR-8512862, by a Digital Equipment Corporation External Research Grant, and by a research grant from the Tandem Computer Corporation. Funding was also provided by a DARPA/NASA sponsored Graduate Research Assistantship in Parallel Processing.

"Tradeoffs in Processing Complex Join Queries via Hashing in Multiprocessor Database Machines" by D.A. Schneider and D.J. DeWitt from *Proc. 16th VLDB Conf.*, 1990, pp. 469-480. Copyright © 1990 by VLDB Endowment, Inc., reprinted with permission.

Degrees of Parallelism

There are three possible ways of utilizing parallelism in a multiprocessor database machine. First, parallelism can be applied to each operator within a query. For example, ten processors can work in parallel to compute a single join or select operation. This form of parallelism is termed **intra-operator** parallelism and has been studied extensively by previous researchers. Second, **inter-operator** parallelism can be employed to execute several operators within the same query concurrently. Finally, **inter-query** parallelism refers to executing several queries simultaneously. In this paper, we specifically address only those issues involved with exploiting inter-operator parallelism for queries composed of many joins. We defer issues of inter-query parallelism to future work.

Query Tree Representations

Instrumental to understanding how to process complex queries is understanding how query plans are generated. A query is compiled into a tree of operators and several different formats exist for structuring this tree of operators. As will be shown, the different formats offer different tradeoffs, both during query optimization and query execution.

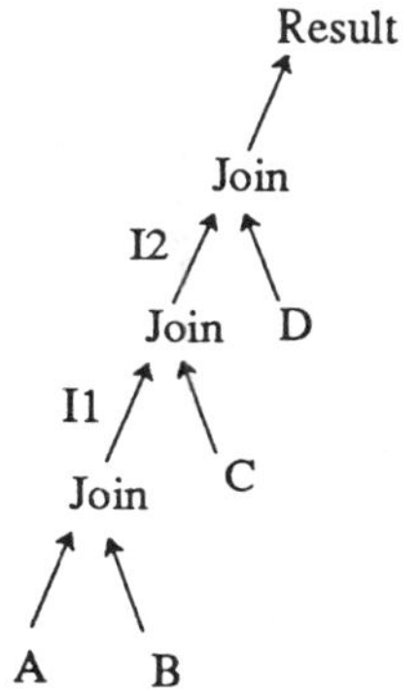

(((A * B) * C) * D)

Left-Deep Query Tree

Figure 1

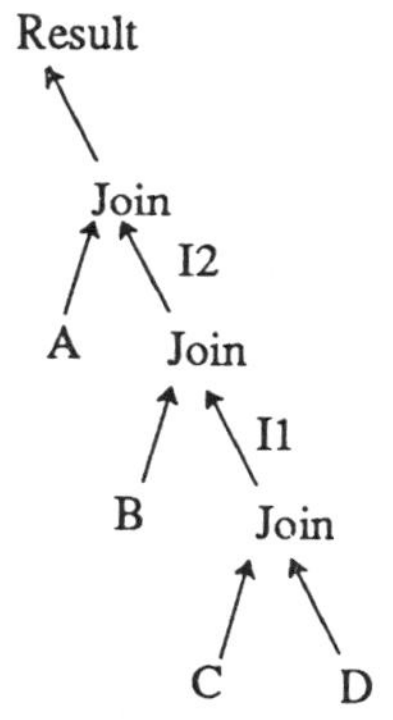

(A * (B * (C * D)))

Right-Deep Query Tree

Figure 2

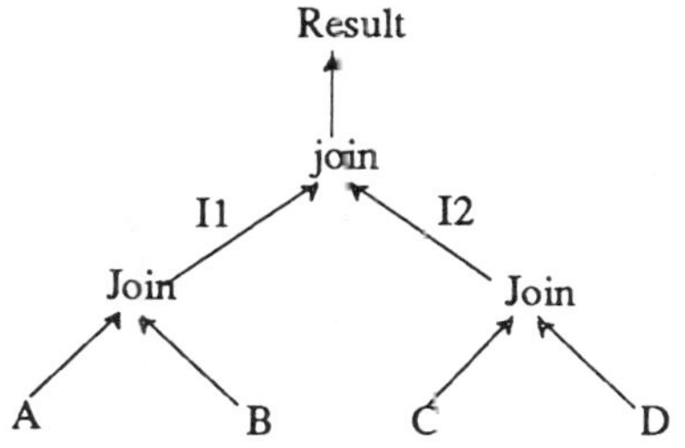

((A * B) * (C * D))

Bushy Query Tree

Figure 3

The different formats that exist for query tree construction range from simple to complex. A ''simple'' query tree format is one in which the format of the tree is restricted in some manner. There are several reasons for wanting to restrict the design of a query tree. For example, during optimization, the space of alternative query plans is searched in order to find the "optimal" query plan. If the format of a query plan is restricted in some manner, this search space will be reduced and optimization will be less expensive. Of course, there is the danger that a restricted query plan will not be capable of representing the optimal query plan.

Query tree formats also offer tradeoffs at runtime. For instance, some tree formats facilitate the use of dataflow scheduling techniques. This improves performance by simplifying scheduling and eliminating the need to store temporary results. Also, different formats dictate different maximum memory requirements. This is important because the performance of hash-based join algorithms depends heavily on the amount of available memory [DEWI84, SCHN89a, SHAP86]. Finally, the format of the query plan is one determinant of the amount of parallelism that can be applied to the query.

Left-deep trees and right-deep trees represent the two extreme options of restricted format query trees. Bushy trees, on the other hand, have no restrictions placed on their construction. Since they comprise the design space between left-deep and right-deep query trees, they have some of the benefits and drawbacks of both strategies. They do have their own problems, though. For instance, it is likely to be harder to synchronize the activity of join operators within an arbitrarily complex bushy tree. We will examine the tradeoffs associated with each of these query tree formats more closely in the following sections. Refer to Figures 1, 2 and 3 for examples of left-deep, right-deep, and bushy query trees, respectively, for the query A join B join C join D. (Note that the character * is used to denote the relational join operator.)

2. Survey of Related Work

[GERB86] describes many of the issues involved in processing hash-based join operations in multiprocessor database machines. Both inter-operator and intra-operator concurrency issues are discussed. In the discussion of inter-operator parallelism, the tradeoffs of left-deep, right-deep and bushy query tree representations with regard to parallelism, pipelined data flow, and resource utilization (primarily memory) are addressed. However, while [GERB86] discusses the basic issues involved in processing complex queries in a multiprocessor environment, it does not explore the tradeoffs between the alternative query tree representation strategies in great depth. [GRAE90] also supports the three alternative query tree formats in the shared-memory database machine Volcano, but the tradeoffs are not discussed in detail. [GRAE87] considers some of the tradeoffs between left-deep and bushy query trees in a single processor environment. Analytic cost functions for hash-join, index join, nested loops join, and sort-merge join are developed and used to compare the average plan execution costs for the different query tree formats.

[STON89] describes how the XPRS project plans on utilizing parallelism in a shared-memory database machine. Optimization during query compilation assumes the entire buffer pool is available, but in order to aid optimization at runtime, the query tree is divided into fragments. At runtime, the desired amount of parallelism for each fragment is weighed against the amount of available memory. If insufficient memory is available, three techniques are described that can be used to reduce memory requirements. First, a fragment can be decomposed into sequential fragments. This requires the spooling of data to temporary files. If further decomposition is not possible, the number of batches used for the Hybrid join algorithm [DEWI84] can be increased. Finally, the level of parallelism applied to the fragment can be reduced.

3. Tradeoffs of Alternative Query Tree Representations

In this section we discuss how each of the alternative query tree formats affects memory consumption, dataflow scheduling, and the ability to exploit parallelism in a multi-way join query. The discussion includes processing queries in the best case (unlimited resources) to more realistic situations where memory is limited.

A good way of comparing the tradeoffs between the alternative query tree representations is through the construction of **operator dependency graphs** for each representation strategy. In the dependency graph for a particular query tree, a subgraph of nodes enclosed by a dashed line represent operators that should be scheduled together for efficient pipelining. The directed lines within these subgraphs indicate the producer/consumer relationship between the operators. The bold directed arcs between subgraphs show which sets of operators must be executed before other sets of operators are executed, thereby determining the maximum level of parallelism and resource requirements (e.g. memory) for the query. Either not scheduling the set of operators enclosed in the subgraphs together or failing to schedule sets of operators according to the dependencies will result in having to spool tuples from the intermediate relations to disk.

The operator dependency graphs presented in this section are based on the use of a hash-join algorithm as the join method. In this paper, we consider two different hash-join methods, Simple hash-join and Hybrid hash-join [DEWI84]. It is assumed that the reader is familiar with these join methods although a brief description of them is included here. For this description, consider the join of relations R and S, where R is the smaller joining relation.

The Simple hash-join method is an optimistic algorithm that assumes that all the tuples from the **smaller**[1] joining relation R (termed the **Building** relation) can be staged into a main memory hash table. If this assumption fails, overflowing tuples from R are dynamically staged to a temporary file on disk. Once all the tuples from R have been processed, the tuples from the **larger** relation S (the **Probing** relation) are processed. As each tuple from S is read from disk, the tuple is either used to probe the hash table containing tuples from R or is written back to disk, if hash-table overflow occurred while building the hash table with R (see [SCHN89a] for more details). If hash-table overflow has occurred, the overflow partitions of R and S are recursively joined using this same procedure.

[1] The smaller relation is always used as the building or inner relation in a hash join algorithm in order to minimize the number of times the outer relation must be read from disk. Also by using the smaller relation as the inner or building relation, one maximizes the probability that the outer relation will only have to be read once.

The Hybrid hash-join algorithm was developed in order to prevent the overflow processing discussed above while utilizing as much memory as is available. The key idea is to recognize a priori that the join will exceed the memory capacity and partition each joining relation into enough disjoint buckets such that each bucket will fit into the available memory. As an enhancement, a portion of the join result is computed while the two joining relations are being partitioned into buckets.

With hash-join algorithms, the computation of the join operation can be viewed as consisting of two phases. First, a hash table is constructed from tuples produced from the left input stream (relation R, in the above examples). In the second phase, tuples from the right input stream (relation S) are used to probe the hash table for matches in order to compute the join. Since the first operation must completely precede the second, the join operator can be viewed as consisting of two separate operators, a **build** operator and a **probe** operator. The dependency graphs model this two phase computation for hash-joins by representing $Join_i$ as consisting of the operators B_i and P_i. The base relations to be joined are represented in the operator dependency graphs as S_i, signifying the scan of relation i.

The reader should keep in mind that intra-operator parallelism issues are being ignored in this paper. That is, when we discuss executing two operators concurrently, we have assumed implicitly that **each** operator will be computed using multiple processors as described in [SCHN89a].

3.1. Left-Deep Query Trees

Figure 4 shows a generic N-join query represented as a left-deep query tree and its associated operator dependency graph. From the dependency graph it is obvious that no scan operators can be executed concurrently. It also follows that the dependencies force the following unique query execution plan:

1) Scan S1 - Build J1
2) Scan S2 - Probe J1 - Build J2
3) Scan S3 - Probe J2 - Build J3
•
•
N) Scan SN - Probe JN-1 - Build JN
N+1) Scan SN+1 - Probe JN

The above schedule demonstrates that at most one scan and two join operators can be active at any point in time. Consider Step N in the above schedule. Prior to the initiation of Scan SN, a hash table was constructed from the output of Join N-1. When

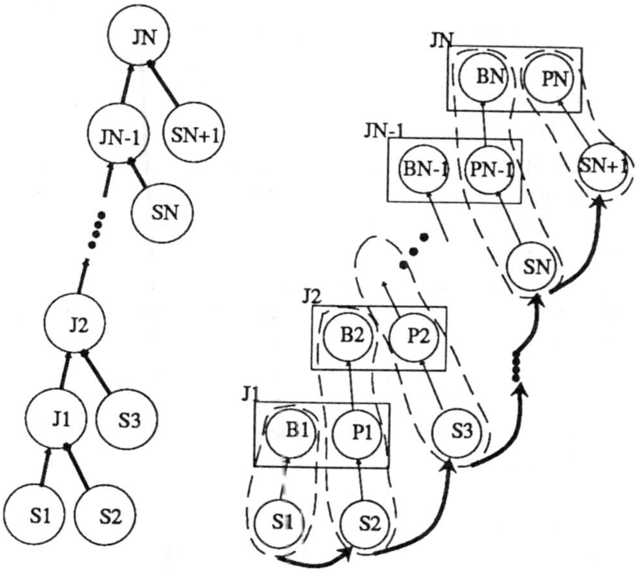

Left-Deep Query Tree and Dependency Graph
Figure 4

the Scan SN is initiated, tuples produced from the scan will immediately probe this hash table to produce join output tuples for Join N. These output tuples will be immediately streamed into a hash table constructed for Join N. The hash table space for Join N-1 can only be reclaimed after all the tuples from scan SN have probed the hash table, computed Join N, and stored the join computation in a new hash table. Thus, the maximum memory requirements of the query at any point in its execution consist of the space needed for the hash tables of any two adjacent join operators.

Limited Memory

Although left-deep query trees require that only the hash tables corresponding to two adjacent join operators be memory resident at any point during the execution of any complex query, the relations staged into the hash tables are the result of intermediate join computations, and hence it is likely to be difficult to predict their size. Furthermore, even if the size of the intermediate relations can be accurately predicted, in a multi-user environment it can not be expected that the optimizer will know the exact amount of memory that will be available when the query is executed. If memory is extremely scarce, sufficient memory may not exist to hold even one of these hash tables. Thus, even though only two join operators are active at any point in time, many issues must be addressed in order to achieve optimal performance.

[GRAE89] proposes a solution to this general problem by having the optimizer generate multiple query plans and then having the runtime system choose the plan most appropriate to the current system environment. A similar mechanism was proposed for Starburst [HAAS89]. One problem with this strategy is that the number of feasible plans may be quite large for the complex join queries we envision. Besides having to generate plans which incorporate the memory requirements of each individual join operator, an optimizer must recognize the consequences of intra-query parallelism. For example, if a join operator is optimized to use most of the memory in the system, the next higher join operator in the query tree will be starved for memory. If it is not possible to modify the query plan at runtime, performance will suffer.

A simpler strategy may be to have the runtime query scheduler adjust the number of buckets for the Hybrid join algorithm in order to react to changes in the amount of memory available. An enhancement to this strategy would be to keep statistics on the size of the intermediate join computations stored in the hash tables and use this information to adjust the number of buckets for join operators higher in the query tree.

3.2. Right-Deep Query Trees

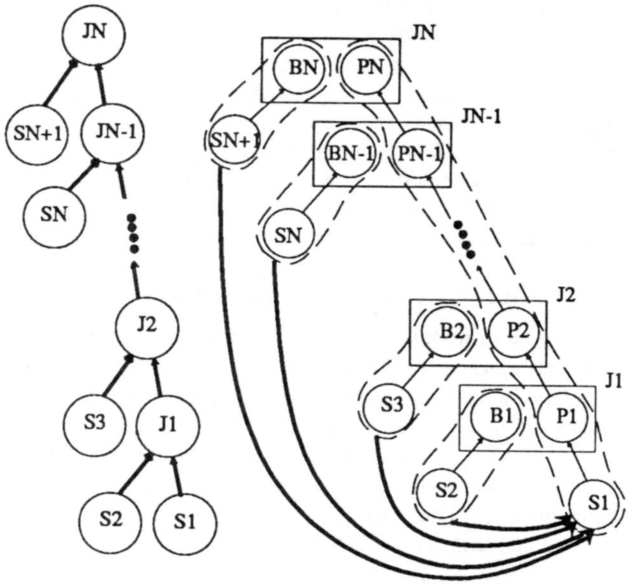

Right-Deep Query Tree and Dependency Graph
Figure 5

Figure 5 shows a generic right-deep query tree for an N-join query and its associated dependency graph. From the dependency graph it can easily be determined which operators can be executed concurrently and the following execution plan can be devised to exploit the highest possible levels of concurrency:

1) Scan S2-Build J1, Scan S3-Build J2, ...,Scan Sn+1-Build Jn
2) Scan S1-Probe J1-Probe J2-...-Probe Jn

From this schedule it is obvious that all the scan operators but S1, and all the build operators can be processed in parallel. After this phase has been completed, the scan S1 is initiated and the resulting tuples will probe the first hash table. All output tuples will then percolate up the tree. As demonstrated, very high levels of parallelism are possible with this strategy (especially since every operator will also generally have intra-operator parallelism applied to it). However, the query will require enough memory to hold the hash tables of **all** N join operators throughout the duration of the query.

A question arises as to the performance implications of scheduling scans S2 through SN+1 concurrently. If these operators access relations which are declustered over the same set of storage sites, initiating all the scans concurrently may be detrimental because of the increased contention at each disk [GHAN89]. However, in a large database machine, it is **not** likely that relations will be declustered over all available storage sites. Further declustering eventually becomes detrimental to performance because the costs of controlling the execution of a query eventually outweigh the benefits of adding additional disk resources [GERB87, COPE88, DEWI88]. In Section 4 we present experimental results which illustrate the performance implications of the data declustering strategy.

Limited Memory

Dealing with limited memory is expected to be a bigger problem with right-deep trees than with left-deep trees because more hash tables must be co-resident in memory. Also, there is little opportunity for runtime query modifications since once the scan on S1 is initiated the data flows through the query tree to completion. However, it is expected that more accurate estimates of memory requirements will be available for a right-deep query tree since the left children (the building relations) will always be base relations (or the result of applying selection predicates to a base relation), while with a left-deep tree the building input to each join is always the result of the preceding join operations.

Several alternative techniques exist for exploiting the potential performance advantages of right-deep query trees when memory is limited. One strategy (similar to that proposed in [STONE89]) involves having the optimizer or runtime scheduler *break* the query tree into disjoint pieces such that the sum of the hash tables for all the joins within each piece are expected to fit into memory. This splitting of the query tree will, of course, require that temporary results be spooled to disk. When the join has been computed up to the boundary between the two pieces, the hash table space currently in use can be reclaimed. The query can then continue execution, this time taking its right-child input from the temporary relation. This scheduling strategy is termed **static right-deep scheduling**.

A more dynamic strategy, called **dynamic bottom-up scheduling**, schedules the scans S2 to SN+1 (Figure 5) in a strict bottom-up manner. The scan S2 is first initiated and the resulting tuples are used to construct a hash table for the join operator J1. After this scan completes the memory manager is queried to check if enough memory exists to stage the tuples expected as a result of the scan S3. If sufficient space exists, scan S3 is initiated. This same procedure is followed for all scans in the query tree until memory is exhausted. If all the scans have been processed, all that remains is for the scan S1 to be initiated to start the process of probing the hash tables. However, in the case that only the scans through S_i can be processed in this first pass, the scan S1 is initiated but now the results of the join computation through join J_{i-1} are stored into a temporary file S1′. Further processing of the query tree proceeds in an identical manner only the first scan to be scheduled is S_{i+1}. Also, the scan to start the generation of the probing tuples is initiated from the temporary file S1′. Although this strategy sacrifices parallelism in scanning the "building" relations, it has some interesting properties when certain filtering techniques are applied [GERB90]. This tradeoff will be analyzed in future work.

Both of these strategies share a common feature of dealing with limited memory by "breaking" the query tree at one or more points. Breaking the query tree has a significant impact on performance because the benefits of data flow processing are lost when the results of the temporary join computation must be spooled to disk. Although, we have assumed that enough memory is available to hold at least each relation individually and, hopefully, several relations simultaneously, this may not always be the case. An alternative approach is to preprocess the input relations in order to reduce memory requirements. This is what the Hybrid join algorithm attempts to do. Below, we discuss the use of the Hybrid join algorithm for processing complex query trees represented as right-deep query trees. We refer to the resulting algorithm as **Right-Deep Hybrid Scheduling**.

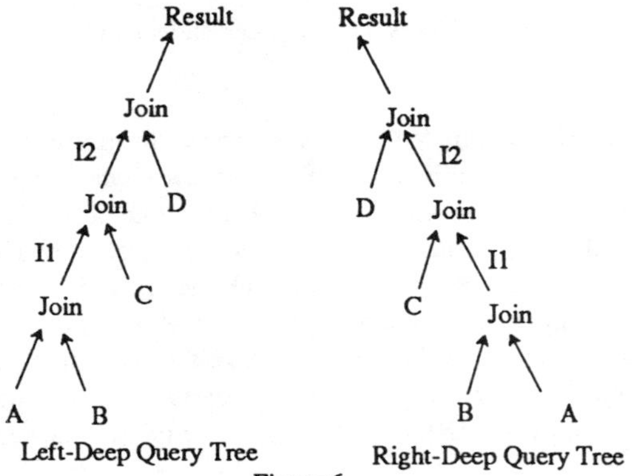

Figure 6

Consider the right-deep join query in Figure 6 and assume that each join will be broken into two buckets, with the first being staged immediately into memory. The first bucket of A (denoted A_{b1}) will join with the first bucket of B to compute the first half of A*B. Since this is a right-deep tree the first inclination would be to probe the hash table for C (actually C_{b1}) with all these output tuples. However, this cannot be done immediately because the join attribute may be different between C and B, in which case the output tuples corresponding to A*B (I1) must be rehashed before they can join with the first bucket of C. Since I1 must use the same hash function as C, I1 must be composed of two buckets (one of which will directly map to memory as a probing segment). Thus, the tuples corresponding to $B_{b1}*A_{b1}$ will be rehashed to $I1_{b1}$ and $I1_{b2}$, with the tuples corresponding to the first bucket (about half the A*B tuples assuming uniformity) immediately probing the hash table built from C_{b1}. Again, the output tuples of this first portion of A*B*C will be written to the buckets $I2_{b1}$ and $I2_{b2}$. Output tuples will thus keep percolating up the tree, but their number will be reduced at each succeeding level based on the number of buckets used by the respective building relation. Query execution will then continue with the join $B_{b2}*A_{b2}$. After all the respective buckets for A*B have been joined, the remaining buckets for C*I1 will be joined. Processing of the entire query tree will proceed in this manner.

With Right-Deep Hybrid Scheduling (RDHS), some tuples will be delivered to the host as a result of joining the first buckets of the two relations at the lowest level of the query tree. This is not possible with an analogous left-deep or bushy query tree. If a user is submitting the query, the quicker feedback will result in a faster response time (even though the time to compute the entire result may be identical). And, in the case of an application program submitting the query, it may be very beneficial to provide the result data sooner and in a more "even" stream as opposed to producing the entire result in one step because the computation of the application can be overlapped with the processing of the join.

Several questions arise as how to best allocate memory for right-deep query trees with the RDHS join algorithm. For correctness it is necessary that the first bucket of EACH of the building relations be resident in memory. However, it is NOT a requirement that all relations be distributed into the same number of buckets. For example, if relation B and D are very large but relation C is small, it would be possible to use only one bucket for relation C while using additional buckets for relations B and D. Hence, the intermediate relation I1 would never be staged to disk in any form, rather it would exist solely as a stream of tuples to the next level in the query tree.

As can be seen, RDHS provides an alternative to the static and dynamic bottom-up scheduling algorithms described above. Whereas these algorithms assumed that enough memory was available to hold at least each relation individually and hopefully several relations simultaneously, the use of the RDHS algorithm potentially reduces the memory requirements while still retaining some dataflow throughout the **entire** query tree. If RDHS can use a single bucket for every relation, it becomes equivalent to the static right-deep scheduling algorithm. It remains an open question as to when one scheduling strategy will outperform the other.

The Case for Right-Deep Query Trees

(1) Right-deep query trees provide the best potential for exploiting parallelism.

(2) In the best case, intermediate join results exist only as a stream of tuples flowing through the query tree.

(3) The size of the "building" relations can be more accurately predicted since the cardinality estimates are based on predicates applied to a base relation as opposed to estimates of the size of intermediate join computations.

(4) Even though bushy trees can potentially re-arrange joins to minimize the size of intermediate relations, a best-case right-deep tree will never store its larger intermediate relations on disk.

(5) Several strategies exist to deal with limited memory situations. "Breaking" the query tree represents a static approach while the dynamic bottom-up scheduling algorithm reacts better to the amount of memory available at run-time. The RDHS strategy can deliver tuples **sooner** and in a more constant stream to the user/application than a similar left-deep query tree can.

(6) Right-deep trees are generally assumed to be the most memory intensive query tree format but this is not always the case. Consider the join of relations A, B, C, and D as shown in Figure 6 for both a left-deep and a right-deep query tree format. Assume the size of all the relations is 10 pages. Furthermore, assume that the size of A*B is 20 pages and the size of A*B*C is 40 pages. At some point during the execution of the left-deep query tree, the results of A*B and A*B*C will simultaneously reside in memory. Thus, 60 pages of memory will be required in order to execute this query. With a right-deep query tree, however, relations B, C and D must reside in memory, but these relations will only consume 30 pages of memory.

(7) The size of intermediate relations may grow with left-deep trees in the case where attributes are added as the result of each additional join. Since the intermediates are stored in memory hash tables, memory requirements will increase. Note that although the width of tuples in the intermediate relations will also increase with right-deep trees, these tuples are only used to probe the hash tables and hence they don't consume memory for the duration of the join.

3.3. Bushy Query Trees

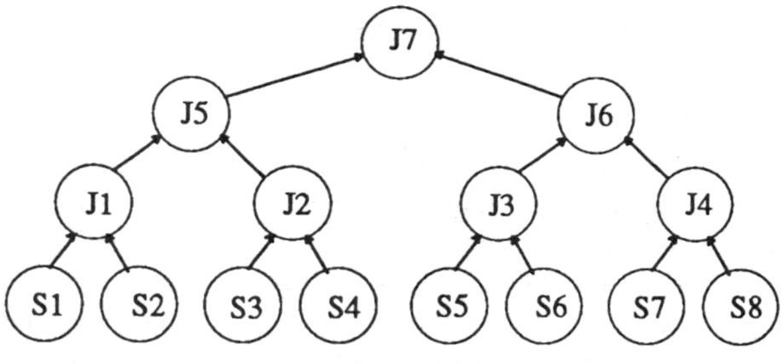

Bushy Query Tree
Figure 7

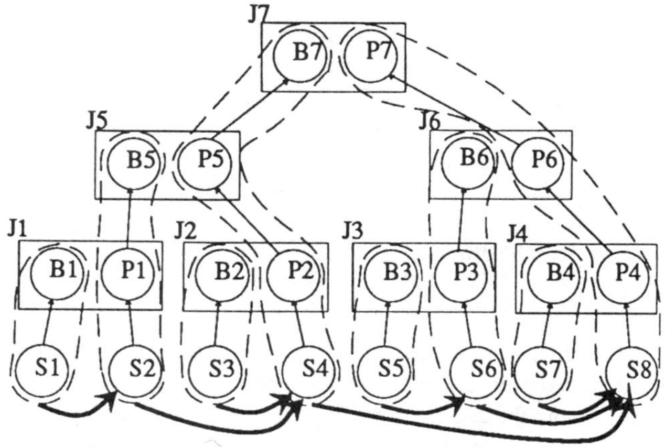

Dependency Graph for a Bushy Query Tree
Figure 8

With more complex query tree representations such as the bushy query tree for the eight-way join shown in Figure 7, several different schedules can be devised to execute the query. A useful way of clarifying the possibilities is again through the construction of an operator dependency graph. Figure 8 contains the dependency graph corresponding to the join query shown in Figure 7. By following the directed arcs it can be shown that the longest path through the graph is comprised of the subgraphs containing the scan operators S1, S2, S4 and S8. Since the subgraphs containing these operators must be executed serially in order to maximize dataflow processing (i.e., to prevent writing tuples to temporary storage), it follows that every execution plan must consist of at least four steps. One possible schedule is:

1) Scan S1-Build J1, Scan S3-Build J2, Scan S5-Build J3, Scan S7-Build J4.
2) Scan S2-Probe J1-Build J5, Scan S6-Probe J3-Build J6.
3) Scan S4-Probe J2-Probe J5-Build J7.
4) Scan S8-Probe J4-Probe J6-Probe J7.

However, notice that non-critical-path operations like Scan S7 and Build J4 could be delayed until Step 3 without violating the dependency requirements. The fact that scheduling options such as the above exist, demonstrates that runtime scheduling is more complicated for bushy trees than for the other two tree formats. As was the case with the other query tree designs, if the order in which operators are scheduled does not obey the dependency constraints, tuples from intermediate relations must be spooled to disk and re-read at the appropriate time.

Limited Memory

By intelligently scheduling operators it is possible to reduce the memory demands of a query represented as a bushy tree. Consider again the previous schedule for executing the 7 join query. After the execution of Step 1, four hash tables will be resident in memory. After Step 2 completes, memory can be reclaimed from the hash tables corresponding to join operators J1 and J3 but new hash tables for join operators J5 and J6 will have been constructed. Only after the execution of Step 3 can the memory requirements be reduced to three hash tables (J7, J6, and J4). However, it may be possible to reduce the memory consumption of the query by constructing a different schedule. Consider the following execution schedule in which we have noted when hash table space can be reclaimed:

1) Scan S1-Build J1.
2) Scan S2-Probe J1-Build J5-Release J1, Scan S3-Build J2.
3) Scan S4-Probe J2-Probe J5-Build J7-Release J2 and J5.
4) Scan S5-Build J3.
5) Scan S6-Probe J3-Build J6-Release J3, Scan S7-Build J4.
6) Scan S8-Probe J4-Probe J6-Probe J7-Release J4, J6 and J7.

Although this execution plan requires six steps instead of four, the maximum memory requirements have been reduced throughout the execution of the query from a maximum of 4 hash tables to a maximum of 3 hash tables. If these types of execution plan modifications are insufficient in reducing memory demands, the techniques described in the last two subsections for left-deep and right-deep query trees can also be employed.

3.4. Issues When Using the Sort-Merge Join Algorithm

The use of hash-join methods affects the preceding discussion on the achievable levels of parallelism associated with the alternative query tree designs. For example, reconsider the left-deep query tree and its associated operator dependency graph in Figure 4. With the sort-merge algorithm as the join method, the scan S1 does not necessarily have to precede the scan S2. For example, the scan and sort of S1 could be scheduled in parallel with the scan and sort of S2. The final merge phase of the join can proceed only when the slower of these two operations is completed. This is in contrast to the strictly serial execution of the two scans in order for a hash join algorithm to work properly.

The modifications to the operator dependency graphs required to support the sort-merge join method can be found in [SCHN89b]. These modifications are very simple but are not presented here due to space limitations. One interesting point to note about using the sort-merge join algorithm is that the left-deep and right-deep query tree representations become equivalent because all the base relations (S1 through SN+1) can be scanned/sorted concurrently in either strategy, whereas with the hash-join algorithm there is an ordering dependency which specifies that the left-child input must be completely consumed before the right-child input can be initiated.

4. An Initial Performance Evaluation of Left-Deep vs. Right-Deep Query Trees

The preceding discussion indicated that a multi-way join query represented in a right-deep query tree can potentially offer significant performance advantages over the same query represented in a left-deep tree. In this section we focus on quantitatively measuring the extent of this performance advantage. The reader should note that the goal of the performance evaluation is to determine the range of possible performance tradeoffs between left-deep and right-deep query trees and does not purport to encompass all possible situations. Rather, the analysis will serve to show the feasibility of the strategies proposed for processing multi-way join queries.

As the experimental vehicle for our analysis we chose the shared-nothing database machine Gamma [DEWI86, DEWI90]. Gamma currently runs on a 32 processor iPSC/2 Intel hypercube [INTE88] with one 330 megabyte MAXTOR 4380 (5 1/4") disk directly attached to each Intel 80386 processor. One deficiency of the iPSC/2's I/O system is that it does not provide DMA support for disk transfers. Rather, disk blocks are instead transferred by the disk controller into a FIFO buffer, from which the CPU must copy the block into memory.[2] A high-speed hypercube connected network topology using specially designed hardware routers is used for communication between processors.

[2]Intel was forced to use such a design because the I/O system was added after the system had been completed and the only way of doing I/O was by using an empty socket on the board which did not have DMA access to memory.

Instead of implementing the scheduling algorithms directly on Gamma and measuring their performance, we chose to build a simulation model of Gamma. There were two reasons for this decision. First, we felt it would be simpler and faster to construct new scheduling algorithms in a simulator than in the actual system. Second, a simulation model allows us to study the different algorithms in hardware configurations much larger than Gamma currently provides.

4.1. Simulation Model

The simulation model of Gamma is constructed as follows. Each node in the multiprocessor system consists of a Disk module, a CPU module, a Query Scheduler module, and multiple instances of an Operator module. Additionally, three stand-alone modules are provided: a Network module, a File Manager module, and a Terminal module. The DeNet simulation language [LIVN88] was used to construct the simulator.

The Disk module schedules disk requests according to an elevator algorithm. In order to accurately reflect the hardware currently being used by Gamma, the disk module interrupts the CPU when there are bytes to be transferred from the I/O channel's FIFO buffer to memory or vice versa. The CPU module enforces a FCFS non-preemptive scheduling paradigm on all requests, with the exception of these byte transfers to/from the disk's FIFO buffer. Operator modules are responsible for modeling the relational operators select and join. These modules repeatedly make requests to the CPU, Disk and Network modules in order to perform their particular operation. The Query Scheduler module implements the algorithms to process left-deep and right-deep query trees. The Network module currently models a fully connected network and the Terminal module provides the entry point of new queries. Finally, the File manager keeps track of how many files are defined, what disks each file is declustered over, and the number of pages of each file on each disk. An assignment of each page in a file to a physical disk address is maintained. This physical assignment of file pages allows for more accurate modeling of sequential as well as random disk accesses.

4.2. Simulation Model Validation

In order to provide more faith in the results from the multiprocessor database machine simulator, we validated the simulator against results produced by Gamma. For the validation procedure, the system was configured to use 18 KByte disk pages and 8 KByte network pages. Costs associated with basic operations on this machine and relevant system parameters are summarized in Table 1.

To validate the simulation model we present the performance of both a 10% selection query and a join query in a system with 5-30 processors with disks. Expanded versions of the Wisconsin Benchmark relations [BITT83] serve as the test database. The selection query retrieves 100,000 tuples from a 1,000,000 tuple relation and stores the resulting tuples back into the database. As shown in Figure 9, the simulation model matches with observed Gamma performance very closely for this query. However, the actual error is greater than implied because Gamma uses a one page readahead mechanism when reading pages from a file sequentially. The performance implications of this mechanism are discussed in more detail below.

Disk Parameters	
Average Seek Time	16 msec
Average Settle Time	2 msec
Average Latency	0-16.67 msec (Unif)
Transfer Rate	1.8 MBytes/sec
Disk Page Size	18 KBytes
Xfer Disk Page from SCSI to mem	9000 instructions
Network Parameters	
Maximum Packet Size	8 KBytes
Send 100 bytes	0.6 msec
Send 8192 bytes	5.6 msec
Cpu Parameters	
Instructions/Second	4,000,000
Read 18K Disk Page	32,800 instructions
Write 18K Disk Page	61,500 instructions
Miscellaneous	
Tuples/Network Packet	36
Tuples/Disk Page	82
Number of Sites	5-30

Simulation Parameters for Model Validation
Table 1

In order to validate join performance in the model, we joined a 1,000,000 tuple relation (200 megabytes) with a 100,000 tuple relation (20 megabytes) to produce a 100,000 tuple result relation (40 megabytes). As illustrated by Figure 9, the simulation model

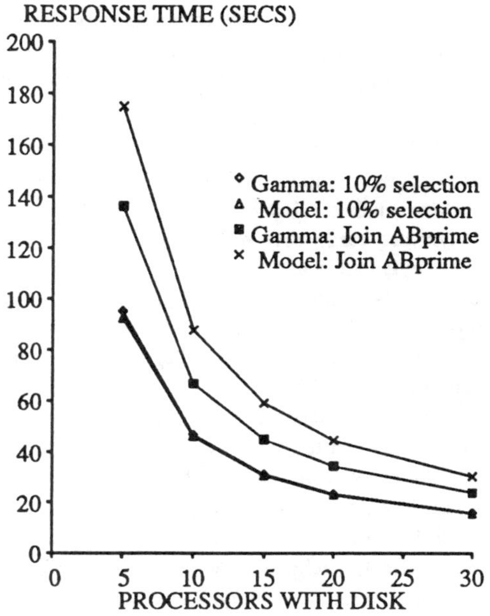

Validation of Selection and Join Performance
Figure 9

overestimates the response time for this query by a constant factor of 20% over the range of 5 to 30 processors with disk. We attribute much of this modeling inaccuracy to be related to Gamma's use of a one page readahead mechanism when scanning a file sequentially. Since join queries are very CPU intensive operations, Gamma can effectively overlap most of the CPU costs of constructing and probing the hash table with the disk I/O necessary for reading the joining relations. This should not imply, though, that the model is overpredicting performance by 20% for the selection query presented in Figure 9. The CPU requirements of this query are much lower and thus the extent of the overlap of CPU and disk processing is much more limited. This claim is further supported by the fact that the simulation model accurately predicts execution times for selection queries which use a non-clustered B-tree access. These queries generate a series of random disk requests and hence readahead is not employed.

4.3. Experimental Design

As stated in the beginning of the section, the experiments were designed to present the range of performance differences between left-deep and right-deep query trees. For the experiments conducted, the query suite consisted of join queries composed of 1, 2, 4, and 8 joins. In order to simplify the analysis, though, the queries were highly constrained. For example, the queries were designed such that the size of the result relation is constant regardless of the number of joins in the query or the query tree representation. This was accomplished by making all relations the same size and by setting the join "probe-ability" factor to 1 for every join in the query tree. That is, each probing tuple joins with exactly one building tuple. Constraining queries in this manner allowed for a direct comparison between a query represented as a left-deep tree and its analogous right-deep tree. Comparing randomly generated queries could be misleading because an optimizer would most certainly produce different plans for the same query given the different query tree formats.

The database was composed of nine 1,000,000 tuple relations and each relation has a selection predicate applied to it which reduces the output cardinality to 500,000 tuples. Since input tuples are 208 bytes wide and attributes are not added with each successive join, the result cardinality of ALL the joins was 500,000 tuples, each 208 bytes wide. All result relations were written back into the database. A parallel version of the Simple hash-join algorithm [DEWI84, SCHN89a] was used as the join method and, unless otherwise stated, enough main memory existed to guarantee that hash table overflow would never occur, regardless of the number of concurrent join operations. In order to more accurately predict performance for "typical" database machines, a 25% buffer pool hit ratio was specified in order to model a disk prefetch mechanism. Response time for the queries is measured from the time the query plan is submitted to the database machine until the query is fully computed.

Four major experiments are reported here. The first experiment considers performance differences in an environment where the declustering of the joining relations forces a high level of resource contention. In the second experiment, the environment is changed to ensure a low level of resource contention. In the third and fourth experiments, the first two experiments are repeated in an environment where memory for joining is limited.

4.3.1. High Resource Contention Environment

In a database machine with a relatively small number of processors, it is likely that large relations will be declustered over all the available nodes. Thus, executing multiple scan and join operators concurrently will result in a high degree of resource contention. For these experiments, the system was configured such that each relation was declustered over 50 nodes. Each join in the query tree was also processed on all 50 nodes.

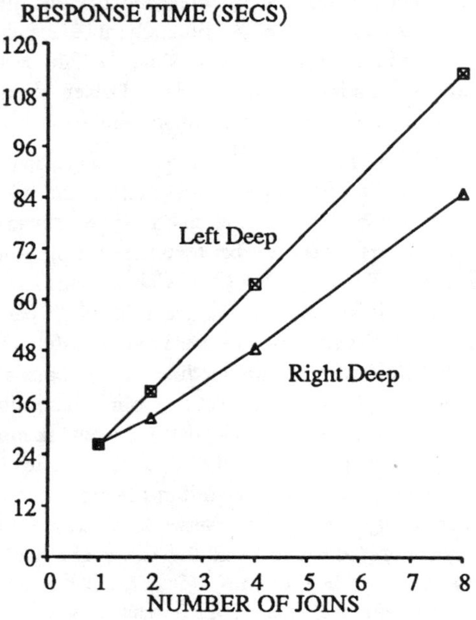

Full Declustering - 50 nodes
Figure 10

The results of these full declustering experiments are shown in Figure 10. For each join query, the performance of the right-deep query tree is approximately 15-20% faster than for its analogous left-deep query tree (left-deep and right-deep query trees are identical for single join queries). This performance improvement occurs because the disks are not fully utilized, and thus executing the scans in parallel for the right-deep trees provides a performance advantage. Note, that the maximal memory requirements for left-deep and right-deep query trees is identical for 1 and 2 join queries, but is twice as high for right-deep queries with 4 joins and four times as high with 8 joins. Thus, when all the relations to be joined are declustered over the same set of nodes, the benefits provided by using right-deep query trees cannot be maintained relative to the amount of memory consumed as the number of joins in the query increases.

4.3.2. Low Resource Contention Environment

In this next set of experiments we repeated the previous experiments in a machine with more processors and where relations are declustered over a subset of nodes and hence, resource contention is reduced when executing several operators concurrently. The system was configured as follows. Each of the nine 1,000,000 tuple relations was declustered over 10 distinct, non-overlapping nodes. Each join was also processed on the 10 processors on which its "building" relation was declustered. Given these conditions, the number of processors actively participating in each query during the scanning of relations and the building/probing of hash tables increased as the number of joins in the query increased. For example, in the 2-join query 30 nodes were used, and in the 8-join query 90 nodes were used. Regardless of the number of joins in the query, each **result** relation was declustered over all 90 nodes.

As illustrated by Figure 11, left-deep query trees are unable to take advantage of the hardware resources that become available as additional joins are added to the query. This is to be expected because relations must be scanned one at a time when a left-deep query tree is employed. However, for right-deep query trees, a nearly constant response time is maintained as the number of joins is increased from one to eight. This may appear startling but can be easily explained given the experimental parameters. Consider the first step in executing the query - scanning the "building" relations and constructing the corresponding hash tables. Since all relations are the same size and have the same selectivity factor applied, and since all the relations are declustered over distinct nodes and the join nodes correspond to the base relation declustering nodes, each scan can be executed completely in parallel and without interference. Thus, the cost of this operation is constant regardless of the number of joins (disregarding the small overhead necessary for initiating the operators).

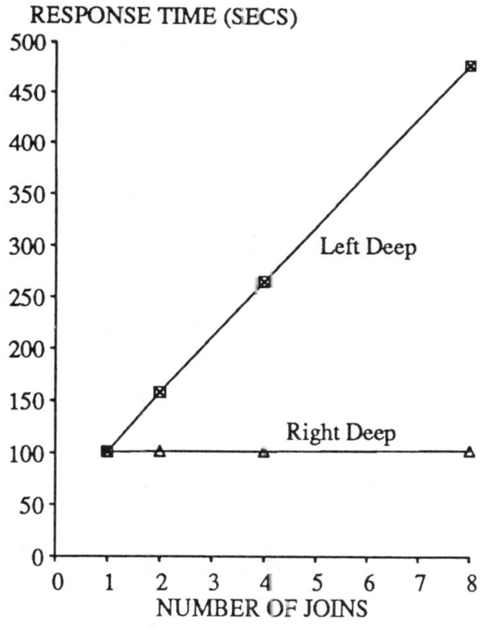

Partial Declustering - 90 nodes
Figure 11

The second phase (the "probing" phase) can scale with the number of joins due to the effect of pipelining. As tuples are produced from a lower join they are immediately sent across the network to participate in the next level of the join. Thus, processing of tuples in different levels of the tree are overlapped. Viewed another way, the throughput of the pipeline is constant regardless of the depth of the join tree and the difference in response time as the number of join levels increases is due to the increased latency to initiate and terminate the pipeline.

The results contained in Figure 11 represent the best-case performance improvements of right-deep query trees. All experimental parameters were set to allow the parallelism potential of the right-deep strategy to be exploited to its fullest. Under more realistic conditions, the performance improvements of right-deep query trees will fall between the extremes presented in Figures 10 and 11. However, it should be noted that the right-deep query with eight joins required four times more memory than any of the left-deep join queries. The results do demonstrate, though, the extreme performance benefits that can be obtained with a right-deep strategy.

4.3.3. Limited Memory Experiments

In this set of experiments we relaxed the assumption that an unlimited amount of memory exists. All query and model parameters are identical to those reported in the previous section with the exception that we only considered the query with 8 joins. High resource and low resource contention (full declustering and disjoint declustering) experiments were again conducted. The static right-deep scheduling strategy (see Section 3.2) was used for processing right-deep query trees.

In order to model a limited memory environment, we modified the aggregate amount of memory available for joining relative to the memory required to stage all eight "building" relations into memory simultaneously. Response time was plotted for left-deep and right-deep strategies for x-axis values ranging from a value of 0.25, where only 2 of the 8 building relations could co-reside in memory, to a value of 1.00, where all 8 building relations can fit in memory simultaneously. X-axis values less than 0.25 would have required resolution of memory overflow for left-deep query trees and are not reported. For the static right-deep strategy it was assumed that the optimizer could perfectly predict scan selectivities and thus could always choose the optimal places to "break" the query tree.

4.3.3.1. Limited Memory - High Resource Contention

In Figure 12, the performance of the left-deep and static right-deep scheduling algorithms are shown as the amount of available memory is varied in an environment where all base relations are declustered across all 50 sites. Three observations should be noted from this figure. First, it is obvious that the left-deep scheduling algorithm is not able to take advantage of memory as it is added. In contrast, the static right-deep scheduling algorithm demonstrates significant performance improvements with additional memory. Next, the cross-over point in the graphs demonstrates the fact that "breaking" the query tree into too many pieces can be detrimental to the performance of right-

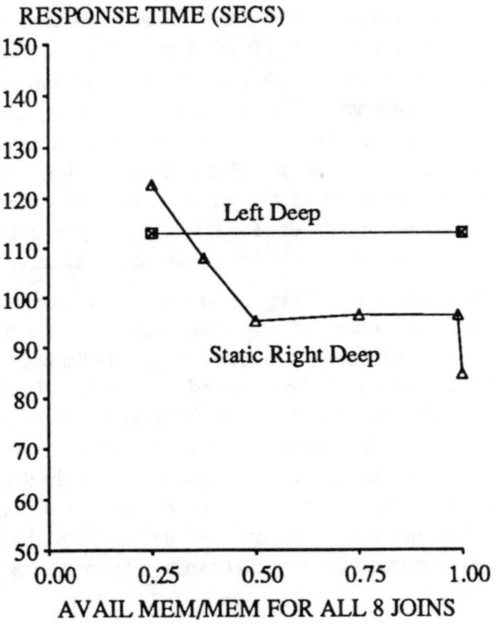

Limited Memory - Full Declustering
Figure 12

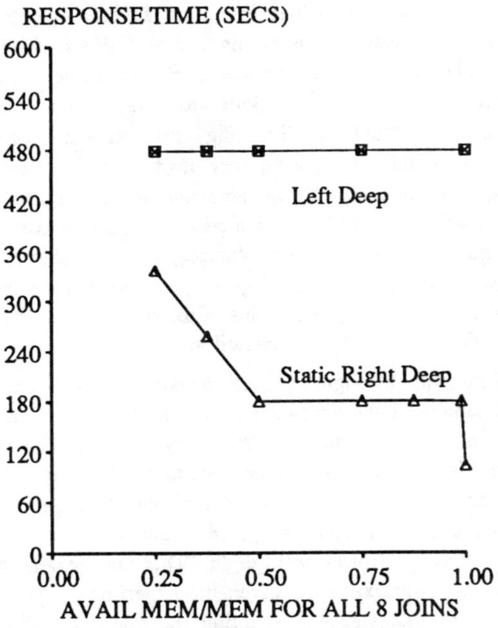

Limited Memory - Partial Declustering
Figure 13

deep scheduling algorithms. For example, at the x-axis value 0.25, the tree had to be broken into three pieces to ensure that the right-deep strategy did not experience memory overflow (requiring the writing and subsequent reading of temporary join computations to and from the disk at three points during query execution). The last point to note is the flatness of the right-deep scheduling graph from 0.5 to just before 1.0. Over this range, the query tree had to be broken into only two pieces. Since the queries produced intermediate relations of a constant size regardless of the number of joins in the query, the placement of the "break" has no effect on performance because the same number of tuples are temporarily staged to disk. Under more likely conditions of growing or diminishing temporary join size results, the selection of the break points for a query will almost certainly have some effect on the execution time of the query. This will be explored in a future performance analysis.

4.3.3.2. Limited Memory - Low Resource Contention

In Figure 13, we present the execution time of the left-deep and right-deep scheduling strategies for the 8-join query when the relations to be joined are declustered over mutually disjoint processors with disks. The simulation parameters are identical to those reported in Section 4.3.2.

The results are very similar to those shown in Figure 12, i.e., the shape of the curves is identical. It is obvious though, that the partial declustering environment offers additional performance advantages for right-deep scheduling strategies even when memory is not unlimited. This is very encouraging because, as stated earlier, it is likely that relations will be partially declustered in database machines with large numbers of processors/disks.

5. Conclusions

In this paper, we have described many of the problems and tradeoffs associated with the task of processing queries composed of many joins in a multiprocessor database machine. In particular, we focused on how the strategy chosen to represent a query tree affects the degree to which parallelism can be applied within a query and the corresponding effects on performance, the resource consumption of the query, and the extent that dataflow processing techniques can be applied. Hash based join methods were assumed for much of this analysis although the sort-merge join method was discussed briefly.

Results obtained from this analysis indicate that the right-deep query representation strategy is well suited to exploit the parallelism inherent in large multiprocessor database machines. As an added benefit, the importance of accurately estimating join selectivities is potentially reduced when using right-deep query trees. These results encouraged us to develop several algorithms for processing queries represented in this query tree format.

In order to quantitatively measure the performance benefits that right-deep query trees can provide over their corresponding left-deep query trees, we constructed a simulation model of a parallel database machine and implemented scheduling algorithms for processing queries represented in these formats. Experimental results from the analysis of these algorithms confirmed that right-deep query trees can offer very significant performance advantages in large database machines. However, the extent of the performance improvement is strongly dictated by the physical placement of the base relations and comes at the cost of increased resource consumption. Furthermore, when memory is limited the performance difference between the scheduling algorithms diminishes.

Our future work includes extending the current study to include a much richer mix of queries, selectivity factors, and base relation cardinalities. We are also interested in studying the performance of the alternative query processing algorithms under multiuser workloads and with skewed data distributions. Although multiuser performance comparisons were beyond the scope of this paper, the memory requirements of a query will serve as a good indicator of potential throughput because memory is so crucial to high performance query processing, especially with the hash-join algorithms. We hope to apply the technique of Adaptive Sampling [LIPT90a, LIPT90b] to help tackle the problem of skew.

Acknowledgments

We would like to thank Jeff Naughton for his many helpful discussions concerning this work.

6. References

[BARU87] Baru, C., O. Frieder, D. Kandlur, and M. Segal, "Join on a Cube: Analysis, Simulation, and Implementation", **Database Machines and Knowledge Base Machines**, M. Kitsuregawa and H. Tanaka (eds), Kluwer Academic Publishers, 1987.

[BITT83] Bitton, D., D.J. DeWitt, and C. Turbyfill, "Benchmarking Database Systems - A Systematic Approach," Proceedings of the 1983 VLDB Conference, Oct., 1983.

[BRAT87] Bratbergsengen, Kjell, "Algebra Operations on a Parallel Computer — Performance Evaluation", **Database Machines and Knowledge Base Machines**, M. Kitsuregawa and H. Tanaka (eds), Kluwer Academic Publishers, 1987.

[COPE88] Copeland, G., W. Alexander, E. Boughter, and T. Keller, "Data Placement in Bubba", Proceedings of the 1988 SIGMOD Conference, June 1988.

[DEWI84] DeWitt, D. J., Katz, R., Olken, F., Shapiro, L., Stonebraker, M. and D. Wood, "Implementation Techniques for Main Memory Database Systems," Proceedings of the 1984 SIGMOD Conference, June, 1984.

[DEWI85] DeWitt, D., and R. Gerber, "Multiprocessor Hash-Based Join Algorithms," Proceedings of the 1985 VLDB Conference, Aug., 1985.

[DEWI86] DeWitt, D., Gerber, R., Graefe, G., Heytens, M., Kumar, K. and M. Muralikrishna, "GAMMA - A High Performance Dataflow Database Machine," Proceedings of the 1986 VLDB Conference, Aug., 1986.

[DEWI88] DeWitt, D., Ghandeharizadeh, S., and D. Schneider, "A Performance Analysis of the Gamma Database Machine", Proceedings of the 1988 SIGMOD Conference, June 1988.

[DEWI90] DeWitt, D., Ghandeharizadeh, S., Schneider, D., Bricker, A., Hsiao, H., and R. Rasmussen, "The Gamma Database Machine Project", IEEE Transactions on Knowledge and Data Engineering, Vol. 2, No. 1, March, 1990.

[GERB86] Gerber, R., "Dataflow Query Processing using Multiprocessor Hash-Partitioned Algorithms," PhD Thesis and Computer Sciences Technical Report #672, University of Wisconsin-Madison, Oct., 1986.

[GERB87] Gerber, R. and D. DeWitt, "The Impact of Hardware and Software Alternatives on the Performance of the Gamma Database Machine", Computer Sciences Technical Report #708, University of Wisconsin-Madison, July, 1987.

[GERB90] R. Gerber, Personal Communication, March 1990.

[GHAN90] Ghandeharizadeh, S., and D.J. DeWitt, "A Multiuser Performance Analysis of Alternative Declustering Strategies", Proceedings of the 6th International Conference on Data Engineering, 1990.

[GRAE87] Graefe, G., "Rule-Based Query Optimization in Extensible Database Systems", Ph.D. Thesis and Computer Sciences Technical Report #724, University of Wisconsin-Madison, Nov., 1987.

[GRAE89] Graefe, G. and K. Ward, "Dynamic Query Evaluation Plans", Proceedings of the 1989 SIGMOD Conference, May 1989.

[GRAE90] Graefe, G., "Encapsulation of Parallelism in the Volcano Query Processing System", Proceedings of the 1990 SIGMOD Conference, May 1990.

[HAAS89] Haas, L., Freytag, J.C., Lohman, G.M., and H. Pirahesh, "Extensible Query Processing in Starburst", Proceedings of the 1989 SIGMOD Conference, May 1989.

[INTE88], Intel Corporation, **iPSC/2 User's Guide**, Intel Corporation Order No. 311532-002, March, 1988.

[KITS88] Kitsuregawa, M., Nakano, M., and M. Takagi, "Query Execution for Large Relations On Functional Disk System," Proceedings of the 5th International Conference on Data Engineering, 1989.

[LIPT90a] Lipton, R. and J. Naughton, "Query Size Estimation by Adaptive Sampling", Proceedings of the ACM SIGACT-SIGMOD-SIGART Symposium on Principles of Database Systems, March 1990.

[LIPT90b] Lipton, R., J. Naughton, and D. Schneider, "Practical Selectivity Estimation through Adaptive Sampling", Proceedings of the 1990 SIGMOD Conference, May, 1990.

[LIVN88] Livny, M., **DeNet User's Guide**, Version 1.0, Computer Sciences Department, University of Wisconsin, Madison, WI, 1988.

[LU85] Lu, H. and M. Carey, "Some Experimental Results on Distributed Join Algorithms in a Local Network", Proceedings of the 1985 VLDB Conference, Aug., 1985.

[SCHN89a] Schneider, D. and D. DeWitt, "A Performance Evaluation of Four Parallel Join Algorithms in a Shared-Nothing Multiprocessor Environment", Proceedings of the 1989 SIGMOD Conference, June 1989.

[SCHN89b] Schneider, D. and D. DeWitt, "Design Tradeoffs of Alternative Query Tree Representations for Multiprocessor Database Machines", Computer Sciences Technical Report #869, University of Wisconsin-Madison, August, 1989.

[SHAP86] Shapiro, L., "Join Processing in Database Systems with Large Main Memories", ACM Transactions on Database Systems, Vol. 11, No. 3, Sept., 1986.

[STON89] Stonebraker, M., P. Aoki, and M. Seltzer, "Parallelism in XPRS", Memorandum No. UCB/ERL M89/16, Feb. 1, 1989.

Exploiting Inter-Operation Parallelism in XPRS *

Wei Hong
Computer Science Division
EECS Department
University of California at Berkeley
Berkeley, CA 94720
hong@postgres.berkeley.edu

Abstract

In this paper, we study the scheduling and optimization problems of parallel query processing using inter-operation parallelism in a shared-memory environment and propose our solutions for XPRS. We first study the scheduling problem of a set or a continuous sequence of independent tasks that are either from a bushy tree plan of a single query or from the plans of multiple queries, and present a clean and simple scheduling algorithm. Our scheduling algorithm achieves maximum resource utilizations by running an IO-bound task and a CPU-bound task in parallel with carefully calculated degrees of parallelism and maintains the maximum resource utilizations by dynamically adjusting the degrees of parallelism of running tasks whenever necessary. Real performance figures are shown to confirm the effectiveness of our scheduling algorithm. We also revisit the optimization problem of parallel execution plans of a single query and extend our previous results to consider inter-operation parallelism by introducing a new cost estimation method to the query optimizer based on our scheduling algorithm.

1 Introduction

There have been growing research efforts in the area of parallel database systems during the past few years. Several research systems have been designed and/or constructed, including *shared-nothing* [STON86] systems such as GAMMA[DEWI90] and BUBBA[COPE88] and shared-memory systems such as XPRS[STON88] and Volcano[GRAE90]. XPRS is a multi-user parallel database management system that we are developing based on the Postgres next-generation DBMS[STON91]. It is implemented on a shared-memory multiprocessor and a disk array as shown in Figure 1. In XPRS, all relations are striped sequentially, block by block, in a round-robin fashion across all the disks in the disk array to allow maximum i/o bandwidth. A shared-memory system has two major advantages over a shared-nothing system. First, there are almost no communication delays because messages are exchanged through shared memory and synchronization can be accomplished by cheap hardware spin locks. Second, the operating system can automatically perform load balancing by allocating the next ready process to the first available processor. Simulation results in [BHID88] show that the potential win of a shared-memory system over a shared-nothing system to be as much as a factor of two. As we will show in this paper, XPRS has been built to fully utilize these advantages of a shared-memory system.

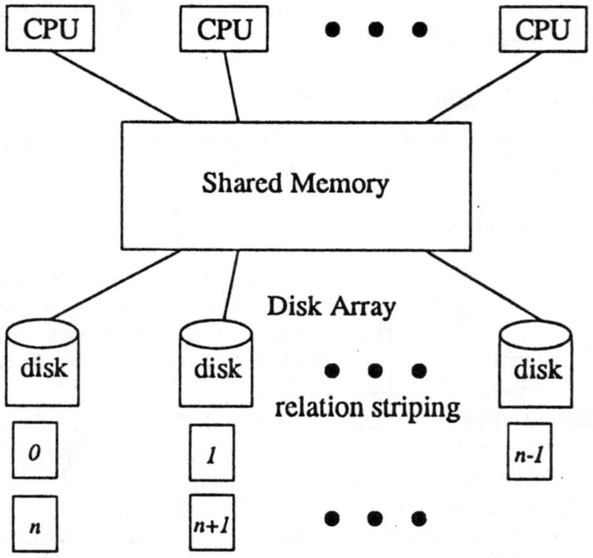

Figure 1: **The Parallel Environment of XPRS**

There are two forms of parallelism that can be exploited in a parallel database system: ***intra-operation*** parallelism and ***inter-operation*** parallelism. Intra-operation parallelism is achieved by partitioning the in-

*This research was sponsored by the National Science Foundation under contract MIP 8715235.

1992 ACM SIGMOD - 6/92/CA, USA
© 1992 ACM 0-89791-522-4/92/0005/0019...$1.50

put data to a certain operation and allocating multiple processors to perform the same operation on subsets of the input data, while inter-operation parallelism is achieved by allocating some processors to one operation and some other processors to another operation. In this paper, we continue our study on parallel query processing in a shared-memory environment which has previously been reported in [HONG91] and present a more complete approach that exploits both intra-operation parallelism and inter-operation parallelism.

[HONG91] is unique in its *two-phase* optimization strategy to overcome the enormous search space in the problem of optimizing parallel query execution plans. In the two-phase optimization strategy, we first, at compile time, optimize sequential query execution plans and then in a second phase, at run time, optimize the parallelizations of the optimal sequential plan chosen in the first phase. Obviously this two-phase optimization strategy greatly reduces the plan search space because it only explores parallelizations of the optimal sequential plan instead of the parallelizations of all possible sequential plans. It is also shown experimentally that this two-phase optimization strategy does not significantly compromise optimality of the resulting parallel plan. However, [HONG91] has only considered intra-operation parallelism and *left-deep tree* plans (i.e., plans that always join the result of a join with a base relation, e.g., $((A \bowtie B) \bowtie C) \bowtie D)$. Due to the sequential nature of left-deep tree plans, no inter-operation parallelism can be exploited within a left-deep tree plan. On the other hand, in a *bushy tree* plan (i.e., plans that allows joins of results of joins, e.g., $(A \bowtie B) \bowtie (C \bowtie D))$, we may be able to perform two joins in parallel before joining them together. In this paper, we will consider bushy tree plans and both intra-operation and inter-operation parallelism. Since the implementation and performance of intra-operation parallelism have already been studied in [HONG91], we will focus on inter-operation parallelism in this paper. Specifically, we will address the following two problems:

- *processor scheduling:* given a set or a continuous sequence of runable operations, what operations to execute in parallel and how many processors to allocate to each parallel operation;
- *query optimization:* how to extend the two-phase optimization algorithm in [HONG91] to handle bushy tree plans and inter-operation parallelism.

Most previous work on parallel query processing has been done on intra-operation parallelism only, e.g., [DEWI90] and [HONG91]. Some recent work has proposed to also apply inter-operation parallelism to query processing. [SCHN90] presents an experimental analysis of the query processing tradeoffs among *left-deep* and *right-deep* tree plans in a shared-nothing enironment. An important finding is that right-deep trees are superior given sufficient memory resources. However, there is no analytical cost expression which can be used by an optimizer to decide whether and when to switch from a left-deep tree to a right-deep tree. Moreover, no algorithms are proposed for determining the degree of parallelism for each parallel operation. [PIRA90] shows through an example query the use of inter-operation parallelism in query processing and models the processor scheduling problem as a modified version of the well-known *bin packing* problem. However, no general scheduling algorithm is proposed. [LU91] proposes an optimization algorithm that considers bushy tree plans and inter-operation parallelism. The algorithm only handles *synchronized* bushy tree plans, i.e., those without pipelining between joins, and uses a greedy algorithm to choose a bushy tree plan that maximizes the opportunities of inter-operation parallelism. Processor scheduling is not specifically addressed in the paper.

In this paper, we present a clean and simple algorithm for processor scheduling given n runable operations. Our main idea is to use inter-operation parallelism to combine IO-bound and CPU-bound tasks to increase system resource utilizations. Our algorithm matches up IO-bound and CPU-bound tasks with appropriate degrees of intra-operation parallelism to make both the processors and the disks operate as close to their full utilizations as possible and thus to minimize the elapsed time. In order to avoid an NP-hard packing problem in the optimization of task schedules, we have also developed a mechanism, taking advantage of the low communication delay of a shared-memory system, to dynamically adjust the degree of intra-operation parallelism of a running task so that the system stays at the IO-CPU balance point as tasks start and finish. Having solved the scheduling problem, we revisit the optimization problem of parallel execution plans of a single query and extend the two-phase optimization strategy to consider bushy tree plans and inter-operation parallelism by introducing a new cost estimation method to the query optimizer based on our scheduling algorithm.

The rest of this paper is organized as follows. Section 2 describes our adaptive processor scheduling algorithm including calculation of IO-CPU balance point, dynamic adjustment to intra-operation parallelism and task reordering heuristics. Section 3 examines variations of our scheduling algorithm and compares their performances through experiment results. Section 4, then extends the two-phase optimization strategy based on our scheduling algorithm, and last, we conclude this paper in Section 5.

2 Adaptive Scheduling Algorithm for XPRS

In this section, we present our adaptive scheduling algorithm for XPRS. First, we describe the architecture of XPRS query processing and define the scheduling prob-

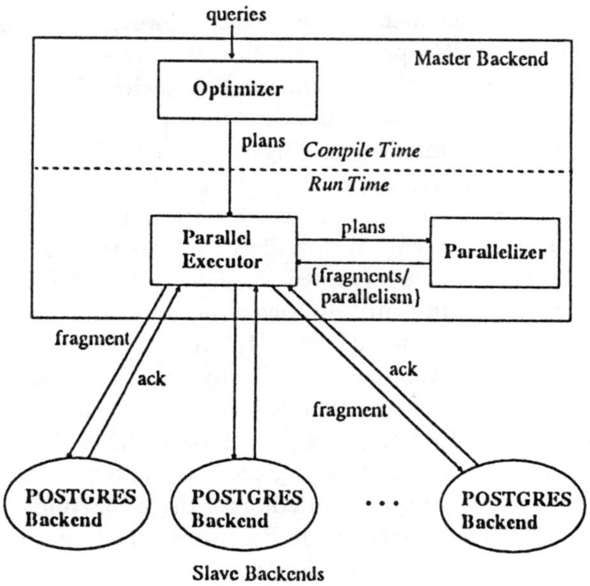

Figure 2: **Architecture of XPRS Query Processing**

lem that we are solving. Then, we describe our classification of IO-bound and CPU-bound tasks and the calculation of the IO-CPU balance point. Then, a mechanism for dynamic adjustment of parallelism is presented. Last, we integrate our ideas into an adaptive scheduling algorithm.

2.1 Problem Definition

The architecture of XPRS query processing is given in Figure 2. There are one master Postgres backend process and multiple slave Postgres backend processes. The master backend is responsible for all the optimization, scheduling and coordination, while the slave backends process whatever tasks assigned to them by the master backend. XPRS query processing consists of two phases. In the first phase, the optimizer takes one or more user queries and generates certain sequential plans for each query.

In the second phase, the parallelizer parallelizes the sequential plans chosen in the first phase. In XPRS, a sequential plan is represented as a binary tree of the basic relational operations, e.g., sequential scan, index scan, nestloop join, mergejoin and hashjoin. First, the sequential plans are decomposed into *plan fragments*, i.e., a group of operations that do not contain any blocking edges. Blocking edges are those between two operations where one operation must wait for the other to finish producing all the tuples before it can proceed. In other words plan fragments are the set of largest pipelineable subgraphes of a sequential plan. Plan fragments are used as the units of parallel execution and are also called *tasks*. By inter-operation parallelism, we in fact mean *inter-fragment* or *inter-task* parallelism.

After identifying all the plan fragments, the parallelizer has to find a processing schedule for the plan fragments and choose a degree of parallelism for each plan fragment. If we only consider intra-operation parallelism, i.e., we only execute one plan fragment at a time, the responsibility of the parallelizer is very simple. As presented in [HONG91], intra-operation parallelism in XPRS achieves near-linear speedup until it runs out of either available processors or the disk bandwidth and there are severe performance penalties for excessive parallelism because of contention on the shared buffer pool. Therefore, the parallelizer only needs to choose a runable plan fragment, i.e., one for which all input data are ready, and choose the maximum parallelism according to the current number of available processors and disk bandwidth. However, the parallelizer's responsibility becomes much more complicated when inter-operation (inter-fragment) parallelism is taken into account. Here is the scheduling problem that we are solving for the parallelizer:

Given n ($n = 1, 2, \ldots, \infty$) runable plan fragments (tasks), $f_1, f_2, \ldots, f_n$, where the plan fragments may be from a bushy tree plan of the same query or from different queries that are simultaneously submitted,
1. decide a processing schedule for $f_1, f_2, \ldots, f_n$;
2. choose a degree of parallelism for each f_i,
such that the total elapsed time of processing $f_1, f_2, \ldots, f_n$ is minimized.

As we will see, our solution to the above described problem works for both a fixed set of tasks or a continuous sequence of tasks. Namely, we also allow n to be infinity in the above description.

2.2 IO-bound and CPU-bound tasks

The key of our solution to the above defined scheduling problem is to combine IO-bound and CPU-bound tasks through inter-operation parallelism so that the utilization of both the processors and the disks is maximized, thus the elapsed time is minimized. Before we describe our solution, we need to define our classification of IO-bound and CPU-bound tasks.

Suppose that if task f_i is processed sequentially, it generates i/o requests at rate C_i (ios/second). When f_i is executed with parallelism x, its i/o rate becomes

$$IO_i(x) = C_i \times x.$$

Suppose that the total disk i/o bandwidth is B (ios/second) and the total number of processors is N.

We define task f_i as *IO-bound* if $C_i > B/N$ and *CPU-bound* if otherwise. Obviously, the function $y = IO_i(x)$ is a straight line with slope C_i. If we draw the line with the rectangle bounded by B and N as in Figure 3, we can see that IO-bound tasks are those corresponding to the lines above the diagonal line and CPU-bound tasks are those corresponding to the lines below the diagonal line.

Since we know the disk block size and we can estimate how many tuples can fit into one disk block and how much CPU time will be spent on each tuple for different

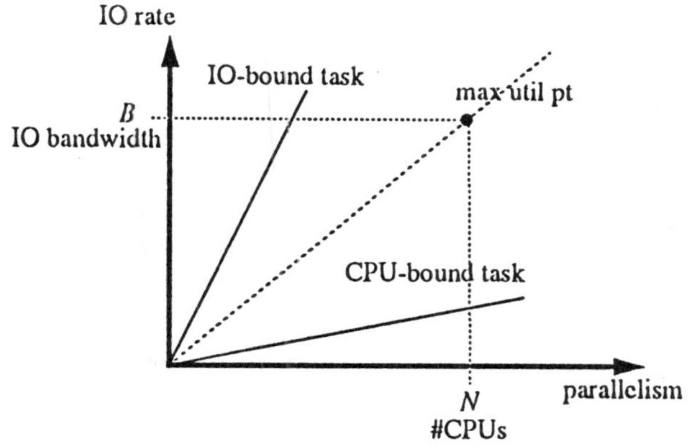

Figure 3: **IO-bound and CPU-bound tasks**

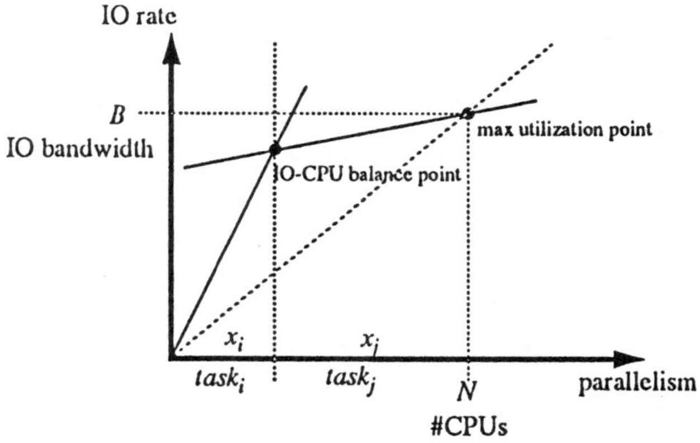

Figure 4: **IO-CPU Balance Point**

database operations, we can estimate the i/o rate, C_i. Therefore, we can do the classification beforehand.

As we can see in Figure 3, the parallelism of a task is limited by the rectangle boundaries and the maximum parallelism of a task is achieved at the intersection between the line corresponding to the task and one of the rectangle boundaries. An IO-bound task will run out of disk bandwidth before it runs out of processors. Its maximum parallelism $maxp(f_i) = B/C_i$. On the other hand, the parallelism of a CPU-bound task is only bounded by the number of processors N, i.e., $maxp(f_i) = N$. In general,

$$maxp(f_i) = min(B/C_i, N).$$

2.3 Calculation of IO-CPU Balance Point

Intuitively, in order to maximize the utilization of both the disks and processors, we want the system to be running at the upper right corner of the rectangle in Figure 3, i.e., the point with coordinate (N, B). Obviously, if we run one task at a time using only intra-operation parallelism, unless the line corresponding to a task is exactly the diagonal line, the system will not be running at the upper right corner of the rectangle. Either some i/o bandwidth or some processors may be wasted.

When we run two tasks f_i with parallelism x_i and f_j with parallelism x_j together, the system is running at the point with coordinate $(x_i + x_j, C_i x_i + C_j x_j)$. We can maximize the system resource utilization by choosing x_i and x_j according to the following equations:

$$\begin{cases} x_i + x_j & = & N \\ C_i x_i + C_j x_j & = & B \end{cases}$$

By solving the above equations, we get,

$$\begin{cases} x_i & = & (B - C_j N)/(C_i - C_j) \\ x_j & = & (C_i N - B)/(C_i - C_j). \end{cases}$$

We call (x_i, x_j) the *IO-CPU balance point* for tasks f_i and f_j.

Suppose that $C_i > C_j$, in order to make x_i and x_j both positive, we must have $C_i > B/N$ and $C_j < B/N$. In other words, valid solutions exist for the above equations if and only if one task is IO-bound and the other CPU-bound. This formula also tells us that one IO-bound task plus one CPU-bound task can always achieve maximum system resource utilization with appropriate parallelism assignment. Although a combination of more than two tasks may also achieve the same effect, it complicates the scheduling algorithm and consumes more memory. Therefore, in exploiting inter-operation parallelism, it is sufficient to only run two tasks at a time, i.e., we never need to run more than two tasks in parallel. This result significantly simplifies the scheduling problem.

Figure 4 gives a graphical interpretation to the above analysis. Given an IO-bound task and a CPU-bound task, if we draw the line corresponding to the IO-bound task through the origin and the line corresponding to the CPU-bound task through the upper right corner of the rectangle, there will always be an intersection within the rectangle between the two lines, which is the IO-CPU balance point. We can see that if we run task i with parallelism x_i and task j with parallelism x_j, the system will be running at the maximum utilization point.

The above calculation assumes that the disk bandwidth B is a predefined constant. However, in reality, disks have two bandwidths, i.e., a sequential i/o bandwidth and a random i/o bandwidth, where the random i/o bandwidth is only about 1/3 of the sequential i/o bandwidth. We have to take this into account and do a more careful calculation for parallelism involving sequential i/o tasks.

Suppose that tasks f_i and f_j both generate sequential i/o's. Let B_s be the sequential i/o bandwidth and B_r be the random i/o bandwidth. Unfortunately the real effective bandwidth B cannot be pre-computed because it depends on the ratio of the time that the disks spend in handling i/o's from each of the tasks and the disk block size used. If we use track-size blocks, even though there may be seeks between the two tasks, each task still sees a close to sequential bandwidth. However, if the block size is too large, it becomes difficult to achieve load balance by distributing data in blocks. Normally, we always use relatively small block sizes, for example, 8K bytes blocks for the current implementation of XPRS. For small block sizes, there are two boundary cases for the effective bandwidth. If the disks spend most of their time handling i/o's from one task, then in effect the disks still do mostly sequential i/o's, so $B \approx B_s$. However, if the disks spend half the time on one task and half on the other, then the disks have to seek between the blocks of one task and those of the other, so $B \approx B_r$. For simplicity, we use a linear interpolation to compute the effective bandwidth in between these two boundary cases. From the above equations, we know that the ratio of i/o time is given by $C_i x_i / C_j x_j$, or $C_j x_j / C_i x_i$. Therefore we can calculate the effective bandwidth B as below,

$$B = \begin{cases} B_r + (1 - C_i x_i / C_j x_j)(B_s - B_r) & \text{if } C_i x_i \leq C_j x_j \\ B_r + (1 - C_j x_j / C_i x_i)(B_s - B_r) & \text{otherwise.} \end{cases}$$

For inter-operation parallelism between two sequential i/o tasks, we need to add this third equation to the above two equations to compute the correct IO-CPU balance point. Similarly, we can also compute the correct IO-CPU balance point between a sequential i/o task and a random i/o task. However, because of the disk bandwidth drop, inter-operation parallelism may lose its advantage over intra-operation parallelism. In other words, for sequential i/o tasks it may be better to run the tasks one by one using only intra-operation parallelism to avoid disk seeking between tasks.

For example, we have run a small experiment on XPRS using two sequential scans. We made sure that one scan is CPU-bound and the other is IO-bound. When we run them separately using intra-operation parallelism only, the total elapsed time is 45 seconds. However, when we run them together using inter-operation parallelism at their IO-CPU balance point, the total elapsed time becomes 65 seconds.

Therefore, in considering running two sequential scan tasks in parallel, we need to compare the estimated time of execution using inter-operation parallelism based on the above equations and the estimated time of execution using only intra-operation parallelism and decide whether inter-operation parallelism is worthwhile.

2.4 Dynamic Adjustment of Parallelism

Even though we have known how to calculate the IO-CPU balance point given an IO-bound task and a CPU-bound task, we have not yet solved the scheduling problem, because by running the two tasks at their IO-CPU balance point only guarantees full resource utilization while both tasks are running, when one task finishes first and there is no other task to fill in the newly available resources, resources are still wasted. Now the question is how to order the execution of tasks so that resource waste is minimized. We can model this problem as a modified version of the bin packing problem or the multiprocessor scheduling problem in combinatorial optimization as in [PIRA90]. However, given the NP-hard complexity of the problem, it will not be efficient to try to solve this problem directly. In XPRS, this combinatorial optimization problem is avoided by a mechanism of dynamic adjustment of intra-operation parallelism taking advantage of the low communication overhead feature in a shared-memory environment.

As described in [HONG91], in XPRS, intra-operation parallelism is implemented in two ways, *page partitioning* and *range partitioning*. In page partitioning, we partition relations across disk page boundaries and assign a subset of disk pages to each participating processors to work on. Specifically, given n processors, processor i processes disk pages $\{p \mid p \ mod \ n = i\}$, where $i = 0, 1, \ldots, n-1$. For example, if we have 3 processors, then processor 0 scans pages $\{0, 3, 6, \ldots\}$, processor 1 scans pages $\{1, 4, 7, \ldots\}$, and processor 2 scans pages $\{2, 5, 8, \ldots\}$. Obviously, using our page partitioning scheme, unless the number of processors that we use is exactly the same as the number of disks in the disk array, the access to each disk is not exactly sequential because of the asynchronousness of the parallel backends. However, although the block requests to each disk are not perfectly sequential, they are always clustered close to each other and thus the seek distances are likely to be very small. Therefore we can still get a close-to-sequential bandwidth which is still much higher than the random bandwidth.

In range partitioning, we partition relations according to the value of a certain attribute. For example, suppose that we want to partition an employee relation between 2 processors. We may have one processor work on tuples with *emp.salary* > 30000 and the other processor work on tuples with *emp.salary* ≤ 30000. We can try to find a balanced range partition with data distribution information in the system catalog or in the root node of an index.

Page partitioning is used for sequential scans while range partitioning is used for index scans. Joins are parallelized using either page partitioning or range partitioning depending on the type of scans in their inner and outer plans. Different parallelism adjustment mechanisms have been designed for page partitioning and range partitioning operations.

Suppose that the current degree of parallelism for a task is n and we want to adjust it to a new degree of n', where n' can be greater than n, which means that we are putting in more available processors to work on this task, or smaller than n, which means that we are taking some processors away from this task to work on another task. We have implemented dynamic parallelism adjustment in XPRS as follows:

- For Page Partitioning

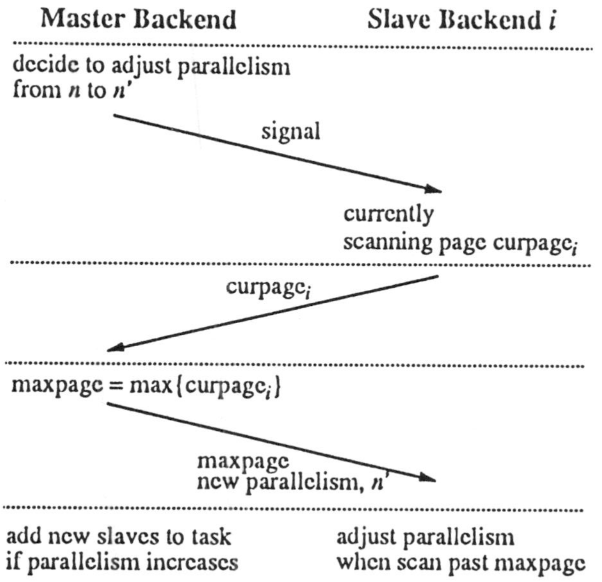

Figure 5: **Page Partitioning Parallelism Adjustment**

The master backend sends a signal to all participating slave backends on the task. Upon receiving the signal, each slave backend, $i = 0, 1, \ldots, n-1$, sends back the current page number $curpage_i$ that it is scanning and then waits for a message from the master backend. After receiving all the page numbers from the slave backends, the master backend computes the maximum page number,

$$maxpage = max\{curpage_i\},\ i = 0, 1, \ldots, n-1.$$

Then the master backend sends *maxpage* and new parallelism n' to all the slave backends, which completes the communications between the master and the slaves for the parallelism adjustment. If $n' > n$, the master backend will start $n' - n$ free slave backends to work on the task and make each of them start scanning after page *maxpage*. After receiving *maxpage* and n', all the slave backends will resume their work until they finish scanning all the pages before *maxpage*, at which point, they will change from scanning every nth page to scanning every n'th page and complete the parallelism adjustment. If $n > n'$, upon scanning past *maxpage*, the slave backends i, $i >= n'-1$ will finish processing the current task and report back to the master backend as available. The communication between the master backend and the slave backends for page partitioning parallelism adjustment is shown in Figure 5.

- For Range Partitioning

  The master backend sends a signal to all the participating slave backends on the task. Upon receiving the signal, each slave backend sends back the intervals of values that remain for them to scan. For example, if a slave backend is assigned to scan for values in interval $[l, h]$ and the current value that is being examined is c, the interval that will be sent back to the master backend is $[c, h]$. After parallelism adjustment, each slave backend may get more than one intervals to scan instead of only one contiguous interval. Upon receiving all the intervals from the slave backends, the master backend redistributes the intervals among n' slave backends and sends each slave backend a set of repartitioned search intervals. If $n' > n$, the master backend will start $n'-n$ free slave backends to work on the task. Meanwhile, the old slave backends will resume their processing with the new search intervals. If $n' < n$, the extra slave backends will finish the processing of the current task and report back to the master backend as available. Figure 6 shows the communications between the master backend and the slave backends for range partitioning parallelism adjustment.

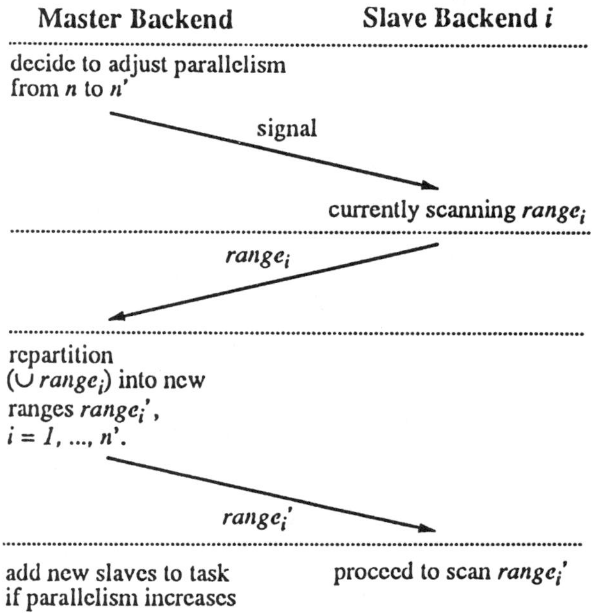

Figure 6: **Range Partitioning Parallelism Adjustment**

As we can see, the efficiency of our parallelism adjustment mechanism depends on the low communication delay advantage of a shared-memory system.

Our dynamic parallelism adjustment mechanism is not only useful for solving the scheduling algorithm, it is also useful for correcting optimizer cost estimation errors. Because of errors in cost estimation models, the optimizer may label an IO-bound task CPU-bound or vice versa, which may cause performance problems. The run time system can detect this error while the mislabeled task is running and adjust it to its correct parallelism.

2.5 Adaptive Scheduling Algorithm

The main idea of our scheduling algorithm is to use our dynamic parallelism adjustment mechanism to keep the system running at the IO-CPU balance point, i.e., at the maximum system resource utilization. At the same time, the algorithm also considers the possibility that inter-operation parallelism may be disadvantageous when sequential i/o is involved because of the disk seeks between tasks, in which case only intra-operation parallelism will be used to take advantage of the sequential disk bandwidth.

Given a set of n runable tasks, $S = \{f_1, f_2, \ldots, f_n\}$, suppose that the sequential execution time of f_i is T_i. And suppose that $T_{intra}(f_i)$ is the execution time of f_i using only intra-operation parallelism and $T_{inter}(f_i, f_j)$ is the execution time of f_i and f_j running at their IO-CPU balance point (x_i, x_j) with inter-operation parallelism. We have,

$$T_{intra}(f_i) = T_i/maxp(f_i),$$

$$T_{inter}(f_i, f_j) = min(T_i/x_i, T_j/x_j) + T_{ij}/maxp_{ij}.$$

where T_{ij} is the execution time of the remaining task when either f_i or f_j finishes first and $maxp_{ij}$ is the maximum intra-operation parallelism of the remaining task. We have,

$$T_{ij} = \begin{cases} T_i - T_j x_i/x_j & \text{if } T_i/x_i > T_j/x_j \\ T_j - T_i x_j/x_i & \text{otherwise,} \end{cases}$$

$$maxp_{ij} = \begin{cases} maxp(f_i) & \text{if } T_i/x_i > T_j/x_j \\ maxp(f_j) & \text{otherwise.} \end{cases}$$

The following is the description of our algorithm.

1. Divide S into S_{io} and S_{cpu} such that $S = S_{io} \bigcup S_{cpu}$, S_{io} contains all the IO-bound tasks and S_{cpu} contains all the CPU-bound tasks.
2. Choose $task_1 \in S_{io}$ and set $S_1 = S_{io}$, or if $S_{io} = \emptyset$, choose $task_1 \in S_{cpu}$ and set $S_1 = S_{cpu}$.
3. Choose $task_2 \in S - S_1$, such that

   $T_{inter}(task_1, task_2) < T_{intra}(task_1) + T_{intra}(task_2)$.
4. If $task_2$ does not exist, run $task_1$ alone with parallelism $maxp(task_1)$ if $task_1$ is a new task, or adjust the current parallelism of $task_1$ to $maxp(task_1)$ if $task_1$ is a running task, set $S = S - \{task_1\}$[1], go to 2 when $task_1$ completes.
5. If $task_2$ exists, calculate the IO-CPU balance point between $task_1$ and $task_2$, (x_1, x_2).
6. Execute $task_1$ with parallelism x_1 if $task_1$ is a new task, or adjust the current parallelism of $task_1$ to x_1 if $task_1$ is a running task; Execute $task_2$ with parallelism x_2.
7. If $task_1$ finishes first while $task_2$ is still running, set $S = S - \{task_1\}$, $task_1 = task_2$, $S_1 = S - S_1$, go to 3.
8. If $task_2$ finishes first while $task_1$ is still running, set $S = S - \{task_2\}$, go to 3.
9. If $S = \emptyset$, algorithm terminates.

[1] When we remove a task from S, we also implicitly remove the task from S_{io} and S_{cpu}.

In the above algorithm, we try to pair up an IO-bound task and a CPU-bound task for inter-operation parallelism only if it is better than running them separately with intra-operation parallelism. If either IO-bound tasks or CPU-bound tasks run out, we will simply execute the remaining tasks with intra-operation parallelism only. We use an obvious strategy to choose the pair of IO-bound and CPU-bound tasks, f_i and f_j, to execute in parallel, namely, to pair up the most IO-bound task, i.e., the task with the greatest i/o rate, and the most CPU-bound task, i.e., the task with the smallest i/o rate. In this way, we can keep the system running closer to the maximum utilization point (the upper-right corner of the rectangle in Figure 4) when either IO-bound or CPU-bound tasks run out first, because the remaining tasks will be those corresponding to lines closer to the diagonal in Figure 4. In a multi-user environment, if we want to minimize the response time of individual queries instead of the the total elapsed time, a shortest-job-first heuristic can be used, i.e., to execute the tasks from the shortest query first.

The above algorithm can be easily extended to handle a continuous sequence of tasks $\{f_1, f_2, f_3, \ldots\}$ instead of a fixed set of tasks. In other words, the above algorithm can also be used for on-line scheduling. All we need to do is to represent S_{io} and S_{cpu} as queues. When a task arrives, it is put into either the S_{io} queue or the S_{cpu} queue according to its i/o rate. For our most IO-bound and most CPU-bound task first strategy, we can easily keep the tasks in the S_{io} queue in descending order of i/o rate and the tasks in the S_{cpu} queue in ascending order of i/o rate. Each time we simply take a task off the head of the task queues. The rest of the algorithm still work as described.

3 Evaluation of Scheduling Algorithms

In this section, we evaluate the performance of our scheduling algorithm described in the previous section through XPRS benchmark experiments. Currently XPRS is implemented on a Sequent Symmetry system with 12 processors and 4 disks running the Dynix operating system. In the experiments, we compare the performance of the following three scheduling algorithms.

- **INTRA-ONLY** – No Inter-Operation Parallelism, i.e., executing tasks one by one using intra-operation parallelism only.

- **INTER-WITHOUT-ADJ** – Inter-Operation Parallelism without Dynamic Adjustment

  This is almost the same as the algorithm in the previous section, except that when one task finishes first, no dynamic parallelism adjustment is performed. The master backend will simply start the task that can get closest to maximum utilization point if executed using the currently available processors in parallel with the running task.

- **INTER-WITH-ADJ** – Inter-Operation Parallelism with Dynamic Adjustment, i.e., the algorithm described in the previous section.

We run the following four workloads against each of the three algorithms:

- all IO-bound tasks,
- all CPU-bound tasks,
- extremely IO-bound tasks with extremely CPU-bound tasks,
- random-mix tasks.

Each workload consists of ten tasks. Since our algorithms only depend on the i/o rate of each task and other details of the operations in the tasks do not affect the performance. we choose all the queries to be one-variable selection queries for simplicity and ease of constructing tasks with specific i/o rates. Hence, all the tasks will be either a sequential scan or an index scan. The length of each task is randomly chosen between scanning 100 tuples and scanning 10,000 tuples. We adjust the i/o rate of each task by varying the size of tuples that are scanned. All relations in the workloads have the same schema:

$$r_i(a = int4, b = text),$$

where attribute b is a variable-size string and is used to adjust the tuple sizes. All queries will be a selection on $r_i.a$. An unclustered index may be created on a to make index scans possible. For sequential scans, the i/o rate is determined by the tuple size. There is a fixed per-tuple overhead (evaluation of query qualifications) after each tuple is read into memory from disks. Therefore, the time between two i/o requests is equal to the time to read in a disk page plus the time to process all the tuples that reside in the read-in disk page. When the tuple size is small, many tuples can be packed into one disk page, thus it takes longer to process all the tuples in a page and the i/o rate is lower, so the task is likely to be CPU-bound. On the other hand, if the tuple size is large, the i/o rate is higher and the task is likely to be IO-bound. For index scans on an unclustered index, however, the i/o rate is always high because index scans can follow the pointer in an index to a qualified tuple on a disk page and hence the time between two i/o requests is small. Therefore, index scans on an unclustered index are most

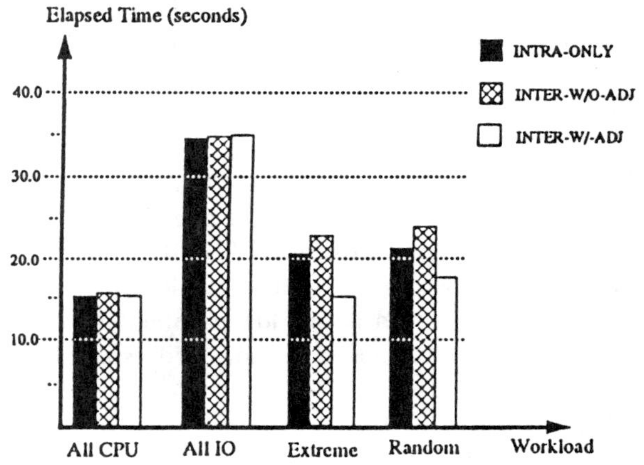

Figure 7: **Experiment Results of Scheduling Algorithms**

likely IO-bound. On the other hand, index scans on a clustered index have more or less the same situation as sequential scans.

In our experiments, the most CPU-bound task is a sequential scan on relation r_{min} in which the b attribute in all the tuples is set to NULL so that the tuple size is the smallest. The most IO-bound task is a sequential scan on relation r_{max} in which the b attribute in all the tuples is set large enough so that each disk page can only hold one tuple. In XPRS, the disk page size is 8K bytes. We have measured the i/o rate of sequential scans on both r_{min} and r_{max}. The r_{min} i/o rate is 5 (ios/second) and the r_{max} i/o rate is 70 (ios/second). All other tasks will have i/o rate in between. We have measured the bandwidth of our disks (bandwidth after file system overhead) to be 97 io's/second for sequential reads, 60 io's/second for almost sequential reads and 35 io's/second for random reads. In parallel executions, we at most see the almost sequential read bandwidth because even for parallel sequential scans, the reads may become unordered due to the asynchronousness of the parallel backends. Since we use 4 disks, we have a total i/o bandwidth of $4 * 60 = 240$ io's/second, and because we use 8 processors in our experiments, according to our definition, those tasks with i/o rate above $240/8 = 30$ io's/second are IO-bound and those below 30 are CPU-bound. We choose the i/o rate of the tasks in our experiments as in the following table.

Type of Tasks	IO Rate (ios/second)
CPU-bound	randomly chosen in [5, 30)
IO-bound	randomly chosen in (30, 60]
Extremely CPU-bound	randomly chosen in [5, 15]
Extremely IO-bound	randomly chosen in [60, 70]

We run each workload in XPRS using each of the above three algorithms and measure the turnaround time of each run. Our experiment result is presented in Figure 7. As we can see, when the workload is all IO-bound or CPU-bound, all three algorithms have roughly the same performance and inter-operation parallelism does not help. It is sufficient to use intra-operation parallelism only in such cases. However, when there is a mixed workload of IO-bound and CPU-bound tasks, our proposed scheduling algorithm INTER-WITH-ADJ can improve performance by as much as 25% over INTRA-ONLY. We can also see that INTER-WITHOUT-ADJ loses to INTRA-ONLY because without parallelism adjustment a task may have to run with a low parallelism even when other tasks have finished and more processors have become available.

4 Optimization of Bushy Tree Plans for Parallelism

In the previous sections, we have studied the scheduling problem of a set or a sequence of runable tasks. Our algorithm can be used regardless of whether the parallel tasks are from a bushy tree plan of the same query or from different queries. In this section, we will concentrate on the optimization problem of parallel execution plans for a single query and propose an optimization strategy based on the scheduling algorithm in the previous sections.

Since we have shown that a proper combination of intra-operation parallelism and inter-operation parallelism wins over only intra-operation parallelism given a workload of mixed IO-bound and CPU-bound tasks. The left-deep-tree-only and intra-operation-parallelism-only optimization strategy proposed in [HONG91] obviously cannot always take full advantage of all available resources and thus cannot guarantee the optimality of the execution plan chosen. However, in a multi-user environment, this problem can be easily solved by combining the two-phase optimization strategy in [HONG91] with our scheduling algorithm. We still find the best parallel plan for each query using only intra-operation parallelism with the algorithm in [HONG91], but we rely on the tasks from different queries submitted by multiple users to achieve maximum resource utilizations using our scheduling algorithm. In this section, we will focus on the optimization problem of a single query in a single-user environment where we have to depend on the tasks within a same plan to achieve IO-CPU balance and where bushy tree plans have to be considered. Our idea is to preserve the same optimization scheme as in [HONG91], but use a new cost estimation method to estimate and compare the costs of bushy tree plans.

Since use of parallelism only helps reduce response time of a query execution, we only consider response time as our cost measurements in the following discussions. For each sequential plan p, let $seqcost(p)$ be the cost of sequential execution of p and $parcost(p,n)$ be the cost of parallel execution of p on n processors. As described before, plan p can be decomposed into a set of plan fragments which are what we call tasks in parallel executions. Unlike the situation in the previous sections, the tasks here have order-dependencies among themselves because some task may take the output of another task as input. However, obviously our scheduling algorithm can be easily modified to deal with the order-dependencies. It only needs to check if a task is ready before choosing it to execute and only execute the ready tasks. Suppose that $F(p) = \{f_1, f_2, \ldots, f_k\}$ is the set of plan fragments (tasks) of plan p. Using the cost estimation methods in conventional query optimization, we can estimate the sequential execution time of each task i, T_i. We can also estimate the number of i/o's of each task i, D_i. Thus, we can estimate the i/o rate of each task i as

$$C_i = D_i/T_i.$$

Let $T_n(S)$ be the elapsed time of executing a set of tasks, S with n processors. We can compute $T_n(S)$ with the following recursive formula:

$$T_n(S) = \begin{cases} T_i/maxp(f_i) + T_n(S - \{f_i\}) \\ \text{if } f_i \text{ is run alone,} \\ \\ min(T_i/x_1, T_j/x_2) + T_n((S - \{f_i, f_j\}) \bigcup \{f_{ij}\}) \\ \text{if } f_i \text{ and } f_j \text{ is run in parallel.} \end{cases}$$

where f_i and f_j are two ready tasks chosen in S according to our scheduling algorithm to execute in parallel at IO-CPU balance point (x_i, x_j), f_{ij} is the remaining task of the longer of f_i and f_j when one of them finishes first. This formula basically simulates each iteration of our scheduling algorithm and computes the total elapsed time of processing all the tasks. We compute parallel execution cost of a plan as,

$$parcost(p, n) = T_n(F(p)).$$

Now for each plan p, we can estimate $parcost(p,n)$ given n and since we are assuming a single-user environment, n is known beforehand. Therefore, we can find the plan that minimizes $parcost(p,n)$. The optimal plan can be found by a conventional query optimization algorithm with $parcost(p,n)$ replacing $seqcost(p)$. Note that the calculation of $parcost(p,n)$ depends on the structure of the entire plan tree of p which makes local pruning, a common complexity-reducing technique in conventional query optimization infeasible. Aside from this factor, we can solve the parallel optimization problem with the same algorithmic complexity as in conventional query optimization.

5 Conclusion

In this paper, we have presented our approach to exploit inter-operation parallelism in a shared-memory environment. We have first studied the scheduling problem of a set or a sequence of independent tasks that are either from a bushy tree plan of a single query or from the plans of multiple queries and proposed a clean and simple scheduling algorithm. Our scheduling algorithm achieves maximum resource utilizations by running two carefully selected tasks in parallel at their IO-CPU balance point, and avoids the combinatorial optimization problem by dynamically adjusting the degree of parallelism of the tasks to keep the system running with maximum resource utilizations. It takes full advantage of the low communication overhead feature of a shared-memory system, which a shared-nothing system does not have. We have also studied the optimization problem of parallel execution plans of a single query and extended our previous result to consider inter-operation parallelism by introducing a cost estimation method for parallel execution costs of a sequential plan based on our scheduling algorithm.

In this paper, we have neglected the memory constraints on parallelism. For example, we cannot run two hashjoins in parallel unless there is enough memory for both hash tables. As future work, we will integrate memory constraints into our scheduling and optimization algorithms. So far, we have only studied the parallel optimization problem of a single query. We also plan to extend our results to deal with optimization of multiple queries for parallel execution.

Acknowledgements

Many thanks go to my advisor Professor Michael Stonebraker, who helped me form the initial ideas of this paper and commented on the first version of this paper. I am very grateful for his support and encouragement to me throughout my research. I also would like to thank the anonymous SIGMOD reviewers for their comments that helped me clarify the presentation of this paper.

References

[BHID88] Bhide, A. and Stonebraker, M., "A Performance Comparison of Two Architectures for Fast Transaction Processing," Proceedings of 1988 International Conference on Data Engineering.

[COPE88] Copeland, G., et. al., "Data Placement in Bubba," Proceedings of 1988 ACM-SIGMOD International Conference on Management of Data, Chicago, IL, June 1988.

[DEWI90] Dewitt, D., et al, "The Gamma Database Machine Project," IEEE Transactions on Knowledge and Data Engineering, Vol. 2, No. 1, March 1990.

[GRAE90] Graefe, G., "Encapsulation of Parallelism in the Volcano Query Processing System," Proceedings of 1990 ACM-SIGMOD International Conference on Management of Data.

[HONG91] Hong, W. and Stonebraker, M., "Optimization of Parallel Query Execution Plans in XPRS," Proceedings of the 1st International Conference on Parallel and Distributed Information Systems, Miami, Florida, December 1991.

[LU91] Lu, H., et al, "Optimization of Multi-Way Join Queries for Parallel Execution," Proceedings of 1991 International Conference on Very Large Data Bases.

[PIRA90] Pirahesh, H., et al, "Parallelism in Relational Database Systems: Architectural Issues and Design Approaches," Proceedings of the 2nd International Symposium on Database in Parallel and Distributed Systems, July 1990.

[SCHN90] Schneider, D. and Dewitt, D., "Tradeoffs in Processing Complex Join Queries via Hashing in Multiprocessor Database Machines," Proceedings of 1990 International Conference on Very Large Data Bases.

[STON86] Stonebraker, M., "The Case for Shared Nothing," Proceedings of 1986 International Conference on Data Engineering.

[STON88] Stonebraker, M., et. al., "The Design of XPRS," Proceedings of 1988 International Conference on Very Large Data Bases.

[STON91] Stonebraker, S., et al, "The Postgres Next Generation DBMS," Communications of ACM, vol. 34 no. 10, pp. 78-92, October 1991.

Query Optimization for Parallel Execution

Sumit Ganguly* Waqar Hasan Ravi Krishnamurthy

Hewlett-Packard Laboratories
1501, Page Mill Road, Palo Alto, CA 94305
email: lastname@hpl.hp.com

Abstract

The decreasing cost of computing makes it economically viable to reduce the response time of decision support queries by using parallel execution to exploit inexpensive resources. This goal poses the following query optimization problem: *Minimize response time subject to constraints on throughput*, which we motivate as the dual of the traditional DBMS problem. We address this novel problem in the context of Select-Project-Join queries by extending the execution space, cost model and search algorithm that are widely used in commercial DBMSs. We incorporate the sources and deterrents of parallelism in the traditional execution space. We show that a cost model can predict response time while accounting for the new aspects due to parallelism. We observe that the response time optimization metric violates a fundamental assumption in the dynamic programming algorithm that is the linchpin in the optimizers of most commercial DBMSs. We extend dynamic programming and show how optimization metrics which correctly predict response time may be designed.

1 Introduction

The Papyrus project[CHK+91] at HP Labs is investigating ways of integrating highly-tuned, customized data managers while preserving their requirements for performance. One source of high performance is parallel execution of queries. While, in its generality, the project seeks to parallelize queries containing arbitrary data manipulation operators, in this paper we focus on the problem of optimizing Select-Project-Join (SPJ) queries for parallel execution.

The need to reduce response time is evident in decision support applications in which human beings pose complex queries and demand interactive responses. For example, a system for stock portfolio managers is capable of running a non-trivial query at the click of a button and graphing the results by many categories of stocks. This is not an isolated example but typifies the tasks in decision making processes. Achieving a reasonable response time has been an important roadblock for these applications.

The decreasing cost of computing makes it economically viable to throw inexpensive resources to achieve the reduction in response times by exploiting parallel query execution. For example hash partitioned sort-merge[SD89] may be used to reduce response time at the expense of extra work done in comparison to vanilla sort-merge. While extra work may be traded for reduced response time, it is unacceptable to minimize response time at any expense.

Todays' commercial database systems aim at maximizing throughput while imposing some limits on response time. For example, the TPC-A benchmark[Gra91] requires that 90% of the queries have a response time of at most 2 seconds. However, this requirement is typically assured, not by incorporating the requirement into the optimizer, but by setting system parameters such as the maximum degree of multi-programming and the frequency of group commit. Assuring response times for other classes of queries will require the optimizer itself to be modified.

The traditional database problem is to maximize throughput subject to constraints on response time. We claim that decision support applications pose the *dual* optimization problem of minimizing response time subject to constraints on throughput.

Optimizing queries for parallel execution is considered an open problem[DG90]. Previous work on minimization of response time in [AHY83] and XPRS[HS91] made restricting assumptions regarding the parallel machine architecture that restrict the applicability of the proposed solutions. The Gamma project[DGS+90, SD89, Sch90] studied many execution strategies but did not address the problem of query optimization.

Any solution to this optimization problem should build on the decade of experience with commercial optimizers.

*Author's permenant address is Dept. of Comp. Sciences, The University of Texas, Austin, TX 78712. sumit@cs.utexas.edu

1992 ACM SIGMOD - 6/92/CA, USA

Taking cue from [SAC+79] we describe our solution to the parallel query optimization problem along the following three dimensions: an *execution space* which defines the syntactic representation of all relevant aspects of an actual execution; a *cost model* which predicts the cost of an execution plan; a *search algorithm* which is used to obtain the minimum cost plan.

The solution described in this paper is applicable to a gamut of parallel machine architectures. Differences across architectures appear as variations in the precise details of the cost model and in the factors considered important in the design of the search metric.

We have extended the traditional execution space to model the sources (such as running different joins in parallel or parallelizing one join) and deterrents of parallel execution (such as data dependence and resource contention). Thus the trade-offs that should be examined by the optimizer have been represented.

We have shown that it is possible to design a cost model that can estimate the above trade-offs in predicting response times. For example, depending on the dataflow dependencies and resource contentions, the response time estimate of a pipelined execution ranges from that of an independent parallel execution to an estimate that is *worse than* that of a sequential execution. This degenerate pipelined execution reflects the penalty for executing operations in a pipelined fashion when there is no available parallelism. Thus, we establish the feasibility of a cost model to be judicious.

We show that response time violates a fundamental property, namely principle of optimality, required by the commercially accepted search algorithm[SAC+79]. While the traditional dynamic programming approach used a total order on work, our extension uses a partial order on a metric that predicts response time. Further we provide an analysis that demonstrates the practicality of this approach.

In summary, we address the problems in designing execution space, cost model, and search algorithm so as to establish the feasibility of a general but practical optimization algorithm for minimizing response time subject to constraints on extra work.

Section 2 presents a precise description of the optimization metric and Section 3 presents an overview of traditional optimizers. In Section 4, we discuss how the execution space models the sources and deterrents of parallelism and Section 5 presents our cost model Section 6 deals with search algorithms and we conclude in Section 7.

2 Parallel Query Optimization : Optimization Metric

The general problem of query optimization may be stated as: Given a query q, a space of execution plans, E, and a cost function $cost(p)$ that assigns a numeric cost to an execution plan $p \in E$, find the minimum cost execution plan that computes q.

We formulate the cost of a query as its response time but place a bound on the amount of "extra" work that can be traded for reducing response time. The bound on extra work is determined by parameters that allow a system administrator control over the work and response-time tradeoff. Our formulation of the query optimization problem is quite novel and we believe, necessary.

Suppose the work and response time costs of the optimal-work plan for query q are W_o and T_o (respectively) and for an arbitrary execution plan p are W_p and T_p. We will consider two ways of limiting the extra work:

- Limit on throughput degradation: The system administrator may specify the factor, k, by which the maximum throughput of the system may be allowed to degrade. The cost of p is T_p if $W_p \leq k * W_o$ and infinite otherwise.

- Cost-benefit ratio: The system administrator may specify a limit, k, on the ratio of the decrease in response time to additional work required. The cost of p is T_p if $\frac{T_o - T_p}{W_p - W_o} \leq k$ and infinite otherwise.

This limit on extra work is incorporated in the search algorithm akin to incorporation of branch and bound techniques.

3 Traditional Optimizer Revisited

Commercial DBMSs are built for optimal throughput and therefore the optimization metric is *work* (total resource consumption). Optimizers in these systems have adopted the framework of the System R optimizer[SAC+79]. The design of such optimizers may be decomposed into three components: Execution Space, Cost Model and Search Algorithm.

Execution Space: Query executions are syntactically represented as *annotated join trees* (also called *plans*). These are *binary* trees in which each internal node is a join operation and each leaf node is a base relation. Annotations of the form *label=value* on nodes permit the important factors of an execution to be modeled. An example annotation for a join node is *join-method=nested-loops*. Other examples of labels are access path, create index, and eliminate duplicates.

The semantics of such trees is intuitive for left-deep trees. We place the semantic constraint that *each tuple of any subtree of a join tree is computed exactly once*. This eliminates some bushy trees that represent the "same" execution as left-deep trees.

Given a query, all trees that compute the query (independent of database state) are considered *legal plans* for the query. Optimizers are designed to only search a finite subset of this infinite space of legal plans. This subset, termed the *search space*, can be syntactically characterized. For example the search space in System R is left-deep join trees with the annotations described in [SAC+79].

Cost Model: The cost model assigns an integer cost to a plan based on some set of assumptions about the statistical distribution of data and the abstract machine that executes plans. A cost function, *cost(plan)* $\rightarrow$ *descriptor*, is *recursively* defined in terms of the descriptors of the left and right subtrees of the plan. The descriptor contains information such as relation size, interesting orderings, and index availability. The cost function is recursive not only for simplicity but so that it may be used in search algorithms based on dynamic programming.

Search Algorithm: This is the algorithm used to search the search space for the plan with minimum cost. A System R style dynamic programming algorithm is reviewed in Section 6.1.1.

4 A Model for Parallel Execution

In this section we delineate important aspects of parallel execution and then present a macro expansion of the traditional annotated join tree to get a new tree called *operator tree* wherein these new aspects are modeled.

4.1 Aspects of Parallel Execution

In addition to modeling important aspects of sequential execution, a model for parallel execution needs to account for the *sources* and *deterrents* of parallelism.

There are essentially two sources of parallelism. (1) Inter-operator parallelism which includes both the data independent parallel execution of a pair of operators (typically subtrees) and data dependent, (i.e., pipelined) parallel execution of a pair of operators. 2) Intra-operator parallelism which refers to the parallelization of a single operation (e.g., sort), that we term cloning.

Two main deterrents of such parallelism are: 1) *Data Dependencies* between operators which arise due to the logical relationship between the operators (e.g., the probe of a hash join cannot begin until the build is completed). 2) *Resource Contention* arising out of several operators running in parallel and competing for the same resource.

4.2 The Operator Tree

In order to accurately model aspects of parallel execution we refine the execution model of join trees to a finer granularity. Each annotated join tree is expanded to a *unique* operator tree by macro-expanding each join node into an operator subtree in a manner described below. Intuitively, the operator tree has nodes which are atomic in the sense that the run-time scheduler cannot subdivide this operation further except for the partitioning the input for cloning. Note that our intention here is only to provide some exemplary aspects of the operator tree model based on which we can discuss the cost model. Therefore it is not complete.

The node *sort-merge*(R_1, R_2)[1] is macro expanded with explicit sorting and merging. For example, if *merge*(*sort*(*Scan*(R_1)), *sort*(*Scan*(R_2))) is the operator tree then the data dependency of the sort operation and the merge operation as well as the independent parallel execution of the two sort operations are explicitly represented here. Note that if R_2 is already sorted then only one sort operation needs to be stated in the operator tree. Similarly, the node *hash-join*(R_1, R_2) can be expanded with explicit reference to the building and then probing of the hash table (e.g., *probe*(*Scan*(R_1), *build*(*Scan*(R_2)))). The *nested-loops* join is expanded with explicit reference to the inflections of this join method such as create-index, duplicate elimination etc. (e.g., *pure-nested-loops*(*Scan*(R_1), *create-index*(*Scan*(R_2)))). Note that a *pure-nested-loops* operator represents an execution of a nested loops without any inflections.

As before, further details of the execution are given as annotations, some of which are given below.

1. The *composition method* annotation for a (child, parent) pair has two possibilities, *pipelined* or *materialized*. It can be set to pipelined if the child can produce partial output, and the parent can consume partial output; otherwise, it is annotated as materialized. Note that this annotation, denoting the method for (child, parent) pair, is associated with the child node which is uniquely defined in an operator tree.

2. The *cloning* annotation is intended to model intra-operator parallelism. This value is a pair (set of resources, the partitioning attribute), representing parallel execution using the attribute partitioned data over the resources. Suppose that a sort-merge node is annotated as being cloned on processes $1, 2, 5, 7$ on the join attribute A. This would represent a hash partitioned sort-merge as described in [SD89].

3. The *data redistribution* between a (child,parent) pair, annotated at the child node, has two possibilities: true or false[2]. This is set to true if it is found necessary to redistribute the output of the child node based on the subsequent cloned operations ; otherwise false.

Example 1 Consider the following join tree *nested-loops*(*sort-merge*(R_1, R_2), R_3)) with the following operator tree for parallel execution:
nested-loops(*merge*(*sort*1(*scan*(R_1)), *sort*2(*scan*(R_2))), *scan*(R_3))

[1] Note that strictly speaking, the operation is *join* and the join-method annotation is sort-merge. For brevity, we use this notation whenever there is no ambiguity.

[2] Note that a more expressive annotation would be needed for practical application. As this is sufficient for this paper, we present the simplest case.

The annotations for this operator tree are given below:

Node	cloning	comp. method	redistr.
$scan(R_1)$	$(\{1,2,3,4\}, A1)$	*pipelined*	*no*
$scan(R_2)$	$(\{1,2\}, A2)$	*pipelined*	*yes*
$scan(R_3)$	$(\{1,2,3,4\}, A3)$	*pipelined*	*no*
sort1	$(\{1,2,3,4\}, A4)$	*materialized*	*no*
sort2	$(\{1,2,3,4\}, A5)$	*materialized*	*no*
merge	$(\{1,2,3,4\}, A6)$	*pipelined*	*no*
n.loops	$(\{1,2,3,4\}, A7)$	–	–

■

5 The Cost Model

We present a cost model primarily to show that the trade-offs — amongst the aspects of parallel execution as it affects the response time — can be represented. We estimate the response time for independent parallel execution (IPE), dependent parallel execution(DPE), parallel execution of cloned operation (CPE) as well as sequential execution (SE) such that the deterrents affect the response time. In particular, the following desiderata for the cost model is put forth:

1. Response time of an IPE degrades to that of a SE depending on the level of resource contention.

2. Response time of a DPE is in the range from that of IPE to a response time worse than that for SE depending on the dataflow dependencies and resource contentions.

3. Response time of a CPE is similar to IPE of the clones.

Note that the DPE may degenerate to an execution that is worse that SE because there is a penalty for executing operations in a pipelined fashion when there is no available parallelism, especially if prohibited by resource contention. This is because, the system necessarily sets up the pipeline and compromises the run time execution of DPE whereas no such penalty occurs for a SE.

The cost model presented below is purely an example that is capable of trading-off the sources and deterrents as per this desiderata. Consequently, this is not intended to be a prescriptive cost model for any parallel execution, and therefore we make simplifying assumptions so long as the above goal of exemplification is not compromised.

We first present the cost model assuming no cloning, or redistribution. Then we will extend it to accommodate these annotations as well. Sans these annotations, the only annotation of interest is the composition method and its effect on parallelism. In short, the execution can be viewed as a traditional execution with parallel access to disks.

The response time (RT) is the metric for the cost model. We assume the usual information in the cost descriptor with the cost estimate in the descriptor representing the response time. In order to account for data dependencies in an operator tree P, especially for pipelined operations, the cost descriptor must have two parts.

1. *First tuple descriptor*, which is a descriptor for those subtrees of P that must be finished before the first tuple of P is output to any subsequent operation. More precisely, given $S1$ the set of subtrees in P, the minimal subset $S2$ of $S1$ that must be finished before the first tuple of $S1$ is output. This is the set of all subtrees of $S1$ that have materialized annotation at the root of the subtree. $S2$ is called the ***materialized front*** of $S1$. In Example 1 $S2$ is the set of subtrees rooted at *sort1* and *sort2*. We refer to the ***residual query*** of $S1$, that is done after the first tuple is computed, as $S1 \ominus S2$.

2. *Last tuple descriptor*, which is a descriptor for the complete execution of P.

The cost portion of the first (last) tuple descriptor is initially represented as an integer tf (resp. tl) denoting the estimated time when the first (resp. last) tuple of the plan is output. We refer to this as the *time descriptor* and is typically denoted by $\mathbf{t} = (tf, tl)$. This will be generalized to include the resource usage in the latter subsection and thus the term *resource descriptor* and this is typically denoted $\vec{r}$. Besides these, we assume the usual statistical information needed for cost estimation, even though we have not explicitly expressed it in the formalism.

We present the cost model in two steps. First, we describe the estimation of response time assuming no resource contention. Therefore, we discuss the estimation of the time descriptor for any query. Then we incorporate the contention on resources into the estimate of the resource descriptor which in turn affects the response time.

5.1 Estimating Resource Contention Free RT

We present an extension to the cost model for traditional DBMS, accounting for data dependencies, intra and inter-operator parallelism assuming there is no resource contention. We introduce three binary operators on time and describe the scenario whose cost each operator is expected to model. We assume that $t1$ and $t2$ represent the completion times of two sets of operators, say $S1$ and $S2$.

1. $t1 \parallel t2$ estimates the response time of IPE of $S1$ and $S2$. Without resource contention, this is $max(t1, t2)$.

2. $t1; t2$ estimates the response time of SE of $S1$ followed by $S2$. Hence, this is $t1 + t2$.

3. $t1 \ominus t2$ estimates the response time for the residual query $S1 \ominus S2$, where $S2$ is assumed to be the materialized front of $S1$ using a DPE of $S2$ piped to $(S1 \ominus S2)$.

This value of $\ominus$ operation depends on the difference between $t1$ and $t2$ and the respective contribution of $S1$

and $S2$ towards the critical path determining the response time. For now we approximate this to be $t1 - t2$, but in the next section when we take the resource usage into account to get a more accurate estimate.

Using these operators we derive the formulae for the two composition methods, namely pipelined and materialized execution as follows:

- Given a pipeline with the producer and consumer time descriptors as $\mathbf{p} = (pf, pl)$ and $\mathbf{c} = (cf, cl)$ respectively, the operator $\mathbf{p} \mid \mathbf{c}$ is the descriptor (tf, tl) for the pipeline given by:
  $tf = (pf; cf)$ $\quad tl = (pf; cf; ((pl \ominus pf) \parallel (cl \ominus cf)))$
  The tf is computed under the assumption that the first tuple is computed at the earliest possible time. The remainder of producer operations run in parallel with the remainder of the consumer operations as reflected in the formula for tl.

- The materialized execution of a subtree whose time descriptor $\mathbf{t} = (tf, tl)$ is computed using the operation $sync(\mathbf{t})$ that sets tf to tl, i.e., $sync(tf, tl) = (tl, tl)$).

The cost of an operator tree is computed recursively using the above formulae. In the base case, the descriptors of the leaves of the tree as well as the join methods are derived in the traditional manner, wherein the response time is the total work required for that operation. Then recursively, given the descriptors $\mathbf{L}, \mathbf{R}$ and **root** for the left/right operands and the root node respectively, the descriptor for the tree may be computed as follows: The materialized frontier of L may run in parallel with the materialized frontier of R to give a time descriptor of $\mathbf{t_1} = (L_f \parallel R_f, L_f \parallel R_f)$, then the residual query of L may run in a pipelined parallel fashion with the residual query of R to give a descriptor of $\mathbf{t_2} = \mathbf{t_1}; (0, L_l \ominus L_f) \mid (0, R_l \ominus R_f)$, and the result of this pipeline is piped to the root node to give $\mathbf{t} = \mathbf{t_2} \mid \mathbf{root}$. This operator is denoted as $tree(\mathbf{L}, \mathbf{R}, \mathbf{root})$. If the root node has only one subtree, then the formula is simply, $\mathbf{L}|\mathbf{root}$. Note that the above formula is also applicable for subtrees that are materialized as well.

Example 2 We continue with Example 1 and estimate the response time. The time descriptor (tf, tl) for each operation in the tree is estimated using traditional approach. For example, creating an index might incur a tf-component that must be done before using the scan. The following table shows, for hypothetical time descriptors of these operation, the computation of the estimate.

Oper.	(tf, tl)	*formula*	*value*
scan R_1	$(0,1)$		$(0,1)$
scan R_2	$(0,3)$		$(0,3)$
scan R_3	$(0,2)$		$(0,2)$
sort1	$(5,5)$	$sync((0,1)\|(5,5))$	$(6,6)$
sort2	$(10,10)$	$sync((0,3)\|(10,10))$	$(13,13)$
merge	$(0,2)$	$tree((6,6),(13,13),(0,2))$	$(13,15)$
n.loops	$(0,2)$	$tree((13,15),(0,2),(0,2))$	$(13,15)$

Now let us relax the assumption that disallowed cloning, and redistribution. The ability to clone a join or a select is captured by changing the time descriptor (tf, tl) by an amount k, the degree of cloning. For example, one simple approach is to take the time descriptor to be $(tf/k, tl/k)$. Needless to say that a more ambitious formulae would take into account the overhead associated with the cloning. The redistribution of data involve network and CPU overhead wherein the network is pipelined to the recipient CPU. Currently, the transfer of data from a producer to a consumer (i.e., between any two operation) has been assumed to be of zero cost. In general, this is not true as suggested by the redistribution cost. This transfer cost needs to quantify the inter-process overhead, communication overhead as well as the potential parallelism available in this transfer. This can be incorporated into the above formulae using the time descriptor for the transfer as well as estimating the response time using the above formulae. In short, the above cost model can be extended to handle other annotations as well.

In summary we have presented a cost model that trades-off the sources and deterrents of parallelism in estimating the response time of a query plan. In this, the overlapped/extra-work that is accrued/incurred by various operations are modeled and the response time is appropriately estimated. All this was done assuming that there was no resource contention. This is relaxed in the next section.

5.2 Modeling Resource Contention

We first present a resource usage model, using which we then present the cost calculus.

5.2.1 Resource Usage Model

Resource usage by a task is modeled by two parameters: t and w, where t is the time after which the resource is freed and w, the work measured as the effective time for which the resource is utilized. For example, suppose that a CPU was used for 10 seconds with an effective work of 5 secs. This means the CPU was busy only 50% of the time. However, in this abstraction, we cannot predict exactly when the busy periods were.

In fact, we make a *uniformity* assumption for this (t, w) abstraction of resource usage. The usage of the resource is uniform over the time period t[3]. Further we assume that the resources are *preemptable* in the sense that they can be time shared. Resources like CPU, disk, network are preemptable whereas memory is not[4]. The following property follows from these assumptions.

> *Property of stretching:* If a plan has a resource usage of (t, w) then it can be made (i.e, using an

[3] As a consequence of this, we lose some ability to model hot spots.

[4] Assuming that time sharing memory by more than one process using virtual memory is prohibitively expensive

appropriate scheduling strategy) to have a resource usage of (mt, w) for any positive number $m > 1$.

Let us assume that resources $r_1, \ldots, r_n$ are used by a certain set of operations (plan). For each of these resources, the usage is modeled by a pair (t_i, w_i). Since we assume that the property of stretching applies, we assume that all the t_is may be assumed to be the same and equal to t. Thus t denotes the response time of the plan and the total work done by the plan is given by $\sum_{i=1}^{n} w_i$. This pair $(t, \vec{w})$, where the components of the vector denotes the work done on that resource, is called a *resource vector*. It is usually denoted by $\vec{r}$. Analogous to the time descriptor, we define *resource descriptor* to be a pair of resource vectors $(\vec{rf}, \vec{rl})$, where $\vec{rf}$ represents the resource vector until the first tuple is output and $\vec{rl}$ represents the resource vector until the last tuple is output.

We use this resource descriptor to estimate the effect of resource contention on the response time.

5.2.2 Cost Calculus

We now extend the calculus of $\|$,; ,$\ominus$ on integers denoting time to resource vectors. In the following let $\vec{r_1} = (t_1, \vec{w_1})$ and $\vec{r_2} = (t_2, \vec{w_2})$ be two arbitrary resource vectors for a set of operations $S1$ and $S2$. The scenarios indicated for the applicability of each of the operators is the same as discussed earlier. The operations $+$ and $-$ on vectors denote the usual co-ordinate wise addition and subtraction.

The operation $\vec{r_1}; \vec{r_2}$ is defined as $\vec{r_1} + \vec{r_2}$ and $\vec{r_1} \ominus \vec{r_2}$ is $\vec{r_1} - \vec{r_2}$. Note that this accurately estimates the subtraction of the materialized front. Therefore, we use the usual vector minus operator instead of the $\ominus$ operator in the formulae. $\vec{r_1} \| \vec{r_2}$ is defined as $(t, \vec{w})$ for each resource i where $t = max(t_1, t_2, max_i(w_1^i + w_2^i))$, for each resource i and $\vec{w} = \vec{w_1} + \vec{w_2}$.

These operations are then used to define *tree* and the pipeline operator $|$ as before, where these take resource descriptors as arguments, rather than time descriptors. The operation of $|$ is slightly altered to take resource contention of the interleaved operations into account so that the resulting estimate is worse than SE if there is high resource contention.

Let p = $(\vec{pf}, \vec{pl})$ and c = $(\vec{cf}, \vec{pl})$ represent the resource descriptors for the producer and consumer of a pipeline respectively. Then, according to the previous formulation, the descriptor for p | c = $(\vec{rf}, \vec{rl})$, where
$\vec{rf} = \vec{pf}; \vec{cf}$ and $\vec{rl} = \vec{pf}; \vec{cf}; ((\vec{pl} - \vec{pf}) \| (\vec{cl} - \vec{cf}))$.
The parallel composition in $\vec{rl}$ is penalized by a (scalar) factor $\delta(k)$ to account for the synchronization overhead of pipelining. Thus $\vec{rl} = \vec{pf}; \vec{cf}; \delta(k) \times ((\vec{pl} - \vec{pf}) \| (\vec{cl} - \vec{cf}))$.

The factor $\delta(k)$ is obtained as follows: Let $(t', \vec{w})$ denote the resource vector for $S1 \| S2$. If t' is close to $t1 + t2$ then it means that the parallel pipelining incurs resource contention. On the other hand, if this t' is close to $max(t1, t2)$ then there is less resource contention. $\delta(k)$ is defined as parametrized linear interpolation of t' between $max(t1, t2)$ and $t1 + t2$; i.e.
$\delta(k) = 1 + k \times (t' - max(t1, t2))/(t1 + t2 - max(t1, t2))$.
In the above formula, k is an adjustable parameter. The linear interpolation may be replaced by other more accurate non linear estimates.

In summary, we have estimated the response time for IPE, DPE and CPE executions wherein the sources and deterrents of parallelism are taken into account.

6 Search

In this section we discuss how, given a query, the search space may be efficiently searched to obtain a query plan with optimal response time.

Starting with a System R style dynamic programming (DP) algorithm, we look at the impact of using response time as the optimization metric. The use of DP requires the problem to satisfy the principle of optimality[Bel57].

We show that response time violates this principle. Further there is no cost metric which correctly predicts response time while satisfying the properties required by DP. We extend DP to solve the problem and discuss how pruning metrics which correctly predict response time may be designed. We show our extended algorithm to have a practical complexity.

We show how limits on the amount of "extra" work may be incorporated and in fact exploited to increase the efficiency of search.

The reader is referred to [GHK92] for proofs of theorems and the extensions of algorithms to the search space of bushy trees.

6.1 Failure of DP

6.1.1 DP Revisited

Figure 1 shows a System R style DP algorithm which searches for an optimal-work plan in the space of left-deep join trees.

Some details of the algorithm are abstracted. The *accessPlan*(R) routine produces the best plan for the relation R; *joinPlan*(p', R) *extends* the join plan p' into another plan p in which the result of p' is joined with the relation R in the best possible way. The bindings available from p' may be exploited in joining with R. The predicate, $\leq_{work}$, is supplied by the cost model[5].

The algorithm proceeds by considering increasingly larger subsets of the set of all relations. Plans for a set of cardinality i are constructed as extensions of the best plan for a set of cardinality $i - 1$. This is possible since the nature of the optimization problem is such that an optimal plan for a set of relations is an extension of an optimal plan for some subset of the set. This property,

[5]Given two plans p_1 and p_2, we define $p_1 \leq_{\alpha} p_2$ and $\alpha(p_1) \leq \alpha(p_2)$ to be equivalent notations. Examples of the $\alpha()$ function are *work*() and the response time function, *RT*().

```
Input: An SPJ query q on relations R_1, ..., R_n
Output: A query plan P_opt for q with optimal work.
for i := 1 to n do
   optPlan({R_i}) := accessPlan(R_i)
for i := 2 to n do {
   for all S ⊆ {R_1, ..., R_n} s.t. ||S|| = i do {
      bestPlan := dummy plan with infinite cost
      for all R_j, S_j s.t S = {R_j} ∪ S_j do {
         p := joinPlan(optPlan(S_j), R_j)
         if p ≤_work bestPlan
            bestPlan := p
      }
      optPlan(S) := bestPlan
   }
}
P_opt := optPlan({R_1, ..., R_n})
```

Figure 1: DP Algorithm for Left-Deep Join Trees

which is often called the *principle of optimality*, is exploited by the algorithm. Optimal plans for subsets are stored in the *optPlan*() array and are reused rather than recomputed .

6.1.2 Fundamental Assumptions in DP

The proof of correctness for the DP algorithm of Figure 1 requires the following assumptions about the cost metric:

• *Principle of Optimality*: If two plans differ only in a subplan then the plan with the better subplan is also the better plan. In particular, for left-deep trees we need the following: if p_1 and p_2 are two plans for the same subquery, then

$$p_1 \leq_{cost} p_2 \Rightarrow (\forall i) joinPlan(p_1, R_i) \leq_{cost} joinPlan(p_2, R_i)$$

• *Total Order*: Plans can be totally ordered based on the cost metric.

$$(\forall p_1 p_2) not(p_1 \leq_{cost} p_2) \Rightarrow (p_2 \leq_{cost} p_1)$$

The cost metric, *work*, is an integer and therefore provides a total order. Whether it satisfies the principle of optimality depends on the choice of the cost model (which in turn depends on the chosen execution space).

For example, consider an execution space that allows nested loops and hash joins as join methods and index scan and relation scan as access methods. In any reasonable cost model for this execution space[6] the cost of the best way of joining a subquery with an additional relation will be dependent only on the subquery and not on the choice of the plan for the subquery. The cost of the join depends only on the logical aspects of the subquery such as available bindings and is independent of the physical plan. More formally, suppose p_1 is a plan for subquery q_1 and $joinwork(q_1, R)$ is the work cost of the best way of joining any relation R with the result of subquery q_1.

Definition (Physical Transparency): A cost model is said to exhibit *physical transparency* iff the following equation holds: $work(joinPlan(p_1, R)) = work(p_1) + joinwork(q_1, R)$

Theorem 1 *The cost metric for work,* $\leq_{work}$*,*
(1) is a total order and
(2) satisfies the principle of optimality under the physical transparency assumption.

A cost model that exhibits physical transparency is *not* reasonable if the execution space includes sort-merge join. It is now possible that the *physical* ordering of tuples produced by a plan may save work for a subsequent sort-merge join. Suppose plans p_1 and p_2 for subquery q are such that $p_1 \leq_{work} p_2$ but p_2 produces tuples in the order needed by a sort-merge join with relation R. It is possible to have $joinPlan(p_2, R) \leq joinPlan(p_1, R)$ if the interesting order produced by p_2 saves a sort pass in the sort-merge join algorithm. Thus the principle of optimality is violated.

Optimizers, such as in System R, retain some plans for subqueries with different "interesting orders" in the hope that they will prove useful by cutting down the cost of some join at a later stage. This *heuristic* solution to the violation of the principle of optimality is generally accepted to be sufficient in practice.

6.1.3 DP and Response Time

One important question is whether it is possible to use the response time metric, $RT(p)$, as the cost metric in DP.

Does response time satisfy the principle of optimality? The not very surprising answer is that it depends on the choice of the cost model. But we believe that any reasonable cost model for response time will violate the principle of optimality quite violently. The intuitive reason is that data dependencies and resource contention between parts of a plan are crucial factors for response time and any cost model that takes them into account will violate the principle of optimality. The following example shows how resource contention leads to a violation of the principle of optimality.

Example 3 Consider a database consisting of the tables $CTR(course, time, room)$ and $CI(course, instructor)$. Suppose CTR has two indexes, a clustered index $I_{CT}(course, time)$ (stored on disk 1) and an unclustered index $I_{CR}(course, room)$ (stored on disk 2) and CI has one index $I_C(course)$ (stored on disk 1).

The query $\pi_{course}(CTR \bowtie CI)$ may be computed purely by scanning indexes. We consider two nested-loops join plans of the form[7] $NL(p, indexScan(I_C))$

[6] The reader is reminded that cost models are built by human beings. Given the quirks of human nature we can only appeal to "reasonableness" when saying that a property of the cost model follows from the choice of the execution space.

[7] For brevity, we use NL to stand for nested-loops in these expressions.

where p is either $p_1 = indexScan(I_{CT})$ or $p_2 = indexScan(I_{CR})$. Suppose the resource vector (considering disk1 and disk2 to be the only significant resources) for p_1 is $\langle(20,20),(0,0)\rangle$; for p_2 is $\langle(0,0),(25,25)\rangle$ and for $NL(*, indexScan(I_C))$ (the join without counting p) is $\langle(40,40),(0,0)\rangle$. Since nested-loops is pipelined, we apply the calculus on resource vectors to obtain the resource usage of $NL(p_1, indexScan(I_C))$ to be $\langle(60,60),(0,0)\rangle$ and that for $NL(p_2, indexScan(I_C))$ to be $\langle(40,40),(25,25)\rangle$.

Applying the definition of response time, $RT(p_1) = 20$ and $RT(p_2) = 25$. However,

$RT(NL(p_1, indexScan(I_C))) = 60$ and

$RT(NL(p_2, indexScan(I_C))) = 40$

showing that response time violates the principle of optimality. ∎

The violation of the principle of optimality due to interesting orderings did pose a problem in the optimization for work. The same principle is violated due to resource contention when optimizing for response time. We expect the problem to be more difficult for response time due to an explosion in the number of causal factors. Resource contention is likely to happen between any two parts of a plan. The resource usage of a plan varies depending on what resources are used for sorting or partitioning intermediate results in addition to variables such as access methods, join methods and join ordering.

A natural question to ask next is whether it is possible to *design a new metric* that correctly predicts response time and satisfies the two properties that we require. Such a metric could then be used for pruning in DP. We will refer to such a metric as a *pruning metric*.

Definition (Correct Prediction): A pruning metric α will be said to *correctly predict* response time iff
$p_1 \leq_\alpha p_2 \Rightarrow p_1 \leq_{RT} p_2$

Theorem 2 *There does not exist any pruning metric that correctly predicts response time, provides a total order and satisfies the principle of optimality.*

The implication of this theorem is that it is not possible to use DP for optimizing response time without relaxing our requirements. We must develop variants of DP based on giving up one of the two fundamental assumptions that we noted. Giving up the principle of optimality essentially amounts to giving up the ability to prune the search space at all and leads us to brute force algorithms for exhaustive search. Therefore the less devastating alternative is the relaxation of requiring a total order.

We show this to be a practical direction by showing

- a generalization of DP that is capable of utilizing a partial order and provides acceptable performance (Section 6.2)
- how pruning metrics which correctly predict response time, provide a partial order and satisfy the principle of optimality may be designed (Section 6.3).

```
Input: An SPJ query q on relations R_1, ..., R_n
Output: A query plan P_opt for q with optimal cost.
1.  for i := 1 to n do
2.     optPlans({R_i}) := accessPlans(R_i)
3.  for i := 2 to n do {
4.     for all S ⊆ {R_1, ..., R_n} s.t. ||S|| = i do {
5.        bestPlans := ∅
6.        for all R_j, S_j s.t S = {R_j} ∪ S_j do {
L1.          for all p ∈ optPlans(S_j) do {
L2.             new := joinPlan(p, R_j)
L3.             if ∄p_better ∈ bestPlans s.t p_better ≤_{α_l} new {
L4.                for all p_d ∈ bestPlans s.t new ≤_{α_l} p_d
L5.                   delete p_d from bestPlans
L6.                insert new into bestPlans
L7.             }
L8.          }
10.       }
11.       optPlans(S) := bestPlans
12.    }
13. }
14. P_opt := bestCost(optPlans({R_1, ..., R_n}))
```

Figure 2: Partial Order DP for Left-Deep Join Trees

6.2 Generalization of DP for Partial Orders

We may define a less-than relation which provides a partial order in l-dimensions as follows: **Definition (l-Dimensional Less Than):** Given two points, $\langle d_1^1, \ldots, d_l^1\rangle$ and $\langle d_1^2, \ldots, d_l^2\rangle$in l-dimensional space, $\leq_l$ is defined as:
$\langle d_1^1, \ldots d_l^1\rangle \leq_l \langle d_1^2, \ldots d_l^2\rangle$ iff $d_i^1 \leq d_i^2$ for $i = 1 \ldots l$

The next section shows that it is possible to design a pruning metric, α, such that $\alpha(plan)$ is an l-dimensional vector[8]. Such pruning metrics will, by design, correctly predict response time as well as satisfy the principle of optimality.

Figure 2 shows the generalization of DP to use a partial order. The important difference from Figure 1 is highlighted: the actions in the innermost loop(lines 7,8,9 in Figure 1) are replaced by new actions (lines L1 through L8 in Figure 2).

The general idea is that instead of one optimal plan for each subset of relations, we keep a *set* of incomparable but optimal plans. These incomparable plans form a unique cover-set for all possible plans.

Plans for a set S of cardinality i are constructed as extensions of plans in the cover-sets for subsets of S of cardinality $i-1$. The cover-set of these plans is computed and retained as the set of optimal plans for S. By the principle of optimality it follows that a cover-set computed in this manner is indeed the cover-set of all possible plans for S.

[8] Given two plans p_1 and p_2, we define $p_1 \leq_{\alpha_l} p_2$ and $\alpha(p_1) \leq_l \alpha(p_2)$ to be equivalent notations.

The final result of the algorithm is obtained by choosing from the set of plans for $\{R_1, \ldots, R_n\}$ with the best cost.

The time and space complexity of the search for optimal plans depends on the size of the set of best plans for each set of relations. Let us assume that this size is k. The time and space complexity of the algorithm may then be shown to be $kn2^{n-1}$ and $k\binom{n}{\lceil \frac{n}{2} \rceil}$ respectively. Whether this is an acceptable complexity depends on the value of k.

Definition (Cover Set): A *cover-set* C for a set of points P with respect to a relation $\leq_p$ is a subset of P such that all points in C are incomparable and every point p' in P is "covered by" some point c' in C (i.e. $c' \leq_p p'$).

Theorem 3 *The expected size of the cover-set (with respect to $\leq_l$) of m randomly chosen points in l-dimensional space is at most $2^l(1-(1-\frac{1}{2^l})^m)$ provided the probability distribution is independent along each dimension.*

The theorem essentially says that 2^l is an upper bound for k. The assumption of independence of dimensions is likely to be optimistic for most pruning metrics. Therefore 2^l is an upper bound under an optimistic assumption.

In summary, if the number of dimensions, l, is kept small then DP with partial orders provides acceptable performance.

6.3 Pruning Metrics and Approximation Techniques

One way of fixing the situation shown in Example 3 is to use the resource vector itself as the pruning metric. The resource vector $rv(p)$, of a plan p, is a l-dimensional vector. Therefore resource vectors may be partially ordered using the $\leq_l$ relation. Obviously, a resource vector correctly predicts response time.

The general idea in designing a pruning metric is to try to make the antecedent in the definition of the principle of optimality false for the cases in which the consequent is false.

For example tuple ordering may be incorporated as an additional dimensions in the pruning metric. This requires a $\leq_{ordering}$ relation over orderings. If an ordering is represented as a sequence of column numbers then the $\leq_{ordering}$ relation may be taken to be "subsequence of". Data dependence and data partitioning may be incorporated in a manner similar to ordering.

However, in order to keep the cost of search acceptable, we must be careful not to have too many dimensions in the pruning metric. If two resources closely track each other, they should be aggregated and modeled as a single resource. For example the RAID system in XPRS[HS91] should be considered to be a single resource since data is hash partitioned on all disks with the intention of keeping each disk equally busy. If a resource is expected to rarely be the bottleneck, it should be ignored. For example resource contention at the disk controller is rarely a problem in a well designed system.

Algorithm	size of space (#plans)	time complexity (#plans considered)	space complexity (max #plans stored)
brute force for left-deep	$n!$	$n!$	1
DP for left-deep	$n!$	$n2^{n-1}$	$\binom{n}{\lceil \frac{n}{2} \rceil}$
p.o. DP for left-deep	$n!$	$n2^{n-1}2^l$	$2^l\binom{n}{\lceil \frac{n}{2} \rceil}$
brute force for bushy	$\frac{(2(n-1))!}{(n-1)!}$	$\frac{(2(n-1))!}{(n-1)!}$	1
DP for bushy	$\frac{(2(n-1))!}{(n-1)!}$	$2^b(3^n\text{-}2^{n+1}$ +n +1)	2^b2^n
p.o. DP for bushy	$\frac{(2(n-1))!}{(n-1)!}$	$2^l2^b(3^n\text{-}2^{n+1}$ +n+1)	$2^l2^b2^n$

Table 1: Comparison of Search Algorithms

6.4 Discussion

Bushy trees offer more scope for independent parallelism since two subtrees may be executed in parallel. The reader is referred to [GHK92] for the DP algorithms extended to the space of bushy trees.

Search over bushy trees is much more costly than over left-deep trees. The complexity of DP increases for two reasons. Firstly and more significantly the space of plans is much larger. Second and less obviously we are now forced to keep plans for all possible bindings of a subquery. This multiplies the complexity by a factor of 2^b (in the worst case) where b is the number of columns in the output of the subquery.

Table 1 summarizes the time and space complexity of several algorithms. We observe that using the search space of bushy trees instead of left-deep trees takes the time complexity of search from $O(2^n)$ to $O(3^n)$. Using a partial order over l dimensions instead of a total order multiplies the time complexity by 2^l.

Work bounds may be easily incorporated in the search algorithm and in fact cut down the search space.

For example, the limit on throughput degradation may be implemented by first running a work-optimizer (such as Figure 1) to obtain, W_o, the optimal work-cost of a query. The chosen pruning metric for the response-time algorithm is simply extended by the work limit giving a more stringent partial order. A similar approach may be taken for incorporating the cost-benefit ratio.

7 Conclusions

In this paper, we have proposed a novel formulation of the query optimization problem: *Minimize response time sub-*

ject to constraints on throughput, which was motivated as the dual of the traditional DBMS problem. We addressed this novel problem in the context of Select-Project-Join queries by extending the execution space, cost model and search algorithm that are widely used in commercial DBMSs. We incorporated the sources and deterrents of parallelism in the traditional execution space. We showed that a cost model can predict response time while accounting for the new aspects due to parallelism. We observed that the response time optimization metric violates a fundamental assumption in dynamic programming algorithm that is the linchpin in the optimizers of most commercial DBMSs. We extended dynamic programming and showed how optimization metrics which correctly predict response time may be designed.

It is a widely held belief that a comprehensive parallel-query optimizer is not available today[DG90]. While we have addressed some of the critical aspects of this problem, there are many open questions. We discuss some of them below.

While we model the sources and deterrents of parallelism in our execution space there are several runtime aspects such as scheduling that are candidates for inclusion. In general, investigating what aspects of the runtime execution should be decided at compile time is an interesting question.

We have addressed the usage of resources that are preemptable (i.e time-sliceable). Incorporating non-preemptable resources such as memory is an open question. Further, our cost model has not quantified the overheads due to pipelining and cloning. This would be necessary in any practical system.

Having observed the drawbacks of the traditional dynamic programming approach, we have presented criteria for designing appropriate pruning metrics. Evaluation of pruning metric alternatives is necessary. We have discussed the search algorithm in the context of left-deep trees. Use of bushy trees is widely believed to provide higher degrees of parallelism. We observe that, even for ten relations, this increases the size of the search space by three orders of magnitude. Consequently use of non-exhaustive search algorithms may be imperative.

Acknowledgements: We thank Marie-Anne Neimat for her advice, encouragement and support from the early stages of this research. We are grateful to Donovan Schneider for sharing his Gamma experience. Thanks are also due to Tim Connors, Curtis Kolovson, Kevin Wilkinson and all other members of the Database Technology Department. We also thank Don Batory, Stefano Ceri, Avi Silberschatz, and Gio Wiederhold for providing useful feedback.

References

[AHY83] P.M.G. Apers, A.R. Hevner, and S.B. Yao. Optimization Algorithms for Distributed Queries. *IEEE Transaction on Software Engineering*, 9(1), 1983.

[Bel57] R.E. Bellman. *Dynamic Programming*. Princeton University Press, 1957.

[CHK+91] T. Connors, W. Hasan, C. Kolovson, M.-A. Neimat, D. Schneider, and K. Wilkinson. The Papyrus integrated data server. In *Proceedings of the First International Conference on Parallel and Distributed Information Systems*, December 1991.

[DG90] D. J. DeWitt and J. Gray. Parallel Database Systems: The Future of Database Processing or a Passing Fad? *ACM-SIGMOD Record*, 19(4):104–112, December 1990.

[DGS+90] D.J. DeWitt, S. Ghandeharizadeh, D. Schneider, A. Bricker, H.-I. Hsiao, and R. Rasmussen. The Gamma database machine project. *IEEE Transactions on Knowledge and Data Engineering*, 2(1), March 1990.

[GHK92] S. Ganguly, W. Hasan, and R. Krishnamurthy. Query Optimization for Parallel Execution. Technical report, HP Laboratories, 1992. HPL-DTD-92-3.

[Gra91] J. Gray. *The Benchmark Handbook for Database and Transaction Processing Systems*. Morgan Kaufmann Publishers, Inc., 1991.

[HS91] W. Hong and M. Stonebraker. Optimization of parallel query execution plans in xprs. In *Proceedings of the First International Conference on Parallel and Distributed Information Systems*, December 1991.

[PMC+90] H. Pirahesh, C. Mohan, J. Cheung, T.S. Liu, and P. Selinger. Parallelism in Relational Data Base Systems: Architectural Issues and Design Approaches. Technical report, IBM Research Division, September 1990. IBM Research Report RJ 7724.

[SAC+79] P. Selinger, M. M. Astrahan, D. D. Chamberlin, R. A. Lorie, and T. G. Price. Access Path Selection in a Relational Database Management System. In *Proceedings of ACM-SIGMOD International Conference on Management of Data*, 1979.

[Sch90] D. A. Schneider. *Complex Query Processing in Multiprocessor Database Machines*. PhD thesis, University of Wisconsin—Madison, September 1990. Computer Sciences Technical Report 965.

[SD89] D. A. Schneider and D. J. DeWitt. A performance evaluation of four parallel join algorithms in a shared-nothing multiprocessor environment. In *ACM SIGMOD*, Portland, Oregon, June 1989.

Chapter 7: Conclusion

In this tutorial, we introduce the general concept of query processing in parallel database systems by providing an overview of work reported in the literature and compiling a representative set of papers by various authors. Due to the breadth of the topic, it is not possible for us to include many equally good papers, and as such, we restricted our discussions to the most basic issues. For example, we covered parallel sort and join in detail but not other operations such as aggregations, intersections, and union. Furthermore, we limit our discussion to relational systems and conventional queries. Parallel processing of other types of queries in nonrelational systems (such as transitive closure and recursive queries in deductive database systems and queries in object-oriented database systems) is not addressed.

Despite the amount of research conducted in parallel query processing and optimization, many important issues require further study. Nevertheless, most of these issues are problems encountered in other database environments too (such as centralized and distributed).[1] In what follows, we outline a number of research problems yet to be solved.

Integrating access methods

As with conventional databases, indexes drastically affect the performance of the parallel processing algorithms. However, unlike conventional databases, instead of a class of access methods, most of the research in parallel query processing considers only hash-based methods. The use of only one access method has the disadvantage of not being able to exploit access patterns and data characteristics. Furthermore, the support of more than one index provides more space for optimization. For example, the performance of the nested-loops join without an index, which is less efficient than the hybrid hash join, could become more efficient than the latter with a hierarchical index.[2] A main reason for not supporting sophisticated indexes is the complexity of maintaining and making use of indexes when data are stored at and processed by more than one processor. More study is required to integrate the various access methods into parallel query processing and optimization algorithms.

The use of bit filtering

Bit filtering has been widely used to reduce data fetching and transfer.[3–6] In a join operation, when the building relation is being scanned and redistributed, the bit filter is created and sent to the nodes where the probing relation resides. Based on the bit filter, the large portion of the probing relation that does not contribute to the final result can often be discarded, thus avoiding unnecessary processing and communication costs. Recently, Chen et al. studied how to interleave bit filters in a bushy plan to further improve its performance. The problem itself is an optimization issue since different interleaving results in a different cost of the plan.[7] Moreover, while bit filtering is typically used for join operations, it can also be applied to other operations such as intersections, semijoin, outer-join, union, and difference.

Adaptive resource management

Most current research assumes some sort of static resource allocation. That is, once a query is executed, the resources allocated to it remain unchanged throughout its execution. It is assumed that a plan for the query remains "optimal" throughout the execution of the query. However, in multiuser environments and/or real-time applications, part of the resources allocated to a query may be relocated to higher priority tasks during its execution. The critical issue then is how do we handle such situations to ensure optimal system performance? Do we suspend the query until resources are available, or do we allow the query to continue to execute with limited resources (which implies that the original plan may no longer be optimal)? In Reference 8, the latter approach is adopted, and a hash-join algorithm is designed to adapt to the current memory and buffer contention each time a new hash table is built. A related problem is the allocation of resources to a variety of queries that include short and complex queries. In Reference 9, the trade-offs of allocating resources among these queries are studied. However, further study is needed in order to have a better understanding of the problems and issues involved and to develop efficient algorithms that will ensure optimal system performance.

Optimization objectives

Although most of the work in parallel query optimization uses the elapsed time as the optimization objective, as it seems to be the major motivation for parallel database systems, some recent works have adopted different cost metrics and hence optimization objectives. In Reference 10, the cost metric used is processing time, which is a weighted sum of the CPU and I/O cost. In Reference 11, the objective is to minimize the elapsed time while placing a bound on the resource consumption that can be traded to reduce the elapsed time.

Selection of the optimization objective is deemed more important in parallel systems than in uniprocessor systems. In uniprocessor systems, there is less contradiction among different objectives and minimizing processing costs usually leads to reducing the response time and improving the throughput. However, in parallel database systems, one can design algorithms that reduce the elapsed time at the expense of increased total processing costs. As a result, the system throughput may decrease. On the other hand, restricting the amount of resources that can be allocated to an individual query may result in a long elapsed time, which may not be tolerable. For example, some urgent queries may have deadlines after which their values are lost. One possible solution is to provide a query optimizer with different adaptive optimization objectives so that the system performance stays satisfactory and is less dependent on applications or even the time when the query is processed.[12]

Search strategy

In Chapter 6, we showed that the search space could be very large for a large number of joins. With such a large search space, exhaustive and dynamic programming methods are prohibitively expensive. Developing efficient and effective heuristics remains an open and challenging field. We discuss some of the areas here.

Generating bushy plans

The class of bushy plans has been conceived to be able to produce better plans, but little effort has been spent in developing heuristics that produce bushy plans. What is worse is that most past efforts assume either no pipelining[13,14] or that the inner relation can fit in the memory.[15] The difficulty with pipelining bushy plans lies in estimating the size of the intermediate results. If the intermediate results are larger than expected, it may break the pipeline and lead to poor performance. It is also not well understood how much we could gain by processing two subplans concurrently. Moreover, it is very hard to schedule two or more subplans such that their result streams are available at the right time and at the right rates. Is it then still wise to use only right-deep-based algorithms that exhibit great potential for pipelining?[16, 17]

Partially declustered relations

Existing work tends to assume that the relations are distributed across all nodes. What would happen if the system comprises clusters, each of which has a number of processors, and each relation is declustered only within a single cluster? How would existing algorithms that do not consider the locality of the relation perform? Could we borrow ideas from distributed database systems and treat each cluster as a site? How could locality information be used to generate plans, and how effective are such plans?

Adaptable search space: Optimization cost vs. quality of plan

There is a trade-off between optimization cost and the quality of the generated plan.[18] A high optimization cost generally entails searching a larger space, which leads to a better plan. However, high optimization cost is unacceptable for interactive applications and ad hoc queries that are executed only once. In such applications, the search space should be effectively pruned to avoid an exhaustive search, and efficient search strategies should be developed. On the other hand, it is imperative to be able to adjust the search space considered by the optimizer for different queries and applications.[19] Applications that are batch-oriented and have repetitive queries could benefit from a larger search space (and hence higher optimization cost) in order to minimize execution time. Even within an application, some queries may benefit more by considering a larger search space than others. For example, if a complex query involves many large relations and its execution time is expected to be high, then a longer optimization time may be tolerated. However, if a query involves only small relations and its execution time is expected to be short, then it might be better to restrict the search space to keep the optimization time short. As such, new algorithms that can adapt to the needs of applications are highly desirable.

Besides developing new algorithms that can adjust the search space parametrically for different queries, the question remains as to how we can use existing algorithms effectively. We have seen several categories of optimization algorithms; namely, exhaustive, dynamic programming, randomized, and polynomial heuristics. For a given query, how do we decide which strategy to use? Can we combine these strategies in some way? For example, polynomial heuristics may be suitable for a large number of relations (> 100) and dynamic programming for a small number of relations (< 15). In addition to the number of relations, the size of the relations and results are important factors to consider. For example, for 15 relations each with 1,000 tuples, it may not be beneficial to spend a long optimization time. On the other hand, 10 relations each with 1,000,000 tuples are expected to have a long processing time and hence a long optimization time may be fine. The problems of critical factors in deciding the choice of algorithms remain unsolved.

Static versus dynamic optimization

Traditionally, databases are used in business data-processing applications where changes made to the database are minor. In such applications, static optimization that involves generating an optimal plan for a query prior to its execution is widely used for four reasons. First, the queries in such applications are usually not very complex. Second, statistics that are used for optimization are fairly accurate. Third, the overhead of optimizing a query at run time is reduced. Fourth, exhaustive optimization techniques that incur relatively high optimization costs may be applied.

However, as DBMS mature, new applications such as real-time and CAD/CAM applications emerge. Such applications pose a great challenge to the database community because of their (1) voluminous data, (2) complex queries composed of large numbers of join operations, and (3) dynamicity of data. To handle such applications, the trend seems to be moving back to the days of the 70s — towards dynamic query evaluation as in References 20 and 21, in which case the optimal plan is selected only at run time. Several reasons account for this:

- A query plan is sensitive to the resources available at run time. Unfortunately, such information is not known at compile time if precompilation is adopted. This is especially so in multiuser systems.

- The distribution of attributes in a relation, especially for intermediate results, is usually not known; neither is the distribution of a relation across the nodes in the system. Data skew poses problems since splitting a relation into subrelations may cause the size of the subrelations to differ drastically.

- Because of the dynamicity of the data, statistics collected are more prone to error. Moreover, error in the estimated intermediate result size may propagate to subsequent operations. For example, the estimate for $R_1 \bowtie R_2$ will affect the estimate for $(R_1 \bowtie R_2) \bowtie R_3$.

While optimizing queries at run time seems to be an alternative solution, it is still not clear how much could be gained by such an approach and how to go about implementing it. For example, in order to minimize the run time overhead, the algorithms used may restrict the search space to the extent that poor-quality plans are generated. We address some of the issues here.

Handling skew

As we have seen in Chapter 5, a large number of skew-handling algorithms have been proposed for single join operations. However, there were very few studies on how to deal with data skew for complex queries.[13,22] The problem is more complicated in multi-way join queries since data skew for intermediate results may not be known during optimization time. There is an urgent need for algorithms that can balance the join load dynamically, that is, during join computation. It may also be beneficial to dynamically rearrange an intermediate relation if the overhead of reorganization is less than its benefit.

Sampling techniques

Sampling techniques have been employed in database applications to estimate query size[23,24] and to estimate percentiles.[25,26] The estimation of percentiles is especially useful in parallel database systems since the estimates can be used to split a relation into approximately equal-sized subrelations to achieve good load balancing across the nodes. In parallel database systems, sampling creates some problems, though. To ensure a random sample, some processors may need to access more samples than others, and this leads to load imbalance during the sampling phase. Reference 27 shows that using stratified random sampling is as effective as simple random sampling and yet minimizes the sampling overhead. The paper also gives a bound on the number of samples to be taken to guarantee a given bound on the skew in the estimated percentiles. However, sampling is expensive since random I/Os have to be used. It is therefore essential to develop approaches that avoid random I/Os.

Precompilation of query evaluation plans

One way of reducing dynamic query optimization cost is to precompile queries as much as possible. The question is: to what extent can we perform precompilation and leave the rest until run time? For example, the two-phase approach discussed in Chapter 6 allows the generated plan to be kept so that repeated execution of the same query may reuse the plan without incurring additional optimization cost. At run time, resources are allocated to the operators of the plan to achieve a minimum elapsed time for the plan. However, the effectiveness of such an approach remains an open question. Another approach is to generate several plans at compile time and allow the query evaluator to choose the most suitable one at run time based on the resource availability.[28,29] The biggest problem with this approach is the number of plans to keep. Restricting the number of plans may not help at all, yet keeping too many plans may be too costly. What, then, is a reasonable number, and which plans should be retained? Recently, the notion of parametric optimization has been used to identify plans that are optimal for subsets of all possible values of the run time parameters.[30] Again, the major problem here is with the number of plans to keep.

Handling complex queries

For complex queries composed of a large number of joins or other operations (> 30), the estimation error may grow drastically. There are two ways to handle this problem:

- The dynamic technique assumes that plans generated using the static approaches are unlikely to perform well. Thus, some form of dynamism must be introduced. For example, only one operation is processed at any one time, using the decomposition technique of Ingres[20,21] to minimize the estimation error. However, this is done at the expense of exploiting data flow between multiple operators. As in Reference 31, we suggest modifying the Ingres decomposition technique[20] to determine and process several operations (< 10) each time, instead of a single operation as in Ingres. To determine the number of operations to be performed, we can borrow ideas from existing algorithms that generate segmented plans.[16,17,32] However, we have yet to see empirical results on this. A related problem is that the optimizer may become a bottleneck, especially in a multiuser environment. How to minimize the optimization overhead becomes an issue with one possible solution being to parallelize the optimization process.

- Static techniques can also be applied. This is achieved by anticipating the possible outcomes of executing subplans and providing multiple alternative subsequent plans.[31] This approach may be feasible for simple queries, but the number of alternative subplans grows drastically for complex queries. Effective ways of limiting the number of alternative subplans have yet to be developed.

Multiple-query optimization

A potentially beneficial direction is to optimize multiple queries at the same time.[33] Existing algorithms that exploit interoperation can be applied, but the problem is slightly different in that optimizing multiple queries provides greater opportunities for load balancing and for exploiting common intermediate results. More importantly, tremendous savings could be made by scanning a relation only once if it is shared by multiple queries.

References

1. G. Graefe, ed., *Database Query Optimization: Proceedings of the ODBF Workshop,* Oregon Graduate Center, CS/E 89-005, May 1989.
2. D. DeWitt, J. Naughton, and J. Burger, "Nested Loops Revisited," *Proc. Second Parallel and Distributed Information Systems Conf.,* IEEE CS Press, Los Alamitos, Calif., 1993, pp. 230-242.
3. E. Babb, "Implementing a Relational Database by Means of Specialized Hardware," *ACM Trans. Database Systems,* Vol. 4, No. 1, Mar. 1979.
4. P.A. Bernstein et al., "Query Processing in a System for Distributed Databases (ssd-1)." *ACM Trans. Database Systems,* Vol. 6, No. 4, Dec. 1981.
5. D.J. DeWitt, "Gamma — A High Performance Dataflow Database Machine," *Proc. 12th Int'l Conf. Very Large Data Bases,* Morgan Kaufman, San Mateo, Calif., 1986, pp. 228-239.
6. D.J. DeWitt, S. Ghandeharizadeh, and D. Schneider, "A Performance Analysis of the Gamma Database Machine," *Proc. Int'l Conf. Management of Data,* Morgan Kaufman, San Mateo, Calif., 1988, pp. 350-360.
7. M.S. Chen, H.I. Hsiao, and P.S. Yu, "Applying Hash Filters to Improving the Execution of Bushy Trees," *Proc. 19th Int'l Conf. Very Large Data Bases,* Morgan Kaufman, San Mateo, Calif., 1993.
8. H. Zeller and J. Gray, "An Adaptive Hash Join Algorithms for Multi-User Environment," *Proc. 16th Int'l Conf. Very Large Data Bases,* Morgan Kaufman, San Mateo, Calif., 1990, pp. 186-197.
9. K.P. Brown et al., "Scheduling Issues for Complex Database Workloads," Technical Report TR-1095, Univ. of Wisconsin-Madison, July 1992.
10. W. Hong and M. Stonebraker, "Optimization of Parallel Query Execution Plans in XPRS," *Proc. First Int'l Conf. Parallel and Distributed Information Systems,* IEEE CS Press, Los Alamitos, Calif., 1991, pp. 218-225.
11. S. Ganguly, W. Hasan, and R. Krishnamurthy, "Query Optimization for Parallel Execution," *Proc. Int'l Conf. Management of Data,* 1992, pp. 9-18.
12. P.G. Selinger, "Five Hard Problems in Query Optimization," in *Database Query Optimization: Proceedings of the ODBF Workshop,* pp. 19-22, Oregon Graduate Center, CS/E 89-005, May 1989.
13. K.A. Hua, Y.L. Lo, and H.C. Young, "Including the Load Balancing Issue in the Optimization of Multi-Way Join Queries for Shared-Nothing Database Computers," *Proc. Second Int'l Conf. Parallel and Distributed Information Systems,* IEEE CS Press, Los Alamitos, Calif., 1993, pp. 74-83.
14. H. Lu, M.C. Shan, and K.L. Tan, "Optimization of Multi-Way Join Queries for Parallel Execution," *Proc. 17th Int'l Conf. Very Large Data Bases,* Morgan Kaufman, San Mateo, Calif., 1991.
15. J. Srivastava and G. Elsesser, "Optimizing Multi-Join Queries in Parallel Relational Databases," *Proc. Second Int'l Conf. Parallel and Distributed Information Systems,* IEEE CS Press, Los Alamitos, Calif., 1993, pp. 84-92.
16. M.S. Chen et al., "Using Segmented Right-Deep Trees for the Execution of Pipelined Hash Joins," *Proc. 18th Int'l Conf. Very Large Data Bases,* Morgan Kaufman, San Mateo, Calif., 1992, pp. 15-26.
17. D.A. Schneider and D.J. DeWitt, "Tradeoffs in Processing Complex Join Queries via Hashing in Multiprocessor Database Machines," *Proc. 16th Int'l Conf. Very Large Data Bases,* Morgan Kaufman, San Mateo, Calif., 1990.
18. R.S.G. Lanzelotte, P. Valduriez, and M. Zait, "On the Effectiveness of Optimization Search Strategies for Parallel Execution Spaces," *Proc. 19th Int'l Conf. Very Large Data Bases,* Morgan Kaufman, San Mateo, Calif., 1993.
19. K. Ono and G. Lohman, "Measuring the Complexity of Join Enumeration in Relational Query Optimization," *Proc. 16th Int'l Conf. Very Large Data Bases,* Morgan Kaufman, San Mateo, Calif., 1990, pp. 314-324.
20. E. Wong and K. Youssefi, "Decomposition — A Strategy for Query Processing," *ACM Trans. Database Systems,* Vol. 1, No. 3, Sept. 1976, pp. 223-241.
21. K. Youssefi and E. Wong, "Query Processing in a Relational Database Management System," *Proc. Fifth Int'l Conf. Very Large Data Bases,* Morgan Kaufman, San Mateo, Calif., 1979, pp. 409-417.
22. K.L. Tan and H. Lu, "Processing Multi-Join Query in Parallel Systems," *Symp. Applied Computing,* IEEE CS Press, Los Alamitos, Calif., 1992.

23. W.-C. Hou, G. Ozsoyoglu, and B.K. Taneja, "Statistical Estimators for Relational Algebra Expressions," *Proc. Seventh ACM Symp. Principles of Database Systems,* Assoc. for Computing Machinery, New York, N.Y., 1988, pp. 276-287.
24. R.J. Lipton, J.F. Naughton, and D.A. Schneider, "Practical Selectivity Estimation through Adaptive Sampling," *Proc. ACM-SIGMOD Int'l Conf. Management of Data,* Assoc. for Computing Machinery, New York, N.Y., 1990.
25. D.J. DeWitt, J.F. Naughton, and D.A. Schneider, "Parallel Sorting on a Shared-Nothing Architecture Using Probabilistic Splitting," *Proc. First Int'l Conf. Parallel and Distributed Information Systems,* IEEE CS Press, Los Alamitos, Calif., 1991, pp. 280-291.
26. D.J. DeWitt, J.F. Naughton, and D.A. Schneider, "A Comparsion of Non-Equijoin Algorithms," *Proc. 17th Int'l Conf. Very Large Data Bases,* Morgan Kaufman, San Mateo, Calif., 1991.
27. S. Seshadri and J.F. Naughton, "Sampling Issues in Parallel Database Systems," *Proc. Third Int'l Conf. Extending Data Base Technology,* 1992.
28. G. Graefe, "Dynamic Query Evaluation Plans," *Proc. ACM-SIGMOD Int'l Conf. Management of Data,* Assoc. for Computing Machinery, New York, N.Y., 1989, pp. 358-366.
29. M. Stonebraker et al., "The Design of XPRS," *Proc. 14th Int'l Conf. Very Large Data Bases*, Morgan Kaufman, San Mateo, Calif., 1988, pp. 318-330.
30. Y.E. Ioannidis and R.T. Ng, "Parametric Query Optimization," *Proc. 18th Int'l Conf. Very Large Data Bases,* Morgan Kaufman, San Mateo, Calif., 1992, pp. 103-114.
31. G. Graefe, "Query Evaluation Techniques for Large Databases," *ACM Computing Surveys* (to appear), 1993.
32. E.J. Shekita, H.C. Young, and K.L. Tan, "Multi-Join Query Optimization for Symmetric Multi-Processors," *Proc. 19th Int'l Conf. Very Large Data Bases,* Morgan Kaufman, San Mateo, Calif., 1993.
33. T.K. Sellis, "Multiple Query Optimization," *ACM Trans. Database Systems,* Vol. 13, No. 1, Mar. 1988.

Bibliography

Akl, S.G. and N. Santroo, "Optimal Parallel Merging and Sorting Without Memory Conflicts," *IEEE Trans. Computers* Vol. 36, No. 11, Nov. 1987, pp. 1367-1369.

Barlos F. and O. Frieder, "A Join Ordering Approach for Multicomputer Relational Databases with Highly Skewed Data," *Proc. 27th Annual Hawaii International Conf. System Sciences,* IEEE CS Press, Los Alamitos, Calif., 1994, pp. 253-262.

Bhide, A., "An Analysis of Three Transaction Processing Architectures," *Proc. 14th Int'l Conf. Very Large Data Bases,* Morgan Kaufman, San Mateo, Calif., 1988, pp. 339-349.

Blasgen, M.W. and K.P. Wilkinson, "Storage and Access in Relational Databases," *IBM System J.,* Vol. 16, No. 4, 1977.

Boral, H., "Parallelism in Bubba," *Proc. First Int'l Symp. Databases in Parallel and Distributed Systems,* IEEE CS Press, Los Alamitos, Calif., 1988, pp. 68-71.

Bultzingsloewen, G.v., "Design and Implementation of Kardamom — A Set-Oriented Data Flow Database Machine," *Proc. Sixth Int'l Workshop on Database Machines,* Springer Lecture Notes, No 368, Springer-Verlag, Heidelberg, Germany, 1989, pp. 18-33.

Bultzingsloewen, G.v., "Optimizing sql Queries for Parallel Execution," *SIGMOD RECORD,* Vol. 18, No. 4, Dec. 1989, pp. 17-22.

Chen, M.S., H.I. Hsiao, and P.S. Yu, "Applying Hash Filters to Improving the Execution of Bushy Trees," *Proc. 19th Int'l Conf. Very Large Data Bases,* Morgan Kaufman, San Mateo, Calif., 1993.

Choi, H.K. and M. Kim, "Hybrid Join: An Improved Sort-Based Join Algorithm," *Information Processing Letters,* Vol. 32, No. 7, 1989, pp. 51-56.

Copeland, G. et al., "Data Placement on Bubba," *Proc. ACM Int'l Conf. Management of Data,* Assoc. for Computing Machinery, New York, N.Y., 1988, pp. 99-108.

DeWitt, D.J., "Direct — A Multiprocessor Organization for Supporting Relational Database Management Systems," *IEEE Trans. Computers,* Vol. 28, June 1979, pp. 395-406.

DeWitt. D.J., "Parallel Database Systems: The Future of High Performance Database Systems," *Comm. of the ACM,* Vol. 35, No. 6, June 1992, pp. 85-98.

DeWitt, D.J., "Gamma — A High Performance Dataflow Database Machine," *Proc. 12th Int'l Conf. Very Large Data Bases,* Morgan Kaufman, San Mateo, Calif., 1986, pp. 228-239.

Dias, D.M., B.R. Iyer, and P.S. Yu, "Tradeoffs Between Coupling Small and Large Processors for Transaction Processing," *IEEE Trans. Computers,* Vol. 37, No. 3, Mar. 1988, pp. 310-320.

Dobosiewicz, W., "Sorting by Distributive Partitioning," *Information Processing Letters,* Vol. 7, No. 1, Jan. 1978, pp. 1-6.

Duppel, N., "Modelling and Optimization of Complex Database Queries in a Shared-Nothing System," *Proc. Third IEEE Symp. Parallel and Distributed Processing,* IEEE CS Press, Los Alamitos, Calif., 1991, pp. 52-59.

Enslow, P.H. Jr., "Multiprocessor Organization — A Survey, *ACM Computing Surveys,* Vol. 9, No. 1, Mar. 1977, pp. 103-129.

Epstein, R., M. Stonebraker, and E. Wong, "Distributed Query Processing in a Relational Database System," *Proc. ACM Int'l Conf. Management of Data,* Assoc. for Computing Machinery, New York, N.Y., 1978, pp. 169-180.

Fishman, D.H., M.Y. Lai, and W.K. Wilkinson, "Overview of the Jasmin Database Machine," *Proc. ACM Int'l Conf. Management of Data,* Assoc. for Computing Machinery, New York, N.Y., 1984, pp. 234-239.

Francis, R.S. and I.D. Mathieson, "A Benchmark Parallel Sort for Shared Memory Multiprocessors," *IEEE Trans. Computers,* Vol. 37, No. 12, Dec. 1988, pp. 1619-1626.

Ganguly, S., W. Hasan, and R. Krishnamurthy, "Query Optimization for Parallel Execution," *Proc. ACM Int'l Conf. Management of Data,* Assoc. for Computing Machinery, New York, N.Y., 1992, pp. 9-18.

Goodman, J.R., "An Investigation of Multiprocessor Structures and Algorithms for Database Management," *Technical Report UCB/ERL,* M81/33, University of California at Berkeley, May 1981.

Graefe, G., ed., "Database Query Optimization: Processings of the ODBF Workshop," Oregon Graduate Center, CS/E 89-005, 1989.

Graefe, G., "Query Evaluation Techniques for Large Databases," *ACM Computing Surveys,* Vol. 25, No. 2, June 1993, pp. 73-170.

Graham, R., "Bounds on Multiprocessing Timing Anomalies," *SIAM J. Computing,* Vol. 1, No. 7, 1969, pp. 416-429.

Gupta, A. et al., "Centralized, De-Centralized and Pipelined Algorithms to Parallelize Joins," Proc. 1993 Int'l Conf. Parallel and Distributed Systems, 1993, pp. 612-621.

Hong, W., "Exploiting Inter-Operation Parallelism in XPRS," *Proc. ACM Int'l Conf. Management of Data,* Assoc. for Computing Machinery New York, N.Y., 1992, pp. 19-28.

Hong, W. and M. Stonebraker, "Optimization of Parallel Query Execution Plans in XPRS," *Proc. First Int'l Conf. Parallel and Distributed Information Systems,* IEEE CS Press, Los Alamitos, Calif., 1991, pp. 218-225.

Hong, W. and M. Stonebraker, "Optimization of Parallel Query Execution Plans in XPRS," *Distributed and Parallel Databases,* Vol. 1, No. 1, Jan. 1993, pp. 218-225.

Hsiao, D.K., *Advanced Database Machine Architecture,* Prentice Hall, Englewood Cliffs, N.J., 1983.

Hsiao, H.I., M.S. Chen, and P.S. Yu. "Processor Allocation for Parallel Execution of Hash Joins," Proc. 1993 Int'l Conf. Parallel and Distributed Systems, 1993, pp. 196-203.

Hurson, A.R., L.L. Miller, and S.H. Pakzad, eds., *Parallel Architectures for Database Systems,* IEEE CS Press, Los Alamitos, Calif., 1989.

Ibaraki, T. and N. Katoh, *Resource Allocation Problems,* MIT Press, Cambridge, Mass., 1988.

Ioannidis, Y.E. and E. Wong, "Query Optimization by Simulated Annealing," *Proc. ACM Int'l Conf. Management of Data,* Assoc. for Computing Machinery, New York, N.Y., 1987, pp. 9-22.

Iyer, B.R. and D.M. Dias, "System Issues in Parallel Sorting for Database Systems," *Proc. Sixth Int'l Conf. Data Eng.,* IEEE CS Press, Los Alamitos, Calif., 1990, pp. 246-255.

Janus, P.J. and E.A. Lamagna, "An Adaptive Method for Unknown Distributions in Distributive Partitioned Sorting," *IEEE Trans. Computers,* Vol. 34, No. 4, Apr. 1985, pp. 367-372.

Keller, A.M. and S. Roy, "Adaptive Parallel Hash Join in Main-Memory Databases," *Proc. First Int'l Conf. Parallel and Distributed Information Systems*, IEEE CS Press, Los Alamitos, Calif., 1991, pp. 58-67.

Kitsuregawa, M. and Y. Ogawa, "Bucket Spreading Parallel Hash: A New, Robust, Parallel Hash Join Method for Data Skew in the Super Database Computer (SDC)," *Proc. 16th Int'l Conf. Very Large Data Bases,* Morgan Kaufman, San Mateo, Calif., 1990, pp. 210-221.

Kitsuregawa, M., S.I. Tsudaka, and M. Nakano, "Parallel Grace Hash Join on Shared-Everything Multiprocessor: Implementation and Performance Evaluation on Symmetry S81," *Proc. Eighth Int'l Conf. Data Eng.,* IEEE CS Press, Los Alamitos, Calif., 1992, pp. 256-265.

Lakshmi, M.S. and P.S. Yu, "Effectiveness of Parallel Joins," *IEEE Trans. Knowledge and Data Eng.,* Vol. 2, No. 3, Sept. 1990, pp. 410-424.

Lakshmi, M.S. and P.S. Yu, "Effectiveness of Parallel Processing in Database Systems," *Computer Systems Science and Eng.*, Vol. 5, No. 2, Apr. 1990, pp. 73-81.

Lakshmivaraham, S., S.K. Dhall, and L.L Miller, "Parallel Sorting Algorithms," *Advances in Computers,* Vol. 23, 1984, pp. 295-354.

Liu, G.S., and H.H. Chen, *Information Systems,* Vol. 13, No. 4, 1988, p. 429.

Lo, M-L et al., "On Optimal Processor Allocation to Support Pipelined Hash Joins," *Proc. ACM Int'l Conf. Management of Data*, Assoc. for Computing Machinery, New York, N.Y., 1993, pp. 69-78.

Lohman, G. et al., "Query Processing in R*," in *Query Processing in Database Systems,* W. Kim, D.S. Reiner, and D.S. Batory, eds., Springer-Verlag, Heidelberg, Germany, 1985, pp. 31-47.

Lorie, R.A. and H.C. Young, "A Low Communication Sort Algorithm for a Parallel Database Machine," *Proc. 15th Int'l Conf. Very Large Data Bases,* Morgan Kaufman, San Mateo, Calif., 1989, pp. 125-134.

Lu, H. and K.L. Tan, "Dynamic and Load-Balanced Task-Oriented Database Query Processing in Parallel Systems," *Proc. Third Int'l Conf. Extending Data Base Technology,* 1992, pp. 357-372.

Lu, H. and K.L. Tan, "Load-Balanced Join Processing in Shared-Nothing Systems," (to appear) *J. Parallel and Distributed Computing,* 1994.

Mehta, M., V. Soloviev, and D.J. DeWitt, "Batch Scheduling in Parallel Database Systems," *Proc. Ninth Int'l Conf. Data Engineering,* 1993, pp. 400-410.

Nakayama, M. and M. Kitsuregawa, "Hash-Partitioned Join Method Using Dynamic Destaging Strategy," *Proc. 14th Int'l Conf. Very Large Data Bases,* Morgan Kaufman, San Mateo, Calif., 1988, pp. 468-478.

Niccum, T.M., J. Srivastava, B. Himatsingka, and J. Li, "A Tree-Decomposition Approach to the Parallel Execution of Relational Query Plans," *Technical Report TR93-16,* Univ. of Minnesota, Computer Science Dept., 1993.

Omiecinski, E. and E. Lin, "Hash-Based and Index-Based Join Algorithms for Cube and Ring Connected Multicomputers," *IEEE Trans. Knowledge and Data Eng.,* Vol. 1, No. 3, Sept. 1989, pp. 329-343.

Omiecinski, E. and E. Lin, "The Adaptive-Hash Join Algorithm for a Hypercube Multicomputer," *IEEE Trans. Parallel and Distributed Systems,* Vol. 3, No. 2, May 1992, pp. 334-349.

Ozkarahan, E., *Database Machines and Database Management,* Prentice Hall, Englewood Cliffs, N.J., 1986.

Ozsu, M.T. and P. Valduriez, *Principles of Distributed Database Systems,* Prentice Hall, Englewood Cliffs, N.J., 1991.

Pirahesh, H. et al., "Parallelism in Relational Data Base Systems: Architectural Issues and Design Approaches," *Proc. Second Int'l Symp. Databases in Parallel and Distributed Systems,* IEEE CS Press, Los Alamitos, Calif., 1990, pp. 4-29.

Qadah, G.Z. and K.B. Irani, "The Join Algorithms on a Shared-Memory Multiprocessor Database Machine," *IEEE Trans. Software Eng.,* Vol. 14, No. 11, Nov. 1988, pp. 1668-1683.

Rahm, E., "Parallel Query Processing in Shared Disk Database Systems," *Proc. Fifth Int'l Workshop on High Performance Transactions Systems,* 1993.

Rahm, E.and R. Marek, "Analysis of Dynamic Load Balancing Strategies for Parallel Shared Nothing Database Systems," *Proc. 19th Int'l Conf. Very Large Data Bases,* 1993.

Rishe, N., S. Navathe, and D. Tal, eds., *Proc. Int'l Conf. Databases, Parallel Architectures and Their Applications,* IEEE CS Press, Los Alamitos, Calif., 1990.

Rosenthal, A. and U.S. Chakravarthy, "Anatomy of a Modular Multiple Query Optimizer," *Proc. 14th Int'l Conf. Very Large Data Bases,* Morgan Kaufman, San Mateo, Calif., 1988, pp. 230-239.

Roussopoulos, N. and L. Tong, "Optimization of Response Time in Parallel Pipelined n-Joins," *Proc. PARBASE Conf.,* IEEE CS Press, Los Alamitos, Calif., 1990, pp. 496-498.

Shasha, D. and T.L. Wang, "Optimizing Equijoin Queries in Distributed Databases Where Relations are Hash Partitioned," *ACM Trans. Database Systems,* Vol. 16, No. 2, June 1991, pp. 279-308.

Stamos, J.W. and H.C. Young, "A Symmetric Fragment and Replicate Algorithm for Distributed Joins," *Technical Report Research Report RJ 7188,* IBM Almaden Research Center, 1989.

Su, Y.W.S., *Database Computers: Principles, Architecture and Techniques,* McGraw-Hill Int'l Edition, Computer Series, 1988.

Tan, K.L. and H. Lu, "Pipeline Processing of Multi-Way Join Queries in Shared Memory Systems," *Proc. 22nd Int'l Conf. Parallel Processing,* Vol. 1, CRC Press, Boca Raton, Florida, 1993, pp. 345-348.

Tan, K.L. and H. Lu. "On Resource Scheduling of Multi-Join Queries in Parallel Database Systems," *Information Processing Letters,* Vol. 48, No. 4, Nov. 1993, pp. 189-195.

Tandom Performance Group, "A Benchmark of Nonstop SQL on the Debit Credit Transaction," *Proc. ACM Int'l Conf. Management of Data,* Assoc. for Computing Machinery, New York, N.Y., 1988, pp. 337-341.

Ubell, M., *The Intelligent Database Machine (IDM),* Springer-Verlag, Berlin/Heidelberg, 1985, pp. 237-247.

Valduriez, P., "Join Indices," *ACM Trans. Database Systems,* Vol. 12, No. 2, June 1987, pp. 218-246.

Valduriez, P., "Parallel Database Systems: The Case for Shared-Something," *Proc. Ninth Int'l Conf. Data Eng.,*" IEEE CS Press, Los Alamitos, Calif., 1991, pp. 460-465.

Varman, P.J., B.R. Iyer, and D.J. Haderle, "An Efficient Multiprocessor Merge Algorithm," *Proc. PARBASE Conf.,* IEEE CS Press, Los Alamitos, Calif., 1990, pp. 276-283.

Walton, C.B., M.L. Pinsonneault, and F. Haddix, "Measurements of Data Skew in Two Databases," *Technical Report TR-90-32,* University of Texas, Austin, October 1990.

Walton, C.B. and A.G. Dale, "Data Skew and the Scalability of Parallel Joins," *Proc. 3rd IEEE Symp. Parallel and Distributed Processing,* IEEE CS Press, Los Alamitos, Calif., 1991, pp. 44-51.

Wolf, J. et al., "Comparative Performance of Parallel Join Algorithms," *Proc. First Int'l Conf. Parallel and Distributed Information Systems,* IEEE CS Press, Los Alamitos, Calif., 1991, pp. 78-88.

Zeller, H. and J. Gray, "An Adaptive Hash Join Algorithms for Multi-User Environment," *Proc. 16th Int'l Conf. Very Large Data Bases*, Morgan Kaufman, San Mateo, Calif., 1990, pp. 186-197.

About the Authors

Hongjun Lu is currently a senior lecturer at the National University of Singapore. His research interests include query processing and optimization in various data/knowledge base management systems, including distributed, parallel, and multidatabase systems. He is also interested in database performance and database application development such as geographical information systems.

Before starting his post-graduate study in 1979, he worked as an engineer at the Chinese Academy of Space Technology. Prior to joining National University of Singapore, he was a principal research scientist at Honeywell Computer Science Center in Minnesota and worked on the very large parallel data flow project.

He received his BS degree in electronic engineering from the Tsinghua University, Beijing, China in 1968, and MS and PhD degrees, both in computer science, from the University of Wisconsin, Madison, in 1980 and 1985, respectively.

He is a member of the Association for Computing Machinery and IEEE Computer Society and actively participates in international professional activities. He is a co-editor of the proceedings *GIS: Technology and Applications* (World-Scientific).

Beng Chin Ooi joined the National University of Singapore in 1989. His research interests include database performance issues, database UI, multi-media databases, and GIS.

He received his BSc.(hon) and PhD in computer science from Monash University, Australia, in 1985 and 1989, respectively. He is the author of *Efficient Query Processing in Geographic Information Systems* (Springer-Verlag), and a co-editor of the proceedings *Advances in Spatial Databases* (Springer-Verlag) and *GIS: Technology and Applications* (World-Scientific).

Kian-Lee Tan, is currently pursuing his PhD degree at the National University of Singapore. His major research interests include query processing and optimization in multiprocessor and distributed systems, and database performance. He received his BS and MS degrees, both in computer science, from the National University of Singapore in 1988 and 1991, respectively.